Microsoft® Windows® 2000 Network Infrastructure Design Special Edition

COURSE TECHNOLOGY
THOMSON LEARNING™

Australia • Canada • Mexico • Singapore • Spain • United Kingdom • United States

COURSE TECHNOLOGY
THOMSON LEARNING™

Microsoft Windows 2000 Network Infrasturcture Design Special Edition

Managing Editor:
Stephen Solomon

Marketing Manager:
Toby Shelton

Production Manager:
Melissa Panagos

Manufacturing Coordinator:
Denise Sandler

Cover Design:
Julie Malone

Printed in Canada

1 2 3 4 5 6 7 8 9 WC 04 03 02 01

For more information, contact Course Technology, 25 Thomson Place, Boston, Massachusetts, 02210.

Or find us on the World Wide Web at: www.course.com

ISBN 0-619-06283-5

Contents

Introduction

BOOK PURPOSE

This book is designed to provide you with the information you need to design a Windows 2000 network infrastructure. This book meets all published criteria for Microsoft's Exam 70-221, Designing a Microsoft Windows 2000 Network Infrastructure.

This book material is appropriate to learners who have experience working in a TCP/IP internetwork environment. Learners should be familiar with Windows 2000 and Windows NT, including Windows 2000 Active Directory domain networks.

While designed to meet all certification requirements, the information provided in this book also will be useful for learners who are not currently certification candidates. This book is appropriate for anyone involved with the network design process. This includes anyone implementing a new network or modifying an existing network environment.

All of the exercises in this manual are identified as optional exercises. You do not need to complete them to be able to complete the book materials in this manual. This manual also includes case studies, which test your comprehension of the material presented. No special hardware requirements are necessary to complete the questions associated with the case studies.

In addition to the exercises included in each chapter of this book, the Special Supplemental Exercises section features more in-depth exercises designed to increase your hands-on proficiency with Windows 2000 network design. The Special Supplemental Exercises include Review Questions, Hands-On Projects, and Case Projects that can be used to reinforce the skills needed for MCSE certification.

BOOK GOALS

This book will provide you with the information you need to complete the following:

- Gather the information needed to modify an existing network design.
- Gather the information needed to create a new network design.
- Identify network topology and security models.
- Collect information relating to business activities and organizational requirements.
- Identify an organization's information technology structure design.
- Identify design constraints that will impact an organization's network design.
- Gather information about Local Area Network (LAN) and Wide Area Network (WAN) topology, routing, communication, and user requirements.

- Identify current network support personnel and support changes required by a new network design.
- List and describe procedures for compiling a network hardware and software inventory.
- Given network communication requirements, determine TCP/IP addressing and subnet requirements.
- Design LAN and WAN links and routing.
- Design a network that integrates Windows 2000 in a heterogeneous networking environment.
- Design a Domain Name System (DNS) network solution.
- Design a Windows Internet Name Service (WINS) network solution.
- Design a Dynamic Host Configuration Protocol (DHCP) network solution.
- Design dial-up networking and demand-dial routing network solutions.
- Design shared Internet access solutions.
- Integrate Virtual Private Networks (VPNs) into a networking solution.
- Identify application and data resource requirements.
- Design a Distributed File System (Dfs) data availability solution.
- Design a plan for deploying your network design.
- Describe requirements for monitoring in a newly implemented network design.

EXERCISES

The exercises in this manual are designed to give you hands-on practice working in both stand-alone and network environments. You may find that there are some exercises that you are unable to complete due to hardware or software requirements. Do not let this stop you from completing the other exercises in this manual. All exercises in this manual are considered optional exercises. It is suggested that you complete the optional exercises when referenced. However, this may not always be convenient. If you need to skip an exercise, you should plan on completing the exercise later when time and circumstances allow. You should be aware that some exercises depend on completion of earlier exercises.

NOTICE:

The exercises in this self-study product are designed to be used on systems and as part of a network designated for training purposes *only*. Practicing the exercises on a LAN or systems that are used for other purposes may cause configuration problems, which could require a reinstallation and/or restoration from a tape backup of the original configuration. Please keep this in mind when working through the exercises.

In addition to the exercises included in each chapter of this book, the section labeled "Special Supplemental Exercises" features more in-depth exercises designed to increase your hands-on proficiency with Windows 2000 network design. This section includes Review Questions, Hands-On Projects, and Case Projects that can be used to reinforce the skills needed for MCSE certification.

SCENARIO-BASED LEARNING

This book uses three case studies that are referenced by several scenario-based learning exercises. An introduction to each case study is provided in Chapter 1, with additional, detailed information added as necessary in subsequent chapters. Based on the information provided, you will be asked to determine the best solution for each of the associated scenario questions. Suggested solutions, as well as the case studies (in their entirety), are provided at the back of the manual.

It is important that you take the time to work through the scenario-based exercises. These are an important supplement to the training materials and are meant to reinforce the textual information in your manual.

SIMULATIONS

Throughout the book, you will see icons asking you to use NEXTSim to practice the concepts you have learned. NEXTSim is an interactive simulation product that provides you with scenario-based training and hands-on experience in a *safe* environment. This tool should be used strictly as a supplement to the book and not to replace the book content. NEXTSim is included on the CD-ROM at the back of this book.

ASSESSMENT

The CD-ROM accompanying this book also includes a limited version of CoursePrep, an exam prep product that replicates the actual MCSE exam environment. CoursePrep can be used to prepare you fully for the MCSE certification exam.

HARDWARE REQUIREMENTS

You will need three systems to complete the exercises in this manual. Each system will need a Pentium 166 (or better) processor, 128 MB (or more) of RAM, a minimum of a 2-GB hard disk partitioned as at least two disk partitions, a CD-ROM drive, an SVGA monitor, a network adapter, and network connection hardware. All data on these systems will be overwritten during the exercises. You will also need the Windows 2000 Server installation files.

INSTRUCTOR'S MATERIALS

The following supplemental materials are available to Instructors who use this book in a classroom environment:

- **Electronic Instructor's Manual.** The Instructor's Manual which accompanies this book includes:
    - Additional instructional material to assist in class preparation, including suggestions for lecture topics, suggested lab activities, tips on setting up the lab for hands-on assignments, and alternative lab setup ideas in situations where lab resources are limited
    - Solutions to all extra materials, including the Review Questions, Hands-on Projects, and Case Projects found in the Special Supplemental Exercises section
- **Course Test Manager 1.3.** Accompanying this book is a pwerful assessment tool known as the Course Test Manager. Designed by Course Technology, this cutting-edge Windows-based testing software helps instructors design and administer tests and pre-tests. In addition to generating tests that can be printed and administered, this full-featured program also has an online testing component that allows students to take tests at the computer and have their tests automatically graded.

ABOUT THE CD-ROM

The CD-ROM accompanying this book includes the following software products:

- NEXTSim, an interactive simulation product that can be used to practice the concepts presented in the book
- CoursePrep, an exam-preparation program that replicates the actual MCSE exam environment

CHAPTER 1

Introduction to Design

MAJOR TOPICS

OBJECTIVES

At the completion of this chapter, you will be able to:

- Describe the basic procedures involved in network design.
- List and describe network components and resources.
- Describe key business information required during network design.
- Describe guidelines for forming a design team.
- Compare and contrast turn-key implementation and phased implementation.
- Describe significant budget concerns as they relate to network design and implementation.
- List and describe what should be included in network design goals.
- List and describe common business models.
- Compare and contrast centralized and decentralized management models.
- Compare and contrast workgroups, Windows NT domains, and Active Directory domains.
- List and describe common network topologies.
- List and describe common network protocols.
- Describe the information-gathering process.

PRE-TEST QUESTIONS

The answers to these questions are in Appendix A at the end of this manual.

1. What is meant by the term *cable plant*?

2. Why are business relationships with other organizations significant to network design?

3. What are advantages of having an interdepartmental network design team?

4. Why is logon security important to your network design?

5. Which of the following network models uses decentralized security management?
   - A. Workgroup
   - B. Windows NT domain
   - C. Active Directory domain

6. What protocol is required for Internet access or implementation of Internet technologies in a private intranet?

INTRODUCTION

Whether building a new network from the ground up or updating an existing network, network design can be an overwhelming task if not managed properly. For most organizations, the network has become a critical part of how they do business. A poorly designed and poorly implemented network can have a significant impact on a company's profitability.

The purpose of this chapter is to provide a few basics to get you started thinking critically about the design process. Later chapters will look at the design process in much more detail, focusing individually on different business and network components.

The chapter opens with an overview of the design process. You will be introduced to some fundamental concerns relating to network design, some of the basic activities you will be required to perform, and guidelines for implementing your design. Most of this discussion will focus specifically on network concerns.

From there, you are introduced to a broader view of the design process. You will be shown the significance of understanding not only your network model and its goals, but your organization's business model and its goals as well. This will also include guidelines for creating a network design team and the importance of having different departments or divisions within your organization represented during the process.

The focus then shifts back to the network with an overview of some information that should already be at least somewhat familiar to you. You are going to be introduced to the network security and physical models that will be referenced during the course. This includes an introduction to common Local Area Network (LAN) topologies and protocols.

Some time is spent discussing, as an overview, the information-gathering process. This is meant as a brief introduction, with more details relating to specific requirements to be presented in later chapters. You will also be introduced to a set of case studies that will be used during scenario-based learning activities throughout the course.

DESIGN PROCESS

Network design is often a long and very involved process. Let's start with a few fundamentals. The following topics are covered in this section:

- About Network Design
- Basic Activities
- After the Design

For now, the discussion is going to remain at an overview level as a general introduction. You'll get more detail as you continue through this chapter and through the course as a whole.

About Network Design

Network design is a little like planning a trip. You (hopefully) know where you are and you have a general idea of where you are heading. The difficult part is figuring out how to get there. You want to find the best possible route, but you have to consider factors that are going to influence your selection. Often, compromises are required along the way.

The same is true of network design. You need to know where you are, where you are going, and how to get there. One of the most common reasons why problems arise is that network design isn't given the emphasis it deserves. There is an understandable rush to get to implementation as quickly as possible. Unfortunately, this often means having to go back and make changes after the fact. If the changes can be identified and made before you get to the implementation phase, you're going to save time, money, effort, and your sanity.

Where You Are

Figuring out where you are isn't as simple a task as you might think. Many networks and many businesses have something in common: they've grown up organically. In other words, there may have been a general plan in place, but for the most part, they've grown up in bits and pieces with little control. Changes have been made on the fly to meet changing conditions. Personnel changes can mean changing visions and goals. Unfortunately, these visions and goals aren't always well communicated, and when personnel leave, their plans and schemes leave with them.

Of course, there's also a reason why the network is there in the first place. The only valid justification for having a network is that it supports your organization. This means that you are also going to have to understand organizational requirements and goals.

That said, you probably have a general idea of where you stand. That's a good place to start, but you're going to need detailed, accurate information before and during the design process. The better your information, the better your design.

About Your Network

Believe it or not, this is probably going to be the easy part. Of course, easy can be a relative term. It's probably a safe assumption that you are more a technical expert than a business expert, though the two don't have to be mutually exclusive. However, most people who deal with networks on a day-to-day basis have some grounding in computer and network technologies.

Poorly documented networks are a fact of life. In the rush to get the network connected and keep it running, documentation tends to be a low-priority afterthought. Even if the documentation is there, it is often incomplete and out of date.

You are going to need to know everything you can about your network, including the following:

- Servers

  Servers are at the core of your network. They provide resources to client workstations and, in the most common network models, are the control point for centralized security management.

- Client workstations

  With Windows-family operating systems, the line tends to blur between client and server machines. The main function of client systems is to give users access to network resources and services. However, clients can also provide services to the network and host shared resources.

- Protocols

  Protocols are the *languages* used when computers communicate over a network. Your network may host multiple protocols, but TCP/IP is generally recognized as the de facto standard for PC networks.

- Topologies

  Topologies describe how computers are linked together in the network. In a large network, especially one that has grown up over time, you may be supporting multiple topologies.

- Cable plant and connection hardware

  The cable plant and connection hardware make up the physical path network systems communicate over. The cable plant refers to the media used to connect systems. Traditionally, this has meant copper or fiber-optic cabling, but wireless communication methods have gained some popularity in recent years. Connectivity devices are used for connecting the transmission media. Common examples are repeaters, switches, bridges, and routers.

- Software and data

  When you think about network components, the tendency is to focus on hardware components only. This is a mistake. Operating systems, user applications, and shared data files are also network components, even if they aren't separate physical devices.

You need to know both the current components that make up your network and how they are related. In a large enterprise networking environment, you are probably going to need some help in gathering all of the information that you need.

Windows-family operating systems provide tools, such as the Windows Diagnostics tool, that can help you inventory individual systems. Products such as Microsoft Systems Management Server can be used to help document and maintain network PCs.

About Your Business

Along with your network, you need to take a close look at your organization and its business practices. Don't be afraid to ask questions or request additional clarification if you're not sure you understand the terms or concepts that you are exposed to during the design or implementation process.

Just like gathering information about your network, you're going to need to collect a lot of information about your organization, including the following:

- Company model

  This includes how your company is organized, its management structure, and so forth. Issues such as whether your company has a centralized or decentralized management structure can become important during the design process. So can issues such as whether work is done based on strict divisional boundaries or if work groups crossing multiple divisions are the rule.

- Geographic distribution

  The locations of any branch or subsidiary offices are going to have a major impact on your network design. You need to determine how communications with remote locations are going to be managed, which often means finding your best compromise between performance and cost.

- Company processes

  This is everything about how your company does business and how information flows through the organization. You are going to have to identify mission-critical activities to ensure that they get the resources that they need. An additional benefit to this analysis is that you will often find ways to improve business processes.

- Relationships

  You need to understand not only who your company does business with, but how information flows between your company and your vendors, partners, and customers. You need to know how they currently communicate with your company and any proposed communication changes that need to be included in the network design.

- Planned changes

  A large number of items can be included in this category. The company's projected growth will have to be reflected in network expansion plans. This includes growth through acquisition, which can include its own special challenges, such as having to integrate different network types.

- Information Technology (IT) management

  Once again, you need to be concerned about both the current management model and any projected changes. Issues such as approval processes, funding, and change management are all critical to designing and implementing a new network model.

This is just a partial list. The complete list, just like the data you collect, is going to be somewhat specific to your organization.

It's very likely that this is an area where you are going to need to ask a lot of questions. You don't necessarily have to be an expert in your business and its requirements, but you are going to want to work with someone who is.

Where You Are Going

Typically, the goal is to change–this usually means either upgrading or adding to–an existing network. You need to have a clear understanding of the changes that are to be made. This is at the core of your design document. In other words, if you don't know where you're going, you're never going to figure out how to get there.

As a starting point, here are some of the most common changes you will encounter:

- Software

  At minimum, you can expect new operating systems. This is one of the most common reasons for making changes to your existing network design. You want to make sure that you're getting the most out of new network and client operating systems.

  You may also be dealing with new user applications at the same time. Typically, you will want to avoid upgrading both operating systems and applications at the same time. Try to keep the variables to a minimum to make it easy to isolate the causes should any problems arise.

- System hardware

  New operating systems often require bringing in new servers. At the very least, you will probably find yourself upgrading existing servers. Hardware requirements for new operating system and server applications tend to increase with each release.

- Communication media

  As users come to rely more on the network and as data file sizes increase, so does the need for additional bandwidth. This is especially a problem with wide-area links, which tend to have a lower available bandwidth than local-area connections.

  You may also find that while you are upgrading the rest of the network is a good time to upgrade older cable plants. If the current network relies heavily on coaxial cable, you will probably find it cost effective in the long run to migrate to twisted-pair cable. You might also want to consider fiber optic for especially high-volume applications, such as network backbones. However, the cost of fiber optic continues to be prohibitive, in most cases, for making connections to user workstations.

A network is going to be a reflection of the organization that it supports and the physical environment it is implemented in. Networking is definitely not a one-size-fits-all world. While you may want to look at other implementations of technologies that you plan to use as a way of getting ideas and suggestions, keep in mind that you are probably going to have to make modifications before it fits your particular needs.

Just like the current network, your planned network must be defined in detail and carefully documented. This will help you identify potential problems and help you ensure that everything is in place before you start implementation. It also means that your network will already be documented when it goes into place. Of course, you will have to update the network documentation on a regular basis if you want it to remain accurate.

How to Get There

This is usually the trickiest part. It can be a difficult balancing act whether you are migrating an existing network or implementing a new network. It is very likely that compromises are going to have to be made along the way. Innovations can come along that weren't available during the design process. Business plans can change to meet changing realities.

This doesn't give you an excuse to not develop a complete implementation plan. You will, however, have to be ready to modify your plan based on business requirements and applicable technological improvements. When making these changes, they must be documented and you must evaluate how they impact the implementation plan as a whole.

Basic Activities

The design and implementation process can be broken down into a series of activities. You probably already have a good idea of what these are. The activities include the following:

- Selecting the design team
- Gathering information
- Compiling the information
- Creating a plan
- Approving the plan
- Implementation

You may find that you have to go back and forth between creating a plan and getting approval a few times before you are ready for implementation. While in most organizations the final approval will lie somewhere with upper management, you are going to want to build acceptance for the plan at all levels of the organization. The more that everyone feels as if they are involved in the planning process, the more likely they are to accept the new network when it is in place.

After the Design

One important factor is going to be your implementation schedule. You have two basic choices. You can either plan on a complete *turn-key* changeover or a gradual phased implementation plan.

Turn-Key Implementation

This option can be tempting. It entails all of the users logging off of one network on Friday and logging back on to a completely new and upgraded network on Monday. This is similar to what Microsoft did when changing all of their corporate servers over to Windows 2000.

Even though tempting, this simply is not feasible for most organizations. The personnel requirements alone are more than most organizations can meet. In addition, you have to worry about what you are going to do if anything goes wrong during the conversion. You may be able to do some limited testing and should do all that you can, but full-scale tests are probably going to be out of the question. You are going to need to have a recovery plan in place as a just-in-case measure. The problem is, are you going to have the personnel and other resources you need to revert back to your old network configuration?

Apart from having the personnel resources available to do the necessary work, you also have to worry about cost. You will have to have everything in place and ready to go beforehand. You will probably want to have spares on hand for critical equipment should you encounter any failures.

This doesn't mean that you have to completely rule out a turn-key implementation. What you have to do, however, is make sure that it is appropriate for your organization. Typically, it is much easier to manage a turn-key implementation for a small organization due to the limited number of users and machines involved. The more complex the organization, the greater the likelihood that attempting a turn-key implementation will be more problems than it is worth.

Phased Implementation

Unless you are implementing a new network from the ground up, you are probably going to want to use a phased implementation. This approach allows you to make gradual changes and have time to test and verify that everything is working properly before moving on to the next phase.

One of the keys to a successful phased implementation is careful planning. You want to keep the impact on the end users to a minimum. You will often have to make changes after hours or during off-peak hours. Of course, even with the best implementation plans, there may be some downtime before you are finished.

DESIGN REQUIREMENTS

Now that you have a general idea of what is going to happen, you can start looking a little closer at some of the specifics. For now, the focus is going to be on some of the activities taking place early in the process. The following topics are covered in this section:

- Design Team
- Design and Implementation Planning
- Business Models
- Management Models

Other areas will be covered in more detail later in this chapter and throughout the course.

Design Team

One of the first things you need to do is select your design team. At least this would be your first step in an ideal world. Let's start with what might happen before looking at what you want to happen. With any luck, you may be able to find a workable compromise somewhere between the two.

No Team

In this scenario, some general goals and guidelines are handed down from above, and you are tasked with coming up with a new network design. You have yourself (and your staff, if any) available as resources for coming up with the design.

The drawbacks to this are obvious. The time and personnel resources available for gathering information are going to be very limited. You are also likely to have a limited perspective, focusing more on technical issues than on business-related issues. The problem isn't that you are not willing to gather the information you need, but that you may not know all of the questions that you need to ask.

There is at least one advantage, as well, especially if you are solely responsible for the design: there's going to be less of a chance of design committee meetings getting bogged down in arguments.

Delegated Team

In this scenario, the team is picked for you and assigned the design project. While usually an improvement over doing everything yourself, this still isn't an ideal situation. How well this is going to work will rely heavily on how well the person picking the design team does his or her work.

Even though you have more resources in this scenario, the team itself can be a disadvantage. If the persons delegated to the team aren't motivated and don't take an active role, they are going to be more of a liability than an asset. Teams created in this manner often contain people who look like they have the time available and aren't necessarily the most appropriate ones to be taking part in the design process.

You do have the advantage of a somewhat broader perspective with a team of this type. If you can get (and keep) the team members motivated to help, you'll have additional resources available that can be assigned information-gathering tasks in their areas of expertise.

Selected Team

If done right, and with proper organizational and management support, this scenario represents your best option for creating a design team. You select personnel from different departments or divisions representing different viewpoints and areas of expertise.

A team of this type gives you a more broad-based view of network requirements. It gives you a way of picking the people who either already have the answer you need or at least know the right questions to ask and where to get the information. If you give team members the option of whether they want to take part, you have a better assurance of at least some level of motivation.

Of course, there are also potential drawbacks. The most obvious one is that you won't be able to get everyone that you want involved on the design team. The best people are usually also the busiest and simply may not have time to take part. If not, have them suggest someone as an alternative. Second best is still better than none at all. You are also going to find yourself having to make compromises throughout the process. Even if you have been supplied with an overall goal, there is often still a lot of room within that goal for personal needs and requests.

Team Suggestions

The team you put together is going to be like the network you are designing. It is going to be specific to your organization and its overall requirements. With that in mind, here are a few suggestions to help you get started. Your design team should include the following:

- Technical personnel

  This one is obvious. You are going to need people who understand both the current technology and the technology that you want to implement. If they don't know the new technology, then they are going to have to learn.

  You are going to want to have all of your network administration and support personnel involved with the process at some level. Even if you don't use their ideas, they need to be given an opportunity to express them. After all, these are the people who will be supporting the new network design.

- Operations personnel

  Operations personnel can take a different definition with different organizations. For the purposes of this course, operations personnel refers to the personnel responsible for all of the organization's support systems, such as phone systems and the network.

  You may think that by including network technical personnel that operations is well represented. This is somewhat true, but you need to bring in persons responsible for other services for their input in how the new network design may impact the company as a whole. Also, operations personnel are often a good source for an accurate description of how information flows within an organization.

- Division representatives

  If at all possible, you are going to want to have each department or division within your company represented. These representatives can let you know how each division is currently using the network and changes that they would like to see made. Focus on items such as software requirements, accessibility needs, and data files.

- Typical end users

  End users are often completely left out of the design process. The thought is that end users have little technical background and don't really understand the technologies that they are using, so their input would be of questionable value.

  However, ignoring end users is a mistake. If the end users aren't kept informed and don't feel as if they have any *ownership* of the network, they aren't going to be happy with its performance. Minor problems are going to be blown into major catastrophes, and anything that happens is going to be blamed on the new network–network related or not.

- Outside consultant

  Your view on outside consultants is going to be influenced by your past experiences and where you sit on the fence. As a network administrator or manager, you may see an outside consultant as an invader in your personal space. If you are a consultant, then you are obviously going to think that a consultant is a good idea.

  If you are implementing unfamiliar technologies or aren't sure what technologies you need to meet your networking requirements, then you should consider involving an outside consultant. At the very least, you may want to use someone to help lay some of the groundwork and get you pointed in the right direction. Keep in mind, however, that there's nothing to keep *anyone* from calling him- or herself a consultant. Get referrals from people that you know and trust before investing part of your budget in outside help.

It would be to your advantage if you can get someone in upper management or at a level where decisions can be made involved on at least an advisory level. This is especially true if the final decision is going to be made by some type of management committee. That way, you would have at least one person on your side going in to the final decision process.

Design and Implementation Planning

You can think of this somewhat as designing your design process. There's some preparation work that has to be done before you start designing the network. You need to decide who is going to be involved in the design process. You need to get input from the final decision makers as to their expectations and any constraints they are placing on the network design.

Understanding the Design Process

Make sure that everyone involved understands the design process and what is required at each phase. This includes the following:

- Information gathering

  You should have a general idea by now of the type of information you are going to need. Make sure that everyone involved with the design team is aware of what is needed and match personnel to the types of information that needs to be collected. Don't forget that this is going to involve both technical and nontechnical information.

- Design

  Once you have a goal in mind and your network and business information in hand, you can start the design process. You need to go into the design process expecting that your first design, and probably your first few designs, are *not* going to represent your best potential solution. Once you have the design team's approval, you still probably have to face the final decision makers. Be ready to justify your design, possibly in great detail, if asked.

- Implementation

  Once the design is approved, you can start getting the components (hardware and software) in place and begin the implementation process. You should remember from the earlier discussion about implementation that a phased implementation is likely going to be the best solution for most organizations. Be ready to revise your plans as necessary.

- Management

  Ongoing management is a fact of life. Immediately after making changes to your network, you'll find that you want to keep a closer eye on network activity than usual. Careful monitoring will be critical. The earlier you can catch any potential problems, the easier they'll be to fix. Also, the feedback you receive from early phases in the implementation may cause you to modify later phases and may force you to rethink major portions of your design.

Plan on personnel changes as you move through different phases of the process. Different skills are going to be required during each phase.

Budget

Sooner or later, money is going to rear its ugly head during the process. You will probably encounter one of the following as your general budgetary guideline:

- How much do you need?

  In this case, the responsibility is placed on you and your team to tell the decision makers how much it's going to cost. They may accept your budget numbers as is, or they may have you go back and re-evaluate the design to see where you can save additional money.

  While this does give you greater freedom in your planning, it also means that you *own* the budget. If you go over budget, you and your team will be expected to take full responsibility since you were the ones who provided the numbers.

- Here's what you have

  This is the more common scenario. You are given general goals and guidelines, then given a maximum budget for implementation. This often means that you are going to spend much of the design process finding compromises between the best-possible technical solution and the amount of money you have available for implementing it.

  Don't think that because the budget was handed to you that you are removed from all responsibility. If there are shortcomings in the new network design or if the project goes over budget, it's still your project and your responsibility.

Either way, coming in at or under budget is generally considered good; coming in over budget is generally considered bad. Designing and implementing a network is a major project. For organizations that use annual performance reviews, you will probably find your review (and raise) directly impacted by how you stay within time and cost constraints.

Staying on Budget

Staying on budget typically means a series of compromises. You are going to have to separate out what you need to do and what you want to do. Set the want-tos aside and forget them for now. You can come back to them later if you have money left in the budget.

Next, set priorities on your need-tos. Critical requirements come first. Less-critical requirements need to fall later on the list. You may find that you simply cannot accomplish all of the goals within the task with the budget you've been provided. This often happens when the persons setting both the goals and the budget have little understanding of the technologies involved or their costs. At this point, your negotiation skills are going to have to come into play.

Negotiating the Project

When you cannot meet your goals within the budget provided, something has to change. Either the goals have to be scaled back or the budget is going to have to be increased.

You need to come into these negotiations well armed with facts. You need to provide costs involved and the benefits expected from the technology solutions. Make sure that you explain the potential pitfalls of scaling back on the technology side to reduce costs.

From a technical standpoint, you're probably not going to get everything you want. Through careful explanation and negotiation, however, you might be able to get everything that you need.

Design Goals

Make sure that you fully understand the design goals before starting the design process. This may seem obvious, but if the design goals are being provided for you, you may find that there are gaps that need to be filled in. Some of these might be left to your discretion, or you may need to go back to the decision makers for additional guidelines. Before going back, you may find that you need to educate the decision makers in some basic technological concepts.

At minimum, the design goals should include the following:

- Functionality
- Security
- Performance and Availability

Let's take a closer look at each of these.

Functionality

In simple terms, once everything is in place, it has to work and it has to work right. However, these criteria need to be clearly defined. You need to know the functionality that is going to be required and how it will be determined, whether or not the functionality requirements are going to be met. Some key issues will include the following:

- User applications

  You need to know what user applications are going to be required, how they are going to be distributed, and how they are going to be maintained.

- Server applications

  Server applications include applications such as Microsoft's SQL Server. You need to determine the resources required to implement and support server-based applications.

- Network services

  Network services is a blanket description for a wide range of services. These can include automated address assignment (DHCP), name resolution, logon validation, remote access, Internet access, and so forth.

Network accessibility is also a key functionality issue but deserves separate mention. Accessibility issues are discussed later in this section.

Security

Security should be a critical issue for any organization. Network security can cover a number of different areas, including the following:

- Logon authentication

  This is the foundation of your network security. There are several potential issues that must be considered here, such as whether to audit logon attempts, how (or if) you will implement intruder lockout, and what types of password policies are going to be required.

- Access security

  There are going to be both local data access and shared data access concerns that must be considered. You must determine the level of protection that is going to be required and how it is going to be implemented.

- Data encryption

  You may find that you want to implement data encryption to ensure even more secure protection of confidential or mission-critical files. You may have to adjust how widespread encryption is implemented based on its impact on network performance.

- Data transmissions

  You need to determine if data encryption is necessary during data transmission. This is usually less of a concern in a local area network environment but can be a critical concern when wide-area links are involved since you have less control over media security.

- Internet access

  How, or even if, you provide Internet access for your users is going to be a critical issue. There is also the issue of allowing access from the Internet into network servers.

Unfortunately, security issues may not get attention until after a problem is discovered. By then, the damage has already been done and all you can do is try to prevent further damage or unauthorized disclosure.

Performance and Availability

Availability and performance tend to go hand in hand. From the standpoint of the end users, these are usually the most critical network issues. Availability simply refers to the users having access to the network and network resources. This is a function of network uptime and availability of connections across wide-area links.

Performance refers to how well the network responds to service requests, such as a request to open and retrieve a data file. There are a large number of variables that can impact network performance, such as server performance, client workstation performance, available network bandwidth, and so forth.

Business Models

It's probably a safe assumption that you're going through this course either to prepare for a certification exam or to get the information you need for a real-world design problem. Either way, your experience probably runs more toward the technical side, or network administration and support, than the business side. With this in mind, let's spend a little time talking about business models.

In truth, there are a lot of variables involved in describing a business model, and it is very seldom that a generic model can be used as a completely accurate description of a business. What you are being provided with here are some general terms, concepts, and guidelines for developing business models, not specific models that you should attempt to apply to your organization.

Sample Models

There are a wide range of potential organizational models that can be used to describe how you do business. Many organizations are actually a hybrid of one or more of these models, meaning that you have to address multiple types of concerns.

This discussion will be limited to a few generalized business models. Later in this chapter, you will be looking at some case studies based on fictitious companies that will help you see a little more about how these models can be applied in *real-world* situations. For the purpose of this course, the focus will be on the following models:

- Service Based
- Manufacturing and Product Development
- Wholesale Warehousing
- Retail Sales

You can probably already see where some of the overlaps can occur. A small manufacturing company may sell its products directly to consumers. A large retail organization may also be involved with warehousing and wholesaling products to other retailers.

Overlapping with the business model is the organizational model. This is similar but focuses on the management model and company organization. This also includes relationships with partners, suppliers, and customers. Both the business model and organizational model must be considered in your network design.

Before moving on to management models, let's take a little closer look at each of these.

Service Based

Service-based organizations is a very broad category, taking in everything from dry cleaners to auto repair and financial organizations. Their requirements are just as varied.

Some companies, dry cleaners, for example, will likely have limited network requirements. They will focus on controller work flow and accounting. They may have few, if any, remote access requirements. Security will be a concern, but not as serious a concern as for many other organizations. Availability may also be less of a concern. Many organizations continue to duplicate their efforts through *paper-and-pencil* tracking, back posting from hard-copy invoices.

Organizations such as financial organizations typically fall at the other end of the spectrum. Remote communication is critical, with a need to keep in contact both with remote offices and with other related organizations. Security, availability, and reliability are going to be critical concerns with no margin for error.

Manufacturing and Product Development

In a manufacturing company, you will often find that you have a wide range of requirements that must be met. One obvious requirement is inventory control for both incoming raw materials and components as well as completed products. One concern that may not be quite so obvious is the need for security. Build lists, material costs, and cost of goods sold are all confidential, mission-critical pieces of information. So are any product design and development plans.

There is typically a significant requirement for remote communications. The organization will need to be in contact with both its suppliers and its customers. Many manufacturing companies also use remote salespeople who need periodic dial-in access.

Wholesale Warehousing

A wholesaler is the middle tier between the manufacturer and the retailer. That means a wholesale company needs secure communications with both, as well as with its field sales and in-house sales personnel. Often, multiple warehouse locations are involved, and inventory orders and customer shipments must be carefully coordinated.

One of the major challenges in this type of organization is identifying information flows since there is so much information going in so many different directions. Real-time accuracy on inventory, invoices, shipments, and such is critical.

Retail Sales

Most people are at least somewhat familiar with this model. Much of the network focus is going to be on inventory control and processing retail sales. The need for sharing information between multiple locations is common. Most retail sales organizations now also support some type of Internet-based sales.

Data access is going to be a major concern in an organization of this type. Data access requirements are typically task related. For example, check-out associates usually just need access to the selling price and possibly to on-hand inventory. Management personnel need to be able to change prices and may need access to employee records.

Management Models

There are two basic management models, though many organizations employ a combination of the two. The basic models are as follows:

- Centralized management

  Centralized management means that there is one central point of control. Specific management tasks are usually delegated to different managers and administrators, but each task is managed from one point for the organization as a whole.

- Decentralized management

  In decentralized management, administrative tasks may be delegated at any level. While this often means less control over management functions, it can allow an organization to respond more quickly to changing conditions.

It's not uncommon to see a mix of management models used. An organization might use tightly controlled centralized management for most activities but allow each department or working group to control access to its own data.

You will need to reflect the business management model, at least to some extent, in your network management model. More specifically, the network must be configured to support the business model, setting security limits to match management responsibilities.

NETWORK MODELS

This is an area where you should be a little more comfortable. Along with the business model, you must carefully consider both the current and proposed network models. The following topics are covered in this section:

- Security Models
- Physical Models
- Network Design Impact

The business model and the network model are going to have a direct impact on each other. Always keep in mind that the network is there to support the business, not the other way around.

Security Models

Basic security issues were discussed to some extent earlier in this chapter. You need to identify your network security requirements and ensure that they are properly implemented. In the process, you want to keep security as transparent to the end user as possible. Use security to control end-user access, but avoid getting the user directly involved in security issues.

The security model you implement is going to be determined by your network resources and security requirements. The Microsoft Windows family supports the following three basic security models:

- Workgroups
- Windows NT Domains
- Active Directory Domains

Let's take a closer look at each of these models.

Workgroups

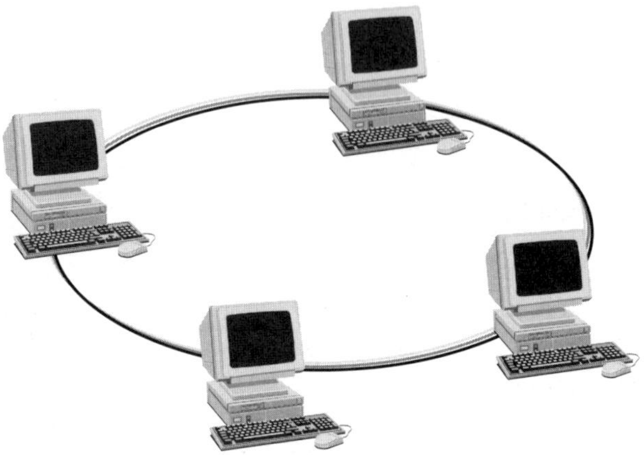

If you've ever dealt with workgroups in Windows 95/98 or Windows NT, you're familiar with the network design shown above. Workgroups, also known as peer-to-peer networks, are effectively the same under Windows 2000.

A workgroup will include two or more systems, typically made up of Windows 2000 Professional systems or a mix of Windows 2000 Professional systems and Windows 2000 Servers. This model is easy to implement when supporting a small number of technically competent users.

One of the distinctive features of a workgroup is that management is decentralized, including security management. Each system has its own list of users and groups. Each system manages its own security rights and permissions. Changes made to one computer, such as adding a new user that you want all of the systems to recognize, must be made to all of the computers in the workgroup. This can cause you to quickly reach a point where security is unmanageable.

Windows NT Domains

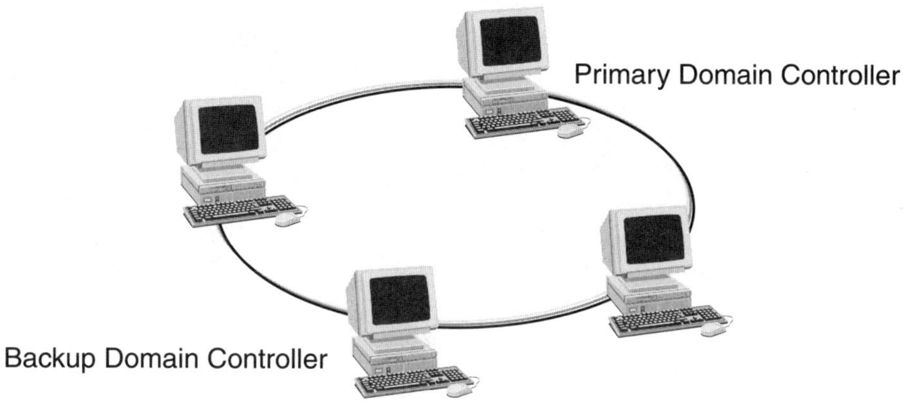

You should already be familiar with Windows NT domains. A Windows NT domain will have a Primary Domain Controller (PDC) and will typically have one or more Backup Domain Controllers (BDCs). The rest of the systems are configured as domain workstations. In this context, member servers are being included as part of the general workstation category.

Management is somewhat centralized in a Windows NT domain. Users and groups are managed at the domain level, specifically at the PDC, and copied out to the BDCs. Due to inherent limitations in the domain controllers, large enterprises often require that multiple domains be established and multiple trust relationships be set up between the domains to support logon and access to each other's resources.

Management is considered to be only *somewhat* centralized because resources are still tied very closely to individual systems. When a user wants to access a resource, not only does the user need appropriate access permissions, but he or she must also know which computer the resource is located on. Browsing to find resources can be a daunting task in a large enterprise environment.

Active Directory Domains

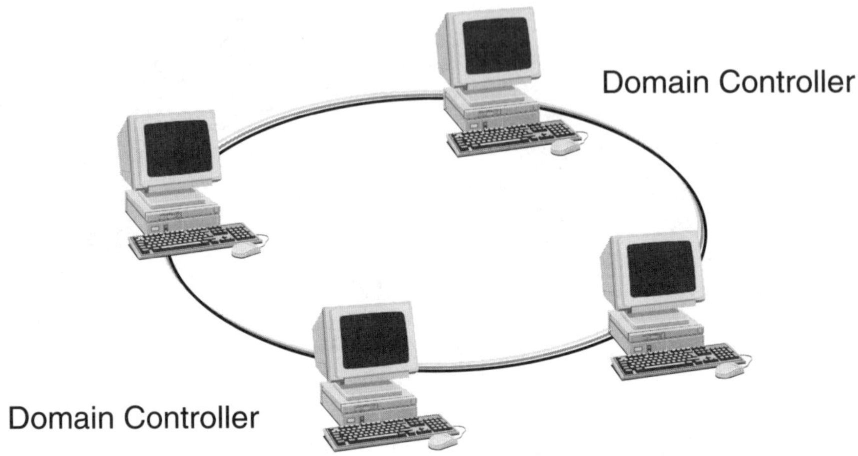

Moving to Windows 2000, you have to forget what you know about domains. Domains have been restructured and redefined. Rather than being identified with the PDC and its BDCs, a Windows 2000 Active Directory domain is based around a central directory database that contains information about all domain objects. The old definitions of PDC and BDC are gone and are replaced by domain controllers that carry copies of the central directory. Changes made to any one of the domain controllers are automatically replicated out to the rest of the domain controllers.

The remaining systems are domain members and can include Windows 2000 Servers configured as member servers. Domain members, including Windows 2000 member servers, do not store directory information.

This new domain model provides centralized management for networks ranging from small LANs to large enterprise networks. The central directory contains not only the users and groups, but all network-shared resources as well. Users no longer need to know where a resource is physically located, but do need to know where it can be found in the directory. Resources can be organized and grouped based on nearly any logical design, making them easy for users to locate. A directory can potentially grow to contain millions of objects.

Physical Models

The physical model describes how computers are connected and how they communicate. This includes the network topology and network protocols. For now, the focus will be on LAN models. Wide Area Network (WAN) models will be introduced later in the course.

The topology is the physical connection between network devices. Your topology selection will be used to determine your transmission media. The network protocol is the *language* used when computers communicate. There are actually two levels of protocols you need to concern yourself with: the low-level access protocol and the higher-level transmission protocol. There may also be a need for remote access protocol support.

Topology

Despite a number of changes in network technology seen in the past few years, most networks still use one of the following topology types:

- Bus
- Ring
- Star

There are other network topologies defined, but most of these are used in specialized applications and are seldom seen in LAN configurations.

Bus Topology

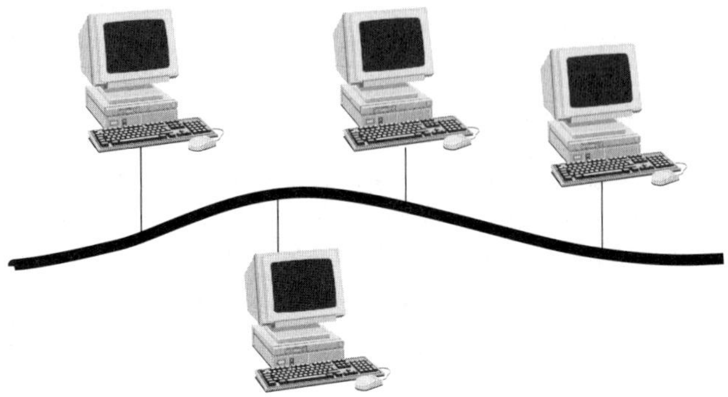

In a bus topology, all network devices connect to a single central communication path. All network devices have equal access to the transmission media, which can lead to a problem of collisions when two or more devices attempt to communicate simultaneously.

Traditionally, this was the preferred topology for Ethernet-based networks, using a coaxial cable as the transmission medium. A bus topology is still sometimes used for backbone applications but is typically only used for device connections in legacy networks.

Ring Topology

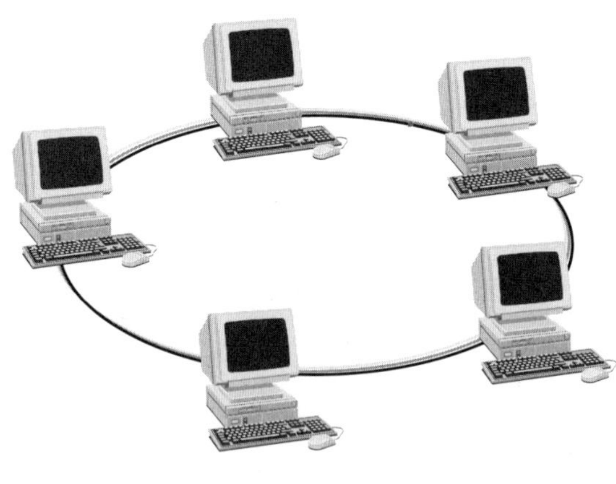

In a ring topology, network devices are connected by one loop, or two loops in some fiber-optic implementations to provide added fault tolerance. Network access and control passes from system to system. Token Ring and FDDI networks operate as rings, though Token-Ring networks are typically wired in such a way as to appear to use a star topology.

Star Topology

In a star topology, network devices connect to central points. These central points can be hubs, switches, or Multistation Access Units (MSAUs). The star topology has become the de facto standard for LAN connections in recent years. It is used with 10BaseT Ethernet. In most applications, Token Ring is also connected in a physical star topology, even though network devices communicate in a ring.

There any many reasons for the star topology's popularity. A star topology is relatively inexpensive to install and to maintain. It is also easy to isolate and makes it easy to identify network failures.

Protocols

For now, the focus is going to be on two types of protocols. These are access protocols and transport (communications) protocols. Both are required for network communications.

Access Protocols

Access protocols are low-level protocols describing the basic requirements for systems to communicate. The two most common access protocols that you are likely to encounter are Ethernet and Token Ring. Of the two, Ethernet is by far the most popular.

For two systems to be able to communicate, both systems must be using the same access protocol. The access protocol you are using is set by the network adapter type installed in network systems. An Ethernet network adapter supports Ethernet communications only, and a Token-Ring network adapter only supports Token Ring.

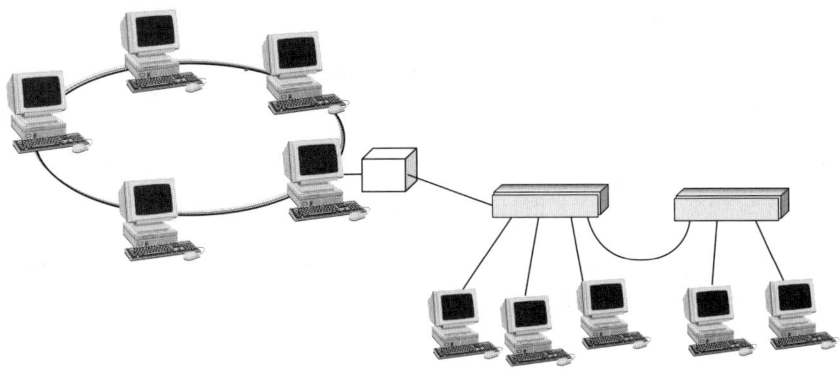

All network devices on a single cable segment will be running the same access protocol. You can, however, bridge between segments running different access protocols, allowing them to communicate.

If at all possible, you are going to want to have all of your network segments running the same access protocol. Running different network protocols adds to your network management overhead. As mentioned before, you want to keep things as simple as possible.

Of course, this isn't always going to be possible. One of the most common causes for having to support multiple access protocols is growth through acquisition. In other words, you may have standardized on Ethernet, but you may have inherited a Token-Ring network that must be integrated into your overall network plan. Even in this situation, you will probably find it cost effective in the long run to eventually migrate the Token-Ring network to your standard Ethernet unless there is a pressing reason why you cannot do so.

Transport Protocols

You will also see the term *communication protocols* used to describe these protocols. These are also what usually come to mind first when the term *protocol* is mentioned. Windows-family operating systems, as well as other PC operating systems, are capable of supporting multiple transport protocols simultaneously.

Common protocols supported by Windows-family operating systems include the following:

- Transport Control Protocol/Internet Protocol (TCP/IP)

  This is the de facto standard for both local- and wide-area networking. This is a routable protocol that gives you a great deal of flexibility in your network design. TCP/IP is required for connectivity with the Internet or to implement Internet technologies on your private network.

- NWLink (IPX/SPX emulation)

  NWLink is Microsoft's implementation of Novell's IPX/SPX protocol. NWLink is required, along with NetWare client software, for communication with NetWare servers running IPX/SPX. NWLink is also required for servers providing services to NetWare clients running IPX/SPX as their only transport protocol.

- NetBIOS Enhanced User Interface (NetBEUI)

  NetBEUI support is provided primarily for communications with legacy support. NetBEUI requires minimal system resources but is designed primarily for small LAN implementations. One of the biggest limitations to NetBEUI is that it does not support routing.

- Data Link Control (DLC)

  DLC was designed to support mainframe communications and is still sometimes used to support communications between PCs and mainframe systems. More often, it has been used for communications with Hewlett-Packard (HP) printers connected directly to the network. It is only required on systems acting as print servers and communicating directly with these printers. More recently, it has become more common for network-connected printers to use TCP/IP rather than DLC as their transport protocol.

- Infrared Data Association (IrDA)

  IrDA is provided here as a reference but is not really applicable for network communications. That doesn't mean that it won't apply somehow to your network. It is commonly used for direct communications with laptop systems, handheld computers, palm-top computers, Personal Digital Assistants (PDAs), and digital cameras.

- AppleTalk

  AppleTalk is a routable protocol used for communications with Apple Macintosh computers. AppleTalk is only required if you need to provide support for Macintosh computers or networks. AppleTalk is supported on Windows 2000 Server systems but not on Windows 2000 Professional systems.

Unlike access protocols, you can support multiple transport protocols on the same cable segment. Two network devices must share at least one common transport protocol in order to communicate. In most cases, you will probably find yourself using TCP/IP as your default–and eventually as your only–protocol.

Network Design Impact

You need to be aware of all access and transport protocols being used on your current network. Once you've done this, you may find that you need to make some changes to improve network efficiency and reduce your management overhead.

Just because you can run multiple transport protocols doesn't mean that you necessarily want to. As you upgrade existing systems or add new systems, only install those protocols that you actually need. This will help to minimize both system resource requirements and the level of background maintenance traffic on your network. This can be especially important over lower-bandwidth remote links.

INFORMATION GATHERING

You should be getting a pretty good idea of the information you are going to need by now. Let's shift our focus slightly and look at how you are going to collect that information and what you are going to do with it once you have it. The following topics are covered in this section:

- Collection and Analysis
- Compilation

This introduction is provided primarily at an introductory level. The course will address information gathering in more detail later in the course.

Collection and Analysis

This can be a long, involved, and tedious process. You need to collect all of the information than you can, then determine what actually applies to or influences your network design.

The Collection Process

By now, you should be able to see the importance of information gathering. You want to find out everything you can about your network, your organizational design, and data flows (both electronic and hard copy) throughout your organization.

It's somewhat likely that you are going to end up collecting more information than you really need. That doesn't mean that you need to scale back your data-collection efforts, just that you will need to filter out inappropriate or unnecessary information once collection is complete and you are preparing to move on to the design process.

The tendency during the collection process is to focus on a short-term view. You are gathering information about current conditions and immediate goals for the network. What you need to do is take a long-term view during the process or you may find that your network design is obsolescent almost as soon as it is in place.

Asking the Right Questions

This can be harder than it sounds. You need to ask questions that will generate as much information as possible. Before you start, write out what you consider to be critical questions. As you are talking to different people, write down any additional questions that come to mind. If you don't write them down, you're going to forget to ask them.

The specific questions you ask will depend on who you are asking. When talking to nontechnical personnel, be sure to word technology-related questions in a way that they can understand.

To help you get started, here are a few sample questions:

- What applications are you currently running?
- What applications do you think you will need in the near future?
- When do you or your users need access to the network?
- When do you or your users *not* need access to the network?
- What data do you maintain that is unique to your department?
- What data do you maintain or access that is shared with other departments?
- What performance problems have you experienced?
- What types of errors have you experienced recently?
- What information do you currently track through hard copy that you would prefer to keep on the network?
- What are your short- and long-term expansion plans?

These should give you a general idea of the types of questions that you are going to be asking. Of course, the questions you need to ask are going to be specific to your organization.

Asking the Right People

In an ideal world, you would be able to talk to every person in your organization to get their input on current processes, suggested changes, and long-term goals. Unfortunately, you are not going to have unlimited time for the information-gathering process. You are going to need to gather everything you can, as quickly as you can, and make your decisions on the information you have available.

In a small organization, talking to everyone might be a possibility. In most organizations, this would be an inefficient use of your available time. Instead, you need to select key persons that can provide the information you need. These can include the following:

- Technical personnel

  You might wonder about this one initially. After all, you are going to have technical personnel involved on the design team. In fact, you may have all of your network and technical personnel involved.

  The problem is that some people may not feel comfortable spontaneously expressing their ideas. Unless you're careful, it's common for one or two people to monopolize any discussion. You should seek your top technical people out individually to get their input.

- Upper-level management

  Upper-level management, if available for discussions, can provide you with a great deal of insight into business practices and the general organizational model. They will also be your best source for information about proposed changes and long-range goals.

  Keep in mind that much of the information you get from upper management will be in the form of a general overview or all-encompassing visions. It will be up to you to seek out or interpolate the details. Also, don't expect them to tell you everything they know. Some information has to be kept confidential for business or legal reasons.

- Mid- to lower-level management

  This is the level where you are going to start gathering your *nuts and bolts* information. These are the people who usually have some of the best understanding of day-to-day information requirements and data flows. They are often your best source for detailed information about short-term goals, though they may be less informed about long-term goals.

  In most cases, these are managers who realize how much they rely on the network. They have a personal interest in the changes you are going to be making and how the changes will impact their job activities.

- End users

  These are the folks that are in the trenches, using the network day in and day out. They may not be able to give you a great deal of insight into where they are going, but they can definitely tell you where they are, their current concerns, and immediate changes they would like to see made. This is your opportunity to get detailed information about what people are doing on the network.

  All too often, end users are not given an appropriate voice in the information-gathering and design process. This is a mistake. Long-term success or failure of the project may depend on how well it is accepted by the end users. If the end users aren't happy, you're going to be spending a lot of time dealing with real and imagined crises.

- Suppliers

  Changes that you make to the network don't necessarily only impact the company users. If business activities require direct communications with suppliers, you may need to bring the suppliers into the conversation at some point. They need to be aware of any changes that might directly affect them. They may also be able to provide you with suggestions on how to improve your remote access plans.

- Customers

  In most cases, you only need to discuss network changes with customers if they are going to be directly impacted by them. These are typically going to be the most difficult people to talk with, and it may not be possible to get feedback from your customers. If not, you need to talk with people who deal directly with the customers to get their impression of customer requirements.

This list is just meant to get you started. You are going to need to develop your own list of specific people you want to talk to based on your organization. Plan on this list evolving during the information-gathering process when the person you initially selected doesn't have the information you need or you need to gather additional details.

Compilation

In simple terms, compilation means putting all of the information you've gathered into a useable format. Your first step is to sift through the information and only keep information that is applicable to your network design requirements. Summarize key points into a format that can be easily distributed. This may seem like a lot of work at this point, but it will pay off in the long run.

You are going to use this information as you develop your network design. You may also need it to justify your overall network design or individual network components. You'll come to appreciate any firm numbers and statistics that you have on hand if you need to negotiate to increase the network budget.

CASE STUDIES

You will be using the case studies in this section throughout the course. They will be referenced by several scenario-based learning exercises. This course will be using, at different times, the following three different case studies, which are covered in this section:

- Things and Stuff
- Barney's Bank
- Fairco Manufacturing

You are going to be provided with a brief introduction to each of these case studies. More detailed information will be added, as necessary, in later chapters. A complete description of each case study company is provided in Appendix C at the end of the manual.

Sample answers to the questions asked at the end of each case study are provided in Appendix B at the end of the manual.

Things and Stuff

Things and Stuff is a retail sales outlet with a single location. The owner hopes to expand to different locations eventually, but there are no definite plans to do so at this time. All sales are walk-in, point-of-sale transactions.

The current network has two Windows NT servers, nine Windows NT workstations, and three Windows 98 systems. The systems are currently configured as a workgroup. The owner would like to upgrade all systems to Windows 2000 Server and Workstation but hasn't decided whether he wants to make any changes to the current LAN configuration.

1. This business is an example of which of the business models described in this chapter?

    ....

    ....

2. From the information given, what are the organization's remote access requirements?

    ....

    ....

Barney's Bank

Barney's Bank is a full-service financial institution with branch offices in various locations in the United States. Barney's Bank also has several wholly owned subsidiaries, with five different locations in Europe. The organization has traditionally grown through acquisition and plans to continue to use this as its primary growth model. Each of the remote offices has limited control over day-to-day decisions, but all major decisions are made from the main office in Corpus Christi, Texas.

From an IT standpoint, the organization is best described as a mismatched and patched-together mess. As new locations have been acquired, the existing networks have been left in place, resulting in a network management and communications nightmare. The network management staff is short-handed and overworked. The organization wants to standardize its network operations, implementing two Active Directory domains configured as part of the same forest. The company will have separate domain namespaces for the United States and Europe.

In response to its competition, Barney's Bank wants to give its users access to account information via the Internet. It is also considering using a Virtual Private Network (VPN) to connect between the main offices in the United States and Europe via the Internet.

1. Barney's Bank most closely matches which management model?

2. From the information you have available, would a turn-key or phased implementation be most appropriate for this organization?

Fairco Manufacturing

Fairco Manufacturing designs, manufactures, and distributes a wide variety of items for department stores in the United States. Sales are wholesale only to retail outlets. The organization employs a large number of outside salespeople who travel to the major customers on established routes.

Fairco Manufacturing has a large LAN configured as a Windows NT domain. Dial-in access is provided to remote warehouses in strategic locations around the country. This is the only remote communication currently in place. Field salespeople either call in, fax, or hand deliver orders to the main office where they are manually posted. Shipping delays can run from 3 to 20 days, and there is a constant problem with back orders due to out-of-stock items.

The organization wants to update and upgrade its network. In the process, it wants to streamline its operations and improve its business processes. One critical requirement is finding a way to reduce the delay between when an order is taken by the outside salesperson and when the order is shipped to the customer.

1. From the information given, what business process (if any) can be improved through use of network and remote access technology when a new network design is implemented?

   ....

   ....

2. All network systems are currently running TCP/IP and NWLink. What changes, if any, would you suggest to network protocol support?

   ....

   ....

SUMMARY

During this chapter, you were introduced to the following:

- Network design fundamentals
- Design goals
- Basic design activities
- Implementation options
- Design team requirements and guidelines
- Design process phases
- Budget concerns
- Common business models
- Common management models
- Workgroups
- Windows NT domains
- Active Directory domains
- Common network topologies
- Common network protocols
- Information-gathering process

The next chapter continues the discussion of information gathering and analysis requirements, focusing on business-related issues.

POST-TEST QUESTIONS

The answers to these questions are in Appendix A at the end of this manual.

1. What is the potential impact of an organization's geographic distribution on network design?

   WAN LINKS, SERVICE POINTS, AND ORGANIZATION

2. Why is system hardware a concern when migrating to a new operating system?

   NEW OS NEED FASTER/NEWER HARDWARE

3. What are the four steps in the basic network design and implementation process?

   INFO GATHER DESIGN IMPLEMENTATION

4. Why is the business management model significant to the network design?

   THE

5. Where is directory information maintained in an Active Directory domain?

   IN A CENTRAL DATABASE

6. Which topology is most common for wiring an Ethernet 10BaseT network?

   STAR

7. What is the most common reason for installing the Data Link Control (DLC) protocol on a network server?

   HP network printers

8. At what level within a corporation would you be most likely to get information about long-range corporate goals?

   Top-Management

CHAPTER 2

Business Environment Requirements

MAJOR TOPICS

OBJECTIVES

At the completion of this chapter, you will be able to:

- Analyze and describe a company's basic business model.
- Analyze and describe how information flows through a company.
- Describe how data is shared by different departments.
- Analyze a company's product life cycle.
- Analyze network design goals.
- Analyze relationships.
- Analyze and manage change.
- Analyze Information Technology (IT) structure.
- Analyze the personnel model.
- Analyze design constraints.
- Analyze priorities and risks.

PRE-TEST QUESTIONS

The answers to these questions are in Appendix A at the end of this manual.

1. In which business model, branch office or subsidiary, are remote offices typically allowed a higher level of autonomy?
2. What is the defining difference between a policy and a procedure?
3. Would the procedural steps for posting customer payments be considered primarily as an information flow analysis or communication flow analysis?

4. What are the two basic models for management decision making?

5. In general, how does the available bandwidth in a remote link compare to LAN bandwidth?

6. Typically, what is the initial network design concern during an acquisition?

7. From the standpoint of network design, what are the basic differences in the challenges of supporting an acquired office and a new office opened through expansion?

8. Data availability is an overriding concern. What type of risk avoidance can be used to address this concern?

INTRODUCTION

With this chapter, you are going to start looking in some detail at the analysis process. In other words, the chapter focuses on information gathering and compilation relating to business and management requirements. Most of the data collection and analysis discussed in this chapter will also directly apply to the technical requirements analysis in the next chapter.

The information and analysis techniques discussed in this chapter are closely related. The information has been broken into separate topics to make it easier for you to follow the discussion. The chapter begins by taking a closer look at the business model. This includes modeling by business type, organization, and geographic scope. Specific topics include policies, procedures, information flow, communication flow, life cycles, and the decision-making process.

From here, the discussion turns to a closer look at the organizational structure. This includes a closer look at management, the impact of relationships, and an introduction to changes and change management.

The Information Technology (IT) structure must also be considered during analysis and design. This includes an analysis of the administration model, technical personnel model, and change management system.

The chapter then looks at the influence of some specific design constraints on network design. This includes laws and regulations, growth constraints, budget constraints, priorities, and risk analysis. Much of the information in this section is provided as a review and reference, providing general design and analysis guidelines.

The case studies introduced in the previous chapter will be used in scenario exercises during this chapter. Full descriptions of each of the fictitious companies are provided in Appendix C at the end of the manual. You may find it helpful to review these for additional background information before completing any of the scenario-based exercises.

BUSINESS MODEL

This chapter's look at the business and management side of the analysis process begins with the business model and business analysis. You were introduced to a few basics in the previous chapter. The following topics are covered in this section:

- Company Model
- Policies and Procedures
- Company Goals

Some of what is discussed here will already be familiar to you from the overviews in the previous chapter.

Company Model

You were introduced to business models based on type of business in the previous chapter. This section will review those models, but it also introduces an additional way of creating a business model based on your business and organizational structure.

Before looking at the models in any level of detail, it's important that you understand that these two types of models are not mutually exclusive. You should use them together to get as complete an understanding as possible of your organization.

For now, the focus will be on describing a few features of each of the models. Later in the chapter, these models will be addressed again with an eye on special needs and how they relate to creating your network model.

Modeling by Type of Business

In the previous chapter, you were introduced to the following four basic business models that relate to type of business:

- Service based
- Manufacturing and product development
- Wholesale warehousing
- Retail sales

Each of these business types will have a wide variety of network needs. Analyzing business needs can be further complicated by the fact that many organizations will cross model boundaries, needing different models to describe the activities of different departments or divisions.

Use these models to help you determine the type of data that is needed for day-to-day operations. This will help you target your communication and information flow analysis.

Modeling by Organizational Structure

Along with modeling by type of business, you need to develop an organizational model. An organizational model addresses additional details about your organization that you will need to know to create an appropriate network design. Models that fall into this category include the following:

- Branch office

  The most obvious analogy when discussing branch offices is to think of a tree. Each branch goes off in its own direction with a limited amount of autonomy but always remains connected to the main trunk of the tree to survive. The branch cannot stand alone.

  The same is generally true of a branch office. A branch office is an extension of the organization. It receives support and guidance from the main office. A branch office will have some level of management autonomy but will still receive its directions from the main office.

- Subsidiary

  A subsidiary is a wholly owned entity. It is owned by its parent organization but has its own business presence, corporate identity, management staff, and so forth. While under the control and guidance of the parent organization, each subsidiary will typically have a high level of autonomy.

  Because of the level of autonomy given to subsidiaries, they often must be treated somewhat as separate organizations during network design. Though they will probably fall under the general corporate guidelines, they are likely to have their own unique, specific network requirements.

In addition to these two organizational models, you need to describe the organization's geographic scope. These scope definitions can apply to either branch offices or subsidiaries. They should also be considered when analyzing access into or out of your network when communicating with vendors, partners, and customers. Specific requirements for communication outside of your organization are addressed later in the chapter.

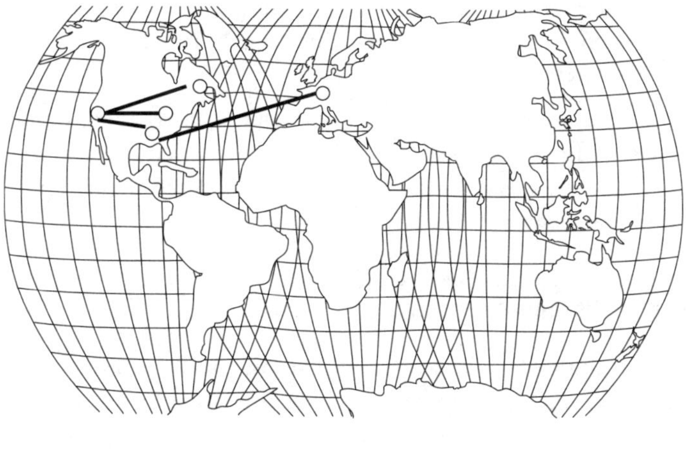

Geographic scope models are somewhat self-explanatory. For the purposes of this course, the following definitions will be used:

- Regional

  This is the hardest geographic scope to define because it encompasses a wide range of potential definitions. As a general definition, a regional scope is a geographic area smaller than a national scope. This could mean a community, a state, a group of states, or any other regional definition. An organization with a single office is usually included in this definition.

- National

  A national scope means that the organization spans all or most of a country. In countries like the United States, this represents a large geographic area. In smaller countries, you are dealing with a smaller area. A national scope in one country could turn out to be significantly smaller than a regional scope in another country.

- International

  An international organization has branch offices or subsidiaries that cross national boundaries. With modern communication technologies, the concerns you are likely to encounter are less due to technical difficulties than political or standards differences.

For the purposes of this course, geographic scope is going to focus primarily on physical offices and field personnel locations. From a strictly networking standpoint, any organization that has set up a Web site could be considered in some ways to have an international scope.

Policies and Procedures

The first thing to do is to define the terms *policies* and *procedures* to ensure that you understand how they are being used in this context. For the purposes of the course, the following definitions will be used:

- Policies

  Policies are high-level descriptions of positions or practices. Policies provide guidelines, often very general in nature. The goal of policies is to define standards and ensure sound and consistent decisions. They describe what is to be done but don't provide details for how the task is to be accomplished.

- Procedures

  Procedures describe the way that a task is accomplished, operating within the guidelines of corporate policy. This is where the specific details are spelled out as to what is required to reach a stated goal.

In summary, policies describe how things are supposed to be done and procedures define how things actually are done. In most organizations, the two officially will closely parallel each other, but that's not always the case. Administrators sometimes have a hard time keeping up with changes to policies dictated by changing procedures in a dynamic business and computing environment.

Policies are important because they define a business framework. However, from a network design standpoint, you are going to be focusing more on procedures. Procedures give you the detailed information you need about business activities and how they are related to the network. They will help you analyze requirements for the following:

- Information flow
- Communication flow
- Life cycles
- Decision making

Before looking at these in detail, let's take a slightly closer look at how policies and procedures are related.

Policy and Procedure Example

You work for a company that sells products through a catalog. Most orders are placed directly with in-house salespeople. Customers call in with their orders and provide payment information. The orders are posted by in-house sales, then routed to the warehouse and accounting, and the product is shipped to the customer.

You have a corporate policy relating to telephone orders that states, "Any order received before 2 p.m. will ship on the same working day."

This is a good policy in that it tells you exactly what is expected. It does not, however, give you any idea how this is going to be accomplished.

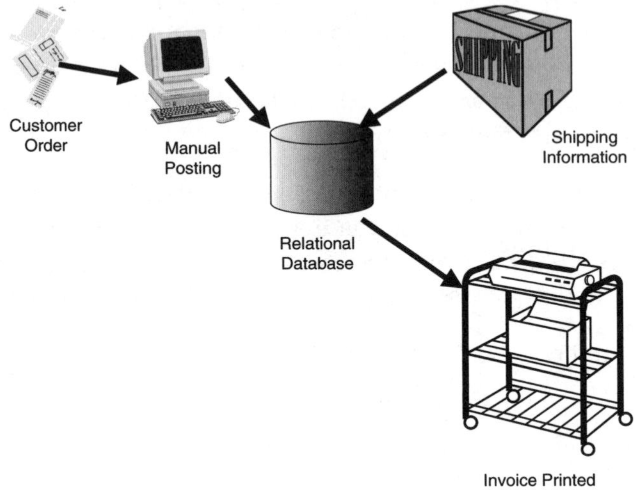

The procedures to accomplish the policy goal might include the following:

1. In-house sales receives telephone call and verifies the customer information or creates a new customer record.
2. In-house sales manually records the products ordered by the customer and the payment information.
3. The order is posted as an invoice by an in-house salesperson and saved to a relational database.
4. A copy of the invoice, containing the products ordered and the customer's shipping address, is printed in the warehouse.
5. A warehouse clerk physically collects the items on the invoice and packages the items for shipping, with the invoice used as the shipping label.
6. A shipping clerk adds shipping information to the copy of the invoice in the relational database and prepares the order for shipment.
7. All packages ready for shipment are picked up by a shipping company at 2 p.m. each working day.

Notice that there was no mention of the accounting department in the work-flow description. That doesn't mean that accounting didn't get updated, but that the update and its related processes didn't apply directly to the task at hand.

As you can see, a procedure statement goes into much more detail than the policy statement. Now for the bad news. In most organizations, these procedures aren't fully documented. In fact, most procedures don't get formally documented at all. Instead, everyone involved *just knows* what needs to be done.

What this means to you is that you and your design staff are going to have to do some detective work. You will have to:

- Identify key policies.

  This is the type of information you can get from published corporate policies or from higher up on the management scale.
- Identify mission-critical (business-critical) procedures.

  You can get most of this information from mid- to lower-level managers with some help from the end users.
- Identify procedural work-flow steps.

  You'll probably get the best information for this from end users, though managers can probably give you some help here as well.

From this information, you can start mapping out information and communication flows.

Information and Communication Flow

It can be hard to draw a solid line between information flow and communication flow. In general, the following working definitions can be used:

- Information flow

  This refers to the flow of data within, into, and out of your organization. Information can be electronic or paper based. If your goal is making your organization efficient, your tasks usually include moving as much of the information flow as possible from paper to electronic.

- Communication flow

  This also refers to data flow, but of a different type. Usually included in this category is *human-based* data such as letters, memos, telephone calls, and so on. This is important to network design because much of this is also electronic in nature. For example, most organizations rely on electronic mail as a critical part of doing business.

This is one of the areas where you may end up with some gaps in your initial analysis. It is difficult to identify all information and communication flows within an organization. One of the reasons for this is that most people go through their normal daily tasks without giving them much thought. When you start asking them to describe what they do and what resources they need, they tend to leave out some of the most common tasks.

Let's start with an overview of information and communication flow analysis. You'll be given some additional details based on business and organization models later in the chapter.

Information Flow

A good place to start looking at information flow is by taking a look at business processes. This will give you a good idea of what kind of information is required and how it moves from point to point within the organization.

You saw an example of this earlier in this section when you stepped through the process for posting an order and getting it shipped out to the customer.

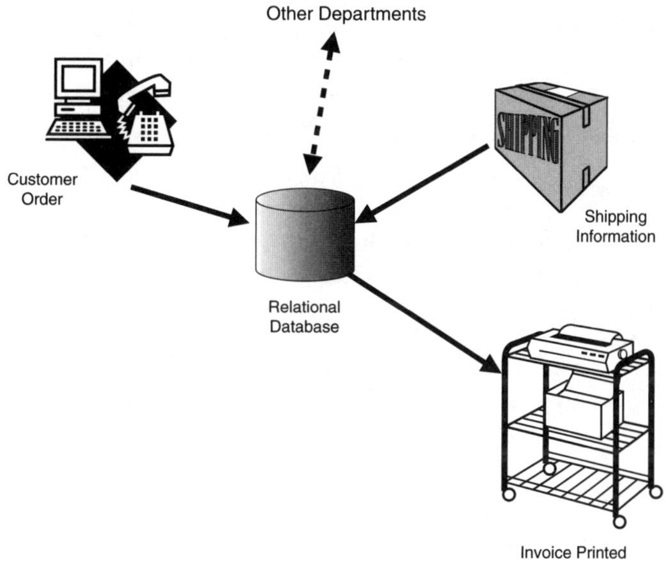

Let's take a look at the information flows represented in the previous figure:

- The customer order going from the posting terminal to a relational database
- The order going from the relational database to be printed as an invoice in the warehouse
- Shipping information going from the warehouse back to the relational database

This is the first part of the analysis. Now you have to determine how the information flow impacts the network design. For what you have documented so far, you are going to need a reliable network connection between:

- In-house sales and the database server
- The warehouse and the database server

You've got a good start, but you still don't have all of the information that you will eventually need. You'll notice that in the figure there is a dotted arrow pointing off to unnamed "Other Departments". Before you were finished, you would still need to determine what other departments are involved and how information flows between those departments and the relational database.

Communication Flow

Communication flow requirements can be a little harder to identify. Also, since many forms of communication are also directly supported by the network, the line between communication flow and information flow can get a little blurred.

You have to avoid letting yourself get caught up in concerns about the blurred definitions and focus on your goal, which is determining network requirements. Areas of confusion can include the following:

- Letters, memos, and other documents

  Handwritten or typed correspondence is the exception in the modern office. You need to determine software, local storage, and network storage requirements for electronic documents. There is often a security requirement as well that can include both access security and data encryption.

- Forms and templates

  These need to be more generally available either within a department or to the organization as a whole. This means shared storage and shared access requirements.

- Reports

  Reports are a form of communication, but there are also information-flow requirements in generating the reports.

- Electronic mail (E-mail)

  Electronic mail has become a mission-critical component in recent years, with a large number of organizations hosting their own mail servers and gateways. E-mail requirements include storage and inbound and outbound access. For the vast majority of mail systems, Internet access is a required component. Even if your organization doesn't host its own mail server, relying instead on a third party such as an Internet Service Provider (ISP), you will still have Internet access requirements.

The communication requirements listed here typically have limited storage and bandwidth requirements. This isn't always the case, however. E-mail storage requirements can become significant, depending on how you've configured message storage and how often users delete old messages.

This is only a partial list of the communication requirements you may encounter. In recent years, additional communication services, such as telephone switches, have merged with the data network and may share common media.

You may find that you have some communication flow requirements that require a significant amount of bandwidth and storage resources. For example, organizations are starting to make more use of streaming video for internal communications and online training. Online video conferencing is also gaining in popularity. These are both areas where the requirements are likely to increase, which means you are going to have to include the increased requirements in your network design.

Losing the Paper Trail

Common goals for network design often include improved efficiency and reduced reliance on hard-copy documents. These areas are also part of your information and communication flow analysis and design.

The basic process is simple. Determine which procedures are currently *paper and pencil* based and see if there is a way to automate them. Many times you will find that the procedure is already at least partially automated and the current processes represent a duplication of effort.

Process Upgrade Example

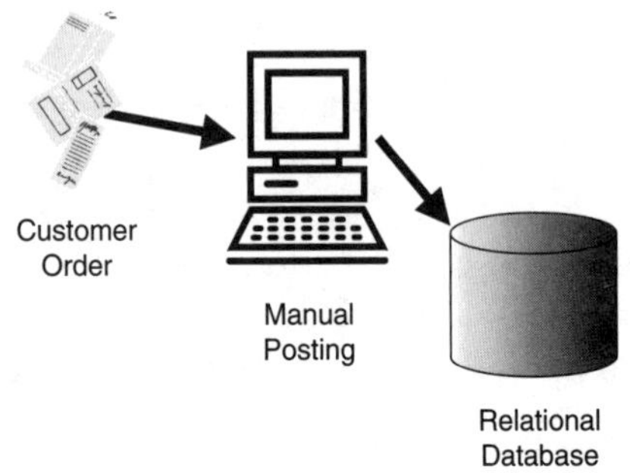

Let's revisit the retail sales example that you've been using in this chapter and expand on the first step. Each of the in-house salespeople records the customer's order on a paper order form. After completing the call, the order is then posted into the database through a data entry form. The potential for improvement should be obvious.

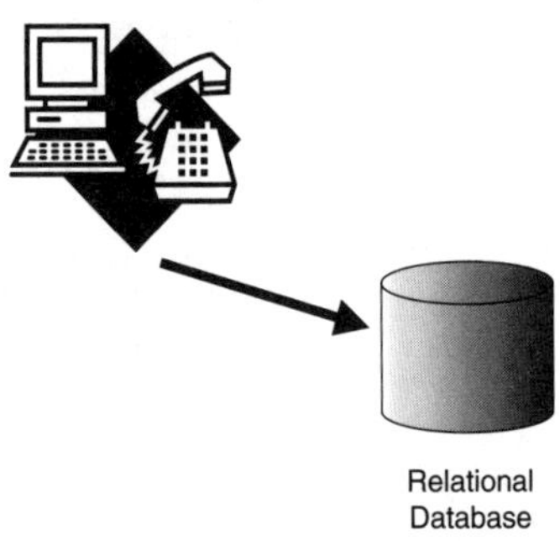

You can improve efficiency by having online forms created so that salespeople can post customer orders directly while they are on the telephone. This eliminates the need to fill out an order form and then post the same information after the fact.

It may sound like you've found the perfect solution, and you may have, but the job isn't finished. You need to consider the impact that the change will have on both the network and on business processes. One concern is going to be database and end-user application performance. Before the creation of online forms, performance wasn't as much of a concern as long as the salespeople posted orders after finishing the call. Delays would be annoying, but probably not much more. The priority for invoice performance changes when they start posting the invoices live. Anyone who has ever placed an order over the phone knows how frustrating it is to sit there waiting while being told, "The computer's really slow today."

This could have serious impacts on the network budget. It may become necessary to upgrade the database server. It might even be necessary to migrate to a different relational database management system, which could mean even more programming requirements as well as data migration concerns. The users are going to have to be retrained, which probably won't come out of your network operations budget, but the overhead generated through additional Help Desk calls might have an impact on the budget.

In short, be careful about proposing *simple* changes until you have done your investigation and analysis. Watch for cascading changes and hidden implementation costs.

Life Cycles

You've probably noticed that a lot of business and network terms are based in the natural world. For instance, files *grow.* A stable software product is said to be *mature*. Product marketing efforts are often based on a product's projected *life span*.

The same is true of product and service life cycles. Unless something unexpected happens along the way, most plants and animals follow the following predictable life cycle:

- They are born.
- They grow and mature.
- They (attempt to) reproduce.
- They die.

The same is true of products and services. They also have somewhat predictable life cycles, outlined as follows, assuming nothing unexpected occurs along the way.

- They are born.

  Starting with an idea and project plan, products and services are defined and created. When the product or service is sold, it is sent out into the world much as a young plant or animal.

- They grow and mature.

  Over time, improvements are made and upgrades offered. New software versions or new product models are released. Additional services are offered or improvements are made to current services.

- They (attempt to) reproduce.

  This one may be stretching it a little, but there is an analogy here. New products are developed based on existing products. You could also consider, as an example of this, collateral or additional sales made based on customer satisfaction or loyalty.

- They die.

  Products wear out and have to be replaced. Service contracts expire or are no longer appropriate. Technological advances and customer preferences change, leaving products abandoned.

Okay, so how does all of this relate to network design analysis? Products and services typically need network support at all phases of the life cycle. In addition, these requirements will change with each phase.

Life Cycle Example

Here's a quick example of what you might encounter. Let's examine how the life cycle might run for a typical product for Fairco Manufacturing, one of the case studies you saw earlier.

Product Birth

This can be a lengthy process that can be broken down into the following phrases:

- Product design and development

  This includes product design and approval, design changes, and the eventual production of one or more product prototypes.

  Two of the biggest concerns during this phase are closely related. You are going to need to be able to share information, but you are going to want to keep all of the information secure to avoid premature disclosure. This means tightly controlled access security. You may also want to use data encryption to provide additional protection for any project files.

- Product manufacture

  Product manufacture includes a number of both information and communication flow concerns. You need to keep up with build lists or build instructions, component orders from suppliers, manufacture schedules, and on-hand inventory. As with product design, data security will also be an overriding concern.

- Product sales

  The initial part of this phase, the product marketing, will probably start concurrent with product manufacture or possibly before. Communication flows are critical, involving getting product information out to the retail outlets that are Fairco's customers.

Keep in mind this is a general overview. The specifics involved will be somewhat unique to each company and each product. The same is true for each of the remaining life cycle phases.

Product Growth

Change is inevitable. Problems can be discovered after manufacture that may require retrofitting. Gradual improvements are made to the product based on consumer requests, technological improvements, and a better understanding of the marketplace.

Changes mean that you need a way of getting the information out to salespeople and to customers. Minor, optional changes to existing products might be posted on a Web site. More serious retrofits might require immediate announcements to distributors and might include direct mailing to registered customers.

Product Reproduction

This is a variation on the product birth phase because it involves the release of a new product. New products are developed based on existing products and consumer requests. The concerns here are much the same as they were for the product birth phase except there is a need for capturing inbound communications for review and evaluation. This could mean tracking telephone call summaries, letters, e-mails, and the like. You will have a concern during this phase in making sure that the necessary lines of communication are in place and can handle the projected traffic.

You are going to be dealing with a mix of electronic and hard-copy data during this phase. You may find that there is a need to convert the hard-copy data into an electronic format for storage and retrieval.

Product Death

You might think that as a product is phased out so are its requirements for network support. It's true that the requirements should be significantly reduced, but there will still be requirements. You will want to archive the information related to the product in case it's needed later for reference. Initially, this may be accomplished through online storage, but may migrate to offline storage eventually.

Decision Making

To understand the decision-making process in an organization, you need to first recognize its management model. The following are two types of management models:

- Centralized

  The most common decision-making process in this model is that information flows up the organizational hierarchy and decisions flow back down. Decisions can be made at different levels within the hierarchy, but there is still a centralized process.

- Decentralized

  This one can be a little more difficult to understand. Typically, this means there is greater autonomy among departments and more decisions can be made locally. The decision-making process is delegated, so you may have the added requirement of finding out who can make network design and implementation decisions.

You need to understand the management model so that requests can be forwarded as appropriate. You also need to understand what is required for a decision to be made.

Some companies, especially smaller organizations and new start-up businesses, tend to have an informal decision-making process. This entails locating the person responsible, telling them what you're planning to do, and getting verbal approval on the spot. Most decisions get documented after the fact, if at all.

Other organizations have a highly structured decision-making process. Before any decision can be made, you have to submit your proposal in writing (or electronic format) along with your supporting documentation. You may be able to submit the request directly to the final decision maker or may find yourself having to forward everything through appropriate channels.

The real world usually falls somewhere in between. Decisions affecting the project and organization as a whole are made through formal channels. This would include items such as overall design goals and budget requirements. Other decisions are made informally at a more localized level, such as how user data storage will be managed and local access requirements.

Centralized Management Concerns

When dealing with centralized management, especially one that is hierarchical in nature, you have to be careful to keep your message from being garbled as it moves up and down through the hierarchy. Make sure that everything is clearly and carefully documented.

Another concern in centralized management is that remote office needs may not be fully understood. In many centralized management structures, there tends to be a *one-size-fits-all* attitude. This can result in business policies and design goals that don't properly address the remote offices.

Decentralized Management Concerns

Coordinating the design and implementation process can be difficult in a decentralized management structure. Depending on the amount of autonomy that has been allowed, you may find very different network standards implemented in different offices or even in different divisions or departments.

One of the biggest concerns in a decentralized management structure is incompatible or mutually exclusive goals and management decisions. It will probably fall on you, as the person in charge of network design, to act as a go-between and negotiate compromises.

Company Goals

There have been some brief references to organizational goals already in the course. In reality, you are dealing with two sets of closely related goals: network design goals, which drive the design process, and the organization's business goals, which will directly affect how the network design goals are implemented.

Network Design Goals

You've seen some guidelines for what you should see in the network design goals. These included the following:

- Functionality
- Security
- Performance and availability

These goals need to be clearly defined, including the criteria to be used to determine whether the goals have been met. One of your tasks will be making sure that the goals can be met and that the judgment criteria are realistic. For example, consider the following performance goal: all users will be upgraded to high-performance workstations.

There are a few problems with this goal. High performance is a relative term. High performance in comparison to what? Whose definition of high performance are you going to use? Your idea of a high-performance workstation may be completely different than the system a graphic artist might have in mind. It's also going to be difficult to set performance criteria to make sure that this goal is met. A better goal would be something along the lines of the following goal: all users will be upgraded to Pentium III systems with at least 64 MB of RAM.

This goal is more clearly defined and it's much easier to tell if the goal has been met. You also have guidelines for starting to determine cost requirements once you've completed the network system inventory.

Business Goals

Business goals are exactly what their name implies. They define what an organization wants to accomplish in the short term and in the long term. Business goals often include the following:

- Increase sales of products and services.
- Reduce cost of sales.
- Reduce operational costs.
- Improve efficiency of business procedures.
- Open additional offices.
- Acquire additional resources.

The list could go on and on. Business goals are generally defined at higher management levels, with the details of the implementation left to lower levels within the organization. Your task is to identify which of these goals impacts network design. You need to look for ways that the network design you develop can help meet the business goals.

Let's take a couple of these as examples, starting with reducing costs. One way of reducing costs is keeping network downtime to a minimum. Downtime is expensive, and the more your organization relies on the network, the more expensive downtime becomes. Quite often any work done while the network is down will have to be reposted or updated once the network becomes available again. Users who rely completely on the network may find themselves assigned *busy work* to keep them occupied.

The network design can also help improve the efficiency of business procedures. During the analysis phase, it is likely that you will find procedures that can be streamlined through automation.

Scenario 2-1: Business Model Analysis

This scenario is based on the case studies introduced earlier in the course. Suggested solutions are provided in Appendix B at the end of this manual. It may be helpful to review the case studies in Appendix C at the end of this manual.

Things and Stuff

Sales information is written to an Access database that daily and weekly reports are generated from.

1. Which business model is represented here?

   ....

   ....

2. Which geographic model is represented here?

   ....

   ....

3. What is the information flow for invoices?

   ....

   ....

Barney's Bank

There is currently no central repository for corporate data. Most periodic reports are compiled from e-mail attachments and hard-copy data sent to the main office weekly.

1. Which business model is represented here?

2. Which geographic model is represented here?

3. What is the primary management model used here?

4. What organizational structure is used for offices within the United States?

Fairco Manufacturing

There are plans in the near future to spin warehouse operations off as a separate subsidiary.

1. Which business model is represented here?

   ....

   ....

2. Which geographic model is represented here?

   ....

   ....

3. A policy was recently issued that turnaround time for customer orders must be improved. What must you know before you can begin to address this policy?

   ....

   ....

ORGANIZATIONAL STRUCTURE

Now that you've got a few more of the basics out of the way, you're ready to take a more detailed look at analysis. The following topics are covered in this section:

- Organization and Management
- Relationships
- Changes

Now the discussion can also include some of the probable network requirements based on the organizational structure.

Organization and Management

Let's start by focusing on organizational structure based on the models already introduced. Now the discussion turns to network design requirements common to each of the models.

Throughout this discussion, you need to realize that these are general requirements provided as examples. The specifics are going to be somewhat unique to each organization. These generalizations will give you a starting point for your own analysis.

Business Model Requirements

An organization's business model will help you get a start on a number of requirements, including information flow, communication flow, and security. Some requirements are going to be common to all of the models. These include the following:

- Electronic mail

  As stated before, e-mail is now considered part of doing business. There is the question of whether to host mail on a private mail server. This decision is more related to organization size and technical staff availability than to the particular business model.

- Data storage

  All organizations have data-storage requirements. Centralized data storage provides a way of making the data available to users as necessary, to control data access, and to ensure data availability through regular backups and data fault tolerance.

- Access security

  Shared data means access control requirements. Basic security requirements will include network logon and shared data access permissions.

In addition to these, there are going to be some requirements more specific to each of the models. There will, of course, be some overlap between the models.

Service Based

A service organization's requirements are going to be determined by the type of service being provided. In general, the requirements will include communication into and out of the organization, tracking of service contracts, account tracking, and so forth.

Security is one of the areas where the level of concern will depend on the type of service provided. A consumer service such as a dry cleaner or automotive repair shop will probably have limited security requirements. A financial service organization will have extremely high security requirements. You will need to determine the type of data involved and work with the decision makers within the organization to develop an appropriate security model.

Service-based organizations can often include branch offices or subsidiaries, which carry their own special needs. Before any design decisions can be made, the organizational model must also be clearly defined.

Manufacturing and Product Development

You saw some examples of this model's requirements when discussing product and service life cycles. There are going to be requirements for both inbound and outbound communications. There will be additional requirements for tracking raw material and finished product inventories. Security will also be a pressing concern.

Whether remote communication with remote locations is a concern will depend on the organization. Most will have needs for communications between different buildings as well as with suppliers and distributors. If the organization has more than one manufacturing location, there will also be significant communication requirements between them.

Wholesale Warehousing

The two most obvious communication flows in this model are between the warehouse and its suppliers and between the warehouse and its customers. Many, if not most, warehouses are older, established organizations, so you are likely to find what may seem to be outdated processes and methods of communications. Activities may be heavily hard-copy based with manual processes followed up by electronic processes after the fact. A major part of your design will likely include updating and streamlining these procedures.

Be careful not to underestimate the security requirements in this model. Inventory costs are closely guarded secrets. Warehouses often have multiple selling prices based on volume and other factors, and these must also be guarded for accidental disclosure.

Retail Sales

This is another model where you are going to see a great deal of variation based on the size of the organization and its geographic structure. Communication flows between remote locations are going to be critical. For example, if one retail outlet doesn't have a product in stock, it needs to be able to quickly check other locations to see if the product is available elsewhere.

Inventory costs and stocking levels are going to be critical concerns. In most cases, there are fewer considerations about selling prices since these are usually posted publicly. Planned price changes and sales promotions are another issue, however. The organization may want to be very careful about releasing that information prematurely.

Performance is often an overriding concern in this environment. One of the keys to making a profit is moving customers through as quickly as possible after they've made their purchase decisions. You will need to identify the processes where network performance is critical and make sure that the necessary resources are made available.

Organizational Model Requirements

Network design requirements are further influenced by organizational models. You need to identify the models followed by the organization, then determine their specific needs.

Take branch offices and subsidiaries, for example. Your first thought might be that the branch offices, as extensions of the main office, face the same network challenges. The truth may be that the offices were acquired through mergers or buyouts and their networks are based on different standards.

Making too many assumptions can also get you in trouble with subsidiaries. You might think that since they typically have more autonomy, you are going to see bigger differences in their networks. Keep in mind, however, that they still answer to the parent organization and may have been given very specific networking guidelines.

Either way, there are going to be communication requirements between the offices. How this is managed is going to be somewhat dictated by the organization's geographic scope.

The common wisdom used to be that the farther you have to go between offices, the more it is going to cost. While this can still be true, you do have additional cost-effective options available. This is especially true if communication requirements can be met by a VPN implemented over the Internet.

Regional Scope

Your requirements for supporting a regional scope are going to depend on how large of an area is defined by the region and where it is located. In a small region, you may find that all of your needs can be met through the local telephone company or other local access companies. As the region grows in size, it will tend to be more like a national scope than a regional scope.

National Scope

There was a time, not long ago, when trying to do anything on a national scale was an implementation nightmare and prohibitively expensive for all but the largest organizations. This has changed somewhat in recent years with the growth of new communication companies offering expanded services. In many cases, you can find one communication company with the resources to handle all of your communication needs.

International Scope

The number of problems you are going to encounter in international communications will depend heavily on where you are going to and coming from. You can run into problems with competing standards, high fees and tariffs, or even the unavailability of your preferred solution. There may also be problems finding qualified technical personnel to help you with your implementation.

This is an area where you may find yourself carefully balancing bandwidth capacity and cost. While possibly not your preferred solution, you may find it necessary to use slower links across national boundaries and provide higher-speed links within each country.

General Communication Concerns

One of your biggest concerns when supporting a Wide Area Network (WAN) with remote links is going to be bandwidth. Remote links typically provide a limited bandwidth in comparison to LAN bandwidth. Not only do you need to find the best, most reliable remote links that you can afford, you may also need to find ways to minimize traffic across the remote links.

You were told earlier that along with design and implementation, you also have to concern yourself with network management. When dealing with remote links, this is going to mean periodically monitoring bandwidth usage levels across the links. You are also going to want to find ways to keep network traffic to a minimum. This means, as much as possible, keeping local traffic local. You'll be shown some techniques for doing this later in the course.

Relationships

For many organizations, relationships with other organizations are going to be another part of the initial analysis and must be considered in the network design. For the purposes of network design, the discussion will be limited to relationships that have a required network communication component.

Business relationships include partners, vendors, and customers. Each has its own access requirements, depending on the business and the type of relationship.

- Partners

  In most partnerships, there is a direct sharing of data. That means that partners will need direct access into at least some portion of the network. You will have to provide for remote access and logon access, and you will also have to set data access controls.

  Partnerships can be transient in nature. You will have to periodically review access requirements and make adjustments as necessary.

- Vendors

  Your vendors are your suppliers. The ordering process has traditionally been a manual process, involving written orders and telephone calls. There has been a migration in Business-to-Business (B2B) relationships with vendors, where orders are posted electronically with minimal human interaction.

  With some vendors, the ordering process entails simply connecting to the vendor's Web site and placing the order. Other vendors, especially warehouses, may have more direct access. Either way, you need to provide for outbound communications with the vendors.

- Customers

  This is the other side of the vendor relationship, where you are acting as the vendor for your customers. If you have migrated to an electronic business (e-business) environment, or are planning to do so in the future, you need to provide inbound access to your customers.

  The nature of the access is going to depend on your business. The most common example is Web access. Customers connect to your Web site and place their orders. For a warehouse organization, you may be supporting direct access to your network for placing orders, though this is going to require carefully designed security controls.

Internet connectivity is going to be discussed in detail later in the course, but it does deserve some special mention before continuing. Providing Web access is more involved than just setting up a Web server and letting it go. You need to provide communications between the Web server and other supporting servers on your network without opening a door directly into your LAN.

When determining the requirements to support business relationships, you must also consider potential changes. You need to look at the direction the organization is wanting to move in and how these changes will impact the network design.

Changes

Change is a fact of life. A business has to change with the marketplace to survive. Your network design must include any planned changes but have enough flexibility built in to let you react to unplanned changes. Business changes can include new services or changes to services offered, changes in business processes, new or evolving partnerships, and acquisitions.

Not only do you have to concern yourself with business changes, but you also have to keep an eye on technological changes. You need to evaluate changing technology to determine when, or even if, it is appropriate to introduce the technology on your network.

One trap that you need to avoid is waiting too long for expected changes. There is sometimes a temptation to avoid implementing a technology because you know that modifications and improvements are on the way. A lot can happen between a product announcement and release, and many announced products either never make it to market or undergo drastic changes before their final release. Make decisions based on what is available now that can meet your networking needs. Otherwise, you might find yourself waiting for innovations to come available.

You also have to avoid the temptation to implement the latest technologies just because they are new. Make sure that there is a valid place for the technology in your network design and that you aren't inventing a need because the technology interests you. In every case, the network is there to support the business, not the other way around. If you cannot make a business case for the technology, then you don't need it.

Acquisitions

Acquisitions almost always present special network challenges. These can usually be managed by the following two transitional phases:

- Initial communications

  Included in most acquisitions is acquisition of an existing network structure. Your first task will usually be to get the acquired network and your current network communicating. Changes in network technologies and operating systems mean that this isn't quite the daunting task that it once was. At minimum, you will have to provide a communication path with sufficient bandwidth to meet information flow requirements.

- Migration

  Once you get the networks communicating, the next task will be bringing the acquired network into line with organizational policies and guidelines. This is usually a more gradual process. The amount of difficulty you encounter will be directly related to the extent of the changes that have to be made.

  You will probably want to treat this as a separate network design project. You have the advantage with this type of project in that you already have a working model to draw from–the existing network.

Planned acquisitions can be included in your network design. Unfortunately, from a planning standpoint, you probably won't hear anything about planned acquisitions until after the fact.

Partnerships

There is usually more advanced warning in partnership relationship changes than with acquisitions. Partnerships are often based on a specific project, or a series of projects, and changes flow with changes in the project's scope and life cycle.

You are going to need to manage inbound and outbound communication requirements. These will usually include network logon and database requirements.

Communication Technologies

You need to investigate the current communication options so that you can make the best choice based on cost and available bandwidth. You also need to keep up to date on changes in communication technologies so that you can take advantage of appropriate technologies.

This has been an area of rapid growth and expansion over recent years. If you are in the process of migrating an existing network, it is likely that you can find ways to improve your current remote access support and links to remote offices. With new companies springing up seemingly every day, you may find that you don't necessarily have to change providers to cut communication costs. Communication service providers are feeling the pressure of increased competition and are often willing to negotiate service fees.

Operating Systems and Network Services

This is another area where you are going to see constant change. As soon as a new operating system is released, rumors surface about the next version, which is already in development. Improvements are made to existing network services, and new services are often rolled out with new operating system versions.

You are going to probably feel pressure from a number of sources to stay upgraded with the latest software versions and service offerings. Before you upgrade, you need to make sure you understand what changes are going to be involved and how they are going to impact your network.

For example, some of the biggest changes you will see with Windows 2000 are directly related to network support. TCP/IP is now the default protocol. The operating system has been optimized for use in an Active Directory domain environment. Should you choose to migrate to an Active Directory domain, you also have to provide Domain Name System (DNS) support.

Scenario 2-2: Analyzing Organizational Structure

During this scenario, you will be answering questions based on the current organizational and network structures in the case study companies. Additional information for each company is presented first, followed by questions relating to all three case studies. Suggested solutions are provided in Appendix B at the end of this manual. It may be helpful to review the case studies in Appendix C at the end of this manual.

Things and Stuff's Current Network

The current network has two Windows NT servers, nine Windows NT workstations, and three Windows 98 systems. The systems are currently configured as a workgroup. There is one person responsible for network management who spends most of his time fixing problems introduced by users attempting to *improve* the network. The network administrator has a set budget but is given free reign in network management within that budget.

Barney's Bank's Current Network

From an IT standpoint, the organization is best described as a mismatched and patched-together mess. As new locations have been acquired, the existing networks have been left in place, resulting in a network management and communications nightmare. The network management staff is short-handed and overworked.

Fairco Manufacturing's Current Network

Fairco Manufacturing has a large LAN configured as a Windows NT domain. Dial-in access is provided to remote warehouses in strategic locations around the country. This is the only remote communication currently in place. Field salespeople either call in, fax, or hand deliver orders to the main office, where they are manually posted. Shipping delays can run from 3 to 20 days, and there is a constant problem with back orders due to out-of-stock items.

Scenario Questions

1. Which of the case study companies has a specified current need for electronic mail?

2. Which of the case study companies currently have remote communication requirements?

3. Which of the case study companies has plans for growth through acquisition?

INFORMATION TECHNOLOGY STRUCTURE

The focus now switches to a specific part of the management structure: IT management and structure. You may be more familiar with the term Information Systems (IS) management.

This introduction looks at the following three key areas:

- Administration
- Personnel Model
- Managing Change

Many organizations, especially smaller companies, do not see IT as a separate management function. Instead, it is integrated into the rest of the management structure, often as part of operations management.

Administration

The IT administration model will typically be the same as an organization's overall management model. In other words, you will usually see either a centralized or decentralized administration model. If there are differences between the management model and the IT administration model, you will usually see a tendency toward more centralization in the IT administration model. Two of the main reasons for this are as follows:

- Need for standardization

  Even when an organization has a decentralized management structure, there is a need for standardization in network implementation and management practices. This causes the IT administration structure to tend to represent a more centralized model, where network administration in remote offices is carefully coordinated.

- Management traditions

  In older, established organizations, the IT administration function is often an extension of or a replacement for mainframe management structures. Mainframe management structures, by their nature, were highly centralized, and the same habits will tend to continue in PC network management.

Of course, it's not that unusual to see mixed administration models employed. For example, you would find that an Active Directory domain structure naturally tends to be a somewhat centralized administration model. At the same time, the Active Directory supports delegation of administration and management tasks, giving you a way of decentralizing selected administration activities.

Administration Changes

While you are in the process of developing a new network design is a good time to review your IT administration model to see if there are improvements you might want to suggest. Depending on the current model and how it is implemented, these could be moving you toward a more or less centralized model, depending on organizational requirements.

Administration model changes are often driven by network changes. When you move to a different network operating system, or even a different operating system version, some changes will have to be made.

For example, you may be migrating from a NetWare 3.12 network to a Windows 2000 Active Directory domain. NetWare 3.12 uses a servercentric administration model. Each network service is administered separately. You have a centralized administration model enforced at the server, but network administration as a whole is somewhat decentralized if you have multiple servers. An Active Directory domain is based on a directory services model. Network services, specifically the domain controllers, are centrally managed as a group. Each server will contain all of the directory information, and changes made at one domain controller will be propagated through replication to other domain controllers.

Active Directory Example

Let's look at an Active Directory domain example and how the domain might be managed. To keep the example relatively simple, assume that the network is based on a single Active Directory domain.

This is a case where the Active Directory itself will cause you to tend toward a centralized management structure. Nearly all management and administration activities are implemented as a function of the Active Directory domain. However, you aren't locked in a strictly centralized model.

Consider this situation. You have a limited network administration staff. Networkwide management activities are assigned to network administrators. These assignments include activities such as setting domainwide security policies, managing domain controllers, and so forth. You might then delegate user management at the department or division level. You could structure the Active Directory hierarchy in such a way to make it easy to give each department control over its own users and resources.

Personnel Model

The administration model can be taken down to another level by looking at the personnel involved in the network administration process. Depending on how your organization is structured, you may see some of the roles combined or might encounter different administration roles. As examples, here are some of the most common roles you are going to see:

- Network administrators

  Network administrators are the ones who are expected to take responsibility for the network. If anything goes wrong, they are expected to fix it or see that it gets fixed. If there are problems with resource access, application support, and so forth, they are expected to take responsibility for the problem.

- Technical support

  The technical support staff deals with the nuts and bolts of the network. They are primarily responsible for the hardware side of the network, which includes servers, client workstations, the cable plant, connection devices, and so on. They may also be responsible for server-based applications.

- End-user support

  End-user support personnel deal more with the software and data side of the network. This includes supporting end-user applications and data file access and may include some security management such as managing logons and passwords.

Some network management activities may be outsourced. With some network devices, it may be more cost effective to contract for maintenance and support than to try to train someone within the support staff. The same may be true for some specialized servers such as Web servers.

These roles must be taken into consideration during the network design process. You are going to want input from the responsible support personnel regarding the current network and their thoughts on the possible effects of proposed changes. You will need to consider which, if any, support duties you will need to outsource in the new network design.

Managing Change

Change is a fact of life in a network environment. Its impact on your organization is often related to how change is managed within your organization. With this in mind, the discussion turns to the following three closely related topics:

- Decision-Making Process
- Change Management
- Funding

As with so many other factors in network design, you have to consider both the current structure and proposed changes. These are all subjects that have been at least touched upon already in the course. The difference now is that the discussion focuses specifically on IT administration and how these topics relate directly to the network.

Decision-Making Process

As with other business-related decisions, the process for making network decisions is going to depend on your IT administration model. The first step is understanding how decisions are made, who is directly responsible for the decisions, and what are the limiting factors.

For example, it may be that the network administrator is considered to have final say on networking issues but must operate within defined budget constraints. If the proposed change is going to cost more than the administrator can authorize, the decision will have to be taken to the next higher level.

Change Management

You need to understand how change is managed within your organization. In the process, you may find yourself suggesting modifications to the change-management procedures.

How change is managed is often related to the number of users that are going to be impacted and how much it is going to cost. Major changes typically have to be documented and approved in writing. Lower-level changes, such as modifications to user access permissions, may be done based on a quick conversation in the hallway. These changes often do not get well documented, assuming that they get documented at all.

To be honest, introducing a structured change-management procedure where there hasn't been one in the past is likely to encounter opposition. People, including the technical staff, will probably see it as additional and unnecessary paperwork. However, it's worth making the effort.

When you have a formal change-management process in place, you are more sure of timely and accurate change documentation. You have a paper trail (though not necessarily tracked on paper) of who made the changes and when. If there are problems at some later point, you know who can tell you exactly what was done and what they encountered at the time.

A formal change-management process can also offer you, as a network administrator, a level of protection. As administrator, you spend most of your time in the hot seat in what can sometimes be a strange version of reality. For example, how would you respond in the following situation (without putting your position in jeopardy)?

> Your supervisor comes into your office obviously upset and starts screaming about changes that were made to local user access permissions. He wants to know what idiot proposed and made the changes, which have now resulted in lost time and money. What your supervisor has conveniently forgotten is that he is the one who demanded the changes and that you made them under protest. Everything was managed through word of mouth, so nothing was formally documented.

A formal change-management process gives you a way of protecting yourself in situations such as this. You can show not only who made the change, but also who proposed the change and who approved it.

Funding

Funding is closely related to change management and to the decision-making process. When changes are made, especially when they require purchase of additional hardware, software, or services, someone is going to have to pay. Network funding can be especially tricky, however, since it impacts the organization as a whole.

Some organizations have a separate network budget, and as long as operations stay within that budget, there are very few concerns. Most budgets, however, are designed to account for day-to-day network management and upkeep activities and not much more. If there are special needs, the expenditures usually require approval from upper management. Believe it or not, this is usually the easiest model to work with.

Another model is one where the network budget is delegated to individual departments based on their (perceived) use of or reliance on the network. Once the budget is established, day-to-day activities usually aren't much of a problem, except each of the department managers may tend to feel as if he or she has direct control over the network staff. The real problem occurs when there are special expenditures and you have to determine who is going to pay for them. This often means ongoing negotiations between the different departments until you can finally get the costs partitioned out.

Scenario 2-3: IT Structure Analysis

During this scenario, you will be looking at the current IT structure for each of the case study companies. Suggested solutions are provided in Appendix B at the end of this manual. It may be helpful to review the case studies in Appendix C at the end of this manual.

Things and Stuff

The current IT structure is informal and limited. The one network administrator is self-taught. This is one of the reasons why there has been no attempt before now to change from a workgroup configuration. The network administrator is responsible for all network management tasks.

Change-management procedures are also informal. The network administrator has free reign to make changes as long as they remain within the network budget. Additional funding must be approved directly by the business owner.

Barney's Bank

The current IT staff includes one IT manager, four network administrators who work out of the Corpus Christi office, and two or more network technicians in each branch and subsidiary office. There have been plans for a 24/7 user Help Desk for more than 5 years, but as of yet, there have been no efforts to implement these plans. Network technicians spend more time working with users than working with the network. Network failures are common and costly.

The network is managed as a separate department. Its funding comes as a prorated amount from other departmental budgets. Any changes to the network at any location are supposed to be documented on a network change order. Any changes to the network that will require additional expenditures must be approved by the executive finance committee. Rather than going through this process, many remote offices have *hidden* network expansion costs in other departmental budgets to make what they saw as critical changes.

Fairco Manufacturing

Fairco Manufacturing currently has one network administrator working with five network technicians. The network technicians also provide Help Desk assistance to network users. The network falls under the Operations department, and any network changes must be approved by the Operations manager. Decisions that require additional funding must be approved by the owner.

Network change decisions are seldom documented. The process is typically managed entirely through verbal approval. The budget for network operations is considered part of the general Operations department budget. There is an ongoing push to keep network expenses for daily operations to a minimum.

Scenario Questions

1. Which of the case study companies officially uses a centralized IT management model?

2. Which of the case study companies has a formal policy for documenting network changes?

3. Which of the case study companies uses a network budget based on other departmental budgets?

4. In which of the case study companies would you expect to see the least amount of network standardization, and why?

5. Which case study company has the least amount of in-house expertise and is most likely to require outside assistance almost immediately in the network design process?

DESIGN CONSTRAINTS

Let's shift the focus a little now and look at some of the constraints to network design that you are likely to encounter. The following topics are covered in this section:

- Laws and Regulations
- Growth Constraints
- Budget Constraints
- Priorities and Risks

Some of these issues have already been mentioned elsewhere in the course. They are included here to give you a combined reference. In this section, the term *constraints* isn't meant to necessarily imply restrictions but, instead, factors that will help define your network design and the framework you are operating in.

Laws and Regulations

Applicable laws and regulations are going to be a consideration for any organization as well as any network design and implementation. This is complicated by the fact that the regulations you must be concerned about are going to depend on the following:

- Organization size

  The simple fact is that there are more laws and regulations that apply to larger businesses than to smaller businesses. As an organization grows, you will likely find that the legal constraints you must be concerned about will also change.

- Type of organization

  There are laws and regulations targeted specifically at different types of businesses. For example, financial organizations such as banks and brokerages have to be concerned about what information they can make available and their safeguards against accidental disclosure.

- Geographic location

  You'll find differences based on where you are located. Regulations vary from city to city and state to state.

- Geographic scope

  The wider your geographic scope, the more regulations you are going to encounter. You may find yourself having to contend with interstate and international communication regulations.

Because of the differences between the laws and regulations as they apply to different business, locations, and so forth, there aren't too many sweeping statements that can be made about regulations. This section will give you an overview of the general areas that are going to be of interest.

You need to understand that you may need to seek legal advice in some situations to make sure that you are in proper compliance. The larger the organization, typically, the greater the need to get legal review of the overall network design and planned changes.

Business Regulations

Let's start by looking at the types of regulations that might apply to your organization. This discussion will be limited to laws and regulations that can have some level of influence on your network design.

One key area of concern is data access. The possible problems with international data access are relatively familiar and have been publicized recently in some high-profile legal cases. If you have international communication links, you need to be aware of what type of information can and cannot be released out of the country.

You might think that you don't have any concerns of this type if you are a regional or national organization, but you do. The concerns are related to definitions of what type of data must be held confidential and what data can be released. For example, being too free and open with financial information, especially other people's financial information, can get you into a great deal of trouble.

E-mail is another matter of potential concern. There have been recent cases in which organizations have embarrassed themselves because of information contained in e-mail messages or due to their inability to provide requested e-mails.

Another common constraint is the requirement to keep business and financial records available for a period of time. Most of these regulations were written with hard-copy records in mind, but you need to allow sufficient storage space for electronic records. If you do not keep the records in online storage, you will need to implement a reliable means of archiving the records.

Network Regulations

For this discussion, the focus will be on regulations that apply directly to the network and will address issues and constraints you exercise some control over. That's because there are some regulations that are going to act as constraints, such as controls over transmission rates, bandwidth usage, and other communications issues that impact you indirectly through your service providers. Computer equipment must meet electronic emission standards, but these standards have to be met before you can purchase the equipment.

The regulations that are most likely to impact your network design are going to be local and regional building codes and safety regulations. These are going to define factors such as the following:

- Cable routing

  This includes regulations such as where cables can be routed, how exposed cables must be covered, and so forth.

- Type of cable used

  The most common regulation you are going to see here is the requirement for plenum cable for all hidden cable runs. You may be required to use plenum cable for all interior cabling.

- Workspace ergonomics

  These regulations address issues such as monitor and keyboard placement, hand and arm rest requirements, and so forth.

If you're only dealing with a single office, then you only have to deal with one set of regulations. It gets more complicated when you are also designing network support for remote offices. You can plan on finding differences in each location. You will have to know and follow regulations and restrictions that are applicable in each remote location.

You may be in a situation where you haven't had to deal with a lot of these regulations in the past and wonder why they should be a concern now. Many regulations do not require you to retrofit existing installations but will apply as soon as you start making other changes to your network design.

Growth Constraints

You have to plan for both immediate and long-term growth. When upgrading your network or installing a new network, it is usually more cost and time effective to include support for growth into your design.

Internal Growth

In this usage, the term *internal growth* refers to growth inside an office. Expansion to other offices, though internal to the organization, is external to your local network's scope.

In an established organization, the rate of growth should be somewhat predictable. It will be difficult to estimate projected growth in a newer organization or when an organization is going through massive restructuring.

Some network factors relating to supporting internal growth include the following:

- Computers

  As you add more users, you are going to need more user workstations. Since performance-to-cost ratios have historically improved with time, it is usually more cost effective to purchase systems on an as-needed basis.

  As you add more users, you are going to need more network server resources. There will be additional user validation requests, data access, name resolution, and other requirements. If you include this into your initial plans, you can implement network servers to meet both current and future requirements. Otherwise, you can find yourself having to add or upgrade your existing servers.

- Cable plant and connection devices

  As new systems are added, you are going to have to provide connectivity. If you are aware of the growth plans, you can set up connectivity devices and preinstall the cable while you are implementing your network design. This is usually more cost effective than having someone come back repeatedly to run cable on an as-needed basis.

- Software

  User systems and servers are going to need software. It's going to be your responsibility to make sure that the software is installed, but also to make sure that it is properly licensed. There are no hard-coded user limits built in to most software. It is up to you to track software usage and ensure that you remain within your license restrictions.

- Support personnel

  This is an area that can be overlooked easily when planning for network growth. As the number of users, servers, and other network resources increases, so do the support requirements. You will need to have a plan in place for bringing in and training additional support personnel to meet this need.

Your network growth plans will be no better than the information they are based on. Accurate growth projections are critical to well-managed network growth.

Expansion

Expansion into a remote office should be given the same consideration as any network design project. You will have to make a complete analysis of network requirements, including the following:

- Number of users
- Applications
- Data storage requirements
- Network services
- Remote communications

Opening a new branch office is an opportunity to get it right the first time. Since you will be installing a new network, you don't have to worry about upgrading or migrating an existing network structure.

That doesn't mean that the design and implementation won't be without their own special challenges. One probable area of concern is remote access. You are likely going to need to find ways to keep communications across the remote link to a minimum, which means providing local support for most network services.

Acquisition

Requirements and concerns during acquisition were discussed earlier in this chapter. As a quick review, network support is typically managed in the following two phases:

- Provide network connectivity to the acquired network.
- Migrate the existing network to meet established networking guidelines.

One of your initial tasks is going to be a complete inventory of the existing network. The guidelines are the same as for your initial inventory for any network design project and will include servers, client workstations, application software, server software, cable plant, and connectivity devices.

Budget Constraints

The budget issue has already been addressed in some detail and will continue to turn up on occasion throughout the course. The network budget is always going to have an influence on network design, implementation, and ongoing network operations.

Actually, you will probably find yourself dealing with two network budgets: an implementation budget and an operations budget. Let's take a little time to talk about each of these.

Implementation Budget

This is the money that you are going to have available to design and implement your network. This budget will need to allow for the following:

- System purchases
- System upgrades
- Software purchases
- Cable plant installation
- Personnel
- Outsourced services

Most of these have already been addressed in the course. Personnel and outsourced services may need a little additional discussion.

A new network doesn't install itself. There are systems to be set up, new software to be installed, cable to be run, connection devices to be set up, and so on. Not only do you have the physical installation process, you also have to test everything to make sure that it is working properly. Implementing a new network is a labor-intensive process.

You will want to make as much use of your network support personnel as possible. There may be a problem, however, in that they are going to still have to make sure that their other support requirements are met. You can avoid interruptions by doing most of the implementation work after hours and weekends, but how many weekends in a row can you work your support personnel?

You will probably find yourself wanting to outsource some of the implementation activities. Likely activities include setting up new systems, where you may be able to negotiate setup in with the purchase price, and pulling new network cabling.

Operations Budget

The operations budget is sometimes overlooked during the network design process. However, you can plan on the operations budget being impacted. When you make changes to the network, there will be changes in what it costs to support the network and network users.

Budget Planning

When estimating the operations budget, you need to consider the network's Total Cost of Ownership (TCO). In other words, you need to consider everything related to network support, maintenance, and repair. This includes the following:

- Remote and dial-up access charges
- Hardware repairs and replacements
- Software upgrades and new software
- Network infrastructure support and maintenance
- Network and end-user support personnel

Each of these can include hidden costs that don't come immediately to mind. Take application software upgrades, for example. In addition to the cost of the upgrade, you have to consider the time required to install the upgrades on the client systems and plan on an increased support call volume until the users are comfortable with the new software.

Reducing TCO

What you may find is that your operations costs can actually drop after the initial breaking-in period for your new network. For example, Windows 2000 includes a number of features that can help to reduce your TCO, such as the following:

- Directory services-based centralized management
- Support for delegated administration
- Dynamic Domain Name System (DDNS) support
- Automated software deployment and maintenance

Before you get too excited about the cost savings, you need to realize that you will probably be implementing these over time. It is more likely that you will see gradual cost savings over time rather than large and immediate reductions in cost.

Priorities and Risks

One of the first points made in this course was that the network is in place to support the business. Because of this, your network design priorities are going to be based on your business priorities. That means that you will have to determine what the business priorities are and how they can be supported through network services.

Assessing Priorities

Business priorities are going to be specific to each business and its goals. Most business priorities fall into the following categories:

- Functionality
- Performance
- Availability
- Security
- Cost

You've probably noticed that this is similar to the list of network goals you saw earlier in the course. Network goals are derived from business priorities. How critical the priority is to your organization determines how much weight it should be given as a network goal.

Functionality

The bottom line is the network has to work. If the network isn't up and operational, nothing else about the network is going to matter. This means that the network has to provide all of the required services. Users have to be able to log on. Applications and data files must be available. Remote offices have to be able to communicate.

That means that you have to make sure all of the background services are in place and that sufficient resources are provided for them to work properly. These include logon authentication, name resolution, routing, and so forth. In addition to these, you have to provide services specific to your organization, such as server-based applications.

Performance

Performance requirements are going to be determined by the services that are most critical to your business. Of course, it may take several different network services to meet a single performance goal.

For example, consider the requirements for point-of-sale invoicing. A customer comes up with his purchases and is ready to check out. The end-user application must be optimized to support posting the purchases quickly and accurately. If the sales information is being written to a centralized database, it must have sufficient resources to keep up with peak posting requirements.

Availability

In a LAN environment, it is generally assumed that the network will always be available and user resources will always be accessible. The requirements may not be as strict across remote links. Availability requirements may be met through on-demand connections.

Depending on how critical of a priority availability is, you can improve availability by providing redundant services. These will be discussed in some detail when looking at risk tolerance.

Security

If security isn't a priority for your organization, it should be. Security includes limiting the access to resources and protecting resources from loss or corruption. Logon security should be part of any network design plan. Regular backups, the most fundamental form of data security, should also have a high priority.

Other security priorities will depend on your organization. These were discussed earlier in the course and include data access security, data encryption, and encrypted communications. In some cases, you may be constrained by regulated minimum security requirements.

Cost

If keeping cost to a minimum is going to be a high priority, then you will have to find ways to cut costs in your network design. Unfortunately, this often means that other areas may suffer. You may be limited in the number of servers you can implement and be forced to have servers perform multiple duties. It could mean having to use lower-cost, lower-bandwidth remote connections, which will impact remote communication support.

Tolerance for Risk

Network failures are a fact of life. Hardware devices break, remote links can be temporarily unavailable, virus infections corrupt data and application files, and so on. You need to assess the amount of risk that can be tolerated by your organization and design your network accordingly.

If network and data availability are critical factors, then your network has a low risk tolerance. Your best solution is to implement risk avoidance. Some key points include the following:

- Redundant servers

  Redundant servers ensure availability of critical network services. These include logon authentication, name resolution, network address assignment, and so forth. Guidelines for implementing redundant servers are discussed later in the course.

- Server clustering

  This is also referred to as failover clustering. If a server fails, its partner in the cluster takes over automatically with no perceived difference to the users. Because of the costs involved, you will want to limit this to your most critical servers, assuming that it even has a place in your network design.

- Data fault tolerance

  Data fault tolerance can be implemented at the server level for Windows NT, Windows 2000, and other third-party network servers. It uses arrays of disks configured to allow server operations to continue and to provide data access in the event of a single drive failure. This can also be implemented through disk fault-tolerant subsystems, such as a RAID 5 disk subsystem.

- Redundant communications

  If communication with remote offices is critical, you may need to consider providing redundant communication links. This will provide for load balancing, spreading the load across multiple links, and give you a higher effective bandwidth. Should a link fail or become temporarily unavailable, you will still be able to communicate with remote offices, though at a lower bandwidth.

These will have to be balanced against cost. Risk-avoidance measures increase the initial cost of implementing the network but can pay off in benefits in the long run. One problem you may find is that they can be difficult to cost justify since they are transparent to network users. You will find it easier to sell the idea of risk avoidance for networks that have experienced critical failures in the past.

Scenario 2-4: Analyzing Design Constraints

You have already seen all of the information you need to answer these scenario questions. Suggested solutions are provided in Appendix B at the end of this manual. It may be helpful to review the case studies in Appendix C at the end of this manual.

1. Barney's Bank falls under the most restrictive guidelines and regulations of any of the case study companies. Why would you assume this?

   ....

   ....

2. Which case study company is most likely to need outside assistance in network design when expanding to a new location, and why?

   ....

   ....

3. Fairco Manufacturing can allow minimal downtime but cannot afford data loss. In addition to regular backups, what is the most cost-effective way that Fairco Manufacturing can protect its data?

4. With which of the case study companies will the budget for a new network design have to be negotiated with the different organizational departments?

5. What is the performance priority for Things and Stuff?

SUMMARY

During this chapter, you were introduced to the following:

- Types of business models
- Organizational structure models
- Geographic models
- Policies and procedures
- Process upgrades
- Information flows
- Communication flows
- Life cycles

- Decision-making process
- Network design goals
- Business design goals
- Relationships
- Changes and change management
- Information Technology (IT) administration
- IT staff model
- Network design constraints and influences

In the next chapter, the focus shifts from business requirements to technical requirements.

POST-TEST QUESTIONS

The answers to these questions are in Appendix A at the end of this manual.

1. Network costs can be roughly broken down into implementation costs and ______________ costs.

2. When should network tasks be outsourced?

3. Name probable network requirements after a product has reached the end of its life cycle.

4. Why can a decentralized IT management structure make network administration and management more difficult in the long run?

5. What can you add to your IT management structure to make a network somewhat self-documenting after initial implementation?

6. Is the following an example of a policy or a procedure?

   A full backup will be run on all network servers weekly.

7. Regulations concerning the physical LAN, such as cable routing requirements, are usually set at which of the geographic scopes described in this chapter?

CHAPTER 3

Technical Environmental Analysis

MAJOR TOPICS

OBJECTIVES

At the completion of this chapter, you will be able to:

- Analyze and describe the structure of a company's LAN.
- Describe the analysis tools that are available to administrators.
- Describe the components of the LAN.
- Describe the characteristics of various WAN technologies.
- Analyze the impact of Network Design on the users.

PRE-TEST QUESTIONS

The answers to these questions are in Appendix A at the end of this manual.

1. What is the addressing difference between a routed and nonrouted LAN?
2. What is the purpose of a backbone in a routed LAN?
3. What Windows 2000 tool can be used to capture network traffic for later analysis?
4. Which Event Viewer log will contain entries generated by auditing logons?
5. What is the bandwidth for Ethernet implemented on RG-58 A/U cable?

6. What two name resolution services would you be likely to see in a Windows 2000 Active Directory domain?

7. What is the data rate for a T1 connection?

8. In a standard WAN environment, how is a user's initial connection to the network made?

9. Why is analysis of the current network support structure important to network design?

10. How are user logons validated in a workgroup?

11. What file system is required for local access security?

12. What type of device is used to filter and manage traffic between a LAN and the Internet?

    ....

    ....

13. What Windows NT utility can provide you with detailed information about system hardware?

    ....

    ....

INTRODUCTION

With this chapter, attention turns specifically to the network and network analysis. The chapter begins with a detailed look at Local Area Network (LAN) information gathering and analysis. This includes an introduction to commonly used monitoring tools that can aid you in the information-gathering process.

From LANs, the emphasis shifts to Wide Area Network (WAN) analysis. This includes a look at connection options for remote links between LANs. Much of the information presented during the LAN analysis discussion will also apply to WAN analysis.

The next topic is user and resource analysis. This is presented as somewhat of an overview. This topic will be covered in more detail in later chapters.

The next two topics review and expand on information-gathering and analysis issues introduced earlier in the course. You are going to take a closer look at network support and network security requirements.

The chapter then focuses on network hardware, specifically network computers. It discusses the process for inventorying your network hardware and introduces some useful tools and utilities.

For now, the focus will be primarily on the current network infrastructure. In subsequent chapters, you will begin looking at what's involved in taking the data you've gathered and creating a new network infrastructure design.

LOCAL AREA NETWORK

For the purposes of this course, technical analysis of the network will begin with the LAN. In your analysis, you will probably find it best to start the same way, even if you are working with a WAN. First look at how each of the LANs are configured, then move up a level to see how they fit together into a WAN.

The following topics are covered in this section:

- LAN Overview
- LAN Analysis
- Topologies, Cable Plant, and Bandwidth
- Protocols
- Network Services

Some of the subjects discussed here will come up again during WAN analysis, but from a slightly different perspective.

LAN Overview

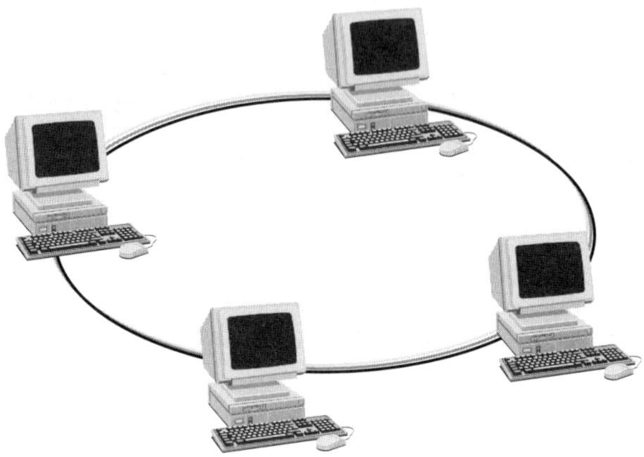

In the simplest terms, a LAN is a group of computers connected together in a way that allows them to communicate. The computers making up a LAN are locally connected. Traditionally, this means that there are no connections across public carriers (such as telephone lines) involved.

While its definition may be relatively simple, a LAN's configuration is not necessarily so. There can be a great deal of variation between LANs. Some common models are presented in this section, but you will also see a number of variations to these models.

For now, the focus will be on analysis, that is, looking at some of the key features of these models. Later in the course, you will be using these models as a reference again, but you will be focusing on benefits and matching models to networking requirements.

Nonrouted LAN

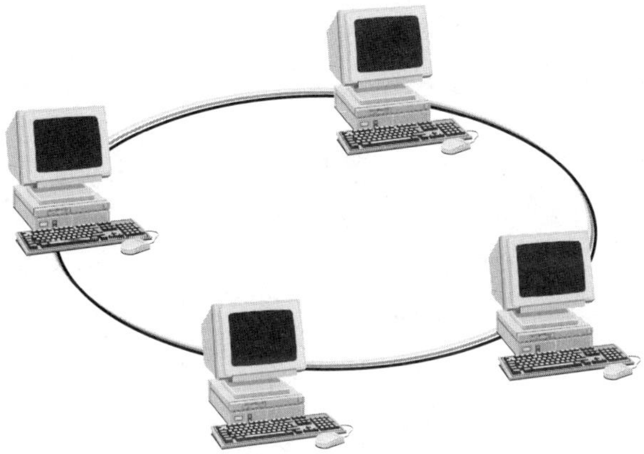

This is the most basic LAN model, with all computers connected on the same network segment. This doesn't necessarily mean that they are all connected to the same cable. In a star topology, each computer would be connected on a separate cable. In a bus topology, there might be multiple cable segments connected by repeaters. However, all network devices are connected as a single logical network with a single network address.

This model supports the use of both routable and nonroutable protocols. Both types of protocols can be used on the same network. Remember, though, that two computers must share a common protocol before they can communicate.

This LAN model is characterized by high bandwidth and high availability. Nothing is done to filter network traffic, so from a communication standpoint, all systems are equally available.

Routed LAN

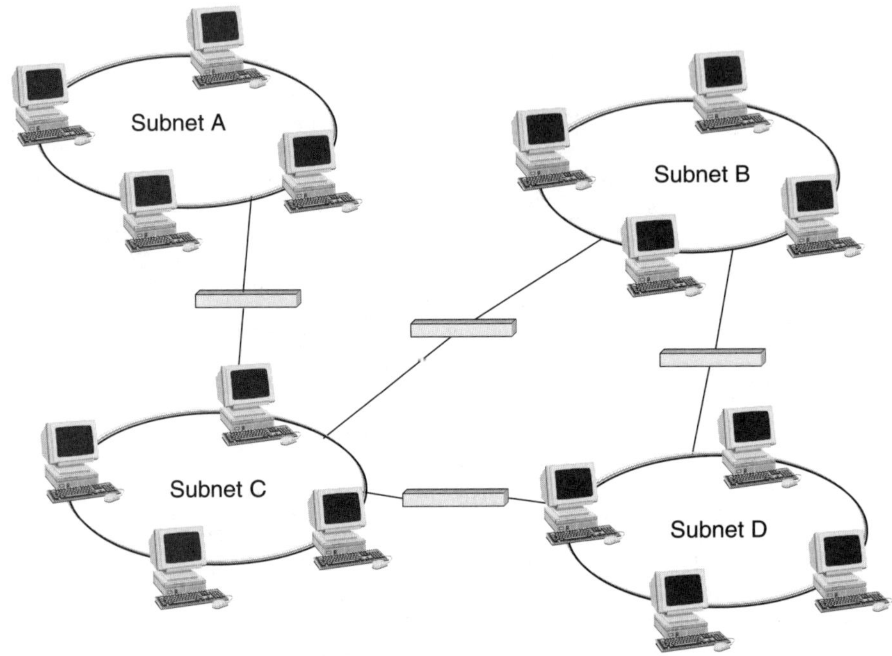

This is where LAN models can start getting a little more complicated. In a routed LAN, the network is broken up into two or more subnetworks, each with its own network address. Routers are used to connect the subnetworks and allow them to communicate.

Routers act to isolate the subnetworks from one another. Traffic having its originating and destination stations in the same subnet is not passed to other subnets. In other words, if a computer in subnet A sends a packet to another computer in subnet A, the traffic stays in subnet A and does not impact the rest of the network. Routers can also be used to provide additional filtering to a network, letting you specify what traffic will or will not be accepted and passed by the router.

This model is characterized by high bandwidth. There is some (usually minimal) performance loss with each hop, that is, each time traffic crosses a router. Traffic between LANs can be filtered, so availability of network resources can be controlled. Other than a few limited examples that will be discussed later in the course, broadcast traffic is not propagated by routers.

Routed LAN with Backbone

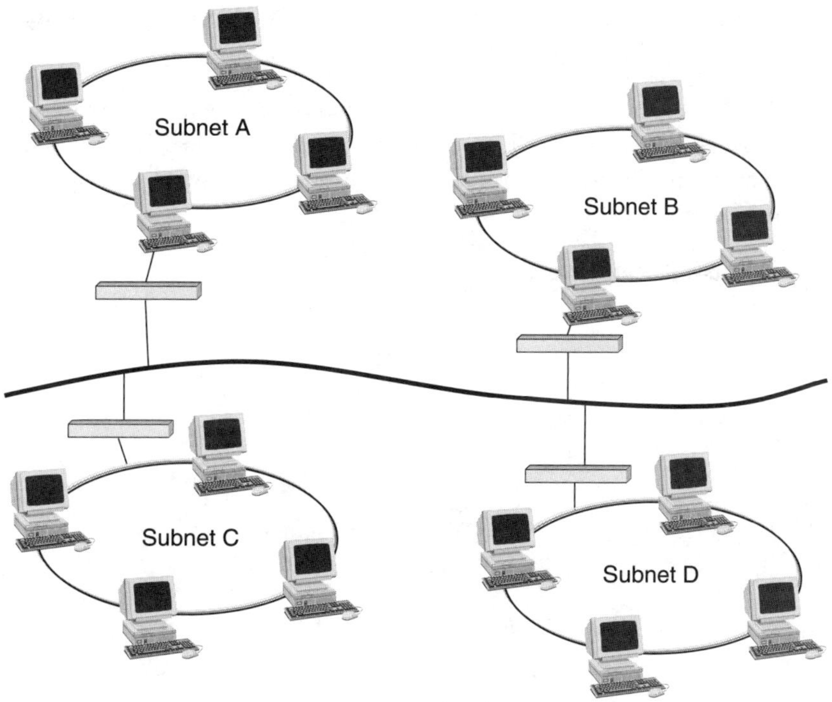

This is a variation on the previous LAN model. Rather than having the subnetworks connecting directly to each other, they are all connected to a backbone cable. The backbone will have its own unique network address and will be seen as a separate logical network.

Each subnetwork will have a unique network address. As with the previous model, traffic local to the subnet is kept within the subnet. Only traffic destined for a different subnet is sent out to the backbone.

In some cases, servers providing resources to the network as a whole may be connected directly to the backbone. For example, you might have a SQL server that all of the subnetworks need to access periodically. You might get a performance improvement by connecting the server directly to the backbone.

The key characteristics are the same as those you saw in the previous model. The model provides high bandwidth, especially across the backbone. There is high, but controllable, availability. Standard broadcast traffic is not propagated by the routers and will not be seen on the backbone.

LANs and Remote Access

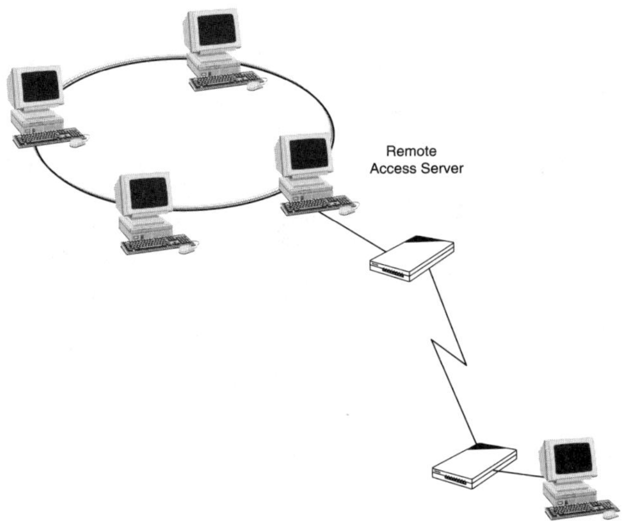

By strict, traditional definitions, this could fall under either LAN or WAN networking. From a practical standpoint, you need to look at the network as a whole before deciding. If you have individual remote system connections, these are usually considered to be an extended part of the LAN. Often, the systems will receive a local network address during logon and will be treated as if part of the LAN. If you are connecting groups of systems, then the configuration will typically be considered a WAN connection.

Most periodic remote connections are made through dial-up connections utilizing the public telephone network. More recently, remote connections through VPNs over the Internet have become more popular. Even with these, however, you are typically dealing with a standard dial-up connection at the client end.

Remote connections of this type are characterized by low bandwidth and periodic on-demand availability.

A Quick Word on WANs

As you will see when the discussion turns to focus on WANs, a WAN is an interconnected collection of LANs. Each of the LANs can be based on any of these models or on a variation. It is common to see a mix of LAN models in a WAN environment.

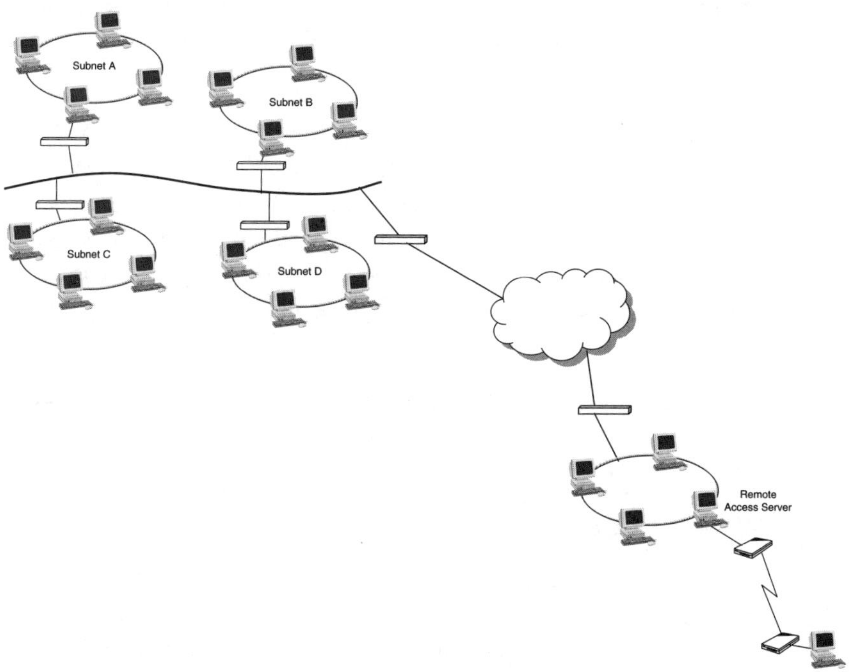

WAN configurations will be discussed in more detail later. For now, it's important to realize that you need to analyze the network environment in each LAN, then in the WAN as a whole.

LAN Analysis

During the LAN analysis process, you will be collecting technical data about your current network. This includes data flows, bandwidth usage, access patterns, server performance, and so forth. Once you have the data, you will need to compile and analyze the raw data to see just how it impacts your network design.

There is an additional reason for LAN analysis that applies more to the implementation phase. You want to be aware of network problems, or potential problems, before you start implementation. Otherwise, you could waste time trying to find out what you did to introduce a problem during implementation when the problem was already there all along.

One thing that you will notice is that the monitoring process can sometimes impact performance. This can be especially noticeable if you are having a server monitor itself, that is, having the server running both the services to be monitored and the monitor tools. However, offloading the monitoring and collection process can also distort your results. This is especially true if you are attempting to get accurate information on network traffic since offloading monitoring to a different system can result in additional traffic.

Since you are going to need to collect a great deal of information about your current LAN, it's important that you have some idea of the tools that you have available and what they can do for you.

Windows 2000 Tools

This discussion will focus primarily on the tools and utilities available with Windows 2000. Most of these are also available for Windows NT systems, though there may be some small differences in how they are implemented and accessed.

The Windows 2000 versions of these tools often have performance or functionality enhancements. If you don't currently have any Windows 2000 Server systems as part of your LAN, making the Windows 2000 monitoring tools available makes a good case for adding or upgrading at least one system.

What follows is an overview of some of the tools and utilities that you will probably find most useful. Key differences between the tools will be pointed out as each tool is discussed.

Network Monitor

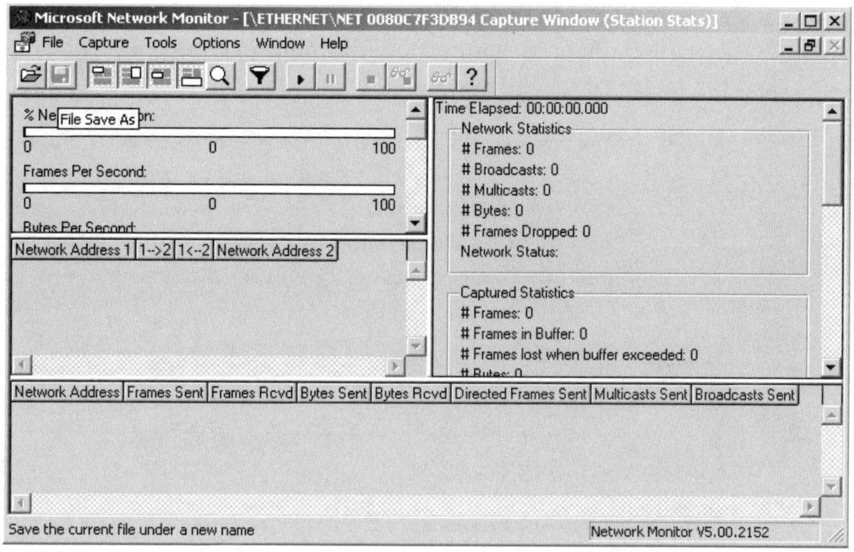

The Network Monitor lets you capture network packets and monitor network traffic. The Network Monitor ships with Windows 2000 Server and Windows NT Server but does not install by default. You can add Network Monitor after operating system installation.

After installation, the Network Monitor is available as part of the **Administrative Tools** menu. The Network Monitor will capture incoming and outgoing packets, placing a time stamp on each based on the elapsed time since you started the capture. In addition to capturing packets, the Network Monitor will decode the packet. This will make it easy for you to view information about the packet, such as the source address, destination address, packet type, and so forth.

Summary network and capture statistics will be displayed while the capture is running. The Network Monitor driver captures the data from the network adapter and passes the data to the Network Monitor. The version of Network Monitor that ships with Windows 2000 can only capture local incoming and outgoing traffic but is still useful for checking traffic for specific systems.

NOTE: *The version of Network Monitor that ships with Microsoft's Systems Management Server allows you to capture traffic from any system with the Network Monitor driver loaded. The Network Monitor driver will forward the data to the system acting as a remote monitor. This will increase the amount of background traffic on your network.*

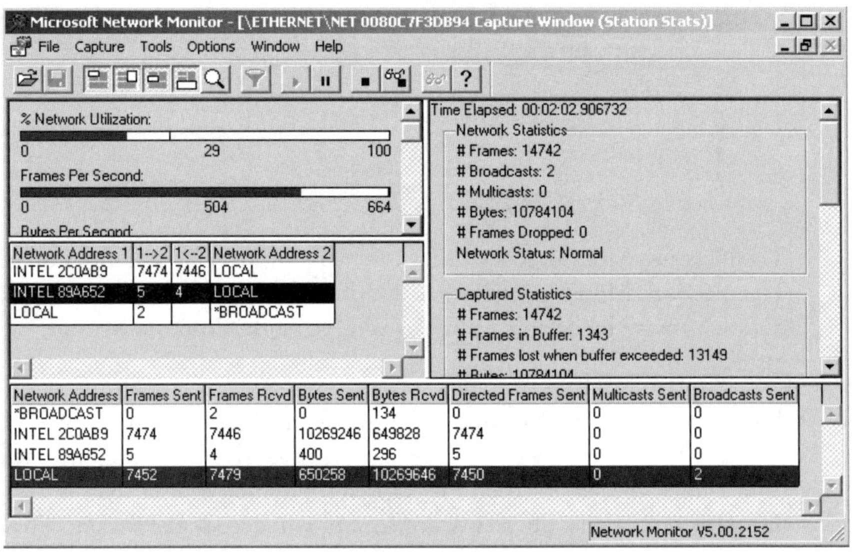

The Network Monitor will immediately start capturing data. While the capture is running, you can see information about the following:

- Current and peak activity
- Totals for local transmissions and received data by source
- Detected network errors

You can pause or stop a running capture. You have the following two choices for stopping a capture:

- Stop

  If you stop the capture, the summary screens will still be displayed. You can choose separately to display more detailed frame information.

- Stop and View

  If you select to stop and view the capture, information about individual frames is displayed.

Capture data can be displayed, filtered to display selected traffic only, and can be saved for later review and analysis.

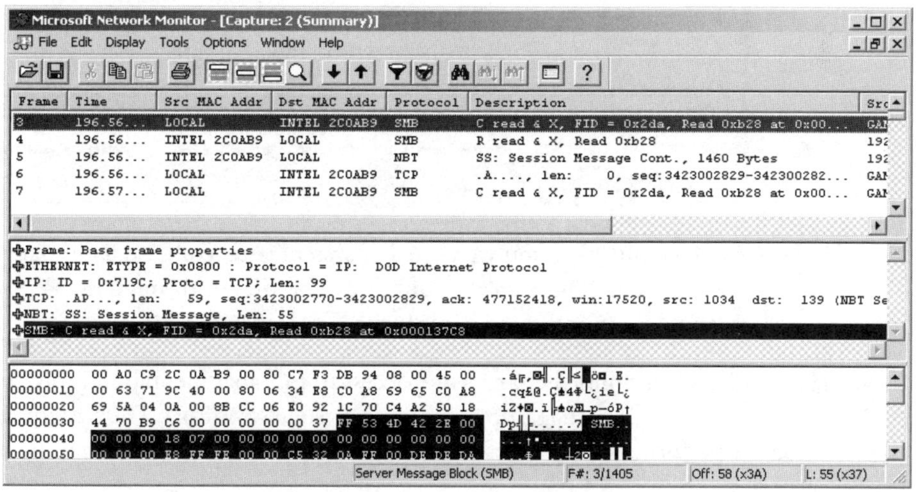

You can view the captured packets down to looking at the contents of each individual packet. You can define filters on the packets that will let you focus on specific traffic matching the filter criteria. You can filter on addresses, protocols, and protocol properties. You can also save the capture for later reference or comparison.

System Monitor

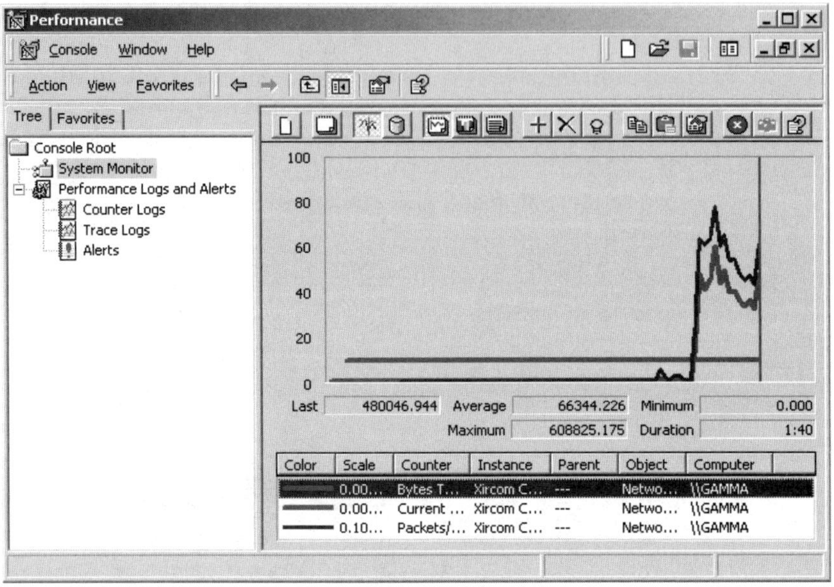

The System Monitor lets you view current system data, collect data for later analysis, and view collected data. The System Monitor can be viewed through the Performance tool, which is launched from the **Administrative Tools** menu.

System Monitor online help provides access to full documentation for System Monitor. It also provides some suggestions for using System Monitor. The System Monitor can monitor performance counters for the local computer or for other computers on the network.

System Monitor supports the following three view options:

- Chart
- Histogram
- Report

The Chart view is the default, and most commonly used, view. It provides near real-time data displayed as a line chart. You are able to view counter data over a short period of time. The time period represented by the window depends on your sampling frequency.

The Histogram view, by default, shows average values. Alternately, you can select to display current, minimum, or maximum values. Only one type of value can be selected, that is, you can't have part of the bars in the bar graph showing average values and others showing current values.

The Chart and Histogram views are both popular because their graphic displays give you a good, immediate overview of system performance. However, that is not all the information they provide. Just below the graphic display is more detailed numeric data. This display is called the value bar. The data displayed is for the currently selected counter and includes the following information:

Last	The last recorded counter value
Average	The average value since the counter was added to System Monitor
Maximum	The maximum value recorded for the counter
Minimum	The minimum value recorded for the counter
Duration	The counter duration

The current counters are listed in the lower portion of the System Monitor window. This is referred to as the System Monitor Legend.

The Report view displays the numeric values of counter data. This is helpful when you want more exact values for comparison or analysis. By default, the values displayed are averages, but you can select to display current values, minimums, or maximums. As with the Histogram view, all counters will display the same type of value.

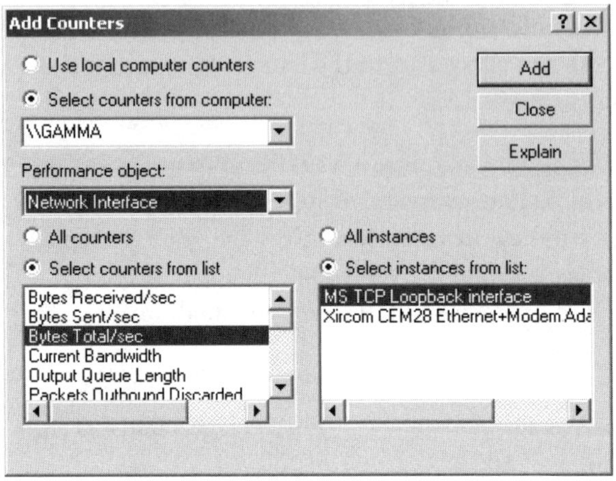

Each performance object will have a set of object-specific performance counters. The performance objects you see listed will depend on the services installed. Installation of some applications and services will cause additional objects and counters to be added to the System Monitor.

You can select to view counters from the local computer or from another computer on your network. You can make performance comparisons between machines by viewing counters concurrently from different machines. If you select **All counters**, all performance counters for the selected performance object will be added to the view.

With some performance counters, you will have multiple instances available. For example, you will have multiple network interface instances available on a system with multiple network adapters. You can choose to display data individually for all instances, for any selected instances, and total counter values for all instances.

Click on **Explain** to view a description of the selected counter. The description will include what is being measured by the counter and how the counter value is generated.

Alerts

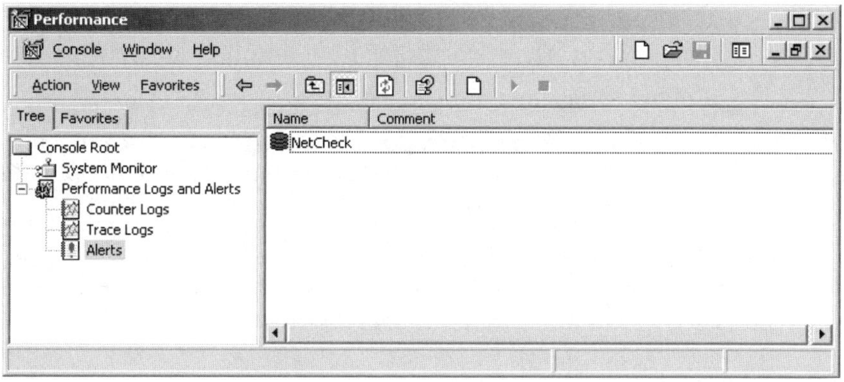

You can use alerts to monitor counters based on threshold limits. When a limit is exceeded, the alert triggers. Alerts are viewed and managed through the Performance tool.

You define alerts based on the same performance counters as are available for the System Monitor. You define an alert by selecting one or more counters and threshold trigger values.

If a counter value exceeds its threshold value, the alert will trigger. If an alert has not triggered, its icon will display in green. The icon color changes to red after the alert triggers. The following actions are available in response to an alert triggering:

- Log an entry in the application event log

  By default, each time an alert triggers, an entry will be written to the Event Viewer Application log.

- Send a network message

  This will send a message to the user, or machine you specify, saying that the alert has triggered.

- Start performance data log

  You can have a Performance log started (so it will begin gathering performance data) automatically when the alert triggers. You can only specify a predefined Performance log. Select the log from the drop-down list provided.

- Run this program

  You can choose to have an executable program or batch file run when the alert triggers. You can specify command-line arguments along with the command to be run. Specify the full path and filename to the executable.

While you won't have much need for alerts during the analysis phase, they can be helpful during the management phase after the new network is installed. It gives you an automated way to watch for potential problems.

Counter Logs

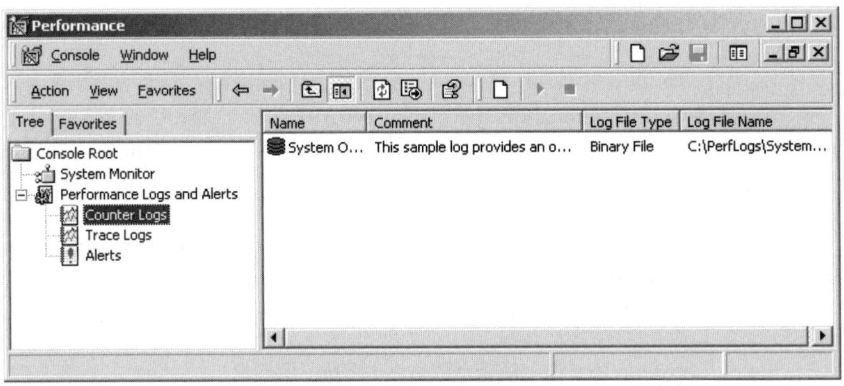

During the analysis phase, it is often helpful to record data sampled from performance counters rather than displaying real-time data. You can do this through the use of counter logs. Counter logs use the same performance objects and counters as System Monitor. They let you record counter values over time for later analysis.

You can create a log file as a tab-delimited text file, comma-delimited text file, binary file, or binary circular file. The default log file type is a binary file. Data logged in a binary file can be viewed through System Monitor. Text files can be viewed through any text editor or other application that accepts text input.

When you create the log file as a binary circular file, the oldest entries can be automatically overwritten when the maximum file size is reached. By default, the log file is able to grow to take all available free disk space on the volume it is located on. Alternately, you can (and usually should) limit the file size.

Trace Logs

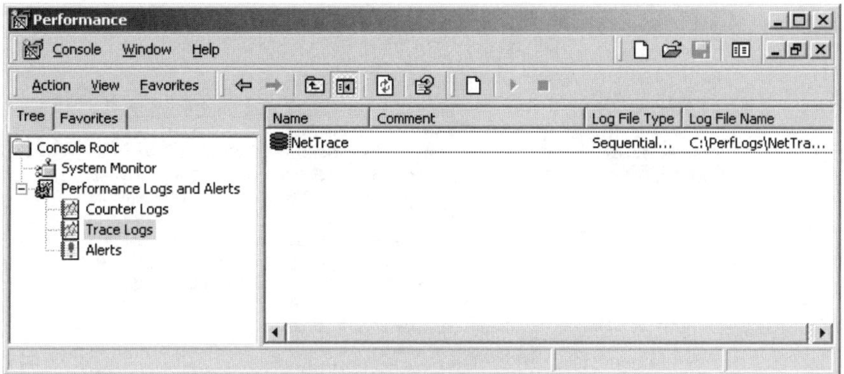

Trace logs were released as a new feature with Windows 2000. Trace logs collect information on system events. One potential use of trace logs is to view associated activities generated by an application or other system activity.

A major difference between trace logs and counter logs is that data is collected from start to finish during events, rather than just sampled. This leads to significantly larger log files and more detail than you will typically need when doing analysis for network design.

There is one significant drawback in that Windows 2000 doesn't provide a tool or utility for viewing trace log data. The data must be parsed to be interpreted, and you will have to provide a parsing tool for this purpose.

Event Viewer

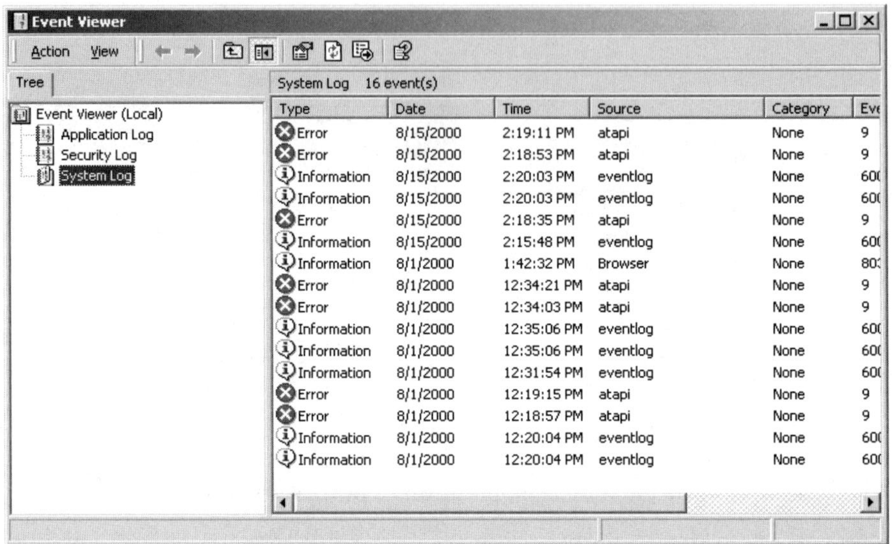

The Event Viewer, which can be launched from the **Administrative Tools** menu, gives you access to a system of Windows 2000 logs. These logs track information, warning, and error messages. The following logs are available by default:

- Application log

  The Application log will contain messages generated by applications. Some services are included under the *applications* umbrella and can add entries to the Application log.

- Security log

  The Security log tracks events generated by auditing selections that you have enabled. You must have administrator permissions to view the content of the Security log.

- System log

  The System log contains service- and hardware-related errors. These can include services that have failed to start or hardware devices that have failed to initialize properly.

The Event Viewer logs are excellent management tools but have limited use when collecting network data for analysis. One possible use is to enable auditing on selected critical folders to gather resource access data.

TCP/IP Tools

It probably comes as no surprise to you that when the discussion turns to protocol planning, the focus will be on TCP/IP. With this in mind, let's discuss a few common TCP/IP tools and utilities. Most of these will be covered in more detail later in the course.

Ipconfig

Ipconfig provides a quick way to view a system's IP configuration, including IP addresses and subnet masks, the primary DNS server, and so forth. It can be used for documenting your system configurations, though the same information is also available through Windows graphic utilities.

After implementing your new network design, Ipconfig can be very helpful in troubleshooting DHCP-related problems. You can use Ipconfig to release and renew automatic IP address assignments.

Ping

Ping is used to test connectivity between two IP hosts. You won't be using Ping much during network analysis, but it is another useful troubleshooting tool that can be used after implementation.

One place where you can use Ping is to look for latency in your network, more in WAN connections than in LAN connections. Ping sends a packet to the remote host and waits for a reply. Part of the information reported on return is the round-trip time, which will give you an idea of links where latency could be a potential problem.

Pathping

Pathping is similar to Ping except that it also returns router information. It can be used for documenting the path between hosts. You need to be aware that in a dynamic routing configuration, the path can change as network conditions change. While of limited use during your initial network analysis, Pathping is another helpful management and troubleshooting tool.

Tracert

Tracert is another tool that will be of more use during management and troubleshooting than during network analysis. Tracert can be used to trace the path a packet takes to its destination. As with Pathping, the path can change in a dynamic routing environment.

Other Tools

Before leaving the subject of analysis tools, it's worth the time to mention a few additional tools that you might find helpful.

Time-Domain Reflectometer (TDR)

A TDR is usually considered a troubleshooting device. It is most commonly used to locate breaks and shorts in network cabling. However, it can also be used to identify cable imperfections. Cable imperfections won't necessarily keep your network from working, but they can prevent your network from operating at an optimum level. They can act to restrict the available bandwidth, throttling your communication capacity. Errors of this type need to be corrected before you start the implementation phase of your network design.

Network Monitors

Third-party network monitors provide the same functionality as the Network Monitor that ships with Windows and Microsoft Systems Management Server. However, they are implemented as separate devices, which means that you are loading down any of your network systems during traffic monitoring.

Network monitors will commonly be used during network analysis to monitor bandwidth usage. Once you know your average and peak bandwidth usage values, you can determine if the current network infrastructure can support projected traffic levels for the new network. You may find that you have to make some changes, such as implementing a higher-speed protocol or segmenting network traffic through subnetting.

Protocol Analyzer

Protocol analyzers perform a wide range of real-time network traffic analysis tasks. You may be more familiar with the term *network analyzers.* Both terms refer to the same type of monitoring device. A protocol analyzer provides all of the functionality described for network monitors and TDRs. In addition, it lets you:

- Identify activity by individual systems.
- Identify network performance trends.
- Set alerts to watch for specific network conditions.
- Identify LAN bottlenecks.

The biggest drawback of protocol analyzers is their cost. A company with a small network will find it difficult, if not impossible, to justify the purchase of a protocol analyzer. You may be able to rent one for a short period of time to complete your analysis. This is a situation where you might consider going to an outside consultant. You may find it an efficient use of your time and money to have someone else come in and do the analysis, then provide you with a report of the results.

Topologies, Cable Plant, and Bandwidth

Network topology, cable plant, and bandwidth are closely related. The network topology describes how the cable plant is physically connected. Your cable plant is going to be a major factor in determining your available bandwidth.

Topologies

As you should remember from the earlier discussion, the common topology types you are likely to see are as follows:

- Bus
- Ring
- Star

You need to be aware that you might encounter a mix of topology types in a large, interconnected LAN.

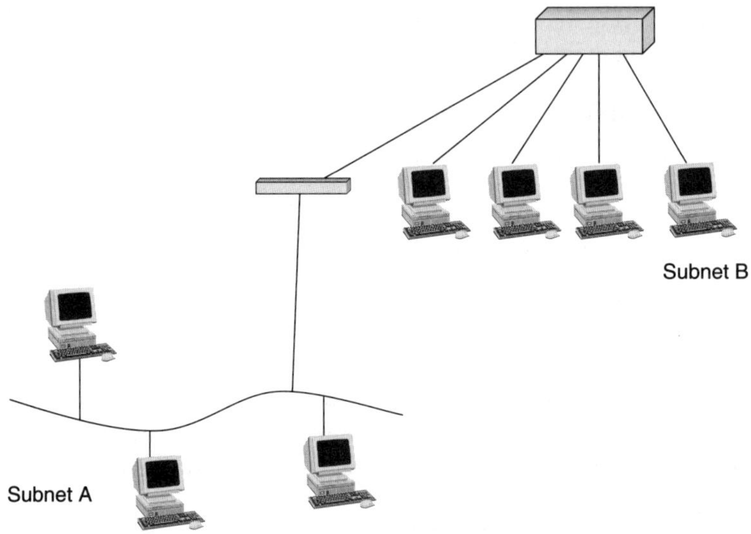

Here's an example you might encounter. In the previous figure, subnet A is your company's original LAN and uses a bus topology. As the company expanded and acquired additional office space, subnet B was installed using a star topology and the two subnets connected by a router.

Part of your design decision will be determining what, if anything, you are going to do about this configuration. You have the option of leaving the LAN configured as is, but you may find it more to your advantage to standardize on one topology.

Cable Plant

Analyzing your cable plant might not be as simple as you first think. This is going to include the following steps:

- Identify cable types.

  You need to know what types of media are currently in use. This will let you determine if you need to replace any of the cable plant when implementing your network design.

- Identify cable routes.

  Cable routes can especially be a problem if your network has grown up over time in a somewhat haphazard fashion. Poorly routed cables can result in less-than-optimal performance and increased support costs.

- Identify connection devices.

  You need to know what connection devices are currently in use. You may find that some of these will have to be replaced as part of the implementation process.

Let's take a look at some of the things that are going to be important during your analysis and physical inspection of the network.

Cable Types

Most cables are labeled in some fashion, usually with the cable identifier stenciled on the casing. Before this can do you any good, however, you need to understand what the cable types are and how they can be used. Let's start with coaxial cable.

Coaxial Cable

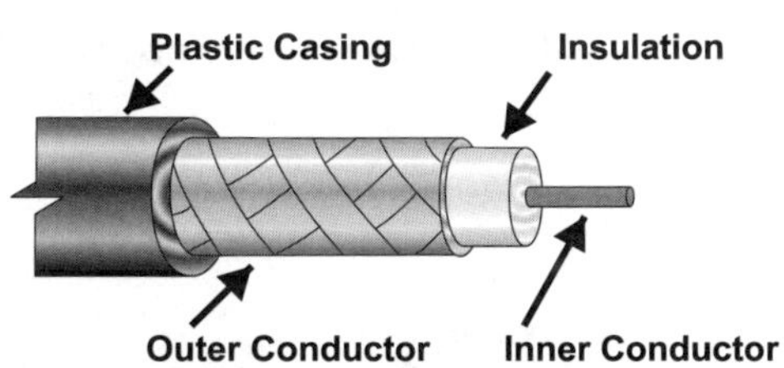

Coaxial cable has a central conducting core that carries the transmission signal. This is covered by a layer of insulation, typically PVC plastic or Teflon, then a copper or aluminum mesh shield to reduce crosstalk between cables and other electronic noise. Finally, the cable is covered with a nonconducting outer shield, either rubber, PVC plastic, or Teflon.

Coaxial cable is used with Ethernet 10Base5 and Ethernet 10Base2 wired in a bus topology. The cable used with 10Base5 is commonly referred to as thicknet cable. The cable designation for thicknet cable is RG-8.

The cable used with Ethernet 10Base2 is commonly called thinnet cable. A cable from the RG-58 coaxial cable family will be used, once again wired in a bus topology. The cables in the RG-58 cable family are as follows:

Cable	Description
RG-58 /U	This is *standard* RG-58, using a solid copper core.
RG-58 A/U	The only difference in this cable is that it has a stranded core rather than a solid core.
RG-58 C/U	This is a military-grade cable but is equivalent to RG-58 A/U in its basic design and characteristics.

ARCNET networks also use coaxial cable, using an RG-62 in this case. ARCNET is sometimes seen in legacy networks but is seldom found in newer networks.

NOTE: A detailed discussion of ARCNET is beyond the scope of this course.

Twisted-pair cable is used for telephone systems, as well as Token Ring and Ethernet 10BaseT.

Shielded Twisted Pair

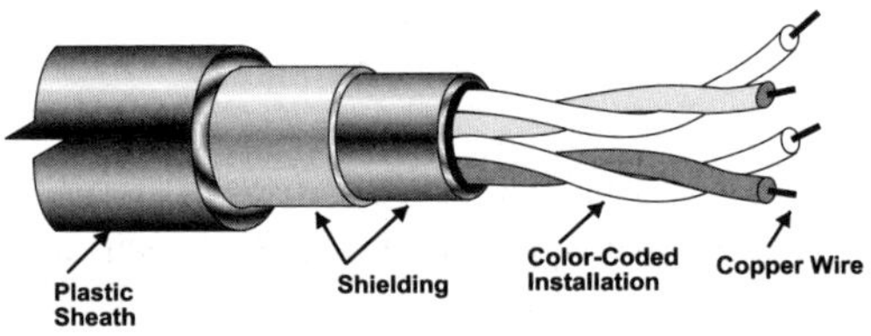

Twisted-pair cable uses pairs of insulated conductors. The pair is given a half twist at a set interval defined by the cable category. The twists help to reduce crosstalk between the cables. A cable will contain one or more twisted pairs of conductors.

Twisted-pair cable is available as Unshielded Twisted Pair (UTP) and Shielded Twisted Pair (STP) cable. STP adds a copper braid jacket or foil wrap around the cables to reduce the effect of electronic noise. However, STP is more expensive than UTP. UTP is most commonly used in network installations unless there is a definite need for STP.

There are five categories of UTP cabling. These are as follows:

Category	Number of Pairs	Description
Category 1	2	Used as telephone cable; the cable is rated for voice transmissions but not data transmissions
Category 2	4	Rated for data transmissions of up to 4 Mbps
Category 3	4	Rated for data transmissions of up to 16 Mbps
Category 4	4	Rated for data transmissions of up to 20 Mbps
Category 5	4	Rated for data transmissions of up to 100 Mbps

Category 2 and Category 3 cables are used for Token-Ring implementations, most using Category 3. Category 4 and Category 5 are commonly used for 10 Mbps Ethernet and 100 Mbps Ethernet, respectively. You may also find installations where Category 3 wiring has been used for 10 Mbps Ethernet.

One of the problems you may find is that the wrong category of cable has been used. This often happens when the network has been upgraded without upgrading the cable.

Sometimes you will find that the cable is labeled with only a manufacturer's part number. If so, you will need to contact the manufacturer to find out how the part number maps to standard cable designations. Many manufacturers make this information available through their Web sites.

Cable Routes

While you are preparing to implement a new network design, it's a good time to check your cable routes. If a cable company installed your network cabling for you, you may have a cable map available that will include most of the cable plant. In most cases, the information available about your cable plant will be based on vague statements such as, "It's up there somewhere," indicating the ceiling.

Tracing the cable route may require some leg work on your part to track down where and how network cables have been run. You will find a TDR or cable test device helpful in this task since they can identify cable lengths. Handheld cable test devices with this feature are readily available and relatively inexpensive.

Some of the things you should watch for while tracing the cable routes include the following:

- Cables routed near sources of electronic noise, such as fluorescent lights, electric motors, and so forth
- Exposed or poorly protected cables in high-traffic areas, leading to cable shorts and opens
- Nonplenum-rated cable where plenum-rated cable is required, including areas such as suspended ceilings and vertical runs through walls
- Cable segments that are longer than their specified maximums

You will also need to identify the type of cable being used in each of the cable routes. If you are planning to upgrade the network to improve bandwidth, you may find yourself replacing a large amount of the network cable.

Connection Devices

Network connection devices include the following:

- Repeaters
- Hubs and Multistation Access Units (MSAUs)
- Switches
- Bridges
- Routers

You need to know where each of these is located in the network and how they connect the cable segments. You also need to know the characteristics of each device. You will need to review the current devices to make sure they are compatible with your network design.

Bandwidth

In a LAN configuration, your available bandwidth will be determined by the following:

- Network adapter

  Network adapters are rated at specific data-transfer rates. Commonly you will find Token Ring adapters that can support 4 Mbps or 16 Mbps and Ethernet adapters that can support 10 Mbps or 100 Mbps. However, you will only be able to support one rate on a network cable segment. For example, if all of your network adapters but one support 10 Mbps and 100 Mbps, but one adapter supports 10 Mbps only, the segment will be using the lower transmission rate.

- Connection devices

  You may also find that your available bandwidth is limited by your connection devices. For example, you may have some older Ethernet 10BaseT hubs that only support 10 Mbps Ethernet.

- Network cable type

  Make sure that you are using a cable type that is rated to support your bandwidth requirements. You may be able to communicate over cable that isn't properly rated, but you will find yourself plagued by intermittent network problems.

- Network cable/cable plant quality

  The quality of your network cable can limit your available bandwidth. This can include problems with poor-quality cable, improperly routed cable, intermittent shorts or opens, and so forth. You can use a TDR or protocol analyzer to help you isolate problems of this type.

A network monitor or protocol analyzer can be used to determine your network bandwidth if you don't already know it. Keep in mind that this bandwidth is shared by all systems on the network segment, so you will also want to determine average and peak bandwidth usage.

Protocols

You were introduced to network protocols earlier in the course. As a quick review, you will most commonly see the following protocols:

- TCP/IP
- IPX/SPX (NWLink)
- NetBEUI
- DLC

You may also see other protocols that have been implemented. For example, you might find that your network is using the Systems Network Architecture (SNA) protocol for communication with IBM mainframe or minicomputer hosts.

Your goal during the analysis phase is to determine what protocols are in use. When you start compiling and analyzing your data, you will need to determine which protocols are actually needed.

Network Services

You need to review the network services currently provided on your network. This includes both what services are there and how they are being implemented. For now, the discussion is going to be kept at somewhat of an overview but with a focus toward eventually implementing a TCP/IP network as an Active Directory domain.

Let's take a look at some general service categories. These include the following:

- Security Services
- Network Address Services
- Name Resolution Services
- Directory Services

Some networks will not need and will not provide all of these services. Your initial goal is to determine what services are implemented on your network.

Security Services

For the purposes of this discussion, security services will focus on two specific categories: logon validation and security validation. In a Windows networking environment, these two are closely related. During logon validation, an access token is generated for the user. The access token is used for security validation when the user attempts to access network resources.

In a workgroup environment, logon and security validation are both handled individually by the peer servers. In a Windows domain environment, validation is managed by the Primary Domain Controller (PDC) and Backup Domain Controllers (BDCs). A Windows 2000 Active Directory domain doesn't identify separate primary and backup domain controllers, identifying them as simply domain controllers.

Logon validation has the biggest impact on network performance. You need to identify the location of your domain controllers and the impact of logon validation on network performance. You will need to monitor network traffic and server performance during peak logon times to determine how well current requirements are met. This will help you determine the changes that need to be made.

Network Address Services

If your network is currently supporting TCP/IP, there's a good chance that you are using Dynamic Host Configuration Protocol (DHCP) servers to manage automatic address assignment. Depending on how DHCP services are configured, the impact on the network is usually minimal after the initial address assignments, but you will need to document the locations of any DHCP servers and will want to monitor server performance to see how well the servers are meeting the current load.

Name Resolution Services

What you find here will depend on your current network configuration. If your LAN is configured as either a workgroup or Windows NT domain on a single subnetwork (a nonrouted network), you may not have any real need for name resolution services before now. If you have a routed network environment, have implemented domain services, or have a mixed environment that includes UNIX systems, name resolution issues have probably come up.

In a Windows networking environment, you will be dealing with the following two name resolution services:

- Domain Name System (DNS)

  DNS is used to provide domain name resolution, allowing host computers to be identified by their Fully Qualified Domain Names (FQDNs). A DNS server can provide an IP address for an FQDN and, in most cases, an FQDN for a requested IP address.

- Windows Internet Name Service (WINS)

  WINS provides resolution for NetBIOS names, providing an IP address for a requested NetBIOS machine name. NetBIOS name resolution is required for supporting legacy Windows-family systems that are not running the Active Directory client and for support of applications that use NetBIOS for peer-to-peer communications.

If you are using name resolution services, you need to document their location and availability as well as monitor performance to see how well the servers are able to meet your network's current requirements.

There are a couple of special points that need to be made in relation to name resolution services. One is that your network can be supporting name resolution without the use of network services. Name resolution support can also be provided through the following locally stored text files:

- HOSTS

  A HOSTS file can be used to support host name-to-IP address resolution. Host names do not have to be FQDNs.

- LMHOSTS

  An LMHOSTS file can be used to support NetBIOS name-to-IP address resolution.

You will usually find these files used in smaller networks with a limited number of computers or where there have been special resolution needs that were supported easily through the use of these files. As a network and the number of computers supported grow, it can become extremely difficult to maintain these files.

NOTE: A detailed discussion of the format, content, and use of HOSTS and LMHOSTS files is beyond the scope of this course.

There is also a chance that you are using a non-Windows DNS server to provide name resolution for your network. There is a good chance of this if your network has included UNIX systems for any length of time. These must also be documented to include not only their location, but the services provided. One issue that is going to come up during the design phase is determining whether you want to integrate or replace these existing servers.

NOTE: DNS name resolution is required for Active Directory domain services. The DNS server must support service (SRV) resource records and dynamic DNS updates.

Directory Services

Windows 2000 implements directory services as Active Directory domains. If your network currently includes Active Directory domains, you need to review the location and availability of domain controllers. Replication traffic usually is not an issue in a LAN environment but can become an issue over WAN links.

Scenario 3-1: LAN Analysis

The purpose of this scenario is to give you practice in LAN analysis. Suggested solutions are provided in Appendix B at the end of this manual. It may be helpful to review the case studies in Appendix C at the end of this manual.

Things and Stuff's Current Network

The network is configured as a 10Base2 Ethernet network. The only protocol in use on the network is NetBEUI. Users logged on to any system can access shared resources from other systems.

1. Is this a routed or nonrouted LAN?

   ....

   ....

2. What would you expect to find as the available bandwidth on the LAN?

   ....

   ....

3. What type of name resolution service servers would be required for this LAN?

   ....

   ....

4. What system or systems are responsible for logon validation?

   ....

   ....

Barney's Bank's Current Network

The main corporate LAN located in the home office is a routed LAN configured as an Active Directory domain. It consists of three subnetworks, all Ethernet, one using a bus topology, and the other two using star topologies. The bus topology subnetwork uses RG-48 A/U coaxial cable. The two subnetworks using a star topology are wired with Category 4 UTP cable. At present, there are two domain controllers in the corporate LAN, both located on the bus topology subnetwork.

1. At minimum, what protocol or protocols would be required on the main corporate LAN?

2. What name resolution services, if any, would be required for this LAN?

3. How does the location of the domain controllers impact performance during logon?

Fairco Manufacturing's Current Network

The LAN is configured as a nonrouted LAN running NWLink and TCP/IP protocols. It is wired in a star topology and was recently rewired using Category 5 UTP. The systems currently have 10 Mbps or 10/100 Mbps Ethernet adapters, about an equal number of each spread evenly around the LAN. The Windows NT domain is set up with one PDC and one BDC. IP name resolution is supported through the use of HOSTS files.

1. What would you expect to find as the current available bandwith on this LAN?

2. Why should you be concerned about scalability for IP name resolution as the network grows?

3. What system or systems are responsible for logon validation?

Exercise 3-1: Hands-On Preparation (Optional)

The purpose of this exercise is to configure your training network for the exercises that follow throughout the book. This exercise assumes that your systems can boot from CD-ROM. If not, you will need to prepare Windows 2000 boot diskettes.

This exercise also assumes that you are installing Windows 2000 Server on systems that already have a copy of a Windows operating system installed. If not, you will see some slightly different prompts than indicated in this exercise.

WARNING!

The data on the destination systems will be overwritten during installation. Back up any data that you want to save before starting this exercise.

All of the hands-on exercises in this course are labeled as optional exercises. You can complete the course without completing any of the exercises; you should, however, consider completing them since they will give you additional practice working with the concepts and technologies discussed during the course. There are no solutions provided for this exercise.

Special Preparation

You will need licensed copies of Windows 2000 Server for the three servers that you will be setting up and configuring during this exercise.

Server Installation

You will be installing three Windows 2000 servers during this exercise. The servers will be named Alpha, Beta, and Gamma. The procedures are the same for all three servers, except where noted in the exercise.

1. Boot your system from a Windows 2000 Installation CD-ROM.
2. When the Welcome screen displays, press *ENTER*.
3. Press *PAGE DOWN* through the Licensing Agreement, then press *F8*.
4. If prompted to repair an existing installation or to install a fresh copy of Windows 2000, press *ESC* to install a new copy.
5. Select drive C: as your destination, then press *ENTER*.
6. If prompted that the partition contains another operating system, press *C* to continue.
7. Select **Format the partition using the NTFS file system** and press *ENTER*.
8. If prompted to verify your action, press *F* to continue and start the format. There will be a delay while the partition is formatted and installation files are copied to the local hard disk. Your system will restart after copying the installation files.
9. After your system restarts, click on **Next** to continue. Setup will detect and install system devices.
10. After hardware detection, leave the regional settings at default and click on **Next**.

11. Enter the name and organization information as appropriate for each system, shown in the following table.

System	Name	Organization
Alpha	Student One	Delta
Beta	Student Two	Delta
Gamma	Student Three	Delta

    Click on **Next** after entering the information.

12. If prompted, enter your product key and click on **Next**.
13. Leave the licensing mode information at default and click on **Next**.
14. Type the following as the computer name:

Installation Order	Name
First system	Alpha
Second system	Beta
Third system	Gamma

    Leave the Administrator password and Confirm password fields blank and click on **Next**.

15. Leave the Windows 2000 components at default and click on **Next**.
16. Set the time zone as appropriate, then click on **Next**.
17. When prompted for network settings, select **Custom settings** and click on **Next**.
18. Select Internet Protocol (TCP/IP) and click on **Properties**.
19. Select **Use the following IP address** and enter IP address information as follows:

System	IP Address	Subnet Mask
Alpha	192.168.105.1	255.255.255.0
Beta	192.168.105.3	255.255.255.0
Gamma	192.168.105.101	255.255.255.0

    Leave the DNS server addresses blank and click on **OK**.

20. Click on **Next**.

21. Type the following as the workgroup name and click on **Next**:

    ```
    DELTA
    ```

22. Remove the installation CD-ROM from the CD-ROM drive and click on **Finish** to complete the installation.
23. After the system restarts, log on as Administrator. Leave the Password field blank.

WIDE AREA NETWORK

Now that you have an idea of what the LAN analysis issues are going to be, the discussion can move on to WAN analysis. The following topics are covered in this section:

- WAN Introduction
- Remote Connections
- WAN Services

The analysis tools discussed in the previous section also apply to WAN analysis.

WAN Introduction

As a working definition, consider a WAN as a collection of LANs that have been connected through public carrier links. As you can probably guess, this definition allows for a great deal of variation between WANs.

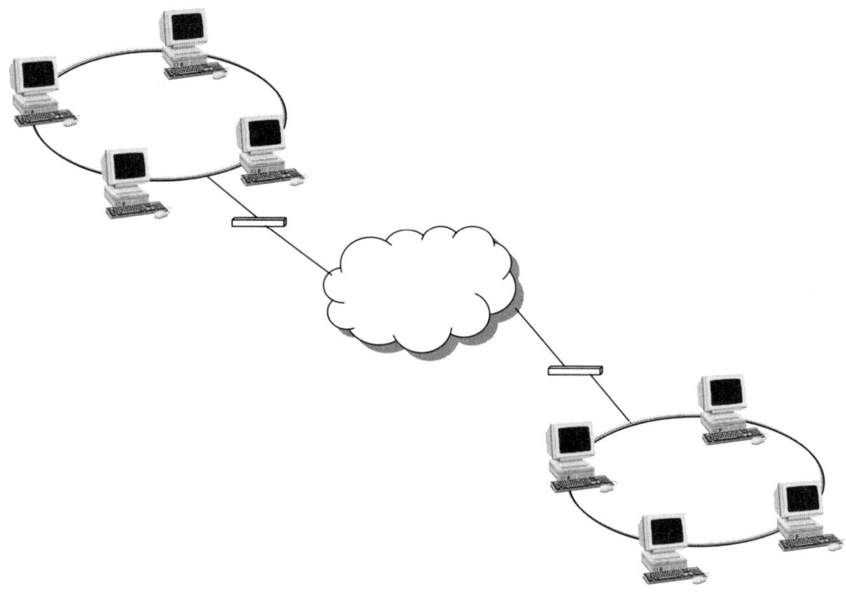

The previous figure represents a simple WAN design. It includes two similarly configured LANs connected by a single communication link. Analysis of a WAN of this type is going to be a relatively simple matter.

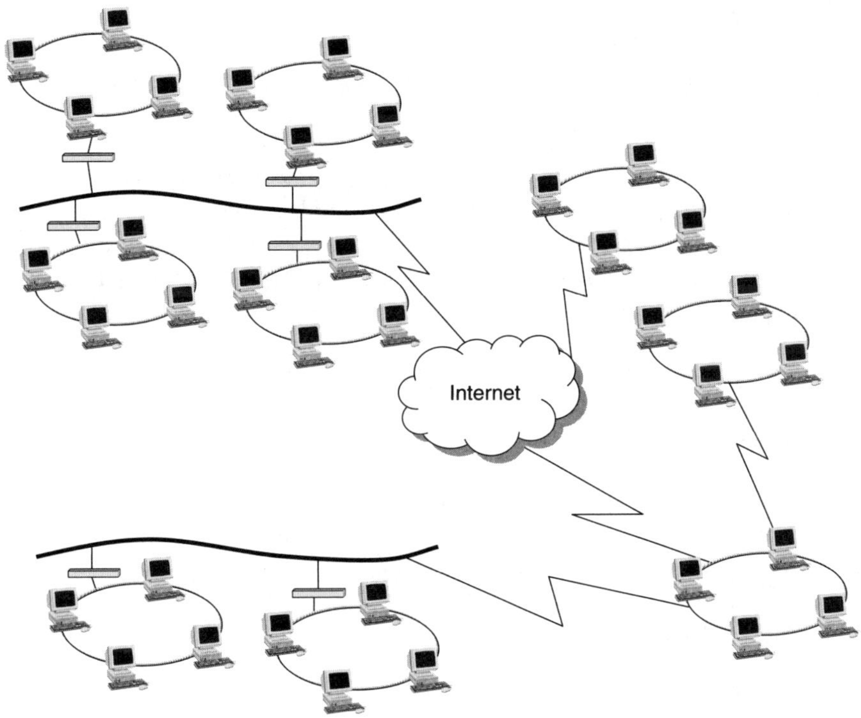

As your WAN becomes more complex, so does the analysis task. LANs can be configured differently and have different service and connection requirements. If multiple communication paths are available, they must be taken into account when determining available bandwidth.

WAN Analysis

A WAN is somewhat similar to a routed LAN except that the connections between LANs are made over remote links. As far as most users are concerned, there is no apparent difference between a LAN and a WAN.

A WAN's scope will be the same as an organization's geographic model, whether it is regional, national, or international. You can have one or more links and may have multiple paths available between LANs. How these links are managed will depend on the type of routers being used. Router characteristics are discussed in detail later in the course.

The first step in WAN analysis is to complete analysis for each of its LANs. From this, you will know what services and resources are being provided locally by the LAN and which are being provided by a remote LAN.

Once you've completed the LAN analysis, you are ready to look at the WAN. This will include the types of links that have been implemented, traffic patterns, available bandwidth, bandwidth usage, and so forth. During the analysis phase, focus on the current WAN configuration. You'll have time to consider improvements during the design phase.

Special Issues

There are some issues that may require a closer look in a WAN environment than they do in a LAN. These include the following:

- Availability

  In a LAN environment, you typically assume 24/7 connectivity, even though you may limit user access to the network through security policy. This won't always be the case with a WAN. You may be using on-demand connections for some of the links to reduce connection costs. You will need to determine the availability supported on each of your links and the costs involved.

- Server placement

  Server placement can be a critical issue in a WAN environment, even more than in a LAN. Some services, such as logon validation, can generate a significant amount of traffic. You need to know where servers are located in the WAN and which of those servers are providing network services to remote LANs.

- Security

  When discussing LANs, the focus was on logon and security validation. These continue to be issues in a WAN, but you have the added issue of communication security. You need to know how inbound and outbound connections are being managed and secured.

  Data transmission security is also an issue. Depending on how your WAN is configured and what types of links you are using, you may have a more likely chance for data to be intercepted during transmission. You need to know what type of encryption is being used, if any, so you can determine what changes need to be made in your new network design.

You will likely find yourself having to coordinate your efforts with technical personnel at each of the remote locations during the analysis process. The technical personnel at each site will have a better idea of how the LAN is configured, what its specific needs are, and what remote access problems they have experienced in the past.

Remote Connections

This is what makes your network a WAN. You need to understand the types of connections that have been implemented, along with the characteristics and potential drawbacks of each of the connection types. During the analysis phase, you are going to focus on the type of connection, bandwidth between locations, and security. You also need to know operational costs related to each of the links. Later, during the design phase, you will use this information to determine the most cost-effective links that provide the capabilities you require.

There are a number of connection options available. Guidelines for selecting a connection option will be discussed later in the course. For now, the discussion will be limited to an overview of some common connection options. This is not meant as a review of all possible connection options, but instead, those options you are most likely to encounter.

Dial-Up Connection

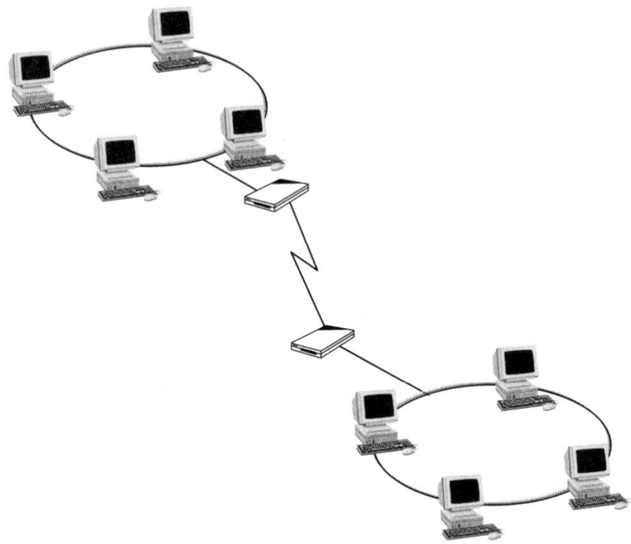

One option for WAN connectivity is to use dial-up connections over the Public Switched Telephone Network (PSTN). In other words, connecting through standard, voice-grade telephone lines.

A dial-up connection requires a modem at each end of the connection. The modem is connected to a modem pool that provides connectivity to the LAN's systems.

Dial-up connections can be used for intermittent connections between LANs where there are minimal bandwidth requirements. You are limited to no more than 56 Kbps. The quality of the circuits linked for the connection can vary with each session, so you may find that some connections will provide a lower bandwidth.

Dial-up connections are seldom used for LAN connections. They are, however, commonly used for remote access connections with individual computers dialing in and connecting to the network.

Dedicated Analog Lines

Dedicated analog-line connections, also referred to as leased lines, use the same general configuration as a dial-up connection. The difference is that the connection remains open all of the time. The circuit quality and bandwidth are somewhat better than for a dial-up connection. However, the dedicated analog lines can only be used when there are limited data communication requirements. Dedicated leased lines are also more expensive than dial-up lines because you are paying for 24-hour availability, whether or not it is being used.

ISDN

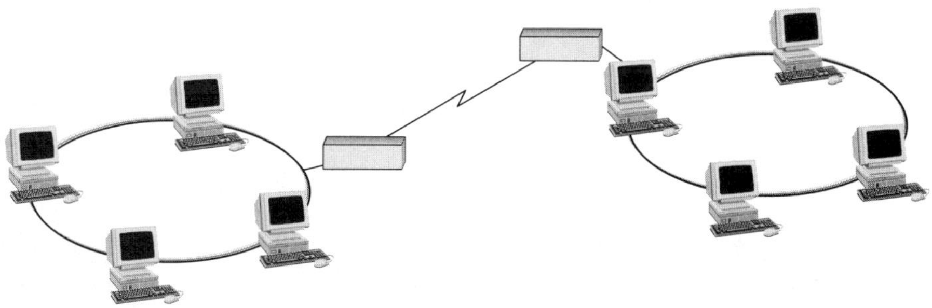

ISDN provides a digital network with support for multiple services, including voice and digital communications. ISDN connections are through multiple 64-Kbps channels. Common connection configurations are Basic Rate ISDN (BRI), which has two 64-Kbps channels, and Primary Rate ISDN (PRI), which has 23 64-Kbps channels.

A Terminal Adapter (TA) is required at each end of the connection. If your company is using ISDN for a WAN connection, it was probably set up by your local telephone company or other communication service vendor.

ISDN is a dial-up service implemented over high-quality telephone lines. Since it is a dial-up service, you will most often find it used where high bandwidth is required, but full-time availability is not needed.

Digital Data Service

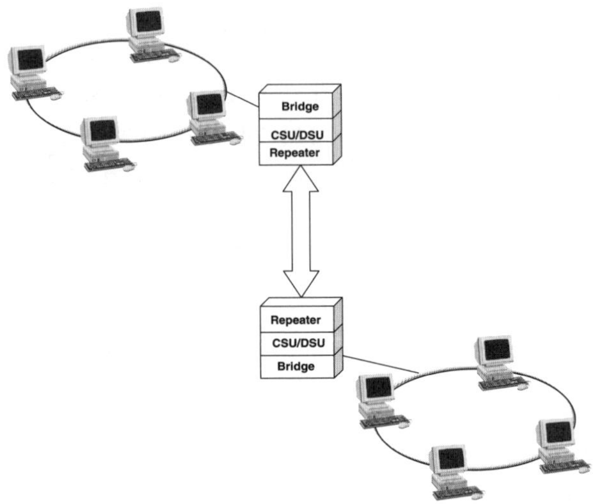

High-speed digital data service is used when high bandwidth and high availability are required. Digital lines are also very reliable, typically providing nearly 99% error-free service.

The T1 service is commonly used when higher-speed data connections are required. A T1 service connection provides a point-to-point connection over high-speed digital service lines. A T1 connection provides a 1.544-Mbps full-duplex transfer rate. The connection is made through a bridge or router to a Channel Service Unit/Data Service Unit (CSU/DSU) and then through a repeater. In case you can't find it, the repeater may not be installed locally. This rate is referred to as a DS-1 signal level.

T1 channels can be combined if higher transmission rates are required. The following table lists service standards and supported data rates.

Signal Level	Carrier	Number of T1 Channels	Data Rate (Mbps)
DS-1	T1	1	1.544
DS-1C	T1C	2	3.152
DS-2	T2	4	6.312
DS-3	T3	28	44.736
DS-4	T4	168	274.760

T1 and T2 carriers can be supported by copper-wire cable, but T3 and T4 require a high-frequency medium, typically fiber optic or microwave. T1 carriers are a United States standard. Outside of the United States, E1 service is usually available with a transmission rate of 2.048 Mbps.

The biggest drawback of digital data service lines is the cost. The cost can be reduced through use of Fractional T1 (FT1) subscriptions in 64-Kbps increments. Fractional T3 is available in 6-Mbps increments.

If you have digital data service lines, you need to know the transmission rate that is provided and how much the service is costing you. You also need to monitor traffic levels to determine bandwidth usage. It may be that you are provided with more bandwidth than is really needed.

X.25

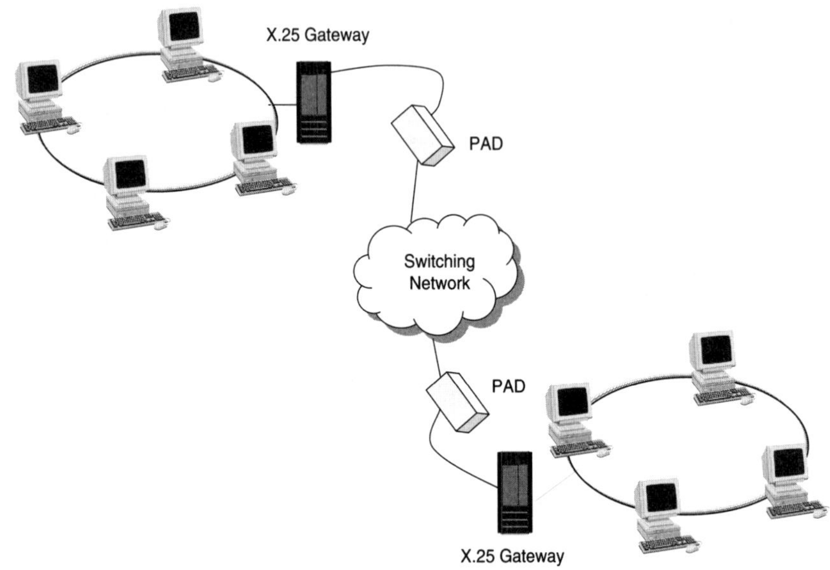

X.25 is a set of standards for sending packet data across a Packet-Switched Data Network (PSDN). X.25 was originally developed to support connecting remote terminals to mainframe hosts. Data is transferred through public data network connections known as virtual circuits. X.25 is designed to provide reliable data transfer even if the media the data is being transferred through is not completely reliable. The circuit path can be constantly changing in an X.25 connection, and the bandwidth can vary.

Connection to the X.25 to the public data network is through a Data Terminal Equipment/Data Communications Equipment (DTE/DCE) interface. This can be provided through an X.25 smart card interface installed in a host computer. When supporting WAN connections, you will typically see each LAN connecting through an X.25, which in turn connects through a Packet Assembler/Disassembler (PAD).

ATM

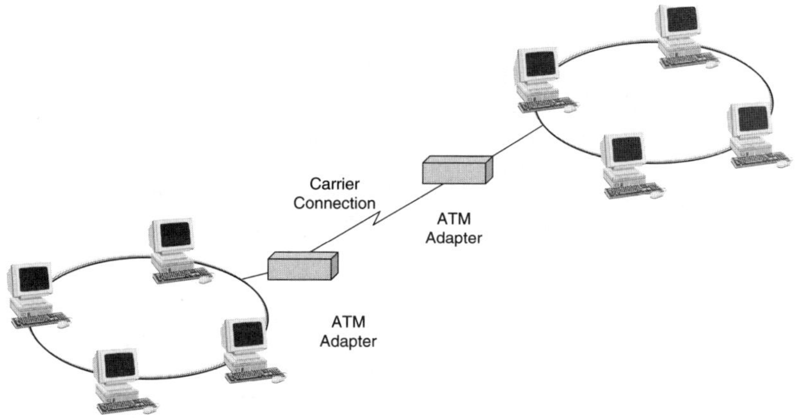

Asynchronous Transfer Mode (ATM) communication is supported over an Asymmetric Digital Subscriber Line (ADSL). ATM is a high-speed transmission technology that transmits data as fixed-length cells. It is well suited to voice, data, and video applications. The connection between LANs is made through an ATM adapter at each end of the connection.

ATM transmission rates are determined by the type of connection used to carry the ATM signal. ATM over ADSL provides 64 Kbps for traffic outbound through the adapter and 1.554 Mbps for inbound traffic. ATM over a T3 line will support 45 Mbps. ATM over fiber-optic lines can support up to 622 Mbps, with 155 Mbps as a typical transmission rate. Your connection type will have been established when the connection hardware was installed and will depend on the carrier options available through your telecommunication service provider.

You are less likely to see ATM in your network than the other options discussed in this section. It has had limited acceptance because of the costs involved, both for the connection hardware and the recurring costs for the connection.

Internet

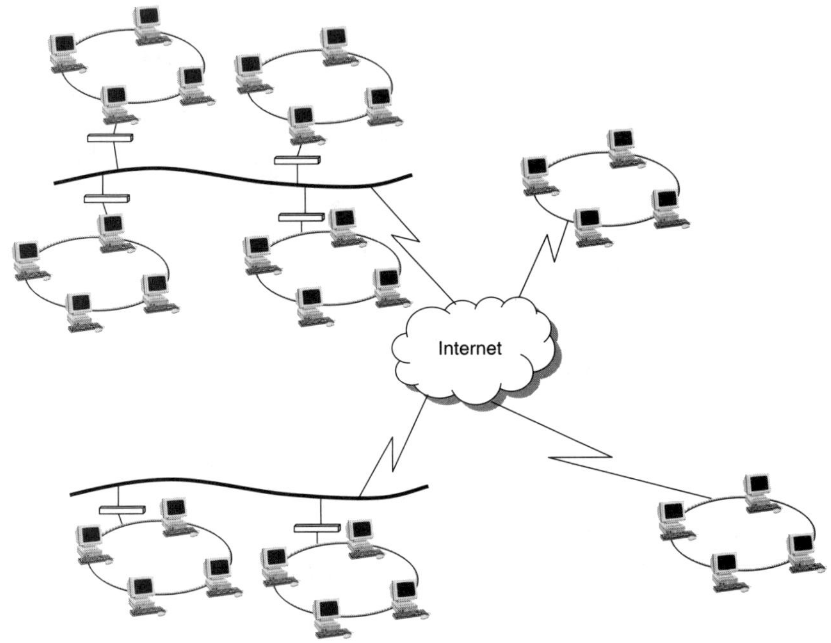

A connection method that has experienced rapid growth and acceptance is using the Internet as your WAN backbone and configuring Virtual Private Network (VPN) connections through the Internet. This connection option provides a great deal of flexibility. Of course, this means you will need to check each LAN's connection individually to see how it is connected to the Internet. Common connections include the following:

- Standard dial-up connection
- ISDN dial-up connection
- Digital Service Line (DSL) connection
- T1 (including FT1, T3, etc.) connection

Availability and bandwidth at the remote LAN will be directly related to the connection type. Remote access and WAN link connections through the Internet will be discussed in detail later in the course. For now, you need to know how the connections are being made and how bandwidth requirements are being met.

About Bandwidth

You've already been told that your available bandwidth is going to depend on the type of connection implemented between LANs. When you have multiple concurrent connections available, the bandwidth is additive.

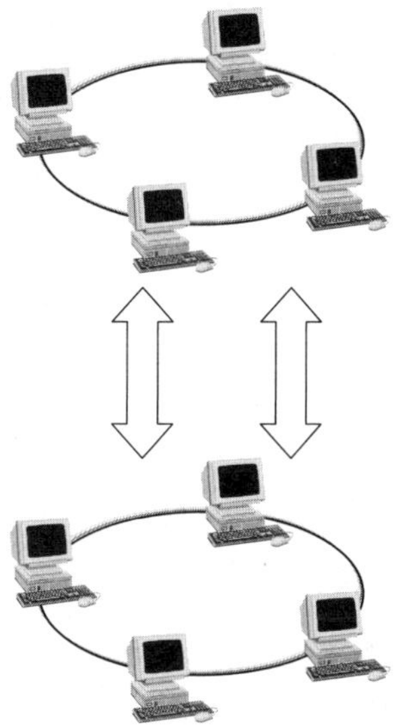

For example, if you have two T1 service connections between two LANs, as shown in the previous figure, your bandwidth is effectively doubled. Now, of course, this is a very simple example. It is more common to have multiple concurrent connections that route through different paths and may have to cross other remote LANs along the way. This additional overhead will act to limit your effective bandwidth.

Along with how much bandwidth is available, you are also interested in knowing how much bandwidth is being used. If you are consistently saturating the available bandwidth, you need to either find ways to reduce communication requirements between LANs or upgrade your connection. If you consistently use only a small portion of the available bandwidth, you may be able to implement a less-expensive connection method.

About Latency

Latency can also be a concern in a WAN environment. In simple terms, latency refers to a delay. Because of the slower link speeds and intervening connection hardware, there will be some level of latency when data is transmitted across remote links. In some situations, this can become a noticeable problem. Delays can cause some time-sensitive applications to fail.

Latency can also occur as a result of server configurations. When you have multiple servers providing the same network service, there will typically be some type of automated update process in use, such as file service replication. Your network is probably configured to avoid immediate updates because of the traffic generated. However, too much of a delay between updates can cause intermittent, hard-to-isolate network problems.

WAN Services

You will be dealing with the same basic service categories in a WAN as you were in a LAN. As a quick review, these are as follows:

- Security services
- Network address services
- Name resolution services
- Directory services

During WAN analysis, the initial temptation may be to immediately start looking for ways to improve network service support. You need to be careful to avoid this and focus instead on the current state of network services. You will have time to look for ways to improve network services during the design phase.

General Analysis

Let's start with a few key points to keep in mind when analyzing the current state of network services.

- Service requirements

  You need to determine what services are required at each of the LANs and how those requirements are currently being met.

- Server placement

  Server placement can be a critical issue in a WAN environment. You need to determine where the servers providing network services are located.

- Server availability

  When services are being provided across remote links, server availability can become a critical concern. For example, if a service is being provided by a demand-dial connection, the latency involved could be impacting overall performance.

- Server performance

  Server performance can become an issue the same as in a LAN environment. Monitor the performance of individual servers to verify that each is able to meet the load requirements. This will also give you an idea of the scalability available through your current services. When you start estimating service requirements in your network design, it will be important to know where you will need to add or upgrade servers.

- Network service traffic

  When some services are being provided by servers on remote LANs, you need to monitor service traffic to determine its effect on available bandwidth. Even if the service is being provided locally, it can be helpful to make occasional spot checks. If the local service is unable to meet the LAN's service requirements, you may find clients making service requests to other LANs.

One way of keeping track of your findings is to sketch out a simple map of your network.

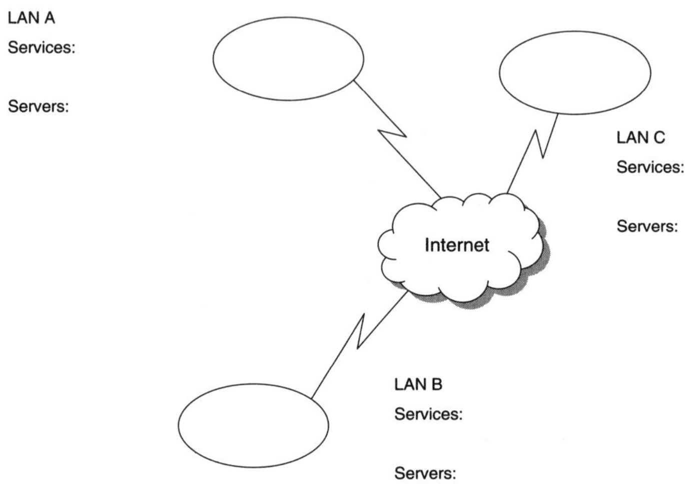

This will also help you to visualize your network configuration and the interaction between individual LANs. Often, the only thing needed is a simple hand-drawn sketch of the network. Products such as Visio not only let you diagram your network, but also make it easy to move objects around inside the drawing when you start the design process.

Network Services

There is no reason to go back through each of the network services in detail. You are dealing with the same service categories, with the same characteristics and basic requirements, as you were during LAN analysis.

- Security services

  As with a LAN, logon and security validation services are going to be a critical part of WAN operations. You need to document the locations of all servers providing these services and the network traffic generated by these services.

- Network address services

  Less traffic is generated by automated address assignment through DHCP than with most of the other services. When documenting server locations, you may find that your WAN is configured to have a single DHCP server provide support for multiple subnetworks. Along with the locations of each of the servers, you need to document the IP address ranges supported by each.

- Name resolution services

  In a routed network environment like a WAN, name resolution services are going to be critical. As with other services, you need to know the location of each of the DNS and WINS servers in your network. With name resolution, there are two traffic patterns you will be concerned about. One is the traffic generated by name resolution requests, initiated by users and user applications. The other is the traffic generated by the replication process used to send updates between name servers.

- Directory services

  You need to know where your domain controllers are located and the amount of traffic generated by user requests and the replication process. You also need to know which servers are configured as Global Catalog servers and are supporting operations master roles.

When monitoring the traffic generated by network services, you are going to be interested in both average and peak traffic values. Monitoring network traffic is one area where you may be limited by your available resources. You can probably get values that will give you a good starting point to work from by using Network Monitor to monitor traffic into and out of your servers.

Scenario 3-2: WAN Analysis

The purpose of this scenario is to introduce you to WAN analysis. Suggested solutions are provided in Appendix B at the end of this manual. It may be helpful to review the case studies in Appendix C at the end of this manual.

Barney's Bank's Current Network

The main corporate LAN located in the home office is a routed LAN configured as an Active Directory domain. It consists of three subnetworks, all Ethernet, one using a bus topology and the other two using star topologies. The bus topology subnetwork uses RG-48 A/U coaxial cable. The two subnetworks using a star topology are wired with Category 4 UTP cable. At present, there are two domain controllers in the corporate LAN, both located on the bus topology subnetwork.

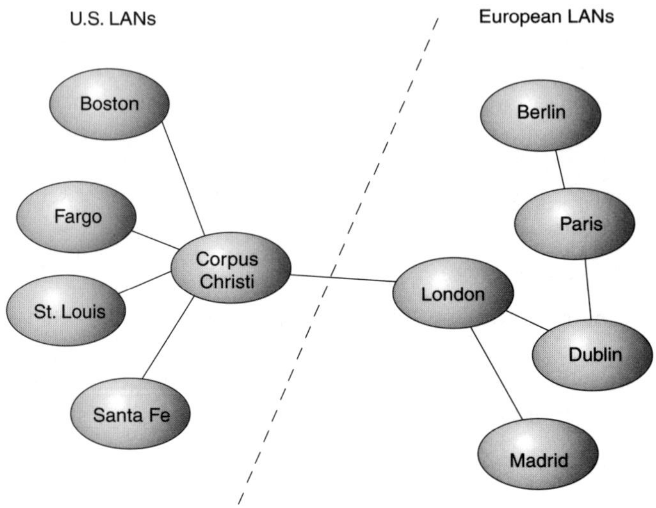

The previous figure is a schematic representation of the current WAN configuration. Except for the LAN in Corpus Christi, all of the LANs are nonrouted LANs. There is an X.25 connection between Corpus Christi and London. The U.S. branch offices connect to the Corpus Christi office through demand-dial ISDN connections. There are E1 connections between all of the European offices as shown in the figure. In addition to the domain controllers in Corpus Christi, there are domain controllers in each of the U.S. offices, in London, and in Dublin. There are DNS servers in Corpus Christi and London. At present, address assignments are managed manually.

1. Across which links will resource and service availability most likely be an ongoing concern?

   ....

   ....

2. Which LANs can locally validate user logons?

   ....

   ....

Exercise 3-2: Continued Preparation (Optional)

The purpose of this exercise is to help you continue preparing your training network to support hands-on practice. You will be installing Active Directory services on one of your network servers during this exercise. There are no solutions provided for this exercise.

Special Preparation

You will need a Windows 2000 Server Installation CD-ROM to complete this exercise.

Active Directory Installation

During this exercise, you will be installing Active Directory services on Alpha. Complete all of the exercise steps on Alpha.

1. Select **Start | Run**.
2. Type the following and click on **OK**:

   ```
   dcpromo
   ```
3. Click on **Next**.
4. Leave **Domain controller in a new domain** selected and click on **Next**.
5. Leave **Create a new domain tree** selected and click on **Next**.
6. Leave **Create a new forest of domain trees** selected and click on **Next**.
7. Type the following as your domain name, then click on **Next**:

   ```
   ndclass.org
   ```
8. Leave the NetBIOS domain name at default and click on **Next**.
9. Leave the database and log locations at default and click on **Next**.
10. Leave the shared system volume location at default and click on **Next**.
11. When warned that the DNS server that handles nsclass.org cannot be contacted, click on **OK**.
12. Leave **Yes, install and configure DNS on this computer (recommended)** selected and click on **Next**.

13. Leave the permissions setting at default and click on **Next**.
14. Leave the password for directory services restore mode blank and click on **Next**.
15. Click on **Next**. It may take several minutes to complete installation. You will be prompted for the Windows 2000 Installation CD-ROM during the file copy and installation.
16. Click on **Finish**.
17. Remove the Windows 2000 Installation CD-ROM and click on **Restart Now**. After restart, log on as Administrator.

USERS AND RESOURCES

User and resource analysis issues are closely related to issues that have already been discussed for LAN and WAN analysis. Much of the information you need about service requirements, data flows, and so forth is going to come from analysis of user requirements.

The following topics are covered in this section:

- User Distribution
- Resource Distribution

The accuracy of the information you collect will be directly related to the tools that you have available and the time you have to invest in monitoring and analysis. You may find it necessary to get typical values as a starting point and leave room in your network design for fine-tuning.

User Distribution

You need to answer the following three basic questions about your network users:

- How many users?
- Where are they located?
- How do they connect to the network?

This may sound easier than it actually is. You are going to need detailed information about your users to make appropriate design decisions.

The three information categories are being used to make it easier to discuss the collection process. In most cases, information gathering for all three categories will be a concurrent process.

User Inventory

You need an accurate inventory of your users. There is more to this than you might first guess because you need more than a raw count. To really be useful, you are going to need to place the users into appropriate categories.

Your specific categories will be based on your user roles. As a starting point, here are some general categories you'll find on most networks:

- Standard users

  Most users will fall into this category. These are the rank-and-file users who probably run no more than two or three concurrent applications, need access to shared data files, and access relatively small personal data files.

  If there is a great deal of variation between requirements for users in different departments or divisions, you may need to break this down into smaller categories based on job responsibilities. For example, you might have sales users, marketing users, accounting users, and so forth.

- Power users

  These are the users running high-end applications or several concurrent applications and needing access to relatively large data files. As with standard users, you may find it appropriate to break power users into smaller categories.

- Temporary personnel

  The number of temporary personnel is often cyclic in nature. For example, your organization might bring in additional help at end of quarter and end of year. You will need to make sure that your network design provides the necessary personnel to support these users.

- Management personnel

  There is often an inverse relationship between management-level and network-access requirements. Upper-level management personnel will have computers but may rarely need access to the network or its resources. This is not always the case, however, and you will find many exceptions to this rule.

- Technical personnel

  You will want to identify all technical support personnel. Their network requirements are often less than many other users on a day-to-day basis, but you will want to be sure to include them in your inventory. One reason for this is because you are going to want to know where they are located when you start analyzing and designing your support and management structure.

While you are collecting your user inventory, you also need to get what information you can about planned personnel changes. You probably won't have too much trouble getting general numbers for increases, but any planned reductions are usually held as confidential information.

User Locations

Not only do you need to know who the users are, you also need to know where they are located. Typically, you will want to count users by the following categories:

- LAN

  You will need a count of users by LAN. This will help you determine network service requirements for the LAN as a whole.

- Subnetwork

  You will also need a count of users by subnetwork. This will impact your network service design. There is also a potential concern on a TCP/IP network of having enough IP addresses available in the subnetwork to support all of your users. You may need to modify your subnetworking scheme or add additional subnetworks as part of your network design.

- Remote users

  These are users that aren't part of any LAN but, instead, connect directly to the network through a remote connection. These are typically intermittent connections of limited duration.

User locations are also going to be important later when you are analyzing resource access requirements.

User Connectivity

User connectivity is going to be based on the user's location. Users that are part of a LAN will connect through the LAN. In a WAN environment, a user will connect through the local LAN and access remote resources through the LAN's remote links. Remote users will either connect through a direct dial-in connection or via the Internet through a VPN connection.

Resource Distribution

Your goal during the analysis phase is simply to determine where resources are located and to determine user access patterns. As part of this, you are going to be watching for resource bottlenecks, but you are not going to concern yourself with optimizing resource access. That will come later during the design phase.

A good place to start is by interviewing representative users. The users can give you an idea of what resources they need to access, but they may not be able to tell you exactly where the resources are located. This is especially true in a domain environment where logical drive assignments have been made for the users and resources have been mapped to appear as part of the domain or as local resources. You may find yourself having to do a little investigative work to find the resources' physical locations.

Not only are you concerned about what resources the users need to access, you also need to know when they need to access the resources. This will give you a start on determining resource access patterns. You will need this information later when you start deciding where to place resources in the redesigned network.

SUPPORT PERSONNEL

You were introduced to support personnel and their roles earlier in the course. This section takes another look at support-related issues, both as a review and to provide some additional information.

This section starts with a general overview, then looks at two ways of analyzing the current support and management structure. The following topics are covered in this section:

- Need for Analysis
- Analysis by Role
- Analysis by Task

There is a great deal of overlap between these two analysis methods. You may find that one is better suited, and the only method needed, for your organization. You should at least initially consider using both since information you might miss through one method may be picked up in the other.

Need for Analysis

It's relatively easy in a small organization to keep track of network support roles and responsibilities. It becomes more difficult as responsibilities are delegated out to a larger number of support personnel. This is especially true in WAN management. You may have a good idea of how your local support structure is organized but only have a general idea of how support is managed at remote locations.

You were introduced to some of the information you need earlier in the course. This included information such as the support hierarchy and change management. In this section, the focus is also on the support hierarchy, but more on how it relates to day-to-day network activities.

You will need to have a good idea of the network support structure before you move on to the network design phase. You need to know what is already in place before you can determine what changes will need to be made in the new design.

Analysis by Role

This is where you are going to start your analysis. A good way to start this analysis is by job titles. Look at the support management structure and hierarchy to see what roles have been defined for your organization. From there, you need to determine the responsibilities that have been assigned to each of these roles.

Before looking at the roles in detail, you need to realize that these are general guidelines and probably will not apply directly to your network. In a smaller organization, you will probably find that these roles have been combined. In larger organizations, you may find a more detailed delegation of tasks. In either, there may be some tasks that have been delegated outside of the support structure, especially when looking at network support at remote offices or subsidiaries.

Network Administrator Role

Network administrators have final responsibility for the network as a whole. They are responsible for making sure that the network is working properly and providing optimal performance for the current hardware and network configuration.

A large part of a network administrator's job is making sure that the day-to-day management tasks get done rather than doing them him or herself. The specific tasks that are delegated to network administrators are going to be unique to each organization. Typically, responsibilities will include the following:

- Network design and planning
- Hardware and software purchase recommendation
- Vendor and service provider negotiations
- Security design and management
- Personnel management

If you have more than one network administrator, these responsibilities may be delegated out to different administrators or shared among the administrators. Either way, there is going to be one person who acts as the lightening rod for the support staff. That's the person who is answerable for all of the support personnel and takes responsibility for anything relating to the network.

Network administrators are also called upon to fill in and help when support resources become overtaxed. An administrator's *hands-on* participation in day-to-day activities is usually determined by job description and personal preference. Many administrators prefer to spend as much time as possible on direct network management tasks in order to keep their technical skills up to par.

Technical Support Role

There are various job titles used to describe this role, such as network support, LAN technician, technical support, and so forth. Some companies simply use network administrator as the job title for everyone who works with the network. In this usage, the technical support role is being used to describe the personnel directly responsible for network and hardware support and maintenance.

There are a large number of tasks that can fall under this category, including the following:

- System maintenance and repair
- Network maintenance
- User and group account administration
- Periodic backups
- Hardware evaluation

Obviously, this is only a partial list, but it should give you a general idea of the kind of responsibilities that go along with this job. You will often find some specialization at this level, with different support personnel assigned different responsibilities. For example, one person may have primary responsibility for maintaining the mail server in addition to his or her other duties. Another might be responsible for maintaining and coordinating DNS servers.

NOTE: Technical support personnel can often provide assistance in the LAN and WAN analysis process.

User Support Role

User support includes handling any user problems that arise. Responsibilities could include the following:

- Troubleshooting application and file problems
- Application procedure assistance
- Application installation and configuration

There will be some overlap between the user support and technical support roles. It can sometimes be difficult to immediately determine whether a problem is software or hardware related, requiring user support and technical support to work closely together. Some organizations will have a single job description that includes both hardware and software support.

You can find a great deal of variation on how organizations provide customer support. Some provide support from a centralized Help Desk or similar department. Others may not have any kind of formal user support in place, forcing users to find help however they can.

NOTE: *User support personnel can often provide assistance in user and resource analysis.*

Analysis by Task

Analysis by task is similar to analysis by role except that it requires you to work from the network up. You start by listing the tasks that have to be performed on the network, then you match those tasks up with support personnel. One way of doing this is through a series of questions, such as the following:

- Who is responsible for maintaining user accounts?
- Who is responsible for managing group membership?
- Who is responsible for daily backups?
- Who is responsible for user workstation repair?
- Who is responsible for monitoring and maintaining remote links?
- Who maintains domain controllers and other services providing network services?

The list can go on and on. Often, you may find that no one in particular has been assigned responsibility for one or more of the issues you raise. Pay close attention to these tasks because it may be necessary to assign formal responsibility as part of your overall network design.

This is a useful exercise in a number of ways. One question will lead to other questions, and you may remember management tasks that you overlooked before. This will also help you locate personnel who have been delegated support tasks but are not part of the *official* support hierarchy.

Exercise 3-3: Network Monitoring Overview (Optional)

The purpose of this exercise is to give you practice in network monitoring. During this exercise, you will be installing and using the Network Monitor. You will also be configuring your remaining systems and Active Directory clients. There are no solutions provided for this exercise.

Special Preparation

You will need the Windows 2000 Server Installation CD-ROM or access to the Windows 2000 Server installation files to complete this exercise.

Active Directory Clients

Complete the following steps on Beta and Delta.

1. Run **Start | Settings | Control Panel** and launch the System utility.
2. Click on **Network Identification.**
3. Click on **Properties.**
4. Click to select **Domain**, type the following as the domain name, then click on **OK**:

   ```
   ndclass
   ```
5. When prompted for a domain username and password, type the following in the Name field, then click on **OK**:

   ```
   Administrator
   ```
6. When the "Welcome to the ndclass domain" message displays, click on **OK.**
7. When warned that you must reboot your computer, click on **OK.**
8. Click on **OK.**
9. When prompted to restart your system, click on **Yes**. After restart, log on as Administrator.

Network Monitor

During this portion of the exercise, you will be installing Network Monitor on Alpha. Complete all steps in this portion of the exercise on Alpha.

10. Open the Control Panel and launch Add/Remove Programs.
11. Click on **Add/Remove Windows Components**.
12. Select Management and Monitoring Tools, but do not place a check in the checkbox, and click on **Details**.
13. Place a check in the **Network Monitor Tools** checkbox, then click on **OK**.
14. Click on **Next**. Insert the Windows 2000 Server Installation CD-ROM in your CD-ROM drive when prompted and click on **OK**.
15. Click on **Finish**.
16. Exit Add/Remove Programs and close the Control Panel.

Monitoring Network Traffic

There are steps to be performed on both Alpha and Beta in this portion of the exercise. During this portion of the exercise, you will be monitoring logon traffic.

Complete on Alpha

17. Run **Start | Programs | Administrative Tools | Network Monitor**.
18. Click on **OK** when prompted to specify a network.
19. Click to select Local Computer, then click on **OK**.
20. Press ***F10*** to start the capture.

Complete on Beta

21. Run **Start | Shutdown**.
22. Select to log off the Administrator from the drop-down list, then click on **OK**.
23. Observe the network traffic on Alpha during logoff.
24. Log on as Administrator. Observe the network traffic on Alpha during logon.

SECURITY REQUIREMENTS

Network security requirements have already been discussed in some detail. During this section, you will take a closer look at current network security. You will also be introduced to some additional security risks that you might not have considered in your current network design.

For the purpose of this discussion, security issues will be divided into the following categories:

- User Access Security
- Data Security
- Secure Communications
- Defense Against Malicious Attacks

As with the other sections in the chapter, your focus is on your current network and current security measures. You'll be looking at requirements for your new network design and suggested security measures later in the chapter.

User Access Security

Issues relating to user access security have already been discussed in some detail. Your goal during information gathering is to understand what security measures are already in place and how well they are meeting current network security needs. You will work from this baseline information to build security into your network design, making changes as necessary.

Logon Validation

User logon validation is your first defense against unauthorized network access. Unauthorized access can take the form of persons attempting to break in who are not part of your organization, typically through a remote connection, or a user attempting to log on with another user's logon name and password.

Security Models

You were introduced to three basic security models earlier in the course. In each of these models, logon validation is managed through username and password, but there are the following differences:

- Workgroup

  In a workgroup, logon validation is handled individually by each system. The user logs on locally to his or her workstation and can be granted access permissions to other workstations in the workgroup. Each workstation maintains its own user and password information.

  This is a decentralized security model that puts control of access security into the hands of the individual users. It should only be used when you have a small number of relatively computer-literate users.

- Windows NT domain

  Logon validation is handled at the domain level. User and password information is maintained at the domain controllers. More specifically, the information is maintained at the PDC and replicated to any BDCs. A user must be able to communicate with a PDC or BDC for his or her home domain in order to log on.

  This is a centralized security system that takes logon security out of the hands of the individual users except that users will typically have control over their own passwords. The user will still be able to log on locally to his or her workstation if no domain controller is available to validate logon, but the user will not have access to domain resources.

- Active Directory domain

  Logon validation is handled at the domain level, with user and password information maintained at the domain controllers. User and password information can be changed at any domain controller and will be replicated to all other domain controllers within the domain. The user must be able to communicate with a domain controller to be able to log on to the domain.

  This is also a centralized security system that takes the control of security out of the hands of individual users. As with the Windows NT domain model, users will typically have control over their own password. Local logon is still an option if no domain controller is available for logon validation, but the user will not be able to use any domain resources.

Logon validation will be based on your current security model.

General Information

You need to collect additional information on how user security is currently being managed. This includes the following:

- Usernames

  Verify that unique usernames are being assigned to each of the network users. A good time for checking this is while you are doing your user inventory, discussed earlier in this chapter. If you find that you have any users sharing usernames for logon, this is one of the first things you are going to want to change when developing your new network design.

- Password policies

  Both Windows NT and Active Directory domains let you set password policies. These let you control minimum password lengths, reuse of passwords, and so forth. Review the current password policy settings. During this review, keep in mind that different policies can be set for different domains, and in an Active Directory domain, different policies can be set at different hierarchical levels.

- Guest account

  Check the status of the Guest account to see whether it is enabled for logon. In most situations, you will want to have the Guest account disabled.

While you are reviewing user and password information, you should also review any corporate guidelines for creating usernames, guidelines provided to users for selecting passwords, and so forth.

Logon Tracking

Successful and failed logon attempts can be tracked through auditing in Windows NT and Active Directory domains. Unless there have been problems with unauthorized logon attempts in the past, you will probably find that logon tracking is not currently being used on the network.

You will find it helpful to be familiar with logon traffic patterns when you start network design. You can enable auditing of logon attempts for a short time to gather some typical logon statistics, then turn off the auditing when you are finished. The logon events are written to the Event Viewer Security log while logon auditing is enabled. After gathering the information you need, you can save the contents of the Security log to a separate file for later review and analysis.

Intruder Detection

As with logon auditing, intruder detection is usually not enabled unless there has been a problem, or a suspected problem, in the past. For the time being, you want to gather information on where and how intruder detection has been enabled through the network. You will want to include standards for intruder detection as part of your security design, based on the current configuration.

Keep in mind that intruder detection, by itself, can only go so far. If an organization has lax security practices, unauthorized access is going to occur without any detections. Intruder detection is activated by the use of a valid username and incorrect password. To work, user accounts must be password protected and users must keep their passwords confidential. Users with blank passwords or who post their passwords on their monitors with sticky notes provide open holes into your network.

Data Security

During data security analysis, you are looking to answer the following three general questions:

- How is data being protected against unauthorized access?
- How is data being protected against deletion or modification?
- How is data being protected in case of system or network failure?

Data protection is going to be somewhat related to where the data is physically located. Data that is stored on individual workstations is almost always more vulnerable than data stored on network servers. There is a tendency for security on individual workstations to be relatively lax. Also, most workstations are *not* backed up on a regular basis, meaning that data can easily be lost should a system failure occur.

Data security issues have already been addressed to some extent earlier in the course. Let's review these concerns and discuss what you may already find in place as protection.

Data Access

As with logon validation, how data access is managed will depend somewhat on the network security model that is currently in place. Let's look at a few specific areas of data access security and what you might find in your network.

Local Access

Like the name implies, local access is managed individually for each computer. Local access control is only available on Windows NT and Windows 2000 systems using the NT File System (NTFS). By default, all local users are given nearly universal access to local file resources. In a large network, it would be unrealistic to think that you could make a complete check of local access security for all user workstations. Instead, you should focus on network servers and on any user workstations that have mission-critical information.

Shared Access

In a workgroup, resource sharing and security are managed at the workstation level. This means that it is in the hands of individual users who may not understand the importance of access security.

In a domain environment, shared data access is more centrally controlled. Data shares from network servers are managed through centralized security, but there is still a possible issue with user-initiated shares. Users with Windows-family operating systems can still act as peer servers within the domain and share their file resources to the network.

You can use Windows Explorer or My Network Places to quickly identify shared folders, grouped by computer. You will want to check the current access security on shared folders and compare this information with what you know about user access requirements so you can determine if share permissions have been set properly.

Data Encryption

An added layer of data protection can be implemented through data encryption. You need to review where data encryption is currently being used. This will let you determine if the current data encryption is really necessary and identify areas where you need to add data encryption into your security plans.

Data Deletion/Modification

As with data access, your primary protection against accidental deletion or modification of files is through access security settings. Review the data you collect on local and shared access to make sure that users aren't being given more access permissions than they actually need.

This is another area where you will want to check on auditing settings. You want to see if deletion or modification attempts are being tracked on critical files, such as shared databases, build plans, customer lists, and so forth. This doesn't do anything to put additional protection on the files, but it does give you a way to track deletion or modification attempts, when they were made, and the user that made the attempt.

Disaster Protection and Recovery

You have more to worry about than accidental (or malicious) attempts on data files. You also have to know what plans are in place in case of workstation, server, or network failures. Potential problems were discussed earlier in the course but are covered again here for added emphasis and to provide an easy reference while discussing data security.

The concerns being addressed during this discussion are system and hard drive failures. Ways to protect against these failures include the following:

- Backups
- Disk Fault Tolerance
- Redundant Servers
- Server Clusters

Let's spend a little time reviewing each of these.

Backups

Regular backups are your first line of defense for both server and workstation failures. If you cannot recover the data any other way, have plans in place that let you go back to your backups. Key issues relating to backups include the following:

- Data backed up

  You need to know which servers and which user workstations, if any, are being backed up. Regular backups are going to be critical. Don't forget that system state data needs to be backed up on, at a minimum, Windows 2000 Server systems providing network services. System state data must be backed up locally.

- Backup methods

  You need to know how the data is being backed up. You need to know if full backups are being run on a periodic basis for, at the very least, all network servers. You also need to know what types of backups are being run between the full backups, if any. Other backup methods include differential backups, incremental backups, and daily backups.

- Backup schedules

  You need to know when backups are being run. This includes the data being backed up at that time and the backup method being used. A complete understanding of the backup schedule will help you understand what will be required during recovery after a failure, including what backups will be required for restoration and how much reposting will be necessary.

Review current backup policies to see if they meet network security requirements and to see what changes will be necessary to support your new network design.

Disk Fault Tolerance

Disk fault tolerance protects you against failure of one disk in a redundant disk array. Disk fault tolerance methods supported by Windows NT and Windows 2000 servers include the following:

- Disk mirroring/duplexing

  In this configuration, you have two disks with identical data. The only difference between disk mirroring and disk duplexing is that in disk mirroring, both disks are connected to the same disk controller, and disk duplexing uses separate disk controllers for each hard disk.

  There is an additional concern when checking for disk mirroring/duplexing. A mirrored (or duplexed) pair can be used as the boot or system drive on a Windows NT or Windows 2000 server. Should the primary disk in the pair fail, a separate boot diskette will be required to start the server. Make sure that boot diskettes are available and contain the necessary files.

- Disk striping with parity (RAID 5)

  Disk striping with parity is a RAID 5 configuration using three or more hard disks. Data and parity information is spread across all of the drives in the array, making it possible to regenerate data should one drive in the array fail. If two or more drives fail, you will have to recover data from backups. Disk striping arrays cannot be used as a server's boot or system drive.

You will need to find where disk fault tolerance is being used and how it is configured. On Windows NT systems, you can get this information through the Disk Administrator utility. On Windows 2000 systems, you will use the Disk Management selection in the Computer Management tool.

Redundant Servers

While gathering information about your network, you are going to be looking at servers providing network services. During this process, you need to document which servers contain redundant data. These can be used as a recovery source in case a network server fails. For example, domain controllers will have redundant domain database information. DNS and WINS servers are commonly configured to have redundant information. DHCP servers, however, have similar information but will have nonoverlapping address scopes.

Server Clusters

Server clusters protect you against server failure through automatic failover support. If a server fails, its partner in the cluster takes over automatically. In addition, you can get performance benefits in a server cluster through load balancing.

Clustered servers are supported for Windows NT Enterprise Edition, Windows 2000 Advanced Server, and Windows NT Datacenter Server. Clustering is also supported for some server applications, such as Microsoft SQL Server, running on these platforms.

Your collection effort will focus on locating where clustered servers have been implemented in your current network. When you start the design process, you will have to determine how these servers will be impacted by the new design.

Secure Communications

Communications security starts with logon validation. You want to make sure that your current remote-access configuration hasn't left a back door open into your network. If it has, this is going to be a critical change item during the network design process.

In addition to logon validation, you need to identify how communication security is currently implemented on your network. This can include the following:

- Encrypted communication

  Encrypted communication methods don't prevent data from being intercepted during transmissions, but they do keep anyone from being able to do anything with the data after it has been captured. You need to document what encryption methods, such as IP Security (IPSec) Protocol, are in use and how they are configured.
- Firewalls

  Firewalls are typically used to prevent direct communications between systems inside and outside of your network. They are used to filter incoming and outgoing traffic. Firewalls can also be used to record information about traffic volume and unauthorized access attempts.

  In a high-security environment, you may also find that firewalls have been implemented internally on your network. This can be done to provide added protection to confidential or critical data.

  Document the firewalls currently in use on your network and how they are being used. Don't forget to use the network traffic data collected by firewalls when analyzing network information flow.
- Proxy servers

  A proxy server is actually a firewall component. A proxy server is specifically responsible for filtering and managing traffic between your LAN and the Internet. It can be used to filter the data that is allowed into your network, as well as outgoing user requests. Document the location of any proxy servers currently implemented on your network and how they are configured.

Communication security is an important component in protecting your network from outside malicious attacks. No organization should consider itself completely safe against outside attacks unless it has no connections outside of its local LAN. Otherwise, you will want to carefully document the protections that are in place so that you can look for ways to improve your communication security.

Defense Against Malicious Attacks

As a final step, you need to consider the types of attacks or security problems that can occur, then look to see if your current security system provides any defense. The following are a few examples to help you get started in your investigation.

- Unauthorized access

  Unauthorized access attacks can take several forms. If someone has a valid username, he or she can try different passwords until finding one that matches. Intruder detection is your best defense against this type of attack. If you haven't secured remote communications, there is the possibility of usernames and passwords being captured if any are being sent as clear text. Encrypted communications will be your best defense in this case.

  Unauthorized access can also result from poor internal security practices. For example, users sometimes have a tendency to write out their passwords and leave them in a convenient location. Users might also not realize the potential impact of telling others their username and password. Protection begins with a clearly defined security policy but needs to be backed up with periodic spot checks.

- Virus infection or Trojan horse

  Viruses can come in through files that users have brought from home, downloaded from the Internet, or otherwise introduced into the network. E-mail-related viruses have been common recently. There are two good defenses against these types of attacks. One is good, up-to-date anti-viral software. Document what software is currently in use (if any) and the procedures used to keep it up to date. The other defense is well-informed users. You need to gauge how well your users understand how virus attacks occur and their potential impact.

- Service-related attacks

  These are attacks against your network, usually accomplished by flooding servers connected to the Internet with service requests until the server crashes. The more visible and well-known your organization, the more likely it is to be attacked. Firewalls can provide a level of defense against this type of attack.

Your goal during information gathering is to list potential attacks and document defenses currently in place. You will use this information later when developing your security design to implement additional defenses, as necessary.

Scenario 3-3: Users, Support Personnel, and Security

The purpose of this scenario is to give you additional practice in analyzing user, network support, and network security. Suggested solutions are available in Appendix B at the end of this manual.

You will need to review the complete case studies in Appendix C before starting this scenario.

1. For which of the case study companies is it most unlikely that intruder detection would discover unauthorized logon attempts?

   ....

   ....

2. Which of the case study companies is currently susceptible to unauthorized logon by someone outside of the company?

   ....

   ....

3. Which company's users have expressed complaints about latency-related problems?

   ....

   ....

4. In which company will network administrators have to work with the largest number of different geographic categories for users?

   ....

   ....

5. Which companies are using backups as their only protection against data loss?

6. What type of network configuration changes can be implemented to improve Fairco Manufacturing's SQL Server replication performance (without modifying the servers' configurations)?

HARDWARE RESOURCES

The discussion now turns to network hardware resources, specifically the computers making up your LAN and WAN. This includes both the current hardware and any planned hardware upgrades or new hardware purchases. The following topics are covered in this section:

- Hardware Inventory
- Consolidating Hardware Information
- Meeting Network Requirements

If you have a current network inventory, it will be a good starting point even if it is not completely up to date. Otherwise, documenting your network hardware can require a significant amount of work.

Hardware Inventory

Much of this discussion is going to parallel some of the points brought out when discussing LAN and WAN analysis. After all, your networked computers are the core network resources.

A complete network inventory can include a great deal of information that you need to collect. Typical items include the following:

- Computer make and model
- Processor(s) and speed
- Physical RAM
- Hard disk storage (total and available)
- Network adapter or other communication device
- Other adapter cards
- Operating system
- Protocol(s)
- Installed applications
- Service packs applied
- Assigned users

You will notice that there are both hardware and software components to the inventory list. Both are required for you to understand your current network requirements and resources available for expansion. With the ongoing growth of user support requirements, scalability is going to be an important issue.

You will want to create your own list of items that are significant to your network and your network inventory.

Organizing Your Inventory

Before beginning the inventory process, or at least early in the process, you must decide how you are going to organize the data. Your first guideline will be the data itself, organizing systems by make and model, process type, and so forth. You also need to track systems by physical location and domain membership.

You will find it useful to put the network inventory into an electronic format that allows for easy sorting and analysis. This usually means using a database program, spreadsheet, or a combination of both.

Inventory Process

Preparing a network inventory can be a daunting task. Of course, you may find that the number of network systems, as well as time and personnel resource constraints, will prevent you from completing an inventory of all servers providing network systems. A full inventory of all network services is critical, but a complete inventory of user workstations may not be required. Instead, you may be able to get the information you need through a representative sampling of user workstations.

One possible solution is to provide users or departmental managers with inventory guidelines and have them perform the inventory of end-user systems themselves. An obvious drawback to this method is that there will be questions about accuracy if the people performing the inventory don't fully understand the technology and what is required.

Inventory Tools

It will help for you to know what tools are available to you to help with the process. One tool in particular is specifically suited to this process, Microsoft's Systems Management Server (SMS). If you have SMS available, it can gather most of the information you need automatically and store the data in a SQL Server database. This makes the information available for easy retrieval and analysis.

If you don't have SMS available, then you are going to have to look at manual collection practices. One utility that is available on Windows NT and Windows 2000 operating systems is Winmsd.

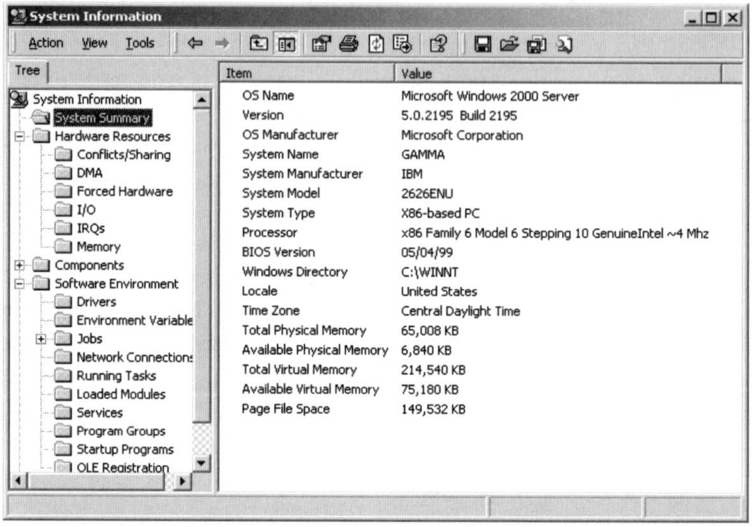

Winmsd, also known as the Windows Diagnostic, provides detailed information about your system configuration. The format is different between the Windows NT and Windows 2000 versions, but the same information is provided. The Windows 2000 version is shown in the previous figure.

Let's take a few minutes to review some of the other tools available by operating system. This will be limited to the most commonly used tools that are likely to provide you with the information you need. These will include the following:

- Windows 9x

  The Control Panel's System utility can provide you with detailed hardware and device driver information. The Control Panel's Add/Remove Programs utility can provide information about installed applications.

- Windows NT

  The Control Panel's System utility can give you a quick summary of system hardware, but Winmsd is your best bet for detailed information. The Control Panel's Add/Remove Programs utility can provide information about installed applications.

- Windows 2000

  In addition to Winmsd, you can use the Computer Management administrative tool to collect detailed system hardware information. The Control Panel's Add/Remove Programs utility can provide information about installed applications.

As you can see, generating a complete inventory can require you to go to different sources on each system.

Consolidating Hardware Information

The information you collect during your network inventory is going to be of even more use when you start consolidating network information and mapping the inventory data to other data that you've collected. In fact, some of the collection activities relating to network data can be completed concurrently, reducing the time and effort required.

This consolidation is going to include the following:

- Network roles

  These map network systems to their roles in the network. Network roles include domain controllers, network service providers, and user workstations.
- Performance data

  You may find this to be less important, but by mapping performance data to hardware inventories, you will have a good start on determining scalability and upgrade requirements.
- Disaster recovery

  This is one that works to tie a great deal of your information together since both the hardware inventory and network role are going to influence disaster recovery requirements.

A flexible storage and recovery system, such as a relational database like Access or SQL Server, is going to become even more important as you start this mapping process. The larger your network, the more likely it is that you are going to need tools of this type to help you with analysis and evaluation.

Meeting Network Requirements

The discussion is going to shift from the pattern that it has been following. You've been focusing primarily on the hardware information that you need to collect. You may find it helpful to spend a little time talking about some additional reasons why this information is going to be important to your network design process.

A new network design usually means additional network services or increased reliance on current network services. You may not be changing the services provided, but you may find that you want (or need) to change how they are provided. For example, assume that you have a network that is using UNIX systems to provide DNS services to the network. You find, during your analysis of the network data, that these systems won't meet the requirements for supporting an Active Directory domain. Instead, you are going to need to install DNS service support on one or more Windows 2000 systems.

Scalability is going to be another area of concern. During the initial analysis, you will be determining how well network services meet the current demand. During the network design process, you need to look at how well the server will meet projected requirements. This will depend on growth projections and on how far into the future you plan for the network design to be serviceable before making additional changes and upgrades.

Operating system and application upgrades are also common when implementing a new network design. You have to be able to:

- Identify candidates for upgrades and new software installations.
- Determine which systems can be upgraded without modification.
- Determine which systems will require hardware upgrades before software upgrades can be installed.

You will often find that it is cheaper to replace rather than upgrade some of your existing systems. If this is the case, you'll want to determine whether there is another appropriate role for these systems in your network.

Scenario 3-4: Hardware Inventory

The purpose of this scenrio is to highlight selected hardware inventory issues. Suggested solutions are provided in Appendix B at the end of this manual. It may be helpful to review the case studies in Appendix C at the end of this manual.

1. Which of the case study companies most clearly defines the current system inventory?

2. With which of the case study companies would you expect to encounter the most logistics-related probems in completing a hardware inventory?

3. For any of the case study companies if it was not possible to do a full hardware inventory on all systems, for which systems should you consider a hardware inventory to be required?

SUMMARY

During this chapter, you were introduced to the following:

- Routed LANs
- Nonrouted LANs
- Remote access
- Monitoring and analysis tools
- TCP/IP tools and utilities
- Cable plant components
- Bandwidth analysis
- Latency
- Network service analysis
- LAN and WAN analysis
- Remote links
- User inventory
- Resource requirements
- Security analysis
- Hardware inventory and analysis

The next chapter takes you out of the information-gathering phase and begins the network design phase. Most of the information presented in the next chapter will be technological overviews and general guidelines, with more details to be provided in later chapters.

POST-TEST QUESTIONS

The answers to these questions are in Appendix A at the end of this manual.

1. What is the maximum bandwidth for a PSTN dial-up connection?

2. What hardware connectivity device is required for support of a LAN supporting multiple network addresses?

3. What UTP category cable can support 100 Mbps Ethernet?

4. What transmission rates are supported by Token Ring?

5. In a WAN environment, what are the benefits of placing services providing network services in each LAN?

6. What are the two most common ISDN connection configurations?

....

....

7. What are the advantages of having multiple links between LANs in a WAN?

....

....

8. From the standpoint of resource usage, why is it important to identify power users?

....

....

9. Why would you want to put an internal firewall in a routed LAN?

....

....

CHAPTER 4

Network Environment Design

MAJOR TOPICS

OBJECTIVES

At the completion of this chapter, you will be able to:

- Identify common characteristics of common topologies.
- Given network requirements, select an appropriate topology.
- Describe concerns when implementing topology changes.
- Given network requirements, select an appropriate protocol.
- Describe the significance of the protocol binding order.
- Given network requirements, select an appropriate LAN design.
- Identify features, benefits, and concerns for a nonrouted LAN.
- Identify features, benefits, and concerns for a routed LAN.
- Describe basic guidelines for WAN design.
- Describe concerns relating to user and resource placement in a LAN or WAN.
- Describe concerns relating to network server placement in a LAN or WAN.
- Identify common WAN configurations.
- Given Internet access requirements, identify an appropriate access option.
- List Internet services commonly implemented in a LAN.

PRE-TEST QUESTIONS

The answers to these questions are in Appendix A at the end of this manual.

1. What type of cable is used with Ethernet 10Base2?

2. What is the maximum number of computers per LAN when using Ethernet 10BaseT?

3. What transmission rates are supported by Token Ring?

....

....

4. Which of the following are nonroutable protocols?

    A. NetBEUI

    B. NWLink

    C. TCP/IP

5. When is NWLink required for connectivity with other LAN systems?

....

....

6. What is the purpose of a default gateway on a TCP/IP network?

....

....

7. How should user workstations, and servers providing resources they need, be configured in a routed LAN?

....

....

8. What is a potential performance drawback of placing duplicate network servers in every LAN in a WAN network?

....

....

9. You need to provide Internet access for one computer. What is typically the easiest and least-expensive way to do this?

   ....

   ....

10. When implementing a Web server, why would you want to place a firewall between the Web server and the rest of your network?

   ....

   ....

INTRODUCTION

The primary course focus shifts with this chapter from information gathering to network design. You will still encounter occasional references to information gathering, but most of the time from here on will be spent on giving you guidelines for designing your Windows 2000 network implementation.

The issues addressed in this chapter are already familiar, but this time they are being approached from a different direction. You are going to be looking at how to put the technologies to work in your network, with guidelines for making appropriate selections.

The chapter starts by diving back into network models. This time, the models will be covered in more detail and you will be given some guidelines for making model selections for your network. Keep in mind that in a large LAN or WAN, you may find yourself needing to implement multiple models.

From there, the discussion drills down in some detail into network technologies and protocols. This includes benefits of and possible concerns about common technologies.

Next, you are introduced to LAN and WAN design. This will include issues that are going to be of concern when developing a network design, and how your design changes can impact your existing network. Most of the information provided in these sections will be more of an overview than a detailed discussion. Detailed discussions of specific network components are provided in later chapters.

The chapter then discusses how you can integrate Internet accessibility into your network design. This discussion will provide you with general guidelines for using the Internet. More detailed information will follow in later chapters.

NETWORK MODELS

You should already feel comfortable with the basic network models described earlier in the course. However, the earlier descriptions were designed primarily to help you recognize your current network model. Now you are going to be given some guidelines for selecting a network model for your network design. The following topics are covered in this chapter:

- Network Model Overview
- Topology Selection
- Implementing Topology Changes
- Remote Access

The discussion focuses on characteristics of, requirements for, and concerns about the models presented. LAN and WAN design is discussed in more detail later in this chapter and throughout the remainder of this course.

Network Model Overview

For most people, the design phase is where the work starts to get interesting. You finally get to start putting the information you've collected to use. As an early word of warning, you are probably going to find the process to be much easier when installing a new network than when updating an existing network. With an existing network, you will often find yourself forced into design decisions based on what is already in place rather than what makes the best sense from a technical standpoint.

Either way, it's best to start with the basics and break the job down into manageable tasks. If you're designing a routed LAN, start by determining what each of the subnetworks is going to look like, then worry about how you are going to connect them. If you're designing a WAN, start with its component LANs. Once you get the LANs right, it's going to be much easier to put the WAN together.

Topology Selection

One of the fundamental design issues is going to be topology. You need to decide how you want to connect the systems together and the types of concerns that might arise. Let's take another look at common topologies, this time with a close look at how they are implemented, their strengths, and their drawbacks.

Bus Topology

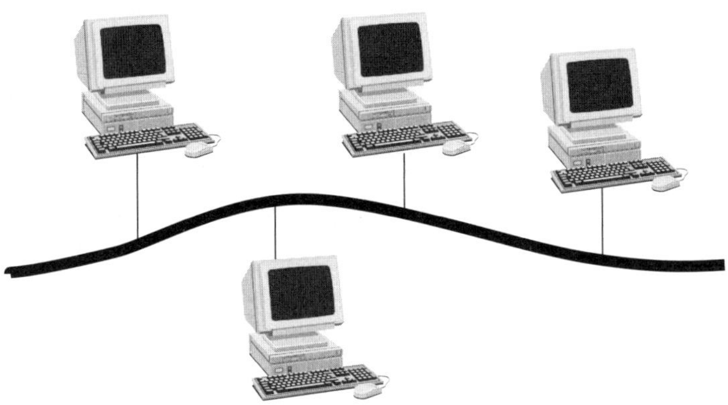

In a bus topology, network devices connect directly to a central coaxial cable. The most common uses of a bus topology are 10Base2 and 10Base5 Ethernet. Available bandwidth, assuming quality cable and proper installation, is 10 Mbps.

A few years ago, this was the most common LAN topology. Let's take a look at some of the specifications for Ethernet 10Base2 to give you a better idea of what to expect from an installation of this type. The specifications include:

- Maximum segment length of 185 meters (607 feet)
- Up to 30 computers per segment
- Up to five segments may be joined using four repeaters, up to 925 meters (3,035 feet)

With combined segments, no more than three segments have computers attached, which means that you are limited to no more than 90 computers on the network before you have to start routing.

Connections to computers are made through BNC connectors. The cable must be terminated at each end with a 50-Ohm terminator.

Benefits

10Base2 in a bus topology is relatively inexpensive and easy to install. Networks are easy to configure because a minimum of connection hardware is involved.

Concerns

You are limited to a 10-Mbps bandwidth, which may not meet the needs of an active network that requires you to move a lot of data around on a regular basis. A bus topology can also be difficult to troubleshoot. An open, a short, or a missing or failing terminator can cause problems all along the cable. At the very least, you will want to have a cable tester available that can locate shorts and opens.

There is also a concern that is inherent to Ethernet. Collisions can be a problem on an active network. A collision occurs when two computers try to communicate at the same time. When this happens, the systems will wait, check to see if the cable is available, and try again. As the number of collisions increases, the network's effective bandwidth is reduced.

Recommendations

You may already have use of bus topology in place as part or all of your network solution. If so, you need to review the information you've gathered about your network to determine if bus topology would meet your current and projected network requirements. This will include a close look at bandwidth usage and projected growth. If available, you should also review network maintenance records. If maintenance expenses have shown a rapid increase, this could be a justification for change.

Bus topology is seldom used in new installations because of the problems with troubleshooting failures, the limited scalability, and the simple fact that it is viewed as old technology. When installing a new network or expanding your network, it is doubtful that you will want to use a bus topology.

Star Topology

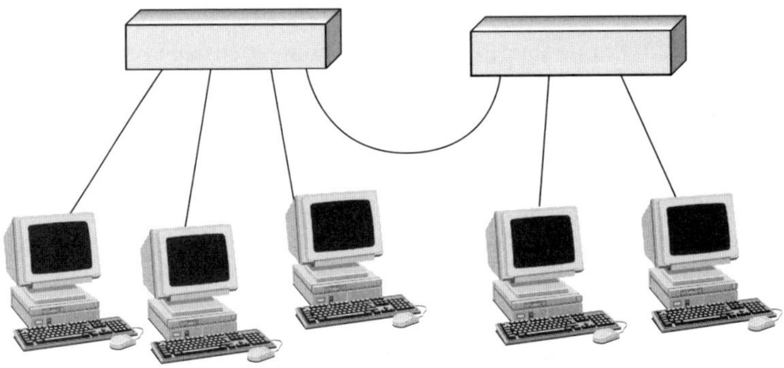

Systems connect to central hubs in a star topology. The network is expanded by connecting additional hubs. Each hub acts as a repeater, boosting the signal before passing it on to the next hub. Hubs may also be connected through a coaxial, twisted-pair, or fiber-optic backbone.

In some implementations, workstations are routed directly back to the wiring closet and connected through distribution panels (patch panels or *punch-down* panels), similar to the panels used for wiring telephone service.

The popularity of star topology implementation has grown with the increased popularity of Ethernet 10BaseT and 100BaseT. 10BaseT supports 10-Mbps transmissions and 100BaseT supports 100 Mbps. Ethernet 10BaseT can use Category 3, 4, or 5 cable. Ethernet 100BaseT uses Category 5 cable. As an example of what to expect, here are some specifications for 10BaseT:

- Maximum 100 meters (328 feet) from hub to transceiver (computer)
- Minimum 2.5 meters (8 feet) from hub to transceiver (computer)
- Up to 1,024 connections per LAN

Computers connect using RJ-45 modular connectors. A transceiver is required at the computer end. Nearly all Ethernet network adapters ship with the transceiver to 10BaseT built in.

NOTE: Token Ring is typically wired as a logical star but acts as a physical ring. This will be discussed as a separate topology later in the section.

Benefits

Since a star topology is wired using twisted-pair cable, usually UTP, installation is typically easy and inexpensive. Because of the modular nature of the connections, most cable plant and connection failures are relatively easy to isolate and troubleshoot.

A star topology can meet most organization's scalability requirements with minimal effort. The technology continues to evolve and improve, making it likely that it can be modified to meet your needs well into the future.

Concerns

UTP cable is susceptible to electronic noise. You may find it necessary to use STP instead of UTP in at least part of your cable runs because of ambient electronic noise. This will increase the cable and labor expenses during installation.

With many hubs (most older), there are still potential concerns about collisions. Collisions can occur at a hub or distribution table and can have the same effect on network performance as in a bus topology network.

If the network is wired with Category 3 or 4 cable, there is also a potential concern about available bandwidth since you are limited to 10BaseT at 10 Mbps. Even if current bandwidth requirements are met, as the requirements increase, it may be necessary to upgrade to Category 5 cable and 100-Mbps network adapters or implement routing to segment network traffic.

Recommendations

This is the most popular topology option for LANs and has been for some time. You will likely find the star topology already in use on your network. You will need to review the result of your information gathering to determine if the network will support your new design as is or if it will have to be upgraded. The most common requirement is upgrading the cable plant to Category 5 cable to support 100 Mbps.

If you are installing or expanding an Ethernet network, a star topology is the most popular choice and will probably be the best fit for your requirements. A star topology can support even the smallest LANs and has the scalability to meet the needs of larger LANs.

Ring Topology

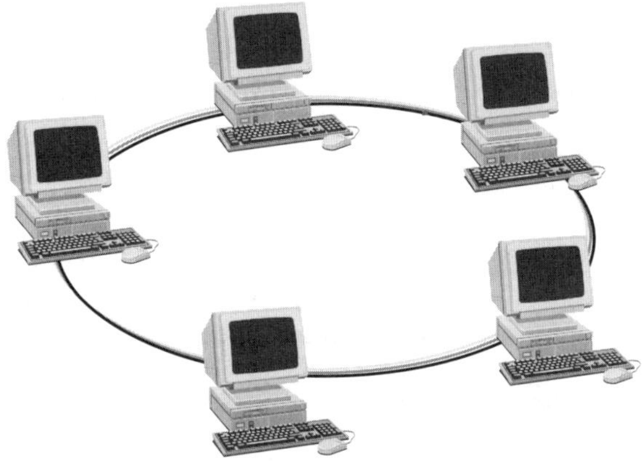

A ring topology is used for Token Ring and Fiber Distributed Data Interface (FDDI) networks. Token Ring is used for PC-based LANs as well as for connections to minicomputers and mainframes. Token Ring is used in IBM's Systems Network Architecture (SNA) networking environments. FDDI is commonly used as a high-speed backbone for campus LANs and moderately sized Metropolitan Area Networks (MANs) or where a high-speed connection is required between computers.

This discussion's focus will be on Token-Ring networks, but a quick overview of FDDI is appropriate at this time as well. Under current specifications, FDDI supports 100 Mbps, has a maximum ring length of 1,000 kilometers (62 miles), and can support up to 500 computer connections. FDDI uses a token-passing technology similar to Token Ring except that it uses dual rings for fault tolerance. If the primary ring should fail, the network can still communicate on the secondary ring.

For standard Token-Ring implementations, the standard ring topology is sometimes referred to as a star-wired ring (or star-ring) topology, indicating that it is wired like a star but works like a ring. Token Ring uses a token-passing technology. Only one computer can communicate on the ring at any time. Each computer in the ring also acts as a repeater since the token is read in then retransmitted out by the system.

There are specifications for 4 Mbps and 16 Mbps Token-Ring implementations. A ring will support either 4 Mbps or 16 Mbps, not both. Token-Ring networks are typically wired using cables based on IBM cabling specifications with IBM Type 1, 2, or 3 cable. You can also find them wired with standard Category 2 or 3 UTP cabling.

The hubs used with Token Ring go by several different names, including Multistation Access Unit (MAU or MSAU) or Smart Multistation Access Unit (SMAU). For the purposes of this course, MAU will be used generically to refer to Token-Ring hubs. When the network has a single MAU, it will loop back internally to create a ring. When multiple MAUs are used, a ring is created by connecting the Ring Out of each MAU to the Ring In of the next in line, ending when it comes back around to the Ring In of the first MAU.

Some technical specifications about Token Ring include the following:

- Maximum 45 meters to 200 meters (148 feet to 656 feet), depending on cable type from MAU to computer
- Maximum 152 meters (500 feet) MAU to MAU
- Minimum 2.5 meters (8 feet) from MAU to computer
- Maximum 33 MAUs per ring
- Maximum 72 computers per UTP network
- Maximum 260 computers per STP network

Connections are made with IBM Media Interface Connectors (MICs), RJ-45 connectors, or RJ-11 connectors.

Benefits

An obvious benefit to Token Ring is that you don't have to worry about collisions because of its token-passing architecture. There is also a level of fault tolerance built in, allowing an MAU to automatically disconnect from a failing computer, bypassing it in the ring. Some MAUs can also detect and bypass when another MAU is failing.

Another benefit is that you may already have Token Ring in place. Token Ring is most commonly found in organizations that have supported (or continue to support) connectivity with IBM minicomputers or mainframes or IBM's SNA networking environment.

Concerns

Bandwidth can become a concern in Token-Ring networks. You are limited to either 4 Mbps or 16 Mbps, which may not provide the amount of bandwidth you will need in order to support future applications.

There may also be scalability concerns. When you reach the maximum limit, 72 computers for UTP or 260 computers for STP, you will need to go to a routed LAN environment to expand your network.

Recommendations

If you have Token Ring in place, you need to answer at least the following three questions:

- Do you support any technologies that require Token Ring?
- Does it meet current and projected bandwidth requirements?
- Does it meet current and projected scalability requirements?

If you are supporting any technologies that require Token Ring, you are going to have to leave it in place, though you may be able to upgrade from 4 Mbps to 16 Mbps Token Ring. Otherwise, you can consider replacing Token Ring if you prefer, but this will require new network adapters, new hubs, and may require new cable. This can become an expensive option.

If you are not currently supporting Token Ring, you need to carefully consider if it will meet your current and projected requirements before deciding on a Token Ring network. The popularity of Token Ring in new installations has declined since the introduction and acceptance of Ethernet 10BaseT and 100BaseT.

Implementing Topology Changes

The decision to change network topology should not be made lightly. Topology changes can be difficult and expensive to implement. Changes to your network topology and how they are implemented can impact the following:

- Network adapters

  This will, of course, depend on the adapters that you are currently using. If your current adapters aren't compatible with the new topology and cable plant, they'll have to be replaced.

- Cabling

  If you are changing to a different topology, say from a bus topology to a star topology, you are going to have to run new network cabling. This could be a requirement even if you are keeping the same topology but upgrading the network to improve bandwidth. For example, moving from 10 Mbps to 100 Mbps Ethernet implemented in a star topology could mean having to run all new Category 5 cable.

- Connection devices

  The same factors apply to connection devices as to cabling. Changing your topology or upgrading your cable plant can mean having to upgrade or replace connection devices as well. This is definitely true when going from a bus topology to a star topology since you are going to need hubs or switches to make connections to the individual systems.

When changing your network topology, get quotes on the hardware costs and the time that will be required to make your changes. Rewiring a network can be an interruption, to put it mildly. You can limit the impact by keeping user downtime to a minimum, but there almost always is going to be some downtime involved.

Making the Change

Make sure that you understand why you are making the change. Don't forget that you may find yourself having to justify the cost of the change, so you need to understand and explain the reasoning behind your decisions. "Because it's the latest technology" isn't going to work in most organizations.

Start by determining what benefits you will derive from the change. Here are a few possibilities to get you started:

- Increased bandwidth

  If your current network cannot meet user and application bandwidth requirements, then you are going to have to make changes. Upgrading to a higher-bandwidth network may be the solution, though you should also consider subnetting (or additional subnetting on a routed LAN) to segment network traffic.
- Better scalability

  If your current network cannot meet your growth requirements, you're going to have to make changes at some point. It's best to make the changes when they can be carefully planned and implemented rather than making them in reaction to critical shortcomings.
- Improved reliability

  This one can be a hard sell if you don't go about it properly. It's hard to justify changes just because something is old. It's much easier to justify the changes if you can point to network failures related to the current topology and cable plant. You have to approach the change as an investment in long-range cost savings.

It should go without saying, but if you are changing your topology because the old one cannot meet your network requirements, you better make sure that the new one will.

Managing the Change

Topology changes typically mean managing a careful balancing act. Carefully consider your priorities before working out an implementation schedule. Start by answering these questions:

- How much user downtime is acceptable?
- How quickly does the new cable plant need to be in place?
- How much can you afford to spend?

The answers will help determine how everything balances out. The less time you have for installing the new cable plant, the more it is going to cost. If you can't afford user downtime, then you're looking at nights and weekends for setting everything up. On a tight budget? Then you will probably have to put up with delays and some user downtime.

Whether you are doing the work using internal resources (the technical staff) is also going to make a difference. Assuming that you have the necessary expertise on staff, then your expenses will be effectively limited to materials and their time. Before making your decision, though, you have to make sure that the people you need are going to be available when you need them. You also need to realize that not everyone is happy with the idea of working nights and weekends in addition to their regular duties.

Bringing in help from the outside can be an effective solution, though it is not without its drawbacks. These can include the following:

- Expense

  You can expect it to cost more when you go outside of the organization. You are also having to pay up front for what might have been treated as hidden costs when doing it yourself, such as employees' salaries for the time spent on the project.

- Time

  You may find that you have less control over the time with an outside contractor. If all of the work is being done during normal work hours, it will have more of an impact on users. You may be able to find a contractor willing to do the work after hours or on weekends, but you can expect to pay a premium for such a service.

- Coordination

  You will probably find yourself having to deal with multiple contractors. This can lead to delays and finger pointing when things don't go well, with you caught in the middle. You may discover that they're willing to talk to you, but not to each other. As a result, you may be left passing messages back and forth with nothing getting accomplished.

It may be possible to have a consultant, one of your vendors, or a contractor act as a general contractor for the project. You'll pay extra, but save yourself time, effort, and headaches. Be sure that the contract spells out your specific expectations of what is to be done, the work schedule, and what you are going to pay.

Remote Access

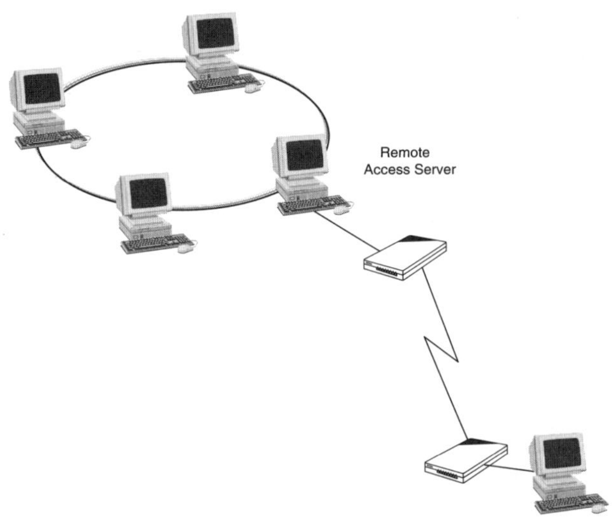

Before leaving network basics, there needs to be a quick discussion about remote access. Specifically, the topic at hand is remote connectivity for individual computers. Remote access will be discussed in detail later in the course. This discussion will be limited to a brief overview.

Remote access gives field employees, such as field salespeople, a way of connecting into the LAN. A remote connection can be configured so that it is almost as if the user has logged on locally but at a severely restricted bandwidth, typically no more than 56 Kbps.

Remote access is commonly used for accessing data files (typically small data files) or online forms and templates, running applications that need to access LAN-based data files, and so forth. It can also be used for remote network management and administration. Remote access should be considered a solution where user connectivity requirements are for periodic, relatively short-duration connections.

The most common connection methods are dial-up or via the Internet through a Virtual Private Network (VPN). Other connection methods, such as ISDN and X.25, are also supported.

A dial-up connection provides greater flexibility since all that is needed is a modem and a way to connect into a telephone line. A VPN provides better security but requires remote users to connect in through an ISP.

NOTE: Remote access connection options are discussed in more detail later in the course.

Scenario 4-1: Topology Design Selection

The purpose of this scenario is to give you practice in evaluating basic concerns and guidelines during network modeling. Suggested solutions are provided in Appendix B at the end of this manual. It may be helpful to review the case studies in Appendix C at the end of this manual.

Things and Stuff's Current Network

The network is configured as a 10Base2 Ethernet network. The only protocol in use on the network is NetBEUI. Users logged on to any system can access shared resources from other systems.

Network Goals

The owner would like to upgrade all systems to Windows 2000 Server and Workstation but hasn't decided whether he wants to make any changes to the current LAN configuration.

The network administrator is of another opinion about network design. He wants to upgrade to a 100BaseT network.

1. If the network administrator's design suggestion is approved, what network hardware replacements will be required?

 ....

 ....

2. What topology will be used if the network administrator's design suggestion is approved?

 ....

 ....

NETWORK TECHNOLOGIES AND PROTOCOLS

Along with deciding on the communication path for your network, you have to decide on how computers are going to communicate. You were introduced to common protocols earlier in the course. This section will review your protocol selections and provide some guidelines for picking the protocol (or protocols) that you need.

The following topics are covered in this section:

- Protocol Overview
- Protocol Selection

This section will provide selection guidelines for a number of common protocols. However, the remainder of this course will focus primarily on configuring your network to support TCP/IP.

Protocol Overview

You were introduced to commonly used protocols earlier in the course. As mentioned, computers must share a common protocol in order to communicate. This is fairly easy to accomplish when using Windows-family operating systems since a Windows-family system can support multiple protocols.

During the information-gathering phase, you are going to determine what protocols are being supported on your network. During the design phase, you are going to decide which protocols your network requires. This decision is going to be influenced by your physical network design, non-Windows and legacy system support requirements, and application requirements.

Common Protocols

Let's start by going back through the protocols that you are most likely to encounter in a LAN environment. These include the following:

- NetBEUI

  You will most commonly find NetBEUI on established networks. It is sometimes there for legacy support but often has been left on the network out of force of habit or because no one thought to remove it.

- NWLink (IPX/SPX)

  You will see NWLink used in mixed Microsoft Windows/Novell NetWare environments. NWLink is used for connecting to a NetWare server and for providing resources directly to NetWare clients. You may also see NWLink when supporting legacy applications that require SPX.

- TCP/IP

  Most networks will be using TCP/IP, either alone or with other protocols. TCP/IP is required when implementing Active Directory domains and when connecting to the Internet.

These are the most common protocols for PC-to-PC communications. However, these aren't the only protocols supported. Let's take a look at some additional protocols you can install on Windows-family systems, specifically Windows 2000 systems.

Additional Protocols

You should also be familiar with these protocols. They are less common and typically only found where they are specifically needed, though that is not always the case. You'll sometimes find them on a network where they've been added just because they were available or because the people setting up network systems weren't that sure of what they were supposed to be doing.

- Data Link Control (DLC)

  You will see DLC installed on systems that need to communicate with Hewlett-Packard printers connected directly to the network. There is less of a need for DLC as more and more printers support TCP/IP. You will sometimes find DLC present when it is no longer needed, simply because no one thought to remove the protocol.

- AppleTalk

  You will see AppleTalk installed on servers that are providing services for Apple Macintosh computers. There is typically no other need for AppleTalk. If not required for Macintosh support, it should be removed.

- SNA

  You will find SNA on servers running Microsoft Host Integration Server. The Host Integration Server was formerly known as, and is still commonly referred to as, SNA Server. SNA Server acts as a gateway between IBM host systems and your LAN.

Any time you find one of these protocols in use when there is no justifiable need, the protocols should be removed. Unneeded protocols add to system overhead and generate unnecessary traffic on the network.

Protocol Selection

You'll know which protocols are in use after you complete the information-gathering phase. This is your starting point, but you are likely to find that some changes need to be made. Review your network configuration and support requirements to determine which protocols you actually need on your network, keeping the number of protocols to a minimum.

Let's take a look at some guidelines for selecting network protocols. After that, we'll discuss installation and configuration procedures.

NetBEUI

NetBEUI was the default protocol for Microsoft LAN Manager and earlier versions of Windows NT. NetBEUI support is provided primarily for backward compatibility.

NetBEUI is a nonroutable protocol designed for use in small networks with a suggested limit of no more than 200 computers. It was originally introduced by IBM in 1985. One reason for its popularity is that at a time when RAM was very limited, NetBEUI required very little memory overhead.

NetBEUI is a broadcast-based protocol, which means that many of its functions are based on broadcast communications. For example, NetBEUI identifies computers by their NetBIOS names and uses broadcasts for name resolution.

NetBEUI Configuration

There are no configurable properties for the NetBEUI protocol. Obviously, this means that NetBEUI has minimal management requirements.

Using NetBEUI

You should only use NetBEUI when supporting legacy systems that are running NetBEUI as their only protocol or when supporting legacy applications that require NetBEUI. Since NetBEUI is a nonroutable protocol, systems running NetBEUI as their only protocol will only be able to access resources in their local subnetwork.

If you don't have a specific need for NetBEUI, it should be removed from any systems it is installed on. You can reduce reliance on NetBEUI by installing a different protocol on systems currently running NetBEUI only (if possible) and by upgrading or replacing applications that require NetBEUI.

NWLink

IPX/SPX has traditionally been the primary protocol for Novell NetWare networks. Windows 2000 provides support for IPX/SPX through NWLink, Microsoft's emulation of IPX/SPX. NWLink is a routable protocol. From a purely technical standpoint, systems running NWLink can access resources located in their local subnetwork or in a remote NWLink (or IPX/SPX) subnetwork.

When you install NWLink, NetBIOS NWLink (NWNBLink) will also be installed automatically. NWNBLink supports NetBIOS applications over IPX/SPX.

NWLink Configuration

NWLink has two key configurable properties: the internal network number and frame type. You will need to set the internal network number to a unique value when providing file and print services to NetWare network clients, when a computer is going to act as an IPX router, or when a computer is supporting any service that relies on the NetWare SAP agent. The internal network number is entered and stored as a hexadecimal value.

The frame type defines how data is formatted before being transmitted on a network. If a computer receives a packet that is using a frame type that it doesn't recognize, it won't be able to read the packet.

Windows 2000 supports the following frame types:

Frame Type	Frame Type Support
802.2	Supported on Ethernet and FDDI fiber optic. This is the default frame type for NetWare 2.2 and NetWare 3.11.
802.3	Supported on Ethernet and FDDI fiber optic. This is the default frame type for NetWare 3.12 and above.
802.5	Supported on Token Ring
SNAP	Supported on Ethernet and Token Ring
Ethernet II	Supported on Ethernet only

By default, when NWLink is first loaded, Windows 2000 will detect automatically the frame type being used on the network. If more than one frame type is detected, Windows 2000 will default to 802.2 as its frame type. If you need to support multiple frame types, you will need to configure them manually.

Using NWLink

You will use NWLink when you need to support connectivity with NetWare network clients and servers. However, installing NWLink doesn't necessarily guarantee communications. Here are some specific examples with their particular requirements:

- Application server

  For example, you might want to add a Windows 2000 server running SQL Server as a database server for a NetWare network. From an operating system standpoint, the only requirement is that you install and configure NWLink. However, the application may need additional configuration or special drivers to support NetWare networks.

- File/print server

  In addition to NWLink, you must install File and Print Services for NetWare to use a Windows 2000 system as a file or print server in a NetWare network.

- Network client/gateway

  In addition to NWLink, you must also have a NetWare client for Windows 2000 systems to access NetWare server resources. Microsoft provides Client Service for NetWare (CSNW) for this purpose on Windows 2000 Professional. Windows 2000 Server ships with Gateway Service for NetWare (GSNW). GSNW allows a server to act as a NetWare client but can also translate resource requests for Windows clients, acting as a gateway and providing the clients NetWare access without having to modify the client systems.

  Each system acting as a NetWare client will have to have NWLink installed. Systems accessing NetWare resources through a GSNW server are not required to support NWLink but must share a common protocol with the GSNW server. The GSNW server, however, must support NWLink.

NWLink is also required if you are supporting any applications that require IPX/SPX. Systems that do not have any of the communication requirements listed previously will not need NWLink. NWLink can be removed from those systems if it is already present.

TCP/IP

TCP/IP has become the de facto standard for PC networks. It is the Windows 2000 default protocol, required for Active Directory domain implementation and required for Internet/intranet access. For now, the discussion will be limited to an overview of TCP/IP. TCP/IP, including supported services and utilities, will be discussed in detail later in the course.

TCP/IP is a suite of protocols rather than one single protocol. The protocols associated with the TCP/IP suite include the following:

Protocol	Description
Internet Protocol (IP)	IP provides connectionless (nonacknowledged) delivery between computer systems. Since this is a connectionless protocol, there is no guarantee of proper sequencing or even arrival at the destination.
Transmission Control Protocol (TCP)	TCP provides acknowledged, connection-oriented communications. It includes fields for packet sequencing and acknowledgement as well as source and destination socket identifiers to allow communications with higher-level protocols.
Internet Group Management Protocol (IGMP)	IGMP provides a form of broadcasting called *multicasting* for communication and passing management information between members of a multicasting group.
Internet Control Message Protocol (ICMP)	ICMP is used to control and manage information transmitted using TCP/IP. It allows nodes to share status and error information. It also helps to reroute messages when a route is busy or has failed.
Address Resolution Protocol/Reverse Address Resolution Protocol (ARP/RARP)	ARP and RARP are maintenance protocols. They are used on a LAN to enable hosts to translate IP addresses to MAC addresses.
User Datagram Protocol (UDP)	UDP is designed for connectionless, unacknowledged communications. UDP also supports optional checksums for verifying header and data integrity.
File Transfer Protocol (FTP)	FTP supports file transport between dissimilar systems. Assuming sufficient rights, directory searches and file operations are supported.
Simple Main Transfer Protocol (SMTP)	SMTP provides a mechanism for exchange of mail information between systems. SMTP is the most widely used service on the Internet.
Simple Network Management Protocol (SNMP)	SNMP uses UDP to send control and management information between TCP/IP hosts.

TCP/IP provides two application interfaces that network applications can use TCP/IP protocol services through. These are Winsock and NetBIOS over TCP/IP (NetBT). Winsock is the standard interface used by socket-based applications. NetBT provides an interface between NetBIOS-based applications and TCP/IP.

Each node (or host) in an IP network will have a 32-bit IP address. This address is divided into four bytes (octets), or a *w.x.y.z* format, as shown in the following example.

206.11.125.1

This actually contains two addresses. These are the network address (or network ID) and host address (or host ID). The network address identifies your network as unique on the Internet, and the host ID identifies your station as unique on the network.

There will be a subnet mask associated with each IP address. The subnet mask identifies which part of the IP address is used as the network address and which is used as the host address. When you assign a host address, you must supply both the IP address and the subnet mask.

NOTE: Subnetting and routing support are covered in detail later in the course.

From a design standpoint, you need to be aware of changes that are planned for TCP/IP. The current 32-bit address scheme was never meant to account for the type of explosive growth that the Internet has experienced over the last few years. A new standard, IP version 6 (IPv6), defines a 128-bit IP address to provide sufficient room for continued expansion. IPv6 is also designed to improve both network performance and security. You can expect a long and gradual transition to IPv6, with the two protocol versions running in parallel until the transition is complete.

TCP/IP Configuration

Configurable properties for TCP/IP include the following:

- IP address

  More accurately, you need to provide an IP address and subnet mask. These values can be entered manually or obtained automatically through the DHCP service. It is typically suggested to use DHCP whenever possible since it reduces your management overhead (and headaches). Some systems, such as domain controllers, DNS servers, WINS servers, IP routers, and DHCP servers will require static (manually configured) IP addresses.

  IP addresses are assigned by a network adapter or other connection device (such as a dial-in modem connection). You can specify multiple IP addresses for any network adapter, making it a multihomed adapter. Reasons for why you might want to do this are discussed later in the course.

- Default gateway

  In a routed network environment, you will define the default gateway that a system should use. When the system generates a packet destined for a different subnetwork, it will direct it to a default gateway, which will then forward the packet on toward its final destination.

- DNS server(s)

  You need to supply the DNS server(s) to be used for name resolution. You can specify one, two, or more DNS servers. When the system cannot contact its primary DNS server for name resolution, or if the primary DNS server is unable to provide name resolution, the system will try the next alternate DNS. When using DHCP to manage IP addresses, DHCP can be configured to provide DNS server information as well.

  Other configurable properties for DNS support include suffixes to use when attempting to resolve a host name and how dynamic DNS registration is managed for the local system.

- WINS server(s)

  As with DNS servers, you can specify one or more WINS servers for NetBIOS name resolution. A computer will automatically register itself with its primary WINS server when the local computer connects to the network. The primary WINS server will be the first WINS server listed for the computer. Whether or not you specify any WINS servers, you can enable or disable the use of the LMHOSTS file for NetBIOS name resolution.

- NetBIOS support

  You have the option of enabling or disabling NetBIOS over TCP/IP support. You can also have NetBIOS support enabled or disabled through DHCP when using DHCP for IP address assignment. NetBIOS over TCP/IP will be required when supporting NetBIOS-based applications.

You can also set options for IP Security and TCP/IP filtering. You can use the IP Security (IPSec) options to decide whether unsecured traffic will be allowed on the network. The TCP/IP filtering properties determine what traffic your system will accept, defaulting to all. You can limit IP traffic by only accepting communications from specified TCP ports or UDP ports. You can also manage filters based on IP protocol.

Using TCP/IP

In a Windows 2000 networking environment, especially in an Active Directory domain, you are going to be using TCP/IP. With TCP/IP currently accepted as the de facto standard for network communication, the question isn't so much when you *should* use TCP/IP, but when you *shouldn't*. It is unlikely that you will not find a situation where you don't need to consider TCP/IP as part of your network solution. In modern, heterogeneous networks, TCP/IP is usually your best bet for finding a common language that all of the computers can speak.

DLC

DLC is only required in limited, specialized implementations. DLC was originally developed by IBM to support mainframe-to-mainframe communications. It was also chosen by Hewlett-Packard (HP) as the protocol for its network-connected printers.

DLC Configuration

There are no configuration properties for DLC, but there is some special setup required when configuring a network-attached printer that uses DLC. You must add an HP network port to your list of printer ports and connection information for the printer.

Using DLC

DLC is only required on the system that will act as a print server and will be sending data to a network-connected printer. You will likely find fewer reasons for using DLC since most network-connected printers and other devices now support more commonly used protocols such as TCP/IP.

AppleTalk

The AppleTalk protocol was developed by Apple Computer Corporation. It was designed specifically to support Macintosh system communication. To provide resources to AppleTalk clients, in addition to AppleTalk, you must also install Windows 2000 Services for Macintosh.

AppleTalk Configuration

AppleTalk networks can be subdivided into zones, similar to dividing a network into subnetworks. Zones are a logical system organization, making it easy to locate and identify systems. The only configurable parameter is, if you are in a network using an AppleTalk zone, you can identify the zone the system will be included in.

Using AppleTalk

You only need to install AppleTalk if you are supporting AppleTalk clients. Even then, AppleTalk is only required on those systems providing resources, acting as an AppleTalk router or acting as a dial-in server for remote access.

Protocol Installation

At some point after you decide on the protocols that you need to support, and on which system, comes the task of installing and configuring the protocol. This discussion will be limited to the procedures of setting up protocol support on Windows 2000 systems. While the procedures will differ somewhat, the requirements and configuration settings are the same for other Windows-family operating systems and, for that matter, most other operating systems.

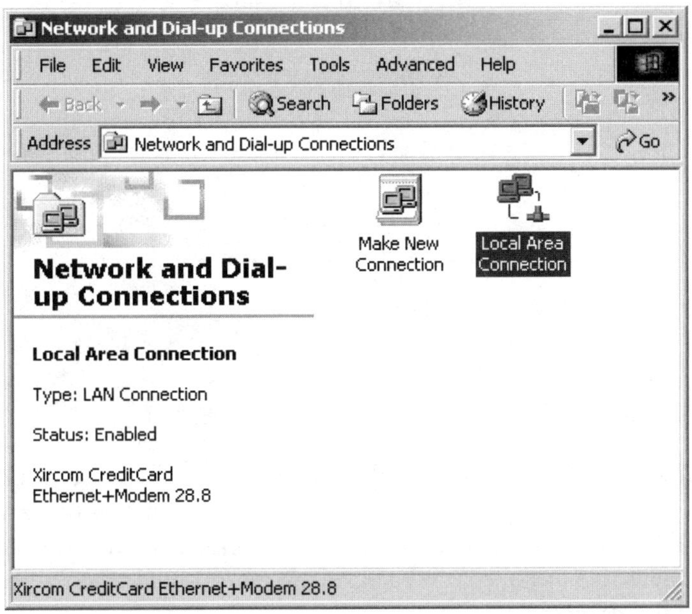

Let's take a look at the general procedures for installing protocols. You view, install, and manage protocols through the Network and Dial-up Connections utility. Launch this utility by running **Start | Settings | Network and Dial-up Connections**. From there, you can right-click on the icon for the system's connection and run **Properties**.

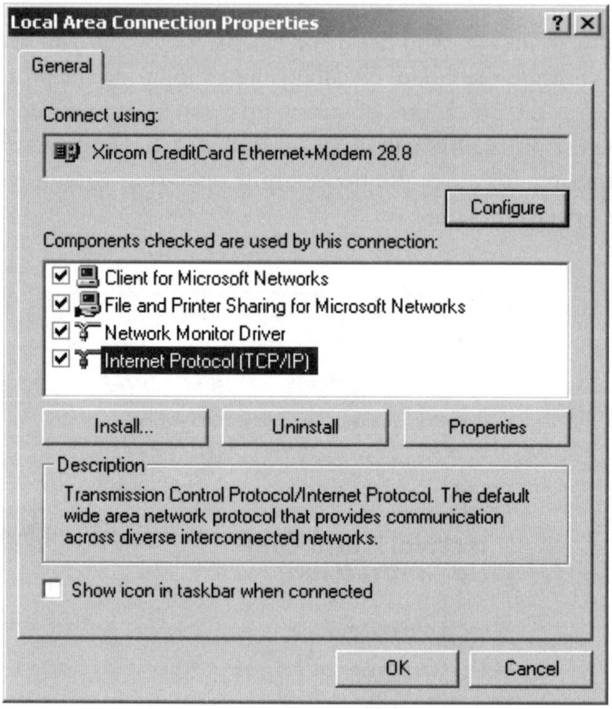

The General page in the Local Area Connection Properties window lists the clients, services, and transport protocols installed for the adapter being used for that connection. The **Install** and **Uninstall** buttons let you install and uninstall components. The **Properties** button lets you manage component properties. Click on **Install** to install an additional protocol.

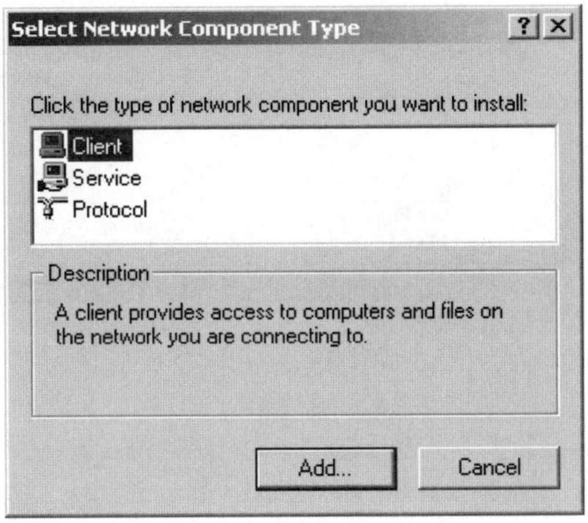

You will be prompted to select the type of component that you want to install, defaulting to Client. To install an additional protocol, click to select Protocol, then click on **Add**.

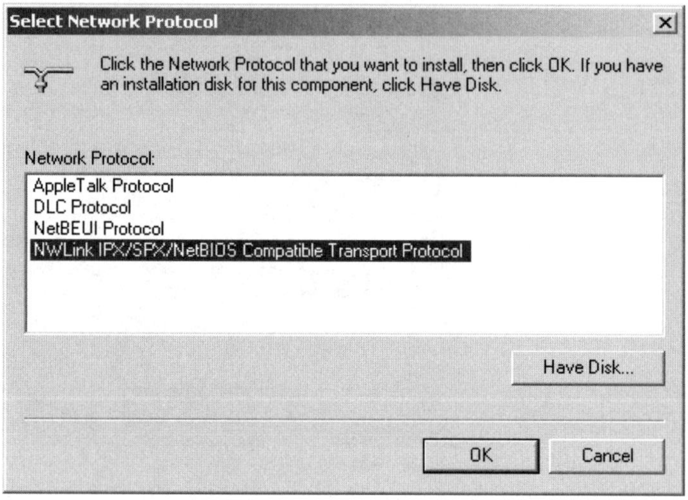

A list of available protocols displays. Only those protocols that are not already installed on the system are listed. Click on the protocol that you want to install, then click on **OK**.

NOTE: Specific procedures and requirements for installing TCP/IP and NWLink are covered in more detail later in the course.

Binding Protocols

When supporting multiple protocols, they bind to all network adapters in a specified order. The same is true of services. Binding order can be significant. When a packet is received, it will be checked by each protocol by binding order. If a system loses its connection with the network, it will attempt to re-establish communications using each protocol, once again going through the protocols in binding order.

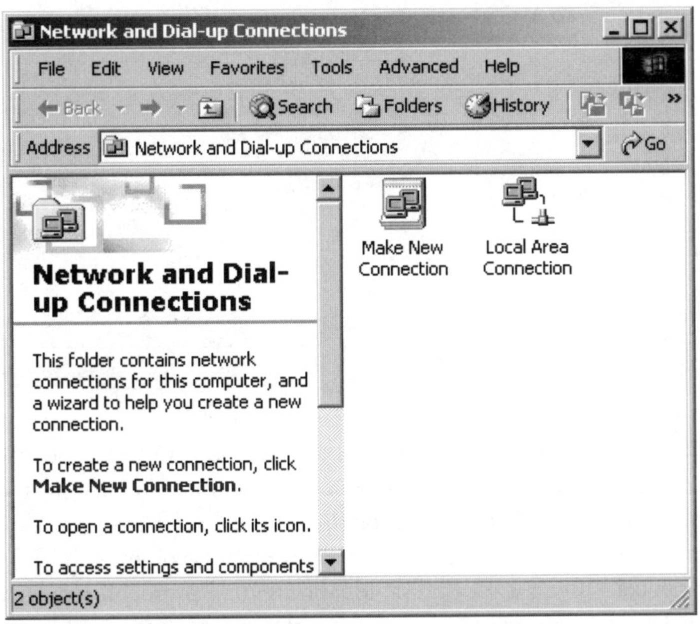

To set the binding order, select the connection you want to manage in Network and Dial-up Connections and run **Advanced | Advanced Settings**.

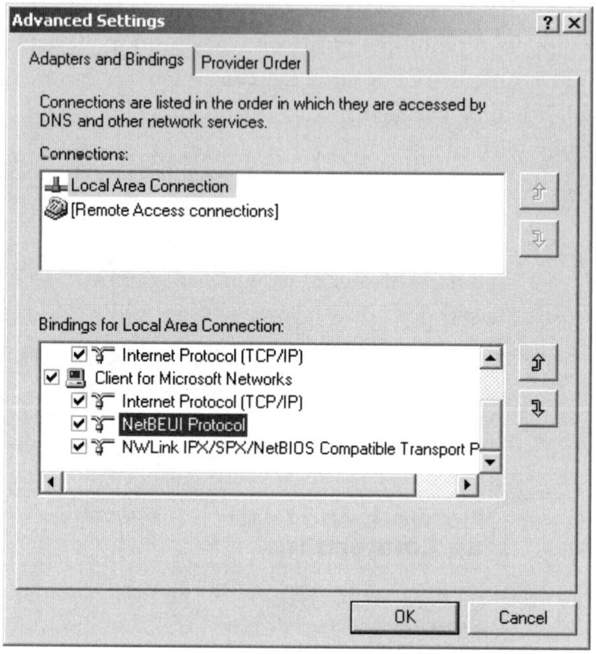

To change the binding order for a protocol, select the protocol and use the up and down arrows at the right to change its relative position. The first protocol listed is your primary (default) protocol and should be the protocol most often used for communications. In a Windows 2000 Active Directory environment, you must have TCP/IP as your primary protocol. If you want to disable binding for a protocol, remove the check from its checkbox. This will leave the protocol installed, but it will not be used for communication.

Multiprotocol Integration

Integrating multiple protocols into your network solution does not necessarily require networkwide changes. Systems do not have to share the same set of protocols, but just need to have one common protocol in order to communicate.

For example, suppose you are supporting a network that includes both Windows 2000 and NetWare 3.12 servers. The Windows 2000 clients are all running TCP/IP. The NetWare clients are running NWLink. There is no need for the two sets of clients to communicate directly, so this configuration meets your needs. Things change, however, when you add a Windows 2000 server running SQL Server 2000 that will be providing services to both Windows 2000 and NetWare clients. This server will have to be running both TCP/IP and NWLink.

NOTE: Specific examples of how you can support multiprotocol integration are provided later in the course.

Scenario 4-2: Protocol Selection

The purpose of this scenario is to give you practice in making network protocol selections. Suggested solutions are provided in Appendix B at the end of this manual. It may be helpful to review the case studies in Appendix C at the end of this manual.

Barney's Bank's Current Network

1. From the information provided in the case study, what protocol is currently in use?

2. Barney's Bank is considering acquiring another office in the United States. The office has a NetWare 3.12 network at present. Users in the new office will need to access data in the main office, but there will be no requirements for accessing data in the office from other locations. Eventually, the NetWare network will be converted to a Windows 2000 Active Directory domain. What protocol changes will need to be made to support this new acquisition?

Fairco Manufacturing's Current Network

The LAN is configured as a nonrouted LAN running NWLink and TCP/IP protocols. It is wired in a star topology and was recently rewired using Category 5 UTP. The systems currently have 10 Mbps or 10/100 Mbps Ethernet adapters, about an equal number of each spread evenly around the LAN. The Windows NT domain is set up with one PDC and one BDC. IP name resolution is supported through the use of HOSTS files.

1. What protocol changes would be required if the network were to be upgraded to a Windows 2000 Active Directory domain?

2. From the information provided, what is the justification for running NWLink on all systems?

Exercise 4-1: Multiprotocol Support (Optional)

The purpose of the exercise is to give you practice in setting up a system to support multiple protocols. Complete all of the steps in this exercise on Alpha. There are no solutions provided for this exercise.

Special Preparation

There is no special preparation required for this exercise.

Protocol Installation

During this portion of the exercise, you will install the NWLink and NetBEUI protocol.

1. Run **Start | Settings | Network and Dial-up Connections.**
2. Right-click on Local Area Connection and run **Properties**.
3. Click on **Install.**
4. Click to select Protocol, then click on **Add.**
5. Select NWLink IPX/SPX/NetBIOS Compatible Transport Protocol and click on **OK.**
6. Click on **Install.**

7. Click to select Protocol, then click on **Add**.
8. Select NetBEUI Protocol and click on **OK**.
9. Click on **Close**.

Protocol Binding Order

During this portion of the exercise, you will modify the protocol binding order.

10. If not already selected, select Local Area Connection and run **Advanced | Advanced Settings**.
11. Locate and select Internet Protocol under File and Printer Sharing for Microsoft Networks.
12. Click on the up arrow to the right of the Bindings list until Internet Protocol (TCP/IP) is moved to the top of the list.
13. Locate and select Internet Protocol under Client for Microsoft Networks.
14. Click on the up arrow to the right of the Bindings list until Internet Protocol (TCP/IP) is moved to the top of the list.
15. Click on **OK**.
16. Exit Network and Dial-up Connections.

LOCAL AREA NETWORKING

Now it's time to use the information you've gathered and your initial design decisions to start mapping out your network. The following topics are covered in this section:

- Network Infrastructure Overview
- Nonrouted LAN
- Routed LAN

The information presented in this section will also apply when talking about WAN design. WAN design will include designing the individual LANs and the remote connections between the LANs.

Network Infrastructure Overview

In simple terms, your network infrastructure refers to everything that makes up your physical LAN. This is going to include the following:

- Cable plant
- Connection devices
- User workstations
- Network servers
- Operating systems and applications
- Protocols

You've already been introduced to some of the selections that you will need to make during network design.

Design Changes

During the design process, you are going to have to decide what changes you need to make to your network. It's best to start with a broad overview of the LAN to give you a road map. This will include information such as the following:

- Number of current users

  You have to make sure that your design provides support for all of your current network users. As much as possible, you are going to want to minimize the noticeable changes and keep user downtime to a minimum during the implementation process.

- Current bandwidth usage

  You need to know if there are any current performance problems that need to be corrected by the network design.

- Projected growth

  Network growth is going to impact user distribution, bandwidth usage, and network service requirements. Accurate growth predictions will make it possible for you to build scalability into your network design.

- Network servers and their locations

  You will need to determine if you have enough servers to meet current requirements and if the servers are in appropriate locations. You may also find that it is possible to combine some servers. Assuming it has sufficient resources, one server can support multiple network services.

Now you know what some of the issues are, so the discussion can move on to the types of changes you may need to propose in your network design. These might include changes to the following:

- Network topology

  These changes have already been addressed. You may find it necessary to implement a new topology or to upgrade your current network.

- Network protocols

  Decide on what protocols you need. These should be the only protocols present on your network. LAN protocols have already been addressed. Remote access protocols will be discussed later in the course.

- Routing

  You need to determine if routing is going to be necessary to provide optimum support. This is going to mean creating subnetworks, then placing users, their resources, and network servers onto the appropriate subnetworks. You are going to need a good understanding of user requirements so that you can estimate projected traffic flows.

- Network services

  Network services changes will depend somewhat on the other changes that you are making to the network. If you're adding Active Directory services, you'll need to make sure that DNS service support is available. If you're implementing routing, you need to decide on where network servers will be located. You may find that you can improve network performance and reduce management overhead by combining services.

- Network management

  While you're making changes to the network, you may find that you need to make changes to the network management structure at the same time. It may be necessary to shift job responsibilities around or add more support personnel.

For now, you need to be aware of the types of issues you may encounter. Each of these issues, along with suggested solutions and design guidelines, will be addressed in more detail later in the course.

Design Impact

You also have to determine how the design changes are going to impact your network. Topology changes can be changing network adapters, connection devices, and your cable plant. If you plan to implement routing, you're going to need routers. Adding new network services means additional support requirements, which could mean having to invest in training or adding support personnel who already understand the services.

You need to compare the old and new network designs and carefully document any differences. Next, determine what is required to make each of these changes.

Also, be ready for surprises. Here are a few things that tend to turn up regularly during network implementation:

- You'll have to work around normal network activities.

  You can be pretty sure that your organization is not going to shut down just so you can make changes to the network. It will be critical to keep the impact on day-to-day user activities to a minimum. Always remember that the network is there to support the organization and that keeping business processes flowing should be your number one priority.

- Transparent changes will be anything but.

  Some changes, such as software upgrades, are supposed to be transparent. That means that the user should have no idea that any change has been made. Even if you are guaranteed that a change is going to be transparent, don't completely trust it. There are likely to be changes that are going to generate user questions and possibly conflict with network activities.

- It's going to take longer than you projected.

  Maybe it would be more accurate to say that it's going to require more hours than you project. You may not have the option of changing the completion date, which means investing more time, more personnel, or both to get the job done on time. This is going to be true whether it's your network or if you've been brought in as a consultant or contractor. As an employee, your next review may be based on project completion. As a contractor or consultant, there may be financial penalties for late completion.

- You're going to forget something important.

  No matter what you might like to think, you're only human. It's very likely that you are going to forget some detail along the way, and it will probably turn out to be something important. Be ready to make changes to your design and implementation *on the fly*, if necessary.

In most cases, you are going to have an overriding goal of keeping network service and availability interruptions to a minimum.

You also have to look ahead to what happens after implementation. For example, you will need to decide what changes have to be made to assignment and scheduling of periodic support activities. You may not need to change backup schedules, but you will probably be backing up more servers. You need to decide if you need to make changes to your auditing selections or to how you make periodic performance checks.

Nonrouted LAN

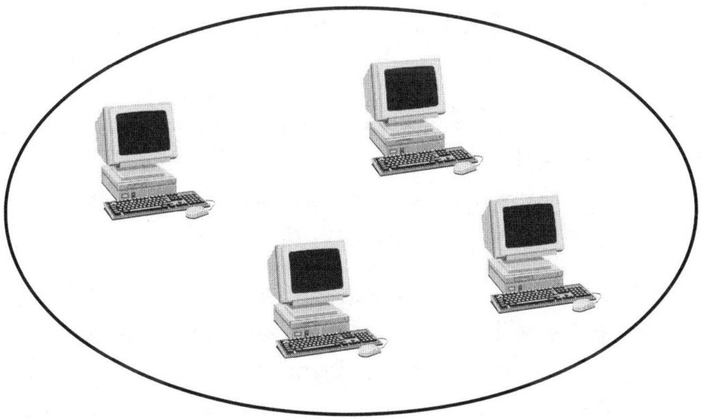

If a nonrouted LAN is going to meet your network requirements, then that's the network model you should use. A nonrouted LAN is typically the easiest, fastest, and least-expensive model to implement.

It is important to make sure that a nonrouted LAN will meet your needs before settling on that as your design. It is much easier to implement routing up front than to try to modify your network later to support routing.

Basic Requirements

The basic design requirements for a nonrouted LAN include the following:

- Topology and cable plant
- User workstations
- Network servers
- Operating systems and applications
- Protocol selections

There are several things you don't have to worry about when using a nonrouted LAN. Latency and resource availability shouldn't be concerns since everything is local to the user workstations. The only network connectivity devices you need are those that are built in to the cable plan, such as repeaters in a bus topology or hubs in a star topology.

There is one issue that has not been addressed yet that does need to be mentioned: the issue of physical placement. The physical placement of user workstations is obvious; you need to put them where the users can reach them. The main concern with workstations is that the placements are ergonomically sound.

Network servers require a little additional thought. If you are modifying an existing network, you've probably already addressed this issue. Otherwise, you have to decide where you are going to put the servers. Access security has been discussed at length already, but there is also an issue of physical security. You will want to provide a location for network servers where they are physically protected against malicious action. A common solution is to set up a secure systems room for network servers. If that is a workable solution for you, find a location that is relatively secure and where you will be able to see if anyone starts to bother with the servers.

LAN Design

The basic LAN design is relatively simple for a nonrouted LAN. All systems are going to be part of the same LAN, so your only cabling concern is providing connections out to the computers' physical locations. Of course, that may not be as easy as it initially seems. You are going to be constrained by the limitations inherent in your topology, as explained below:

- Bus topology

  You will be constrained by the total cable length and number of computers per segment. Keep in mind that on Ethernet 10Base2, you can have up to five cable segments, but computers can only be attached to three of those segments.

- Star topology

  The main thing you'll need to watch here is maximum cable lengths. This may mean having to set up hubs at different locations to stay within those limits.

You also have to be careful about the physical location of the cable plant. Network cabling should be routed to avoid sources of electrical noise and traffic areas. As much as possible, cable should be routed through suspended ceilings, raised floors, walls, and conduit installed specifically for LAN cabling.

Possible Concerns

Before settling on a nonrouted LAN as your design, you need to be aware of some of the potential concerns associated with it. The primary concerns will relate to scalability and performance.

You are going to have physical limits imposed on the network by your topology. These were mentioned earlier in the chapter, but as a quick review, you will be limited to:

- 90 computers in an Ethernet 10Base2 bus LAN
- 1,024 computers in an Ethernet 10BaseT star LAN
- 72 computers in a 4-Mbps Token-Ring LAN
- 260 computers in a 16-Mbps Token-Ring LAN

Make sure that the topology you've selected is going to meet your growth requirements. Otherwise, you are going to be forced into a routed LAN.

There is a good chance that you'll start running into performance problems before you reach the maximum computer limits on your LAN. You may see some performance degradation as you approach the maximum limits in a Token-Ring LAN, but the problems will likely be even more noticeable in an Ethernet LAN.

Routed LAN

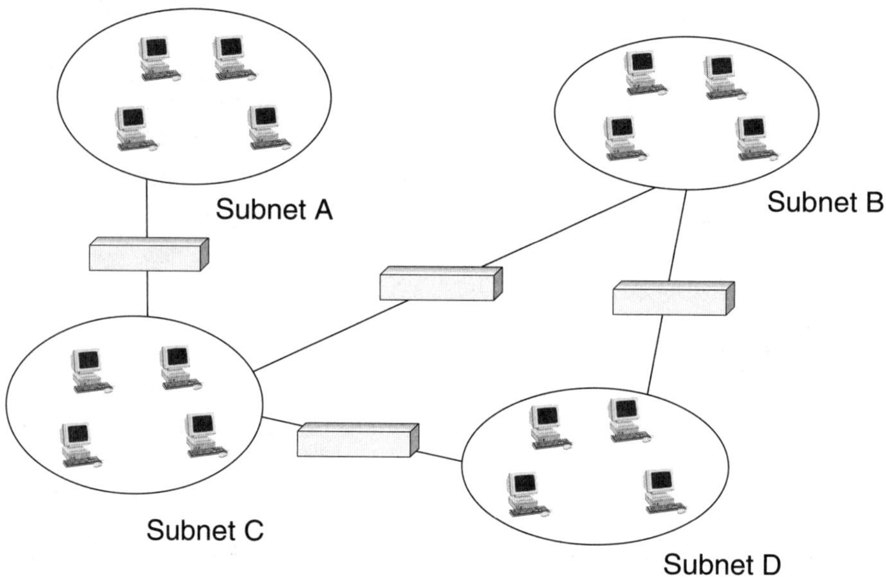

It comes down to a fairly simple decision. If a nonrouted LAN cannot meet your current or projected network requirements, then you are going to have to use a routed LAN.

While designing the physical network, you may find it easier to think of each subnetwork as a separate LAN. Optimize the design for each of the subnetworks, then decide how they need to be connected. You'll be using much the same process in WAN design.

Basic Requirements

The basic requirements start out the same as for a nonrouted LAN. Of course, you do have an additional hardware requirement. You will need to provide routers to connect the subnetworks. This can be done by purchasing routers designed specifically for this purpose or by using Windows 2000 (or Windows NT) servers as routers.

You do need to determine whether you are going to directly connect the subnetworks or if you are going to tie the subnetworks together to a backbone. It is often easier to design a routed network around a backbone, but you have the potential concern that, should the backbone fail, none of the subnetworks will be able to communicate.

LAN Design

The LAN design process is going to be more complicated when designing a routed network. One of your goals will be to keep the traffic going through the routers to a minimum.

For now, the discussion will be limited to an overview of design issues and concerns. The issues presented here will be discussed in more detail later in the course. Issues that need to be considered include the following:

- Resource access

  You are going to be concerned about user and resource placement. As much as possible, users and the resources they need should be placed on the same subnetwork. This will improve availability and reduce traffic through the routers. The information you collected about users and their resource requirements will be invaluable during this phase.

- Server placement

  You are going to have to balance server traffic against performance and availability. You might think that the obvious solution is to place at least one of each type of network service server you need in each subnetwork. While that does give you a high degree of availability, it can also lead to significant increases in router traffic. Domain controllers, DNS servers, and WINS servers will need to keep each other updated through replication as changes are made in their databases.

- Availability

  You can assume that each subnetwork is going to need resources from other subnetworks on a periodic basis. While availability shouldn't be a serious problem most of the time, you do need to realize that routers can represent a single point of failure.

Latency shouldn't be a significant problem in a routed LAN. If you design user and resource placement properly, bandwidth usage in each of the subnetworks should improve over a nonrouted LAN since you are segmenting the LAN traffic.

Possible Concerns

There are a number of concerns when designing a routed LAN. When compared to a nonrouted LAN, the design process is going to be more complicated because there are more design issues involved. The implementation is typically more expensive because more network hardware is involved. Ongoing support costs also increase, mainly because there are more things that can go wrong. Let's take a moment to address some other issues you might encounter.

Protocol Selection

Computers that need to communicate with other subnetworks will have to be running a routable protocol. In other words, you will have to use either TCP/IP or NWLink. For the majority of networks, you can assume that you will be using TCP/IP.

Based on your protocol selection, you have to decide how network systems are going to be configured and supported. You have to design your subnetwork and computer addressing, including how addresses will be assigned and maintained.

Routing

There are a number of issues relating to routing, beginning with the routes you are going to establish. Remember that a single route between two subnetworks means a potential single point of failure. Should the router fail, the subnetwork will not be able to communicate. If you provide multiple routes, then you must also provide additional routers and the physical connections between them.

As already mentioned, one of your design goals should be minimizing traffic through the routers. You will also want to monitor router traffic periodically. Too much traffic and your routers can become bottlenecks, degrading network performance.

Availability and Latency

Availability and latency issues typically will not be serious concerns, but once again, it is going to depend on your network design.

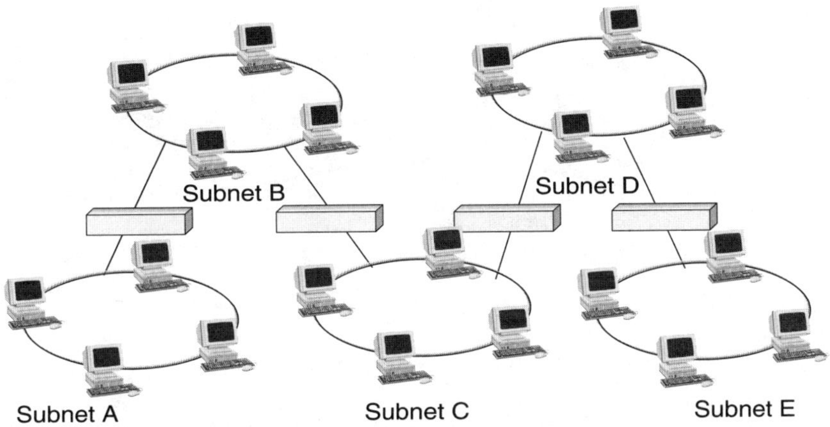

Consider the LAN in the previous figure. It should be obvious that this is a less-than-optimal design. If a computer in Subnet A wants to send a packet to a computer in Subnet E, it must pass through four hops (cross four routers) and go through three subnetworks. This could lead to latency problems for some applications. A failure anywhere along the way would cause availability problems.

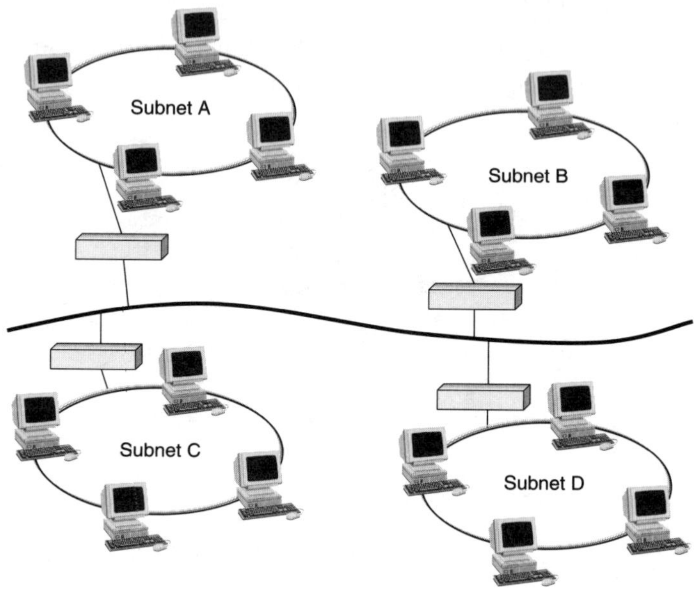

This time, the figure shows a routed LAN with its subnetworks connecting through a backbone. Latency should not be a concern with this configuration. There is a potential problem with availability, however. If the backbone fails, none of the systems will be able to communicate.

Scenario 4-3: LAN Design

The purpose of this scenario is to give you practice in developing a LAN design. Suggested solutions are provided in Appendix B at the end of this manual. It may be helpful to review the case studies in Appendix C at the end of this manual.

Things and Stuff

1. Which LAN model would be best suited for this network and why?

2. Refering to question 1, what network hardware changes would be required by the selected LAN model?

Fairco Manufacturing

1. What LAN model would be used if Fairco Manufacturing wanted to isolate warehouse traffic from the rest of the network?

2. Refering to question 1, what additional network hardware would be required?

    ....

    ....

3. Refering to question 1, how would you need to place domain controllers to minimize traffic between the warehouse systems and the rest of the network?

    ....

    ....

WIDE AREA NETWORKING

Now the discussion turns to WAN design. As with LAN design, the discussion will be kept to an overview of design guidelines and concerns. The following topics are covered in this section:

- WAN Design
- Remote Connection Design

A detailed discussion of WAN design issues will follow in later chapters.

WAN Design

At the core of a good WAN design are well-designed and implemented LANs. Many of the issues you face in WAN design are identical to those you face when designing a routed LAN except that you are dealing with a much larger geographic scope.

Unlike LANs, it would be difficult to provide standard WAN models. The only blanket statement you can make about a WAN is that it is composed of LANs communicating through remote connections. This simple statement leads to any number of variations. Issues that will impact your design include the following:

- LAN configurations
- Geographic scope
- Remote connection types
- Remote connection configuration

A WAN's design will be shaped by the organization that it is supporting. User and resource distribution are going to be key factors, as is the organization's geographic scope. You are likely to find yourself dealing with a broader range of user requirements and conflicting expectations. You are more likely to run into regulatory constraints that will also influence the final WAN design.

Design Basics

Start with your LANs. You have to get the LAN designs right. Your LAN designs must also take in a broader scope. The basic LAN concerns are the same, but now you have to consider the impact of your LAN design on the rest of the WAN.

The process is somewhat analogous to designing a routed LAN, except now you need to consider each LAN as a somewhat autonomous entity. You will have to work with the support structures and personnel in place at the remote LANs. You will need to rely more on their expertise and understanding of their particular requirements.

You will have to be especially careful about LAN changes that are going to require changes in the remote support structure. These changes are likely to be met with opposition and may require careful negotiation. Even if you have the authorization to hand down decisions and expect them to be implemented, you will probably want to show some discretion when dealing with remote offices.

For the purposes of this discussion, each remote LAN will be considered as a whole. Though you will be concerned about issues surrounding local routing requirements in your network design, this discussion won't be addressing those issues.

Users and Resources

From a LAN and WAN perspective, user placement is pretty simple. All users in the remote office will be part of the remote LAN. They will access the network through their local LAN connection.

Resource access might need more careful consideration. Users will have direct and easy access to resources located in their local LAN, but you also have to consider resources located on other LANs. You need to determine whether the resource is located on the appropriate LAN. In other words, is the resource on the same LAN as the majority of the users who need to access it? If not, you need to consider moving files and resources into more appropriate locations.

There is also the issue of resources that users from several different LANs need to access. This is a common issue with data files that need to be referenced on a regular basis. If the files are relatively static, you should consider placing copies in each of the remote LANs where they are needed. You can update the files on an as-needed basis through replication. If the files are more dynamic in nature, you may want to leave the files on one LAN. It's possible that more traffic will be generated by file replication, which is used to keep the copies updated, than is generated through user access.

Network Services

The issue is much the same as it was in a routed LAN. The first temptation, once again, is going to be to place one of each type of server providing network services in each location. To some extent, that may be a possible solution, but you need to compare the traffic generated by users accessing the services, the traffic generated through replicated updates, and the server and service performance.

You best solution will probably fall somewhere between a server in every LAN and centralized support for network services. If you have an Active Directory domain, for example, you will probably want to have at least one domain controller located physically in each LAN. However, you might find it more efficient to use one or two strategically placed servers to support DHCP address assignments.

Availability and Latency

Latency and availability issues are more likely to come up in a WAN environment than in a LAN. This is primarily due to the nature of the remote connections. Bandwidth over remote connections is typically much less than over a local connection, which can mean delays in retrieving data files. Demand-dial connections can be even more susceptible to both availability and latency problems.

One way of keeping availability problems to a minimum is the same as you saw for a routed LAN. If availability is a major concern, you may need to provide multiple connection paths between LANs. This may not be possible, however, due to the costs involved.

Potential Concerns

As your network grows, the possibility of failures increases right along with it. The potential concerns addressed here are not meant to influence your decision as to whether you want to implement a WAN. That decision was made for you by your organization's geographic scope and network support requirements. Instead, these concerns are mentioned so that you can be aware of some of the problems you might encounter and can be thinking about possible solutions.

Management Control

One concern is your technical support structure. You are going to have less direct, hands-on access to the remote LANs and will have to rely on remote support personnel. You will have to be able to depend on remote personnel following established network policies, but it will be your responsibility to make sure that the policies are appropriate to their environment and requirements.

Another, potentially bigger, problem is that there are some things that are completely out of your direct control. When you move to a WAN environment, you no longer own all of the network infrastructure; you are having to work with other companies to provide you with remote links. Some of these providers are going to be more responsive to your needs than others.

Bandwidth

Your bandwidth across remote links is typically going to be much less than the bandwidth in each of the local LANs. This means that keeping traffic between the LANs to manageable levels is a critical concern. You may find yourself having to make adjustments to server placements, network service support, and so forth after the network is in place and you can start gathering traffic statistics.

Domain Support

You are going to have similar concerns when supporting Windows NT domains, Active Directory domains, or both. How complicated the issue becomes depends on the number of domains you are supporting and how the domains are structured.

A single domain environment is fairly easy, at least from the standpoint of understanding what you need to do. Each user must have access to a domain controller in order to be able to log on to the network. This can be a domain controller on the local LAN or one the user connects to over a remote link.

In most cases, it will pay off to set up local domain controllers due to the amount of traffic that is generated by user support requirements. Of course, there are always exceptions to the rule. If you only have a few users in one of your remote locations, you could find that user support generates less traffic than that generated by server updates.

It gets more complicated when you are supporting multiple domains. Your domain design structure can look completely different than your physical network structure. Domain users can potentially turn up in any LAN. In this case, you will need domain membership as part of the information you gather about your users.

The same issue remains as before: where to put the domain controllers. It is complicated by the fact that you not only need to consider whether to provide local domain controllers for a LAN, but you also have to consider which domains you need to support. The guidelines remain the same as mentioned earlier. You have to balance performance and bandwidth usage to see which option is more effective. As a general rule of thumb, if you are only supporting a few domain members as part of a LAN, you probably don't need a local domain controller.

Remote Connection Design

You were introduced to common remote connection types earlier in the course. Those will not be addressed again during this discussion but will be covered in more detail later in the course.

For now, the discussion is going to focus more on how the physical connections are going to be routed–in other words, where the connection points are going to be and how they are going to interconnect.

Designing Remote Connections

When you start designing your WAN connections, you are going to find that some of the connections look similar to the topology models discussed earlier. The configurations presented here are representative of some of the more common configurations you might see but are not meant as complete descriptions of all that you could see. You could see variations on any of these configurations as well as a large number of other configurations not addressed here.

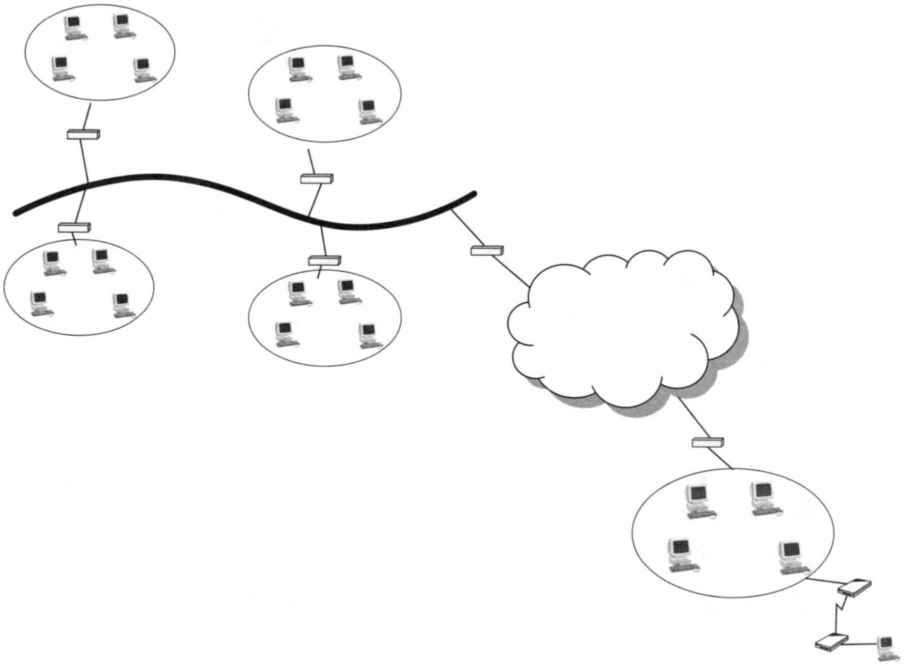

The simplest design is when you only have two LANs that need to be connected. All you need is a single link between the LANs. However, you may find it necessary to use multiple links to increase your bandwidth and to provide redundancy in case one of the links fails.

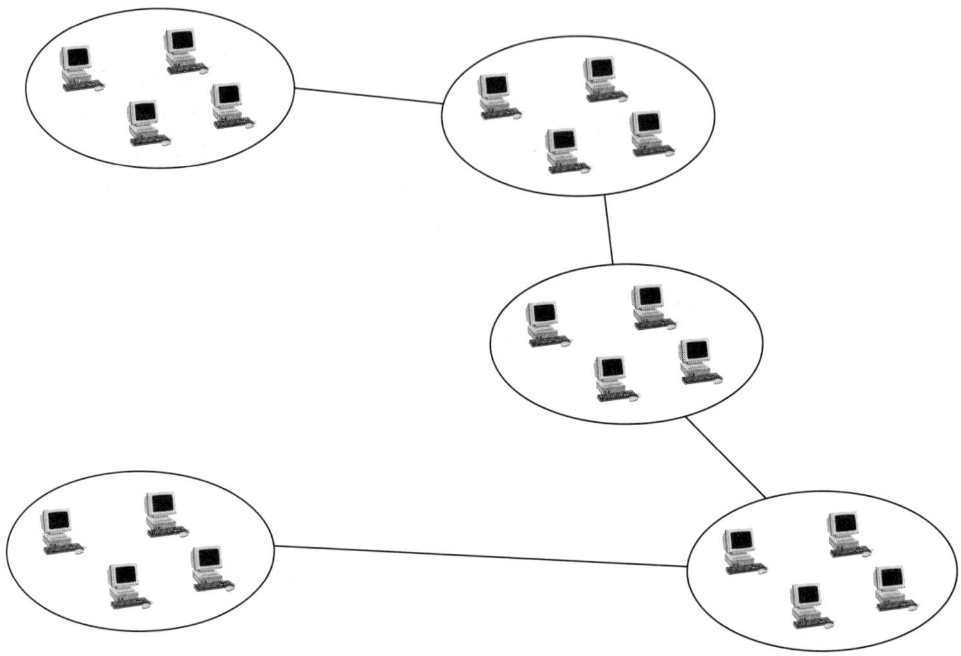

The configuration gets more complicated as the number of LANs that you need to connect increases. The configuration in the previous figure may look something like a LAN bus topology, but it isn't. It's a daisy-chain configuration, like you would see in traditional AppleTalk networks. Traffic feeds through each link and each LAN on its way from end to end.

While this configuration is relatively easy to set up and inexpensive, you need to carefully watch the potential concerns. As traffic moves from end to end, you are going to encounter increased latency. Also, a failure anywhere in the daisy chain is going to isolate the LANs on either side of the failure.

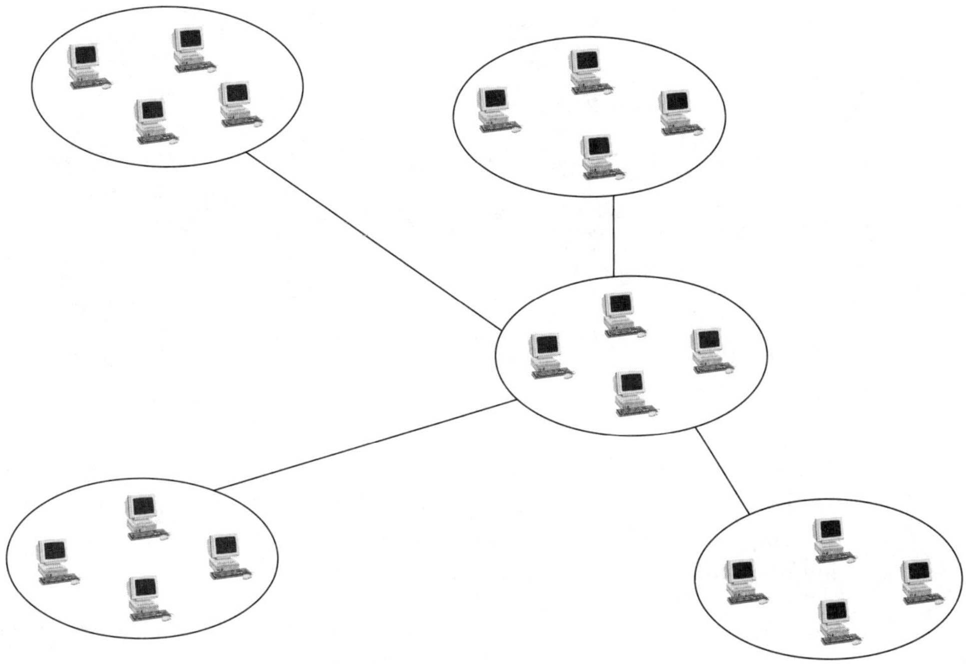

The previous configuration is effectively the same as a star LAN topology. All of the remote LANs connect into one central LAN. This is also relatively easy and inexpensive to set up. If any one link fails, it will only impact the LAN connected through that link. However, a failure at the central LAN could impact communication to all remote links.

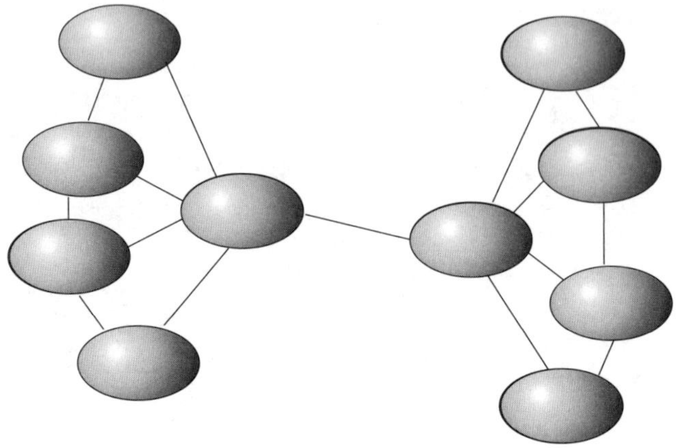

As a quick example of a variation you might see, above is another *star*, but with a few modifications. You now have two central points, with outlying remote LANs connected to each. You also have a secondary path between each set of remote LANs, providing another communication path in case of failure.

One concern with this model is the link between the two *hubs*. The traffic pattern for traffic between the two sets of remote LANs must be carefully analyzed to avoid saturating the link between the *hubs*.

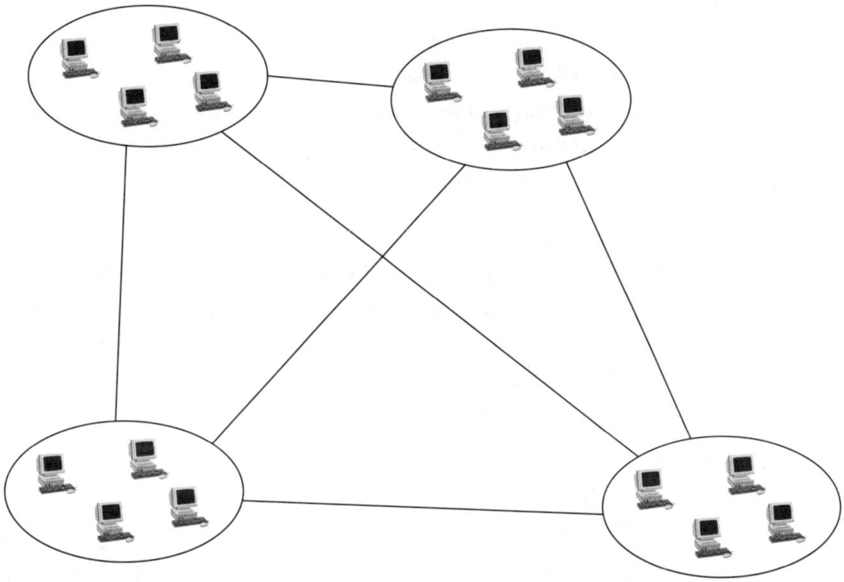

The previous figure represents a mesh configuration, with interconnections between all of the LANs. This gives you a high level of availability, thanks to the number of alternate routes available, and can increase the effective available bandwidth since traffic can be routed through less-congested paths.

The biggest drawback of this configuration is going to be cost. Not only will this be expensive to implement, but expansion costs also increase rapidly. For example, if you have a WAN with four LANS connected in a mesh, you need six remote links. Add a fifth LAN, and the number of links jumps to ten. Add another LAN, and you're up to needing fifteen links for a full mesh.

Picking the Right Configuration

This is not a situation where you want to drop all of your options into a hat, close your eyes, and pick your WAN configuration. It is going to take careful consideration of the network traffic data that you've collected and assumptions about projected changes to traffic patterns. You need to identify the high-traffic links, which are the LANs that have the most communication requirements.

Here's a situation to consider. Assume your home office is in Denver. You have remote offices in Boston, San Francisco, and Dallas. All of the remote offices need to be in regular communication with the home office. The Dallas office seldom needs to access resources from either Boston or San Francisco. Boston and San Francisco, however, need to share data on a regular basis. You want to keep the data going through Denver to a minimum. How could you resolve this situation?

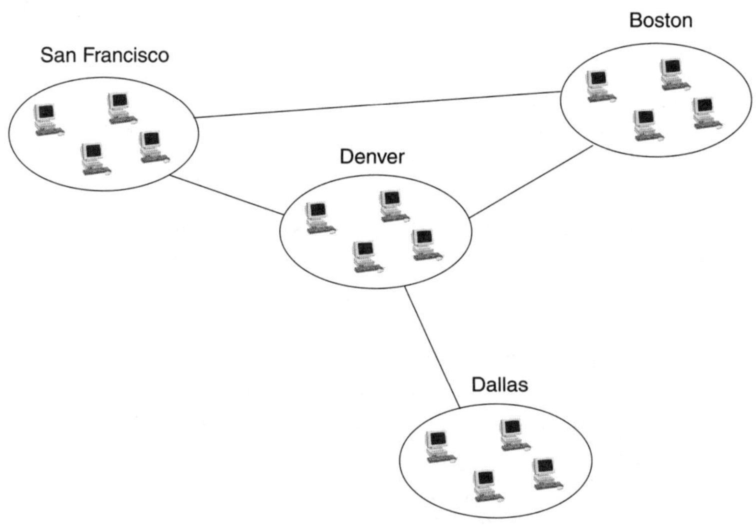

One way is to use a variation of a star configuration. Boston, San Francisco, and Dallas all have direct connections into Denver. There is also a direct link between Boston and San Francisco, which allows them to communicate without having to route all of the traffic through the Denver LAN.

Implementation Concerns

Many of the implementation concerns have already been mentioned. Careful analysis of traffic patterns will be a critical concern during the design phase. Traffic monitoring and analysis will be critical concerns during and after implementation.

You are more likely to feel the pressure to get it right the first time when implementing WAN links than when working with a LAN. It's going to be a concern during LAN implementation, but probably not like you'll encounter with a WAN. Remote links are more expensive to implement than links between subnetworks. It is even more costly in time and money if you have to go back and make changes.

Scenario 4-4: WAN Design

The purpose of this scenario is to give you practice in WAN design basics. Suggested solutions are provided in Appendix B at the end of this manual. It may be helpful to review the case studies in Appendix C at the end of this manual.

Barney's Bank's Network Goals

The organization wants to standardize its network operations, implementing two Active Directory domains configured as part of the same forest. The company will have separate domain namespaces for the United States and Europe.

In response to its competition, Barney's Bank wants to give its users access to account information via the Internet. It is also considering using a virtual private network to connect between the main offices in the United States and Europe via the Internet.

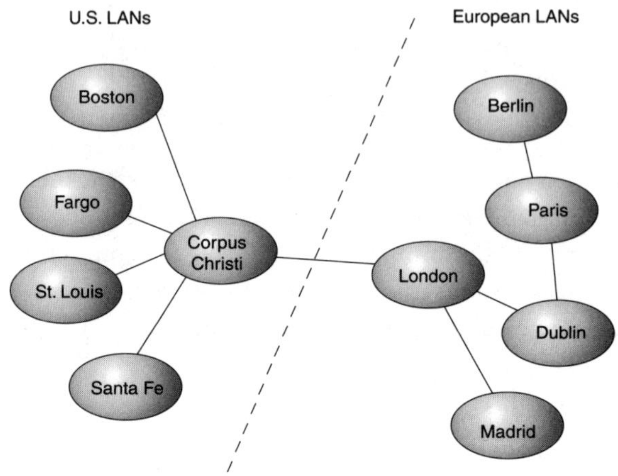

Current Network

1. Assuming no more than five users in each of the offices other than Corpus Christi and London, where would you be likely to place servers providing network services?

 ....

 ....

2. You need to minimize latency between the two main offices (Corpus Christi and London) and the remote offices they support. There is no need for direct communication between remote offices. Sketch the redesigned WAN below.

Fairco Manufacturing's Network Users

Users on the corporate LAN have few complaints about the network. Most of the data they need is located local to the corporate LAN.

Warehouse users are less happy with the way things are currently run. The warehouses currently have two or more stand-alone systems. Only one of the systems in each location, a Windows NT server running SQL Server 6.5, is provided with a modem for remote access. Users will use this system periodically during the day to check stock in the main warehouse. The systems also dial in automatically each night to send and receive database changes through SQL Server replication. Some nights, the replication is still running when users arrive in the morning.

1. How would you redesign the network to correct what the warehouse users see as communication problems?

2. Assuming that you cannot do anything to change the amount of data that must be transferred during SQL Server replication, what can you do to help ensure that replication is completed by morning?

3. Assuming there are three remote warehouses, sketch out your WAN design based on your answers to questions 1 and 2.

USING THE INTERNET

The Internet is reaching a point where it is almost a universal part of doing business. This section introduces some of the ways you might use the Internet in your network design. The following topics are covered in this section:

- Internet Access
- Internet Services
- Remote Connectivity

This discussion will be limited to an overview and is only meant to introduce you to some of the ways that you might use the Internet. The topics introduced here will be covered in more detail later in the course.

Internet Access

Not too many years ago, there was little justification for giving employees access to the Internet. That has changed recently. There are several reasons for this change, including the following:

- Information gathering

  The Internet provides access to a wealth of information on nearly any subject that you can imagine. It has even gotten to the point that the Internet may be the only way to easily find some of the information you need.

- Supplier contacts

  Internet-based business (e-business) has exploded in recent years. It seems as if everyone has a Web site, and everyone's got something to sell. This is often the easiest, and sometimes the least-expensive, way to get detailed product information and to place orders.

- Product/service support

  Many companies are now using the Internet as the core of their customer and technical support. Product support, references, tips, frequently asked questions, and other information are posted on Web sites. Often, the preferred method of contacting customer or technical support for additional information is through the Web site or by an e-mail message initiated through the Web site.

- E-mail services

  Many companies don't have a need to host their own e-mail service and wouldn't have the technical expertise available if they did. Instead, they use e-mail provided by their ISP or other provider, which means that users need to connect to the Internet to get their mail.

The question now typically isn't if employees need access to the Internet, but how that access is going to be provided.

Direct Connection

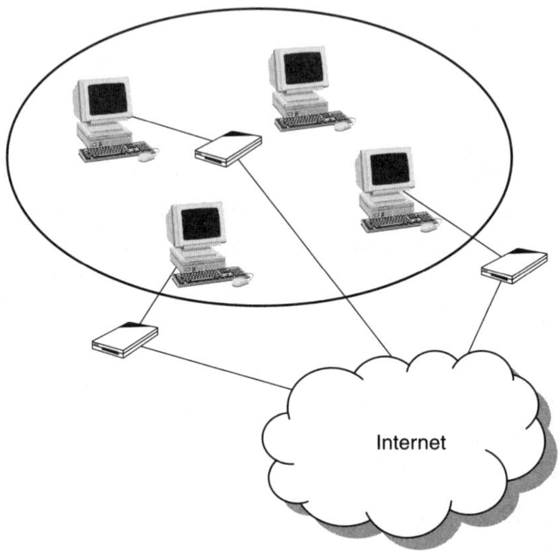

One way to provide Internet access is to provide telephone lines and modems for all of the users who have connection requirements. This was common when only a handful of people in an organization needed to access the Internet. It is still used in some companies that only have a few employees or haven't found a need for more universal access.

This solution has lost favor in most organizations. It is too expensive and too hard to manage. It can also represent a threat to network security since each user connection represents a potential open door into your network.

Shared Connection

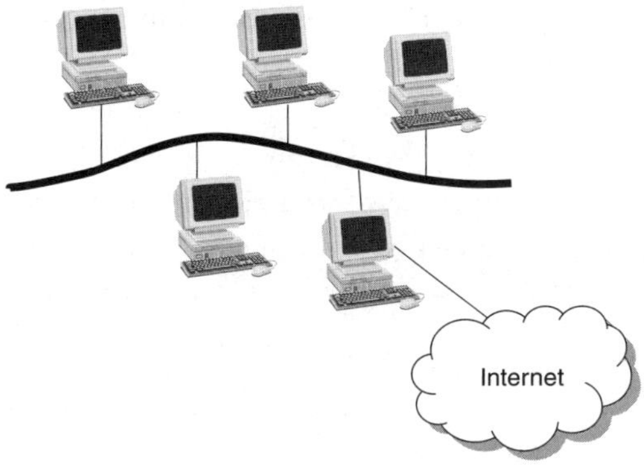

It is much more common to see a LAN using a shared connection to the Internet. One or more systems or connection devices connect directly to the Internet. Users connect through these devices, via the LAN, to the Internet.

Network Address Translation (NAT)

NAT provides a way of sharing an Internet connection between a small number of users, reducing the number of direct connections to the Internet. The Internet connection can be made with one or more public Internet addresses that are shared by the computers connecting through NAT.

NAT is a component of Windows 2000 Server Routing and Remote Access. You need a Windows 2000 system with a network adapter configured for connection to the local LAN and a connection device for connecting to the Internet. Since you are going to have multiple users sharing the connection, you need to consider a higher-bandwidth connection such as ISDN, DSL, a cable modem, or a Fractional T1 connection.

While on the subject, Internet Connection Sharing (ICS) deserves a quick mention. ICS is similar to NAT. It is easier to configure, but that ease has a price. ICS supports less features than NAT. It can only support one public IP address for the Internet connection and has a fixed range of addresses for internal hosts.

With either NAT or ICS, hosts (network computers) connect to the computer running NAT or ICS through the local LAN. Both are suitable for use with a limited number of user connections but cannot handle the volume required in larger LANs.

Proxy Server

You were introduced to proxy servers earlier in the course. A proxy server is a firewall component providing address translation and traffic filtering. A proxy server gives you a way of supporting a larger number of concurrent connections than NAT or ICS. Users connect through the LAN to the proxy server and through the proxy server to the Internet.

Internet Services

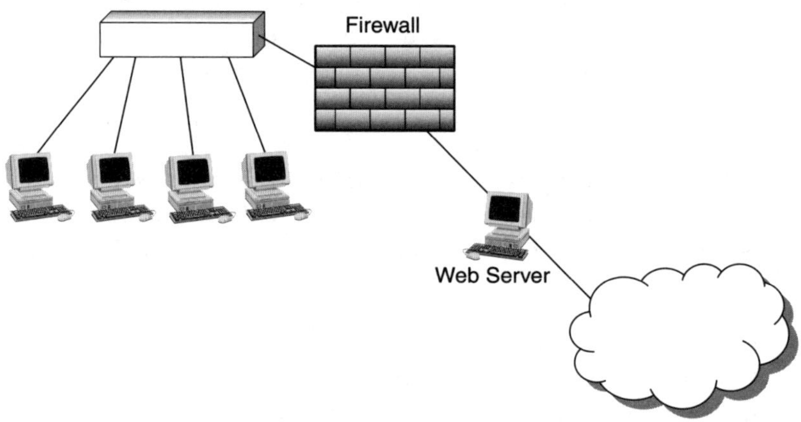

If you aren't already, you've probably considered hosting Internet services as part of your private network. The two most common Internet services that you will see integrated with a network are as follows:

- Web server

  Products such as Microsoft Internet Information Server (IIS) have made it relatively easy for companies to host their own Web sites. This gives them direct control over the Web server, its contents, and how it is maintained.

- Mail server

  As mail volume increases, many companies have found it cost effective to host their own mail servers. This gives them control over their e-mail and how it is managed. This can also add a level of security by providing features such as virus detection and mail filtering.

You will want to place a firewall between the Web server or mail server and the rest of your private LAN. This is done for security reasons to provide isolation between your LAN and the Internet.

It has also become common to include one or more Web servers as part of a private intranet. The term *intranet* is used to refer to a private TCP/IP-based network.

Remote Connectivity

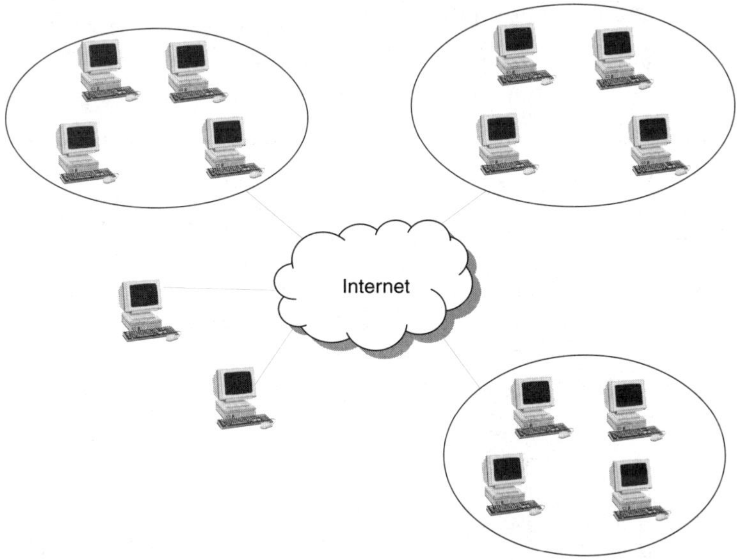

The possibility of using the Internet for making remote connections was mentioned earlier in the course. This subject will also be addressed in detail later in the course, but it deserves a mention while on the subject of Internet access.

Remote connections can be made using the Internet through the following:

- Remote client access

  One use of the Internet is to support remote client links. You set up an Internet connection at the LAN end, and each user connects through a local ISP at the remote end. Connection costs are often significantly reduced.

- WAN links

  Many companies are now using the Internet as their corporate backbone. This typically requires higher-speed connections into the Internet than are necessary for remote client support.

Connections through the Internet are made via a secure VPN. How VPN works and guidelines for setting up VPN connections are discussed in detail later in the course.

SUMMARY

During this chapter, you were introduced to the following:

- Bus topology
- Star topology
- Ring topology
- Topology selection
- Topology changes
- Common protocols
- Protocol selection
- Binding protocols
- Nonrouted LANs
- Routed LANs
- WAN design
- WAN configurations
- Remote links
- Internet access
- Internet services

The next chapter begins a detailed look at TCP/IP design and configuration. This will include both LAN- and WAN-related design issues.

POST-TEST QUESTIONS

The answers to these questions are in Appendix A at the end of this manual.

1. What are advantages of a WAN design that provides multiple links between LANs?

2. You are connecting six LANs in a mesh configuration. How many links are required?

3. Your network currently uses 4-Mbps Token Ring. What is the maximum number of computers that can be connected to the ring?

4. What is the maximum cable length between a hub and computer on a 10BaseT network?

5. DNS and WINS are services that support what protocol?

6. When defining an IP address, what is the purpose of the subnet mask?

....

....

7. Why should users and the resources they need be placed on the same subnetwork in a routed LAN?

....

....

8. Why is Network Address Translation (NAT) used?

....

....

CHAPTER 5

TCP/IP Implementation

MAJOR TOPICS

OBJECTIVES

At the completion of this chapter, you will be able to:

- List and describe the layers that make up the TCP/IP architectural model.
- List and describe protocols and services implemented at each layer of the TCP/IP architectural model.
- Describe initial design decisions to be made during TCP/IP design.
- List and describe TCP/IP features and benefits.
- Describe the purpose and use of IP addresses and subnet masks.
- Given an IP address and user support requirements, select an appropriate subnet mask.
- List the IP addresses reserved as private addresses.
- Determine whether a public or private IP address should be used in a network solution.
- Describe the purpose and use of routers in a TCP/IP network.
- Compare and contrast static and dynamic routers.
- Compare and contrast RIP for IP and OSPF.
- Describe ways of improving security, performance, and availability in a routed LAN design.
- Describe the procedures for installing routing support.
- List and describe concerns when integrating a routing design into an existing network.
- Describe the tools and utilities available when integrating Novell NetWare and Windows 2000 networks.
- Describe the purpose and use of Microsoft Host Integration Server (SNA Server).

PRE-TEST QUESTIONS

The answers to these questions are in Appendix A at the end of this manual.

1. What service can be used to provide automatic assignment and management of IP addresses?

2. A host needs to send a packet to a remote host on a different subnet. The sending host does not know the path to the remote host. Where would the packet initially be sent?

3. What support is provided by a WINS server?

4. Under what circumstances can you use private IP addresses?

5. What is meant by *router metrics*?

6. You have the following address and subnet mask. How many subnets will this combination support?

   IP address: 190.101.210.0

   Subnet mask: 255.255.255.224

   ....

   ....

7. What is supernetting?

   ....

   ....

8. You have a network with multiple redundant paths and regularly changing traffic patterns. What router protocol should you use for dynamic router updates?

   ....

   ....

9. Why is periodic monitoring of subnet traffic after implementation of a network design important?

   ....

   ....

10. You want to provide access to resources on a NetWare server. The server is using the IPX/SPX protocol. You do not want to install NWLink on all of your Windows clients. What Windows 2000 service can provide a solution to this?

    ....

    ....

11. What Windows 2000 service can be used to provide multiple clients access to an IBM host system?

    ....

    ....

INTRODUCTION

This chapter begins your closer look at TCP/IP. The chapter opens with an introduction to TCP/IP and commonly used TCP/IP utilities. You will also be given some initial guidelines for TCP/IP implementation.

From there, the discussion moves on to what is often a critical part of your network design: IP addressing and subnetting. You will first be introduced to IP addresses and their use, then be given the guidelines and information you need for designing the subnetworks for a routed LAN.

Once you've made your network addressing decisions, you have to decide how you are going to implement routing. This look at routing design will include issues relating to both LAN and WAN routing configurations.

The chapter then discusses some guidelines for integrating TCP/IP with your existing network. This includes some guidelines for peaceful coexistence between TCP/IP and other network protocols.

TCP/IP INTRODUCTION

It's best to begin at the beginning, and that's what you'll be doing in this section. You will be introduced to some TCP/IP fundamentals and general implementation guidelines. The following topics are covered in this section:

- TCP/IP Overview
- TCP/IP Features and Benefits
- Configuring TCP/IP

With TCP/IP generally accepted as the standard for both LAN and WAN networking, a good TCP/IP foundation is critical.

TCP/IP Overview

It is rare to find a network where TCP/IP isn't at least part of the networking solution. TCP/IP has become the network protocol of choice because of the wide range of features and benefits it offers. Since TCP/IP was designed with the requirements of a routed network environment in mind, it provides the support needed for today's enterprise networks. Since it is supported by most popular operating systems, it has become a key element in implementing heterogeneous networks.

Before getting into the nuts and bolts of configuring and using TCP/IP, you will find it helpful to understand the architecture and components that make up TCP/IP. This foundation will help you see how the pieces fit together and help you understand some of the configuration, support, and management options that you are going to see along the way throughout the rest of the course.

Before discussing TCP/IP architecture, however, Request For Comment (RFC) documents need to be introduced. You cannot get very far into TCP/IP without running into references to RFCs. TCP/IP is a dynamic entity and continues to be reviewed, revised, and improved by the Internet Engineering Task Force (IETF). This is done through RFCs, which are used to define the Internet, its services, and components, including TCP/IP. Actually, RFCs include a wide range of topics, from technical specifications to tutorial and reference documents.

Architectural Model

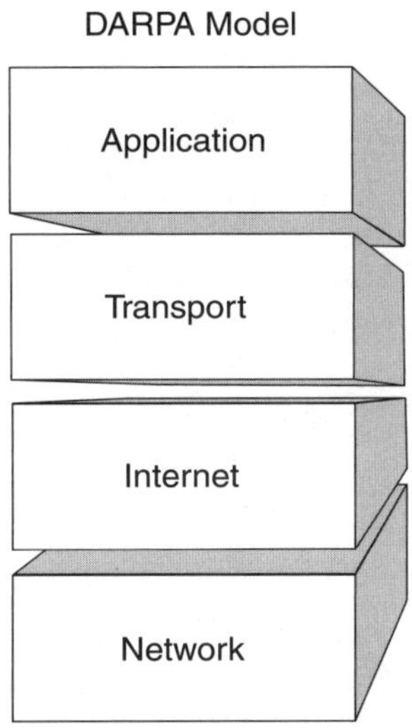

TCP/IP is based on a relatively simple networking model, known as the Defense Advanced Research Projects Agency (DARPA) model. This model makes it easier to talk about TCP/IP components, where they are located in the network hierarchy, and how they are related.

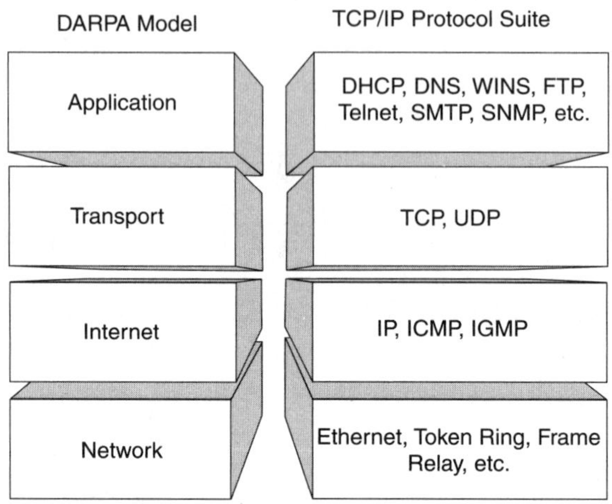

Different TCP/IP protocol suite components are implemented at different layers within the DARPA model. Let's take a little closer look at what is defined at each of these layers.

- Network layer

  The Network layer, sometimes called the Network Interface, defines the physical connection to the network and the relationship between TCP/IP and low-level protocols such as Ethernet and Token Ring.

- Internet layer

  The Internet layer is responsible for end-to-end communication between two computer systems. Routing control is managed at this level, but there is nothing implemented at this layer to guarantee successful communications.

- Transport layer

  Reliable communication between systems is implemented at the Transport layer.

- Application layer

  Applications, users, and high-level services are implemented at this layer.

There's no need to spend any time on the Network layer right now. You were given an introduction to these components in the earlier chapters. However, an overview of the protocols and services implemented in the remaining layers is in order.

Internet Layer Protocols

The Internet layer protocols include the following:

- Internet Protocol (IP)

  IP is the workhorse of the TCP/IP protocol suite. Other protocols use IP as the delivery mechanism. IP provides a connectionless delivery between computer systems. This means that IP doesn't do anything to check that the packet was received by the destination system. There is no guarantee of delivery or proper sequencing. This functionality is provided by higher-level protocols.

- Internet Control Message Protocol (ICMP)

  ICMP is used to help control and manage packet transmissions. ICMP doesn't do anything to help make IP more reliable, but it does help with error reporting. It allows hosts to share status and error information. This information can be passed to higher-level protocols to help them detect and resolve transmission problems.

- Internet Group Management Protocol (IGMP)

  IGMP is used with IP multicast, supporting one-to-many delivery service. It is similar to broadcast transmissions in that a single message is sent to multiple destinations. However, broadcast transmissions are not propagated by routers and will only be seen by hosts on the local subnetwork. IGMP allows for messages to be forwarded by routers to multiple recipients.

- Address Resolution Protocol/Reverse Address Resolution Protocol (ARP/RARP)

  ARP and RARP are TCP/IP maintenance protocols. ARP is used to request a host's MAC address when its IP address is known. RARP is used when the destination host's MAC address is known and the IP address is needed. A host's MAC address is its unique, low-level address. The MAC address is assigned by the network adapter manufacturer and is stored on a PC's network adapter.

Routing occurs based on the destination address information stored in packets at this layer.

Transport Layer Protocols

Transport layer protocols provide reliability to TCP/IP communications. These include the following:

- Transmission Control Protocol (TCP)

  TCP uses IP as its underlying protocol carrier. TCP provides acknowledged, connection-oriented communications. It includes fields for packet sequencing and acknowledgment as well as source and destination socket identifiers to allow communication with higher-level protocols. TCP provides guaranteed delivery, proper sequencing, and integrity. TCP can request data retransmissions if errors occur during transmission.

- User Datagram Protocol (UDP)

  UDP also uses IP as its underlying protocol carrier. UDP is designed for connectionless, unacknowledged communications, but it does support error detection. A UDP packet can include optional checksums for verifying header and data integrity. A UDP packet will also include source and destination socket identifiers.

For example, when you transfer files between two hosts, TCP is used to control communications during file transfer. It verifies that packets are delivered and is responsible for getting packets back into sequence should they get out of sequence during transmission.

Application Layer Protocols and Services

The protocols and services provided by this layer are being enhanced and improved on a regular basis. This list is representative of the Application layer protocols and services but is not a complete list of everything that is implemented at this layer.

Application layer protocols and services include the following:

- Telnet

  Telnet is a simple remote terminal emulation application, allowing one host to connect to and run a session on another host. Telnet uses TCP for acknowledged communication.

- Domain Name System (DNS)

  DNS servers provide host name-to-IP address mappings. In many cases, they also provide IP address-to-host name mappings. DNS service support is required for Active Directory domain implementation.

- Windows Internet Name Service (WINS)

  WINS servers provide NetBIOS name-to-IP address mappings. This is required when supporting systems or applications that use NetBIOS names to communicate.

- Dynamic Host Configuration Protocol (DHCP)

  The DHCP service is used to provide automatic address assignment and host address management. The DHCP server can also provide a DHCP client with TCP/IP configuration information, such as the client's default gateway and primary DNS server assignments.

- Simple Mail Transfer Protocol (SMTP)

  SMTP provides a mechanism for exchanging mail between systems. It is not concerned with mail format but, instead, is just concerned about the transfer process. This is the most widely used mail transfer service on the Internet.

- Simple Network Management Protocol (SNMP)

  SNMP uses UDP packets to send control and management information between hosts. It can be used to collect management statistics and trap error events from a wide variety of devices. Remote device control, configuration, and management are supported through the use of an SNMP management station.

- File Transfer Protocol (FTP)

  FTP supports file transfers between dissimilar systems. Telnet is used for initial authentication, and TCP is used for data transfers.

- HyperText Transfer Protocol (HTTP)

  HTTP is an application protocol used for communication between host computers, specifically between an HTTP server (Web server) and an HTTP client (Web browser). HTTP specifications define the structure and formatting of Web pages.

You can also consider the Microsoft Internet Information Server (IIS) as a service that is implemented at the Application layer. While it can be argued that this isn't completely accurate, the services and protocols supported by IIS are part of the Application layer. Servers supported by IIS include Web services and FTP services.

Printing and diagnostic utilities are also supported at the Application layer. A detailed discussion of TCP/IP printing utilities is beyond the scope of this course. Selected utilities will be discussed in more detail during this section and later in the course.

Initial Design Decisions

Let's take a little while to discuss some of the initial design decisions you will need to make when implementing TCP/IP. Some of these decisions are outside of the scope of the current discussion but will be covered in detail later in the course.

Some of your initial decisions will relate to the following:

- Addressing requirements

  If you are going to be connecting directly to the Internet, you are going to need a registered IP address. If you won't be connecting to the Internet, or will be connecting through address translation, you can use addresses set aside as private IP addresses to meet your internal addressing requirements.

- IP address management

  You need to decide how you are going to manage IP addresses. The basic decision is whether you are going to manage addresses manually or automatically through DHCP. Even if you plan to use DHCP to manage IP addresses, you will still need to manually assign IP addresses for some systems such as domain controllers.

- Routing requirements

  If you are implementing a routed LAN or a WAN, you need to decide how routing is going to be supported. You need to identify your routes and configure your routers to meet your needs.

- TCP/IP service support

  You have to determine what TCP/IP services you need to support, such as DNS, WINS, and so forth. You need to decide how many servers you are going to need, whether to combine services to reduce the number of servers required, and where the servers are going to be located on the network.

When you make your initial design decisions, keep in mind that networking requirements can evolve with time. Whenever possible, you are going to want to build some flexibility into your design. You'll find your task easier in the long run if you establish policies and guidelines for IP network design as part of your initial design process.

TCP/IP Features and Benefits

You usually see features and benefits described when someone is trying to sell you something. It's unlikely that there's any need to *sell* you on TCP/IP, since network technology requirements are probably going to force you to use TCP/IP whether you want to or not. The pressure is definitely on to move you in that direction. For example, TCP/IP is the only protocol installed during a fresh installation of Windows 2000.

Despite the fact that it probably isn't necessary to convince you that you need TCP/IP, it doesn't hurt to have some idea of what is going to be available to you in a TCP/IP network. You've already seen a list of supported protocols and some of the services you are most likely to encounter. Let's move the discussion along by looking at a few additional features.

Features and benefits tend to go hand in hand. Features of something describe what it provides for you, and benefits of something describe why it is important to you. Let's look at some of the features that are likely to be of special interest to you.

IP Addressing

You were introduced to a few basics about IP addressing earlier in the course. TCP/IP lets you design your host and subnetwork addressing to meet your particular networking requirements.

Once you have your subnetwork design, you can use DHCP to automatically manage IP address assignments for most of your hosts.

With Windows 2000, IP address assignment is especially easy on a nonrouted network. You don't necessarily have to use a DHCP for IP address assignment. Instead, you can use Automatic Private IP Addressing (APIPA) to assign IP addresses automatically for you.

> *NOTE: APIPA can only be used on nonrouted networks that do not connect directly to the Internet.*

Connectivity

With its acceptance as a networking standard and broad-based support, TCP/IP is an ideal method for connecting dissimilar systems. TCP/IP also provides Internet connectivity, both for access of Internet services and as a means of supporting remote connections through the use of VPNs.

Security

TCP/IP provides support for authentication, filtering, and data encryption. Authentication is used to manage access to TCP/IP services. You do need to be careful because some services, such as FTP, use clear-text authentication. This means that the username and password are not encrypted before transmission. Filtering lets you control traffic into or out of a network or subnetwork. Filtering can be implemented through software routers or through firewalls. Encrypted transmission methods are available for both local and remote data transmissions.

Transmission Control

TCP/IP supports a number of transmission control mechanisms, most of which are implemented behind the scenes. There have also been a number of improvements for Windows-family systems that are implemented as part of Windows 2000. These include the following:

- Selective Acknowledgment (SACK)

  Traditionally, when a missing packet was discovered during transmission, this meant having to resend that packet and all packets that followed the missing packet. SACK allows retransmission requests for the missing packet only, reducing the amount of traffic generated by retransmissions.

- Large TCP windows

  The maximum TCP window size support has been increased with Windows 2000. The window size impacts the amount of data that can be sent and received before acknowledgment is required. This enhancement improves transmission performance, especially in a WAN environment.

TCP/IP also supports Round Trip Time (RTT) estimation, which is a method of estimating the transmission time between a sending and receiving host. This is used in determining the optimum time to wait before retransmitting missing packets. As with large TCP windows, this will benefit WAN communication performance.

Quality of Service (QoS)

QoS is used to provide high-quality service to selected applications through control and management of network elements such as routers and switches. QoS gives a network administrator a means to provide support for applications, such as streaming video, that have high resource requirements without necessarily having to expand or upgrade the network infrastructure. Several manufacturers are working together to provide the infrastructure to support QoS implementation.

Communication Protocols

TCP/IP supports specialized protocols for remote transmission, including for connection to and through the Internet. These include the following:

- Point-to-Point Tunneling Protocol (PPTP)
- Layer 2 Tunneling Protocol (L2TP)

Specific protocol features and the use of PPTP and L2TP are discussed later in the course. In addition to these, encrypted transmission is supported through IP Security (IPSec). IPSec can provide secure communications through a VPN.

Utilities Overview

One of the strengths of TCP/IP is the wide array of utilities that it provides for monitoring, testing, and troubleshooting. For now, the discussion will be limited to an overview of some of the utilities that you would most likely be using during network design and monitoring.

Hostname

Hostname returns the common name of the computer it is run on. The syntax for this command is as follows:

```
hostname
```

The command does not support any option switches.

Ping

Ping is one of the most commonly used TCP/IP utilities. It allows you to check your connection with another computer. The syntax for this command is as follows:

```
ping [-t] [-a] [-n count] [-l length] [-f] [-i ttl] [-v tos]
  [-r count] [-s count] [[-j computer_list]|[-k computer_list]]
  [-w timeout] destination_list
```

The most common use of **Ping** is to run it without additional options and with a single computer name or IP address specified. For example, you could run the following:

```
ping brigadoon
```

To run by IP address, you could run the following:

```
ping 200.200.200.5
```

Ping supports the following option switches:

Option	Description
-t	The **-t** option causes the specified computer to be pinged until the command is interrupted.
-a	Use this option to resolve addresses to computer names, displaying the computer names in the command output.
-n	By default, **Ping** will send four echo packets. You can use the **-n** option to specify a different count.
-l	By default, the packet length used is 32 bytes. The **-l** option lets you specify a length of up to 65,527 bytes.
-f	This sets a "Do not Fragment" flag on the packet. This keeps gateways (routers) from fragmenting the packet or breaking into smaller packets for transmission.
-i	The **-i** option sets the packet's Time to Live (TTL), or the number of hops (routers) the packet may cross before it is discarded.
-v	The **-v** option sets the type of service for the packet. This is the packet precedence, ranging from routine to network control.
-r	Use the **-r** option to record the packet's route. You can record from one to nine hops.
-s	The **-s** option displays time stamp information for the number of hops specified.
-j	You can use the **-j** option to route the packet through a series (up to nine) of computers. The computers can be separated by gateways.

Option	Description
-k	This is similar to the **-j** option except that the computers in the list cannot be separated by gateways.
-w	This lets you set a timeout interval in milliseconds.

Ipconfig

The **Ipconfig** command lets you view current TCP/IP configuration information. It also works with DHCP assignments at the local computer. The syntax for the command is as follows:

```
ipconfig [/all|/renew [adapter]|/release [adapter]]
```

Run **Ipconfig** without any information to view a summary of TCP/IP configuration information that includes IP address, subnet mask, and default gateway. The **/all** option switch causes additional configuration properties to display.

When using DHCP, you can use the **/release** option switch to release all DHCP configuration information for a system. You can also specify to release DHCP configuration information for a single adapter. The **/renew** option renews the DHCP configuration for the system or specified adapter.

*NOTE: The **/release** and **/renew** options are only available on DHCP clients.*

Netstat

The **Netstat** command lets you display connection information for the system it is run on, along with TCP/IP protocol statistics. The syntax for this command is in the following table:

```
netstat [-a] [-e] [-n] [-p protocol] [-r] [interval]
```

The command option switches are defined in the following table.

Option	Description
-a	Server connections are normally not shown when you run **Netstat**. Include **-a** if you want all connections, including server connections, to display.
-e	Use the **-e** option to display Ethernet statistics. This can be used with the **-s** option.
-n	Rather than resolving addresses to names, addresses and ports are displayed numerically.
-s	Statistics are grouped by TCP/IP suite protocol. By default, TCP, IP, UDP, and ICMP are included.
-p	Connections are displayed for the specified protocol. Unless **-s** is also used, only TCP and UDP are available. Used with **-s**, you can choose from TCP, IP, UDP, or ICMP.
-r	Use this option to display the contents of the routing table. This is where information about known routes is stored.

You can specify an *interval* value if you want output to keep updating at the interval you specify. When you're through, press *CONTROL+B* to interrupt **Netstat.**

Tracert

The Tracert utility is used to discover the routers between a host and its intended destination. Tracert uses ICMP Echo Request packets to identify routers. Because of this, the packets can potentially be blocked by firewalls or filtering routers and may provide incomplete path information.

The general syntax for this command is as follows:

```
Tracert [-d] [-h max_hops] [-j host_list] [-w timeout]
```

The option switches are defined in the following table.

Option	Description
-d	Use this option if you do not want IP addresses of routers resolved to host names.
-h	This sets the maximum number of hops that may be used to reach the destination.
-j	You can use this option with a list of host names to specify source routing.
-w	This sets the timeout value for replies.

Pathping

You can think of **Pathping** as a combination of the **Ping** and **Tracert** commands. This wouldn't be completely accurate since **Pathping** supports additional features, but this analogy gives you a good idea of what **Pathping** is and how it is used. **Pathping** can be used to trace the route to a destination host but is also able to return additional transmission information.

The general syntax for **Pathping** is as follows:

```
Pathping [-n] [-h max_hops] [-g destination_list] [-p ping_timeout]
  [-q num_queries] [-R] [-T] [-w timeout]
```

The option switches are defined in the following table.

Option	Description
-n	Use this option if you do not want IP addresses resolved to host names.
-h	Use this option to set the maximum number of hops to the destination.
-g	This lets you enter IP addresses or host names for source routing.
-p	Enter the number of milliseconds to delay between pings.
-q	This sets the number of queries per hop.
-R	This will cause a check to be made to see if each router supports Resource Reservation Protocol (RSVP). RSVP allows a computer to reserve bandwidth for a data stream. The **-R** option is used to test for QoS connectivity.
-T	This will attach a Layer 2 priority tag to each packet sent out. This is used to test for Layer 2 priority configuration at each router, which is another test for QoS connectivity.
-w	This sets the timeout, in milliseconds, to wait for a reply.

Route

The **Route** command is used to view and modify the IP routing table contained in each router. The general syntax for the **Route** command is as follows:

```
Route [-f] [-p] [print|add|delete|change [mask netmask] [gateway]
  [metric metric_value] [if interface]]
```

The options are defined in the following table.

Option	Description
-f	Use this option to clear all gateway options from the routing table.
-p	Use this option with the **add** command to make the route persistent. The route will be added to the routing table and stored in the Registry.
print	Specify **print** to print the contents of the routing table.
add	Specify **add**, followed by the destination and a gateway, to add a route to the routing table.
delete	Specify **delete** with an IP address to remove the destination from the routing table.
change	Specify **change** to change information about a route currently in the routing table.
mask	You can use **mask** to specify a subnet mask for a destination. **Mask** is only used with the **add** and **change** commands. The default mask value is 255.255.255.255.
metric	You can use **metric** to specify the cost, in hops, to reach the destination. **Metric** is only used with the **add** and **change** commands.
if	This is used with **add** or **change** to identify the interface the destination is available through.

Route design and router implementation are introduced later in this chapter.

Configuring TCP/IP

You were shown how to install TCP/IP in the previous chapter. Now you get to see how to view and modify TCP/IP properties. You will be coming back to some of these property settings periodically during the rest of the course.

Launch **Network and Dial-up Connections** from the **Settings** menu. From there, right-click on Local Area Connection (or the LAN connection you want to manage) and run **Properties.** When the Local Area Connection Properties window displays, select Internet Protocol (TCP/IP) and click on **Properties.**

NOTE: *You were shown how to open the Local Area Connection Properties window earlier in the course.*

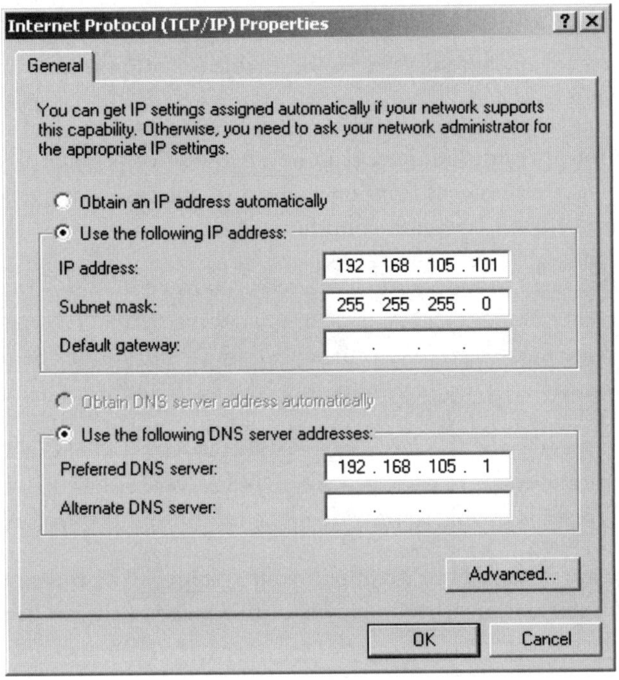

The General page lets you set IP address and DNS server information. IP addresses can either be set automatically or obtained automatically through the DHCP service. If you select to obtain IP addresses automatically, you are not prompted for any address information.

The previous figure shows TCP/IP configured for a static IP address. While it is typically easier to manage systems through dynamic address assignments, there are some situations where you need static IP addresses. Servers filling roles such as DHCP servers, DNS servers, WINS servers, and IP gateways (IP routers) need static addresses so that other systems always know how to locate them by address.

You should use caution when using static IP addresses. By default, there is nothing to keep you from overwriting your own IP address. This can lead to conflicts with existing systems or can cause a system to be unable to communicate because an invalid address has been entered.

Additionally, static addresses can be a real headache when supporting mobile systems. When a system moves from one subnet to another, you have to manually change its IP address before it is able to communicate.

You also need to supply the DNS server(s) to be used for name resolution. In simple terms, the DNS server is a database matching textual host names to IP addresses. Host names are more convenient for people to use but cannot be used by computers to communicate. They have to be resolved as IP addresses before any data can be sent.

The General page also lets you specify a primary and alternate DNS server. When the system cannot contact the primary DNS server for name resolution, or if the primary DNS server is unable to provide name resolution, the system will try the alternate DNS.

If you are using DHCP to obtain your system's IP address, DHCP can provide DNS server information as well. However, this means that you need to specify the DNS server addresses at the DHCP server.

Click on the **Advanced** button to set additional TCP/IP properties.

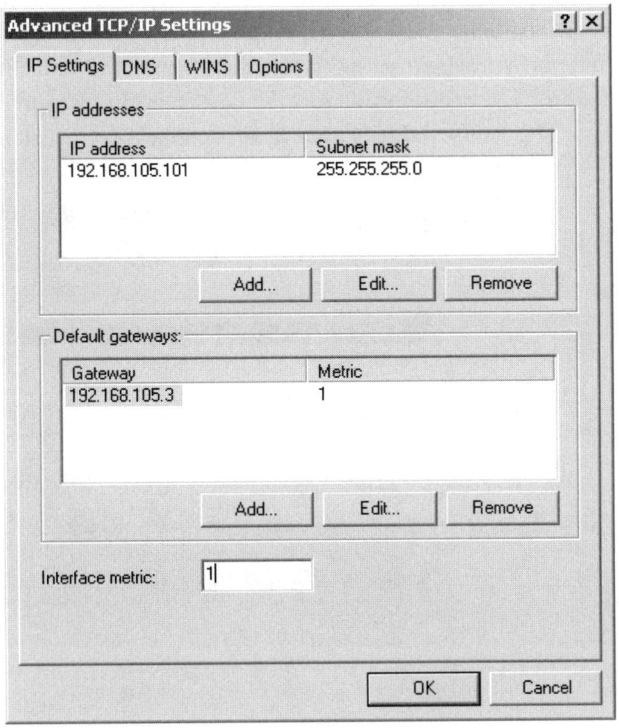

The IP Settings page lets you define additional IP addresses for an adapter and specify default gateway information.

You can specify multiple IP addresses for a network adapter. You would do this if you needed multiple IP addresses to communicate. For example, you could have two different subnetworks (computers having different network addresses) communicating on the same cable segment. The two subnets would be effectively invisible to each other, ignoring each other's packets. If you wanted a machine to be able to communicate with hosts on either subnet, you could provide it with addresses for both networks. You can define any number of additional network addresses.

In a routed network environment, you can define the default gateway that a system should use. When the system generates a packet destined for a different subnetwork, it will direct it to a default gateway, which will then forward the packet on toward its final destination. The metric value sets the cost in hops, or routers crossed, for using this gateway. The metric value is used in making best-route calculations.

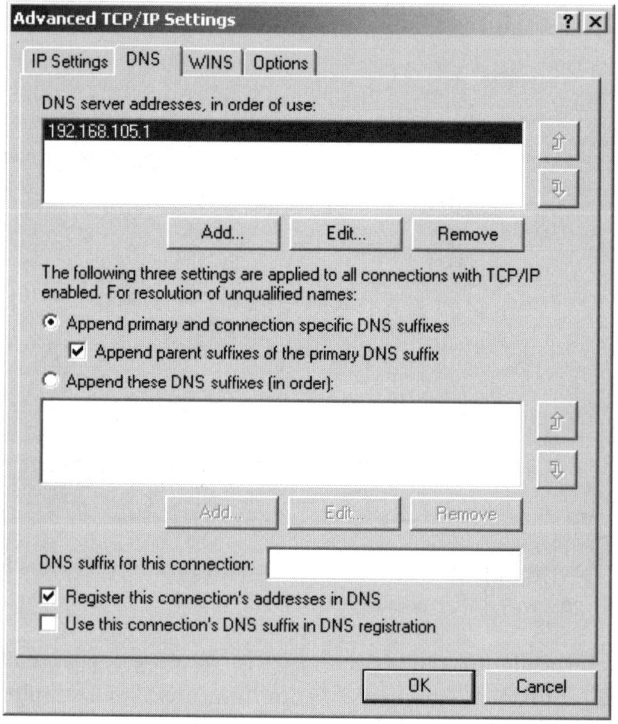

You can configure additional DNS properties through the DNS page. You can list additional DNS servers. The DNS servers will be queried, in order, until a server is found that can resolve a requested DNS name.

Name resolution is based on Fully Qualified Domain Names (FQDNs). In most cases, applications and utilities do not require FQDNs. The next set of options lets you determine how a suffix is appended to an unqualified name.

By default, **Append primary and connection specific DNS suffixes** is selected. The DNS domain suffix of the primary DNS will be appended when resolving an unqualified name. For example, if your domain suffix is ops.mycomp.com and you are looking for comp33, an attempt will be made to resolve the name as follows:

```
comp33.ops.mycomp.com
```

The connection-specific area of that selection refers to the DNS suffix for this connection field. If you enter a suffix value here, there will also be an attempt made to resolve the name using that suffix. For example, if you entered dev.mycomp.com and the initial attempt failed, an attempt would be made using the following:

```
comp33.dev.mycomp.com
```

If you check the **Append parent suffixes of the primary DNS suffix**, then resolution is also attempted using the parent suffix. In the previous example, there would also be an attempt to resolve the name as follows:

```
comp33.mycomp.com
```

Alternately, you can specify the suffixes to be appended and the order they will be used in.

Select **Append these DNS suffixes (in order)** if you want to specify the suffixes to be used. You can use the **Add**, **Edit**, and **Remove** buttons to manage the suffixes. Use the up and down arrows to the right of the window to change the order the suffixes are applied in.

The last two selections on the DNS page deal with dynamic DNS registration, that is, if and how the computer is registered in the DNS database. By default, the connection's address(es) will be registered in DNS. You can choose whether to include the connection's suffix when registering.

If you choose to register a connection in DNS, by default, it will be registered by the computer's full name. This is true whether or not you choose to register the connection's suffix. When selected, that is done in addition to registering the address for the computer's FQDN.

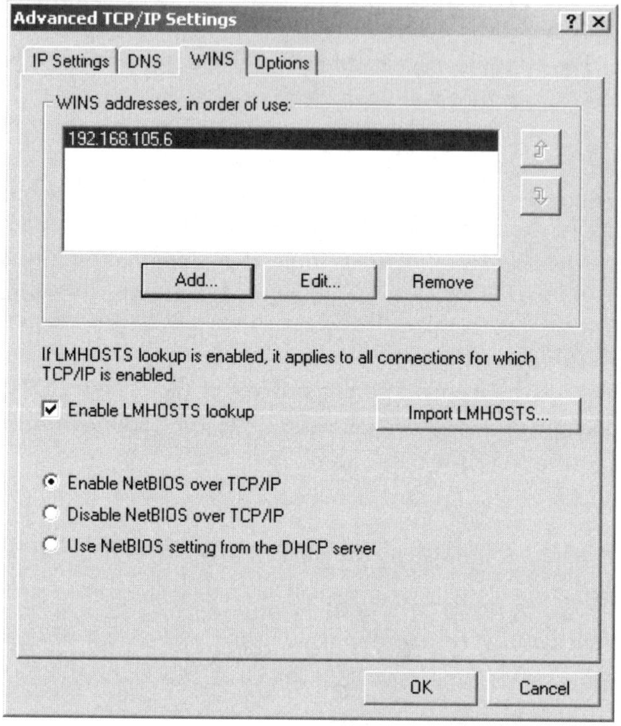

Windows Internet Name Service (WINS) is used for resolving NetBIOS names to IP addresses. The WINS page lets you manage NetBIOS name resolution as well as NetBIOS support for the connection.

NetBIOS name resolution was traditionally managed through NetBIOS broadcasts. This became a problem as networks grew because routers don't propagate broadcasts. The only names that could be resolved through broadcast were those of computers on the local subnet.

The LMHOSTS file and WINS let you resolve names outside of the current subnet. The LMHOSTS file is a text file that maps NetBIOS names to IP addresses. You can also place entries in the LMHOSTS file to have it reference other LMHOSTS files.

NetBIOS name management is automated through WINS. Computers register themselves with the WINS server, which can then be queried directly for name resolution.

You also have selections on the WINS page allowing you to decide whether to enable or disable NetBIOS over TCP/IP support. NetBIOS is going to be required if you are supporting any NetBIOS-based applications. You can set the option yourself or allow the option to be set by DHCP.

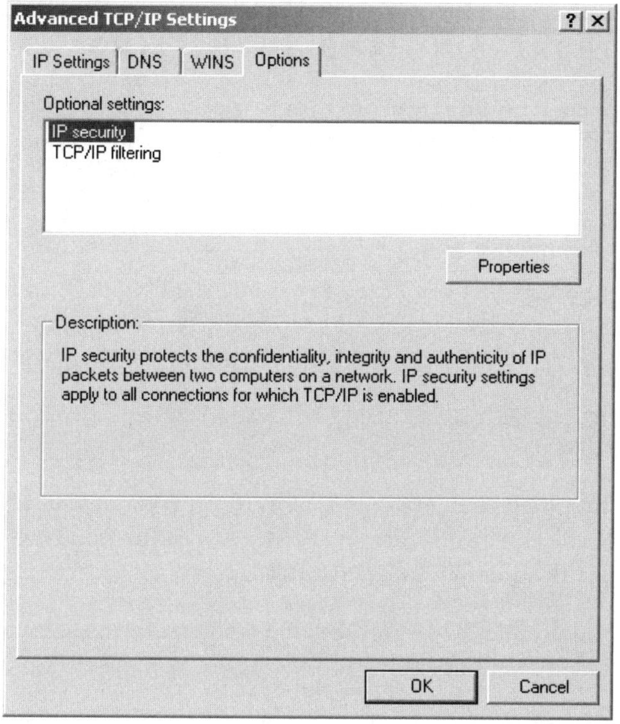

The Options page lets you set configuration properties for TCP/IP options. Specifically, you can set options for IP security and TCP/IP filtering.

You can use the IP Security (IPSec) options to decide whether unsecured traffic will be allowed on the network. The TCP/IP filtering properties determine what traffic your system will accept, defaulting to all. You can limit IP traffic by only accepting communications from specified TCP ports or UDP ports. You also manage filters based on IP protocol.

TCP/IP ADDRESSING AND SUBNETTING

Now the discussion is ready to turn to specifics, starting with IP addressing and subnetting. The following topics are covered in this section:

- IP Addressing
- Subnetting

It is important that you have a firm understanding of IP address use and the process for designing subnetworks. After that, the discussion can move on to connecting the subnetworks to create a routed LAN or, for that matter, a WAN.

IP Addressing

Each host (network device) in a TCP/IP network must be given a unique IP address for each installed network adapter. As you saw earlier, you have the option of defining multiple IP addresses for a network adapter.

An IP address is a 32-bit address that is written as four octets (bytes) in a dotted-decimal notation. For example:

```
192.168.105.1
```

Each address will also have a subnet mask that determines which part of the address is used as the network address and which is used as the host address. You've already seen the following subnet mask used during this course:

```
255.255.255.0
```

That much you've already seen. What you also need to know is where the address numbers are coming from and how the subnet mask values are determined.

Public and Private Addresses

One of the first design decisions you will have to make is whether you are going to use public or private IP addresses. Public addresses are managed by the Internet registry and maintained by the IETF. Public addresses are required for connecting to the Internet.

If you need to connect to the Internet, you are going to need at least one public address. If you have sufficient public addresses available, you can configure your entire network using public addresses. You will need to use public addresses if a large number of hosts on your network require direct access to the Internet.

There are going to be concerns, however, when using public addresses. These include the following:

- Scalability

  You have to make sure that you have enough public addresses available to meet both current and projected host requirements. If you run out, you cannot expand until you either acquire additional public addresses or go to a mix of public and private addresses.

- Security

  When you use public addresses, all hosts have access to the Internet. This also means that, unless you include security measures into your design, all hosts are accessible from the Internet. You are going to want to isolate your private network from the Internet through a firewall or other security device.

- Expense

  Leasing a large number of public addresses can get expensive over time. If you need more addresses, the cost increases.

Private addresses have been set aside for use on private networks. Private addresses are not recognized by the Internet. Private addresses can be used for hosts, and even complete subnetworks, that don't need direct access to the Internet. There's no real expense involved for the addresses; there are enough available to provide effectively unlimited scalability, and you have a level of security built in since the hosts are invisible to the Internet.

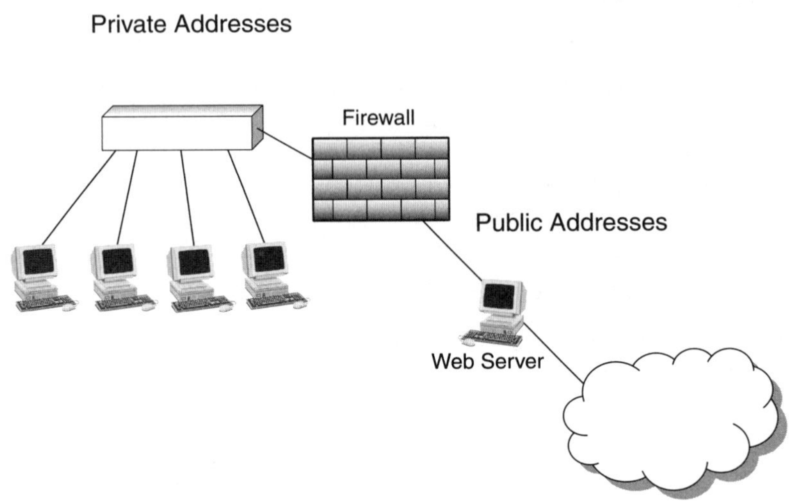

Of course, nothing is perfect. If you do need some kind of Internet access, you'll need a public address. Any hosts communicating directly with the Internet, such as Web servers, will need public addresses. Also, any hosts providing network address translation for shared user access to the Internet will need public addresses.

What it often comes down to in the real world is that the most cost-effective way of meeting your address requirements is going to be using both public and private addresses. The key is to use them effectively.

Public Address Classes

If your network is going to be connecting to the Internet, you're going to need a registered IP address. IP addresses are organized into classes identified as Class A through Class E.

Class	Range	Default Subnet Mask	Description
A	1.xxx.xxx.xxx through 126.xxx.xxx.xxx	255.0.0.0	A Class A address can support up to 16,777,214 hosts.
B	128.0.xxx.xxx through 191.255.xxx.xxx	255.255.0.0	A Class B address can support up to 65,534 hosts.
C	192.0.0.xxx through 223.255.255.xxx	255.255.255	A Class C address can support up to 254 hosts.
D	224.xxx.xxx.xxx through 239.xxx.xxx.xxx	Not applicable	Class D addresses are used for defining multicast groups.
E	240.xxx.xxx.xxx through 255.xxx.xxx.xxx	Not applicable	This class is reserved for experimental purposes.

Host addresses cannot be all ones or all zeros. For example, if you had a Class C address of 192.0.0.xxx, your valid IP address range, assuming the default subnet mask, is as follows:

192.0.0.1 through 192.0.0.254

In theory, you can apply for public addresses from the Internet registry. Realistically, you are going to end up leasing your addresses from your communications provider. You can lease one or more Class C addresses, which you can then configure to meet your addressing requirements.

Private Addresses

If you're not connecting to the Internet or connecting through an application gateway that remaps host addresses, you can use private IP addresses on your subnetworks. The Internet Assigned Numbers Authority (IANA) has set aside three sets of addresses for use as private network addresses. These are as follows:

10.0.0.0 through 10.255.255.255

172.16.0.0 through 172.31.255.255

192.168.0.0 through 192.168.255.255

Looking at these ranges, you've probably noticed that exercises in this course are using private IP addresses. Any routers connecting directly to the Internet should be configured to filter out these addresses.

Special Addresses

There are a couple of special addresses that also need to be mentioned while on the subject. Addresses with an initial octet of 127 are reserved for loopback testing, which is used in a self-test function when a host wants to communicate with itself. For example, if you wanted to test to see if the TCP/IP stack loaded correctly on your computer, you could run the following at a command prompt:

```
ping 127.0.0.1
```

Another special address that you might see turning up occasionally is the following:

255.255.255.255

This address is used for a local broadcast, that is, a broadcast to all hosts on the local subnetwork. Except for some special cases to be discussed later, transmissions with 255.255.255.255 as a destination address will not be passed on by routers to other subnetworks.

Subnetting

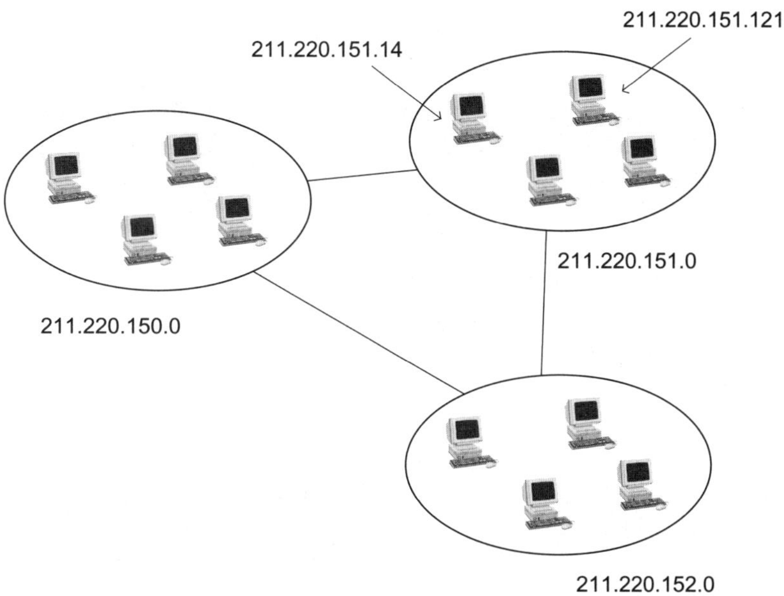

As mentioned previously, the subnet mask breaks an IP address down into its network address and host address. The network address is shared by all hosts that are part of the same subnetwork. The host address will be unique for each host in the subnetwork.

When discussing subnets, you need to realize that you can have physical subnetworks and logical subnetworks. Physical subnetworks are physically located on separate segments of the cable plant and only connect through a router. Logical subnets coexist on the same cable segment but are still effectively invisible to each other unless a router is also provided on the segment.

NOTE: *You will get a chance to work directly with logical subnetworks in an exercise later in the course.*

From a design perspective, you are going to need to create subnet masks that:

- Make optimal use of available IP addresses.
- Allow for host scalability.
- Allow for subnetwork scalability.

This means going back to the information you gathered about users, server distribution, and expected growth. You will want to know how quickly the user population will be growing and where the users will be located. You also need to know about expected office expansions or acquisitions so that they can be included in your design plans.

Subnetting Fundamentals

There are a number of reasons why you are going to want to use subnetting. These include the following:

- Traffic control

  You can use subnets to help manage bandwidth usage in your network. By strategically placing users and the resources they need, you can keep the majority of the traffic local to the subnet. If you reach a point where you're overloading a segment, you can further divide the users to place them and their resources on separate subnets.

- Optimal address use

  A Class C address supports up to 254 hosts. If you have a need for smaller groups of hosts, you can subnet a single Class C address to give you multiple subnets.

- WAN design

  In order to support routing, each remote LAN must be configured as a separate subnet. Therefore, you'll need at least one subnet for each WAN connection.

When you want to communicate with a host in a different subnet, you need to know its IP address, subnet mask, and a default gateway. In a TCP/IP network, the term *gateway* refers to a router.

Role of Routers

Routers are used to connect subnets and to control traffic between subnets. A router will evaluate each packet to determine how it should be managed. If the packet destination is on the local subnet or is a broadcast packet, it won't be passed by the router. If the packet destination is on a remote subnet and the router knows the route to take, it will pass the packet along to the next hop. If the packet destination is on a remote subnet and the router doesn't know the route to take, it will pass the packet to its default gateway.

Setting Realistic Limits

Like it or not, the real world is going to intrude on your well-laid subnet design. The easy way to design local subnets would be to look at where the users are physically located, divide them more or less equally, and there you have it. Unfortunately, all users are not the same, nor are all network servers. You need to take their individual requirements into consideration.

You will need to design your subnets to match your network design specifications. This means keeping within limits on the following:

- Traffic within a subnet

  You have to design your user, resource, and server placement so that you don't generate more traffic on the subnet than its bandwidth can support. This means periodically monitoring traffic inside the subnet.

- Traffic between subnets

  You also have to watch the traffic between subnets. This is especially true if you have a router that is connected to more than two subnets. You need to monitor the router periodically to make sure that it isn't being saturated and becoming a bottleneck to network communications.

- Router metrics

  You also are going to be concerned about the maximum number of hops between subnets. The more hops that a packet has to cross, the greater latency introduced due to additional processing overhead at the router.

You will need accurate information on user requirements, information flow, and router performance in order to create an effectively routed network design.

Defining Subnets

Subnets are defined by modifying the subnet mask value. Let's start with a few general guidelines for defining standard subnet masks:

- The subnet mask must be greater than or equal to the default subnet mask.
- Subnet masks are defined by adding contiguous bits to the default subnet mask.
- The additional network address bits beyond the default subnet mask cannot be all ones or all zeros.

A little later, you'll see some additional examples that go beyond these basics. For now, the focus is on simple subnetting. The following table lists the subnet masks that can be used with a Class C address.

Subnet Mask	Max. Subnets	Max. Hosts/Subnet
255.255.255.0	1	254
255.255.255.192	2	62
255.255.255.224	6	30
255.255.255.240	14	14
255.255.255.248	30	6
255.255.255.252	62	2

To see what is going on, we need to look at the binary value of the subnet mask. Since the fourth octet is used to subnet a Class C address, that's where we'll focus. Let's take a look at 255.255.255.224 as an example. The binary value of 224 is the following:

11100000

The three most significant bits of the fourth octet are being used as part of the network address. Values of all zeros and all ones are not allowed. Assuming a Class C address of 192.100.100.0, that gives you the following network addresses:

Binary Value	Network Address
00100000	192.100.100.32
01000000	192.100.100.64
01100000	192.100.100.96
10000000	192.100.100.128
10100000	192.100.100.160
11000000	192.100.100.192

The remaining five binary digits define the host address. Once again, values of all zeros and all ones are not allowed. Here are the host address ranges:

Network Address	Min. Host (Binary)	Min. Host Address	Max. Host (Binary)	Max. Host Address
192.100.100.32	00100001	192.100.100.33	00111110	192.100.100.62
192.100.100.64	01000001	192.100.100.65	01011110	192.100.100.94
192.100.100.96	01100001	192.100.100.97	01111110	192.100.100.126
192.100.100.128	10000001	192.100.100.129	10011110	192.100.100.159
192.100.100.160	10100001	192.100.100.161	10111110	192.100.100.190
192.100.100.192	11000001	192.100.100.193	11011110	192.100.100.222

Other subnet masks can be broken down into network addresses and host addresses in the same fashion.

Additional Address Structures

Before leaving the subject of IP addresses, there are two more subnetting schemes that need to be mentioned. These won't be covered in the same level of detail, but you do need to be aware of them should you need them at some time in your future network design efforts.

While the subnetting method described earlier in this section will meet many networks' requirements, that won't always be the case. The following are two additional methods that allow you to optimize your use of IP addresses:

- Variable-Length Subnetting
- Supernetting

These methods cannot be used on all networks. In order to use either of these methods, your network routers must support RIP version 2 (RIP-2), Open Shortest Path First (OSPF), or Border Gateway Protocol (BGP).

> *NOTE: Routing protocols are discussed later in this chapter.*

Let's take a brief look at each of these.

Variable-Length Subnetting

Variable-length subnetting can be used with any IP address class. Effectively, variable length subnetting allows you to subdivide one of your subnetworks. To see how this can work, let's take a look at a quick example.

Assume that you have a Class C address of 220.0.0.0 and are using 255.255.255.192 as your subnet mask. This gives you the following subnet addresses:

220.0.0.64

220.0.0.128

You now have two subnets that can support 62 hosts each. Now suppose that you need that many host addresses on one subnetwork, but you have three additional subnets that only need to support ten to fifteen hosts each. You can add another Class C address, but most of the available addresses would be wasted in the process. Instead, you can use different subnet masks and vary the subnetting. The following table shows how this would work.

Network Address	Subnet Mask	Max. # of Hosts	Min. Host Address	Max. Host Address
220.0.0.64	255.255.255.192	62	220.0.0.64	220.0.0.126
220.0.0.128	255.255.255.224	30	220.0.0.129	220.0.0.158
220.0.0.160	255.255.255.224	30	220.0.0.161	220.0.0.190
220.0.0.192	255.255.255.224	30	220.0.0.193	220.0.0.222

This way, you're able to meet your subnetting requirements with a minimum of waste.

Supernetting

Supernetting uses a technique called Classless Interdomain Routing (CIDR) to combine a range of Class C addresses into a single subnet. This is used when your subnet requires more hosts than are supported by a single Class C address. The following are the two requirements for the Class C addresses used:

- The Class C addresses must be sequential.
- The number of Class C addresses used must be equal to a power of 2 (2, 4, 8, etc.)

Supernetting is accomplished by setting bit values for the least-significant bits in the third octet of the subnet mask to zero.

Let's look at an example. You have a range of Class C addresses from 220.1.144.0 through 220.1.147.0 that you want to combine through supernetting, creating a CIDR block. You need to look at the binary values of the third octet of these addresses, as shown in the following table.

Decimal	Binary
144	10010000
147	10010011

Notice that only the two least-significant bits of the binary value change in this range. Those are the bits that need to be set to zero in the subnet mask, giving you a binary value of the following:

11111100

This is a decimal value of 252, making your subnet mask the following:

255.255.252.0

Since you are combining four Class C addresses, this would support a subnet with up to 1,016 hosts.

Scenario 5-1: Subnet Requirements

The purpose of this scenario is to give you practice in working with IP addresses and subnet masks. Suggested solutions are provided in Appendix B at the end of this manual. It may be helpful to review the case studies in Appendix C at the end of this manual.

Barney's Bank

1. From the information provided, what is the minimum number of subnets that will be required to support all offices?

2. Each of the European offices currently has 30 to 35 systems, with projected growth of ten to fifteen systems per office. What is the minimum number of Class C addresses that can be used to support the European offices?

3. You are considering use of variable-length subnetting to get the best use of available addresses. What router concerns must be considered when implementing this as a solution?

Fairco Manufacturing

You are considering the following network solution. Answer the following questions based on this solution.

You have decided to configure the main office as two subnets in order to segment the warehouse traffic. Four warehouse offices will be connecting to the main office through 24/7 links. You want to use a single Class C address to support all of the offices. Your routers will not support variable-length subnets.

1. What subnet mask would you use to get a maximum number of hosts per subnet?

   ....

   ....

2. What is the maximum number of hosts that can be supported on each subnet?

   ....

   ....

Exercise 5-1: Subnetting (Optional)

The purpose of this exercise is to give you practice working with subnetting. Answers to the questions asked in this exercise are provided in Appendix B at the end of the manual.

Special Preparation

There is no special preparation required for this exercise.

Address Assignments

During this portion of the exercise, you will be changing the assigned IP address on Beta. All steps will be completed on Beta.

1. Open a command prompt and run the following:

   ```
   ping 192.168.105.1
   ```

   What happens?

   ....

   ....

2. Open Network and Dial-up Connections.
3. Right-click on Local Area Connection and run **Properties**.
4. Click on Internet Protocol (TCP/IP), then click on **Properties**.
5. Type the following in the IP address field:
   ```
   192.168.100.3
   ```
6. Click on **OK**, then on **OK** again.
7. Exit Network and Dial-up Connections.
8. Execute the following in your open command prompt:
   ```
   ping 192.168.105.1
   ```
   What happens?

   ....

   ....

9. Why did you get a different result than before?

   ....

   ....

ROUTING

Now that you know something about subnetting, it's time to move on to routing design. The following topics are covered in this section:

- Routing Fundamentals
- Routing Protocols
- Routing Design
- Implementing Software Routing
- Testing and Monitoring

This section will focus on routing in a LAN environment. Routing requirements for a WAN can involve a number of additional special issues. These issues will be discussed later in the course.

Routing Fundamentals

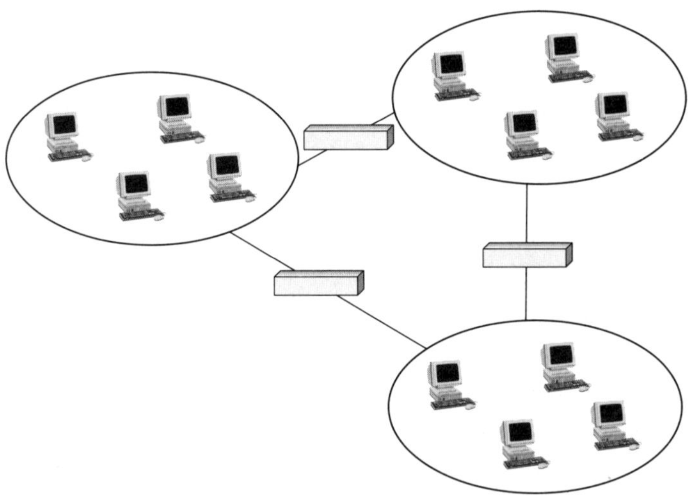

Routing is the process of moving packets between subnetworks to get them to their proper destination. Each router keeps an internal table of known routes that it uses for determining the route to send a packet by.

Some key points to keep in mind about routers include the following:

- A router connects two or more subnetworks.
- A router can be configured to support a single protocol or multiple protocols.
- A router will process only packets specifically addressing it as a destination.
- Packets destined for a locally connected subnetwork are passed to that subnetwork.
- Packets destined for a remote subnetwork are passed to the next router in the path.

Routers are intelligent devices. Many can dynamically determine the best route to a destination subnetwork, compensating for changing network conditions. A router can also inform an originating host if problems occur during transmissions.

A packet will have a destination IP address and a Time-to-Live (TTL) value. As a packet crosses each hop (each router in the path to the destination), the TTL value is decremented by one. When the TTL value reaches zero, the destination is assumed to be unreachable and an ICMP message is sent back to the originating host.

Routing Table

Each router maintains a routing table that is used to determine the path to a remote destination. The routing table will contain:

- The destination subnet IP address
- The destination subnet mask
- The router interface (network adapter) to be used to get to the destination
- The IP address of the next hop (next router) in the path to the destination
- The metric value for the path (number of hops to the destination)

If a packet is destined for the local subnet, it is ignored by the router. If a packet is received by the router that is destined for a subnet it is directly connected to, it will pass the packet along to that subnet. The routing process for packets that are destined for remote subnets depends on whether the router recognizes the subnet address. The router will pass the packet along to the next hop in the path, based on its routing table, when the path is known. Otherwise, it will send the packet to its default gateway for further routing.

Routers can be either static, where the routing table is built manually, or dynamic, capable of building the routing table automatically from updates received from other routers. Dynamic routers are by far the most common type of routers.

The **Route** command can be used to view the contents of a routing table by running the following at a command prompt:

```
route print
```

The **Route** command can also be used to add static entries to a Windows 2000 router's routing table.

NOTE: The procedures for entering manual updates are beyond the scope of this course.

Static Routers

Static routers are more difficult to maintain and less efficient than dynamic routers. Routing table entries must be entered manually. In a large network, this can become a time-consuming process. If there are any changes to the network that impact routing, such as changes to subnets or physical router locations, each router must be updated manually to reflect these changes. Static routers cannot respond to changing network conditions automatically.

Dynamic Routers

Dynamic routers communicate with each other to update their routing tables. Routing protocols are used for this purpose and are specific to the routing function. For example, the routing protocols that are commonly used by IP routers include the following:

- OSPF
- RIP version 2 for Internet Protocol (RIP for IP)

The updates received through these routing protocols are used by a router to build its routing table. They are also used to modify the routing table as network conditions change. These aren't the only TCP/IP routing protocols, but they are routing protocols supported by Windows 2000.

*NOTE: Windows 2000 can support both RIP and OSPF in the same network and even in the same system. However, you should **not** configure both for the same interface (network adapter).*

Routing Protocols

Selecting your routing protocols will be part of your network design process. To do this, you need to understand the routing protocols that are available to you.

OSPF

The OSPF routing protocol is designed for sharing routing information between routers on a large internetwork. It provides a way of passing automatic routing information updates between routers. OSPF requires little network overhead.

OSPF routers maintain a network map that is updated any time a change in network topology is detected. The information is propagated through all of the routers in the network.

An OSPF router is able to determine the best route for a packet based on the information stored in the network map. Routes can be recalculated to account for changing network conditions, so two packets going to the same destination may not necessarily use the same route. Routes calculated through OSPF will not contain loops.

NOTE: OSPF is not supported in demand-dial connection configurations.

RIP Version 2 for Internet Protocol (RIP for IP)

The Routing Information Protocol (RIP) is designed for use in small to medium network environments. RIP for IP is easy to deploy but does not scale well to support large networks.

Each RIP router will build a routing table that includes the networks it is physically connected to. Periodically, it will send an announcement containing its routing table to any other RIP routers local to networks it can reach. Any new route information is added to the local route table and passed along. With RIP version 1, IP broadcast packets are used. RIP version 2 uses multicast broadcast packets. Windows 2000 Routing and Remote Access supports both RIP version 1 and RIP version 2. You will need to use RIP version 2 if you need to support the following:

- CIDR (supernetting)
- Variable-length subnet masks
- Multicast router table updates
- Simple password authentication between routers

As a network grows, the traffic generated by the update broadcasts can become significant. This method of updates leads to a long reaction time to topology changes, up to several minutes. In addition, a RIP router can only support fifteen hops (passing a packet through fifteen routers). If a network is sixteen or more hops away, it cannot be reached by a RIP router. There is a difference, however, in Windows 2000 Routing and Remote Access for RIP. Because it considers all non-RIP-learned routes (like locally connected networks or static entries) as a hop count of two, you are effectively limited to no more than fourteen hops to your destination.

Routing Design

The process for designing routing for a LAN is similar to that discussed earlier in the course for designing a WAN. The basic requirements and concerns are much the same. The biggest difference, at least from a fundamental design standpoint, is that you are connecting through high-speed local LAN links rather than remote links.

Of course, there are going to be differences in how you design LAN and WAN routing. There are issues specific to each. For example, there is no reason to consider requirements for demand-dial connections in LAN routing. This section focuses on LAN routing design. WAN routing design issues are covered later in the course.

Designing for Security

Let's look at a couple of ways of providing security for your network design. You are going to be given an introduction at this time, with more information about routing security to be provided later in the course.

Packet Filtering

TCP/IP filtering can actually be implemented down to the host level or at the router level. One reason for filtering at the host level is to provide protection for a specialized server. With TCP/IP filtering, you set filter criteria and specify whether to pass or block packets based on that criteria. You can filter based on the following:

- IP protocol
- Source IP address range
- Destination IP address range
- TCP port number
- UDP port number

There are restrictions on filtering by IP protocol. You cannot filter out TCP or UDP traffic except by specific port number. You cannot filter out any ICMP, IGMP, or IPSec traffic.

You can use filtering to create screened subnets in your network design. This means that you are limiting the traffic into or out of the subnet (or both). You might, for example, set up a subnet supporting a research and development department as a screened subnet. If you do, you will need to test extensively to make sure that the filtering does not interfere with critical network services.

IPSec

IPSec can be used to provide protection for communication between hosts in a LAN, between routers in a WAN, or between a remote client and a LAN. One of the benefits of IPSec is that it is completely transparent to the user. In other words, the user doesn't have to do anything to initiate secure communication and won't even know that secure communication is being used.

You can only use IPSec if:

- All routers to be secured support IPSec.
- Router authentication is through machine-based certificates.
- Machine-based certificates can be issued through an Active Directory or Public Key Infrastructure (PKI).

You can use IPSec to provide source authentication with or without encryption. An Authentication Header (AH) is used for authentication without encryption. The Encapsulating Security Payload (ESP) is used when you want to provide both authentication and data encryption.

Designing for Availability and Performance

This issue was discussed earlier with WAN design. You can improve availability between subnets by providing multiple routes. This can be through multiple links between two locations or by providing redundant paths. If you are going to use either multiple links or redundant paths, you need to use OSPF routers to make the connections.

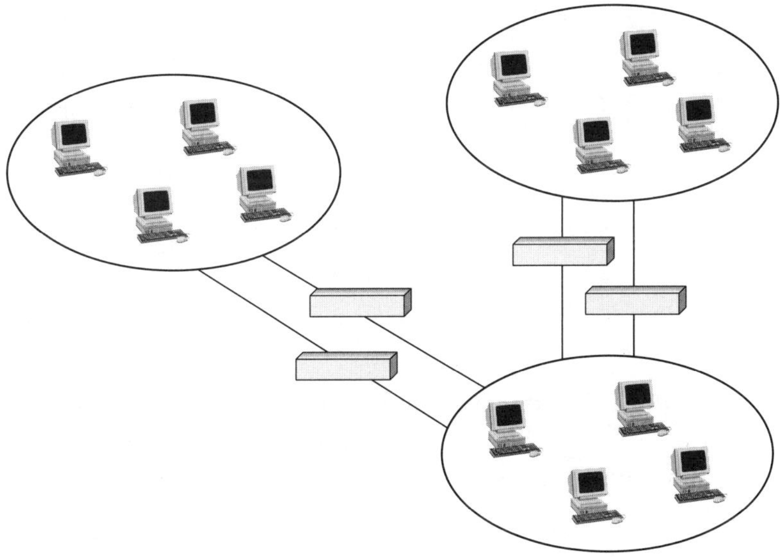

Multiple links means using two or more direct links between the subnets. This increases the bandwidth, allows you to balance the load between the routers, and provides redundancy in case of failure.

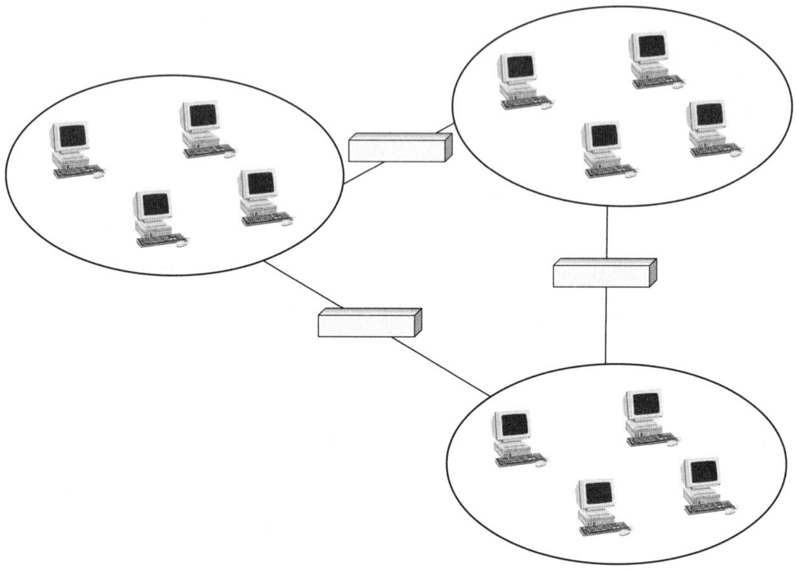

Using redundant paths is effectively much the same as providing multiple links except that you are using indirect links. This does increase effective bandwidth, but you do have to consider the latency introduced by having multiple hops.

When using Windows 2000 Server systems as routers, you should strongly consider dedicating the servers to that task. That will improve availability since you don't have the worry of another application crashing the server. Performance is also improved since the server doesn't have to share its resources among multiple applications.

Router Protocol Selection

When using Windows 2000 Server systems as routers, you will need to determine what routing protocol you are going to use. You've already been introduced to RIP and OSPF and some of the characteristics of each. Now you need to select one for your network.

Using RIP

You can use RIP for IP if you have a relatively small, stable network. You will need to use RIP for IP if you need to provide compatibility with an existing RIP network. You should only use RIP with a Windows 2000 router if packets will need to cross no more than fourteen hops to get to their destination.

Using OSPF

Use OSPF if you have a large network environment (more than 50 subnetworks) or if your network regularly experiences changes in available routes, route congestion, and so forth. You will also need to use OSPF where there are redundant paths between subnets or if existing routers in the network use OSPF.

An OSPF router design can be subdivided into the following:

- OSPF Autonomous System (AS)

  An OSPF AS is defined as all directly connected network segments and their routers.
- OSPF area

  This is a collection of routers connecting contiguous network segments through a common area known as a backbone area using Area Border Routers (ABRs).
- OSPF network

  This represents individual network segments connected by one or more OSPF routers.

Quality of Service (QoS)

QoS implementation will be discussed in some detail later in the course, but it does deserve a mention while talking about LAN routing design. QoS is a way of improving bandwidth availability and support for applications that have high bandwidth requirements.

This is important because routers operate on a first-come, first-served basis, sort of like a toll booth. Packets for applications with time-sensitive data requirements like streaming video or video conferencing are stuck in line waiting with the rest of the traffic. QoS lets you identify high-priority traffic and reserve a portion of the bandwidth for its use. However, before considering implementing QoS, make sure that:

- QoS is supported by the application(s).
- All routers in the path support RSVP.

Of course, you also want to make sure that your application actually needs to have bandwidth reserved for its data needs. This is more likely to be an issue across WAN links than in a routed LAN.

Sample Designs

It would be impossible to present a generic *best design* for all situations. Each network is different, with different traffic flows and user requirements. Instead, let's take a look at some samples to give you a general idea of how LANs can be configured. You've seen different variations of these before during the course.

While you are looking at these designs, you need to keep some basic guidelines in mind, including the following:

- Keep users grouped with their resources.
- Minimize traffic between subnets.
- Minimize the number of hops to any destination.

Now, let's look at the samples.

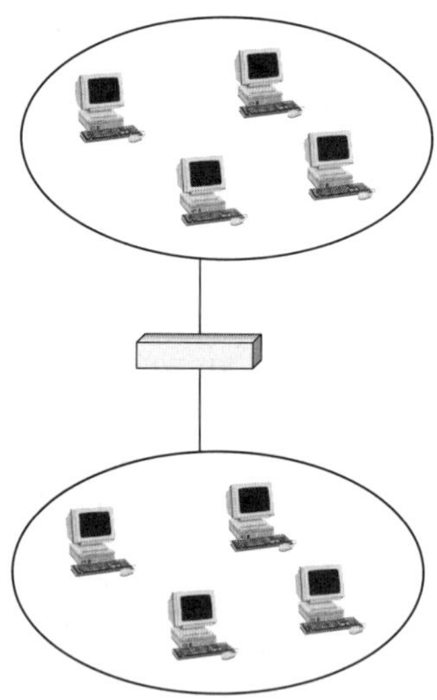

Here's a simple design of two subnets and a single router. Depending on the amount of traffic between the subnets, you may need to add a second router as a second link. You can balance the traffic between the routers through the default gateway assignments, assigning each router to half of the clients.

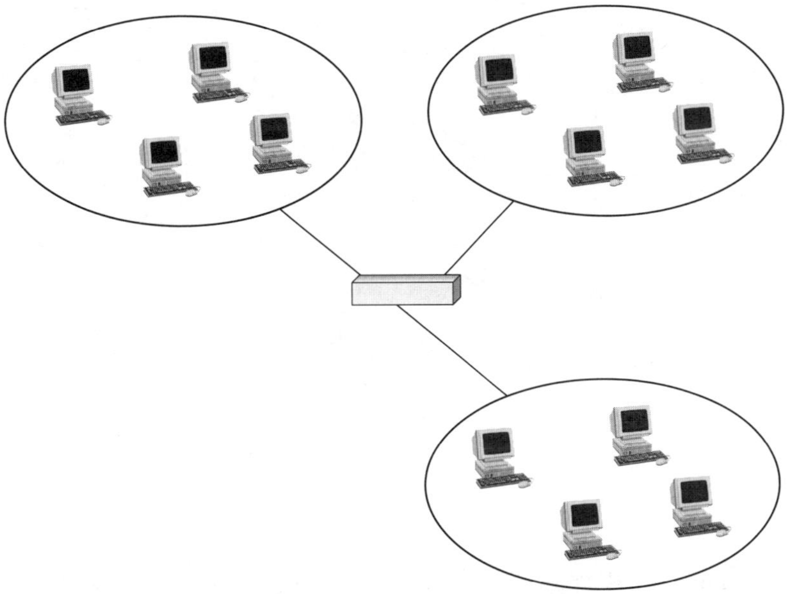

Another model you will see occasionally, especially when you only have a few subnets to support, is to use a router as a hub directly connecting to all of the subnets. This will require periodic monitoring of both network traffic and router hardware performance statistics. As with the single link discussed previously, you can always scale this model by adding more routers.

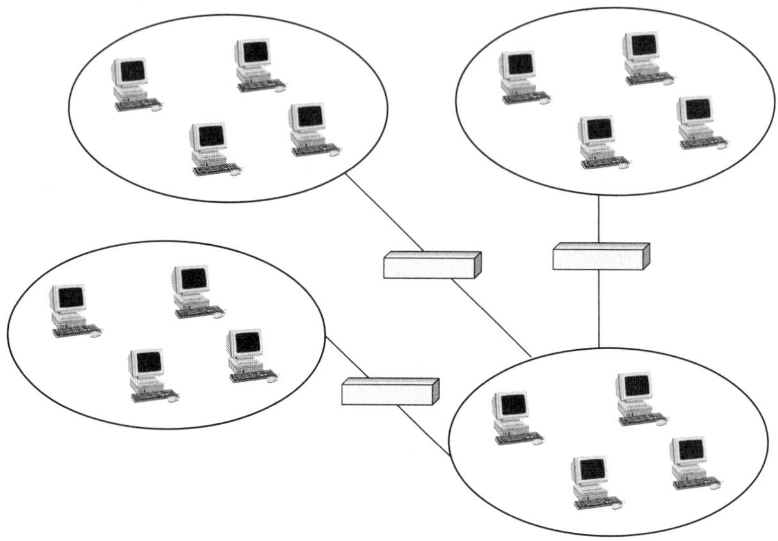

You may see the previous model occasionally, but it is not one of the more popular models. In this model, one subnet acts as the network hub, with separate routers to each of the other subnets. This means that you only have one hop to the *hub*, but two hops to get to any of the *spokes*. This model can easily lead to excessive traffic on the *hub* subnetwork.

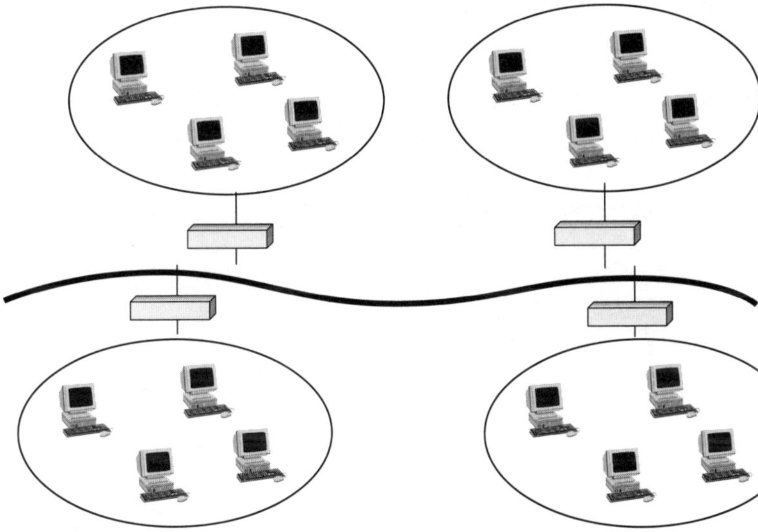

One of the most common solutions when you need to link multiple subnets is to connect them all to a backbone. This configuration has no more than two hops between any two subnets. You will still need to monitor traffic on each of the routers and on the backbone.

Implementing Software Routing

It's time to take a quick look at the procedures for setting up a router. For now, this will be limited to the procedures for setting up a simple LAN router. You'll be introduced to some variations to this simple router later in the course.

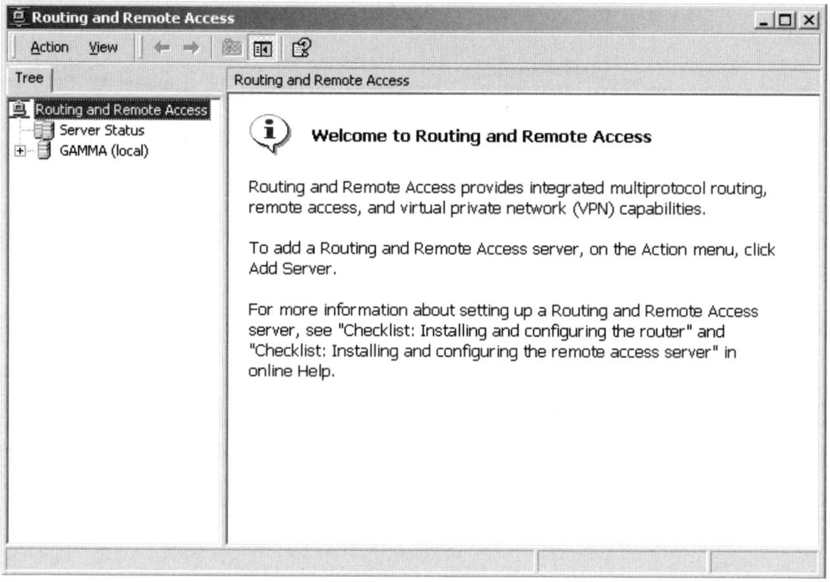

Routing is installed through the Routing and Remote Access tool, which is launched from the **Administrative Tools** menu. If the server that you want to configure as a router is not listed, you can run **Add Server** from the **Action** menu or after right-clicking on Server Status. The next step is to select the server and run **Configure and Enable Routing and Remote Access** from the **Action** menu or after right-clicking on the server. This will launch the Routing and Remote Access Server Setup Wizard.

Click on **Next** to continue past the Welcome screen.

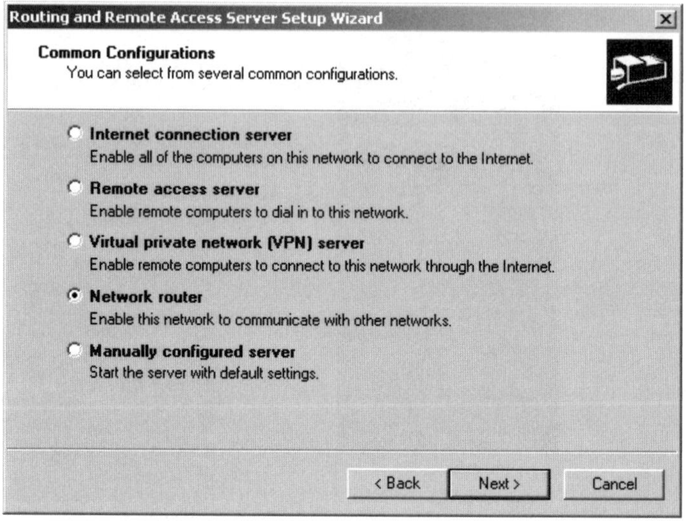

You are prompted to choose from a set of common configurations. Your choices are as follows:

- Internet connection server
- Remote access server
- Virtual private network (VPN) server
- Network router
- Manually configured server

The focus for now is on configuring a network router. After selecting **Network router**, click on **Next** to continue.

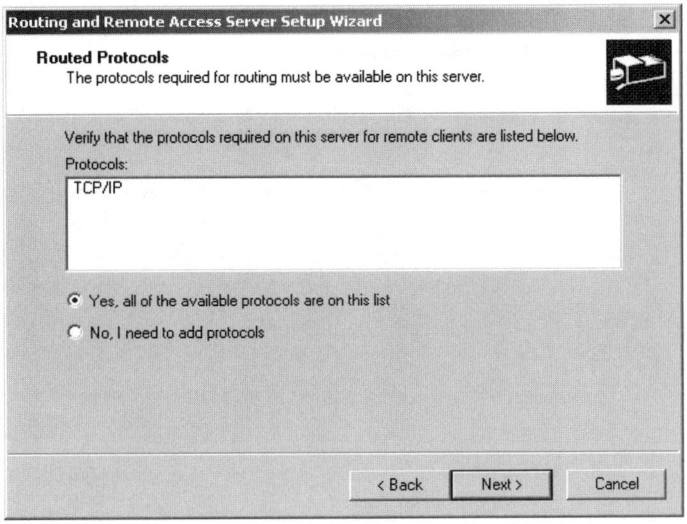

You are prompted to verify that the routable protocols you need to support your clients are listed. The list will contain the routable protocols installed on your system. If you select **No, I need to add protocols** and click on **Next**, you will receive a warning that the wizard cannot continue until the protocols are installed, and you will be prompted to exit. Make your selection and click on **Next**.

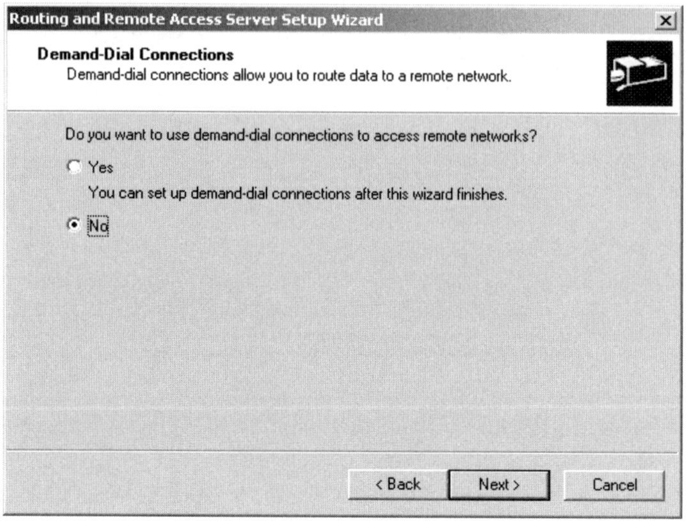

You are prompted to choose whether demand-dial connections are going to be used for connections with remote networks. Since you are setting up a local router, there is no need for demand-dial connections. Leave **No** selected and click on **Next**.

You are ready to complete the wizard and install routing. You are instructed to do the following before using the router that you are creating:

- Ensure that all interfaces have addresses.
- Install and set up routing protocols on each interface.

Click on **Finish** to configure your system as a router. The system will start and initialize the Routing and Remote Access Service (RRAS).

Testing and Monitoring

The monitoring process begins before you ever start the design process if you already have a routed LAN. You need to know what the current traffic patterns are before you can begin to estimate the traffic requirements in your new network.

Testing and monitoring is also going to be critical after implementation. You will want to do extensive testing as soon as possible after implementation to make sure that everything is working properly. You will want to continue with periodic monitoring to give you advanced warning if any problems start to show up.

Testing

The first thing you need to do is make sure that your design is working. The first thing is to test communication between subnets. You can do this with the Ping utility. Working from each subnet, ping locations in the other subnets by their IP addresses. This will let you know that the packets are getting through. If not, you'll need to test each step along the way. You can use Tracert or Pathping to try to determine where the failure is occurring.

One of the most common problems you'll find on a new implementation is that you either haven't configured hosts with a default gateway address or you've entered the wrong default gateway option. This is done so that the host can send the packet directly to the default gateway. Otherwise, the packet won't get forwarded by the router.

Once you have that initial testing out of the way, you need to test communications with user and network applications. Make sure your design is going to work with the applications that you are supporting.

Monitoring

Once you set the users loose on the network, you are going to have to worry about periodic monitoring. You want to make sure that your network is up to traffic requirements being placed on it. You also have to make sure that your routers are up to the job.

Traffic Monitoring

You can use Network Monitor to monitor network traffic, just like you did during information gathering. You need to check the following:

- Subnet traffic

  You have to monitor subnet traffic to make sure that you're not overloading the available bandwidth on the local LAN. If you are, then you either have to upgrade the subnet's infrastructure or reduce the traffic level. Reducing the traffic level usually means reshuffling your users and resources or adding additional subnets.

- Router traffic

  Monitor the traffic through the router to make sure that you don't have excessive traffic going across the links. This is where Network Monitor filtering can come in handy. You can look for the systems generating most of the traffic (source and destination) to see if you might need to relocate some network resources.

You may also find it helpful to set up alerts on the router to watch for error conditions or other performance concerns. You can use counters from the network interface performance object. You can monitor separate sets of counters for each network interface installed in the router.

Router Performance Monitoring

The System Monitor can also be used to monitor router performance statistics. You should watch periodically for signs of processor or memory bottlenecks at the router.

Processor bottlenecks occur when the processor can't keep up with interrupts and processing requests. Use the following counters to check for processor bottlenecks:

Object	Counter	Description
Processor	%Processor Time	This is the percentage of time that the processor spends executing a non-Idle thread, in other words, the percentage of the time that the processor is working. Commonly seeing a value of more than 85% indicates a bottleneck.
Processor	Interrupts/sec	This is the number of interrupts handled by the processor per second. Microsoft suggests that this value should be 1,500 or less for current processors.
System	Processor Queue Length	Monitor the _Total instance when monitoring this counter. The counter reports the current value for the number of threads in the processor queue. A consistent value of greater than 2 indicates a processor bottleneck.

If there is a problem with processor performance, your options are somewhat limited. You may be able to upgrade the processor or add an additional processor. If not, then you need to find a way to reduce the processor load. That means running fewer applications, running fewer services, or offloading some of the work to another server. If possible, you may need to consider adding another server to share network resource requirements. Run the router as a dedicated router or add another router so that you can balance the load between them.

Counters to monitor if you suspect a memory bottleneck include the following:

Object	Counter	Description
Memory	Available Bytes	This is the amount of physical memory available. If this consistently drops below 4 MB, there is a possibility of excessive paging.
Memory	Pages/sec	This is the number of pages read from or written to the hard disk as a result of page faults. A memory bottleneck is indicated by a consistent value of 20 or greater.
Paging File	%Usage	This is the percentage of the available paging file that is currently in use. A value of 70% indicates a need to increase the size of the paging file, the amount of physical RAM, or both.

This is one area where providing more resources (throwing more memory at it) can help, but it shouldn't necessarily be your first reaction. You can reduce memory requirements by reducing the number of applications and services running concurrently on the server. Size and placement of the paging file are also possible concerns.

A few points to keep in mind when creating the paging file include the following:

- Suggested minimum

  You should set the minimum size of the paging file to at least as large as the suggested minimum. Setting the paging file to a smaller size can result in performance problems and can prevent Windows 2000 from being able to generate a memory dump (crash dump) in case of a Stop error.

- Minimum size

  Observe the paging file size with the system under a typical load. If this file expands beyond the minimum size, this is the size you should actually use as your minimum. Increasing the size of the paging file on the fly is relatively inefficient and should be avoided, if possible.

- File placement

  If you have multiple physical hard disks available, you should make an effort to balance the disk load. Place the paging file on a less-active hard disk.

You can sometimes improve performance by creating the paging file on multiple hard disks.

Scenario 5-2: Routing Requirements

The purpose of this scenario is to give you practice in determining routing requirements. Suggested solutions are provided in Appendix B at the end of this manual. It may be helpful to review the case studies in Appendix C at the end of this manual.

Barney's Bank's Current Network

You are considering a solution that will leave the current home office subnetworks physically untouched.

1. Sketch the network routing configuration that would require the fewest routers.

2. Logon activity from the star-routed subnetworks is causing excessive router traffic. How can you reduce router traffic without introducing additional routers?

....

....

Exercise 5-2: Routing (Optional)

The purpose of this exercise is to give you practice setting up software routing. Answers to questions in this exercise are provided in Appendix B.

Special Preparation

There is no special preparation required for this exercise.

Router Installation

Complete the following steps on Gamma.

1. Open Network and Dial-up Connections.
2. Right-click on Local Area Connection and run **Properties.**
3. Select Internet Protocol (TCP/IP) and run **Properties.**
4. Click on **Advanced.**
5. On the IP Settings page, click on **Add** under the list of IP addresses.
6. Enter the following in the IP address field and press ***TAB***:

   `192.168.100.101`
7. Click on **Add**, then on **OK** three times.
8. Exit Network and Dial-up Connections.
9. Launch **Routing and Remote Access** from the **Administrative Tools** menu.
10. Right-click on Gamma and run **Configure and Enable Routing and Remote Access.**
11. Click on **Next.**
12. Select **Network router**, then click on **Next.**
13. Click on **Next**, then on **Next** again.
14. Click on **Finish.**

Client Host Configuration

This portion of the exercise has a section to be completed on Beta and a section to be completed on Alpha.

Beta

15. Open Network and Dial-up Access.
16. Right-click on Local Area Connection and run **Properties.**
17. Select Internet Protocol (TCP/IP) and run **Properties.**
18. Type the following in the Default gateway field, then click on **OK**:
    `192.168.100.101`
19. Click on **OK** twice.
20. Open a command prompt and execute the following:
    `ping 192.168.105.1`
    What happens?

    ....

    ....

Alpha

21. Open a command prompt and execute the following:
    `ping 192.168.100.3`
    What happens and why?

    ....

    ....

22. Open Network and Dial-up Access.
23. Right-click on Local Area Connection and run **Properties.**
24. Select Internet Protocol (TCP/IP) and run **Properties.**
25. Type the following in the Default gateway field, then click on **OK**:
    `192.168.100.101`

26. Click on **OK** twice.
27. Execute the following:

```
ping 192.168.100.3
```

What happens?

....

....

NETWORK INTEGRATION

It can sometimes be difficult to integrate your network design with the requirements placed on it by the real world. One such issue is integrating your network design with an existing network. The following topics are covered in this section:

- Existing Network Integration
- NetWare Integration
- SNA Integration

This section will not provide you with step-by-step guidelines for implementation but will provide you with general guidelines for integrating your network design. This discussion focuses primarily on LAN concerns, but most of the information is directly applicable to WAN integration.

Existing Network Integration

Sometimes it may seem that the easiest thing to do would be to throw out the old network and start over from scratch. What you often find yourself doing is making compromises with the current network design to find a cost-effective, workable solution, even if it isn't the best possible solution.

You will be gathering information about your current network before the design phase. One of your goals will be deciding what you can keep and what you have to replace, weighing performance against the cost of implementation.

User Physical Placement

There may be little you can do about where users are physically located. This can make it difficult to group users and resources without having to rewire your cable plant. If most of the wiring terminates in one central location, the job is a little easier. However, you are going to need to create an accurate map of your cable plant since you won't be able to assume that two users who are sitting next to each other are necessarily on the same subnet.

Router Requirements

You are going to have to consider any existing routers in your routing design. The following are two keys points to keep in mind:

- Router type

  If you want your dynamic routers to be able to keep each other updated, they are going to have to use the same routing protocol. In short, you will use RIP routers if that is what is already in place or OSPF routers if that's what you have.

- Subnetting support

  Your current routers can impact your subnet design. You cannot use variable-length subnetting or supernetting unless your routers support RIP version 2, OSPF, or BGP.

A decision to use existing routers doesn't necessarily require you to use them in their present locations. You may find that you can improve the design by relocating some of the routers within the network.

NetWare Integration

One of the most common situations you are going to encounter is the need to integrate Windows and Novell NetWare. It may be a process of connecting to the networks so that they can communicate, but more commonly, it means supporting both on the same network or subnetwork.

Let's begin with some fundamental requirements. These include the following:

- Protocol requirements

  NetWare usually means IPX/SPX protocol. That means that you are going to be supporting both IPX/SPX and TCP/IP on your network. Any Windows systems that need access to both a Windows domain (or network) and NetWare resources will need to be running both TCP/IP and NWLink.

  The possible exception is NetWare 5.0 servers. NetWare 5.0 servers default to using TCP/IP instead of IPX/SPX. However, if you want to use the Windows 2000 connection services, Client Service for NetWare (CSNW) or Gateway Service for NetWare (GSNW), you will have to enable IPX/SPX support at the NetWare 5.0 server.

- Routing requirements

  A routed LAN (or a WAN) environment with NWLink means that you will also have IPX/SPX routing requirements. These requirements are usually best met through the use of multiprotocol routing. Windows 2000 Server systems configured as routers support multiprotocol routing.

- Access requirements

  You are likely to have access requirements going both ways, with Windows clients that need access to NetWare resources and NetWare clients that need to access Windows resources. You have a number of options available for how these can be managed.

Let's take some time to take a little closer look at the access requirements.

NWLink

You've already been introduced to the NWLink protocol. You may find it helpful, however, to go over a few additional points, including the following:

- IPX

  IPX is a connectionless protocol that controls packet addressing and routing. This function should sound familiar since it is the same function provided by IP in the TCP/IP protocol suite.

- SPX

  SPX provides the same functionality for NWLink (and IPX/SPX) as TCP provides in the TCP/IP protocol suite. SPX provides connection-oriented services and guaranteed delivery over IPX.

- RIP over IPX (RIPX)

  RIPX does the same job as RIP for IP except that it is used for updating IPX/SPX routers. Routing is handled a little differently from the client point of view in an IPX network. Windows-based NetWare clients will broadcast a RIP GetLocalTarget route request to retrieve route information from available routers. Each router will respond with a single best router. The initiating workstation will compare and select a route, then send the packet to the router that provided the selected route.

- Service Advertising Protocol (SAP)

  SAP is used to advertise and collect information about services available in an IPX network. SAP broadcasts are only used to locate resources when bindery or NetWare Directory Services (NDS) queries fail.

Support for NetBIOS applications is also supported by NWLink with NetBIOS over IPX.

Windows Client Access

First, you need to understand how client descriptions are being used in this course. A Windows client refers to a system that is running Windows client software for connection with Windows-based servers. A NetWare client is a system running NetWare client software such as the Novell Client for Windows 2000. Just because a system is a Windows system doesn't mean that it cannot be configured as a NetWare client.

There are two basic options for Windows 2000 clients that want to access NetWare server resources:

- Client Service for NetWare (CSNW)
- Gateway Service for NetWare (GSNW)

Client Service for NetWare (CSNW)

CSNW allows Windows 2000 Professional (and Windows NT Workstation) clients to directly connect to NetWare servers, acting as a NetWare client. Each Windows 2000 Professional system connects individually to the NetWare server, which means that each user will need a valid NetWare user account and password. This is somewhat of a disadvantage since you have to manage both Windows and NetWare accounts for each user. However, the performance is better than you will get with GSNW since you don't have to contend with the latency introduced by the gateway server.

You should consider using CSNW for NetWare connectivity when:

- Planning to continue to use NetWare services as part of your networking solution.
- Performance is an overriding concern.
- You want to enforce individual client-level security at the NetWare server.

This solution will mean that all clients that need NetWare server access will be running both TCP/IP and NWLink.

Gateway Service for NetWare (GSNW)

GSNW provides Windows clients with indirect access to NetWare services. One Windows 2000 Server system, configured as a GSNW server, connects to the NetWare server(s) and its file and print resources. It is then able to reshare the resources as if they were local to the Windows 2000 Server system. There is nothing to indicate to the Windows clients that the resources are not located on the Windows 2000 Server system, and you don't have to make any changes to the Windows client configurations.

You will need to install GSNW on one or more Windows 2000 Server systems to provide client access. You will also have to modify the NetWare servers involved. Each server will need an NTGATEWAY group with at least one user that has sufficient permissions to access the necessary resources on the NetWare server. The gateway can be configured to connect to NetWare bindery services, NDS, or both. The only Windows systems that need to be running NWLink in this case are the gateways.

You will want to use GSNW when:

- Planning to migrate from the NetWare servers, to avoid having to reconfigure the clients twice.
- You want to minimize IPX/SPX traffic on the network.
- You want to keep your management overhead to a minimum.

Working through a server configured with GSNW does increase latency when accessing NetWare resources. When supporting time-critical applications, you will want to test and verify that this latency doesn't cause your applications to fail.

NetWare Client Access

Some server applications, such as Microsoft's SQL Server, provide direct access to NetWare clients. All you need to do is install NWLink at the server and make sure that the server application is properly configured to support NetWare clients.

If you want to provide NetWare clients with access to file or print resources on Windows servers, you are going to have to install File and Print Services for NetWare (FPNW) and NWLink at the Windows server. This will give NetWare clients running IPX/SPX access to the resources you select to share and make available to them.

NOTE: FPNW does not ship with Windows 2000 but may be purchased separately.

Directory Service Migration Tool

A brief mention of the Directory Service Migration Tool is in order while on the subject of NetWare integration. This tool lets you migrate user accounts, group accounts, files, and permission settings from a NetWare server to a Windows 2000 Server system. The Directory Service Migration Tool can be invaluable if your eventual goal is replacing NetWare servers with Windows 2000.

SNA Integration

Another situation that you need to consider is connectivity requirements with an SNA networking environment and with IBM host systems. One of the traditional solutions for this was to configure individual PCs for host access. However, it is difficult to scale this solution since it requires an ever-increasing number of connections at the host. This solution can quickly become prohibitively expensive.

A solution that will meet most organizations' connectivity requirements is Microsoft's Host Integration Server (or SNA Server, as it is still commonly called). SNA Server provides connectivity with IBM hosts running either the SNA protocol or TCP/IP. For hosts running the SNA protocol, SNA is only required between the SNA Server and the host connection. Windows clients that are accessing the IBM host via the SNA Server can be running any protocol in common with the SNA Server. In fact, SNA Server running on Windows 2000 provides connectivity for the following client protocols:

- TCP/IP
- NWLink (or IPX/SPX)
- NetBEUI
- Banyan VINES IP
- AppleTalk

Access to the IBM host is supported over LAN connections or WAN links to the SNA server. Support is also provided for remote access clients through Windows 2000 Routing and Remote Access services.

You can provide improved availability and load balancing by using multiple SNA servers. Let's look at a couple of basic connection models.

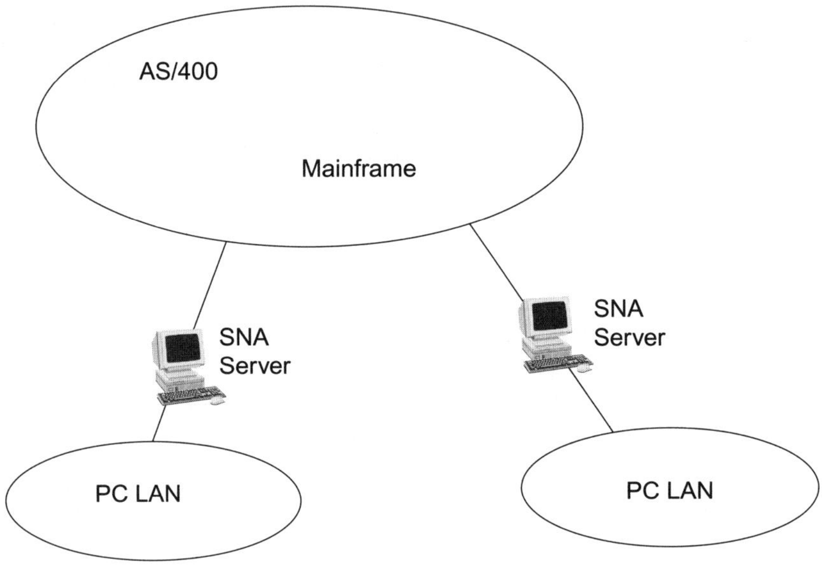

In a LAN environment, you will typically have one or more SNA servers as direct gateways to the SNA environment and IBM hosts. Resources accessed through the SNA server will appear as if they are originating from the Windows 2000 server.

You can use a similar configuration for supporting WAN connections. You can place an SNA server in each remote location and have it connect directly to the host.

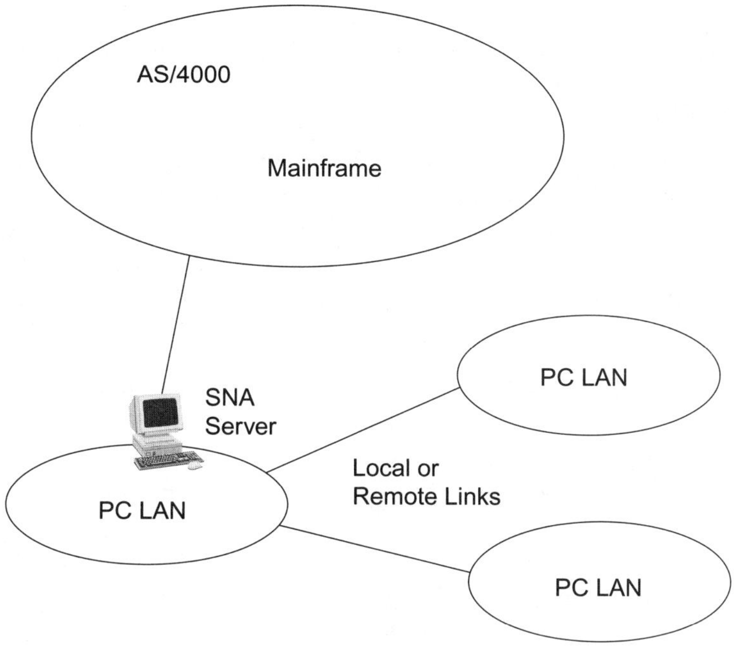

Another WAN solution is to have the SNA server connections made locally to the IBM host, then have the WAN connect remotely to the SNA servers. When using this connection method, you must consider in your network design plans the local traffic that will be generated.

Scenario 5-3: Network Integration

The purpose of this scenario is to give you practice in network integration design. The scenarios in this problem are *not* based on the case studies you have been using during the course. Suggested solutions are provided in Appendix B at the end of this manual.

Scenario 1

You have a nonrouted Novell NetWare network. You have a single NetWare 3.12 server. You are in the process of converting to a Windows 2000 Active Directory domain. You are installing two Windows 2000 Server systems as domain controllers and ten Windows 2000 Professional systems as clients. Until the conversion process is complete, the Windows 2000 Professional systems will need to access file resources on the NetWare server.

1. How can you provide the Windows 2000 Professional systems access to the NetWare server without adding NWLink support?

   ....

   ....

2. Referring to your solution to question 1, what changes will have to be made to the Windows 2000 Professional systems?

   ....

   ....

3. How does your solution to question 1 change your network's routing requirements?

   ....

   ....

Scenario 2

You are planning to use SNA Server to connect your routed LAN to an IBM host. The PCs on the LAN are currently using TCP/IP protocol.

1. Assuming minimal access requirements, what is the minimum number of SNA servers required for this solution?

2. What protocol changes must be made to the LAN PCs?

SUMMARY

During this chapter, you were introduced to the following:

- TCP/IP architectural model
- TCP/IP protocols and services
- TCP/IP utilities
- TCP/IP features and benefits
- Configuring TCP/IP
- IP address classes
- Public and private addresses
- Subnetting
- Subnet planning
- Supernetting

- Variable-length subnetting
- Routing design
- Static routers
- Dynamic routers
- Router protocols
- Testing and monitoring
- Network integration
- NetWare integration
- SNA Server

The next chapter continues your detailed look at TCP/IP design and implementation, focusing on TCP/IP services.

POST-TEST QUESTIONS

The answers to these questions are in Appendix A at the end of this manual.

1. When is a public IP address required?

2. Using the default subnet mask, how many hosts can a Class C address support?

3. What TCP/IP utilities can be used to trace the path between two remote hosts?

4. A destination address of 255.255.255.255 is used for what kind of transmission?

5. All of your routers are Windows 2000 Server systems configured as routers through Routing and Remote Access. All routers are configured as a RIP for IP router. What is the maximum number of hops that will be supported to a remote destination?

6. What security feature would you enable on a router to limit the type of traffic passed between two subnets?

7. Traffic levels between two subnets are causing the router between the subnets to fail. There is nothing you can do to reduce the traffic levels. What can you do to correct this situation?

8. You install a new host in a subnet. You can ping any local host but get a "Destination not available" message when you try to ping a remote host. What is most likely wrong?

9. You have two Windows 2000 Professional hosts that need to access resources on a local NetWare server. The NetWare server is not scheduled for replacement. How should you configure the Windows 2000 systems for access?

....

....

10. What client protocols are supported by SNA Server?

....

....

CHAPTER 6

TCP/IP Services

MAJOR TOPICS

OBJECTIVES

At the completion of this chapter, you will be able to:

- Identify key server resources when optimizing for network service support.
- Describe how domain names are structured.
- Describe the purpose and use of DNS servers.
- List the DNS requirements for implementing Active Directory services.
- Describe how forward lookup queries are resolved.
- Compare and contrast the DNS database storage options.
- Describe the purpose and use of DNS zones.
- List and describe concerns when integrating Active Directory and non-Active Directory DNS servers.
- Describe how DNS zone information is replicated for Active Directory-integrated and standard zones.
- Optimize a DNS design for availability, performance, and security.
- Design a DNS solution for integrating DNS service support with the Internet.
- Describe when WINS servers are needed as part of a network design.
- Describe how WINS is used to resolve NetBIOS names.
- Identify when a WINS server is needed as part of a network design.
- Given network requirements, design a WINS replication solution.
- Design a DHCP solution based on a single DHCP server.
- Design a DHCP solution based on multiple DHCP servers.
- Optimize a DHCP design for performance and availability.
- Describe guidelines for integrating network services.

PRE-TEST QUESTIONS

The answers to these questions are in Appendix A at the end of this manual.

1. What service is provided by a WINS server?

2. What type of resource record support is required when deploying an Active Directory domain?

3. How is replication managed for an Active Directory-integrated DNS zone?

4. What is the minimum number of name servers required in a DNS zone?

5. DNS replication traffic over a low-bandwidth link is causing intermittent network failures. You are going to have to remove the DNS server from the remote location but want to keep traffic generated from name resolution queries to a minimum. How would you solve this problem?

6. What type of zone is required if you want DNS to support secure dynamic updates?

....

....

7. How can you modify a static WINS mapping?

....

....

8. What type of WINS replication would you use if you wanted the receiving WINS server to control the replication schedule?

....

....

9. You have a nonrouted LAN with NetBIOS name resolution requirements. What is the minimum number of WINS servers required to support these requirements?

....

....

10. You have a network configured with multiple DHCP servers. Which of your DHCP servers will respond to a client request for an IP address?

....

....

11. One of your DHCP clients is overriding the primary WINS server supplied by the DHCP server. What is the most likely cause?

....

....

12. What would be your justification for placing a second DHCP server in a nonrouted LAN?

13. What will be the impact on network traffic if you shorten the address lease period?

14. How can a WINS server be used to support DNS name resolutions?

INTRODUCTION

This chapter continues the detailed discussion of TCP/IP protocol suite features. The discussion now turns to network services supported by TCP/IP and designing for their optimal use.

The chapter begins with an introduction to TCP/IP services. Most of this information should already be familiar to you and is provided here as a review before looking at the services in detail.

The first service discussed in the chapter is the Domain Name System (DNS) service. You will see how to configure DNS support in your network as well as how to integrate with existing DNS servers. This also includes a review of DNS names and how they are structured.

From DNS, the focus shifts to another name resolution service, Windows Internet Name Service (WINS). You will be introduced to when you need to implement WINS and guidelines for server placement.

The Dynamic Host Configuration Protocol (DHCP) service is then discussed in detail. You will see how to set up support for routed and nonrouted network environments, guidelines for server placement, and the use of WINS Proxy Agents.

Server integration is then discussed. This is actually two different subjects under the same heading. First, you will be given guidelines for having TCP/IP services support one another. Then the discussion will turn to how and why you might combine multiple services on a single server.

There is another difference between this and the previous two chapters. In the previous two chapters, the primary focus was on LAN design issues. This chapter addresses both LAN and WAN design issues.

SERVICES INTRODUCTION

You should already be somewhat familiar with the services discussed in this chapter. Just to make sure, this section provides you with a quick review of some key points, along with a little new information. The following topics are covered in this section:

- Design Fundamentals
- TCP/IP Services
- Installing and Configuring Services

Installation and configuration are not focused on in this course. An overview is being provided as a reference and to help introduce some of the issues you will encounter during implementation.

Design Fundamentals

This chapter looks at design concerns, constraints, and guidelines for the following three TCP/IP services:

- Domain Name System (DNS) service
- Windows Internet Name Service (WINS)
- Dynamic Host Configuration Protocol (DHCP) service

The technologies employed by these services are not unique to Windows 2000 or even to the Windows operating system family. This chapter, however, will focus primarily on developing a design around Windows 2000's implementation of these services. Where appropriate, concerns about non-Windows service providers and clients will also be included.

Server Guidelines

From a design requirements standpoint, you may find it easier to think of each of the services discussed in this chapter as a server application. These services are similar to server applications in that they require the same resources, though the level of resource requirements varies with each service. These server resources include the following:

- Processor
- Memory
- Disk space

A difference between services and applications is that services run in the background. You can't necessarily tell by looking at a server's desktop what network services it is providing, if any. Many server applications run in the foreground, but there has been a gradual shift toward implementing what have traditionally been considered applications as services.

What this means is that server selection and configuration are going to be important issues. You have to select servers that can provide the resources that these services need. This also means periodic monitoring or use of alerts to make sure that the servers continue to meet service requirements.

Design Issues

The design issues and guidelines are the same as you've addressed already in network design. They include the following:

- User distribution
- Availability
- Performance
- Scalability
- Bandwidth usage

These issues will be addressed again during this chapter, but specifically in the context of network services.

TCP/IP Services

These are services that are already familiar to you. Their basic features and functions have been discussed at different times during the course. However, a quick review will be helpful before looking at each of these services in detail.

Domain Name System (DNS) Service

You have to be careful with the term *domain*. Its definition is context sensitive. In the context of DNS, a domain is a part of the DNS database. Don't confuse this with a Windows 2000 domain, which is an administrative group of network devices, or a Windows NT domain, which is another administrative entity. Unless otherwise specified, any reference to domains in this chapter refers to DNS domains.

DNS resolves IP host names to IP addresses. IP host names are typically easier for most people to remember when trying to connect to another system. If you've had any experience with Web or FTP sites on the public Internet, you're already familiar with domain names.

Proper DNS design is going to require you to understand a number of concepts, some of which may be new to you. These include the following:

- Domain name structure
- DNS database options
- DNS zones
- DNS replication

Since DNS is a requirement for Active Directory implementation, you can plan on it being a significant part of most network designs. There's a good chance that your current network already has one or more DNS servers, though they may not be running on Windows 2000, so integration or replacement is another issue you will have to contend with. You may also need to implement connectivity with Internet DNS servers.

Windows Internet Name Service (WINS)

WINS provides a means for resolving NetBIOS machine names to IP addresses. Traditionally, NetBIOS names were resolved through broadcasts. Since broadcasts were propagated by routers, that meant you could only resolve NetBIOS names for your local subnetwork. The LMHOSTS file provides a way around this. The LMHOSTS file is a text file that relates NetBIOS names to IP addresses. WINS provides a solution for automating management of NetBIOS names and name resolution.

Some of the design issues relating to WINS include the following:

- Justification for WINS
- WINS replication

Unlike DNS, WINS is not a requirement for supporting Active Directory, but it will likely be a requirement if you plan to leave an existing network configuration intact or if you are migrating from Windows NT domain or workgroup structure. WINS may be required if you are supporting a mixed network that includes Windows 98 and Windows NT clients that communicate using NetBIOS names.

Dynamic Host Configuration Protocol (DHCP) Service

DHCP gives you a way of minimizing your IP address management by automatically assigning IP addresses to clients as they start. In addition to providing the client with an IP address and subnet mask, the DHCP server can also configure additional optional values such as the default gateway, DNS server address, and WINS server address.

Issues of special concern in DHCP design include the following:

- Supporting non-Windows clients
- Supporting mobile clients
- Routed network requirements
- Lease periods

You won't be required to use DHCP as part of your network design, but you should at least give it serious consideration. DHCP can significantly reduce your management overhead, especially in a volatile networking environment.

Installing and Configuring Services

A detailed discussion of the procedures for installing and configuring each of the network services discussed in this chapter is beyond the scope of this course. The primary focus is on design rather than implementation procedures. However, it will be helpful if you know the basic installation procedures and the tools available for managing services. You will also be given a chance to work with some of these during hands-on exercises later in the course.

Installation Basics

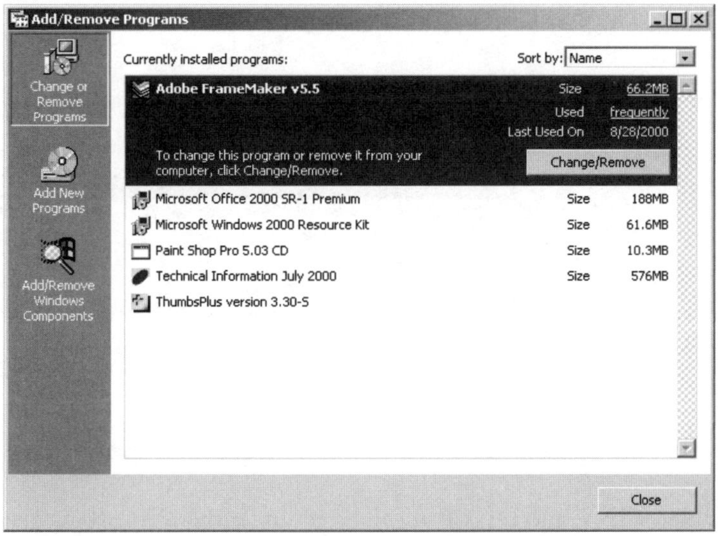

The Control Panel's Add/Remove Programs utility is used to install network services. After launching Add/Remove Programs, click on **Add/Remove Windows Components** to display a list of available components.

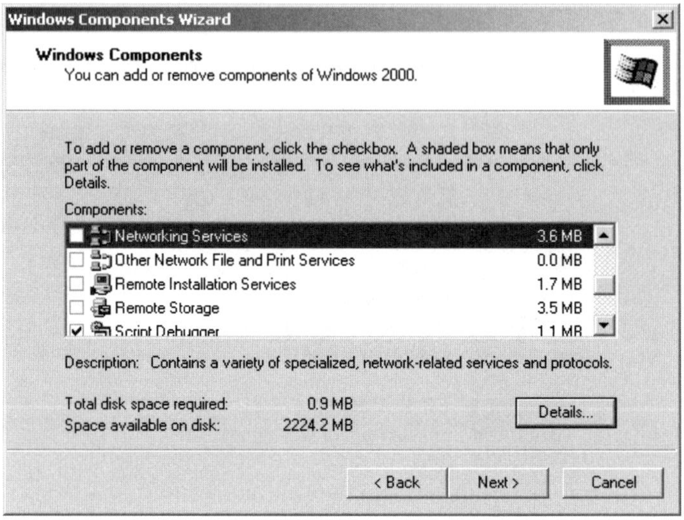

DNS, WINS, and DHCP are all listed under the Networking Services components. If you place a check in the **Networking Services** checkbox, all components will be selected. If you highlight Networking Services and click on **Details**, you can pick the services that you want to install.

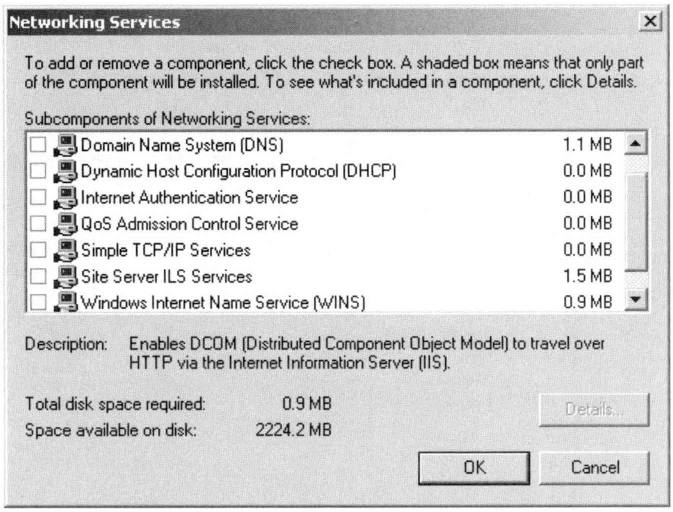

All you need to do to select a service is place a check in its checkbox. You can choose to install multiple services. The necessary files will be copied to your hard disk, and the selected services will be installed. You will need to have a copy of the Windows 2000 Server Installation CD-ROM or access to installation source files when installing services. You are not required to restart your server after installing network services.

Management Tools

Installation is only part of the process of implementing network services. The services must also be configured.

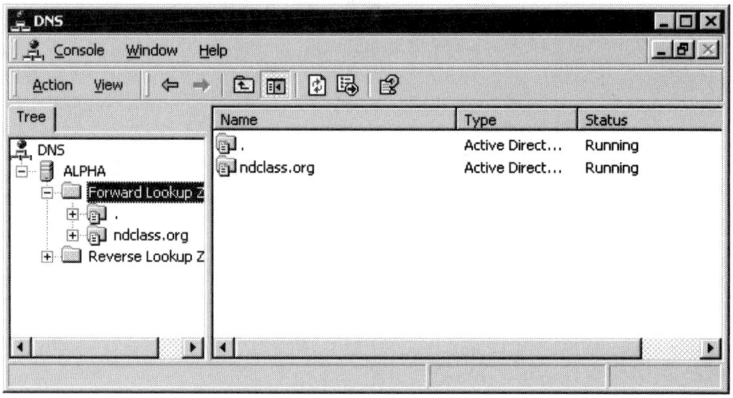

The DNS Administrative Tool is used to manage DNS servers. When first launched, only the local server will be displayed. You can connect to other DNS servers in your network, letting you manage the servers from one central location.

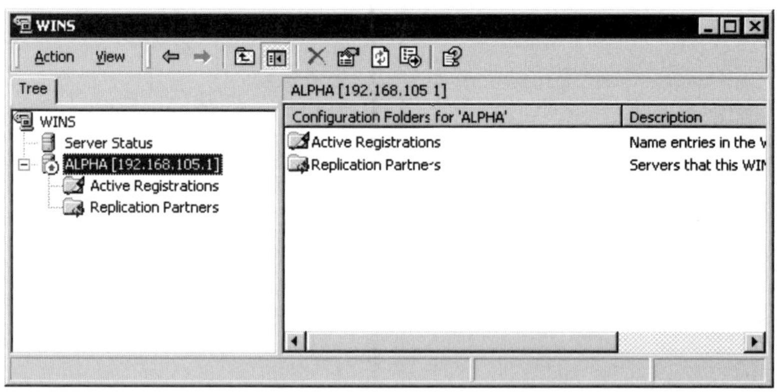

The WINS Administrative Tool provides a centralized point of management for your network's WINS servers. You can set WINS properties and view performance statistics through the WINS tool.

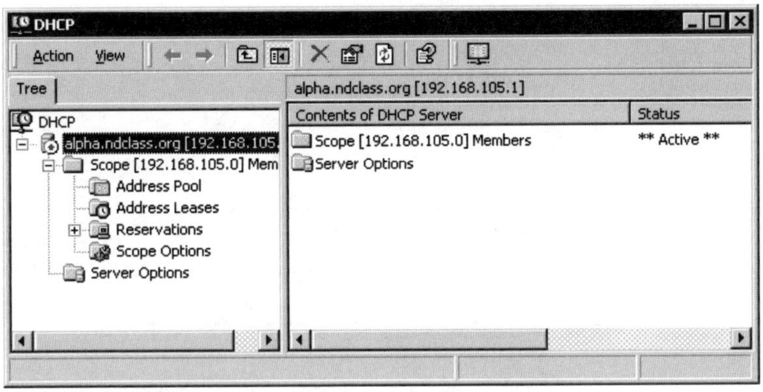

The DHCP Administrative Tool is used to manage DHCP servers. You will use the DHCP tool to define scopes, set DHCP properties, and authorize DHCP servers.

DNS

The discussion now turns to specific network services, beginning with DNS. The following topics are covered in this section:

- Domain Name Organization
- DNS Fundamentals
- DNS Database
- DNS Zones
- DNS Design

The DNS service is going to be a vital component of nearly any network design that uses TCP/IP.

Domain Name Organization

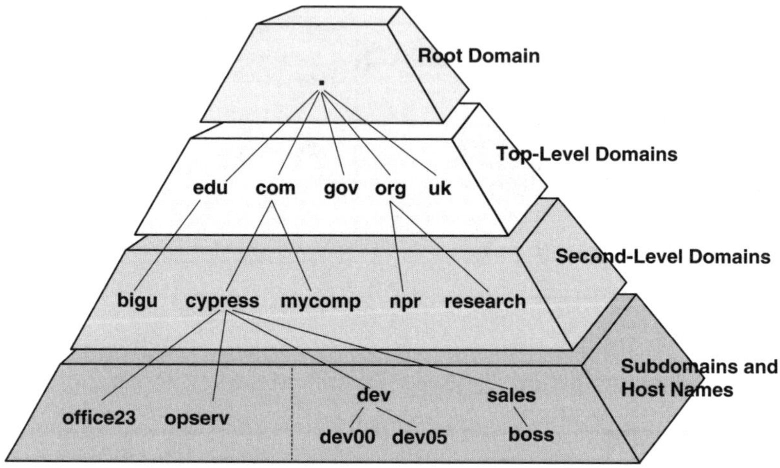

Since DNS is used for name resolution, a good place to start is a quick look at host names. DNS domain names are based on a hierarchical structure known as the domain namespace. A domain's name uniquely identifies the domain and locates the domain within the domain namespace. A host's Fully Qualified Domain Name (FQDN) accurately describes its position in the hierarchy, including the period, which represents the root domain. Let's see how these names are organized.

Root Domain

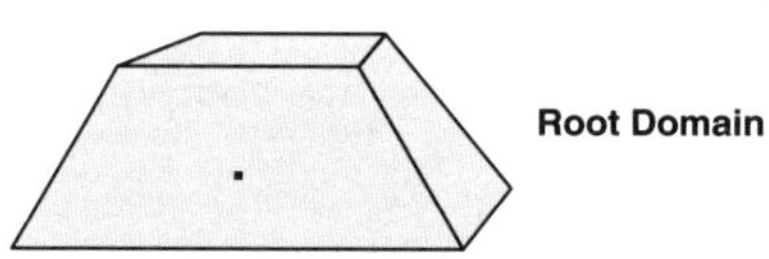

The root domain, represented by a period (.), sits at the top of the domain hierarchy. When navigating the Internet, the root domain is typically assumed and is not included when entering host names. The root domain contains top-level domains.

Top-Level Domains

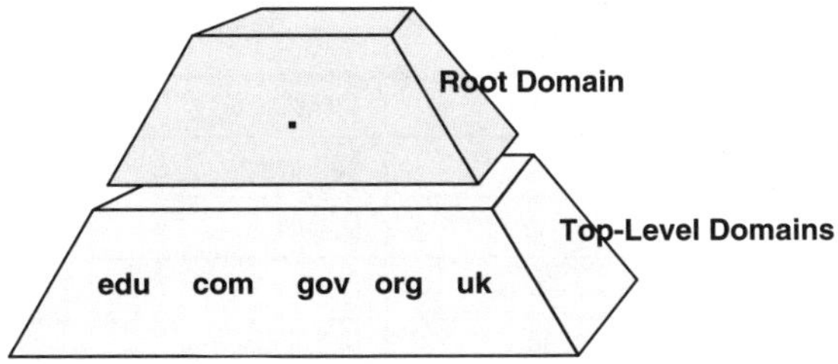

Top-level domains have two- or three-character names. They organize domains by category or by geographic region. Common category domains include the following:

Domain	Description
com	This will typically include companies and for-profit organizations. For example, Microsoft corporation's domain is microsoft.com.
edu	The edu name is used to identify educational institutions, typically colleges and universities. For example, Massachusetts Institute of Technology has a domain name of mit.edu.
gov	This category is reserved for United States government organizations, such as nasa.gov for the National Aeronautic and Space Administration.
mil	United States military organizations use this category, such as af.mil for the United States Air Force.
net	This category is used for Internet gateways and administrative hosts. Many ISPs fall into this category, with names such as ldd.net.
org	Nonprofit organizations and other organizations that can't be easily categorized end up in this category. For example, National Public Radio has a domain name of npr.org.
int	You may sometimes see international organizations use .int as their top-level domain. One example of this is nato.int.

Geographic domains are organized by country. Some examples include the following:

Domain	Description
us	United States
au	Australia
ca	Canada
fr	France
uk	United Kingdom

Top-level domains can contain second-level domains and host names. Much of the time, they will contain second-level domains.

Second-Level Domains

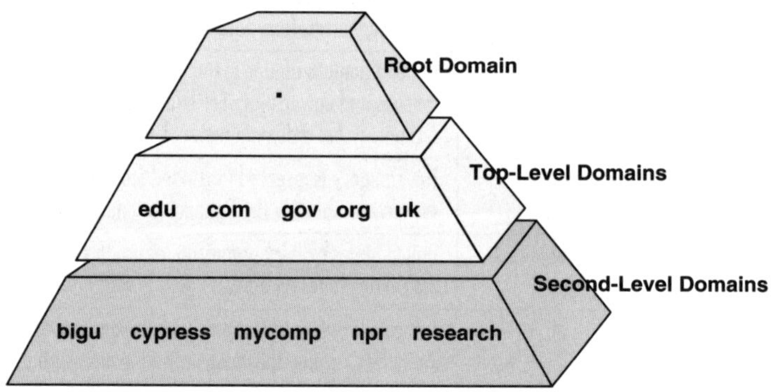

This level allows you to identify yourself or your organization. If you are going to be connecting to the Internet, you must register your unique second-level domain name. Second-level domains can contain subdomains and hosts.

Additional Domains and Hosts

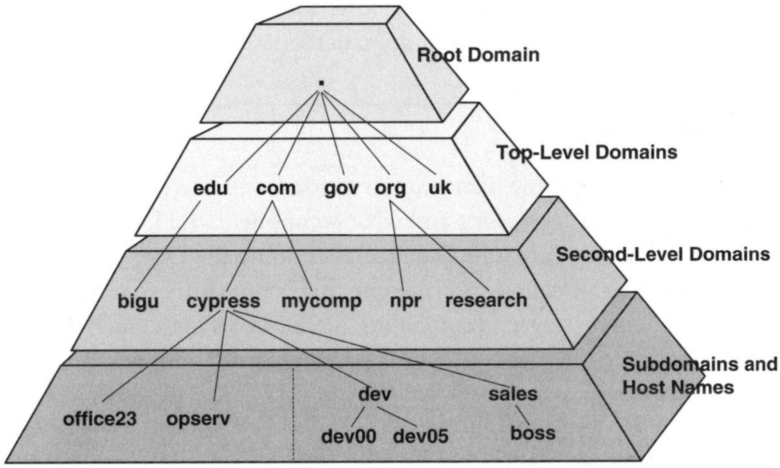

At this level, you take over control of the domain namespace. You decide what subdomains and hosts you are going to support and have complete control over how they are named, within limits. Each FQDN must be unique within the domain namespace.

You are limited to no more than 63 characters for a domain name, including the periods. An FQDN is limited to no more than 255 characters. Both the ASCII and Unicode character sets are supported for domain names. However, you are limited in the characters that you can use. Domain names may include the following:

- Lower-case alphabet (a-z)
- Upper-case alphabet (A-Z)
- Numbers (0-9)
- Hyphen (-)

When installing TCP/IP, a computer's name will be used as its default host name. Any special characters not supported by DNS that are embedded in the computer name will be replaced by hyphens when stored as a host name. Even though upper-case characters can be used in domain names, domain names are not case sensitive.

DNS Fundamentals

Now that you see how names are structured, you need to understand how domain names are resolved to IP addresses and what components are involved. Let's start with DNS servers. The accurate term for a server running the DNS server is *name server*. In a local network environment, especially one that is not connected to the Internet, it's easy to think of a name server as containing the DNS database, including all host names and their IP addresses. More accurately, a name server contains an applicable portion of the DNS database.

Entries in the DNS database are known as resource records. Resource records associate domain host names with network resources, most noticeably, IP addresses. Each name server will contain resource records for the domain namespace for which it can respond to client queries. This is also referred to as the domain the name server is authoritative for.

You can have one or more name servers supporting your network. In a large network, you may have multiple servers and different database files. Looking out into the Internet at large, there are additional name servers, including name servers for root and each of the top-level organizations.

You are not limited to only using Windows 2000 DNS servers on your network. Other DNS servers can be used in conjunction with or in place of Windows 2000 DNS servers. If you are designing a network for an Active Directory domain and choose to use a name server other than the Windows 2000 DNS server service, it should support the following features:

- SRV records

  Service records, map services, and the servers they are offered from

- Dynamic update protocol

  Dynamic update protocol is required for Dynamic DNS support, allowing servers and clients to automatically add records to the DNS database. If not supported, the DNS database will have to be updated manually.

- Incremental zone transfers

  Name servers that support incremental zone transfers allow for replication of new and updated resource records only. Without incremental zone transfers, updates require transfer of the entire zone database.

SRV record support is required for Active Directory domains. Dynamic update protocol and incremental zone transfer support is optional but is strongly suggested. These are all supported by Microsoft's DNS server service.

NOTE: DNS zones and zone transfers are discussed in detail later in this section.

Name Resolution Queries

The following are the two types of name resolution queries:

- Forward lookup query

  A forward lookup query is used when the host name is known and you want to find its IP address.

- Reverse lookup query

  A reverse lookup query is used to map a known host IP address to a host name.

It's important to know how queries are serviced. You need to understand the data flow involved since supporting the traffic generated by name resolution will need to be considered as part of your network design.

Forward Lookup Query

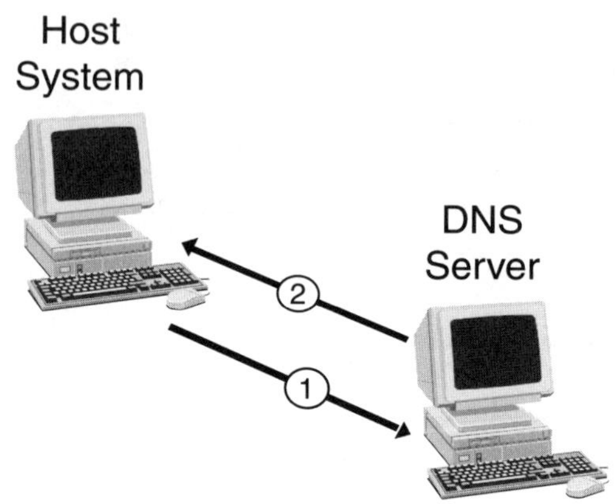

This example illustrates the resolving of a local host name. For example:

1. When a client needs to resolve a host name, it will query its primary DNS server.
2. The DNS server will return the IP address for the requested host.

Now let's look at an Internet example to get a good idea of what happens during a more involved forward lookup query. Let's say you wanted to find a Web server that is not part of your local domain at www.mycorp.com.

You can specify multiple DNS servers for each of your client systems. These can include local DNS servers and, if you choose, DNS servers for commonly accessed domains. The client will first attempt to query these servers to resolve any host names. DNS servers can be configured manually for each client or, if you prefer, automatically by supplying the configuration options through DHCP.

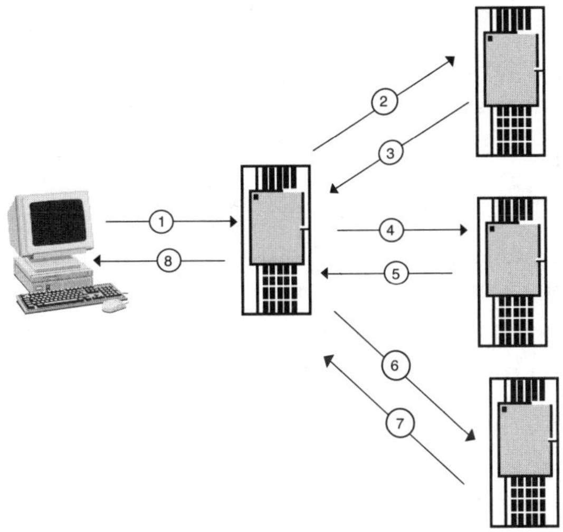

When a request is made that cannot be resolved locally, the following steps are taken:

1. There is an attempt to resolve the name locally at the client's primary DNS server.
2. If the local DNS name server cannot resolve the request and doesn't support the requested domain, the request is forwarded to a root name server.
3. The root name server sends a referral, in this case, a list of com name servers, back to the local name server.
4. The local name server next sends a request to a com name server.
5. The com name server responds with a referral to the mycorp.com name server.
6. The local name server sends the request to the mycorp.com name server.
7. The mycorp.com name server returns the IP address for www.mycorp.com.
8. When the local name server receives the IP address, it forwards it on to the requesting client.

As you can see, there can be a number of requests required to resolve a single name.

To keep traffic to a minimum, the local name server will locally cache the results of its queries. This also makes it possible for the local name server to respond quicker to other queries for addressing in the same domain namespace. Cached entries are only maintained for a limited amount of time. The time that an entry will remain cached is defined by a TTL parameter, defaulting to 60 minutes.

Reverse Lookup Query

The DNS database is designed and optimized for resolving host names to IP addresses. Some applications and troubleshooting utilities, however, require the ability to go from an IP address back to a host name. To make this possible without having to go through an address-by-address search, a second-level domain called in-addr.arpa is used.

The in-addr.arpa domain and its subdomains are organized by IP address and subnet mask rather than host and domain name. The IP address dotted-decimal value is used for naming subdomains of the in-addr.arpa domain, but the octet order is reversed. For example, if you have a Class C address of 192.23.131.0 and are using a subnet mask of 255.255.255.0, the reverse lookup subdomain for this would be as follows:

```
131.23.192.in-addr.arpa
```

DNS Database

Resource records are stored in the DNS database. Actually, a DNS server can support multiple DNS databases, referred to as zone databases, allowing it to service host name resolution requests from multiple lookup zones. You have a choice over where and how these databases are managed.

Storage Options

A DNS name server must have at least one forward lookup zone. You will be prompted to select from the following three zone configuration options when creating a forward lookup zone:

- Active Directory integrated

  This is the master (authoritative) copy of a new zone. Zone database file storage and replication will be supported through Active Directory services. The zone database file is replicated as part of Active Directory store replication. An Active Directory-integrated zone name server can only be created on a domain controller. Active Directory-integrated zones can only be created in an Active Directory domain.

- Standard primary

  This is the master (authoritative) copy of a zone database file stored as a standard text file. The database is stored on and maintained at the computer the zone was created on. You would use this option when you need to exchange DNS data with other servers that only support text-based storage.

- Standard secondary

  This is a replica of an existing zone database file, stored as a read-only text file on the system it is created on. The secondary will receive zone data from an authoritative database file.

A reverse lookup zone is considered optional but is required by some troubleshooting tools. The same zone types are supported as for forward lookup zones: Active Directory-integrated, standard primary, and standard secondary.

These are important because the type of zone (its storage method) determines how it is updated. Active Directory-integrated zones are updated as part of the Active Directory domain replication process. It is managed and controlled with the rest of Active Directory replication. When you use standard primary and secondary zones, zone updates are used to keep the databases up to date. You will have to consider traffic requirements for zone updates in your network design.

Standard DNS Database Files

If you create an Active Directory-integrated domain, the database is stored as part of the Active Directory. When you create a standard zone, the DNS database is stored as a text file. The default location and filename for the DNS database is as follows:

```
\%systemroot%\system32\dns\domain_name.dns
```

For a domain named remote.sscorp.com, this would be the following:

```
\%systemroot%\system32\dns\remote.sscorp.com.dns
```

Since this is a standard text file, it can be viewed and modified with any text editor. On a Windows 2000 Server system running the DNS service, it is suggested that you use the DNS Administrative Tool to modify a DNS database. Changes to the DNS database will be made to the authoritative database on the primary name server, identified by the SOA resource record in the DNS database. The changes are then replicated to update other DNS servers.

Dynamic DNS (DDNS)

While on the subject of DNS databases, you need to be introduced to Dynamic DNS (DDNS). DDNS supports automatic client updates to DNS database records. This keeps you from having to manually update the database every time a host is added or a host's IP address changes. By default, Windows 2000 DNS server is configured to support DDNS.

Each client will attempt to register the following two resource records:

- An A (host) record

  The A record provides the host name-to-IP address mapping.
- A PTR (pointer) record

  The pointer record references the IP address to the name mapping of the computer. This creates an integrated registration.

A client will initiate a DDNS update by first using an SOA query to locate the primary DNS server and zone authoritative. It will next send a query to verify if the registration already exists. If not, the client will send a dynamic update package to the server to create and register its record. If the update fails, the client will continue to attempt to make the update, first after a 5-minute delay, then after an additional 10 minutes, and then every 50 minutes if the registration continues to fail.

You can synchronize DNS and DHCP to verify that mapping information is properly updated in the DNS database. When DHCP assigns an IP address to a client, the client will register its A record and the DHCP server will generate the PTR record. When a lease expires, which means that a client system is no longer allowed to use an assigned IP address, the DHCP server will remove both the A and PTR records.

The traffic generated by DDNS updates should not be especially significant once your network design is up and running.

DNS Zones

The term *zone* could possibly cause some confusion. You've seen references to forward and reverse lookup zones. You will also see zones used to refer to divisions in the DNS database. These divisions are typically made to make the domain namespace more manageable. The divisions are still defined by a forward lookup zone.

Zones are logical organizations based on domain namespace. Since domain namespace isn't limited by geographic location, it is possible that the hosts in a particular zone could be spread out over a wide geographic scope.

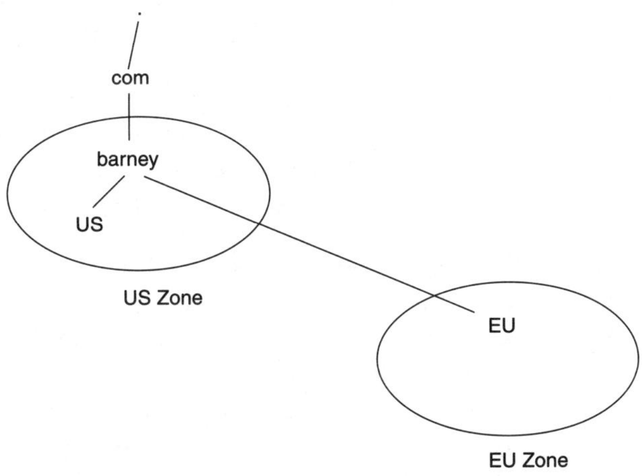

When defining zone hierarchy, the topmost zone will be the zone's root domain. Each additional zone you define will represent a contiguous namespace. The zone's DNS database will only include IP mappings for the DNS domain and any subdomains included in that zone. DNS zone information, the zone database for each zone, can be stored as either a standard text file or in the Active Directory. A DNS server must be running on a domain controller for it to be able to store DNS information in the Active Directory.

In the previous figure, a DNS domain is divided into two zones. The US Zone will contain resource records for barney.com and US.barney.com. EU.barney.com has been placed in its own zone, EU Zone. It is still a subdomain of the barney.com domain, but its resource records are stored separately in the EU Zone database.

Zone Name Servers

Each zone will have at least one name server–its primary name server. It's strongly suggested that each zone has at least two name services to provide redundancy in case of a failure. Large zones spread across large, routed networks can justify having multiple name servers. Multiple name servers provide a level of fault tolerance to your domain namespace. Multiple name servers can reduce the load requirements on any one server and can help improve performance, especially in a WAN environment. It's not uncommon to see a name server in each physical location.

Zones are logical organizations based on domain namespace. Geographically, zone hosts can be widely dispersed. If you have several hosts in one remote location, you can improve performance of name resolution and minimize traffic over the WAN link by also placing a name server in that location.

Unless you are using Active Directory-integrated zones, each zone will have one name server that contains the primary zone database file for that zone. Any additional name servers will have a copy of this master zone database, known as a secondary zone database file. When you set up an additional name server in a zone, it will receive a copy of the primary zone database file through a process known as zone transfer. Any changes made to the zone are made at the server containing the primary zone database file and will be applied later to the secondary zone database files through updates. A name server containing a secondary zone database file will periodically query the server with the primary zone database file to see if there have been any updates.

You may find it appropriate to set up caching-only name servers in some locations. As mentioned previously, a name server will cache name resolution information it receives in case it is needed again. You may find it appropriate to place caching-only servers in some locations that have limited name resolution requirements. Caching-only name servers do not keep a copy of the zone database. Instead, they make name resolution queries and cache the results.

Since a caching-only name server doesn't have a copy of the zone database, it won't be receiving periodic updates. Instead, it will be building its cache of host names and IP addresses gradually. Avoiding the traffic generated by zone transfers and opting instead to gather the information through queries may be preferable when dealing with a low-bandwidth link.

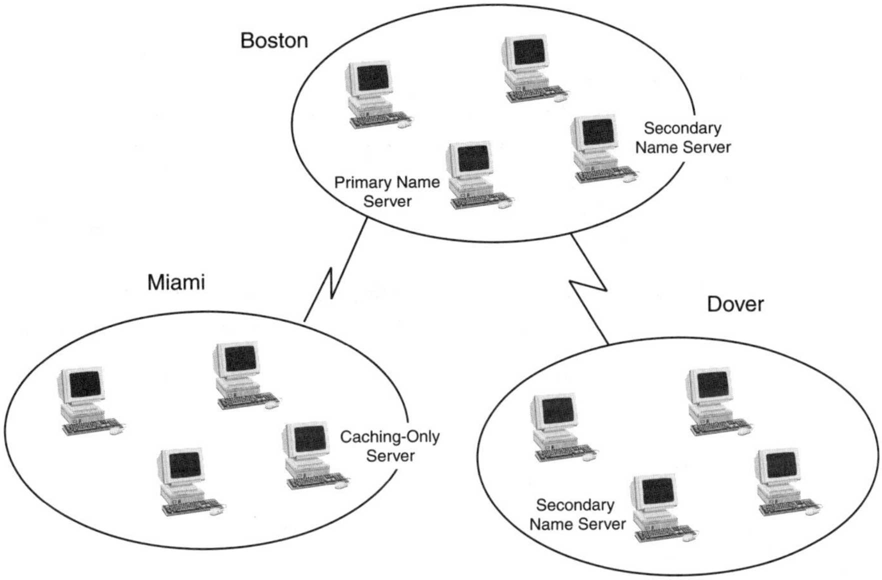

Here's a possible configuration. In the previous figure, the primary name server and a secondary name server are located in Boston. The Dover office has a large number of users and is connected to the Boston office through a high-bandwidth link. A secondary name server has been placed in the Dover office to improve accessibility and performance. The Miami office only has a few users and connects to Boston through a low-bandwidth link. A caching-only name server has been placed in Miami to keep from overloading the link with zone update traffic.

Zone Integration

When implementing Active Directory services in an existing network, you may find yourself in a situation where you want (or need) to continue to use an existing DNS server. The problem is that the server may not support SRV records, which are required for Active Directory. Also, the server may not support DDNS, which would require you to manage resource records manually.

Integrating Non-Active Directory Servers

First, you need to know which servers fall into these categories. Rather than trying to list all of the DNS servers that do not support SRV resource records and dynamic updates, it's easier to list those that do.

SRV records are supported by the following DNS servers:

- BIND 4.9.6 or later
- Windows NT 4 with Service Pack 4 or later
- Windows 2000

SRV record support is specified in the IETF Internet-Draft "A DNS RR for specifying the location of services (DNS SRV)".

Dynamic updates are supported by the following DNS servers:

- BIND 8.1.2
- Windows 2000

If you are using a non-Microsoft server that isn't on this list, then you will have to implement a workaround. How you do this depends on whether you want to:

- Use an existing zone name as your Active Directory domain name.
- Use a delegated zone name as your Active Directory domain name.

You will need to decide which of these options is the most appropriate solution, considering your needs and preferences.

Zone Replication

The process for transferring information between name servers and keeping servers synchronized depends on the type of zones supported by the name servers. Active Directory-integrated zones are supported differently than standard zones.

Active Directory-Integrated Zones

Active Directory-integrated zone updates use Active Directory replication and are based on a multiple-master model. Rather than residing on any one name server, the master copy of the DNS database is stored in the Active Directory and is replicated to all domain controllers.

There are a number of advantages to this model. The zone database can be updated by any domain controller running DNS server services. Updates from any domain controller are written to the master copy in the Active Directory and are automatically replicated to all other domain controllers. When a new zone is added to the Active Directory, it is automatically replicated to all domain controllers.

Active Directory-integrated zones also provide better overall performance and require less overhead than standard zones. You don't have to worry about managing DNS replication separately since it is managed through Active Directory replication. Network traffic is kept to a minimum because only changes are replicated between domain controllers. You also have an additional level of security available when using Active Directory-integrated zones, allowing you to specify which users and groups will be allowed to update zone and resource record properties.

Standard Zones

Zone replication, through zone transfers, is managed separately from Active Directory replication when using standard zones. Zone transfers are used for replication between the primary zone and any secondary zones and for maintaining proper synchronization between name servers. Zone transfers occur when:

- A new secondary server is added to the zone.
- The zone's refresh interval time expires.
- A notify list has been defined for the zone and changes have been made to the primary zone.

The following are the two types of zone transfers:

- Full Zone Transfer (AXFR)
- Incremental Zone Transfer (IXFR)

Let's take a closer look at each of these.

Full Zone Transfer (AXFR)

When a secondary DNS server is added to an existing zone, it is necessary to transfer a full copy of the DNS database to the new server. This is done through AXFR. Many non-Windows 2000 DNS servers also use AXFR for zone updates. In other words, the only way to update and synchronize secondary servers is by transferring a fresh copy of the full DNS database.

Incremental Zone Transfer (IXFR)

Windows 2000 DNS servers, as well as many third-party servers, also support IXFR as described in RFC 1995. When using IXFR, a secondary server is able to pull just the changes to the zone database rather than the entire database. The source server in an IXFR zone transfer can be the primary server or another secondary server. The source server was defined when the secondary zone was first defined.

Zone transfers are initiated by the destination (secondary) server. The first step in an IXFR transfer is to determine the differences between the source and destination versions of the zone database. As an aid to this, a serial number is maintained in the SOA resource record. This is updated any time a change is made to the zone database. If the SOA serial number is the same on both the source and destination, no changes have occurred and there is no need for a zone transfer.

If the source serial number is greater than the destination serial number, an IXFR transfer will occur. The source server keeps track of incremental changes, and only those changes made since the last update have to be replicated. This reduces the amount of network traffic required for zone transfers.

DNS Design

Now that you have DNS concepts out of the way, it's time to focus on integrating DNS support in your network design. You'll be looking at ways of meeting specific network requirements through different DNS design options.

Some issues that will influence your design include the following:

- Active Directory support

  If you need to support Active Directory services, you will have to use a DNS name server, such as Windows 2000 DNS services, that supports SRV resource records. Active Directory gives you the option, however, of creating Active Directory-integrated zones.

- Users and remote locations

  You need to refer to your user inventory to see how many users you need to support in each remote location. Typically, you will want to place at least one DNS server in each remote location. If a location has an especially large number of users, you may find that you need to add a second DNS server. If it has an especially small number of users, then you may want to use a caching-only server.

- Remote links

  The bandwidth between remote locations can be a concern on a very active network. There may be concerns about whether the link can support the traffic generated by zone transfers.

- Exiting DNS servers

  If you plan to leave existing DNS servers in place, you will need to know what features they support. You may find that your current servers will prevent you from implementing features such as DDNS or incremental zone transfers.

There will also be concerns about integrating DNS with other TCP/IP services. These concerns will be discussed later in this course.

Designing for Availability

There are two primary issues when discussing DNS availability. You want to make sure that:

- A DNS server is available to service queries.
- The database on the DNS server is up to date.

Let's look at some ways you can make sure that these goals are met.

Server Availability

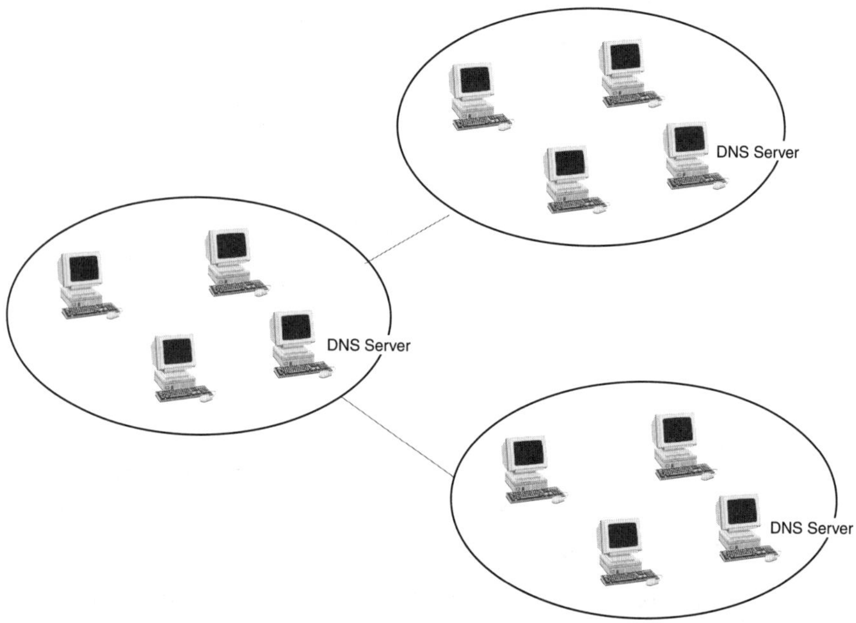

One way of designing for server availability is to place at least one DNS server in each location. This makes a DNS server readily available in each LAN. Clients in each LAN should have a local DNS server configured as their primary DNS server. Should any of your remote links fail, client queries will still be serviced by the local server. You can configure remote DNS servers as secondary DNS servers in case the local DNS server becomes unavailable. This will offer protection in case of a server failure or if a server is overloaded and cannot respond to requests.

Server Fault Tolerance

You've already seen one way of providing DNS support in case of a server failure. By setting up DNS servers in each remote location, you have redundancy built in to your design.

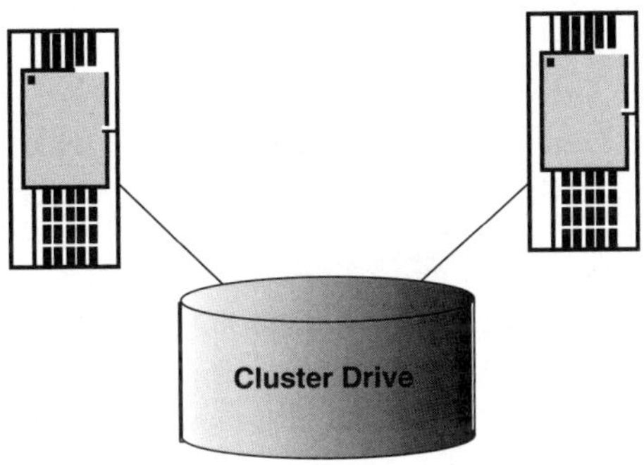

You can improve the availability of any DNS server through the use of server clustering. Server clustering is supported for Windows 2000 Advanced Server and Windows 2000 Datacenter Server. Server clustering uses two servers connected locally to a shared cluster drive. Should either server fail, the other server takes over automatically.

DNS server is supported through server clustering even though it is not a cluster-aware application. If using standard zones, you must store the DNS database(s) on the cluster drive to ensure availability.

Latency

In a very active network, there can be a concern about the latency between when an update is made to the DNS database and when that update gets sent out to the remaining name servers in the zone. The solution is the same whether using Active Directory-integrated or standard zones:

- Use incremental updates.
- Adjust the update schedule to limit latency.

Active Directory-integrated zones already use incremental updates through Active Directory replication. Standard zone name servers must be configured to use incremental zone transfers. With either, you must adjust the update schedule (or replication schedule) to limit latency. Keep in mind that increased updates can have a detrimental impact on bandwidth usage and availability.

Designing for Performance

There are two performance issues that you need to consider in your network design. You want to keep the time required to resolve a query to a minimum and you want to limit the amount of traffic generated by replication, especially across remote links.

These issues can sometimes work in direct conflict with each other. The best way of ensuring quick response to queries is to place a DNS server in every remote location. However, when you do this, you are going to increase the amount of traffic across the links due to replication.

Reducing Network Traffic

You need to compare the traffic generated by name resolution queries against the traffic generated by replication. If name resolution queries generate significantly less traffic, you can either service the request from another LAN or install a local caching-only server. A caching-only server is typically a preferred solution since it will cache the results of queries, making them locally available. On low-bandwidth links, you may find that you need to use a caching-only server because the traffic generated by zone updates overloads the link.

Another way of reducing network traffic in a hierarchical namespace is to use delegated zones. This reduces the size of the DNS database and the amount of data required for zone updates. This does require you to add more DNS servers. This solution can only be used in a hierarchical namespace since a DNS domain cannot be broken into multiple zones. However, if you have multiple subdomains, they can be placed in separate zones and will contain only the resource records applicable to their subdomain.

You can also reduce the impact, if not the volume, of network traffic through careful scheduling. You can schedule zone transfers to occur during off-peak periods, minimizing the impact on network operations. Before doing this, to avoid overloading the available bandwidth, you need to see if there are any other off-peak transmissions scheduled. You also have to make sure that the increased latency inherent in this design is acceptable.

Improving Query Response

The first step in improving query response has already been introduced: placing a DNS server in each remote location. Assuming that you've already done that and you are still having server-related performance problems in one (or more) of your domains, you still have the following options available:

- Upgrade/replace the server

  If the server doesn't have the resources necessary to meet your needs, one option is to upgrade or replace the server.

- Add more servers

  If you add more local DNS servers, you can implement load balancing. This will share the load between the DNS servers.

Be sure to watch for general network performance issues as well. If there are other complaints about network performance, there may not be any problem with your DNS server(s).

Non-Windows 2000 Integration

You were introduced to issues relating to integrating with non-Windows 2000 DNS servers earlier in this section. You can continue to use existing BIND and Windows NT DNS servers if they meet your needs. You need to be aware of the features that these DNS servers do not support. Support concerns include the following:

- Active Directory-integrated zones

  BIND and Windows NT DNS servers do not support Active Directory-integrated zones.

- SRV resource records

  SRV resource record support is required for implementing Active Directory services. Windows NT servers do not support SRV resource records. BIND versions earlier than 4.9.6 do not support SRV resource records.

- Dynamic DNS (dynamic updates)

  Windows NT DNS servers do not support dynamic updates. BIND versions earlier than 8.1.2 do not support dynamic updates.
- Unicode character support

  Windows NT and BIND DNS servers do not support Unicode characters. They only support RFC-compliant ANSI characters. To support zone transfers, you will have to restrict Windows 2000 DNS servers to RFC-compliant characters.

If your network design can operate within these restrictions, then you will be able to continue to use existing non-Windows 2000 DNS servers. If not, you may need to replace your current DNS servers.

Once you've decided that you are going to continue to use your existing DNS servers, at least for a time, you have to decide how you are going to deploy your Windows 2000 DNS servers. The method you use will depend on your eventual design goals.

Additional DNS Servers

When adding Windows 2000 DNS servers as additional name servers in an existing standard zone, they will be configured as secondary zone servers. This will have no impact on the existing namespace since you aren't making any changes to the existing DNS servers.

There is a special concern if you are going to be adding Active Directory domain support to your network. You won't be able to use the Active Directory Installation Wizard to set up your first domain controller in this situation because the wizard defaults to creating an Active Directory-integrated zone on the first domain controller. Instead, when installing the Windows 2000 Server system that will be your first domain controller, set it up as a secondary zone server in an existing zone. You will want to configure the Windows 2000 Server system to provide dynamic updates to the primary zone name server. Once you have the server set up as a secondary zone server, you can run **Dcpromo** to promote the Windows 2000 Server system.

If the primary zone name server doesn't support dynamic updates, it will have to be updated manually after promoting the Windows 2000 Server system. If the primary zone server doesn't support SRV resource records, it cannot be used to support Active Directory. However, there is another option available, which is adding a new zone.

Network Division/Expansion

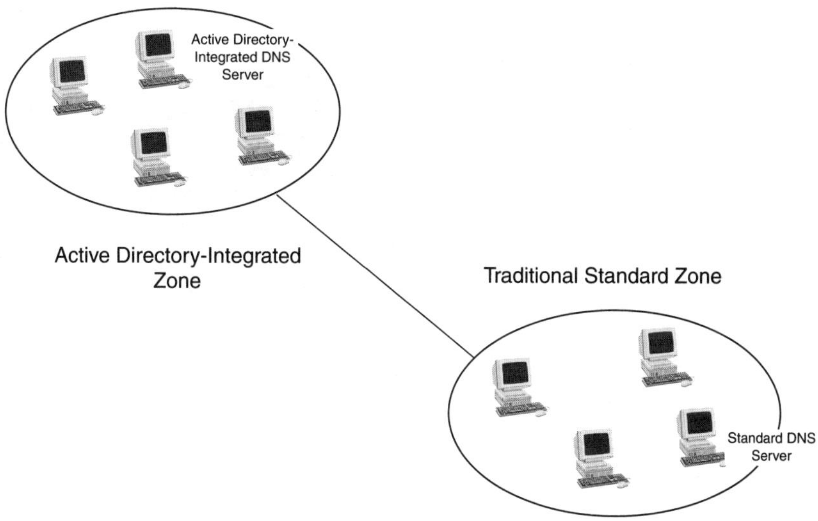

One option you can consider is creating a new zone for your Active Directory domain and leaving the old zone in place. This will have minimal impact on the existing namespace and give you the functionality that you need to support Active Directory services. The Active Directory domain namespace could be created as a subdomain of your organization's root domain.

Internet Integration

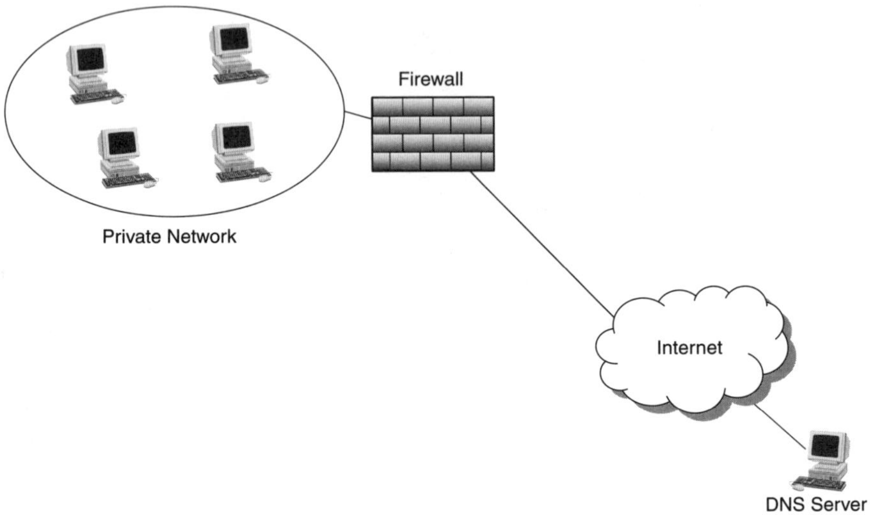

You need to address the following two issues regarding integrating your DNS solution with the Internet:

- Forwarding DNS queries to the Internet
- Responding to DNS queries from the Internet

You can configure your local DNS server to forward queries to the Internet. A common solution is to use DNS servers provided by your ISP. These DNS servers will be able to forward requests that they cannot resolve, as necessary. The other option is to go to the source yourself and forward the requests to Internet DNS servers.

Responding to requests from the Internet can be a little more complicated. If you only have a few stable resource names, you can usually have your ISP place entries for the services on a DNS server supported by your ISP.

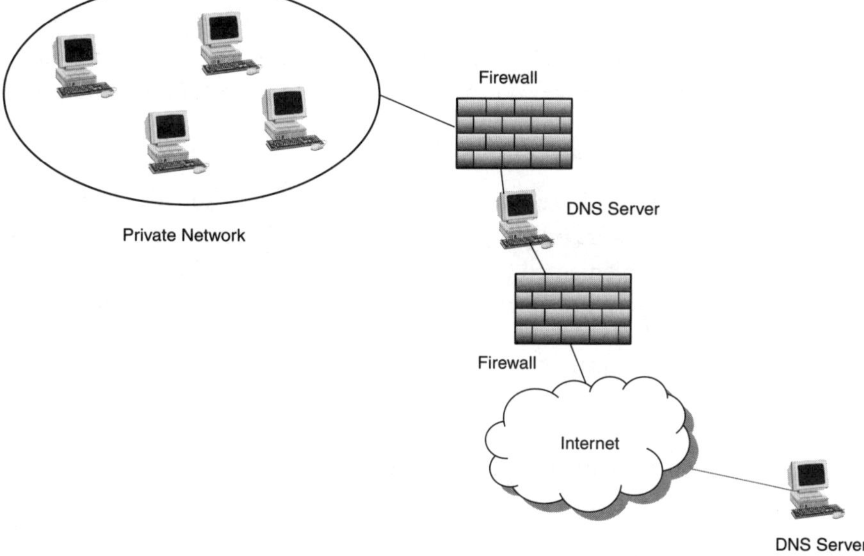

If you have a larger number of resource names that need support if resource names change frequently, or if you simply want to manage your resources yourself, you can set up a DNS server to respond to Internet requests. You will want to set this server up in a screened subnet, separate from your private network and protected from the Internet. For security reasons, you should use a secondary zone server for this purpose since it has a read-only copy of the DNS database. This will prevent Internet-based users from making updates that will be replicated through your DNS servers.

You need to place a firewall between the DNS server and the Internet to keep anyone from making unauthorized changes to the server. You are setting up a separate DNS server for this purpose because you don't want to expose your full DNS database to the Internet. This could allow persons outside of your organization to retrieve host name and IP address information about hosts inside your private network. This could lead to unauthorized access and other breaches in your security.

Designing for Security

The means of securing your DNS design will depend on whether you are designing security for a public or private network. Of course, you could end up having to design solutions for both since your network can include both public and private subnets.

Private Subnet Security

You can secure a private subnet by controlling updates made to DDNS zones. Secure, dynamic updates are only supported for Active Directory-integrated zones, so this feature can only be implemented in an Active Directory domain. This is because dynamic update security is implemented through Active Directory security.

You can assign update permissions to:

- An entire zone
- Resource records within a zone
- Users
- Computers
- Security groups

Windows 2000 clients can update resource records directly. Non-Windows 2000 clients will need to be updated through DHCP dynamic updates. On a large network, you will likely find it easier to manage update permissions through DHCP updates rather than setting permissions through users, computers, and groups.

Public Subnet Security

Public DNS updates can be a concern when you are using a public carrier for WAN links. For example, you may be using the Internet for remote links and passing zone updates across the Internet.

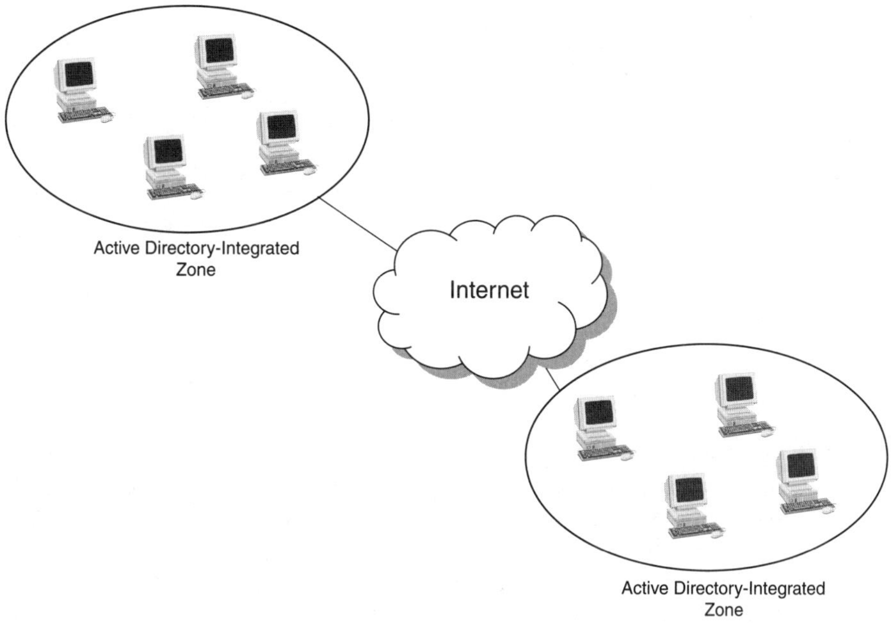

This usually isn't much of a concern when using Active Directory-integrated zones. Since the zones are updated through Active Directory replication, there are a number of security features built in to the process. All DNS servers must be registered with the Active Directory so you don't have to worry about unknown servers intercepting the updates. Updates will only be sent to other Active Directory-integrated zones that are registered with the Active Directory domain. Replication traffic is encrypted, so even if it can be intercepted, it cannot be used.

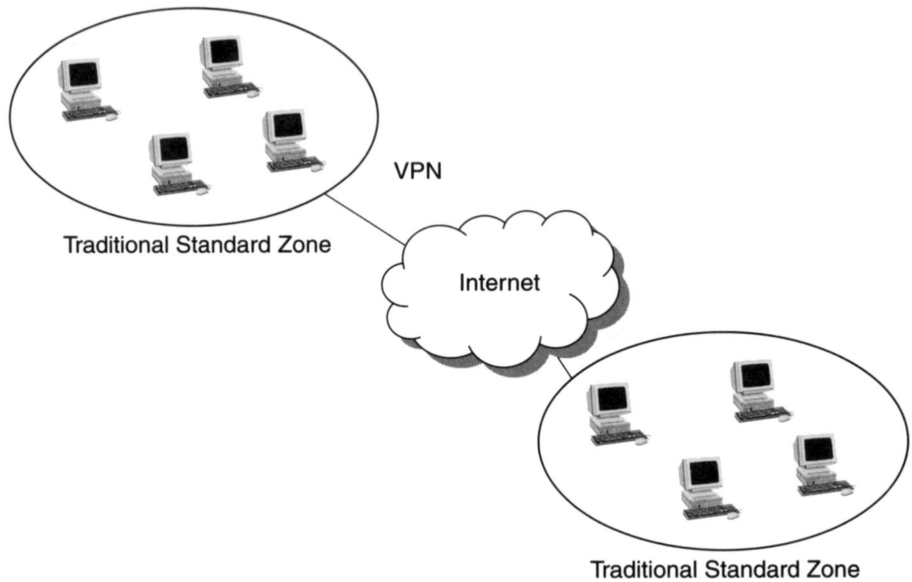

If you are using standard zones, you will want to implement added security. You will want to require authentication when establishing communications and use the highest level of encryption available. PPTP provides encryption, but only between the two endpoints of the VPN tunnel. For full end-to-end (computer-to-computer) encryption, you will want to use L2TP and IPSec.

NOTE: VPN security issues are discussed in detail later in the course.

DNS Monitoring

You have the ability to monitor and log DNS server activity. Monitoring and logging options are set at the server level through the DNS server property pages. Logging options are set through the Logging properties page. The log file is stored in the DNS folder, as follows:

```
\%systemroot%\system32\dns\dns.log
```

The following logging options are available:

Logging Option	Description
Query	All client queries will be logged.
Notify	Notification messages received by the DNS server service from other servers are logged.
Update	All dynamic updates received from other computers are logged.
Questions	The content of the question section of each DNS query message processed by the server is logged.
Answers	The content of the answer section of each query message processed by the server is logged.
Send	This selection will log the number of DNS query messages sent by the DNS server service.
Receive	This selection will log the number of DNS query messages received by the DNS server service.
UDP	This will log the number of DNS requests received through a UDP port.
TCP	This will log the number of DNS requests received through a TCP port.
Full packets	The number of full packets written and sent by the DNS server service will be logged.
Write through	This will log the number of packets written through and back to the zone by the DNS server service.

Debug logging options are disabled by default. This is because the logging process is resource intensive and can adversely affect server performance. You should enable logging on an as-needed basis and disable logging when no longer needed.

Monitoring options are also set through server properties pages. The Monitoring properties page lets you test server response to query requests. These can be run as manual tests or can run automatically on a schedule that you specify. By default, monitoring is disabled and should only be used on an as-needed basis. The traffic generated by monitoring can have an adverse impact on network performance.

Scenario 6-1: DNS Design

The purpose of this scenario is to give you practice designing DNS solutions for your case study companies. Suggested solutions are provided in Appendix B at the end of this manual. It may be helpful to review the case studies in Appendix C at the end of this manual.

Things and Stuff

1. What DNS integration concerns will you have when adding Windows 2000 DNS servers to the existing network?

   ....

   ....

2. If you decide to upgrade the network to an Active Directory domain, what type of zone would provide redundancy and the shortest delay in recovery should a DNS server fail?

   ....

   ....

3. What can you do to have resource records for the current network systems added dynamically to the DNS database?

   ....

   ....

Barney's Bank

1. You want to use multiple zones in your design. How can you configure the zones, based on the information you've been given?

2. What is your primary concern about existing DNS servers when converting to an Active Directory domain?

3. Why would you not want to use caching-only servers in the remote U.S. offices?

4. You are going to leave the DNS server in London in place. You are considering changing the links between London and the other European offices by using VPN tunnels through the Internet. What is available to you that will provide end-to-end encryption of zone updates?

Fairco Manufacturing

Low-bandwidth, high-availability links are being considered between the main office and remote warehouses. Users in the remote warehouses will seldom have a need to access remote resources. How would you provide DNS support to the remote warehouses while minimizing bandwidth requirements?

....

....

Exercise 6-1: DNS Fundamentals (Optional)

The purpose of this exercise is to introduce you to some DNS fundamentals. Complete all of the steps in this exercise on Alpha. There are no solutions provided for this exercise.

Special Preparation

There is no special preparation required for this exercise.

DNS Overview

1. Launch the **DNS** tool from the **Administrative Tools** menu.
2. Expand Alpha, then expand Forward Lookup Zones.
3. Right-click on ndclass.org and run **Properties**.
4. Select Yes from the Allow dynamic updates? drop-down list.
5. Click on **OK**.
6. Right-click on Alpha and run **Properties**.
7. Select the **Monitoring** tab to display the Monitoring properties page.
8. Place a check in the **A simple query against this DNS server** checkbox.
9. Click on **Test Now**.
10. Click on **Cancel**.
11. Exit the DNS tool.

WINS

The course now turns to the WINS service and NetBIOS name resolution. Even with the move away from NetBIOS names and NetBIOS-based applications, legacy support is likely to remain an issue in the foreseeable future. The following topics are covered in this section:

- WINS Introduction
- NetBIOS Name Resolution
- WINS Replication
- WINS Design

If you don't have any NetBIOS name resolution requirements in your network, then you won't need to include any WINS servers in your design.

WINS Introduction

WINS provides a means for resolving NetBIOS machine names to IP addresses. WINS may be required if you are supporting a mixed network that includes Windows 98 and Windows NT clients that communicate using NetBIOS names.

You may find that there is a need for WINS during early implementation of your network design. Once you've completed implementing the network changes, if you find that WINS is no longer required, support can be dropped and the system resources dedicated to meet other network needs.

Traditionally, NetBIOS names were resolved through broadcasts. Since broadcasts are not propagated by routers, that meant you could only resolve NetBIOS names for your local subnetwork. The LMHOSTS file provides a way around this. The LMHOSTS file is a text file that relates NetBIOS names to IP addresses.

WINS automates the process by allowing WINS clients to register their NetBIOS names and IP addresses with a WINS server. WINS servers also let you manually add static entries to the database. In larger networks, where multiple WINS servers are required, you can configure the WINS servers to automatically update each others' databases through replication.

WINS Clients

The following operating systems can be configured as WINS clients:

- Windows 2000
- Window NT Server and Workstation, version 3.5 or later
- Windows 95/Windows 98
- Windows for Workgroups version 3.11 with Microsoft TCP/IP-32
- MS-DOS running Microsoft Network Client version 3.0 and the real-mode TCP/IP driver
- MS-DOS running LAN Manager version 2.2c for MS-DOS

To configure a system as a WINS client, you must identify the primary WINS server. You have the option of specifying a secondary WINS server as well.

Automatic Name Registration

WINS clients will automatically register themselves at the WINS server(s) in your network. When a WINS client starts, it will send a name registration request to its primary WINS server. If the server is available and the name is not already registered by another WINS client, the WINS server will inform the client that the name was registered successfully. The name will be registered with a Time-to-Live (TTL) value, during which time the client will need to refresh its name registration if it wants to keep the name.

If a client is unable to find its primary WINS server, it will make two additional attempts. After the third failed attempt, the client will attempt to register with its secondary WINS server, if any.

If the client's name is already present in the WINS database, the WINS server will send a request to the registered machine to verify that the machine is still present on the network. Three requests will be sent. If the machine is multihomed, requests will be sent to all of the machine's IP addresses. If the name's owner responds, the client's registration request is denied. If the name's owner doesn't respond, the client will be able to register the name.

When a client registers its name, it is given a timed lease. It will be able to continue using the name during the lease period. To keep using the name beyond the lease period, the client must renew its lease. The procedures for renewing are based on the TTL value of the lease at the following times:

- At one-eighth of the TTL

  The client will attempt to contact its primary WINS server to renew its lease. If the client does not receive a response, it will continue trying every 2 minutes until it reaches the halfway point in the TTL.

- At one-half TTL

  If there is a secondary WINS server configured, the client will try to renew with that server, making an attempt at one-eighth TTL intervals. If unable to contact the secondary WINS server, the client will revert to its primary.

- After renewing the lease.

  If WINS is able to renew its lease, the client will receive a new TTL from the WINS server. Each subsequent attempt to renew the lease will be made at one half of the TTL time.

If a WINS client is shut down properly, it will send a message to the WINS server during shutdown to release its name. The WINS server will verify the client name and IP address in the release request against its database. If they match, the name is released and a response is sent to the client. If they don't match, the name will not be released.

Static Mappings

WINS clients will register themselves automatically with the WINS server. Non-WINS clients are a different matter. If you want them included in the WINS database, they have to be added manually. When you enter a static mapping, you will be prompted for the computer's NetBIOS name, NetBIOS scope, type of mapping, and IP address. NetBIOS scope is an optional field and should only be filled in if you are using NetBIOS scopes on your network.

> *NOTE: Microsoft discourages the use of NetBIOS scopes. A discussion of NetBIOS scopes is beyond the scope of this course.*

The following five type selections are available when creating a static mapping:

Mapping Type	Description
Unique	This is used for mapping a single IP address. This is the mapping you will use to map a computer name for a computer that has a single IP address.
Group	This maps the name to a group of computers, with no limit as to the number of computers you can include in the group. Group member IP addresses are not stored in the WINS database.
Domain Name	This is used for mapping a domain group of up to 25 members. If you enter more than 25 IP addresses, the oldest entries are overwritten.
Internet Group	This defines a group of up to 25 members used to identify group resources for reference and browsing.
Multihomed	This is used for mapping a multihomed computer, letting you map multiple IP addresses to one computer name. You can include up to 25 IP addresses.

The WINS server makes an effort to verify that the NetBIOS names and IP addresses entered as static mappings actually exist. Once entered, a static mapping cannot be modified. The only way to change a static mapping is to delete and re-create the record.

NetBIOS Name Resolution

You've seen how names get into the WINS database. Now let's see how name resolution requests are resolved.

Name Resolution

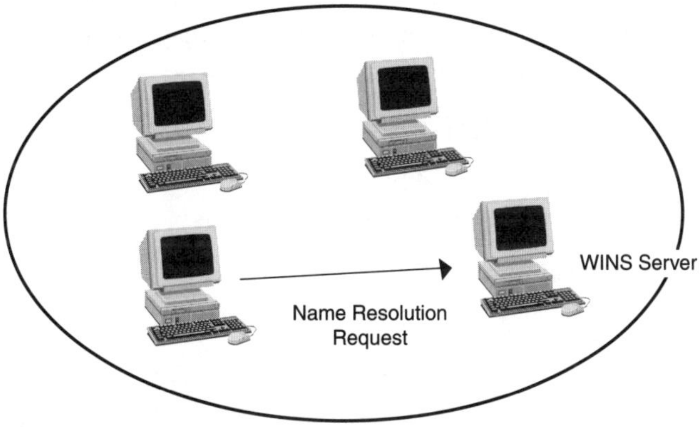

If a machine is not configured as a WINS client, the primary method for resolving names is through broadcasts. The machine will first check its local cache of resolved names, and if not found there, it will send a network broadcast to try to resolve the name. This changes when a machine is configured as a WINS client. Here are the steps that a WINS client will take for name resolution:

- The client will check its local NetBIOS name cache.

  Recently resolved names and IP addresses will be stored in the cache. If the client finds the name it needs, there is no reason for it to go any farther.

- The client will send a query request to the WINS server.

  The client will first try to resolve the name with its primary WINS server. If the primary WINS server doesn't respond after three tries, the client will try to resolve the name with the secondary WINS server (if any).

If the name is resolved by either WINS server, the IP address is returned to the client. If a WINS server cannot be contacted or if the name cannot be resolved from the WINS database, the client will receive a message that the name does not exist. At this point, the client will try using a network broadcast to resolve the name.

Since WINS name resolution requests are sent as directed messages addressed to the WINS server, they can be forwarded by routers. That means that the WINS server doesn't have to be on the same subnet as its clients. In networks where there are minimal NetBIOS name resolution requirements, you may find that your requirements can be met by a single WINS server.

You can also integrate WINS and DNS name resolution on your network, letting DNS forward requests to WINS and WINS forward requests to DNS. This will be discussed in some detail later in the chapter.

WINS Proxy Agent

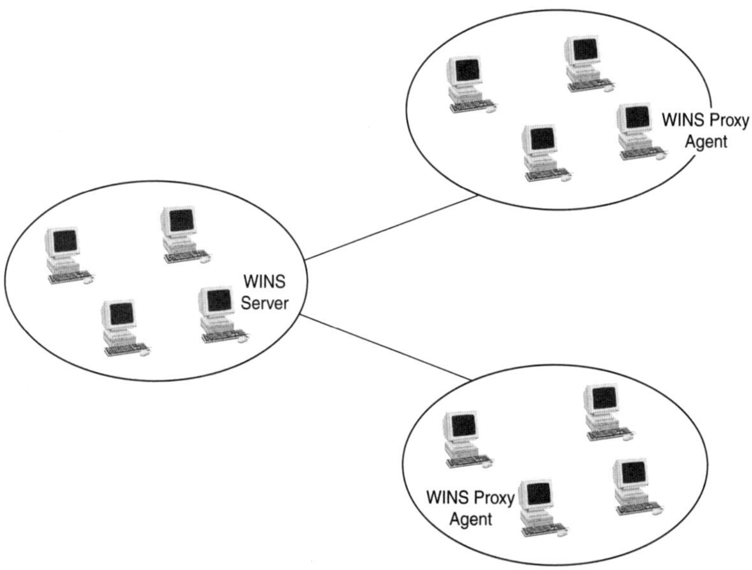

WINS Proxy Agents provide support for non-WINS clients on your network.

A WINS Proxy Agent can support the following:

- Name registration broadcasts

  The WINS Proxy Agent will forward name registration request broadcasts made by non-WINS clients to the WINS server. This is done for verification only to check that the name is not already in the WINS database. The name will not be registered by the WINS server.

- Name resolution broadcasts

  The WINS Proxy Agent will attempt to service name resolution requests from non-WINS clients. The proxy server will check the request against its internal cache and, if not in the cache, forward the request to the WINS server. If the name is found, the IP address is returned to the WINS Proxy Agent, which will then return the IP address to the requesting client.

Windows for Workgroups, Windows 95/Windows 98, Windows NT, and Windows 2000 systems can be configured as WINS Proxy Agents. A system that is already configured as a WINS server cannot be configured as a WINS Proxy Agent.

WINS Replication

WINS replication is used to let WINS servers update each other with new name registrations. This adds a level of redundancy and fault tolerance to WINS support. It also increases the amount of network traffic generated by WINS.

When designing WINS replication, you will need to balance bandwidth loading against concerns about convergence. Convergence refers to the latency in updating all WINS servers to the point where they all contain the same data.

Justifying WINS Replication

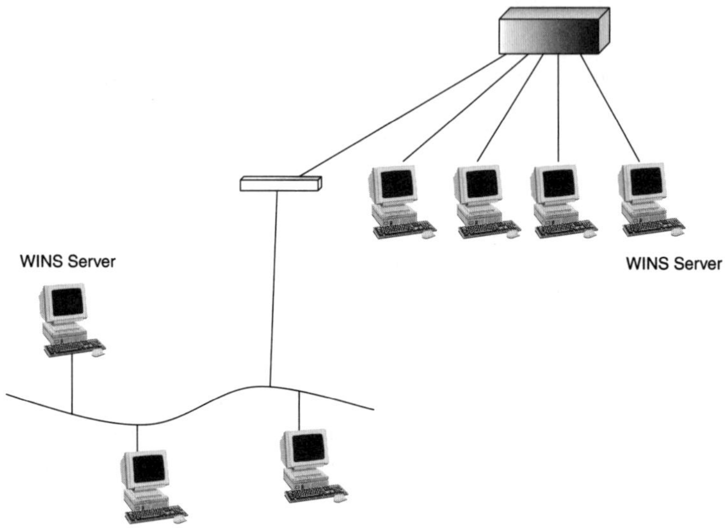

One reason for implementing WINS replication is to provide redundancy. In the previous figure, either WINS server would be able to meet the network's NetBIOS name resolution needs. Even if your name resolution requirements can be met by a single WINS server, you should consider installing a second server to provide redundancy. Updates made to either server will be added to the other, and should either server fail, you still have WINS support available.

When your network design needs multiple WINS servers, you will want to use replication to keep the WINS databases updated. Replication over low-bandwidth links can be scheduled for off-peak hours. This will ensure that the updates occur but will mean increased latency.

Replication Partners

Replication is configured through replication partners. Two types of partners are supported.

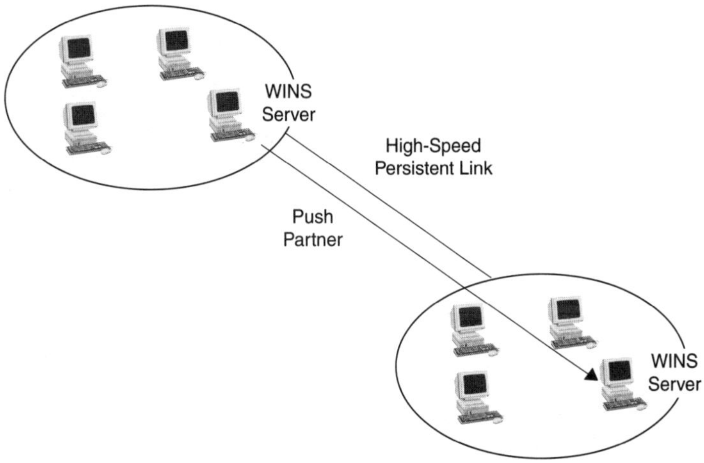

A push partner sends updates out to its replication partner. Updates occur based on a count of changes made to the WINS database at the initiating WINS server. This configuration is more commonly used with well-connected partners when you want to keep latency to a minimum.

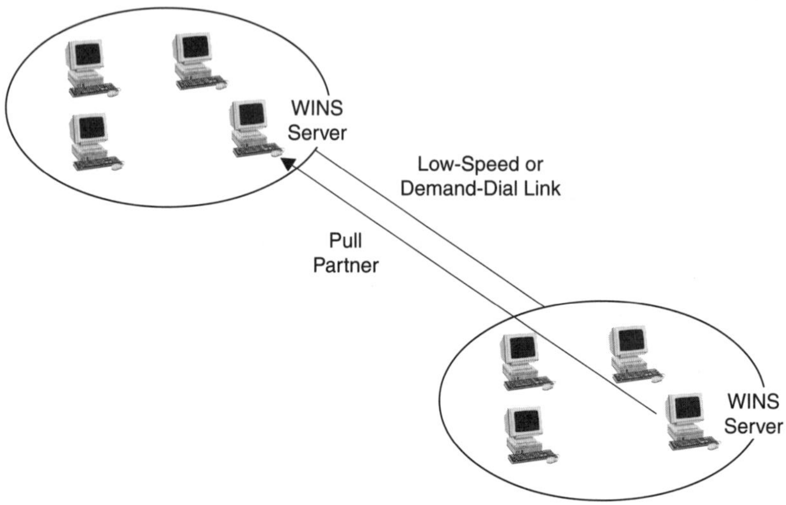

A pull partner requests updates from its replication partner. Updates occur based on an update schedule, with the requesting server polling its partners at a periodic interval. This method is commonly used when WINS servers are connected through a lower-bandwidth link so that updates can be scheduled during off-peak times.

WINS Design

You will find that the issues for developing a WINS design are much the same as those discussed for designing DNS deployment. You are going to have concerns about the following:

- Availability
- Performance
- Security
- Bandwidth usage
- Latency

There are going to be issues about the number of WINS servers that you need and their physical locations. You will have to determine how replication is going to be managed and by what schedule. You also need to consider if you need to include WINS Proxy Agents and where they should be located.

Before looking at these design issues and some suggested guidelines, there is one point that needs to be brought out. You don't necessarily need to have any WINS servers, even if you are supporting clients that need NetBIOS name resolution support.

No WINS

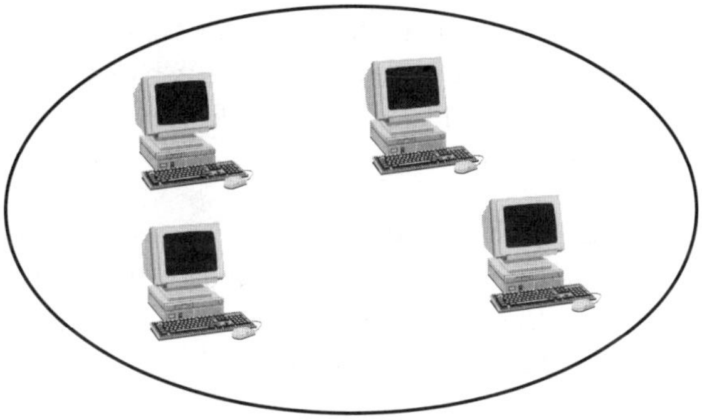

If you have a small nonrouted LAN with no remote links, there is seldom any requirement for a WINS server. Without a WINS server, a host that needs to resolve a NetBIOS name will broadcast a name request and receive an answer back from the requested host. If the requesting system doesn't get an answer back, it assumes that the host name doesn't exist. Two transmissions are required to resolve the name. With a WINS server, the requesting host will send a request to the WINS server and receive a response. If the name cannot be resolved, the requesting host will then broadcast a resolution request and wait for a reply. As you can see, having a WINS server on a nonrouted LAN can potentially increase traffic.

Design Guidelines

A single WINS server can, in theory, support thousands of WINS clients. The actual number of clients that can be supported by a WINS server will depend on the server's hardware configuration, other applications (or services) running on the server, and your network configuration.

In a smaller network, you may find that you can easily have a Windows 2000 Server configured as a combined server, acting as a WINS server while concurrently supporting other network services. In a larger network, you may find you need a dedicated WINS server, but an even better solution might be to use multiple combined servers.

When designing your WINS deployment, you will probably find that the design parallels your DNS design, though you may find that WINS will be deployed on a smaller scale. The number and placement of WINS servers will be determined by performance, availability, and redundancy requirements.

Designing for Availability

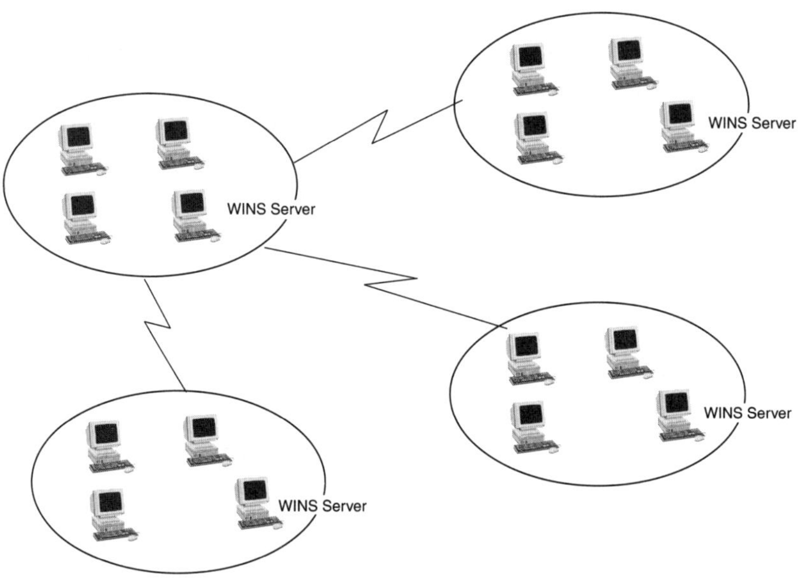

Your first reaction to optimizing availability is to place at least one WINS server in each LAN. While this does provide easy access to WINS servers, it causes a potential concern about the traffic that will be generated by WINS replication.

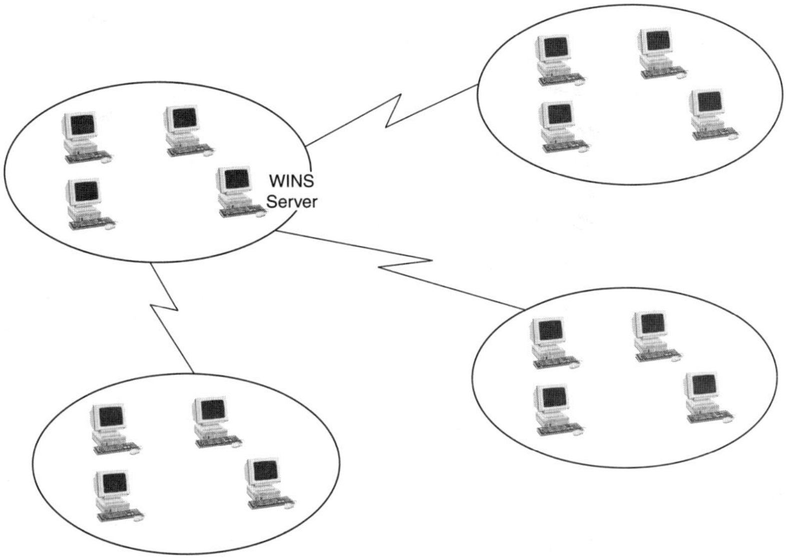

Another possibility is to place WINS servers in strategic locations rather than in all LANs. This option works well when each LAN is somewhat self-sufficient; that is, the LAN supplies most of the resources that the users need. You will need to periodically monitor the traffic generated by name resolution requests from each of the LANs to determine when (or if) placing a WINS server in the remote LAN is a better use of your resources.

Of course, if you only place WINS servers in some of your LANs, there comes the question of how to support non-WINS clients. One option, if supported by your routers, is to enable forwarding of NetBIOS broadcasts. This is usually not an acceptable option due to the increased traffic this can generate, impacting both LAN and remote link performance. If you have a small number of non-WINS clients, you may consider use of the LMHOSTS file to resolve NetBIOS names for hosts that aren't part of the local network. Unfortunately, this method gets progressively harder to manage as your network grows.

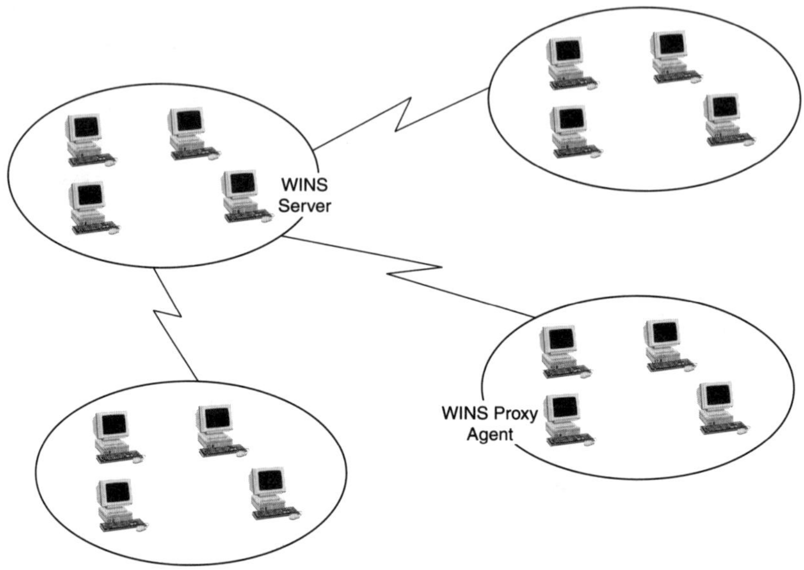

You should consider a WINS Proxy Agent as a potential solution to this problem. In most cases, a single WINS Proxy Agent in each routed segment will be sufficient to meet name resolution requirements. If you do include multiple WINS Proxy Agents, you need to be aware that all proxy agents in a subnet will respond to NetBIOS name resolution broadcasts and will all send a resolution request to the WINS server. The added traffic requirements must be considered in your network design.

If you are concerned about the continued availability of a specific WINS server, you can provide fault tolerance through server clustering. This works the same as when implementing DNS server services on a server cluster. Should either server fail, the remaining server will handle name resolution requests. However, it is unlikely that you will find a need to use server clustering as part of your WINS design solution.

Designing for Performance

You need to consider three performance factors in your WINS design. You want to minimize the response delay for name resolution, minimize convergence, and minimize network traffic. Unfortunately, these three goals can come in direct conflict with each other. For example, minimizing convergence means minimizing the period between replication updates. The more often updates are replicated, the more traffic you generate.

Optimizing Name Resolution

You will get the best performance on name resolution from well-connected WINS servers. In short, that means placing a WINS server in each LAN. As described earlier, that may not be the most practical solution for your network design, and you may need to come to a comfortable compromise.

The performance issues for any individual WINS server are much the same as for any other network service provider. If the server is not meeting performance expectations, you can use the Windows 2000 System Monitor to determine the cause of the bottleneck and respond appropriately. If you cannot upgrade the server to improve performance, then you need to consider either replacing the server or adding more local WINS servers.

Minimizing Convergence

You minimize convergence by minimizing update latency. In other words, you have to replicate changes more frequently. When this is a primary concern, you can often minimize convergence by configuring WINS servers as push/pull partners. That will cause replication to be initiated when the count reaches the change threshold on any server and on a set periodic schedule.

Minimizing Traffic

You will need to monitor network activity to determine whether more traffic is being generated from name resolution requests or from WINS replication traffic. If more traffic is generated through name resolution, increase the number of WINS servers, placing at least one server in each LAN. If the majority of the traffic is from replication, you can reduce the number of WINS servers and have one WINS server support multiple LANs. You can also lessen the impact of replication traffic by using pull partners and scheduling replication for off-peak periods.

Another way of minimizing traffic requirements is to increase the TTL for name registrations. By default, this value is set to six days. Increasing this value means that clients need to register with a WINS server less often.

Burst Handling

Windows 2000 WINS servers include a feature called burst handling. Burst handling is also supported on Windows NT 4.0 Server systems with Service Pack 3 or later applied. A burst is when a large number of WINS clients attempts name registration at the same time. For example, you could see a burst when everyone comes in on Monday morning and starts their systems. High traffic levels of this type could end up overloading a server and keeping it from responding to name registration requests. This will cause the client to retry, generating even more name registration. Needless to say, this can result in a significant performance hit on a WINS server.

Burst handling allows the WINS server to respond with a positive reply even though a client's name and IP address information have not yet been written to the WINS database. Burst handling is initiated when the server's burst queue reaches a configured value. By default, this limit is set to 300 registration requests. The responses will be associated with relatively short TTL values ranging from 5 to 50 minutes. TTL values are varied between clients, spreading out the registration traffic.

Replication Design

You will need to give some thought to how you want to configure WINS replication when supporting multiple WINS servers. You've already been told about push and pull replication partners, which are used to determine which server is responsible for initiating updates. However, WINS replication design must address the issue of data flow during replication.

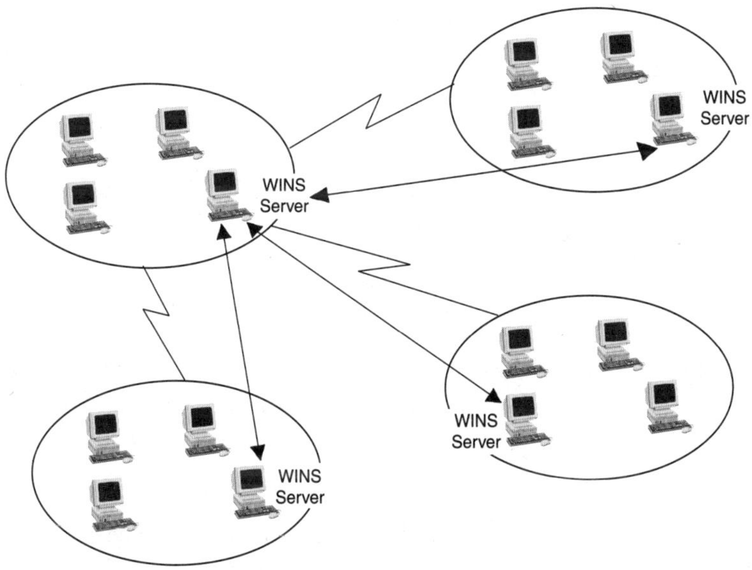

One method is to use one WINS server as a *master* server. Updates come in to the master server from the *spoke* servers. The updates are then passed out from the master to the spokes.

One of the advantages of this design is that it is easy to set up different replication schedules for each of the WINS servers. You can use a mix of both push and pull partners, selecting the best match for each link.

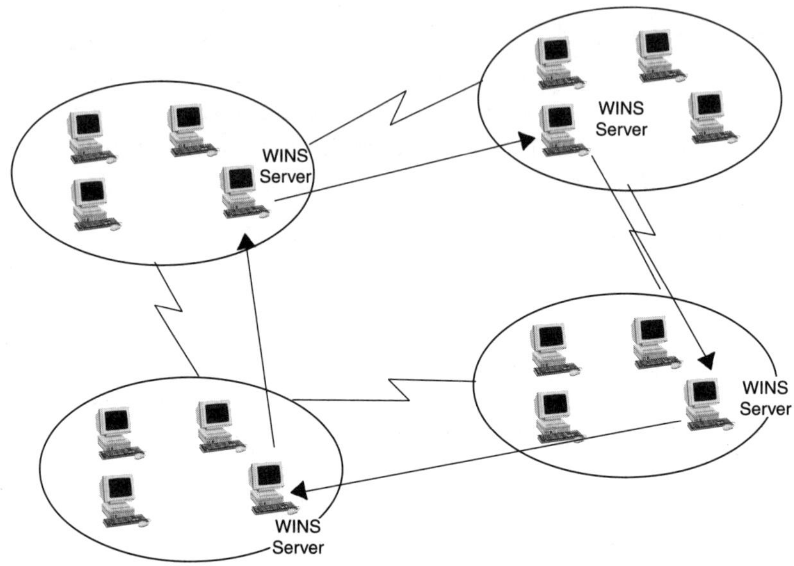

Another common method is to use round-robin updates. This follows a model similar to a Token-Ring network. Updates are passed from one WINS server to the next, with each adding its own updates along the way. The update cycle loops back around itself to the originating system.

You will want to exercise some caution in how update schedules are set. This is often easiest to manage with pull updates timed to occur sequentially.

As shown in the following figure, WINS servers can be connected in a mesh configuration, with each server updating every other server. This configuration is seldom used because it can be difficult to set up and maintain. It can also result in higher levels of traffic, especially if you aren't using a mesh routing design.

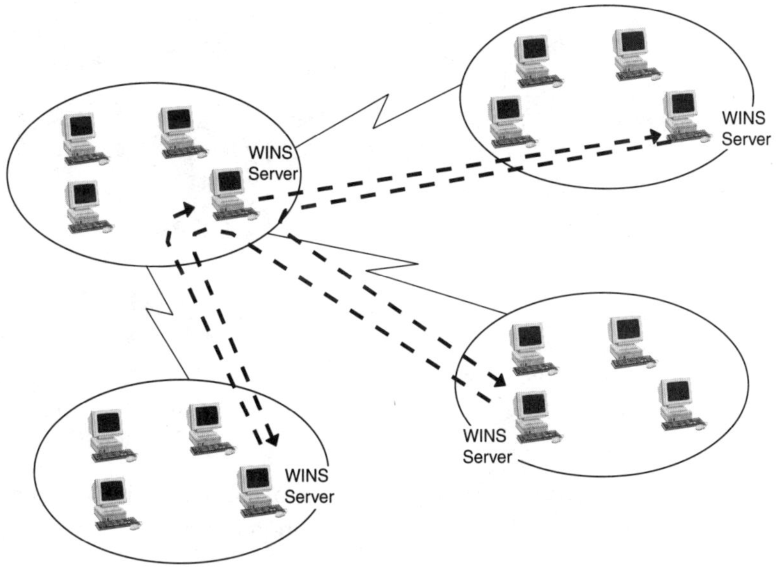

Your replication design doesn't have to duplicate your LAN or WAN routing model. For example, you can have your WAN configured around a central LAN operating as a hub and still use round-robin updates. When you do this, however, each update will have to pass through the hub LAN, increasing network traffic across remote links. In most cases, you can keep traffic to a minimum by having your replication design based on your routing design.

Designing for Security

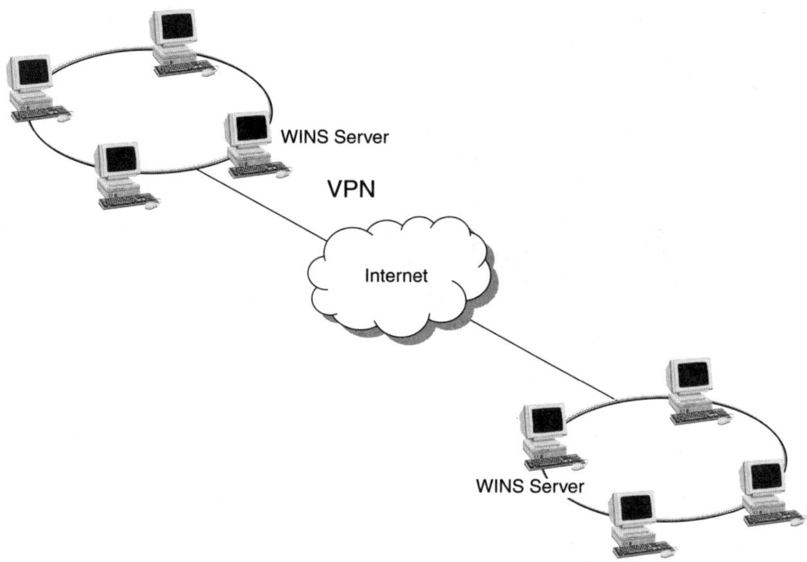

You have the same potential security concerns during replication as during DNS zone updates. You have to worry about interception of traffic across a public carrier like the Internet. The same solution also applies.

You will want to require authentication when establishing communications and use the highest level of encryption available. PPTP provides encryption, but only between the two endpoints of the VPN tunnel. For full end-to-end (computer-to-computer) encryption, you will want to use L2TP and IPSec.

Monitoring WINS

Monitoring network traffic and WINS server performance have been addressed at different times during this section. A quick review will be helpful to remind you of your potential periodic review requirements.

- Network traffic

  You are watching for two types of traffic, name resolution traffic and WINS replication traffic. The best solution usually means finding an acceptable compromise between the two.

- Server performance

  As with any network service provider, you will want to periodically monitor WINS servers to make sure that the servers themselves aren't becoming a bottleneck to performance.

These are the same issues that you saw with DNS servers. As with DNS servers, you may find it helpful to augment periodic monitoring with use of alerts to watch critical performance areas.

The WINS Administrative Tool can display WINS server statistics, including information such as the number of registrations, number of queries, success and failure information, and so forth. You can also directly query the WINS database to see if a NetBIOS name is present.

Scenario 6-2: WINS Design

The purpose of this scenario is to give you practice in resolving WINS design issues. Suggested solutions are provided in Appendix B at the end of the manual. You should review the case studies in Appendix C before starting this scenario.

Things and Stuff

1. After TCP/IP support has been added to the network, what is the minimum number of WINS servers that will be required to meet NetBIOS name resolution requirements?

   ....

   ....

2. Assuming that WINS support is deployed in this network, which of the current network systems can be configured as WINS clients and will be able to register their NetBIOS names and IP addresses?

   ....

   ....

Barney's Bank

1. You've been directed to deploy no more than two WINS servers. You want to keep name resolution and WINS replication to a minimum. Where will you place the WINS servers?

   ....

   ....

2. What change will need to be made to remote U.S. office links to improve availability?

   ....

   ....

Exercise 6-2: WINS Introduction (Optional)

The purpose of this exercise is to give you a brief introduction to WINS. Complete all of the steps in this exercise on Alpha. There are no solutions provided for this exercise.

Special Preparation

There is no special preparation required to complete this exercise. You will need to have a copy of the Windows 2000 Server Installation CD-ROM or access to the Windows 2000 installation files to complete this exercise.

WINS Installation

During this portion of the exercise, you will be installing WINS.

1. Open the Control Panel and launch Add/Remove Programs.
2. Click on **Add/Remove Windows Components**.
3. Select Networking Services and click on **Details**.
4. Place a check in the **Windows Internet Name Service (WINS)** checkbox and click on **OK**.
5. Click on **Next**. You may be prompted for the Windows 2000 Installation CD-ROM during the file copy.
6. Click on **Finish**.
7. Exit Add/Remove Programs and exit the Control Panel.

WINS Overview

This portion of the exercise introduces you to the WINS Administrative Tool.

8. Launch the **WINS** tool from the **Administrative Tools** menu.
9. Right-click on Alpha and run **Properties**.
10. Click on the **Intervals** tab. This is where the TTL and associated values for name registration are set.

11. Click on the **Advanced** tab. This is where burst handling is configured.
12. Click on **Cancel**.
13. Exit the DNS tool.

DHCP

The discussion now moves on to DHCP. DHCP can significantly reduce the amount of time spent in managing IP addresses. The following topics are covered in this section:

- DHCP Introduction
- DHCP Management
- DHCP Design

For all but the smallest networks, you are likely to find a place for DHCP in your network design.

DHCP Introduction

DHCP gives you a way of minimizing your IP address management by automatically assigning IP addresses to clients as they start. In addition to providing the client with an IP address and subnet mask, the DHCP server can also configure additional optional values such as the default gateway, DNS server address, and WINS server address.

Client systems lease addresses from the DHCP server for a specified period of time and are given the option of renewing the address lease. A Windows-based DHCP client will request a DHCP lease:

- When TCP/IP is initialized for the first time on a DHCP client.
- When a DHCP client requests a specific IP address and is declined.
- When a DHCP client has released its IP address and needs a new address.

If a computer is configured with multiple network adapters, it will be necessary for each adapter to request a separate DHCP lease. The leases are assigned individually by adapter.

BootP clients can request and receive IP addresses from DHCP servers. However, BootP clients do not recognize IP lease periods. Some systems will require static IP addresses and cannot be configured as DHCP clients. These include DHCP servers, DNS servers, and WINS servers.

IP Address Assignment

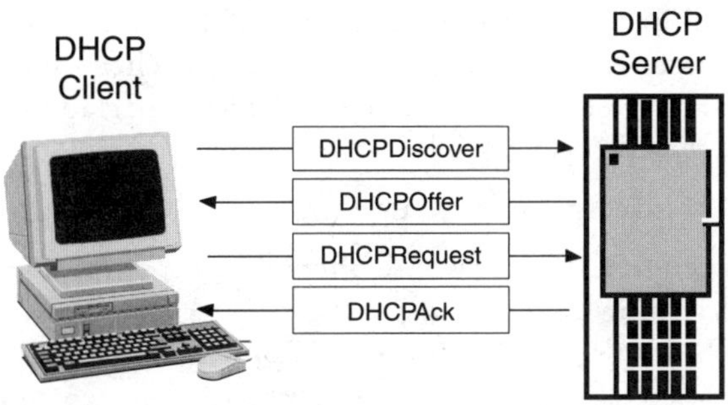

DHCP assignment is a four-step process:

- Client request

  The client broadcasts a DHCPDiscover message. This requests the location of a DHCP server and requests an IP address assignment. The message includes the computer's name and hardware (MAC) address. The client will use 0.0.0.0 as its source address for the broadcast and 255.255.255.255 as the destination.

- Server offer

  Any DHCP server that receives the request and has a valid IP address available for assignment will respond with a DHCPOffer message. The message will contain the following:

  - Client hardware address
  - IP address and subnet mask
  - Lease period
  - DHCP server IP address

  The response is sent as a broadcast. The server will reserve the address until the client either accepts or rejects the offer.

- Client acceptance

  The next step is for the client to accept the IP address. If the client receives multiple offers (from different DHCP servers), the client will accept the first offer it receives. After accepting an offer, the client responds by broadcasting a DHCPRequest message that includes the IP address of the server whose offer was accepted.

- Server acceptance/rejection

  The DHCP server whose offer was accepted will broadcast a DHCPAck message as acknowledgment to the client. The message will include a valid lease for the IP address. It may also contain option configuration settings for the client.

If the lease process is unsuccessful, the DHCP server will broadcast a DHCPNAck message. This can happen if a client has moved to a different subnetwork or if the client is trying to lease a specific IP address that is no longer available.

It is common for a Windows DHCP client to attempt to lease a specific IP address. By default, a DHCP client does not release its lease when it is shut down. When an existing DHCP client starts, it will attempt to lease the last IP address again from the DHCP server that originally offered the address. The client will make this attempt even if there is time remaining on its lease.

> *NOTE:* *You have the option of having DHCP force clients to release assigned IP addresses during shutdown.*

Address Renewal

A client will attempt to renew its IP address lease before the lease period expires. At 50% of the lease time, the client will issue a DHCPRequest message sent directly to the DHCP server the address is leased from. If the server is available, it will respond with a DHCPAck message, renewing the lease and providing any updated configuration options.

If the client cannot contact the original DHCP server, it will broadcast DHCPRequest at 87.5% of the lease time. This is broadcast in an attempt to reach any DHCP server. Any server can respond with a DHCPAck message to renew or a DHCPNAck message to deny renewal. If the client receives a DHCPNAck or if the lease period expires, the client will start the lease process over from the beginning.

You can use the **Ipconfig** command to force release and renewal of a client's lease. To release a lease, run the following:

```
ipconfig /release
```

The client will send a DHCPRelease message to the server, which will release its lease and make its IP address available for assignment.

To initiate the lease process used to receive or renew a lease, run the following:

```
ipconfig /renew
```

Multicast IP Addresses

Though not a focus of this course, you should be aware that the Windows 2000 DHCP service also supports the Multicast Address Dynamic Client Allocation Protocol (MADCAP). MADCAP is used to support address assignment for multicast clients, allowing them to join multicast groups.

DHCP Management

Before the discussion can move on to DHCP design, you need to be introduced to a few key points about DHCP management. After installing DHCP, you have to configure the server before it is ready for use. This includes:

- Creating a DHCP scope

  A scope defines the IP addresses that the server has available for assignment. A DHCP server can support multiple scopes.
- Setting DHCP options

  Along with assigning IP addresses, a DHCP server can set selected client options.
- Authorizing the DHCP server

  This is required for DHCP servers used in an Active Directory domain. Before a DHCP server can assign IP addresses, it must be authorized in Active Directory services.

You also have the option of setting up reserved addresses for specific clients. This will cause the client to always receive the same IP address.

Scope Overview

Scopes are used to define the IP address range and client configuration options provided for a subnet.

Address Range

Each scope will have a name and be defined by the following:

- Starting IP address
- Ending IP address
- Subnet mask

The subnet mask can be entered by length (the number of 1s in the subnet mask) or by entering the subnet mask octets. For example, a subnet mask of 255.255.255.0 could also be expressed as a length value of 24.

You can also define any addresses to be excluded from the scope. If there are any addresses within the scope limits that have been assigned as static addresses, they must be excluded from the scope to avoid having duplicate IP addresses in the subnetwork. For example, you would need to exclude addresses assigned to domain controllers, DNS servers, WINS servers, DHCP servers, and so forth.

Lease Period

The lease duration is also defined by scope. The lease duration defaults to 8 days. You can modify the lease duration to fit your specific needs. If you have a network that includes a large number of mobile or dial-in clients, then you will probably want to use a shorter lease duration to make sure you have addresses available for assignment when you need them. In a relatively stable network, you can increase the lease period.

Client Options

As mentioned previously during the course, you can define client options to be assigned through DHCP. Commonly specified options include the following:

Option	Description
Router	This option is used to specify the client gateways (routers). One or more routers may be specified and are identified by IP address. If only one router is specified, it will be the default gateway. If multiple routers are included, the first router will be the default gateway.
DNS Servers	You can specify one or more DNS servers by IP address. The first DNS server listed will be the primary DNS server.
DNS Domain Name	This lets you enter the domain name to be used for client host name resolution.
WINS/NBNS Servers	Use this option to identify the WINS servers that clients in the subnet managed by this scope should use. The first WINS server listed will be the primary WINS server.
WINS/NBT Node Type	This specifies the NetBIOS name resolution method to be used by the client.

Locally configured options take precedence over those supplied through DHCP. That means, for example, if a WINS server has been specified locally on a client, the WINS server value provided by the DHCP server will be ignored.

Once a scope is defined, it must be activated. Until it is activated, the scope cannot be used to make IP address assignments. DHCP servers deploying in an Active Directory domain must also be authorized to provide IP addresses to the domain.

Reservations

You can reserve an address to make sure that a DHCP client will always receive the same address. When defining a reservation, you must supply the reservation name, IP address to be assigned, and the client's MAC (hardware) address. Reservations are supported for DHCP and BootP clients.

Multiple Scopes

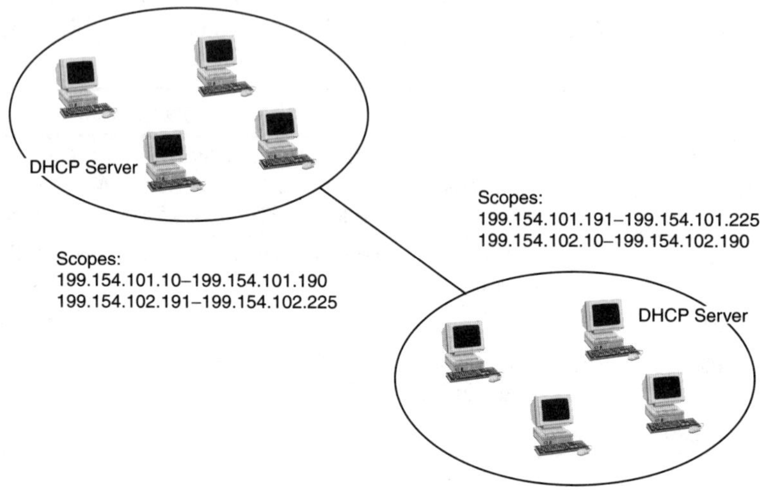

A DHCP server can support multiple scopes. This gives you the ability to support multiple subnets from a single DHCP server. However, any router between the DHCP server and the subnets it supports must be configured as a DHCP Relay Agent (to support BootP routing). This is done so that the router will forward the client's DHCPDiscover packet. The router will embed its IP address in the DHCPDiscover packet. This is used to identify the source subnet so that DHCP servers can see if they support a scope for that subnet.

DHCP Authorization

Authorization is required for DHCP servers that will be used in Active Directory domains. This is done to prevent rogue DHCP servers, a term for unauthorized DCHP servers, from joining the network and providing IP addresses to DHCP clients.

When the DHCP service starts on a DHCP server that is part of an Active Directory domain, the Active Directory is queried to see if it is an authorized server. If not, the DHCP service will be shut down on that server.

DHCP Design

As you have seen in this section, there are a number of factors that must be taken into consideration in your DHCP design. Your design will be influenced by whether you have a routed or nonrouted LAN environment, your routing and remote connection configuration, and client support requirements.

Using Multiple DHCP Servers

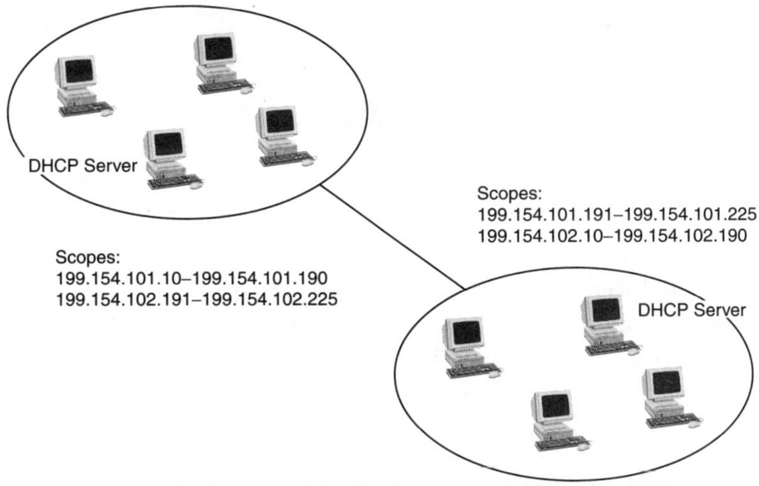

You may find that you want to use multiple DHCP servers to improve availability and reduce traffic across links. There is an added advantage in that you can add a level of fault tolerance to your design at the same time.

As mentioned previously, a DHCP server can have multiple scopes. As part of your design, you can define scopes on different DHCP servers for the same subnet. Should one DHCP server be unavailable, the other would be able to service IP address requests.

When setting up multiple DHCP servers, you must be careful that the scopes you define on each server do not overlap. Each server must be configured with remote IP addresses. The general rule of thumb is to place 75% of the available addresses on the server that will act as the primary DHCP server for the subnet. Place the remaining 25% of available addresses on the other DHCP server.

Nonrouted Network Design

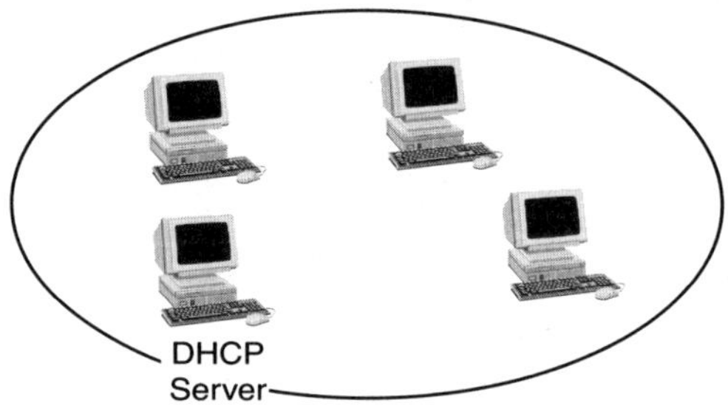

DHCP design for a nonrouted network is relatively easy. You only have one set of IP addresses and, therefore, only one scope you need to be concerned about. You don't have to worry about supporting DHCP traffic through routers since there are no routers in the network.

You may find, however, that you want to include a second DHCP server in your design. You would do this if the user service requirements are more than can be supported by a single server or if you wanted to provide fault tolerance in case of a DHCP server failure.

Routed Network Design

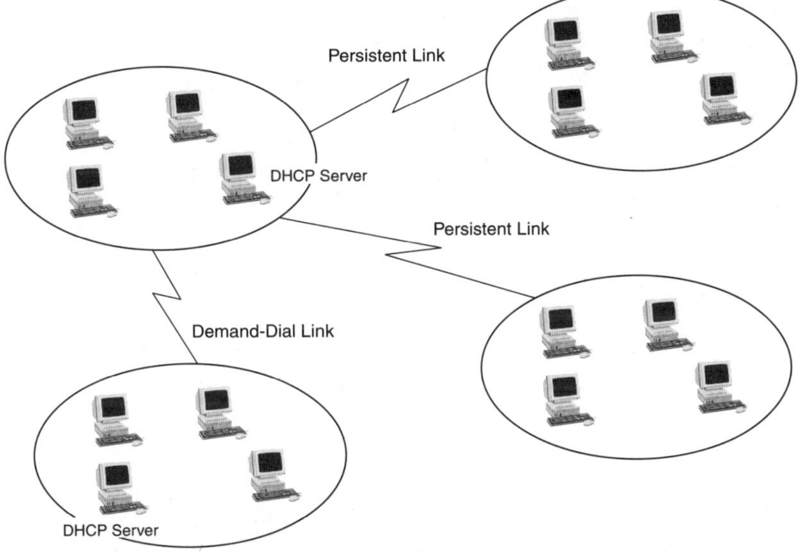

A routed network design can be a little more challenging. You are going to need to refer to your user inventory so that you understand user distribution within the network. You will need to determine how many DHCP servers you need and where they are going to be placed. This decision is going to be influenced by the type of links between LANs in a WAN environment. Limit DHCP traffic to high-speed persistent links only. You will want to provide a local DHCP server even if a LAN has a relatively small number of users to avoid overloading slower links with DHCP traffic or when a LAN is connected by demand-dial routing links.

Don't forget that there is also a potential concern with routers. If a client needs to communicate with a DHCP server that is not located in its local subnet in order to get an IP address assignment, each router in the path must be configured to support the DHCP Relay Agent.

Designing for Availability

Many of the issues relating to availability have already been discussed during this section. To ensure availability, you should only have DHCP servers supporting multiple subnets only if connected to the subnets through high-speed persistent connections. Otherwise, you need to place a DHCP server in each of the subnets.

Fault tolerance is provided through distributed scopes, placing scopes for the subnet on two or more DHCP servers. You can provide fault tolerance for any DHCP server through server clustering, the same as for DNS and WINS servers. You may want to consider this option when supporting multiple subnets from a single DHCP server.

Designing for Performance

Several performance issues have already been addressed during this section. Let's take a moment to quickly look at a few of these as a review.

- Address lease period

  You want to set the lease period to match your system requirements. Use longer lease periods in a stable network to reduce traffic and the load on your DHCP servers. Use shorter lease periods when supporting mobile users to free up addresses more quickly.

- Local DHCP servers

  You can improve performance by keeping DHCP servers local to their clients.

- Server response time

  Server performance can become an issue with DHCP, the same as it can with any other network service. You can use System Monitor for periodic checks and define alerts for critical components.

When supporting multiple subnets from one DHCP server, you will also want to periodically monitor network performance to make sure that you aren't overloading any of the links.

Designing for Security

You can secure your DHCP design if implemented in an Active Directory domain. DHCP servers must be authorized before they are recognized by the Active Directory. If a server isn't authorized, the server won't be able to start the DHCP service. There are also periodic checks made of running DHCP servers. If a server is removed from the authorized server list, the DHCP service will be shut down. These checks only apply to Windows 2000 DHCP servers. Other DHCP servers, such as Windows NT DHCP servers, will start whether they are authorized or not.

When a network design for an Active Directory domain includes multiple DHCP servers, the first DHCP server must be installed on a domain controller or a Windows 2000 member server. You will also need to configure any routers between DHCP servers as DHCP Relay Agents to allow the DHCP servers to communicate.

You can also control DHCP server management in an Active Directory environment. You can allow or deny access permissions to users or groups to keep unauthorized users from making changes to DHCP server configurations.

Scenario 6-3: DHCP Design

The purpose of this scenario is to give you practice designing a DNS solution. Suggested solutions are provided in Appendix B at the end of this manual. It may be helpful to review the case studies in Appendix C at the end of this manual.

Barney's Bank

1. You are planning to use one DHCP server to support the London and the remote European offices. How must routers be configured to support this solution?

   ....

   ....

2. Given the current network configuration, what is the minimum number of DHCP servers that will be required to support the three subnets in Corpus Christi?

....

....

3. Given the current network configuration, what is the minimum number of DHCP servers that will be required to support all of the U.S. offices?

....

....

Fairco Manufacturing

1. You've decided to convert the network to an Active Directory domain. The first network change you have planned is to install a Windows NT 4.0 Server system that will be supporting WINS and DHCP during the conversion. What changes will you have to make to the DHCP server after installing Active Directory services to allow the DHCP server to continue providing IP address assignments?

....

....

2. You are going to be adding persistent links to the remote warehouse sites. Each remote warehouse is configuerd as a separate subnet. Assuming two to three systems at each remote warehouse, how would you manage IP addresses to minimize management overhead and network traffic?

....

....

Exercise 6-3: Implementing DHCP (Optional)

The purpose of this exercise is to give you practice implementing DHCP. There are no solutions provided for this exercise.

Special Requirements

There are no special requirements for this exercise.

DHCP Installation

During this portion of the exercise, you will be installing the DHCP server on Alpha.

1. Open the Control Panel and launch the Add/Remove Programs utility.
2. Click on **Add/Remove Windows Components**.
3. Click to select Network Services, then click on **Details**.
4. Place a check in the **Dynamic Host Configuration Protocol** (DHCP) checkbox and click on **OK**.
5. Click on **Next**. You may be prompted for the Windows 2000 Server Installation CD-ROM during the file copy.
6. Click on **Finish**.
7. Exit Add/Remove Programs and close the Control Panel.

DHCP Configuration

During this portion of the exercise, you will configure a scope for the DHCP service running on Alpha and prepare the DHCP server for use in an Active Directory domain.

8. Launch the **DHCP** tool from the **Administrative Tools** menu.
9. Right-click on your server and run **New Scope**.
10. Click on **Next**.
11. Type the following in the Name field and click on **Next**:

```
Members
```

12. Type the following as the Start IP address:

```
192.168.105.200
```

13. Type the following as the End IP address:

```
192.168.105.250
```

14. Click on **Next.**
15. Click on **Next.**
16. Change the lease duration to 4 days and click on **Next.**
17. Select **No, I will configure these options later** and click on **Next.**
18. Click on **Finish.**
19. Right-click on your scope and run **Activate.**
20. Right-click on your server name and run **Authorize.**
21. Exit the DHCP tool.

Client Configuration

During this portion of the exercise, you will configure your remaining servers and DHCP clients. Complete the following steps on both Beta and Gamma.

22. Open Network and Dial-up Connections.
23. Right-click on Local Area Connection and run **Properties.**
24. Select Internet Protocol (TCP/IP), then click on **Properties.**
25. Click to select **Obtain an IP address automatically**, then click on **OK.**
26. Click on **OK.**
27. Exit Network and Dial-up Connections.
28. Open a command prompt and run the following:

```
ipconfig
```

The system should now have an IP address from the configured scope.

SERVICE INTEGRATION

This section ties up a few loose ends relating to network service support. The following topics are covered in this section:

- Integrating Network Services
- Combining Network Services

Some of the information presented in this section was introduced earlier in the chapter.

Integrating Network Services

This discussion is provided as a review to highlight a few key points, which were mentioned earlier in the chapter, for integrating network services.

Dynamic Updates

DHCP can be configured to automatically update your DNS database for you. This will keep the host and IP address information up to date, even though a DHCP client's IP address can change.

As an added benefit, this is a way of supplying dynamic updates for clients that cannot update the DNS database for themselves. Windows 2000 systems can update DNS entries themselves. For other operating systems, as long as they are DHCP clients, you can let DHCP provide the updates for them.

Update options are set through the DNS properties pages. The default is to only allow secure updates, giving you a way of controlling security on DNS updates. You can configure a list of servers authorized to initiate dynamic updates. This can include secondary name servers, domain controllers, DHCP servers, and WINS servers. By default, network name servers and clients can initiate automatic updates. You can also allow all updates or allow no updates, which will disable dynamic DNS updates.

Secure updates can become an issue when using DHCP. DHCP can only make dynamic updates if the DHCP server is a member of a special security group, the DnsUpdateProxy group, or unless you set the dynamic updates option to allow for updates from any source.

NOTE: DHCP servers can also register client NetBIOS names in the WINS database.

DNS and WINS

You have the option of having DNS queries that DNS cannot resolve forwarded to a WINS server for resolution. If the WINS server can resolve the requested name, the information will be passed back to the DNS server. This can be configured on a zone-by-zone basis.

The WINS properties page of the DNS properties pages lets you enable WINS to be used for forward lookup for names that cannot be resolved through a DNS query. This can be used to simplify name resolution management when operating in a mixed-mode environment with other operating systems. To use WINS for forward lookup, you will need to provide IP address information for the WINS servers(s) to be queried. You can also set how long information from a WINS query can be cached.

Combining Network Services

You may find that you can improve your network design by combining network services. Combining services also gives you additional options for optimizing your use of network resources. For example, you may find failure of either your primary DNS server or primary WINS server is a critical concern. It could be that your most cost-effective solution is to use clustered servers, but install both your DNS and WINS servers on the same server cluster. Services that are not cluster aware, such as DNS, must have any critical files stored on the shared cluster drive.

Combining services can be a way of reducing network traffic. As you've seen in this chapter, there are several situations where network servers share or pass information. You can reduce traffic by combining them on the same server. Examples include:

- Combining DHCP and DNS for dynamic updates
- Combining DHCP and WINS for WINS database updates
- Combining DNS and WINS for forwarded resolution queries

There is a potentially serious drawback to combining services, however. When you combine services, they are going to be contending for the same server resources. You will need to make sure that your server can provide enough resources to support all of the services that are running. DNS, WINS, and DHCP all have relatively high disk resource requirements, but relatively low memory requirements. Of the three, DHCP has the highest processor resource requirements, followed by DNS, and then WINS.

Scenario 6-4: Service Integration

The purpose of this scenario is to give you practice in dealing with issues relating to service integration. Suggested solutions are provided in Appendix B at the end of this manual. It may be helpful to review the case studies in Appendix C at the end of this manual.

Barney's Bank

1. You have set up an Active Directory domain as a separate DNS zone, configured as an Active Directory-integrated zone. The DNS servers are configured to allow secure updates only. Your DHCP servers have been authorized in the Active Directory. What else must you do before the DNS servers will accept updates from the DHCP servers?

2. Your network design requires both DNS and WINS servers. During the early deployment phases, a majority of the Windows NT and Windows 98 systems will retain their static IP addresses. Primary WINS and DNS server addresses will be added manually for the systems. What do you need to do to ensure that DNS queries for these systems will be correctly resolved?

SUMMARY

During this chapter, you were introduced to the following:

- TCP/IP network services
- Network service installation
- Domain name organization
- Domain Name System (DNS) servers
- Forward and reverse lookup zones and queries
- DNS databases
- DNS zones
- DNS zone replication
- DNS design, monitoring, and optimization
- NetBIOS name resolution
- Windows Internet Name Service (WINS)
- WINS Proxy Agents
- WINS replication
- WINS design, monitoring, and optimization
- WINS replication design
- Burst handling
- Dynamic Host Configuration Protocol (DHCP)
- IP address assignments
- DHCP scopes
- DHCP design, monitoring, and optimization
- DHCP Relay Agents
- Network service integration
- Combining network services

The next chapter addresses wide area networking and remote access. This includes a detailed look at how the Internet can fit into your network design.

Stop now and complete the following NEXTSim exercises on the Interactive Learning CD-ROM:

Windows 2000 Network Infrastructure Design

TCP/IP Services

Install and Configure DHCP

POST-TEST QUESTIONS

The answers to these questions are in Appendix A at the end of this manual.

1. You are concerned about a potential processor bottleneck on a DHCP server. How can you arrange to be notified automatically if performance counters exceed what you consider necessary operating parameters?

 ....

 ....

2. You configure a Windows 2000 DNS server to support a standard secondary zone. What type of zone transfer will be used to create the zone database on the server?

 ....

 ....

3. A Windows 2000 server is brought online and is registering itself with its primary DNS server. What types of resource records will be created if the registration is successful?

 ....

 ....

4. What types of resource records are created when a DHCP server registers a DHCP client with a DNS server?

....

....

5. You are deploying DNS servers in a WAN. You want to optimize the design for DNS availability at each LAN. How would you do this?

....

....

6. You will be exposing a DNS server to the Internet to provide name resolution for resources you are providing Internet access to. How can you secure this server against outside mischief?

....

....

7. You have a routed LAN with three subnets that is supported by a single WINS server. What do you need to do to provide NetBIOS name resolution for non-WINS client systems in the other two subnets?

....

....

8. What types of network traffic do you need to monitor to detemine the load generated by WINS NetBIOS name resolution?

....

....

9. WINS replication traffic is being sent over the Internet. What protocol option will provide end-to-end encryption?

....

....

10. You want to minimize the traffic generated by WINS client name resolution requests and responses in your WAN. How would you do this?

11. Your nonrouted LAN is set up as an Active Directory domain. You have installed and configured a DHCP server. You defined and activated a scope, but none of your DHCP clients are receiving IP addresses. What is most likely wrong?

12. You want to use DHCP to manage IP address assignments in your routed LAN. Systems in the subnet local to the DHCP server are receiving address assignments but not any of the other DHCP clients. Assuming that the scopes have all been set up correctly, what is most likely wrong?

13. You have one central office and three remote offices. There is a LAN in each location. The remote offices connect to the central office through an ISDN demand-dial connection. What is the minimum number of DHCP servers you will need to efficiently support this network?

....

....

14. How do changes to the DHCP lease period impact network traffic?

....

....

CHAPTER 7

Wide Area Design

MAJOR TOPICS

OBJECTIVES

At the completion of this chapter, you will be able to:

- Identify when to use persistent or demand-dial connections.
- Describe how user population influences Wide Area Network (WAN) design.
- Describe the basic network requirements for access and data security.
- List and describe the protocols and services that can be configured through the Routing and Remote Access Service (RRAS).
- List and describe the Windows 2000 client connection options.
- List and describe the protocols supported for remote user access.
- List and describe the authentication and encryption methods supported for remote user access.
- Design remote user access solutions for routed and nonrouted LANs and WANs.
- List guidelines for optimizing remote user access performance and security.
- Describe the purpose and use of remote access policies.
- Describe the purpose and use of the Remote Authentication Dial-In User Service (RADIUS).
- Design a network solution using RADIUS for user authentication.
- Describe the purpose and use of the Network Address Translation (NAT) protocol.
- List guidelines for implementing NAT servers.
- Design a NAT solution for Internet access.
- List guidelines for optimizing NAT performance and security.
- Describe the purpose and use of Microsoft Proxy Server.
- Design a Proxy Server solution for Internet access.
- List guidelines for optimizing Proxy Server performance and security.
- Describe the VPN tunnel types and how tunnels are established.
- List and describe the protocols that can be used with VPN.
- Include a mail server in a network design.
- Include a Web server in a network design.

PRE-TEST QUESTIONS

The answers to these questions are in Appendix A at the end of this manual.

1. You are adding an NAT server to a nonrouted LAN. The NAT server will connect to the Internet using a standard modem. Which, if any, NAT server connections will be persistent connections?

2. You are deploying DHCP in a routed network environment. Each DHCP server will be supporting multiple subnets. What additional requirement does this place on your routers?

3. What protocols are supported by RRAS demand-dial routing?

4. What is the default protocol for Windows 2000 remote user access dial-in connections?

5. What type of remote access authentication must you use if you want to support encryption through IPSec?

....

....

6. What purpose is the PPP Multilink Protocol used for?

....

....

7. What service do you want to install if you want to configure a Windows 2000 server as a RADIUS server?

....

....

8. When will a remote access client system connect directly to a RADIUS server for authentication?

....

....

9. What is the minimum number of network interfaces required on an NAT server?

....

....

10. You want to design a network solution that will support a Remote Procedure Call (RPC)-based application through a shared connection to the Internet. What would you use to provide this support?

....

....

11. In addition to IP filtering, what options do you have available through NAT to control Internet user access to private network resources?

....

....

12. Proxy Server can support clients running what LAN protocols?

....

....

13. What is the minimum number of network interfaces required on a proxy server?

....

....

14. When would you enable the Guest account on a proxy server?

....

....

15. What type of tunnel is used when a remote access client establishes a VPN connection with a remote access server?

....

....

16. What is used to provide encryption for an L2TP VPN connection?

....

....

17. By default, how will Proxy Server handle resource requests for a Web server located on your private network?

....

....

INTRODUCTION

This chapter focuses on some remaining wide area networking issues. The chapter begins with an overview of WAN design issues. This includes some information presented in earlier chapters, combined here to give you a more concise reference.

From there, the chapter turns to a general look at access services. This includes a slightly more detailed look at the Routing and Remote Access Service (RRAS) as an introduction to WAN and Internet services. You will also be introduced to client connection services.

Remote user access is covered in detail, including design concerns for remote access servers and client connection issues. During this discussion, issues relating to demand-dial configurations for LAN-to-LAN connections are also addressed. You will also be introduced to the Remote Authentication Dial-In User Service (RADIUS). You will see how to use RADIUS to centralize authentication management.

The chapter next addresses a couple of Internet-specific services and design issues. The first of these is the Network Address Translation (NAT) protocol and the use of NAT servers to provide Internet access. This is followed by an introduction to Microsoft Proxy Server as a more secure Internet access method.

The use of Virtual Private Networks (VPNs) as a way of implementing secure communications is also addressed during this chapter. While VPNs can be used in both a local routed LAN and Internet-based connections, the focus is on securing communications through the Internet.

The chapter then looks briefly at two additional services. You will be provided with an overview and general guidelines for implementing mail and Web servers as part of your network design solution.

WIDE AREA DESIGN FUNDAMENTALS

You were introduced to some suggested WAN configurations earlier in the course. You will need to select a WAN topology based on your connectivity requirements, resource access requirements, and budget constraints. The following topics are covered in this section:

- Connection Options
- Network Services
- Network Security

This review is being provided to lay the groundwork for a more detailed discussion of some of the technologies involved in wide area design.

Connection Options

Earlier in the course, you were told about connection options from the standpoint of establishing the physical connection between LANs. This discussion focuses on design decisions that will help you determine what type of physical connection option to use.

Persistent Connections

A persistent connection refers to a connection that is always open and available. You would use a persistent connection where high availability is an issue. As a general rule, the more centralized your organizational structure, the more likely you are to use persistent connections since they lend themselves well to centralized management.

The biggest drawback to persistent connections is usually their cost. It can be more expensive to have an around-the-clock open connection than connecting on an as-needed basis.

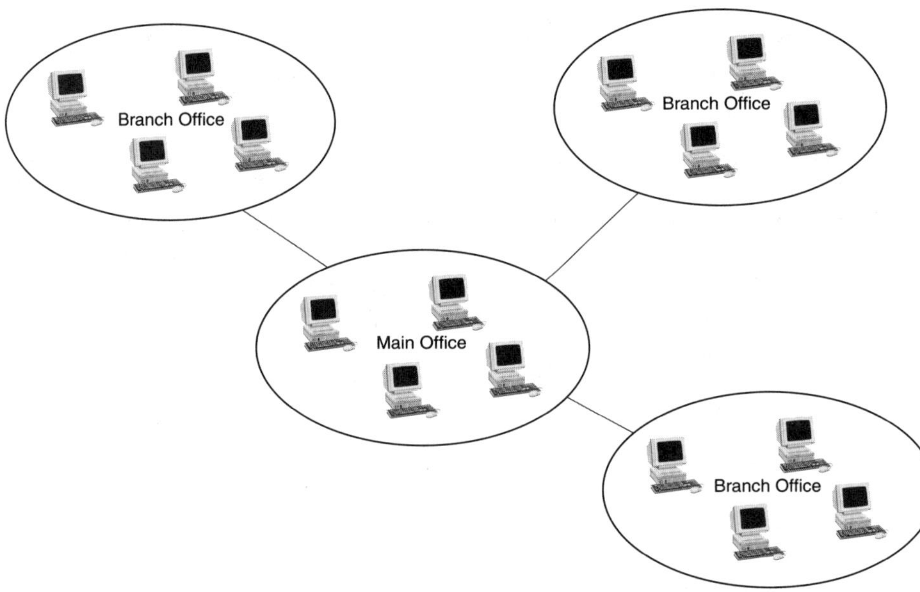

For example, assume you are responsible for network support for a locally owned bank with offices in various locations within the city. The branch offices need immediate access to customer and account records that are maintained in the main office. The branch offices will need persistent links to the main office to facilitate this access.

Demand-Dial Connections

With a demand-dial connection, the connection is made only when a system needs to communicate with another LAN. This connection method has lower availability and higher latency than a persistent connection. Latency can become a problem in some applications since timeout failures may occur while waiting for the connection to be made.

You also need to keep an eye on costs. A demand-dial connection costs less when you only need periodic connectivity, but the costs can go up as the frequency of connections increases. You may reach a point where a persistent connection becomes more cost effective.

You might wonder why you would want to use a direct dial-up solution rather than connecting via a VPN through the Internet. One potential problem is that your data transmission rate through an Internet connection can vary. This may be unacceptable for some application requirements.

> *NOTE:* *The use of VPN connections in WAN designs is discussed in detail later in this chapter.*

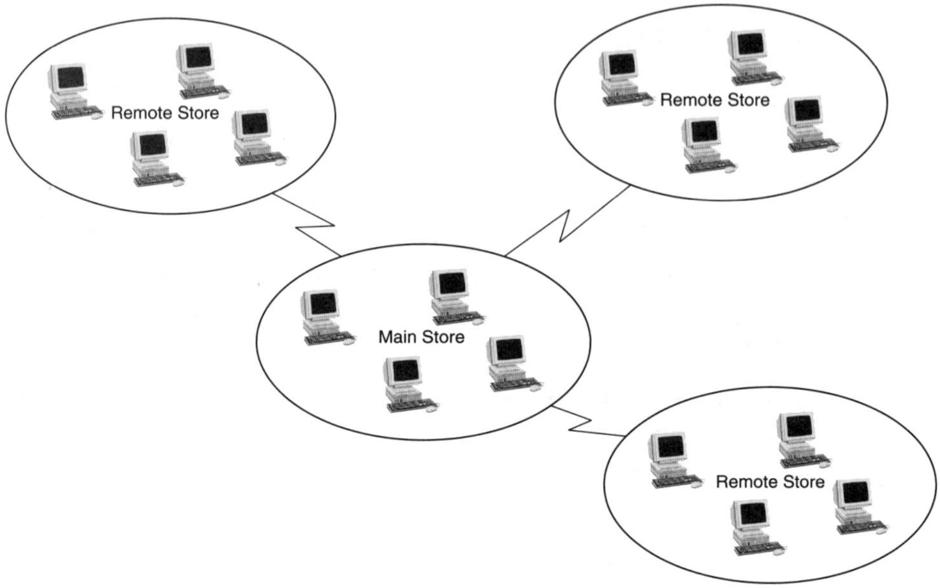

For example, assume a retail organization has three stores. A server running SQL Server in each location keeps track of that store's inventory and sales. There are only two situations where one store needs to contact another store. One is for inventory lookup. If an item is out of stock locally, a check is made to see if the item is available in another store. The other is for SQL Server replication. Each evening, the main store calls the other stores to retrieve inventory and sales changes.

User Population

User population and resource requirements will have a direct impact on how you design connectivity for a WAN. The information you gather about traffic patterns will become very important during this part of the process. You will need to pay special attention to traffic volume and traffic frequency.

Traffic Volume

High traffic volume typically means that you need a high-bandwidth connection. You also need to determine if latency is going to be a serious concern. It is possible to have requirements to support high traffic levels for short periods of time where latency is considered as part of the design.

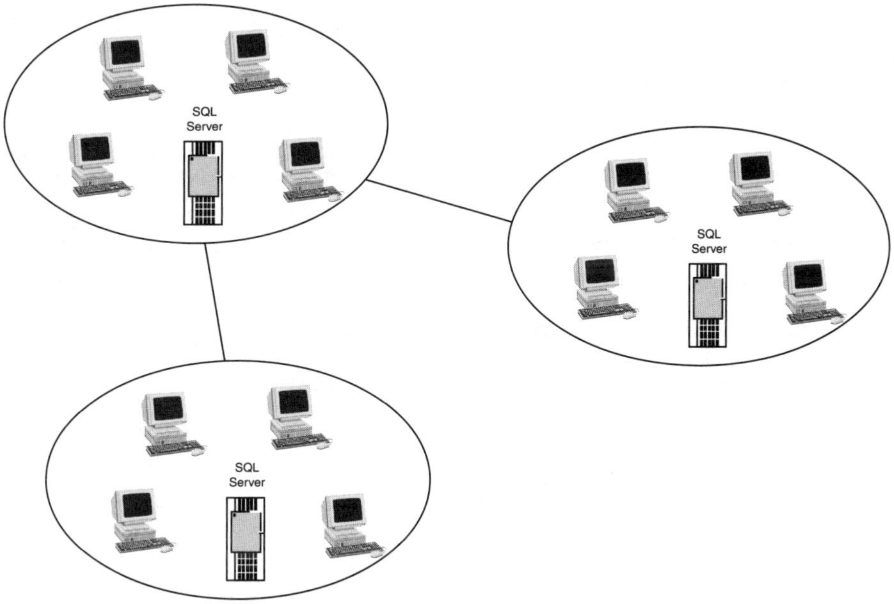

You could see this in a distributed database application. You have database servers in different locations that need to update each other through nightly replication. High-bandwidth connections are needed during the process to make sure that it completes before the start of the next business day. However, other than making sure replication completes in time, latency isn't going to be a concern in this scenario.

Traffic Frequency

Traffic frequency and traffic volume aren't necessarily related. You can have high frequency requirements, or a need to communicate across links on a regular basis, and still have a low traffic volume if very little data is transferred with each transmission.

Traffic frequency will play an important role in deciding between a persistent or a demand-dial connection. The higher the frequency, the more likely that you're going to need a persistent connection to meet your needs.

User Connections

You will have to decide how user connections are going to be connected to the WAN. Most remote links are going to justify router-to-router connections, providing access to all users in each LAN. There are going to be some circumstances, however, where you are going to need to provide remote access to individual users, including those who spend time traveling for business and those telecommuters who need periodic network access.

Network Services

You were introduced to network service design issues earlier in the course. This included both LAN- and WAN-related design issues. Let's take a few minutes to focus on some key issues specific to WAN design.

DNS

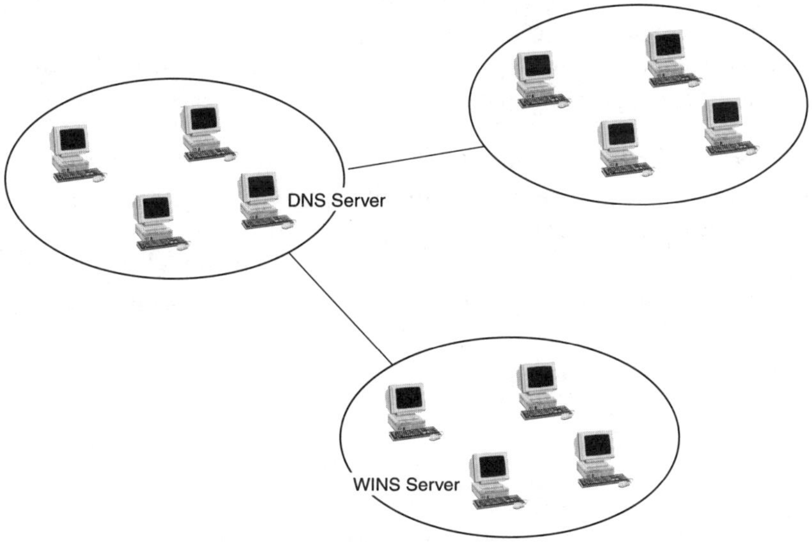

You can be relatively sure that DNS is going to be part of any WAN design. DNS is the most efficient way of managing host name-to-IP address resolution and is a requirement for implementing Active Directory services.

The number and placement of DNS servers is going to depend on the number of users in each location, connection types, and DNS-related traffic. One DNS server can support more than one location, but you are going to want to limit this to persistent links. The latency across demand-dial links can become excessive. In a mixed network environment, unresolved name queries can be forwarded to a WINS server. Once again, availability is going to be an issue. You have to make sure there is a path available to the WINS server.

If the traffic generated by lookups and dynamic updates is going to be less than that generated by zone updates, you will want to consider handling the load through a remote link or setting up a local caching-only server. If zone updates are going to generate less traffic, place a separate DNS server in the remote location. You can use DNS zones to control and manage replication traffic.

Security can become an issue when using standard DNS zones. You will probably want to encrypt any zone-update traffic that is being routed over a public carrier. There is also a security issue when you need to expose a DNS server to the public Internet. The DNS server should be set up in a screen subnet, with firewalls between the DNS server and the Internet and between the DNS server and your private LAN.

WINS

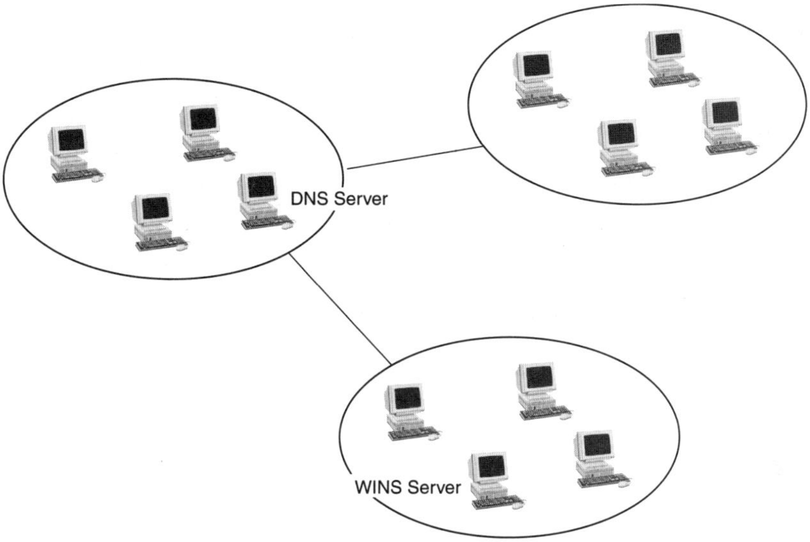

WINS support will only be an issue if you have systems or applications that use NetBIOS names. If you don't, you won't have any need for a WINS server. You will also likely find that you don't need a WINS server in a nonrouted LAN environment.

The issues are much the same as for DNS servers. You need to resolve number and placement issues for WINS servers. Designs that include multiple WINS servers bring up issues about designing WINS replication support, along with concerns about latency and convergence.

If you don't plan to put a WINS server in every location, you need to determine if you have any systems that cannot be configured as WINS clients but that will need NetBIOS name resolution support. You will need to set up at least one WINS Proxy Agent in each of those locations.

DHCP

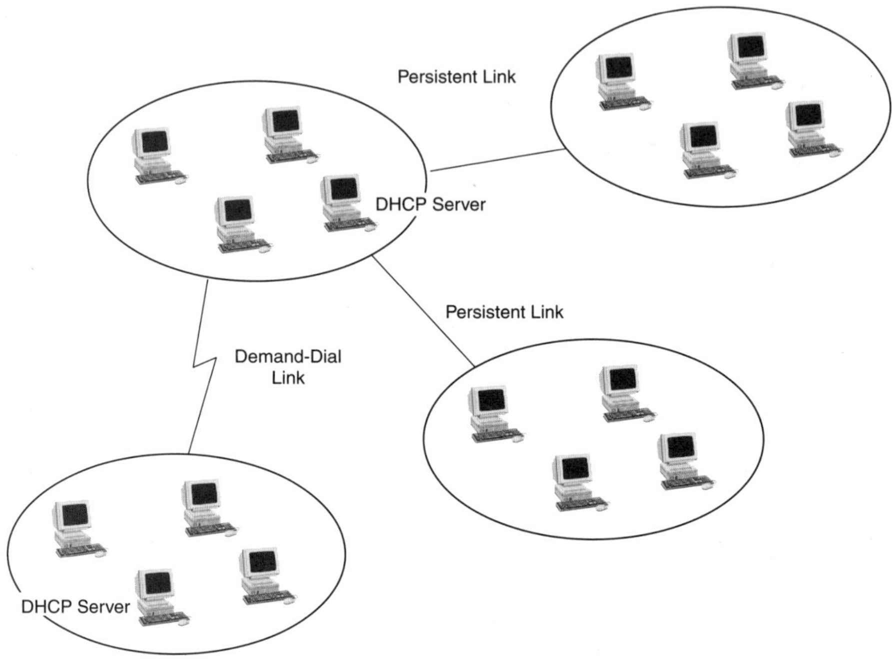

DHCP can significantly reduce your management overhead in all but the smallest network designs. You will need to determine how many DHCP servers you are going to need and where they should be placed. Even though a DHCP server can be used to manage addresses for multiple subnets, there needs to be a persistent high-bandwidth connection between each remote subnet and the DHCP server. Also, any routers along the way will have to be configured as DHCP Relay Agents.

You will have to decide how you want to manage scopes. When using multiple DHCP servers, you may want to improve fault tolerance by splitting part of the scope off to a different DHCP server. You also have to decide which, if any, client options you want to configure through DHCP.

As an added benefit, DHCP can automatically update both the DNS and WINS databases. This is important to keeping both DNS and WINS information accurate since WINS client IP addresses can change.

Network Security

A number of network security issues have already been introduced in this course. Security will continue to be an important part of the discussion throughout the course, with targeted discussions focusing on specific security areas. For now, this look at security will be limited to a quick overview of general security areas. This is provided as a road map of where some of the security discussions are going to be leading.

Access Security

There are several issues relating to access security that must be addressed in your WAN design. These will include the following:

- Local logon validation

  You need to provide logon validation for users who are accessing the network by logging on at their local LAN. In most cases, you are going to want to provide local logon validation, both because of the amount of traffic generated during logon and because of concerns about latency. For a Windows 2000 Active Directory domain, this means placing a domain controller in each location and having to consider Active Directory replication traffic in your network design.

- Remote access security

  If you are going to support remote user access, you have to determine how access security is going to be managed. This includes logon validation, but goes beyond that with issues such as whether users will be able to dial in directly, how usernames and passwords are going to be passed, whether users will have access to the network or to the remote access server only, and so forth.

- Internet access

  This issue was addressed in some detail earlier and will be addressed again during this chapter. You have to determine which users need Internet access and how that access is going to be provided while protecting your private network against unauthorized access.

Never forget that user access controls are going to be your network's first line of defense.

Data Access Security

Local and shared access security were introduced in some detail earlier in the course. In a WAN environment, there is going to be a special emphasis on shared access security. Some points to keep in mind in an Active Directory domain include the following:

- Use groups to manage security.

  As much as possible, assign access permissions through security groups rather than making explicit assignments to individual users. Group assignments are much easier to manage in the long run.

- Leave Guest disabled.

  Unless you have a justifiable requirement for the Guest account, it should be left disabled. The Guest account, if enabled, can become a dangerous backdoor into your network.

- Grant only required access permissions.

  If you grant too few permissions, your users are going to let you know. If you provide too much access, you may not find out until after the damage has already been done.

You should also consider auditing access to critical or confidential data files.

ACCESS SERVICES

This section provides a brief overview and introduction to some connectivity options and connection services. Connection services applicable to this course will be discussed in more detail later. This section will also include a brief introduction to client connection options. The following topics are covered in this section:

- Routing and Remote Access Service (RRAS) Overview
- RRAS Configurations
- Client Connection Options

You had a brief introduction to Routing and Remote Access earlier in the course when setting up an IP router. Now you are going to see the other services supported through this utility.

Routing and Remote Access Service (RRAS) Overview

You are going to be using the Routing and Remote Access tool extensively in setting up and managing your network. Even though the specific procedural steps involved in installing each of the Routing and Remote Access options is beyond the scope of this course, you will probably find an introduction to its features and functionality useful.

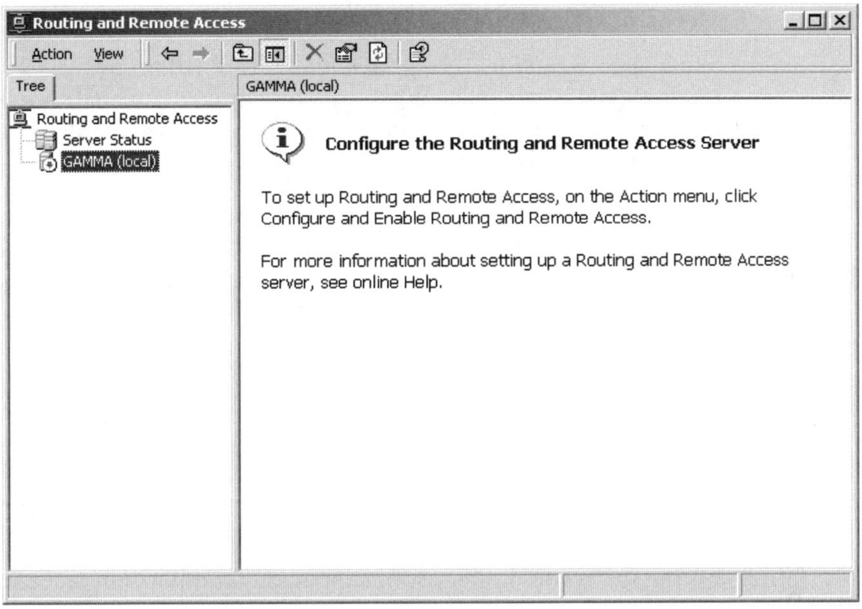

Windows 2000 combines support for multiprotocol routing and remote access in a single server. RRAS allows a single server to support both local area network and remote routing, including support for demand-dial connections. This also means that both routing and remote access can be managed through a single utility, the Routing and Remote Access Administrative Tool.

In addition to being fully integrated with the Windows 2000 operating system, RRAS also supports Application Programming Interfaces (APIs) that make it possible to develop custom networking solutions. RRAS supports a wide array of protocols and access methods.

Supported Configurations

RRAS supports the following three basic configurations:

- Multiprotocol router

  Simultaneous routing is supported for TCP/IP (IP routing), NWLink (IPX routing), and AppleTalk. When you initially configure RRAS to support multiprotocol routing, support is automatically added for all of the routable protocols currently installed on the server.

- Demand-dial router

  A Windows 2000 Server system configured as a demand-dial router can support routing over a dial-up or persistent connection. This includes support for VPN routing. The router can act as either the calling or answering router. Routing is supported for IP and IPX.

- Remote access

  A Windows 2000 Server system configured as a remote access server can support remote client access. Remote clients can be dial-in clients or VPN clients. Remote access is supported for clients running IP, IPX, NetBEUI, or AppleTalk. RRAS supports both server and client configurations.

RRAS has the ability to simultaneously support any combination of these configurations.

Multiprotocol Routing

RRAS supports concurrent multiprotocol routing. Along with AppleTalk and IPX routing, RRAS supports unicast and multicast IP routing.

AppleTalk Routing

Windows 2000 supports routing for AppleTalk internetworks. The basic concept is the same as for supporting any routable protocol. AppleTalk packets are forwarded between small networks (subnetworks) by the router. The routing table is maintained through the Routing Table Maintenance Protocol (RTMP).

IP Routing

When you refer to IP routing, it would usually be more accurate to use the term unicast IP routing. This is the type of router that was introduced in the previous chapter. Unicast routing refers to a two-way, point-to-point connection between two computers. Most often, routing is managed as a series of unicast routing connections.

Routing tables can be managed and updated through static (manually configured) addresses, RIP, OSP, and ICMP router discovery. A unicast router can be configured as a DHCP Relay Agent and supports IP packet filtering. It can also be configured to support Network Address Translation (NAT).

NOTE: NAT is discussed in some detail later in this chapter.

Multicast IP Routing

Multicast IP routing is typically used when you need real-time data delivery to multiple hosts. The traffic is sent to a single host but can be processed by multiple hosts configured to listen for multicast IP traffic.

NOTE: A detailed discussion of multicast IP routing is beyond the scope of this course.

IPX Routing

IPX routing is typically required in a mixed Windows 2000 and Novell NetWare environment. It supports routing of packets in an IPX internetwork environment. RIP for IPX is supported, which is vector-based routing as was discussed for RIP for IP routing earlier in the course. It also supports SAP advertising and packet filtering.

Demand-Dial Routing

Typically, when you think of router connections, you think of them being made between local subnets or across persistent WAN connections. Demand-dial routing supports connections over persistent links but also supports on-demand links where the connection is made with the remote router when packet routing is required. Demand-dial routing also supports connecting to the Internet and IP and IPX routing.

Remote Access and VPN

RRAS allows clients to connect from remote locations, typically through dial-up connections. You can also use RRAS to configure a VPN server. Both remote access and VPN are discussed later in this chapter.

RRAS Configurations

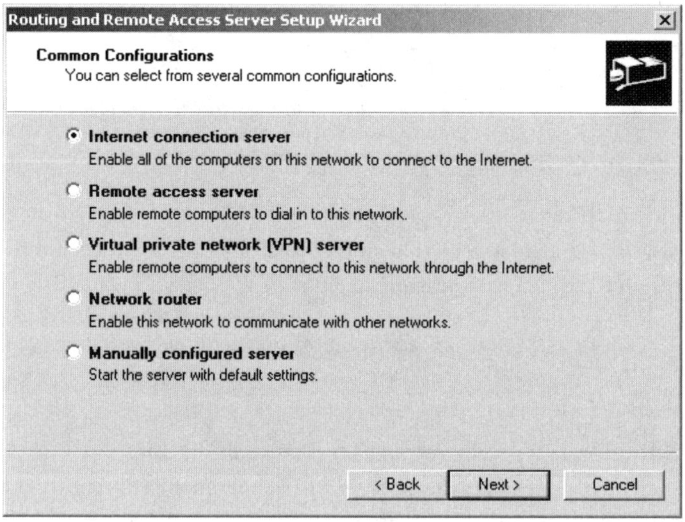

The Routing and Remote Access Server Setup Wizard is designed to step you through the process of setting up support for a selected common configuration. A detailed look at the steps involved in setting up each of these options is beyond the scope of this course, but you should at least be aware of the options that are available. Later in this chapter, you will see how selected options can be integrated into your network design.

The following common configurations are supported:

- Internet connection server
- Remote access server
- Virtual private network (VPN) server
- Network router
- Manually configured server

If the server is going to be used for a single purpose, make your choice from the list. Even if it's going to be supporting multiple roles, you may find it easier to install RRAS to match its primary role, then modify server RRAS properties to fine-tune the server's support.

Internet Connection Server

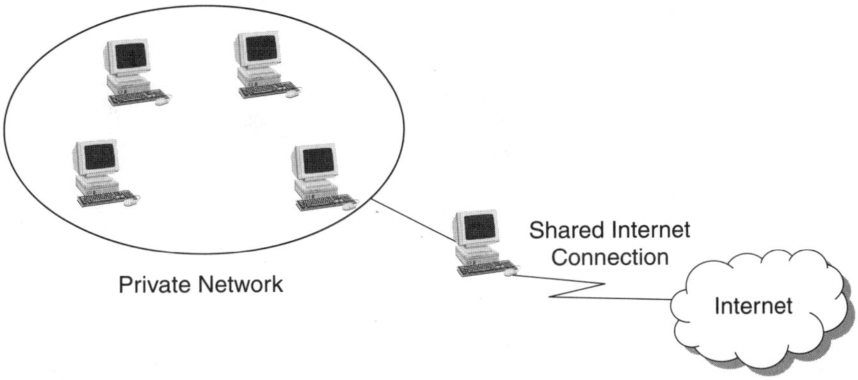

This selection lets you set up a shared Internet connection based on your network requirements. The connection options were introduced earlier in the course. As a reminder, they are as follows:

- Internet Connection Sharing (ICS)

  You would use ICS when you are connecting a small LAN with limited connectivity requirements to the Internet.

- Network Address Translation (NAT)

  You would use the NAT routing protocol when you have more extensive connection requirements. The NAT routing protocol can be used when you need to support multiple network connections and also supports demand-dial routing configurations.

A detailed discussion of ICS is beyond the scope of this course. The NAT routing protocol and its use will be discussed later in this chapter.

Remote Access Server

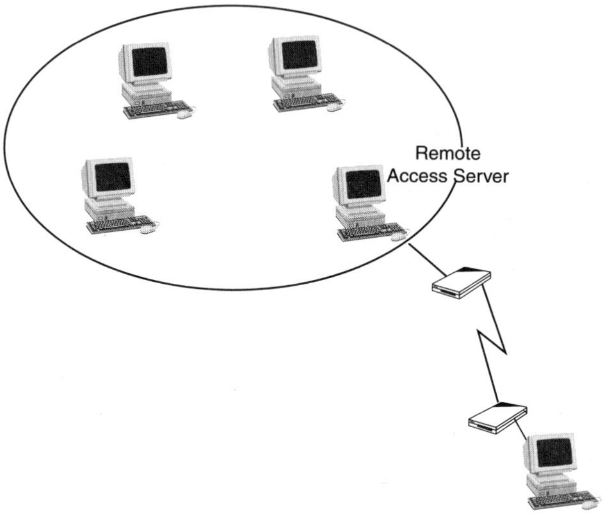

A remote access server provides support for remote clients to connect to the network through a standard dial-in line or other connection option. Remote access server use will be discussed in more detail during this chapter.

Virtual Private Network (VPN) Server

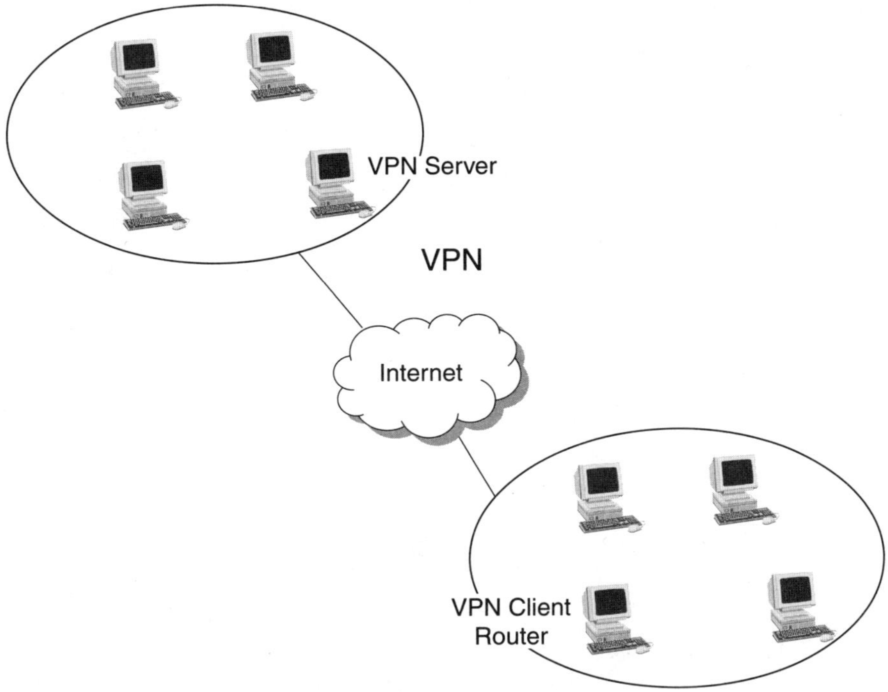

VPNs have already been mentioned during this course as one of your WAN connectivity options for connecting through a remote router. You can also support remote client connections through a VPN. VPN connections provide a way of connecting to your network through the Internet. Use of VPNs for network connectivity will be discussed in more detail during this chapter.

Network Router

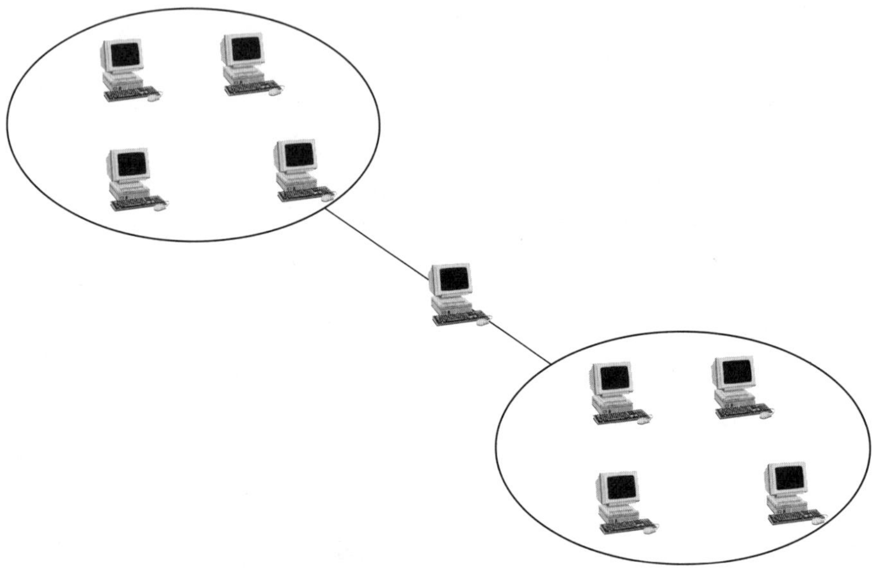

You've already been introduced to the RRAS multiprotocol router. This is the most common RRAS configuration and is used in both LAN and WAN configurations. The advantage of a multiprotocol router is that you only need one router, in most situations, to handle all of your protocol routing requirements.

Manually Configured Server

This option installs routing and remote access but doesn't configure the system for any particular configuration. The system is configured with default settings that you can then change through system properties.

Client Connection Options

While looking at an overview of your connection options, let's take a little while to look at the client side. Client connection options are configured through the Network Connection Wizard, which is launched from Network and Dial-up Connections.

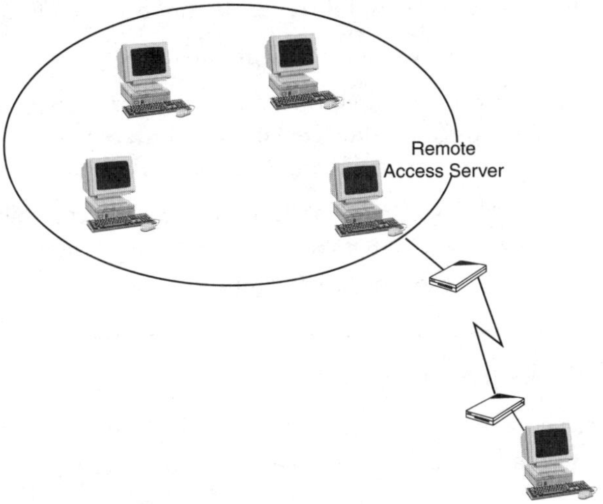

The following client connection options are supported:

- Dial-up connection to a private network

  Use this selection to configure a computer as a remote access client. You can configure the system to connect through a dial-up modem connection, dial-up ISDN connection, or infrared port.

- Dial-up connection to the Internet

  This selection lets you configure a computer's Internet connection. It lets you enter the information needed to connect to your ISP, including username, password, and TCP/IP configuration settings.

- Connect to a private network through the Internet

  You can use this selection to configure a computer to connect to a VPN server through the Internet. You must provide the host name or IP address of the VPN server you want to connect to.

- Accept incoming connections

  This option is used to configure the computer to accept incoming connections. Dial-up, Internet, and direct cable connections are supported.

- Connect directly to another computer

  Use this option to establish a direct connection with another computer either through a directly connected cable or infrared port. You can identify your system as either the host (supplying information) or guest (receiving information).

You cannot use the Network Connection Wizard to configure incoming connections on Active Directory domain members or domain controllers. Instead, you must use RRAS to configure support for incoming connections.

REMOTE USER ACCESS

The focus now turns to implementing remote access solutions, starting with remote user access. The following topics are covered in this section:

- Remote Access Introduction
- Design Decisions

This discussion also provides some additional guidelines for implementing demand-dial routers as part of a WAN connectivity solution.

Remote Access Introduction

Before going into details about implementing a remote access solution, it's best to get some of the basics out of the way. The better you understand what is supported through remote access, the better you will be able to make design decisions.

Remote Access Protocols

A remote access server supports inbound connections through the following two protocol options:

- Point-to-Point Protocol (PPP)

  PPP is the de facto connection protocol for remote access connections. PPP is a set of industry-standard remote access protocols. A PPP client, assuming proper authorization, can connect to any PPP remote access server, not just Windows 2000 RAS servers. PPP supports a variety of authentication methods, data encryption, and data compression.

- Microsoft Remote Access Protocol

  Asynchronous NetBEUI (AsyBEUI) support is provided to allow legacy remote access clients that do not support connecting through PPP a way to connect to the remote access server.

There is also limited support provided for Serial Line Internet Protocol (SLIP). A remote access server can dial out with SLIP but does not support incoming SLIP connections.

LAN Protocols

Once the connection is made through the remote server, the remote client accesses network resources through its LAN protocol. LAN protocols supported by Windows 2000 remote access servers include TCP/IP, IPX, NetBEUI, and AppleTalk.

User Authentication

Security is going to be a major issue with client connections. An open telephone line can mean an open door into your network if not properly protected. This protection begins with user authentication.

This discussion focuses on the authentication methods supported by PPP. Remote access, implemented through Windows 2000, supports the following:

- Extensible Authentication Protocol (EAP)
- Microsoft Encrypted Authentication (MS-CHAP)

- Microsoft Encrypted Authentication Version 2 (MS-CHAP v2)
- Encrypted Authentication (CHAP)
- Shiva Password Authentication Protocol (SPAP)
- Unencrypted Password (PAP)

In addition, you can also configure a remote access server to access unauthenticated connections.

Windows 2000 remote access gives you the option of using mutual authentication. With mutual authentication, the server and client authenticate each other's credentials. Mutual authentication is only supported by EAP-Transport Level Security (EAP-TLS) and MS-CHAP v2. If a Windows 2000 remote access client supports only EAP-TLS and MS-CHAP v2 as its remote access authentication protocols, mutual authentication is required.

Extensible Authentication Protocol (EAP)

EAP is supported for Windows authentication. EAP supports passing EAP messages to a RADIUS server for authentication. EAP supports multiple authentication types. Two are supported for Windows 2000 authentication: EAP-Message Digest 5 Challenge Handshake Authentication Protocol (EAP-MD5 CHAP) and EAP-TLS. The client and server must both support the same EAP authentication type for authentication to occur.

NOTE: RADIUS is covered in more detail later in this chapter.

EAP-MD5 CHAP uses challenges and responses sent as EAP messages between the client and server. It is typically used to support authentication based on usernames and passwords.

EAP-TLS is used with certificate-based security. For example, you would use EAP-TLS if you were using smart cards for logon and authentication. EAP-TLS is only supported if your RAS server is part of an Active Directory domain.

Microsoft Encrypted Authentication (MS-CHAP)

MS-CHAP uses a challenge and response handshake for authentication. The server begins the authentication process by sending a challenge that includes a challenge string and session identifier to the client. The client responds with a username, session identifier, password, and a nonreversible encryption of the challenge string that it received from the server. The server will check and authenticate the response, if valid.

Microsoft Encrypted Authentication Version 2 (MS-CHAP v2)

MS-CHAP v2 provides some enhancements to MS-CHAP, including the following:

- LAN Manager-encoded responses are not supported, improving security.
- LAN Manager-encoded password changes are not supported, also as an improvement to security.
- Mutual authentication is supported.
- The cryptographic key used for encrypting data is based on the user's password and the challenge string rather than on the password only.
- Separate cryptographic keys are generated for transmitted and received data.

During MS-CHAP v2 authentication, the server sends a challenge string that includes a session identifier and challenge string. The client responds with the username and a peer challenge string that it generates. The client also sends a one-way encryption of its peer challenge string, the server challenge string, the session identifier, and the user's password. The server checks this response, then informs the client if authentication was successful and sends a response based on its challenge string, the peer challenge string, the client's encrypted response, and the user's password. The client must now authenticate the server's response. The client will not use the connection if unable to authenticate the server's response.

Encrypted Authentication (CHAP)

CHAP is an industry-standard challenge and authentication handshake. You will need to enable CHAP on your server when supporting non-Microsoft clients that use CHAP for authentication. When using CHAP as your authentication method, user passwords must be in a reverse encrypted form.

Shiva Password Authentication Protocol (SPAP)

SPAP provides more security than using clear-text passwords but is not as secure as other methods such as CHAP or MS-CHAP. You will need to use SPAP when connecting a Windows 2000 system as a client to a Shiva LANRover or when allowing Shiva clients access to your RAS server. SPAP requires the use of reverse encrypted passwords.

Unencrypted Password (PAP)

PAP will typically only be used if a server and client cannot negotiate a more secure authentication method. PAP uses clear-text passwords, so there is a possibility of passwords being compromised.

Security Features

While on the subject of security, let's take a look at a couple of key security features. Additional features will be discussed later in the chapter.

Remote Access Account Lockout

Remote access account lockout allows you to limit the number of authentication attempts a client can make before the client is denied remote access. You can specify:

- The number of failed attempts
- Failed attempts counter reset

This is very similar to user account lockout, discussed previously in the course. The server will count the number of failed attempts, and when the maximum is reached, any connection attempts by that user are denied. A successful authentication will reset the counter to zero. The counter reset value will reset the counter after a delay that you set, allowing the user account to be used again for remote access.

Data Encryption

There are two basic encryption options supported for remote access communications. Encryption is supported for Windows 2000, Windows NT 4.0, Windows 95, and Windows 98 clients. The supported encryption methods are as follows:

- Microsoft Point-to-Point Encryption (MPPE) protocol

  Windows 2000 remote access supports data encryption over dial-up links using EAP-TLS, MS-CHAP, or MS-CHAP v2 authentication. Encryption is supported for PPP or PPTP connections. MPPE encryption is based on a secret key generated during user authentication and known to the server and client. Encryption can be required when a secure password is required for MS-CHAP and MS-CHAP v2 authentication. You can also require authentication when using EAP-TLS smart card authentication. MPPE does not require a machine certificate infrastructure.

- L2TP over IPSec

  L2TP and IPSec are covered in some detail later in this chapter when discussing VPN connections. For now, you should know that IPSec can be used for encryption over an L2TP connection. Machine-based certificates are used to provide additional security by making it harder for an unauthorized computer to impersonate an authorized computer. You must be using CHAP, MS-CHAP, MS-CHAP v2, or EAP-TLS authentication if you want to support L2TP over IPSec.

The data encryption method you use will be determined by the connection protocol. PPTP and L2TP are used for VPN connections. A direct dial-in connection uses PPP, so MPPE will be used as the encryption method.

Design Decisions

You should already be getting an idea of some of the design decisions you are going to have to make. Before looking at design in any detail, the following general design points need to be discussed:

- Need for remote access

  You need to make sure that remote client access is the appropriate solution. If you need to support several clients in one location, a LAN-based connection might be a better solution.

- Connection type

  Standard telephone lines and modems are still a common connection method. You have the option, however, of using ISDN or X.25 for client connections if a higher bandwidth is required. Connections can be through a direct dial-in to the server or through a VPN.

- Authentication method

  Earlier in this chapter, you were introduced to the authentication methods supported for remote access. You have the option of using RADIUS for central authentication and authorization of RAS clients. You need to already have at least one RADIUS server set up if you want to use RADIUS. The default is to not use RADIUS.

  You need to select an authentication method best matched to your needs. Your choices may be restricted by some of the clients you are supporting.

- IP address assignment

  You can have IP addresses assigned automatically through DHCP, or you can set a specific range of addresses to be used by remote clients. You must configure the remote access server as a DHCP Relay Agent if you want to have DHCP manage client addresses.

  If you select to specify a range of addresses, you will need to supply an address range. Make sure that the address range does not include any assigned addresses and does not overlap any DHCP scopes. If you prefer, client IP addresses can also be managed through use of manually assigned static addresses.

- Resource access

  You have the option of limited access to the resources available locally on the remote access server or to the WAN at large.

Other issues are much the same as when designing a routed LAN. You are going to want to limit the traffic across the remote link. You will need to review the LAN protocols being used by the remote client to determine whether they are actually required.

Client Overview

Part of designing your remote access solution is knowing what clients you can support. Windows 2000 remote access supports the following clients:

- Windows 2000
- Windows NT version 3.5 or later
- Windows 95/Windows 98
- Windows for Workgroups
- MS-DOS
- Microsoft LAN Manager
- Third-party PPP remote access clients

You will find your management overhead reduced if you can manage users from a central location rather than individually for each server. If your servers are part of an Active Directory domain, you can set up the users as Active Directory user accounts. Otherwise, you have the option of setting up a RADIUS server to centralize user management.

You have the option of enabling Internet Connection Sharing (ICS) through a client connection. This will allow other users to access external resources, including the remote server and LAN, through your connection. If you select to enable ICS, you are also prompted to enable on-demand dialing, effectively making the remote client into a demand-dial router for its local LAN.

As an added benefit, Windows remote access clients can also be used to connect to other PPP-based remote access servers. This includes devices such as NetWare connect and UNIX-based SLIP and PPP servers. This means that the same client can be used, should circumstances require, for connecting to other networks.

Service Integration

The remote access service can be integrated with other services. While this might be obvious, considering what you've already seen about the support provided for services, it is worth mentioning. You will need to consider how you will want to integrate remote access services with other services in your network design. This includes the following:

- DNS

  The DNS database can be updated dynamically with IP address information for remote clients, the same as for local clients. Remote clients can also query DNS servers for their name resolution needs.

- WINS

  Remote clients can be registered automatically with a WINS server in the same manner as local clients. Name resolution is the same for remote clients as for local clients.

- DHCP

  You can manage remote access assignments through DHCP. If the remote access server is configured as a DHCP Relay Agent, clients can get their addresses directly from a DHCP server. Otherwise, the remote access server can lease addresses in blocks of ten from the DHCP server for assignment to clients.

- RADIUS

  RADIUS integration provides centralized management for multiple remote access servers. This includes distributed authentication for clients, centralized management of remote access policies, and logging of authentication attempts.

Depending on your remote access server's hardware configuration and user support requirements, you may be able to combine services on the server. If you do, you will need to periodically monitor server resources to make sure the server is providing optimal support for all of the services it is running.

Remote Access and Nonrouted LANs

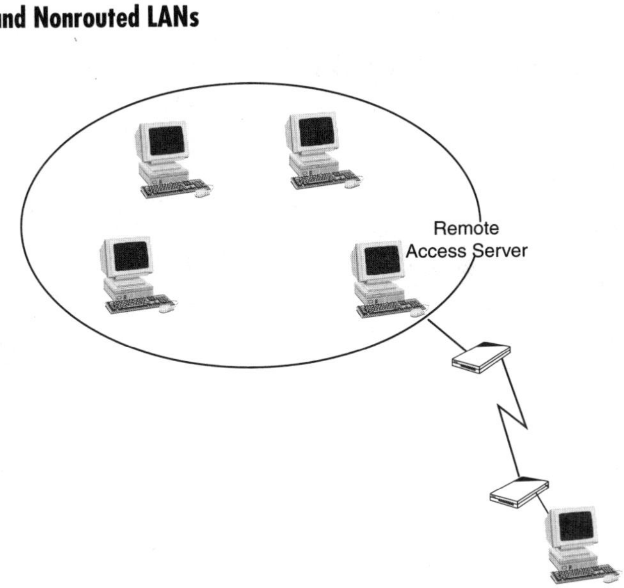

Most of the discussion in this section, and the chapter as a whole, has been about WAN support. This isn't meant to imply that you can't provide remote access support from what is otherwise a nonrouted LAN.

You will need to determine the number of concurrent client connections that are going to be required and the connection types to be used. You will need to consider both the bandwidth requirements for the remote clients and the effect that their added traffic will have on LAN bandwidth usage.

IP address options are the same as for any client. You can use static IP addresses, have addresses assigned through DHCP, or provide a pool of addresses through the remote access server. If you are using Automatic Private IP Addressing (APIPA) addresses for the LAN, you can also use the same addressing option for your remote clients.

Remote Access and Routed LANs

Even though the focus right now is on remote client access, let's take a look at a couple of closely related issues. First, this discussion will address setting up for client access, then it's going to provide some additional details on implementing demand-dial routers as a way of connecting LANs.

Client Access Configuration

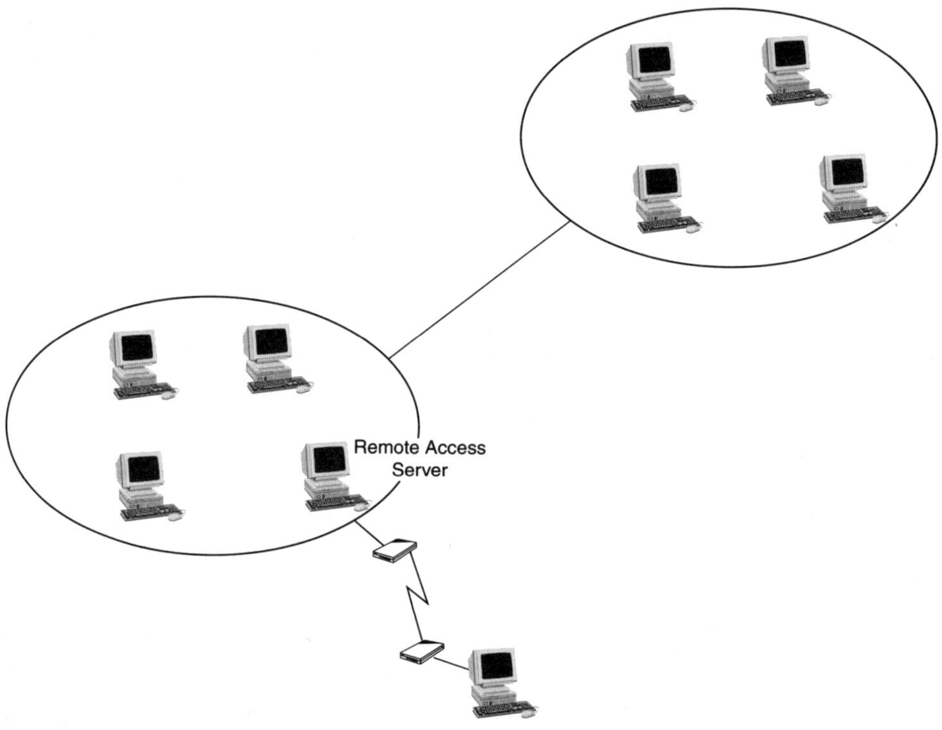

The issues start out the same as for a nonrouted LAN. You have to determine how many clients are going to need concurrent access and the connections that are going to be required to support them. You need to estimate how much additional traffic remote access clients are going to generate on the LAN they are connecting to. You also have to decide how to implement service integration.

There are also going to be issues that relate directly to the WAN environment. You have to determine where you are going to place the remote access server or servers. You are going to want to make a best effort to put remote access servers on the same LANs as the resources the clients are going to need to access. Security concerns may also impact your server placement. Security design concerns are covered later in this section.

Demand-Dial Configuration

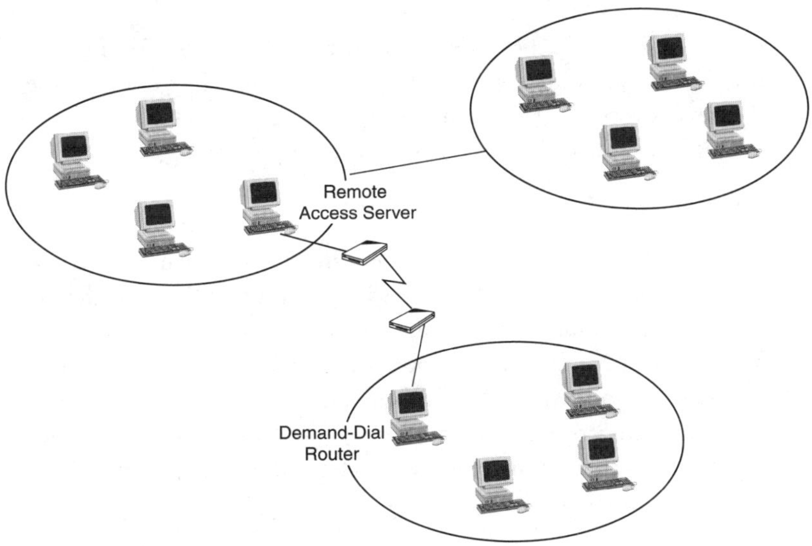

Your remote access server can also be used as a LAN router. While on the subject of remote access and dial-up communications, it's a good time to talk in a little more detail about demand-dial routing support. Many of the same issues apply as were discussed for setting up for remote client support. You still need to carefully consider router placement and the impact of the additional traffic on each connected LAN.

If you set up a default remote access server, LAN routing is not enabled by default. You will have to enable support through the remote access server properties. You will have to enable at least one port for demand-dial routing. You can configure a remote access server for incoming connections only or to support incoming and outgoing connections. When you set up to support outgoing connections, you will have to provide the number to call when connecting to a remote router. You must provide a primary number and have the option of providing alternate numbers to be used if the server is unable to connect with the primary number.

You can select the LAN protocols to be routed through this interface. You can select to add a user account to support other routers dialing in. You have the option of sending a plaintext password if you are unable to connect through a secure authentication method. You also have the option of scripting the connection.

Designing for Performance

Performance and availability issues are similar to those discussed for other network services. One solution discussed earlier for other services was the use of multiple servers. The same solution applies to remote access as a way of avoiding having a single point of failure. It can even be more important to provide multiple remote access servers at different locations, given that problems with the public telephone network could prevent you from connecting to one location. This also gives you a potential cost savings if remote access servers can be located to limit the need for long-distance calls when connecting to the servers.

Remote access performance can be influenced by several factors, including the following:

- Server performance

  The issues here are the same as for other network services. You need to make sure that the server has the resources necessary to support the remote client load. If not, you will need to upgrade or replace the server or provide multiple servers for load balancing.

- Client connection

  This one should be obvious. Communications with the client are going to be limited by the client connection's transmission rate.

- Server connection

  The server's connection to the network can sometimes become a bottleneck, especially when the server is supporting multiple high-volume remote access clients.

As remote client and remote LAN requirements increase, the load placed on remote access resources will also increase.

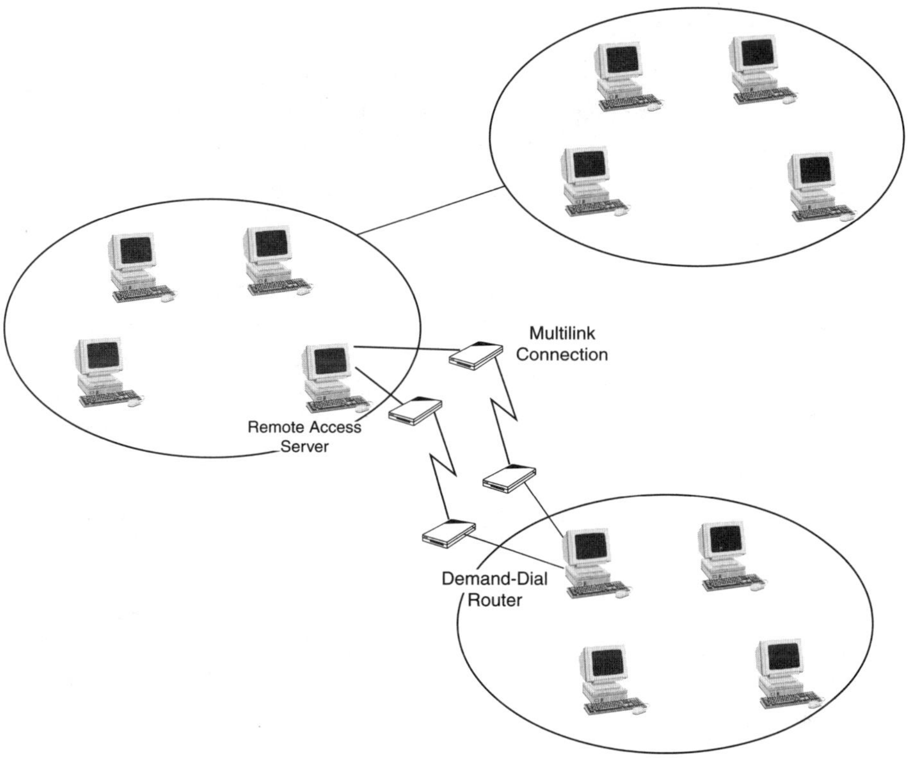

PPP Multilink Protocol (MP) is one possible solution to help improve performance over dial-up connections. MP allows remote access clients and demand-dial routers to combine multiple physical connections into one logical connection when connecting to the server. For example, if a remote client has two dial-up modems, it could be configured to use both to support one connection when connecting to the server. This increases the bandwidth for the connection.

If you select to support multilink connections, the default is to use Bandwidth Allocation Protocol (BAP) and Bandwidth Allocation Control Protocol (BACP) to negotiate adding or removing multiple physical connections.

Designing for Security

You've already been introduced to some of the security features built into remote access. A key decision is going to be how to handle authentication. You were introduced to authentication options earlier in the chapter. You will be shown how to include RADIUS in your design later in the chapter.

Resource Access

You have the option of limiting remote clients to resources available from the remote access server. This will prevent them from accessing other resources in the WAN. You can limit clients to resources on the subnet the remote access server is located in or specify static routes to identify the subnets the remote user will have access to.

Server Placement

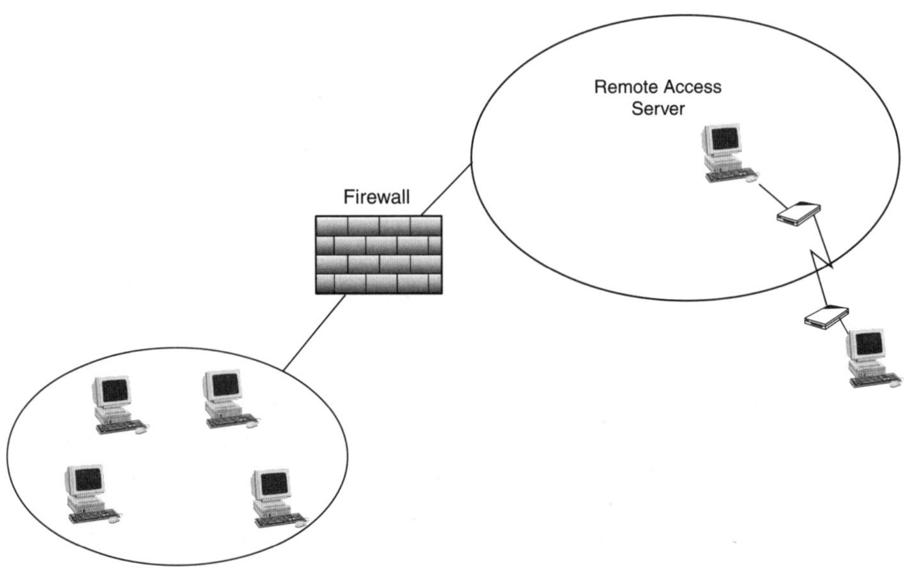

You can control security by remote access or VPN server placement. If you are restricting users to resources available from the remote access server only, you can place the server (or servers) on a private subnet. For added security, you can use a firewall, a proxy server, or IP filtering to screen the subnet from the rest of the network.

There are other justifications, in addition to that already given, to placing remote access servers in a screened subnet. If clients are connecting through a VPN tunnel, a screened subnet placement is suggested. You will also want to place any remote access server that is providing data to the public Internet as a combined service in a screened subnet. If users need access to resources in addition to those available from the remote access server, those resources should also be placed in the same screened subnet.

Using VPN

VPN technology and connection options will be discussed in detail later in this chapter. It is still important to mention, while on the subject of remote client access, that client access can be established through a VPN. This gives you a way of building a high level of security into your network design.

Without going into too much detail, VPN connections can be established through compulsory tunnels or voluntary tunnels. These tunnel types will be contrasted in detail later, but from the standpoint of management remote access, they are described briefly as follows:

- Compulsory tunnel

  A compulsory tunnel is initiated by the remote access server, and client support for tunneling is not required.
- Voluntary tunnel

  The tunnel connection is initiated by the client, and the client must support tunneling protocols.

Remote Access Policies

Another way of managing remote access security is through remote access policies. As mentioned earlier, connections must be authenticated and authorized. Whether a connection is accepted after authorization will depend on the user account properties and remote access policies.

Policies can be managed on a per-server basis. You also have the option, if you are using RADIUS authentication, to create centralized access policies on your IAS server. One policy will be defined for you automatically. You have the option of defining others as needed. Remote access policies are used to set conditions for allowing or denying access.

When you create a policy, you define conditions for access. You can select whether users matching the conditions are granted or denied access. You can set access conditions by selected attributes such as group membership, type of connection, type of authentication or encryption requested, or time of day and day of week.

If your remote access server is part of a native-mode Active Directory domain, you can also create per-user remote access policies. Per-user policies are not supported for remote access servers that are part of a mixed-mode domain or a Windows NT domain.

You can also set policies for dial-in constraints, IP address, multilink support, authentication, encryption, and selected additional properties that are identified by Microsoft as advanced properties.

Dial-In Constraints

Through dial-in constraints, you can set policies to:

- Disconnect automatically if the connection is idle for longer than the specified timeout period.
- Limit the maximum length of the session to a specified time period.
- Restrict access based on day and time of day.
- Limit dial-in access to a single phone number.
- Restrict the dial-in media that access will be allowed through.

For example, you might be supporting several remote users and trying to keep the number of concurrent connections to a minimum. One way to help do this is to impose a limit on the maximum session length, 20 minutes, for example. If the user isn't finished by that time, the session will be ended by the server.

IP Address

You can set how IP addresses are assigned through policy definition. The options are as follows:

- The server supplies the client's IP address.
- The client must request an IP address.
- The IP address policy is determined by the server settings.

You can also set filtering for incoming or outgoing packets. You will be prompted for the destination filter for incoming packets or source filter for outgoing packets. You will be prompted to support the source or destination IP address and subnet mask for filtering as well as the specific TCP/IP protocol the filter will be applied to. This gives you a way of building additional security protection into your design.

Multilink Support

Multilink support allows you to dial in simultaneously over multiple lines, providing a higher effective bandwidth for the connection. The default is to default to the server settings, but you can also choose to enable or disable multilink through policy settings. If you allow multilink, you can also limit the number of physical ports that can be used by the connection.

Bandwidth Allocation Protocol (BAP), which allows you to configure BAP settings, was also mentioned earlier. You can set the parameters for dropping one of the lines in a multilink connection based on average bandwidth usage over a period of time.

Authentication

You were introduced to the authentication options earlier in this chapter. Authentication options can be set through server options or through remote access properties.

Encryption

You can set the levels of encryption supported by the profile. By default, basic and strong encryption as well as no encryption (clear text) are supported. If you do not want to allow any clear-text transfers for a profile, you must explicitly enable encryption.

Advanced Properties

The advanced properties let you specify connection attributes to be returned to the server.

Even if you are using a policy to deny access, you have the option of defining a profile for the policy. Policy conditions can be overridden on a per-user basis, meaning that a user might still be allowed access even if the user account meets the policy conditions. In that case, any profile properties that you have defined would still be applied to the user.

Client Security Settings

The remote access permission setting lets you explicitly allow or deny access for the user. The default is to use the remote access policy to control access, as you saw previously in the chapter.

You can verify the caller ID to require a user to always call in from the same number. If the number doesn't match, the connection is denied. To use the option, caller ID must be supported by the caller, the remote access server, and the phone system between the two. If not, the connection will be denied.

You can also control access security through callback options. By default, the client dials in and a connection is established with the server. With callback, after the client calls in, the connection will be dropped and the server will call the client. You can have the server call back to a number specified at that time or require the server to always call back to a specified number.

You define a static IP address for the connection and it gives you the option of applying static routes. The default is to receive an IP address automatically when the connection is established. You can use static routes to limit the subnets a remote access client will have access to.

Scenario 7-1: Remote Access Design

The purpose of this scenario is to give you practice in designing a remote access solution. Suggested solutions are provided in Appendix B at the end of this manual. It may be helpful to review the case studies in Appendix C at the end of this manual.

Fairco Manufacturing

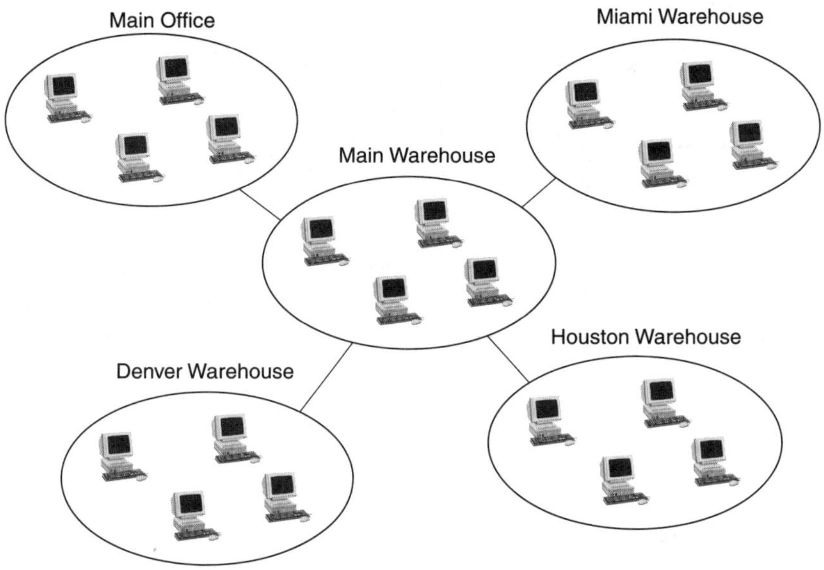

The previous figure represents a proposed network design for Fairco Manufacturing. All of the links shown are persistent links. You are planning to deploy one remote access server to allow field salespeople to dial in.

1. In which LAN will you most likely place the remote access server?

   ....

   ....

2. You don't want to have to configure multiple modems or multiport adapters to support concurrent access for multiple salespeople. How will you configure remote access support?

   ....

   ....

3. You want to be able to centrally manage the conditions that will be used to determine if a connection will be accepted. How can you do this?

   ....

   ....

REMOTE AUTHENTICATION DIAL-IN USER SERVICE (RADIUS)

You have seen a number of references to RADIUS throughout this course. This section addresses including RADIUS as part of your remote access design solution. The following topics are covered in this section:

- RADIUS Overview
- RADIUS Design

You may be unfamiliar with RADIUS, given its relatively new introduction as a Windows family-supported service. While you may not see a place for RADIUS in your immediate network design plans, you should at least be aware of RADIUS as a potential solution to networking requirements.

RADIUS Overview

Let's start with a quick description. RADIUS provides a means of managing secure authentication and accounting for remote users. It is an industry-standard client/server protocol. In a Windows 2000 network, RADIUS is used when needed to provide for user authentication outside a private network.

On a Windows 2000 system, the server side is provided through the Internet Authentication Service (IAS). The client side is configured through Routing and Remote Access, with a remote access server acting as the RADIUS client.

Using RADIUS

RADIUS makes it easier to implement and support remote access in a heterogeneous networking environment. It makes it possible to separate remote access support from remote authentication support, running each on different computers. Communication between these computers is provided through the RADIUS protocol.

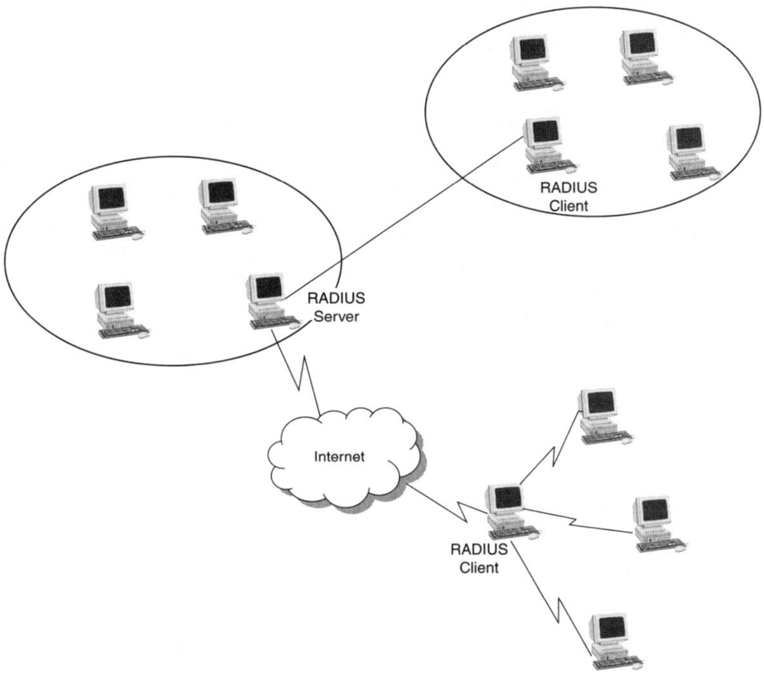

Your remote access server is the RADIUS client. It's supporting the same function as before, providing access to remote resources. This means that the same features are supported for remote client access as were discussed earlier, including support for the following:

- A variety of connection methods
- A variety of authentication protocols
- Encrypted data transmissions
- Multiple LAN protocols

RADIUS Authentication

The difference is that authentication is the responsibility of the RADIUS server.

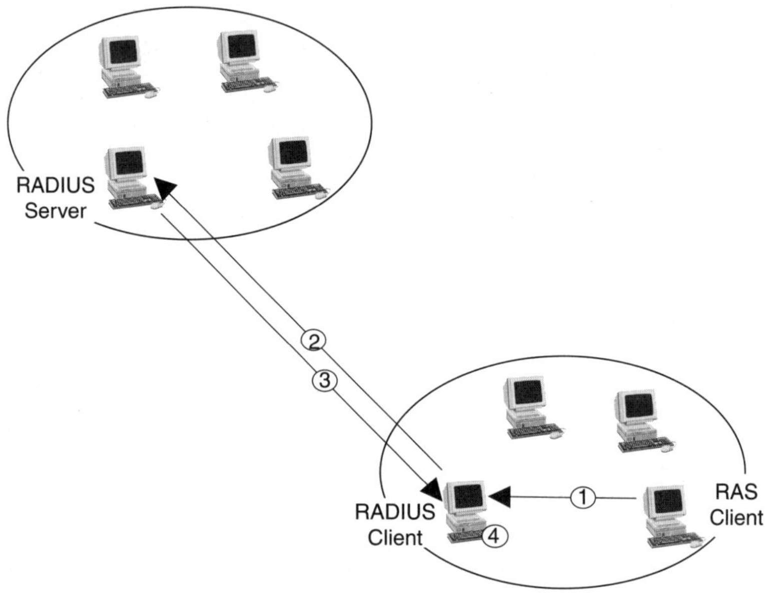

The basic flow for establishing and authenticating a connection is as follows:

1. A user connects to the RADIUS client and requests authentication.
2. The authentication request is forwarded from the RADIUS client to the RADIUS server.
3. The RADIUS server validates the access request and passes the results back to the RADIUS client.
4. The RADIUS client allows or denies access based on the RADIUS server's response.

The same authentication protocols are supported as were mentioned earlier for remote access servers. The same guidelines also apply for selecting an appropriate authentication protocol.

There is also the issue of authentication between the RADIUS client and server when a connection is established. Authentication can be through RADIUS secrets, IPSec machine certificates, or VPN tunnels. RADIUS secrets may need a little extra explanation. The secret is a simple password known by both the server and the client. The secret password is used for mutual authentication and is used in encrypting the remote access user's password before sending it for authentication.

A RADIUS server can be configured to support multiple RADIUS clients. Also, a RADIUS client can be configured to contact an alternate RADIUS server if its primary server is not available. A RADIUS server can be configured to authenticate accounts that are part of an Active Directory domain or Windows NT 4.0 domain. Mixed- and native-mode Active Directory domains are both supported. One domain will be identified as the default domain for authentication. If a user needs to be authenticated by a different domain, the remote access user must explicitly specify the domain.

Implementing RADIUS

From what you've seen already during this chapter, your first guess might be that RADIUS support is installed through Routing and Remote Access. However, when you consider that RADIUS installs as a service, you will likely come to your second, and correct, guess. RADIUS support installs through the Control Panel's Add/Remove Programs utility as one of the available Windows Networking Services components. Install Internet Authentication Service (IAS) to implement RADIUS.

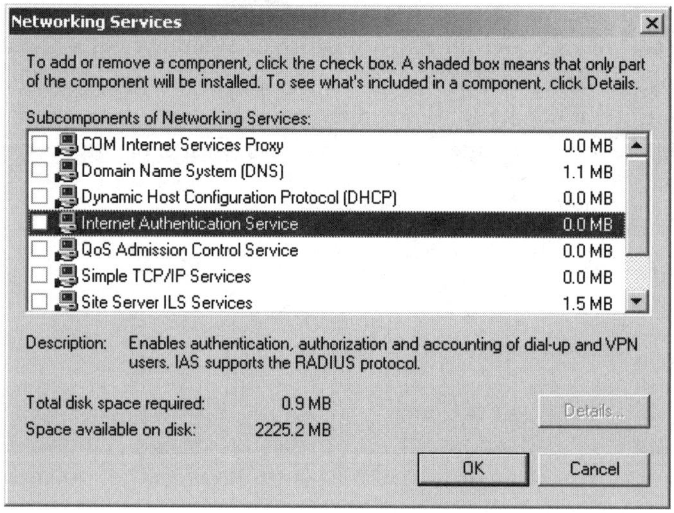

As with other services, installation is just the first step. After installation, you have to configure IAS properties through the Internet Authentication Service tool, which is added to the **Administrative Tools** menu during installation. You can:

- Register the service in the Active Directory.
- Add RADIUS clients.
- Set logging options.
- View RADIUS logs.
- Set remote access policies.

Remote access policies are used in the same way as the policies discussed earlier for remote access servers. You can set the conditions to be met and whether a condition is used to allow or deny access.

RADIUS Integration

Because RADIUS is an industry-standard protocol, Windows 2000-based RADIUS clients and servers can be integrated with other RADIUS clients and servers. The only requirement is that they adhere to the protocol specifications defined in RFCs 2138 and 2139.

RADIUS Design

As with any one component of your network design, you need to consider your current network and connectivity requirements before you start designing a RADIUS-based solution. These include the following:

- Number and location of remote clients

  You need to know the geographic locations of your remote clients. This will determine where you will be placing your RADIUS clients and will influence placement of RADIUS servers. You also need to know the number of remote clients at each location so you can determine the number of RADIUS clients you will need to install.

- Authentication source

  You will have to identify the domain (Active Directory or Windows NT 4.0) that will be used as the default source to authenticate remote access users.

- Access tracking requirements

  RADIUS gives you the ability to track successful and failed authorization attempts. You can also track the amount of time that a RADIUS client is connected.

Connection time may or may not be an issue for you. It will be for some organizations. For example, if you were charging for other organizations to access resources on your LAN, connection time would be one way of tracking time online. Tracking connection time also provides you with additional network usage statistics that you may find helpful when monitoring and optimizing network performance.

RADIUS Client

Keeping in mind that RADIUS clients are remote access servers, you have to deal with the same issues on client placement and configuration as were discussed earlier in the chapter. This includes issues such as the following:

- RADIUS Client Placement
- Connection Type
- LAN Protocols

Let's take a closer look at each of these issues.

RADIUS Client Placement

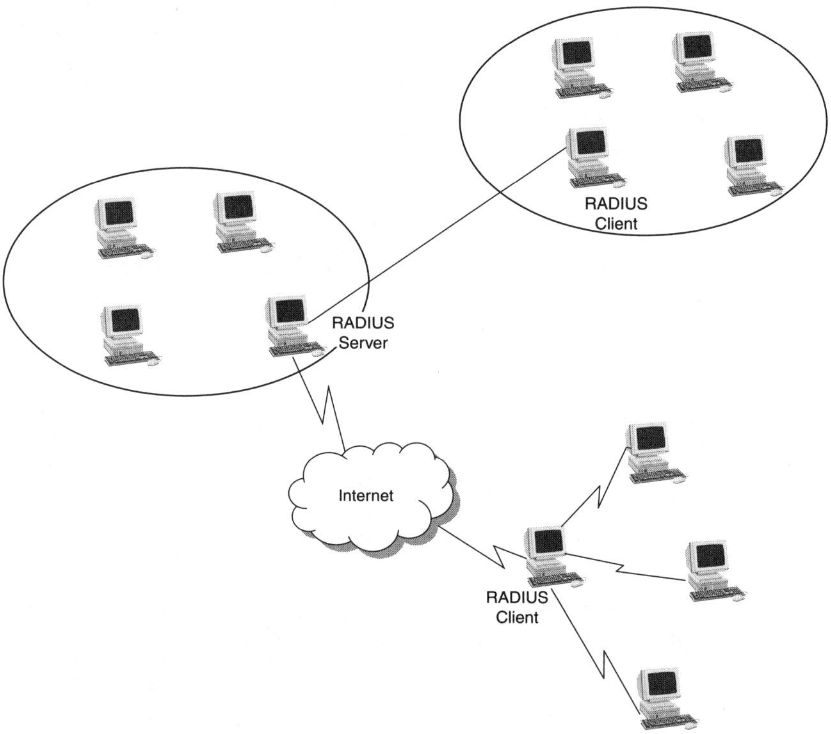

Just as was the case with other remote access servers, you will want to have your RADIUS clients placed geographically as close as possible to your remote access users. This will help you keep access charges to a minimum. You can also use a RADIUS client to provide connectivity for a remote LAN. The RADIUS client provides routing for local LAN clients.

A RADIUS server is being used for authentication for two sets of users in the previous figure. One set is on a LAN that includes a RADIUS client that works with the RADIUS server to provide authentication and access.

The other set of users is individual users who are not part of a LAN. The users are located in the same general geographic area. A RADIUS client has been set up near the remote users. Users connect to the RADIUS client through dial-up connections. The RADIUS client connects to the RADIUS server through a VPN connection.

Connection Type

You need to decide how remote access client connections are going to be supported. You can support dial-up connections, VPN connections, or both for remote users connecting to your RADIUS client.

A direct dial-in connection lets you use additional remote access security features such as callback or caller ID. You will need to provide enough incoming lines and modems or communication ports to support your remote users.

You also have the option of having remote users connect through a VPN connection. You will need to choose your communications protocol, either PPTP or L2TP, as well as the level of encryption that you want to support over the connection. Keep in mind that data transfer rates can vary over a VPN connection, so you will want to test and verify that a VPN connection can support your client applications.

LAN Protocols

You will need to select the LAN protocols that you are going to support. A RADIUS client supports the same LAN protocol options that were listed for a remote access server. The protocols you need to support will be determined by the protocols that are running on the remote access clients. Remote access clients should be configured to only use those protocols necessary to support resource access or protocol-specific applications.

RADIUS Server

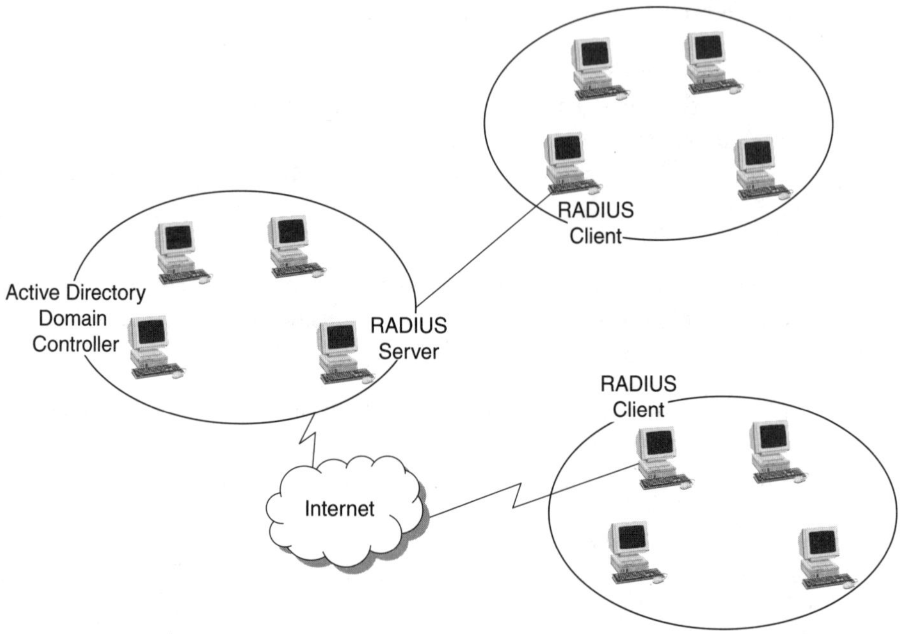

You will want to place your RADIUS server so that it is well-connected to the server that will be providing remote client authentication. For example, in an Active Directory domain, you would want to have your RADIUS server physically located on the same subnet as an Active Directory domain controller.

You have to decide how you are going to support connections between RADIUS clients and servers. Since the traffic between users and the resources they need to access is passed through the RADIUS client and server, you have to make sure that the connection can support the traffic volume. In most cases, you are going to want to have a persistent connection between the RADIUS client and server.

Designing for Performance

You have to consider both RADIUS client and RADIUS server performance in your network design. RADIUS client performance issues are the same as those discussed for remote access server performance.

The RADIUS server acts as the intermediary system between remote access clients and the network resources that they need to access. This means that you are going to need sufficient bandwidth between the RADIUS client and server to support authentication traffic and the traffic generated by resource access.

You will need to periodically monitor RADIUS server performance and should consider use of multiple servers to provide load balancing and fault tolerance. As support requirements increase, you may find it necessary to upgrade or replace some of your busier RADIUS servers. If you are using RADIUS accounting, you can relieve some of the strain on a server by reducing the amount of information recorded during RADIUS accounting.

Designing for Security

As you saw with remote access, user access can be controlled through user access properties and remote access policies. Remote access policy management is centralized at the RADIUS server. Policies on the RADIUS server are applied when a remote access user is authenticated. Any remote access policies created on the RADIUS client are ignored.

When defining the connection between the RADIUS client and server, you can select the level of encryption for passing authentication information and for passing user data. The same encryption methods are supported between the RADIUS client and server as were described earlier for encryption between a remote access user and remote access server. You can use either MPPE or IPSec as your encryption method.

You can use screened subnets to improve security in your RADIUS implementation design. When using screened subnets, RADIUS clients are placed outside the screened subnet and RADIUS servers are placed inside the screened subnet. This will prevent user accounts and remote access policies from being exposed outside of your private network. This configuration requires that the RADIUS client and server communicate through VPN or IPSec tunnels.

Scenario 7-2: RADIUS Design

The purpose of this scenario is to give you practice in designing a RADIUS authentication solution. Suggested solutions are provided in Appendix B at the end of this manual. It may be helpful to review the case studies in Appendix C at the end of this manual.

Fairco Manufacturing

1. You are considering a network design where a LAN will be set up at each remote warehouse. You want to use RADIUS authentication to authenticate remote users. What changes will you have to make to the current security model before you can deploy your RADIUS solution?

   ....

   ....

2. Where would you place your RADIUS server?

   ....

   ....

3. Where would you place your RADIUS client or clients?

   ....

   ....

4. What type of connection will you need to use between the remote warehouses and the main office?

   ....

   ....

NETWORK ADDRESS TRANSLATION (NAT)

Starting with this section, attention is focused on technologies and services that can be implemented to support Internet access. First among these is the use of NAT. The following topics are covered in this section:

- NAT Overview
- NAT Design

You were given a brief introduction to NAT earlier in the course. This section is designed to provide you with additional details about how you can use NAT in your network design.

NAT Overview

To be completely accurate, NAT is a protocol supported through Windows 2000 Routing and Remote Access. For the sake of simplicity, NAT will be used throughout this section and through the remainder of this course to refer to the NAT protocol.

NAT is one of the solutions available to you for providing network users with Internet access. In most network environments, you are *not* going to want to provide access to the Internet on a user-by-user basis. Not only is this not the most cost-effective solution, it can become a serious threat to network security.

NAT Features

NAT is used to keep private network addresses private. It translates one or more public IP addresses to the private IP addresses used on your LAN. In other words, it sets a translation mapping between public and private addresses. NAT can also provide IP address and configuration options to its clients on your private network and can forward DNS name resolution requests to both local DNS servers and DNS servers on the Internet.

Not only does NAT provide network users access to the Internet, it also protects your private network resources from unauthorized access from the Internet. Any requests made by Internet users for network resources must be forwarded through NAT. Internet users cannot directly access your private network resources.

NAT Configuration

Let's take a look at a few configuration issues and guidelines for NAT servers. Considering the configuration issues that have been discussed for other services during this course, you probably already have a good idea of the configuration issues that will need to be addressed when implementing NAT.

Hardware Configuration

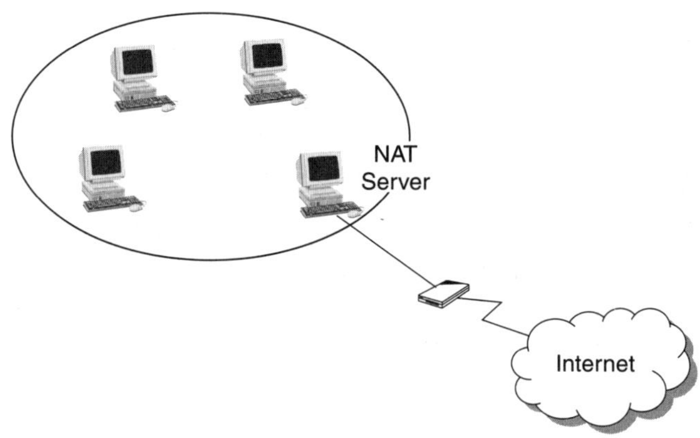

A NAT server must be configured with at least two network interfaces. You need one to provide connectivity to your private network and one to provide connectivity to the Internet. Each network interface must be configured with an IP address and subnet mask. The IP address and subnet mask values must be compatible with the subnet each interface is connected to, the same as any subnet host.

Configuring IP Address Assignment

If you are using automatic address assignment, you will find configuration requirements for both the NAT server and its clients. You will need to configure the local subnet's clients to support automatic address assignment, just as you would if you were setting them up as a DHCP client. Any system that can be configured as a DHCP client will also be supported by NAT.

At the server side, you need to specify an IP address range and subnet mask. You also have the option of using APIPA addresses. If you choose to use APIPA addresses, you will need to configure the NAT server with a static address taken from that address range.

Configuring DNS Forwarding

The ability to forward DNS name resolution queries is available if you need to use it. It won't be needed if you are setting up an NAT server on a nonrouted LAN or if there is local DNS name server support.

NAT Integration

There are some potential concerns and configuration issues that must be considered when integrating NAT into an existing network. Two key issues are IP address management and protocol support.

IP Address Management

NAT provides IP address and configuration information for your private network hosts. This includes IP address, subnet mask, and other configuration options such as default gateway, primary DNS server, and so forth. Because of this, you cannot have DHCP servers configured with scopes to provide IP configuration for any subnet that is using NAT.

Protocol Support

There are a large number of protocols that are *not* supported by NAT. The only LAN protocol supported by NAT is IP. In addition, NAT does not support the following:

- Kerberos v5
- Internet Protocol Security (IPSec)
- Lightweight Directory Access Protocol (LDAP)
- Simple Network Management Protocol (SNMP)
- Microsoft Remote Procedure Call (RPC)

This is only a partial list of the protocols that are not supported. Obviously, if you need to provide support for applications requiring any protocol that is not supported, you are not going to be able to use NAT.

NAT Design

You need to determine if NAT meets your Internet access design requirements and if it is required for Internet access. NAT can be used when supporting nonrouted users. This doesn't mean that you can use NAT in a routed environment, but that you will be setting up NAT for each subnet with Internet access requirements.

As mentioned earlier, NAT provides limited protocol support. You cannot use NAT if any of your applications require protocols not supported by NAT. An alternate solution in this case would be Microsoft Proxy Server.

NAT is only supported on networks where hosts are configured with private IP addresses. If your network hosts are configured with public IP addresses, you don't have to use address translation to connect to the Internet, though you are going to want to filter traffic between your private network and the Internet.

Once you've decided that you are going to use NAT, you have to decide what features you are going to implement. An NAT server can provide IP address assignment, much as a DHCP server can provide name resolution by forwarding name resolution queries to a DNS server.

NAT Server Placement

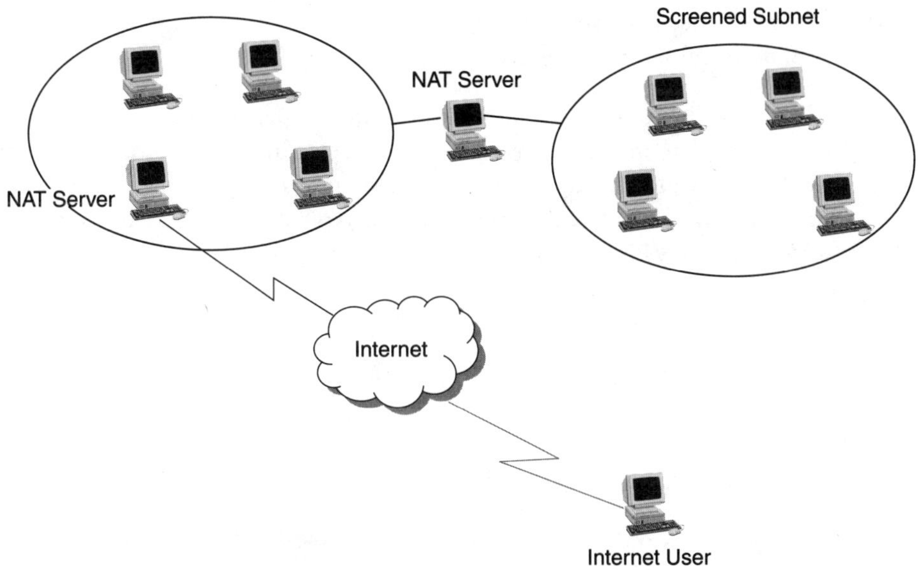

One point about NAT server placement is going to be obvious. You are going to place an NAT server on the same subnet as the hosts that need Internet access. However, you can also use NAT to provide Internet users with screened access to selected resources on your private network. You can even use NAT between private subnets to create screened subnets.

Designing for Performance

You have two transmission rates that you have to consider when configuring an NAT server. On one side, you have the interface that is connecting to your private network and, on the other, the interface connecting to the Internet.

The connection to your private network will be a persistent connection. Its transmission rate will be determined by the network segment's transmission rate. The connection to the Internet can be set up as either a persistent or nonpersistent connection. That transmission rate will be determined by the type of connection used. NAT supports use of dial-up and VPN connections.

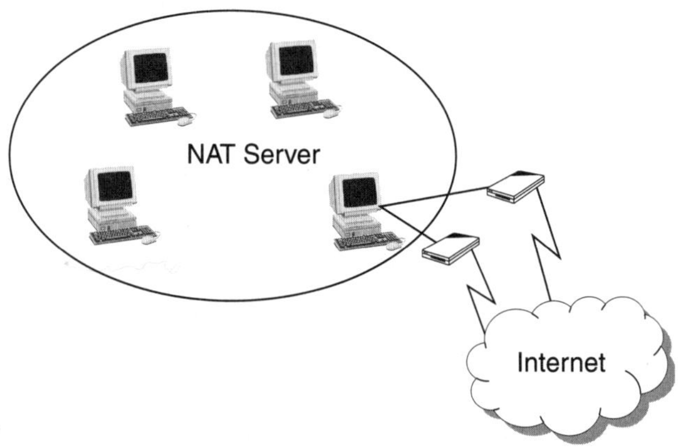

If you are going to have a bottleneck, it's probably going to be with the Internet connection. You can improve performance over the Internet connection by using a persistent connection and avoiding the connection time inherent in a demand-dial connection. You can also improve performance by providing multiple connections to the Internet.

The issue with transmission rates is the same as you've already seen repeated during this course. You have to make sure that your transmission rates are going to be able to support incoming and outgoing traffic requirements. Don't forget to consider the impact of the additional traffic generated by your NAT server on your local network segment.

Issues relating to NAT server performance are the same as you've seen before for other network service servers. Make sure that your server has the resources necessary to support NAT. Also, remember that combining services on a server can put a strain on available resources.

Designing for Security

It is important to understand how you are limited with NAT as well as how NAT can be configured to enhance security. You were told earlier that NAT security is somewhat limited. One of these limitations is that you cannot restrict Internet access on a user-by-user basis.

Of course, there are security features that are supported by NAT that you may find helpful in your network design. Since NAT is implemented as a Routing and Remote Access protocol, IP filtering is supported. As a reminder, IP filtering is used to control traffic coming into or going out of a routed network. Filtering options were discussed earlier in this course. You can apply filters to the private network interface, Internet interface, or both.

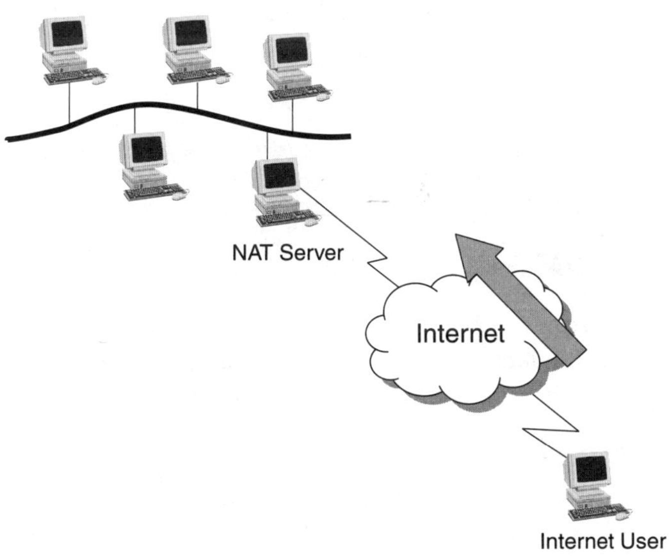

In addition to filtering, you can provide additional protection for your private network's resources through use of address pools and special port mappings. By default, Internet users will not be allowed any access to your private network's resources. However, you have the option of configuring access to selected resources through NAT.

If your NAT server is configured with multiple public IP addresses, you can place addresses in an address pool that can be used for supporting access to private resources. NAT will evaluate resource requests and forward them to servers on the private network as appropriate. This option cannot be used when you need to restrict access to ports on the resource server since the requester is given access to all IP ports on the resource server.

The other option is to define special port mappings. You are required to use this solution if you want to provide access to private resources and only have one public IP address configured on the NAT server. This enables you to examine the IP address and port number of a request coming in from the Internet, then forwards the request to the IP address and specific port number on the resource server. Each shared resource requires a separate special port mapping.

NOTE: Unless you have a specific requirement to provide resources to Internet users, leave NAT configured with the default selection (no access).

Scenario 7-3: NAT Design

The purpose of this scenario is to give you practice in resolving NAT design issues. Suggested solutions are provided in Appendix B at the end of this manual. It may be helpful to review the case studies in Appendix C at the end of this manual.

Things and Stuff

1. You are considering the use of NAT to provide LAN users with Internet access. What changes would have to be made to the current network design to support this?

   ....

   ....

2. How would you decide what range of IP addresses to use for LAN host addresses?

   ....

   ....

MICROSOFT PROXY SERVER

This section continues the focus on Internet connectivity, this time with an introduction to Microsoft's Proxy Server 2.0. While this is not quite as in-depth as some of the service introductions you've seen in this course, it will still provide you with enough information to start determining if there is a place for Proxy Server in your network design. The following topics are covered in this section:

- Proxy Server Overview
- Proxy Server Design

In the previous section, you were told that Proxy Server is a potential alternative when NAT cannot meet your Internet access requirements. Now you will be able to see why.

Proxy Server Overview

Microsoft Proxy Server allows you to provide network users access to the Internet and Internet users access to resources on your private network. Proxy Server security features give you a great deal of control over inbound and outbound access, making it possible for you to protect your private network from unauthorized access or access to unauthorized resources.

While this may sound like a description of NAT, Proxy Server is a more secure and robust solution. It includes features beyond those supported by NAT. However, unlike other network services that have been discussed in this course, Proxy Server does not ship with Windows 2000. It is available as a separate product that is supported by Windows 2000.

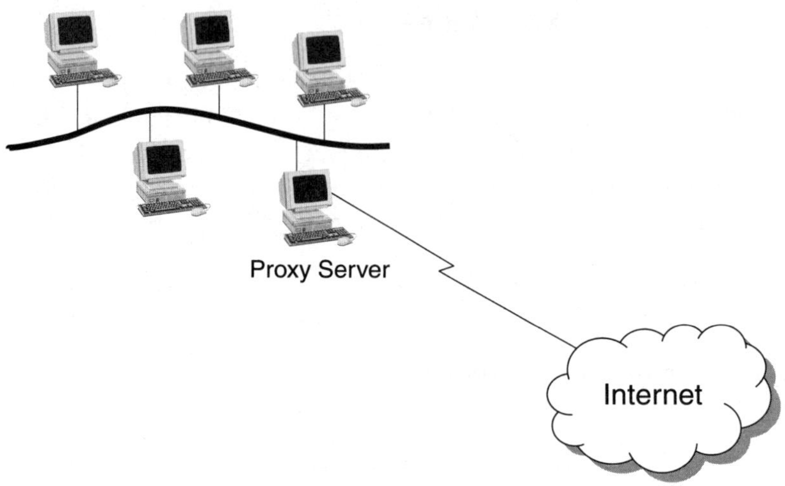

The fundamental purpose of Proxy Server is the same as that of NAT–to keep your private network private. You can use Proxy Server to control inbound and outbound traffic between your private network and the public Internet. It can also be used to set up screened subnets within your private network.

Proxy Server adds a great deal of flexibility to your network design. It supports both TCP/IP and IPX/SPX clients, which means you can provide IPX/SPX clients access to the Internet without having to install TCP/IP support. You can also use Proxy Server to perform IPX/SPX-to-TCP/IP translation in support of your private network. This application of Proxy Server doesn't require a connection to the Internet.

Using Proxy Server

Proxy Server gives you the ability to select which users in your private network are going to be allowed Internet access. This means that you can limit access to only those users who have a real need to access the Internet rather than throwing Internet access open to all users. Proxy Server supports filtering, letting you select the IP packets to be passed or discarded based on IP address and port numbers.

By its design, Proxy Server can also improve performance when commonly accessed Internet resources are requested. When requested FTP or HTTP resources are retrieved from the Internet, they are passed to the requesting client and cached locally at the proxy server. Should the same resource be requested again while still in the cache, the proxy server will service the request from its own cache rather than going back out to the Internet to retrieve the resource. If a proxy server is being used just for caching purposes, it can be configured with a single network interface connecting it to the private network. If requested data isn't locally cached by a proxy server, the request can be forwarded to another network proxy server.

Proxy Server can also route resource requests from Internet users to appropriate resource servers on your private network. It will intercept and evaluate incoming Uniform Resource Locator (URL) requests. Requests that map to private network resources, if allowed, will be forwarded as appropriate.

Proxy Server Configuration

Let's take a moment to go over some configuration issues. These include issues relating to both server and client configuration.

Hardware Configuration

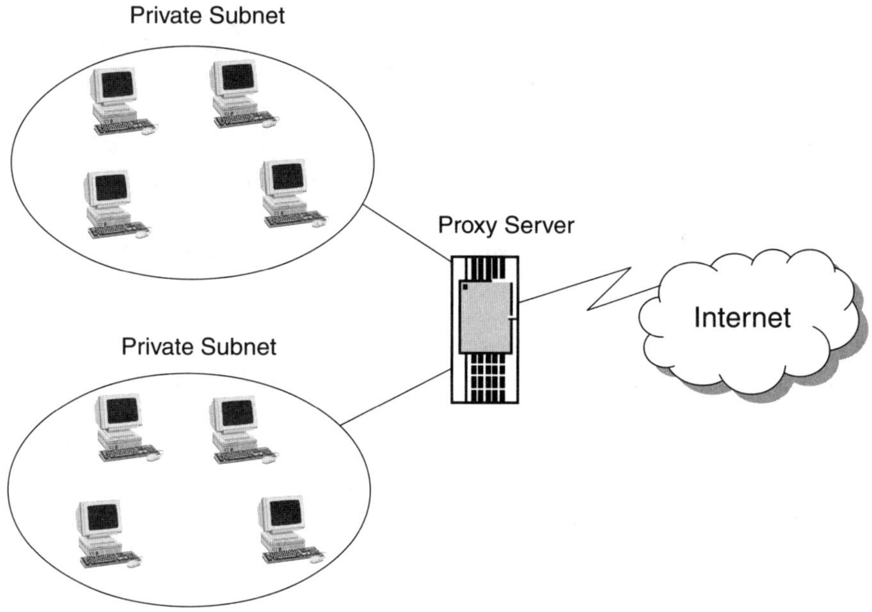

Each proxy server must be configured with at least one network interface. Proxy servers that only provide cache or IPX/SPX-to-TCP/IP translation will only require one network interface. Proxy servers providing a connection between your private network and the Internet will need at least two network interfaces but may have additional network interfaces installed.

The hardware configuration issues are much the same as they were when setting up an NAT server. Each network interface will have to be configured with appropriate IP address and subnet mask values.

IP Address Configuration

You will need to identify a range of IP addresses for the proxy server. This will be a range of IP addresses from those used on the private network. Local clients will communicate with the proxy server through these addresses. The addresses are stored on the proxy server in its Local Address Table (LAT). The proxy server compares the addresses on requests with the addresses in the LAT to identify Internet requests.

Client Configuration

You are not required to install any special Proxy Server client software on your client systems. You have the option of configuring the client systems with the proxy server's IP address as the default gateway address. Any requests for resources that are not on the local subnet will be forwarded to the proxy server. This is going to generate extra traffic in a routed network environment since requests for resources local on other subnets in the private network will have to be routed through the proxy server and on to the appropriate subnet.

You can reduce private network traffic by configuring Proxy Server clients with client software that will send only requests for Internet resources to the proxy server. Each client that has a copy of one of the supported client software options installed will have a local copy of the proxy server's LAT, which is used in determining if requests should be forwarded to the proxy server.

Client software options include the following:

- Proxy Server client

  The Proxy Server client supports IP traffic on any operating system that supports the WinSock standard. It can also be used on IPX/SPX-based private networks.
- Microsoft Internet Explorer (IE) 5.0 (or later)

  IE can be used when client access requirements are limited to FTP and HTTP traffic. IE is readily available for Windows-family operating systems.
- SOCKS

  SOCKS can be used on operating systems that run SOCKS-compatible applications. Supported operating systems include UNIX and Apple Macintosh.

Each of these client options also includes some filtering capabilities.

Proxy Server Integration

Proxy Server can be easily integrated into existing networks. When deployed in a Windows 2000 Active Directory domain, a single domain logon also provides access to the Internet through the proxy server.

Proxy Server Design

You should consider Proxy Server as an Internet access solution in situations where direct user access and NAT cannot meet your access requirements. Unlike NAT, Proxy Server lets you control Internet access on a user-by-user basis. You can also control Internet access to private resources on a resource-by-resource basis. It can be used in both routed and nonrouted network environments and is well suited to networks that encompass a large geographic scope.

Proxy Server is also a potential solution to screened subnet requirements. The same security features that can be used to isolate your private network from the Internet can also be used to isolate one subnet from other subnets in your private network.

Proxy Server Placement

Part of your network design process will be determining where you are going to physically place proxy servers in the network. You are going to want to minimize the additional traffic generated by Proxy Server, but you don't want to compromise network security in the process. Your placement must provide access for all Proxy Server clients and must give the proxy server a path to resources being shared with the Internet.

Inside the Network

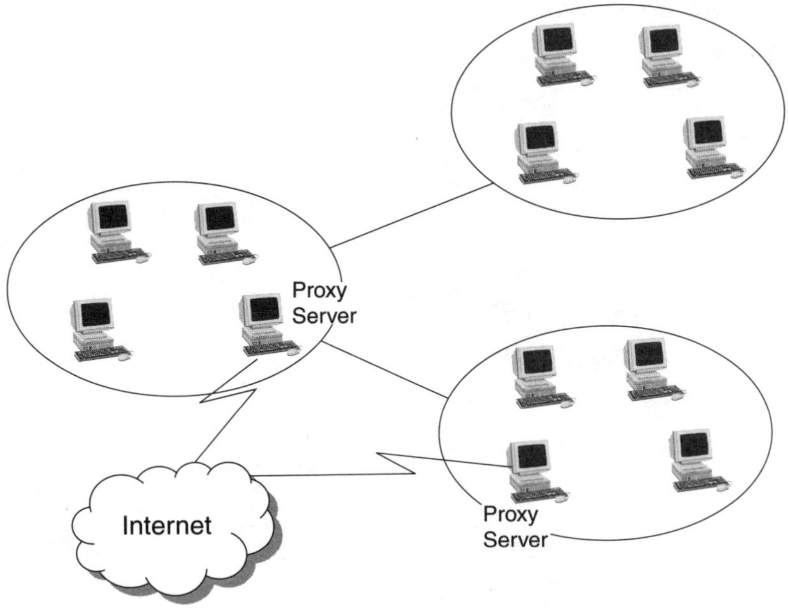

One option is to deploy Proxy Server as a directly connected part of your private network. This will improve communication performance between the proxy server and its clients.

The number of proxy servers you need to deploy will depend on the load generated by Internet access. In a routed network environment, you may want to place proxy servers on multiple subnets.

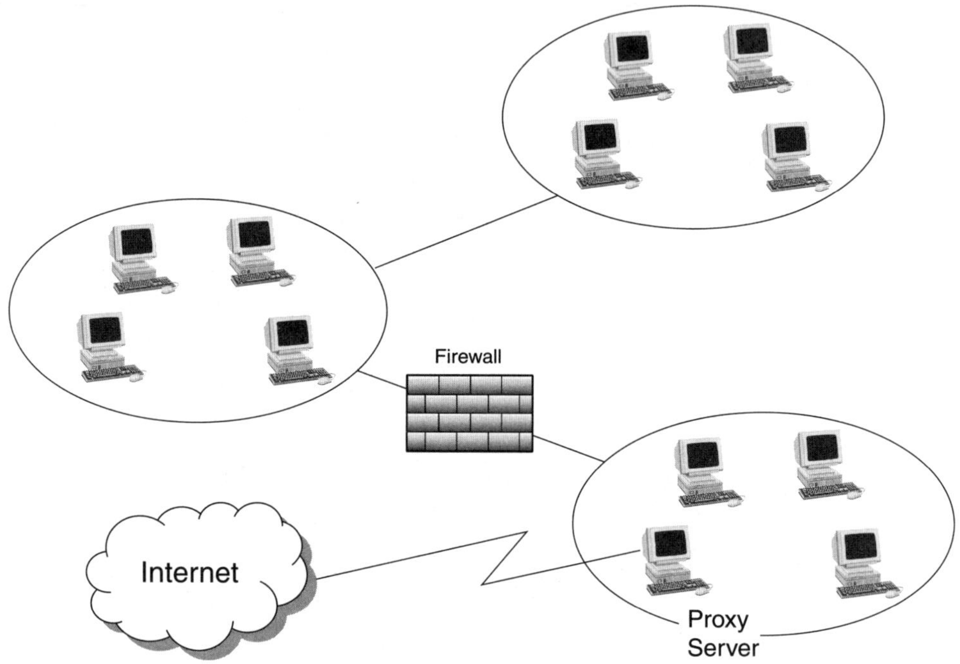

You should be aware that deploying a proxy server directly in your private network may carry some additional design overhead. You should consider setting up the subnets a proxy server is deployed in as screened subnets to provide additional security.

Outside the Network

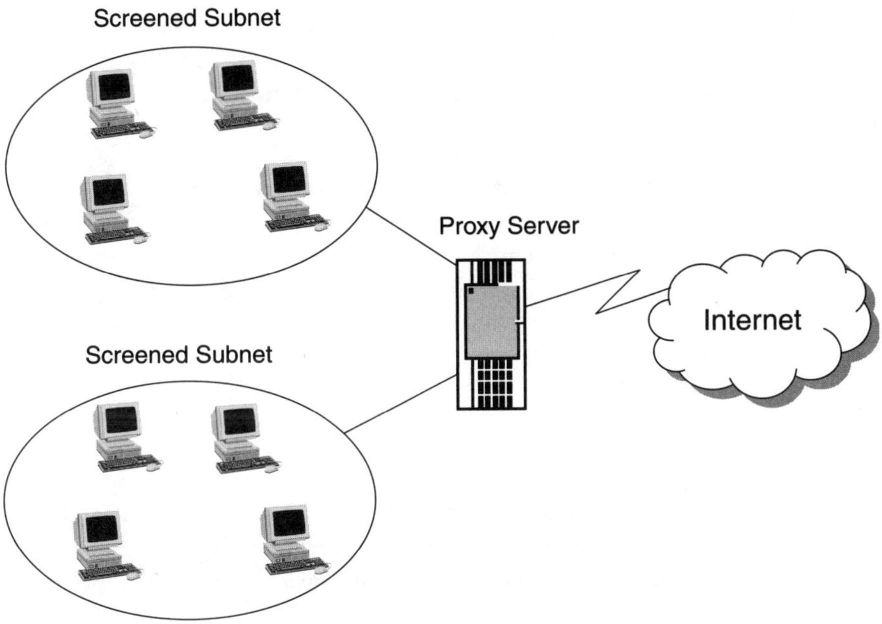

You can also improve security while still providing inbound and outbound access by deploying a proxy server just outside of your private network. In this configuration, the proxy server provides communication between the Internet and private network subnets, isolating the private network from the Internet.

You can set up multiple screened subnets by using either a single proxy server with multiple network adapters or by setting up multiple proxy servers, one for each subnet. Use of a single proxy server provides you with centralized management, but there is a potential concern about system performance due to the strain placed on server resources. Multiple proxy servers make it easier to maximize performance but do result in a somewhat decentralized management model.

Designing for Performance

There are at least two transmission rates that must be considered when working with a proxy server to provide Internet access: the connection between the proxy server and your private network, and the connection between the proxy server and the Internet. Keep in mind, however, that you might have multiple connections configured on either side.

A connection to your private network will be a persistent connection. Its transmission rate will be determined by the network segment's transmission rate. A connection to the Internet can be set up as either a persistent or nonpersistent connection. That transmission rate will be determined by the type of connection used.

If you are going to have a bottleneck, it's probably going to be your connection with the Internet. You can improve performance over the Internet connection by using a persistent connection and by providing multiple connections to the Internet.

The issue with transmission rates is the same as you've already seen repeated during this course. You have to make sure that your transmission rates are going to be able to support incoming and outgoing traffic requirements. Don't forget to consider the impact of the additional traffic generated by your proxy server on your local network segment.

Optimizing Individual Proxy Servers

It shouldn't be necessary to go back over hardware performance issues and bottlenecks. These have been discussed at length throughout the course. There is, however, an issue that is specific to Proxy Server that can impact performance, which is the way that caching is implemented.

Proxy Server supports two caching options. By default, a proxy server is configured to use active caching. Active caching automatically updates cached information based on the number of requests and the detected frequency of changes.

Passive caching doesn't automatically update cached information. Instead, the cache is only updated when requested information is retrieved from the Internet. Passive caching requires less processor overhead than active caching but does require more disk space.

Optimizing Multiple Proxy Servers

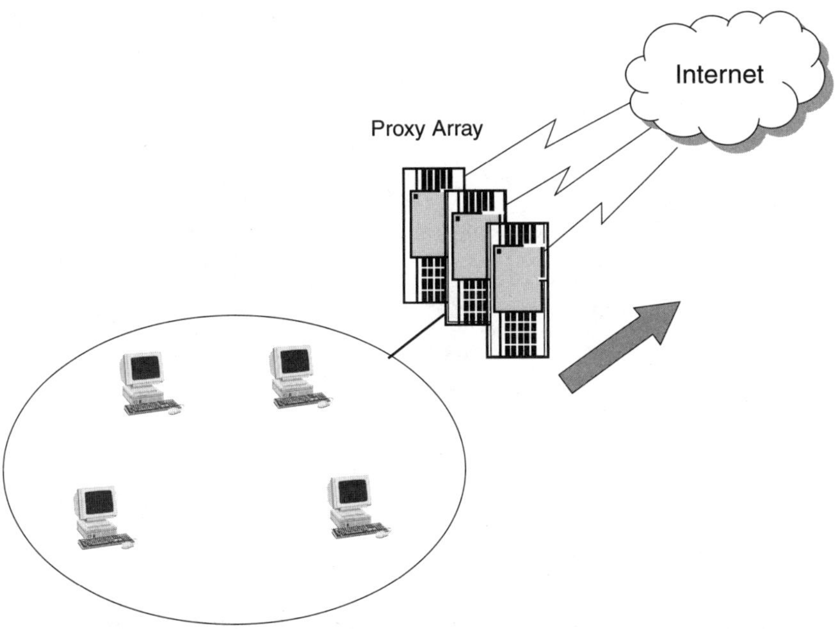

One way of improving performance and availability for outgoing requests is through the use of multiple proxy servers configured as a Proxy Array. This provides load balancing through the use of multiple servers and fault tolerance should any of the servers fail.

All members of the Proxy Array must be identified by the same Proxy Array name. They must also be members of the same Active Directory domain and must be configured as part of the same site. This is because the configuration information for all of the servers in the array is stored in the Active Directory database.

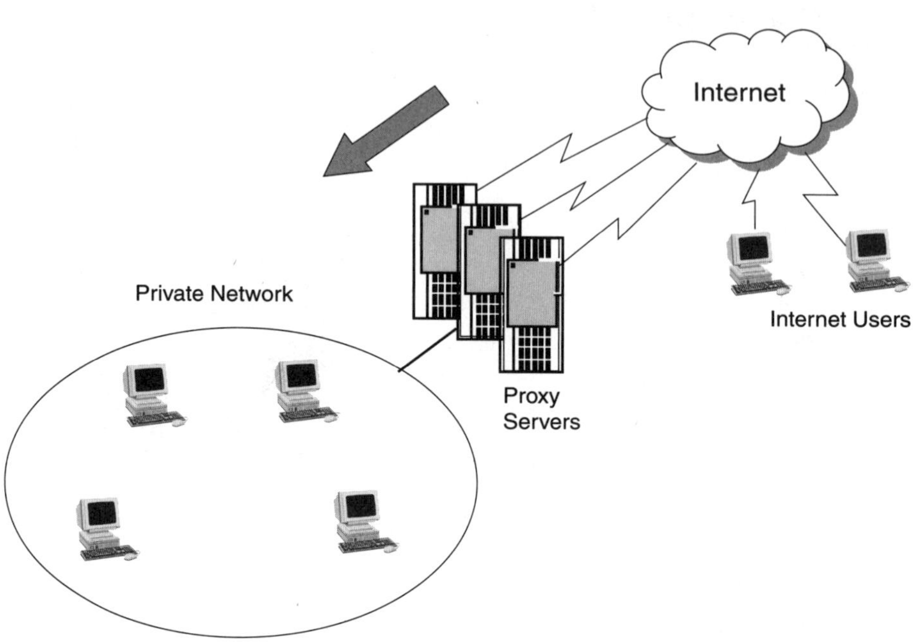

You also have other options for improving performance and availability through the use of multiple proxy servers. You can specify a round-robin DNS entry for each of the proxy servers or implement Network Load Balancing.

Outbound traffic will benefit most from the use of Proxy Array. Inbound traffic performance will be optimized through the use of round-robin DNS entries or Network Load Balancing.

> *NOTE:* *Round-robin DNS entries and Network Load Balancing are discussed later in this course.*

Designing for Security

Security is one of the primary reasons for using Proxy Server to control communications between your private network and the Internet. Let's look at some specific security issues and how they are addressed by Proxy Server.

User Access Control

How user access control is managed is somewhat dependent on the network environment Proxy Server is deployed in. In an Active Directory domain, Proxy Server is integrated with Active Directory to provide access control through a single logon. Internet access is controlled through Active Directory permissions, giving you the ability to manage access through group membership or through explicit assignments to individual users.

This is one situation where you may find it appropriate to enable the Guest account. Though normally not suggested, you can enable the Guest account to allow access to non-Active Directory domain clients that are part of a heterogeneous networking environment.

In a non-Active Directory network, you will be installing Proxy Server on a stand-alone Windows 2000 system. Access will be controlled through local users and groups created on the proxy server. You can simplify access by enabling the Guest account and thereby allowing anonymous access to the proxy server.

> *NOTE: In either case, enabling the Guest account for anonymous access means that you are no longer controlling access on a user-by-user basis.*

Packet Filtering

You can use packet filtering to control both inbound and outbound traffic through your proxy server. This gives you a way of controlling user access to Internet-based resources and Internet user access to local resource providers. Filtering can be based on the following:

- Traffic direction

  You can choose to filter inbound traffic only, outbound traffic only, or both.

- Protocol

  You can filter based on specific protocols within the TCP/IP protocol suite.

- IP address

  Filtering can be based on local and remote IP addresses. Filtering can be based on a range of addresses or on specific individual addresses.

- Port numbers

  You can also filter packets based on local and remote TCP and UDP port numbers. Filtering can be based on any port number, limited to specific port numbers, or can include a range of unknown port numbers.

You must also specify whether packet criteria are used to forward or deny requests.

Scenario 7-4: Using Proxy Server

The purpose of this scenario is to give you practice in resolving Proxy Server design issues. Suggested solutions are provided in Appendix B at the end of this manual. It may be helpful to review the case studies in Appendix C at the end of this manual.

Barney's Bank

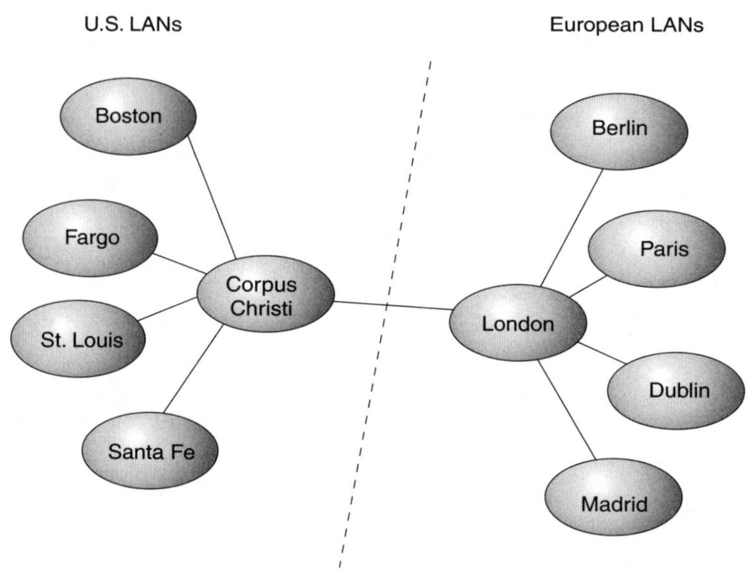

The previous figure represents a proposed network design for Barney's Bank. All links shown in the figure are persistent links.

1. You are considering a Proxy Server solution that will use two proxy servers shared by multiple LANs. One of your primary concerns is minimizing the traffic required to authorize Internet access requests. Where would you place the proxy servers to minimize WAN traffic?

2. The European remote LANs have several non-Windows Active Directory domain hosts. How can you configure your solution to authorize Internet access for those hosts with a minimum of management overhead?

3. Barney's Bank is acquiring a new location that currently has a NetWare 3.12 network. As part of the initial conversion process, you want to install a proxy server to provide IPX/SPX to TCP/IP translation for that LAN. The LAN has no Internet access requirements. What are the hardware connectivity requirements in this situation?

VIRTUAL PRIVATE NETWORK (VPN)

With the number of references to VPN connections during the course so far, you probably have a good idea already of its purpose and use. This section provides you with more detailed information about VPN. The following topics are covered in this section:

- VPN Concepts
- VPN and Tunneling
- VPN Protocols
- VPN Management
- VPN Design

This discussion about VPN is structured a little differently than earlier discussions during this course about implementing network and Internet services. With the earlier discussions, the emphasis was on solution design. VPN is a potential part of that solution design, providing a secure path for communications. The earlier discussions focused on what communication paths were needed. Now you'll be looking at an option for implementing those paths.

VPN Concepts

A VPN provides secure communication support for your network. VPN connections are typically discussed in the context of remote connections through the Internet. One of the advantages of this type of connection is that a dial-up connection that would otherwise require a long-distance call can be serviced through a local call to an Internet Service Provider (ISP). However, that's not the only way of using VPN in your network design. VPN connections can be used in any situation where you need a secure communication path. This can include providing security when passing confidential data between local subnets on your private network.

This discussion about the use of VPN technology is going to focus on providing a secure communication path through the Internet. Though some of the implementation details will differ when using VPNs in a local private network, the concepts are the same.

Connection Overview

Let's start with an overview of remote connectivity options. There are two connection options for connecting to a VPN server:

- Single-user connection

  A single user can connect as a VPN client via the network. This is similar to a remote access client connecting to a standard remote access server except that the client dials in to its ISP rather than dialing the remote access server directly.

- Network connection

  You also have the option of configuring a remote router as a VPN client. The router connects to the VPN server through the Internet. Remote network clients access resources through the router.

The VPN server's connection to the Internet must be through a persistent connection. Depending on traffic requirements, the connection is typically made through a T1, Fractional T1, or Frame Relay connection. When configuring the WAN adapter that connects to the dedicated line, it will need to be configured with an IP address and subnet mask. This can be an address assigned to your domain or one provided by your ISP. You will also need to configure the adapter with the ISP's default gateway.

Clients can connect through a persistent or nonpersistent (dial-up) connection to the Internet. A persistent connection is more commonly used when connecting a remote router. A dial-up connection is typically used to support a single-user connection but can be used to support a small remote network with limited bandwidth requirements.

Remote client (individual or router) addresses can be configured as static addresses, can be assigned from an address pool, or can be assigned through DHCP.

Authentication and Authorization

Essentially, the same authentication and authorization options as discussed previously for remote access servers are supported for VPNs. You can configure the VPN server to use Windows authentication or RADIUS authentication.

Access security remains as critical an issue, if not more so, as when supporting dial-in remote access. The only thing really keeping the public Internet out of your network is your access security.

Access can be authorized by user or by group. User access is authorized through user properties. Group access is authorized through remote access policy.

VPN and Tunneling

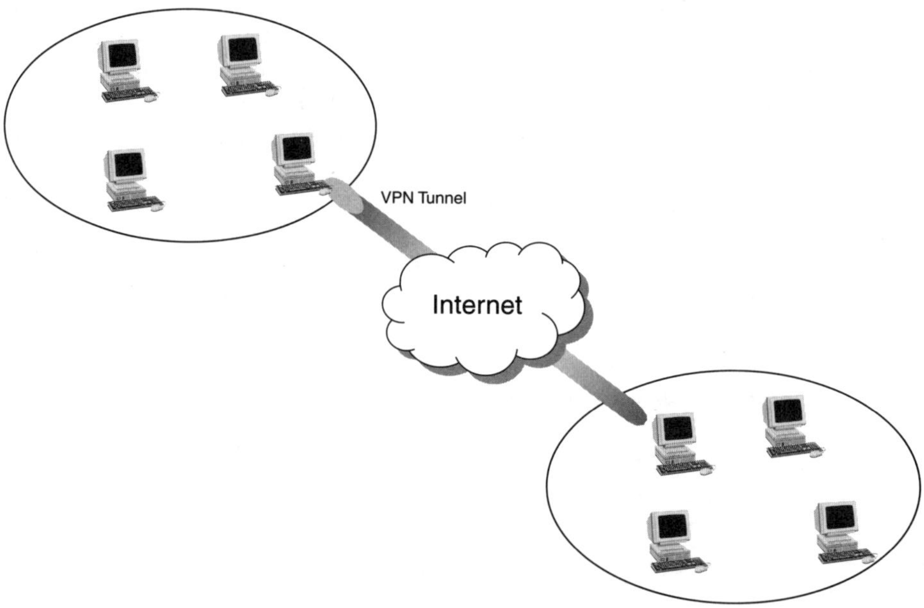

During VPN transmissions, data packets must be encapsulated with an additional header before being transferred across the Internet. They are then de-encapsulated at the receiving end. This process of encapsulating and transmitting data is known as tunneling. The path that the data travels is known as a tunnel. Tunneling is supported through tunneling protocols that support tunnel maintenance and tunnel data transfer. For a server and client to communicate, they must share a common tunneling protocol.

Tunnel Maintenance

The first step in tunneling is creating the tunnel. Tunnel creation is initiated by the tunnel client. The tunnel server will request authentication from the client. The client must be authenticated and authorized before the server will allow a tunnel connection. Once the tunnel is established, the client and server can begin transferring data.

Some tunneling technologies, including those used by Windows 2000 VPNs (PPTP and L2TP), require tunnel maintenance after the tunnel has been created. When no data is being transferred, each end of the tunnel will periodically poll the other end to determine its state and to keep the tunnel open.

Either end of the tunnel can terminate the tunnel. This is typically done through an exchange of tunnel termination messages.

Tunnel Data Transfer

Data cannot be transferred until the tunnel has been created. After the tunnel is created, the tunnel data transfer protocol is responsible for encapsulating and de-encapsulating data. After the data has been de-encapsulated, it can either be processed by the local system or forwarded through the local network as appropriate.

Tunnel Types

There are two basic tunnel types: voluntary tunnels and compulsory tunnels. Voluntary tunnels are created through user interaction at the client computer. Compulsory tunnels are created automatically without user intervention or knowledge.

Voluntary Tunnels

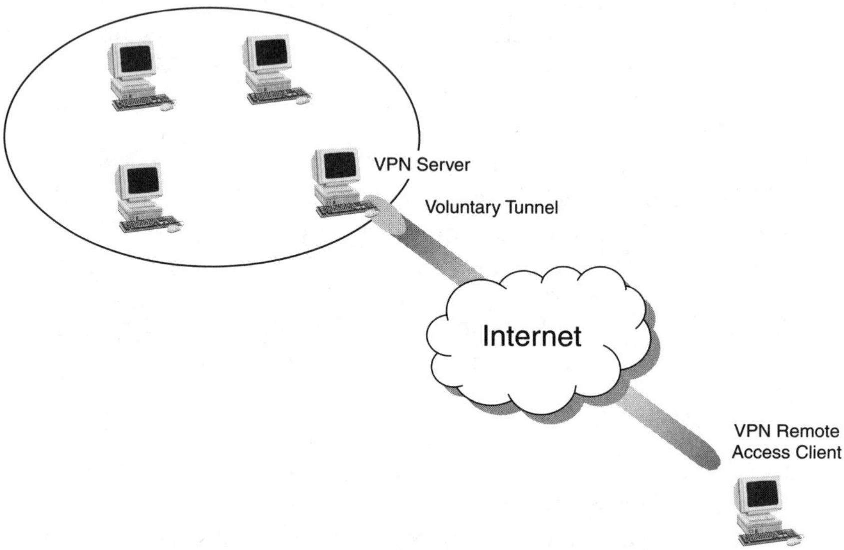

A voluntary tunnel can be created if the client system is already connected to an internetwork (such as the Internet) or if the client establishes a dial-up connection to the internetwork that will be used for transferring data. The client workstation creates the tunnel to the target server. Individual VPN clients are an example of using voluntary tunnels.

Compulsory Tunnels

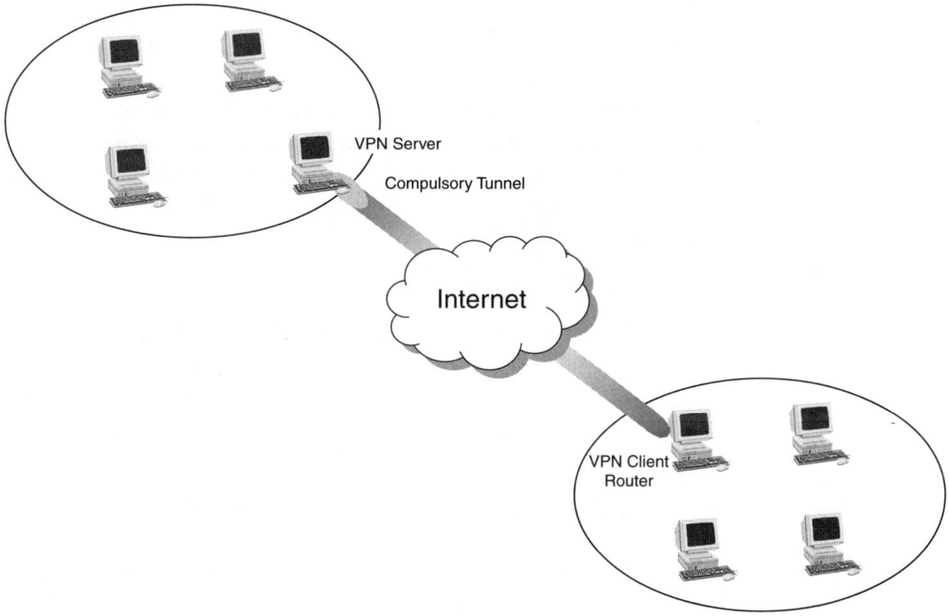

A user's computer is not the endpoint in a compulsory tunnel. Instead, there is another system the user's computer can communicate with. The device that establishes the tunnel with the target server is known as an access concentrator. That device, a network router, for example, establishes the tunnel and acts as the tunnel endpoint. Since the user's computer isn't involved in establishing the tunnel, it doesn't need to have a tunneling protocol installed.

There are two types of compulsory tunnels:

- Static compulsory tunnels

  Static compulsory tunnels can be configured as either automatic tunnels or realm-based tunnels. An automatic tunnel uses dedicated local access lines to have each client automatically tunneled to a specific access concentrator. Realm-based tunneling does not require dedicated lines or communication equipment. Instead, a portion of the user's name is used to determine the tunneling destination. This portion of the user's name is known as the realm. All users in the same realm will be tunneled to the same destination.

- Dynamic compulsory tunnels

  You have the option of making tunneling selections on a per-user basis with dynamic compulsory tunneling. This gives you a great deal of flexibility since tunnel destinations can be based on specific user properties. Dynamic compulsory tunneling does not require the client to be connected through a dedicated line.

  User information for determining dial-up client tunneling is stored in a database. The database can be local to the access concentrator or may be maintained in a RADIUS server.

VPN Protocols

Before going any further in this discussion about VPN, you need to be introduced to the VPN protocols. PPTP, L2TP, and IPSec have already been mentioned during this course. Another protocol supported by VPN that has not been mentioned yet is IP-IP.

Point-to-Point Tunneling Protocol (PPTP)

PPTP can be used for data transmission over an IP internetwork (such as the Internet). It can also be used to support private LAN-to-LAN communications. A TCP connection is used for tunnel maintenance.

PPTP is an extension of PPP and supports the same authentication methods as listed earlier in the chapter for remote access. If encryption is needed over a connection, it is provided by PPP, and the encrypted data is passed through the internetwork by PPTP. The same is true of compression support.

PPTP can only be used to transfer data across an IP internetwork. This won't be a limited factor when using VPNs for connections through the Internet. It does mean, however, that PPTP can only be used on local TCP/IP networks.

Data encryption is only supported for the EAP-TLS, MS-CHAP, and MS-CHAP v2 authentication protocols. There may be an additional concern in some situations about using PPTP because of the way data is encrypted. Data encryption occurs only between the two endpoints of the tunnel.

NOTE: End-to-end security can be established through use of IPSec. IPSec is discussed later in this section.

Layer 2 Tunneling Protocol (L2TP)

L2TP encapsulates and transmits PPP packets over IP, X.25, Frame Relay, or ATM. However, when used with Windows 2000, L2TP can only be used for an IP network. L2TP supports VPNs as an Internet tunneling protocol. As with PPTP, it can also be used for private LAN-to-LAN networking.

L2TP supports tunnel authentication, using the same authentication methods as supported for PPP. Tunnel maintenance is supported through UDP and L2TP messages. L2TP can encapsulate packets compressed with PPP compression, but PPP encryption is not supported. Instead, IPSec is used for data encryption.

IPSec

IPSec is a set of secured transfer standards. It can encapsulate and encrypt IP datagrams through IPSec Encapsulating Security Payload (ESP) Tunnel mode. The encapsulated and encrypted packet is then encapsulated by the tunnel protocol for transmission.

IP in IP (IP-IP)

IP-IP is typically used for tunneling multicast traffic through network segments that do not support multicast routing. It works by encapsulating an IP packet with another IP header. Tunnel maintenance is supported through ICMP messages.

VPN Management

Most of the VPN management procedures are the same as those discussed for RAS servers. The following are a few key points:

- Connection management

  As with other types of connections, the Internet connection properties are set through Network and Dial-up Connections. This is where you will enter and manage information such as your local IP address and subnet mask, username and password for connecting to the Internet, and so forth.

- Policies and profiles

  Policies and profiles are used in the same manner as they are with routers and remote access servers. The same policy and profile options are available.

- Authentication

  As was mentioned before, you have the same authentication types available. You will have to configure your VPN server to support either Windows authentication or RADIUS authentication.

- User management

  If at all possible, you want to avoid managing users individually on each server, especially if you are supporting multiple servers. You should manage user information from a central location, either by using Active Directory users and groups or by setting up a RADIUS (IAS) server.

User access can be managed either by user or by group. As with RAS clients, by-user access can be managed through user properties. As you saw previously, you can allow access, deny access, or manage access through properties.

You can also manage VPN access by group through the use of a policy. You saw an example of a Group Policy previously in the course. You can create a Security group to contain all users who need to be allowed VPN access and create a policy to allow that group access.

VPN Design

This topic isn't so much about VPN design as it is about finding where VPN best fits into your design. A number of potential security applications have been mentioned already in this course. These have included providing security for the following:

- User resource access
- LAN-to-LAN communication
- DNS zone replication
- WINS replication

That partial list should give you a good idea of how many situations there are where you might want to use a VPN server.

Designing for Performance

There isn't any need to go into a great deal of detail about performance issues. It would simply be a repetition of the performance issues addressed for remote access servers and remote routers. As a brief reminder, key performance areas are as follows:

- Private network bandwidth and usage
- Internet connection bandwidth and usage
- Server hardware resources

As with other routing solutions, you can improve performance and availability through the use of multiple VPN servers.

Designing for Security

VPN server placement and security design issues overlap and can be discussed at the same time. When you are deciding where to place VPN servers, start by thinking where you would place routers and remote access servers. The basic issues are the same, including the following:

- Minimizing private network traffic
- Minimizing remote traffic
- Availability to remote hosts
- Availability to servers

Since VPN is used as a way of protecting data from unauthorized interception, your security requirements are also going to have a significant impact on server placement.

One option is placing the VPN server in a screened subnet. This solution works especially well when you want to use VPN to support traffic such as replication updates. You can often place the server you are supporting in the same screened subnet as the VPN server. If you have sufficient server resources, you may even be able to have them both running on the same machine.

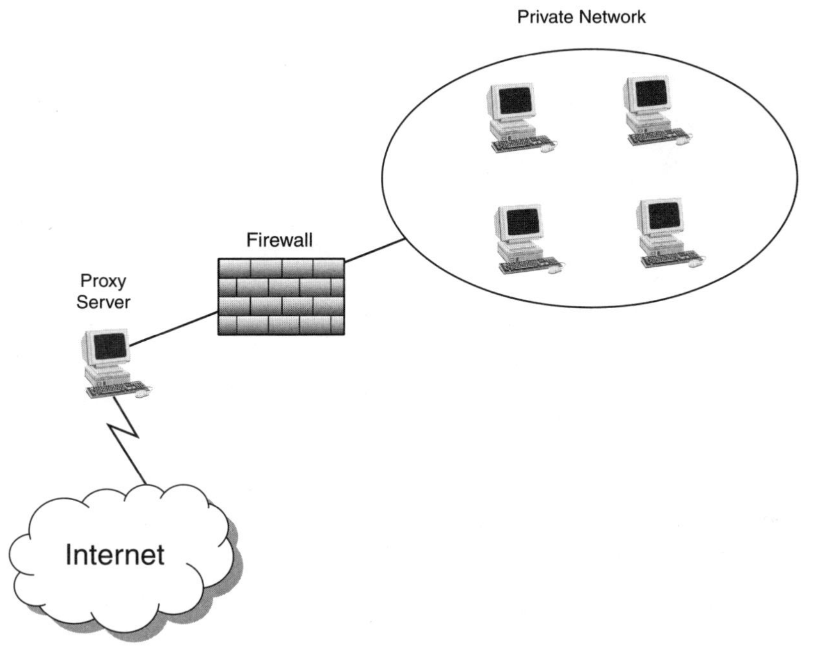

It is common to use a VPN server in combination with a firewall to provide additional security. You can place the VPN server outside the firewall if exposing the server to the Internet won't compromise your network security. Typically, you will want to install VPN on a stand-alone Windows 2000 server in this configuration. The firewall isolates your private network from the Internet, and you can configure your network so that the VPN server is the only way through the firewall.

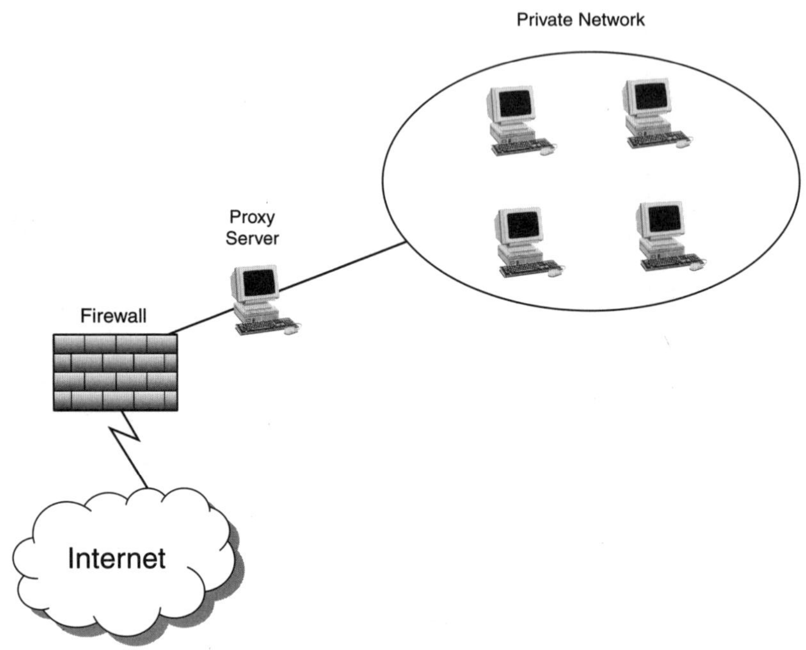

If exposing your VPN server to the Internet can compromise security, you have the option of placing it inside the firewall. This does make setting up filtering more complicated at the firewall since you must allow PPTP- and L2TP-based traffic for the VPN IP address range.

INTERNET TECHNOLOGY SUPPORT

This section ties up a few loose ends relating to deploying Internet technologies as part of your network design. This chapter provides some additional information on implementing mail and Web services. The following topics are covered in this section:

- General Design Issues
- Mail Services
- Web Services

These were introduced earlier in the course. During this section, you will be provided with some additional guidelines for deployment.

General Design Issues

The same general design issues apply here as have applied in the other network design scenarios discussed during this chapter.

- Traffic concerns

  You are going to want to minimize traffic across links as much as possible or find ways to increase your available bandwidth to support the traffic load such as implementing multiple connections.

- Server performance

  Server performance continues to be an important issue. You have to make sure that your servers have sufficient resources to support the services they are running. You may find it necessary to upgrade or replace servers that aren't up to the task.

- Security

  Security remains a critical concern. You will need to consider server placement carefully to avoid compromising security. You will also need to isolate your private network from the public Internet.

You will want to periodically monitor both network bandwidth usages and critical server resources to make sure that they continue to provide optimal support.

Mail Services

Products such as Microsoft Exchange Server make it possible for you to manage your own e-mail services. Many network designs can be supported by a single mail server. In a routed network environment, especially one with a large geographic scope, you will probably find that you can improve availability and performance by deploying multiple mail servers.

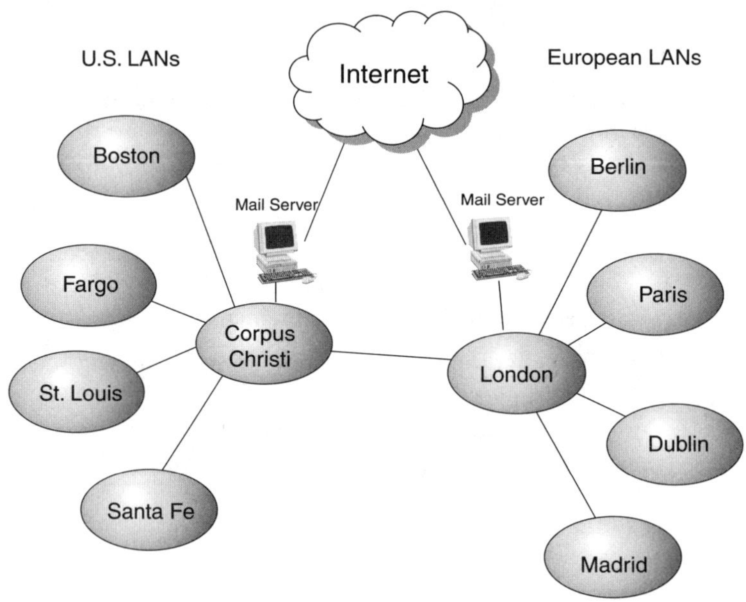

The previous figure shows one possible deployment option. Two mail servers have been deployed, one to service U.S. users and one to service European users. Each mail server will have its own connection to the Internet.

Web Services

Things can get a little more complicated when using a product such as Microsoft's Internet Information Server (IIS) to provide Web services. A Web server is usually thought of as providing resources to the public Internet. However, there has been a trend to include one or more Web servers as part of your private network solution as well. Determine if you need to support internal users, external users, or both. Once that has been decided, you'll have to decide how many Web servers you are going to need and where you are going to locate them on your network.

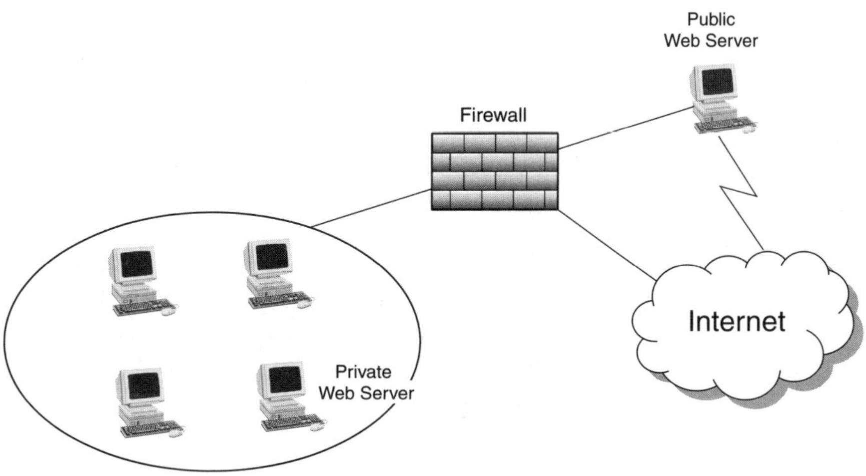

Though not always the case, the general rule is that you will be deploying Web servers that support your intranet inside your network and public Web servers outside of your private network. For public Web servers, there is the additional consideration of whether they should be deployed in front of or behind a firewall. If directly exposing the Web server doesn't compromise your security, then you have the option of deploying it outside a firewall. If you are concerned about compromising security or want to provide additional protection for your Web server, it should be deployed behind a firewall.

Proxy Server Integration

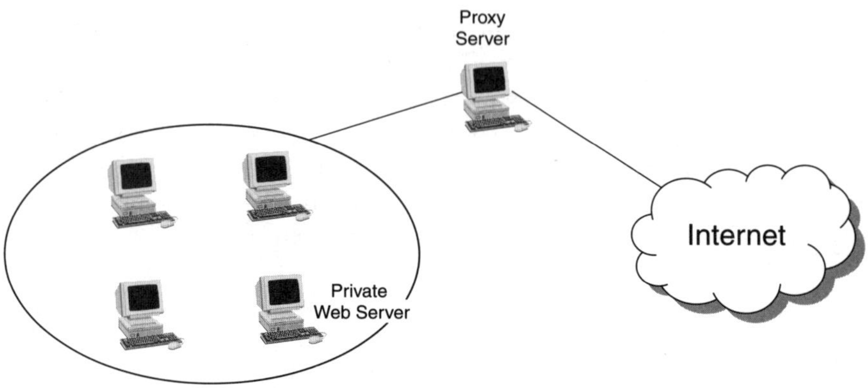

You can use Microsoft Proxy Server to manage access to Web servers on your private network. This gives you a way of having one Web server provide both private and public resources. You can have Proxy Server evaluate inbound service requests and then forward or deny the requests as appropriate.

By default, all requests to Web servers on your private network are denied. You have the option of passing the requests to specific Web servers or forwarding all requests to a default Web server installed on your proxy server. When forwarding requests, you have the ability to remap the requested URL to a different URL on your private network, effectively hiding your Web servers from direct access.

Scenario 7-5: Internet Services

The purpose of this scenario is to give you practice in making design decisions about the deployment of Internet services. Suggested solutions are provided in Appendix B at the end of this manual. It may be helpful to review the case studies in Appendix C at the end of this manual.

Barney's Bank

1. As part of your initial testing, you set up a Web server in one of the Corpus Christi LANs and connect to the LAN through a proxy server. By default, what Web service requests will get forwarded to the Web server?

2. You want to make a Web server publicly available but also provide some protection to the Web server from possible attacks from the Internet. Where should you place your firewall in relation to the Web server?

SUMMARY

During this chapter, you were introduced to the following:

- Persistent and demand-dial connections
- WAN design guidelines
- Routing and Remote Access Service (RRAS)
- RRAS configurations
- Windows 2000 client connection options
- Remote user access, including the following:
  - Protocols
  - Authentication
  - Encryption
  - Clients
- Remote access server design guidelines
- Remote LAN access guidelines
- Remote Authentication Dial-In User Service (RADIUS)
- RADIUS authentication process
- RADIUS design guidelines
- Network Address Translation (NAT) protocol
- NAT features
- NAT configuration
- NAT design guidelines
- Microsoft Proxy Server
- Proxy Server features
- Proxy Server design guidelines
- Virtual Private Network (VPN)
- Tunneling concepts
- VPN protocols

- VPN implementation guidelines
- Mail services
- Web services

The next chapter addresses issues relating to application support in a network environment. It will include issues relating to both user and server applications.

Stop now and complete the following NEXTSim exercises on the Interactive Learning CD-ROM:

Windows 2000 Network Infrastructure Design

Wide Area Design

Install and Configure RADIUS

POST-TEST QUESTIONS

The answers to these questions are in Appendix A at the end of this manual.

1. You need to have a guaranteed bandwidth between two remote LANs. What kind of connection would you use between the LANs?

2. You have two SQL Server systems set up, each in a separate remote LAN. You want to make sure that replication updates between the servers are not intercepted. You also want to keep the solution as cost effective as possible. What kind of connection would you use?

3. You select the **Internet connection server** option in RRAS. What server configuration options will be available?

4. You are configuring a host as a VPN client. What Network and Dial-up Connection configuration option should you select?

5. What LAN protocols are supported by a Windows 2000 remote access server?

6. What service can be used to centrally manage authentication for a large number of remote access servers?

7. What is the significance of enabling ICS on a remote access client?

8. What is a RADIUS secret?

9. What sources can be used for RADIUS authentication?

10. You are adding an NAT server to a screened subnet with a single link to the rest of your network. How can you ensure that DHCP servers located in other subnets will not be able to assign IP addresses to hosts in the screened subnet, even if an appropriate scope is defined on the DHCP servers?

11. What protocols are supported by Proxy Server?

....

....

12. You have configured three proxy servers as a Proxy Array. The change had no impact on inbound traffic. What is most likely wrong?

....

....

13. You want to be able to use VPN tunneling across an ATM connection. What tunneling protocol would you use?

....

....

14. You want to provide Web services in your private network as a way to improve organizational communications. Where should you place the Web server?

....

....

CHAPTER 8

Designing Resource Availability

MAJOR TOPICS

OBJECTIVES

At the completion of this chapter, you will be able to:

- List and describe areas of concern when designing application support.
- Given an application type, describe its data and bandwidth requirements.
- Compare and contrast the use of centralized and decentralized application resources.
- Given network requirements, design a data resource solution.
- Describe the purpose and use of Quality of Service (QoS).
- Describe resource design concerns when planning for network growth.
- Describe the purpose and use of Distributed File System (Dfs).
- Compare and contrast stand-alone and domain Dfs roots.
- Given network requirements, design a Dfs solution.

PRE-TEST QUESTIONS

The answers to these questions are in Appendix A at the end of this manual.

1. Why are protocol requirements a concern in a network that uses NAT servers to create screened subnets?

2. What are the peak bandwidth usage times for traditional applications such as word processors?

3. What is meant by a well-connected link between application servers?

4. From the standpoint of data recovery, why is centralized data storage preferred over decentralized data storage?

5. How many Dfs roots can be configured on a single server?

6. How is replication managed for a domain Dfs root?

7. When will you be required to use a stand-alone Dfs root?

INTRODUCTION

In this chapter, attention turns to applications and application resources, specifically application data and support. You will be given general resource requirements for different types of applications along with guidelines for designing an application solution.

The discussion then focuses on resource requirements. Centralized and decentralized resource management are compared, with a look at concerns inherent in each. You will be provided with resource solution guidelines and be given a short introduction to Quality of Service (QoS) support.

The chapter then looks at using Distributed File System (Dfs) support as part of your network data design solution. You will be introduced to the use of stand-alone and domain Dfs roots, as well as the use of Dfs replicas and links. You will be given some general guidelines for selecting the type of Dfs root to use in your network design.

APPLICATION REQUIREMENTS

At the beginning of this course, you were told that the main reason for having a network is to support your organization. Since then, the discussion has addressed designing a network to fit your organization, but there hasn't been much emphasis on support other than through network services. The discussion now turns to one of the primary ways a network supports an organization: by providing an environment for applications. The following topics are covered in this section:

- Application Overview
- Traditional Applications
- Server Applications
- Time-Critical Applications
- Application Guidelines

This discussion will mention some applications as examples but does not focus on any specific applications. The goal is to have you recognize the needs of types of applications. With the changes and enhancements to PC applications, lines have gotten blurred, and you will find that many applications can fall into multiple categories.

Application Overview

In order to design an appropriate environment for your applications, you have to understand the applications' requirements. This means having a complete inventory of the applications used on your network and the locations of data files and other resources required by the applications. In an Active Directory domain environment, you also have to consider the potential requirements for automated distribution and management of applications.

Some potential areas of concern include the following:

- Storage requirements

  Most applications have data requirements. You need to know where data is currently stored on your network so that you can make recommendations for possible changes.
- Bandwidth requirements

  The most obvious bandwidth requirement relates directly to storage locations. If the application data files are stored in a central location, then they will have to be sent to the user over the network. However, there are going to be other data transmission requirements that are not directly related to stored data files.

- Protocol support

  Some applications may have special protocol requirements, such as Remote Procedure Calls (RPCs). You need to provide communication paths that will support these protocol requirements. For example, you already know that NAT servers don't support RPCs.

- Network service support

  Many applications may have both direct and indirect needs for network service support. Indirect needs are when the application doesn't make a specific request for services but does make a request to the operating system it is running on, which results in a request for services.

This section looks at the requirements you are likely to encounter for some general types of applications. This is not meant as a complete list of the types of applications you might have to support but is provided as an example to get you started thinking about application design. This discussion will include a brief look at data requirements, but data and other resource requirements are covered in more detail later in the chapter.

Traditional Applications

The term *traditional applications* is being used to refer to common business applications. These include applications such as word processors, spreadsheets, graphic arts, and the like. The application is typically installed locally on the end-user's system.

Data Requirements

Access to application data is going to be a primary concern with traditional applications. There is an added concern in that you may have only limited control over where data files are being stored. With most applications, you can provide guidelines for data file storage but cannot prevent users from ignoring the guidelines and storing the files in a different location.

Part of the job here can include education. Many users have a mistaken impression that their data files are *safer* if they keep them on their local system. The truth is, this will typically put the data files at risk. In most networks, local user systems seldom, if ever, get backed up. Also, most users are lax about local access security, leaving files open to unauthorized access.

Bandwidth Requirements

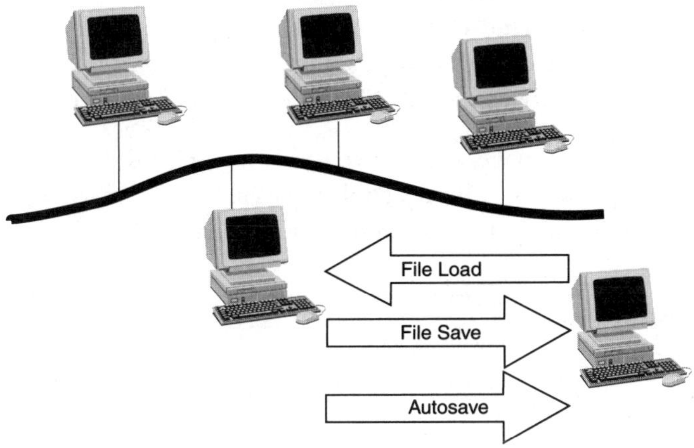

Bandwidth requirements for traditional applications usually come in bursts. These bursts include the following:

- File load
- File save
- Autosave

If you collect network performance data over time, you can get a good idea of your bandwidth requirements. Watch for recurring peaks such as those that might occur at the start of the business day.

Special Concerns

If you are storing data files on network servers, you are going to have network resource requirements, specifically name resolution requirements. You also need to look at the type of traffic generated by your applications to determine if there are going to be any conflicts with network communication devices, IP filter configurations, and so forth.

You also have to make sure that you truly understand the applications that you are supporting. Most traditional applications are in fact anything but traditional. New features and functionality are placing additional strains on network resources.

Server Applications

The term *server application* is not as descriptive as it once was. An application server may not necessarily require a server operating system and may be implemented on workstation operating systems, such as Windows NT Workstation, Windows 2000 Professional, or Windows 9x.

Application Models

There are two basic server application models. These are the traditional client/server applications and multitier applications. Over the past few years, Microsoft has used a number of terms to refer to multitier applications, but the fundamental model has remained somewhat consistent.

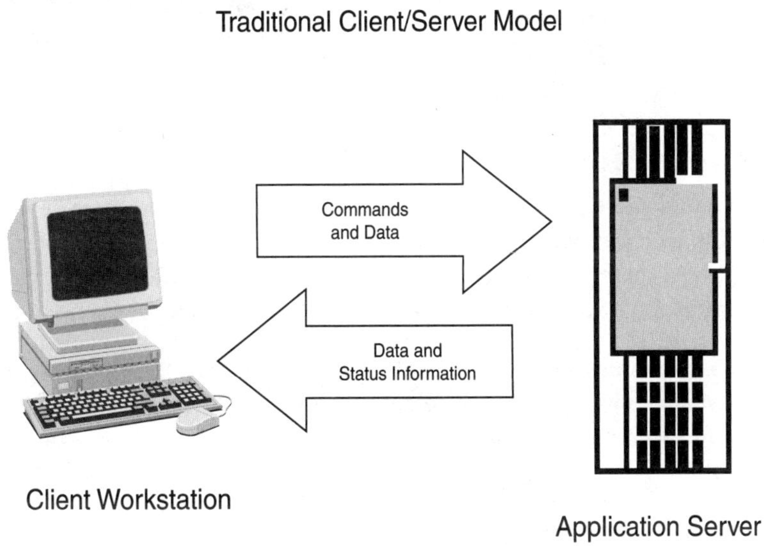

In a traditional client/server application, there is an application running on the server that provides data and resources to the clients. The client provides the end-user interface and is responsible for presenting data in a way that is meaningful to the user. Most of the traffic results from users passing data and commands to the server, and the server responding with data and status messages to the client.

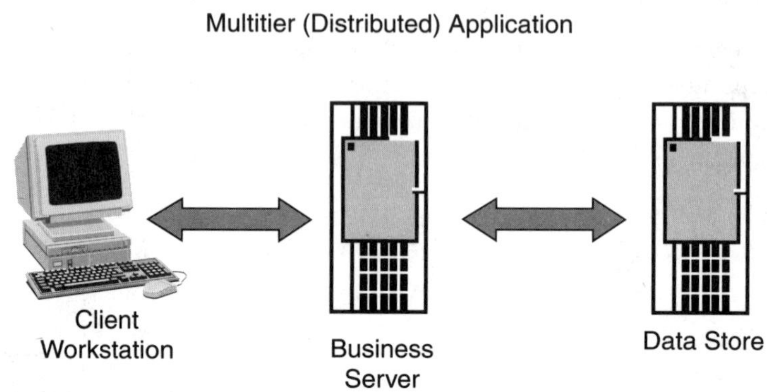

In a multitier application, the application is divided into three or more levels. There is still a server providing data and services and a client providing the end-user interface. In between these there is one or more levels providing additional services such as the application of business rules for passing data between the client and server.

To make things a little more confusing, the number of layers doesn't necessarily define the number of systems that are going to be involved. For example, if you have enough resources at the server, you may decide to deploy the business components on the application server.

Application Requirements

The data requirements for both application models are primarily at the application server. You have to make sure that application servers have sufficient storage to meet application needs. There is also a potential concern of the application server becoming a performance bottleneck. Periodic monitoring of application servers will be an ongoing activity.

Server Placement and Availability

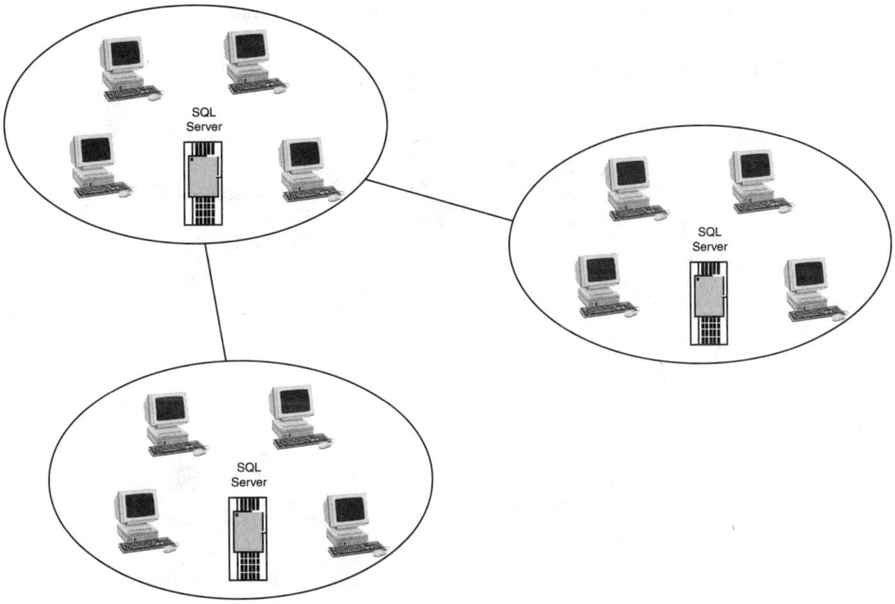

Server-based applications are common in routed network environments. Server placement and availability are going to be important to your network design. The general guidelines are going to be similar to those addressed for servers providing network services. You are going to want to place application servers as close as possible to the users who need to access them.

One factor that can influence your design is that some applications require well-connected clients or well-connected links between servers. A well-connected link refers to a high-bandwidth, high-availability connection and is usually meant to imply a local area network link. This requirement could mean having to use more servers than you would initially assume.

Assuming that you've done your preliminary information gathering, the traffic generated by server applications is relatively predictable. There is the traffic passing between clients and servers and, in a multiserver application, update traffic passing between servers.

Remote Communication Requirements

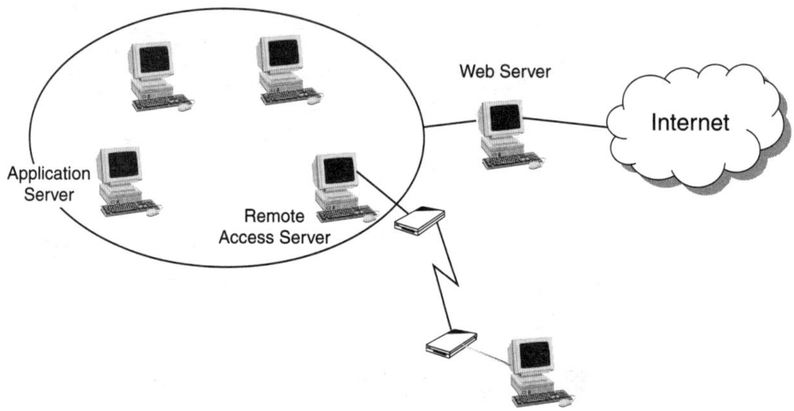

Providing support for remote clients is often a concern when designing a server application environment. This could mean having to support clients connecting to the application server through a remote access server or through an Internet browser-based application. Potential concerns include the following:

- Available bandwidth

  Make sure that the remote link can provide the bandwidth necessary to support the application.

- Data communication security

  There is a potential concern about data being intercepted. This means implementing data encryption. This is a situation where VPNs are often an appropriate solution.

- Firewalls and filtering

  Make sure that your firewalls, proxy servers, screening routers, and the like are configured to pass application traffic. If the application has special protocol requirements, you will have to make sure that these are compatible with your routers and security devices.

Server applications are typically mission-critical applications. You are going to want to test any new devices or services that you are introducing to an existing network to make sure that they are compatible with your applications.

Time-Critical Applications

Time-critical applications include applications where any delays in packet delivery are going to be noticeable and may cause the application to fail. These include applications such as voice applications and streaming video. While there are going to be potential concerns about storage requirements and availability, the biggest concerns are going to be bandwidth and latency.

Time-critical applications, in this usage of the term, require large amounts of data being delivered in a timely manner. This means that enough bandwidth needs to be available to support the application. Of course, there is the concern that the application is sharing the bandwidth with other network activities.

A possible solution is the use of Quality of Service (QoS) as part of your network design. QoS lets you identify some of your network traffic, such as data for streaming video, as high-priority traffic. You can allocate part of your bandwidth for this traffic, giving it priority when passing through routers and other connection devices.

Application Guidelines

The same general guidelines for design and implementation that have been discussed throughout this course also apply to application design. You will want to design application support to maximum availability, performance, and security. At the same time, you will be working to keep the traffic generated by your applications, especially across remote links, to a minimum.

Some applications may have direct requirements for network services such as DNS or WINS. Make sure that these are available, as necessary, for your applications.

Make sure that you are using network-aware applications. This isn't a problem with newer applications but may be an issue when supporting older legacy applications.

Scenario 8-1: Application Support

The purpose of this scenario is to give you practice in identifying application design issues. Suggested solutions are provided in Appendix B at the end of this manual. It may be helpful to review the case studies in Appendix C at the end of this manual.

1. Which of the case study companies has identified a need for supporting a server-based application?

   ....

   ....

2. Which of the case study companies has identified resource problems related to generating periodic reports?

   ....

   ....

3. For which of the case study companies would you expect requirements for supporting traditional applications?

   ....

   ....

RESOURCE REQUIREMENTS

This section addresses application resource requirements, design, and management. The primary focus is on designing appropriate data resource solutions. The following topics are covered in this section:

- Resource Distribution
- Resource Design

Some of the issues addressed in this section were introduced earlier in the course.

Resource Distribution

Resource placement will be an important part of your network design. Obviously, resources will have to be available to the users that need them, but there are other issues that have to be considered as well. You need to consider the impact of server-based resources on bandwidth usage. You have to plan for both access security and physical security of your data. As with other components in your network design, you will probably find yourself making compromises to find a workable solution.

Decentralized Resources

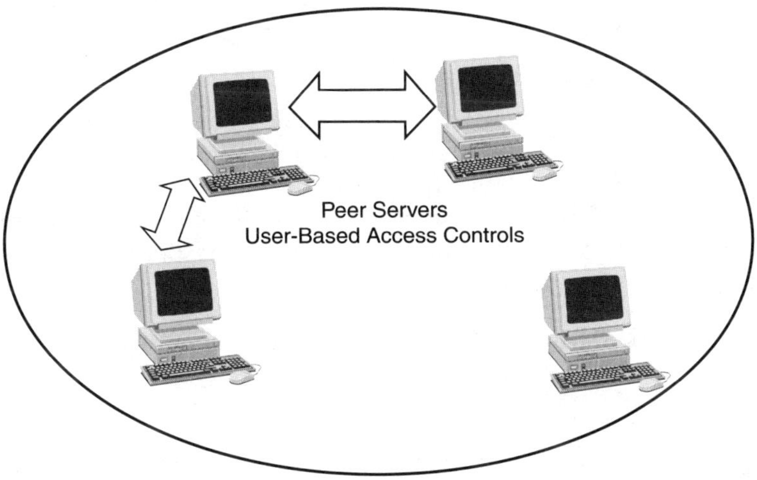

One option is decentralized data management–in other words, keeping data that is needed by the user local to the user's system. Local data access doesn't generate any network traffic and doesn't require the network for data access. In the case of a network failure, the user should still be able to log on locally and access his or her data.

That doesn't mean that you can't have shared data in a decentralized storage model. A peer-to-peer workgroup is a common example of a decentralized storage model, with the users taking responsibility for file sharing and remote access security for the data on their systems. Access to shared data depends on the network, and accessing the shared data will generate network traffic.

There are quite a number of potential drawbacks to this solution, however, including the following:

- Access security

  If the users' systems haven't been configured to limit local access, there is a possibility of the data being compromised through unauthorized access. This is also an issue if the users have shared folders from their system to the network.

- Physical security

  Most locally stored data is under an ongoing threat of potential loss or degradation. Most organizations find that there is too much overhead involved in running decentralized backups of user data. Most users are unwilling to make an effort to back up their own data. On top of this, only server versions of Windows-family operating systems support disk fault tolerance.

- Availability

  Unless shared to the network, local data is exactly that–local to the system and not available from anywhere else.

- Disaster recovery

  Except for known critical data, most disaster recovery plans do not include any plans for recovering local data. If users haven't taken the initiative for backing up data, it will likely be unrecoverable after a serious system failure.

If used at all, decentralized storage should be limited to private data files.

Decentralized data means decentralized management. More of the responsibility is placed on the users. This may not be a serious concern when you have experienced users, but less-experienced or less-computer literate users can introduce problems through their management efforts.

Centralized Resources

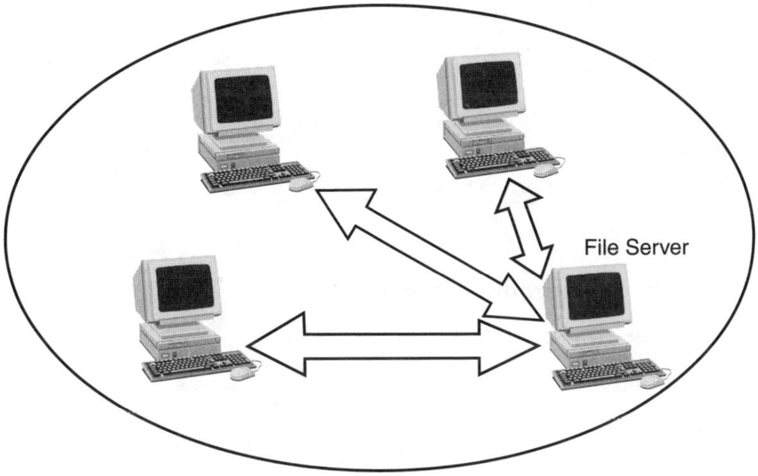

The most common solution is to keep most, if not all, data files on network servers. This is one of the primary justifications for installing a network in the first place. Data can be backed up on a regular basis. Further data security can be implemented through disk fault tolerance. Network servers are typically included in network disaster recovery plans.

The data is made available to network users through network shares, which is also how you establish data access security. This leads to potential issues with availability and bandwidth usage. Data is only available when the server is available. A server or network failure means that the data isn't available.

You also have to move the data back and forth between the server and the client. This means an additional impact on bandwidth usage every time a user opens or saves a data file. There is also the additional traffic generated by some applications with autosave, or saving a backup copy of the file while you are working. If supported by your application, you can reduce network traffic by having these backup files created and saved on your local hard disk.

Centralized data means centralized management. This can add to your administrative staff's management overhead. In some cases, you may find it appropriate to delegate some of the data management tasks.

Real-World Solutions

Most real-world solutions are built around a mix of centralized and decentralized storage. Part of your job is deciding when to use each storage method. Typically, you will use centralized storage for the following types of data:

- Shared data
- Data that is difficult to re-create
- Mission-critical data
- Confidential data

On the other hand, you would use decentralized storage for the following types of data:

- Personal data
- Easily re-created data
- Noncritical data

One category of data that has not been addressed is the data associated with server applications. This is typically stored on the application server and managed by the application server administrators.

Resource Design

The focus now turns specifically to centralized resources. You should have a good idea of what is going to be required here. During this course, you've already seen all of the issues related to this.

Designing for Performance

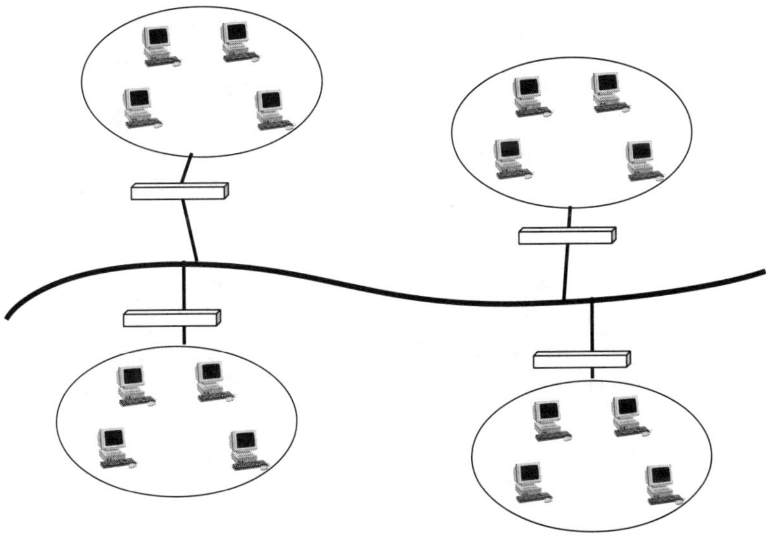

In general, the performance issues are the same as those for network services. The bottom line is that you have to make resources available to your users, and you want, as much as possible, to optimize resource usage.

Server Performance

As with any other type of server, you are going to need to match a file server's hardware configuration to its operational requirements. File servers will typically only need one network adapter. Disk resources–both disk size and disk speed–are going to be critical.

You may find that your network solution can include combining file services on the same system with other network services. This is especially true if file access requirements tend to be intermittent requests for relatively small data files.

Server Placement

You have to put your servers where they can be accessed by your users. You want the placement of your servers to optimize performance and minimize traffic. As much as possible, keep resources local to the users that need them. If the resources have to be placed in a remote subnet or LAN, keep the number of hops between the users and resources to a minimum.

Server availability, except in cases of network or server failure, will typically not be an issue for resources that are accessed through a LAN. You will need to provide appropriate access paths for remote users, realizing that there are more conditions that can cause a server to be unavailable, such as link failures, inability to get an available dial-up line, and so forth.

Network Traffic

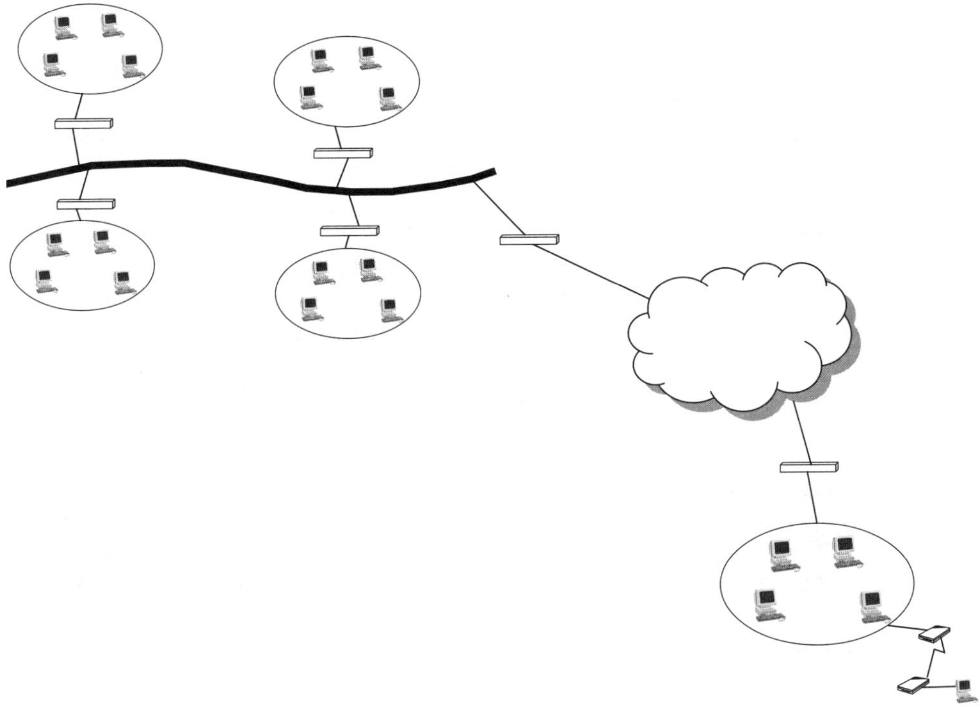

You need to monitor bandwidth usage in local LANs and across remote links. If you start to load down the bandwidth on a local subnet, you may need to consider additional subnetting to balance the network load. If you are loading down remote links, you should consider:

- Implementing faster links.
- Implementing additional connections.

- Providing a local data resource.
- Managing data locations and access through the Dfs.

The latency caused by the connection time during remote access or when using demand-dial routers can cause some applications to fail with timeout errors. You should test extensively before attempting to support an application over a dial-up link. QoS, which is discussed in the next section, is one way of increasing the percentage of your bandwidth.

Real-time applications are especially sensitive to bandwidth and latency issues. Depending on how you structure your tests, advanced testing may not uncover all of your potential problems unless you make the effort to simulate the requirement to share the available bandwidth with other network applications. You will typically want to use persistent connections and keep the number of hops to a minimum to reduce latency. If you are required to use a dial-up link, you need to establish the remote connection before starting your real-time application.

Quality of Service (QoS)

QoS has been mentioned as a way of improving support for real-time and resource-intensive applications. You were given a brief introduction to QoS at the beginning of the course. You may find it helpful, however, to have some additional information about QoS before deciding where, or if, QoS fits into your network design.

The Quality of Service referred to here is that you are guaranteeing a quality of service, or preferential access to network resources, to selected applications. Windows 2000 includes the Generic QoS API as a subset of the WinSock 2 API, which allows applications to invoke QoS services. QoS works by allocating bandwidth to an application's packets. As packets are received by routers, they are sorted into queues based on priority, with QoS high-priority packets going into a special queue that is serviced based on a preferential schedule.

QoS may not be an appropriate solution for your performance concerns. The applications you want to implement bandwidth allocation for must support QoS, and all routers in the data path must support the Resource Reservation Protocol (RSVP). RSVP is used by sending and receiving devices to establish reserved bandwidth for your application.

Designing for Security

The types of security issues you are going to face have already been addressed during this course. As a quick review, these will include the following:

- Data access security

  This can be further broken down into controlling network access and controlling data access. The primary ways of controlling network access are logon controls and remote user authentication. Data access is controlled through access permissions. Additional data access controls can be implemented through IP filtering and the use of firewalls.

- Communication security

  Encrypted communication can be used over both local and remote links. You can use IPSec to encrypt local traffic. Remote traffic can be encrypted through the use of VPNs with either encrypted PPTP or L2TP over IPSec.

- Physical data security

  Physical data security is implemented through the use of backups and data fault tolerance. For mission-critical data, you may want to consider server clustering as an additional option.

You need to include disaster recovery planning as part of your physical data security plans.

Designing for Growth

If you think back to the initial chapters in this course, part of the information you needed to gather before starting the design process was expected network growth. Your network's projected growth is going to impact your network design. You will want your design to provide sufficient resources to meet immediate and near-term needs. You will need to make your design scalable to meet the additional resource requirements that come with network growth.

Continuing network growth can force changes such as the following:

- Additional subnetworking of existing subnets
- New subnets or remote LANs
- Additional resource servers
- Higher-speed remote links
- Replacement of demand-dial links with persistent links

If the need for potential growth and expansion is designed into your network, it will be much easier to implement when the time comes.

Scenario 8-2: Resource Design and Deployment

The purpose of this scenario is to give you practice in identifying resource design requirements. Suggested solutions are provided in Appendix B at the end of the manual. You should review the case studies in Appendix C before starting this scenario.

1. Which of the case study companies has expressed a need to consider expansion of its geographic scope as part of its projected growth?

   ....

   ....

2. Which case study company is most obviously using completely decentralized storage management?

   ....

   ....

3. Which of the case study companies has expressed a definite need for QoS?

   ....

   ....

4. Which of the case study companies is most likely to encounter security-related problems based on their current design?

   ....

   ....

DISTRIBUTED FILE SYSTEM (DFS) DESIGN

Introduced with Windows 2000, Dfs provides a way of organizing and accessing shared folders. The following topics are covered in this section:

- Dfs Overview
- Dfs Roots
- Dfs Design

As you will see during this section, Dfs simplifies user access to files and folders.

Dfs Overview

Dfs lets you set up a single tree, known as a Dfs root, as a point of reference for locating and accessing shared folders. The Dfs is a hierarchical structure with links to shared folders. Users can access shared folders through the Dfs hierarchical tree. This means that the users don't need to know where the files are physically located or the full share path to the folders.

NOTE: *The Dfs Service is installed automatically when you install Windows 2000 Server. It cannot be removed from the operating system.*

Dfs Structure

Before looking at Dfs structure, let's take a look at what you might have without using Dfs.

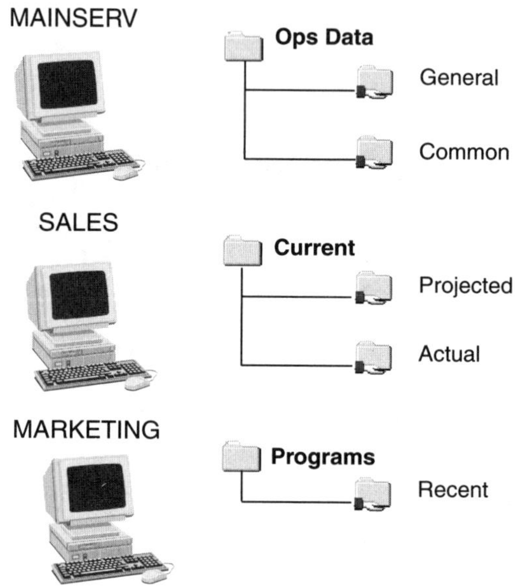

In the previous figure, there are three servers with shared folders. To connect to a shared folder, the user must know (or at least recognize) both the server and the share name. As a network grows in size and complexity, it can become more difficult for users to locate the folders and files that they need.

To take this a little further, what if there were data in each of these folders that was required when generating weekly sales reports? The user would have to locate each of the servers and shared folders. Should one of the servers fail and its data be moved to a different server, things become more complicated for the user, at least for a little while.

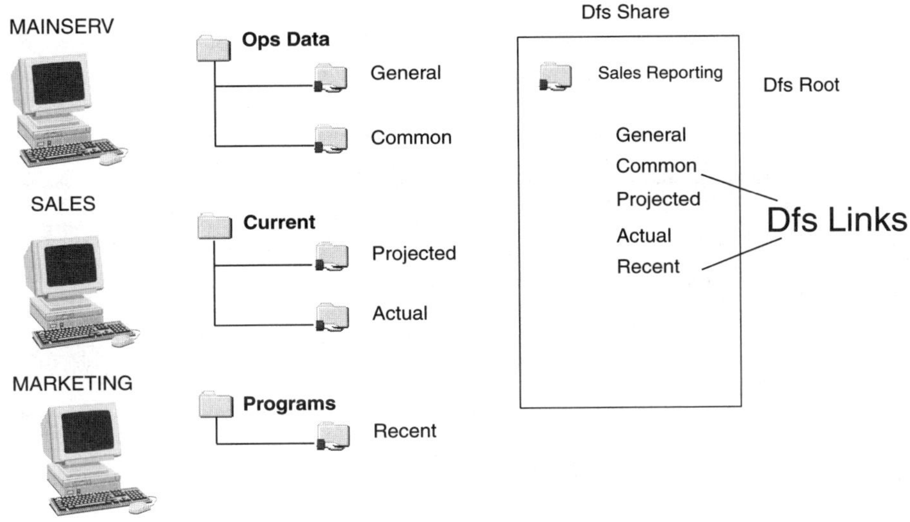

With Dfs, the user can access all of these folders through a single share point. Locating the necessary folders and data becomes significantly easier for the user.

To set up Dfs, the first step is to set up a Dfs root. You can then define multiple links to shared folders, called Dfs links or child nodes, under the Dfs root. If it becomes necessary to replace a server, you can update the Dfs links to the new shares. The user never has to be aware of the change.

Dfs Restrictions

There are a few restrictions that you need to know when planning how you are going to implement Dfs. These include the following:

Dfs Feature	Limit
Number of Dfs roots per server	One
Number of Dfs roots per domain	Unlimited, up to the number of servers in the domain
Maximum characters per file path	260
Maximum alternates per volume	32
Maximum number of volumes per domain/enterprise	Limited by system resource (available servers, one per server)

Now that you've seen the restrictions, let's look at some key points about Dfs and the benefits it provides.

Key Points

Dfs can make life simpler for network administrators and users. Resources are accessed through a single namespace, the Dfs root, rather than by mapping local drive IDs to multiple servers and shares. As previously mentioned, servers can be replaced without impacting the user, and the Dfs can be expanded as necessary to include additional servers and shares. Dfs can also be integrated with IIS.

Security

Linking to a share through Dfs does not affect network security. Dfs links are managed the same way as any shared folder is managed.

Performance and Reliability

Dfs lets you set up alternate physical locations for files, providing a level of load balancing. Frequently accessed resources are cached with Dfs clients, allowing the client to connect more quickly to the requested server.

Clients

Windows 2000 and Windows NT clients can access Dfs shares without modification. Windows 95 and Windows 98 clients must have the Dfs Service for Microsoft Network Client installed in order to access a Dfs share.

Dfs Roots

Windows 2000 supports two Dfs root configurations: stand-alone Dfs root and domain Dfs root. You will sometimes see a domain Dfs root referred to as a fault-tolerant Dfs root.

As far as users are concerned, a Dfs root looks like any other shared folder. Users connect to a Dfs root in the same fashion as they would connect to any other share and can access the Dfs root and its links by mapping a drive ID or by using the UNC path. The UNC path to a Dfs root is as follows:

```
\\server_name\Dfs_root
```

One advantage should be obvious: the user can map a single logical drive to the Dfs root and access all of the links through that drive rather than having to map a drive for each of the individual shares.

Stand-Alone Dfs Root

A stand-alone Dfs root is somewhat limited. The Dfs topology is stored on a single computer. It doesn't provide any type of replication or backup. Because of this, it represents a possible single point of failure. It also only permits a single level of Dfs links. A stand-alone Dfs root can be located on any supported file system, but an NTFS volume is suggested.

You will have to identify the server that will act as host for the Dfs root when creating a stand-alone Dfs root. You also have to identify the shared folder that will be used as the Dfs root share.

Domain Dfs Root

A domain Dfs root provides features in addition to those supported by a stand-alone Dfs root. The Dfs root is stored in Active Directory services and replicated to participating Dfs root servers. This gives you a way to recover the Dfs tree topology should a root be offline. You can also replicate Dfs resources, allowing the client to be connected to an alternate resource if necessary, adding a level of fault tolerance to resources as well as the Dfs topology. Replication uses the domain's Active Directory replication topology.

There is an additional restriction when installing a domain Dfs root. A domain Dfs root must be located on an NTFS 5.0 volume. Also, you cannot directly convert an existing stand-alone Dfs root to a domain Dfs root. You must first delete the existing stand-alone Dfs root.

> *NOTE: Replication is supported by the Windows 2000 File Replication Service (FRS).*

Instead of identifying just a host server, you have to identify the host Active Directory domain and host server when creating a domain Dfs root. You will also have to identify the root share.

Fault tolerance is achieved for a domain Dfs root's topology through the use of root replicas. A root replica is a copy of the Dfs root created on a different server. Replication is disabled by default. If you decide to enable replication, the first share that replication is enabled for will be configured as the master (or primary) copy.

Dfs Links

Before you define any links, the only resources available to clients are folders directly under the Dfs root share. You can add links, which are other shared folders, to the root. These links will appear to the client as folders directly under the Dfs root. There is nothing to identify the links to the client as being physically located on a different server.

You must specify the share to which a link is being established to create a Dfs link. Clients will see the link listed by the link name that was specified when the link was created, not the folder's share name. An accessed link, by default, is cached locally by the client for 30 minutes.

When using a dynamic Dfs hierarchy, you can define Dfs link replicas. These are copies of link data hosted on different servers.

Dfs Design

It's important to remember during Dfs design that Dfs links are used for the logical organization of shared data. The shared folder the link is created for, along with its data, remains in the same physical location. Traffic generated by users accessing the linked data must be accounted for in your network design. You also need to consider root placement. If the deployment of multiple root locations best fits your network design, you can do this with multiple stand-alone roots or, in an Active Directory domain, multiple root replicas. That brings you to your other decision: whether you want to use a stand-alone Dfs root or domain Dfs root. The decision may be made for you.

Stand-Alone Dfs Root

If you don't have an Active Directory domain, you will be required to use one or more stand-alone Dfs roots. Each Dfs root must be managed separately, and there is no fault tolerance support for the Dfs hierarchy.

Domain Dfs Root

You will likely find that one or more Dfs roots will be the more appropriate solution in an Active Directory domain environment. The domain Dfs hierarchy is fault tolerant, and improved availability is provided through the use of root replicas.

Designing for Performance

Dfs centralizes your resource management and provides you with a great deal of flexibility to meet changing conditions. You can add and remove Dfs links without impacting other links in the hierarchy. Data can be moved between servers without changing link names, making the moves transparent to the end user and applications.

Dfs makes it easy to configure your network to account for low-bandwidth and nonpersistent links. Copies of commonly accessed data can be kept on alternate servers that are local to the remote users. These alternate servers are configured as Dfs link replicas and provide both local access and fault tolerance.

Scenario 8-3: Dfs Design

The purpose of this scenario is to give you practice in resolving Dfs design issues. Suggested solutions are provided in Appendix B at the end of this manual. It may be helpful to review the case studies in Appendix C at the end of this manual.

Barney's Bank

1. Given the current network design, what type of Dfs roots can be implemented?

   ....

   ....

2. You want to implement centralized management for data resources for the U.S. offices. You are planning to do this through the use of Dfs. Data is being transferred to servers in Corpus Christi. How can you minimize traffic across remote links for the data most often accessed by the remote offices and maintained through centralized management?

   ....

   ....

Fairco Manufacturing

1. Given the current network design, what type of Dfs roots can be implemented?

   ....

   ....

2. What type of fault tolerance could be automatically built into the Dfs hierarchy?

   ....

   ....

SUMMARY

During this chapter, you were introduced to the following:

- Application requirements
- Application types
- Server application models
- Decentralized resources
- Centralized resources
- Resource solution design
- Quality of Service (QoS)
- Distributed File System (Dfs) features
- Dfs roots
- Dfs links
- Dfs replicas
- Dfs design

The next chapter ties up some loose ends relating to network design. It discusses design rollout as well as monitoring and management.

Stop now and complete the following NEXTSim exercises on the Interactive Learning CD-ROM:

Windows 2000 Network Infrastructure Design

Implementation and Management

Configure Distributed Management to an OU

POST-TEST QUESTIONS

The answers to these questions are in Appendix A at the end of this manual.

1. What type of name resolution support would be required for a NetBIOS-based application running on a TCP/IP network?

2. You are implementing a server-based application that will include remote users. Remote access traffic passes through a firewall. How does this impact your firewall configuration?

3. When using a decentralized data storage model that doesn't include sharing data from workstations, what concerns do you have about security, if any?

4. What protocol is used by QoS to establish reserved bandwidth for an application?

5. A server that was hosting a shared folder failed. The folder was configured as a Dfs link. You've recovered the failed server's files to a different server. What must you do to repair the link?

6. You are supporting a WAN with some low-bandwidth links. How can you use Dfs to improve file access for the remote LANs with low-bandwidth links?

7. Your WAN is expected to experience rapid growth and expansion. What type of Dfs root provides the most flexibility and scalability with minimal management overhead?

CHAPTER 9

Implementation and Management

MAJOR TOPICS

OBJECTIVES

At the completion of this chapter, you will be able to:

- Explain why network maintenance may be necessary before starting implementation.
- Describe guidelines for testing a network design before implementation.
- Describe guidelines for setting deployment schedules.
- Explain how check lists can aid the implementation process.
- Describe how dependencies can impact a phased implementation.
- List and describe Windows 2000 monitoring tools.
- List network hardware components that require periodic monitoring.
- List network software components that require periodic monitoring.
- List and describe Windows 2000 network Administrative Tools.
- Describe general guidelines for optimizing network performance.
- Identify when Network Load Balancing (NLB) can be used to improve network performance.
- Identify when round-robin DNS can be used to improve network performance.

PRE-TEST QUESTIONS

The answers to these questions are in Appendix A at the end of this manual.

1. Why should you check for network problems before starting implementation of a new network design?

2. How can check lists aid in the implementation process?

3. How can unattended installations streamline the installation process?

4. You want to collect sampled performance statistics over 2 days and save the information as a baseline for later reference. What Windows 2000 tool will let you do this?

5. What command-line utility can be used to have a DHCP host release and renew its IP address assignment?

6. What protocol is used by clients communicating with a Global Catalog server?

....

....

7. What administration tool would you use to modify RADIUS server properties?

....

....

8. What resource record entries do you need to make to use round-robin DNS for load balancing?

....

....

INTRODUCTION

This chapter addresses deployment, management, and monitoring issues. You are already familiar with most of the information that is presented in this chapter. It has been presented in bits and pieces throughout the earlier chapters. This chapter pulls the information together as a more concise reference while helping to present the *big picture* of network implementation.

The assumption is, at this point, that you've completed your initial network design. You are now ready to plan your deployment schedule and look ahead to the activities that will follow implementation of your new network design. The chapter starts, however, with a step back and has you first check your current network before starting implementation. The discussion then moves on to your implementation plans, including creating deployment schedules and using check lists to help manage the process.

After this, attention turns to network monitoring and management. There will be monitoring requirements after implementation to make sure that your new network design is working as expected. There will also be ongoing periodic monitoring requirements throughout the life of your network. A review of monitoring tools and an overview of management utilities are included in the discussion.

Finally, the chapter spends a little time reviewing a few key points about network optimization. This will include some of the tips you were given earlier when discussing optimizing network services.

DESIGN ROLLOUT

Once you've completed your network design, you're ready to starting moving on to the deployment phase. This section talks about implementing your network design. The following topics are covered in this section:

- Network Review
- Preparing for Implementation
- Deployment Guidelines

A thorough deployment design is just as important to successful implementation as a thorough network design.

Network Review

Your network design is finally finished. You have approval and funding and you're ready to go. While you may be tempted to dive into implementation, a final review of your network will be a good investment of your time.

Current Network Status

You should be intimately familiar with your current network by the time you've finished your network design. Despite this, one last check is still in order before moving on to the next phase. You need to be aware if any changes have been implemented on the network since you started the design process.

In a small LAN, this isn't likely to be much of a problem. If any changes have been made to the network, you were probably either involved in overseeing the changes or might have even made the changes yourself. Even in a routed LAN, you will probably have a good idea of what's been happening on the network. After all, someone had to make the changes, and most, if not all, of the technical staff has likely been involved with the design process. Someone who has worked on the design should be personally aware of any major network changes.

This can be a little more difficult in a WAN environment. As mentioned previously, network management tends to be more decentralized in a WAN environment, whether or not it was planned that way. You need to double-check personally with the technical staff at each of the remote LAN locations to see if there have been any recent changes.

For example, part of your design may include upgrading Windows NT 4.0 Workstation systems to Windows 2000 Professional systems. You could find that some of the remote technical staff decided to take matters into their own hands and move the process ahead by starting the upgrades ahead of time. This may not necessarily be a bad thing, but you need to know this because it can impact your deployment schedule. You may find that you now have more time to address other rollout issues since part of the job has already been completed for you.

Network Maintenance

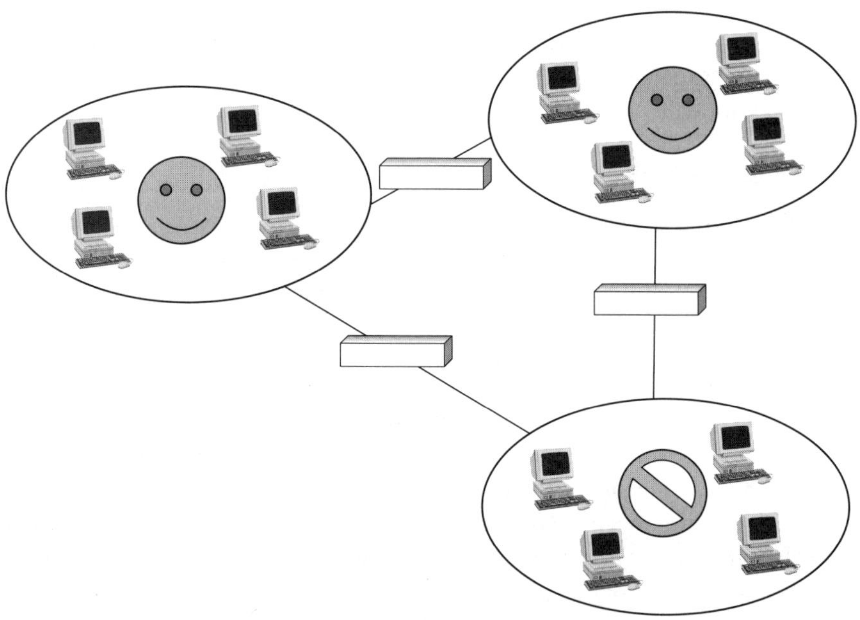

You'll find that deployment goes much faster and easier if you can give your network a clean bill of health before you start the process. Admittedly, it's probably unrealistic to run diagnostics on every network system before you start the deployment phase. However, a few key checks can save you a lot of wasted time and effort later in the process.

The first step is to identify critical resources. Start with the network cable plant and connection devices. If you don't do anything else, you should at least check your network cabling with an inexpensive cable tester to see if there are any obvious problems. Obviously, you shouldn't need to worry about testing cable segments and network devices that are going to be replaced during the rollout.

Next, make a quick check of critical systems that you will either be retaining as part of your network design or will be upgrading during the implementation phase. Critical systems include the following:

- Domain controllers
- DNS servers
- WINS server
- DHCP servers
- File servers
- Application servers

The other systems that you need to check depend on your current and planned network. For example, if you are supporting both Windows and NetWare networks, you would want to check any gateway systems running Gateway Service for NetWare (GSNW) or Windows servers providing services to NetWare clients.

Once again, running system diagnostics may not be practical. There are still checks you can make to help you find any obvious errors. On Windows NT and Windows 2000 systems, review each system's event logs. Watch for failures and warning messages.

Justifying the Review

You may be wondering why you should invest all this time when you're getting ready to change everything over anyway. The fact that you *are* planning to change everything over is exactly why you need to be making these checks.

You are going to want to keep variables to a minimum during implementation. This will make it easier to isolate and correct any problems you introduce while deploying your network design, and you can depend on some problems arising during the process. The last thing you need to do is to spend time trying to determine if you are fighting a problem that you introduced or if the problem was already there.

Preparing for Implementation

Your deployment plans are going to be an important part of your network design. It's not enough to just know what you are going to do. You also need to decide and document how you are going to implement the changes and by what schedule.

Start by reviewing any priorities that might be defined in the network design goals. Some upgrades and other changes may be seen as more important to organizational business requirements than others. Whenever possible, these are going to be your priority.

You will often have to step back a step or two from the network design goals before you can determine what has to be done first. For example, it may be a priority design goal for you to redistribute network servers and users. You currently have a nonrouted LAN and are going to be breaking the LAN into three subnetworks.

Now, let's look at a *what if* that will impact your deployment plans. If all of the systems currently use NetBEUI as their only protocol, you are going to need to either replace or supplement NetBEUI with a routable protocol before you can do anything else.

Testing

You are going to want to test as extensively as possible before you start implementing your design. That said, there are going to be real-world restrictions placed on your testing. You are going to be limited as to how much money and time you can invest in testing. You may have a hard time justifying the idea of extensive testing.

The bottom line is that you are going to have to make your best effort based on what you have available. If at all possible, you are going to want to set up a test network so you can do some of your testing without being connected to your production network. Should you have to do some (or all) of your testing on your production network, you are going to need to make a best effort to test during off-peak hours.

What you need to test depends on the changes that you are making to your network. Some items that you might need to test include the following:

- Application compatibility

  You need to test any new applications that you are deploying and the compatibility of existing applications with your new network design. If your applications require direct network service support, make sure that they get what they need from your network servers.

- Router/firewall configuration

  You may only be able to perform limited testing in this area. You may be able to emulate a routed LAN, but it's going to be more difficult to run realistic tests of a WAN environment. The remote link requirements can be cost prohibitive, and even if available, it could mean trying to coordinate testing schedules with remote locations.

  That doesn't mean that there isn't anything that you can do. For example, you can test compatibility with applications that are going to be generating routed traffic. You may also be able to run some limited Internet connectivity tests.

- Network service support

  You probably won't be able to test a lot of the things that you would like to test, such as server performance under a load, load balancing design, or replication and updates. There are some things that will probably be easier to test, such as integration with non-Windows 2000 servers and integration between network services.

- Security configuration

  Some security configuration changes are going to be easier to test than others. A complete test of your security system is going to be unrealistic, but you can test items such as application support, Web access, and remote user access. As long as you have the telephone lines available, you should be able to test dial-in access with both ends of the connection physically located in your office.

You may not have a need, or a means, to test all of these items. On the other hand, you may have additional tests that are going to be required because of new technologies that you are implementing.

Before you start, decide what you need to test and develop a written test plan. Make specific assignments to the people that are going to be running the tests to ensure that you are going to get the information that you need. Set a test schedule and, barring unforeseen problems, stick to it.

Test Network

It should be obvious that, except in very rare situations, you are not going to be able to exactly duplicate your network in a test environment. What you are going to want to do is set up a test network that is as representative of your network as possible.

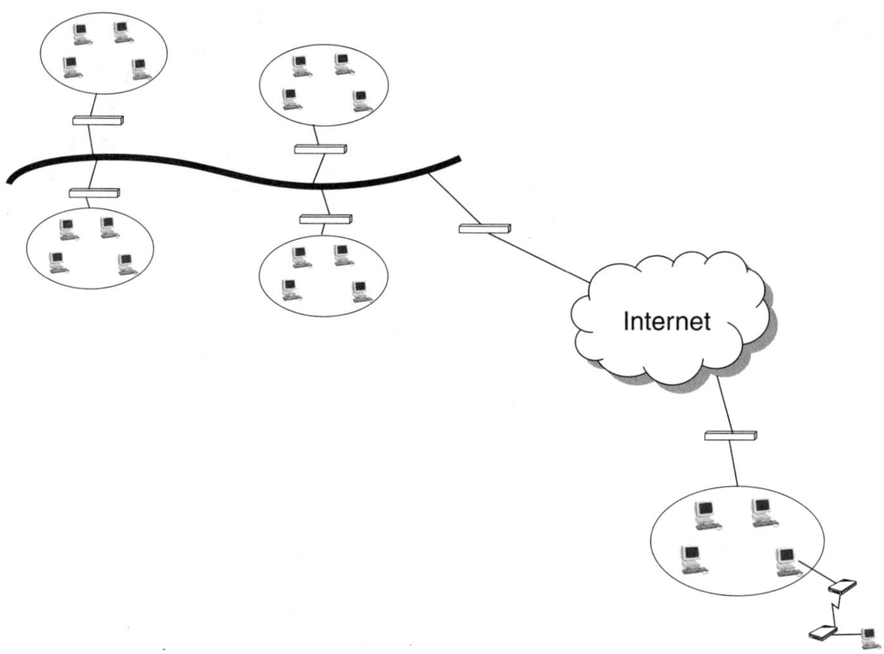

Let's look at a possible example. The previous figure represents your proposed network design. Assume you want to test to make sure that application traffic is being routed properly and that your remote access configuration is going to give users the correct level of access.

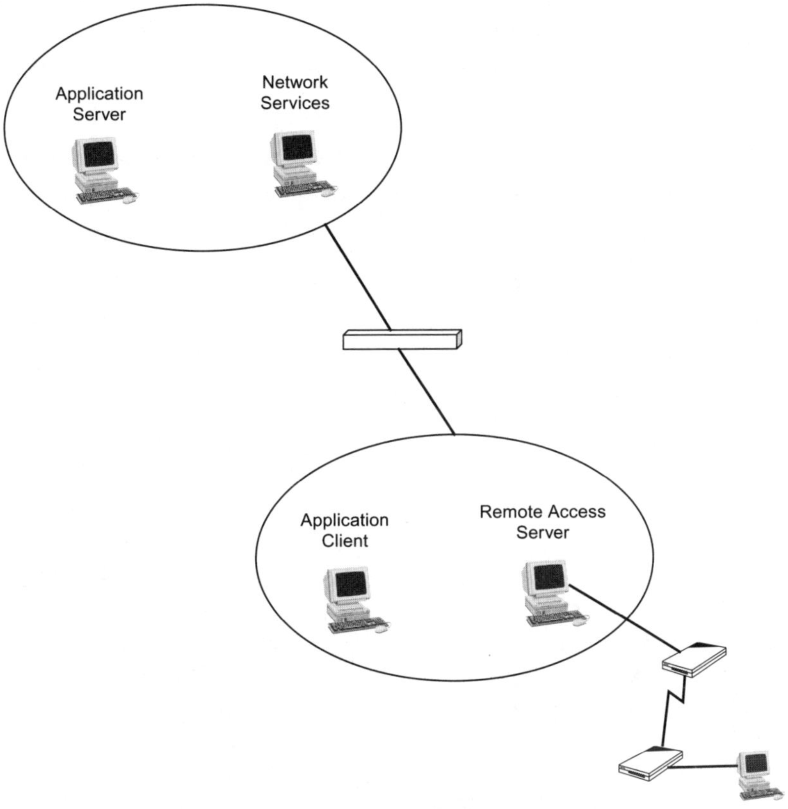

The previous figure represents a possible test network configuration. The testing that you are planning to perform on this network won't put a significant load on network servers, so you can probably get away with combining all of your network services on one or two physical servers. This will let you test communication through the router with your application server and includes a remote access server.

Of course, this test network will only work for specific network and service tests, but it should give you a general idea of what you need to do. You have to design your test network to give you a test platform for what you consider the most critical components and technologies.

Testing is going to help, but it's extremely unlikely that you are going to be able to resolve all of your problems on a test network. You are, after all, working in a different configuration. It's doubtful that you are going to be able to generate the same traffic levels, in either volume or variety, that you will have to support on your production network.

Deployment Schedules

You will have to set a deployment schedule and publish the schedule to everyone that is going to be impacted by the deployment process. Internally, this will include your technical staff, users, and managers. Coordinating the schedule may be the easy part of the process, though, if you are also having to work with outside contractors. You can get vendors and outside contractors to agree to a schedule, but there is little that smaller organizations can do to force them to adhere to the schedule other than threatening not to pay.

When you set your deployment schedule, you need to realize that business activities are going to be planned around your deployment activities. This will be done to minimize the impact on day-to-day business. This means that you are going to have to make every effort you can to stay on schedule and to let everyone else know as early as possible when changes are made to the schedule.

Check Lists

Check lists can be a key part of a successful implementation. While some people may look at preparing check lists as a waste of time, they can pay off in the long run. Check lists help in a number of ways, including:

- Helping you not to skip any steps
- Providing procedural steps for consistent operating system and application installation
- Providing procedural steps for consistent server and workstation configuration
- Providing a *who did what* paper trail should problems surface at a later date

Check lists can be especially important in a large routed LAN or distributed WAN environment. The more people you have involved in the implementation process, the bigger the chance that variations can creep in between systems. Check lists are one of the best ways of providing consistency guidelines.

Deployment Guidelines

You were introduced to a couple of general deployment methods earlier in the course. You were given the choice of a complete switch-over or a phased deployment. Most organizations don't have the personnel or other resources to shut down the old network on Friday evening and greet the users with a new network on Monday morning. Considering real-world constraints, you are most likely going to be using a phased implementation.

Managing Phased Implementation

You've already been introduced to what's involved in managing phased implementation. Now you just need to put it all together to create your deployment road map.

The basic steps involved will include the following:

- Identify priorities.

  These were probably given to you as part of your network design goals. Real-world requirements may force you to make some shifts in priorities.

- Identify dependencies.

  These are all of the *A before B* components of your design. For example, you cannot implement routing until you've installed a routable protocol. You cannot convert all of your workstations into DHCP clients until the DHCP servers are in place. Try to identify all dependencies before you start.

- Create a deployment schedule.

  Map out your deployment schedule and distribute it to anyone who will be directly impacted by deployment activities. Be sure to clearly identify critical items such as planned downtime.

- Prepare check lists.

  Prepare check lists for everyone who is going to be taking part in the deployment process. This will help to minimize isolation and repair time should problems arise during or after installation.

Once everything is in place, you're ready to start. You are going to want to test during the implementation process and monitor the network carefully after implementation. Once it looks like everything is working right, you can shift to a more periodic monitoring schedule.

Deployment Concerns

Phased implementation isn't always easy. In fact, managing a phased implementation can be frustrating at times. You end up spending weeks, or even months, supporting a mix of operating systems, applications, network topologies, and other network components that seem to be in a constant state of flux. You no more than raise one set of user issues before you have to start on the next set of questions and concerns.

Many areas of concern have already been addressed. Here are a few, as a quick summary:

- Network services

  You may find yourself having to integrate network services support or have parallel services running until the implementation is complete.

- Network operating systems

  Living with a mix of network operating systems can turn out to be a short-term situation or something that you need to deal with for the life of your network. Either way, you'll need to provide support to share resources between the different network operating systems.

- Network clients

  If you are supporting different network operating systems, you are also going to be supporting different network clients. Often, you may be having to support different types of network clients, such as Microsoft and Novell, on a single client workstation.

- Client operating systems

  It's not unusual to see a mix of different clients on a network, such as Windows-family and Apple/Macintosh clients. Even within the Windows family, the different Windows versions have different features and support requirements.

You are going to want to work toward reducing the number of variables such as network and client operating systems. Simplifying your network will reduce your management overhead.

Making Life Easier

There are some things you can do to make the implementation process easier to manage. These include:

- Unattended operating system installation

  You can use unattended installation to simplify Windows 2000 installation and upgrade. Microsoft has developed several options for how you can manage the unattended installation process so that you can select the option that best suits your needs.

- Automated software distribution and management

  You can also automate software installation and upgrade through Windows 2000 Windows Installer Service and Active Directory Group Policy settings. This can significantly reduce the time and effort required to distribute end-user software.

The larger the network, the more you can benefit from unattended operating system installation and automated software distribution. You will have to invest some time in setting these up beforehand, but the investment can more than pay for itself in time saved during implementation. There is an added benefit in that this will ensure consistent installations.

Scenario 9-1: Designing Deployment

The purpose of this scenario is to give you additional practice working with deployment issues. Suggested solutions are provided in Appendix B at the end of this manual. It may be helpful to review the case studies in Appendix C at the end of this manual.

Things and Stuff

1. You've decided to organize the network as an Active Directory domain. What system upgrades are going to be required before you can start organizing your domain?

   ....

   ....

2. In addition to Active Directory services, what network service will be required by this conversion?

   ....

   ....

Barney's Bank

You have 60 Windows NT workstations in Corpus Christi that need to be upgraded to Windows 2000 Professional systems. What can you do to provide consistent installations but minimize the installation time required for users or your support staff?

SERVICE MONITORING AND MANAGEMENT

This section focuses on two monitoring requirements: closely monitoring network activity immediately after implementation and periodically monitoring performance on an ongoing basis. The following topics are covered in this section:

- Monitoring Overview
- Ongoing Management

This section also includes an introduction to selected Windows 2000 Administrative Tools.

Monitoring Overview

As you've seen, a Windows 2000 network can be a relatively complicated environment as it requires you to support multiple closely related network services. Any problems that occur can have a ripple effect throughout the network. Keeping it all running right can sometimes feel like an overwhelming task.

Part of keeping a network in top form is making sure that it is working right in the first place. This means testing the performance of network components during and after implementation. After the network is in place, you are going to want to include periodic monitoring as part of your ongoing management practices. Periodic monitoring can help you detect minor network problems before they become serious failures. During the monitoring process, you are going to be looking closely at individual components, but you have to be careful not to lose site of the overall goal of network management.

If you're wondering what you need to monitor, the short answer is everything. While that's not a very informative answer, it is very close to the truth. It's a little easier to see, though, if you break it down into a few details. For the purpose of this course, monitoring is being separated into two major categories: hardware monitoring and software monitoring. These are being used for convenience. As you will see, there is a great deal of overlap between the items in these categories.

Before looking at individual components and services, let's start by reviewing some Windows 2000 monitoring tools.

Monitoring Tools

You've already been introduced to several of the tools that you are going to be using to monitor network performance and reliability. Think back to the discussions about the information-gathering phase. You need to collect much the same information and will be using the same tools as during that phase. The information collected during information gathering can be used as an initial baseline for comparison against your network after your changes have been implemented. Information collected immediately after implementation provides a second baseline, which can be used to monitor changes to your network over time.

Let's take a few moments to review some of the monitoring tools that are available to you. This is not meant to be a complete list of all of the available tools, nor does this discussion provide detailed procedural instructions for using the tools. Instead, it is an overview provided to help you identify some of the most commonly used tools and situations where they are appropriate choices for performance monitoring.

System Monitor

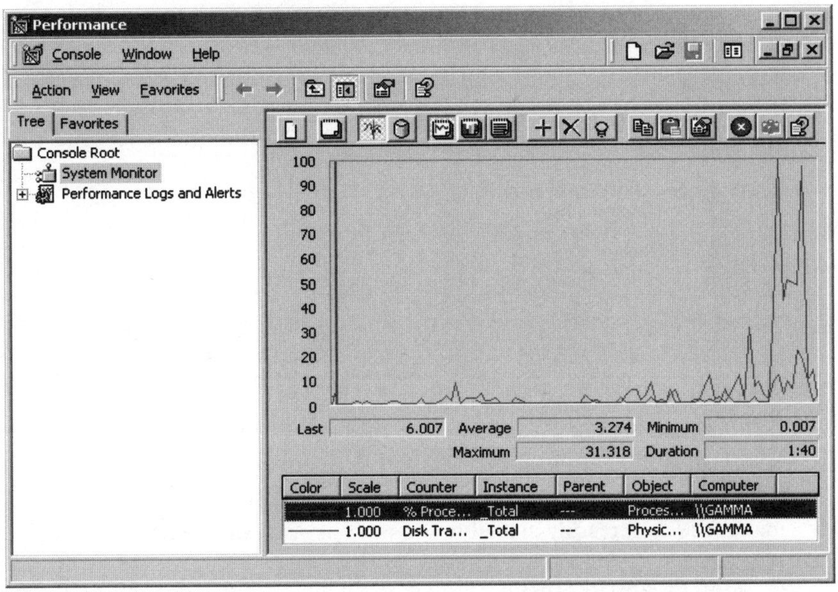

You were introduced to the System Monitor earlier in the course as an information-gathering tool. The System Monitor is implemented on Windows 2000 as part of the Performance tool. It is also going to be one of your primary tools for monitoring network and individual server performance after implementation.

You will primarily use System Monitor to collect near real-time performance data and average performance data over a limited period of time. You typically will not leave System Monitor running for an extended period of time.

Performance Logs and Alerts

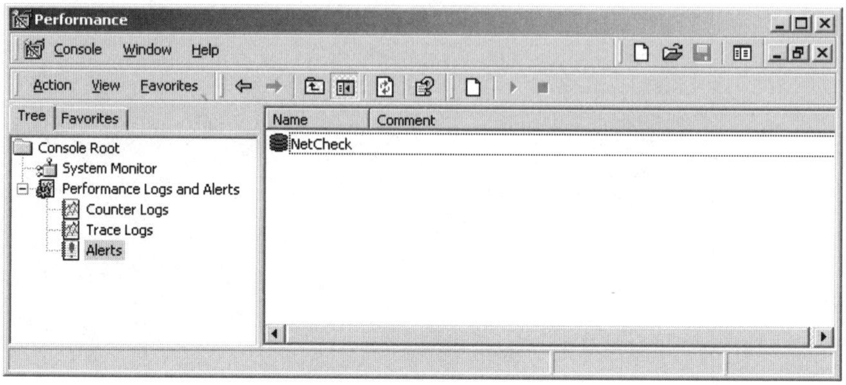

Performance logs and alerts are also available through the Performance tool. Windows 2000 supports two types of performance logs: counter logs and trace logs. Both are used for collecting and recording performance data over a period of time. This makes the data readily available for analysis and comparison.

A counter log works by sampling performance counters over a period of time. The same data is collected as when you use System Monitor except that the values are being written to a log file. You should use counter logs when you want to collect baseline values or other performance data over a period of time. For example, if you are trying to gather information on daily performance patterns, a counter log would probably be the most appropriate tool to use.

Trace logs are also used to gather data over time. A major difference between trace logs and counter logs is that trace log data is collected from start to finish during events rather than just sampled. Trace logs are used to collect information on selected system events. One potential use of trace logs is to view associated activities generated by an application or other system activity. You could then, for example, use the information to see if application activity was related to network performance problems.

You can use alerts to monitor performance counter values in comparison to threshold performance limits that you have specified. When a limit is exceeded, the alert triggers. You define an alert by selecting one or more counters and threshold trigger values. Threshold values can be specified as either minimum or maximum values.

You can choose to have the system perform one or more of the following when an alert triggers:

- Log an event to the Application event log.
- Send a network message.
- Start a Performance data log.
- Run an executable program.

Select the actions that are most appropriate to the event.

Event Viewer Logs

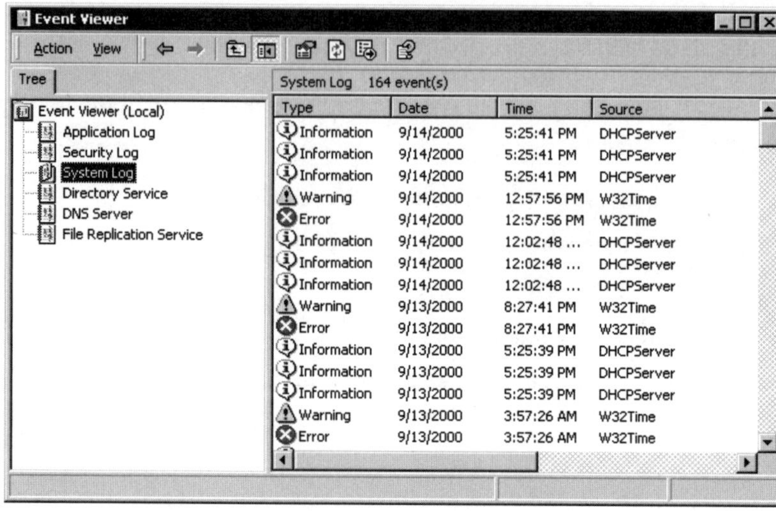

You can learn a great deal about what's happening on a system through the Event Viewer logs. The logs contain informational, warning, and error messages generated by system, service, and application events. The Security log will contain success audit and failure audit events. The logs you may see include the following:

- Application log

  Applications can be written to write events to the Application log. More important to this course, however, is that some network services, including DHCP, WINS, and IPSec, will also write events to the log. When having problems with any of these services, the Application log is one of the first places to check.

- Security log

  Audit events are written to the Security log. This means that only those events you have enabled logging for will be seen in the Security log. For example, you can select to log failed logon attempts if you suspect that someone is trying to break in to your system.

- System log

  Check the System log for system warning and error event messages. Many service errors are also written to the System log. If you suspect a hardware problem, such as a failing network adapter, this is one of the first places to check.

- Directory Service log

  Events relating to the Active Directory database are written to the Directory Service log. You will only see this log on Active Directory domain controllers. This is a good source of information about Active Directory activity.

- DNS Server log

  Only DNS servers will have a DNS log. DNS-related events are written to this log. If you suspect problems with DNS, or if you are having problems with automated IP address assignments, this is a good place to start looking for an idea of what is wrong.

- File Replication Service log

  Events relating to SYSVOL replication are written to the File Replication Service log. This is a good place to start when you suspect replication errors such as group policies not getting updated properly.

The Application, Security, and System logs are present on all Windows 2000 systems. The remaining logs will only be present on systems with those services installed.

Simple Network Management Protocol (SNMP) Events

SNMP uses SNMP managers and agents working together to view and manage system configuration information. The components supported are defined through files called Management Information Bases (MIBs). Managers can query SNMP agents for status information and receive alerts (called traps) from the agents. Agents respond to SNMP manager commands and generate alerts.

You have the option of installing the SNMP agent on your network's Windows 2000 (and Windows NT) systems. Microsoft does not currently provide an SNMP manager for Windows 2000. Implementation of an SNMP manager will require third-party software.

Network Monitor

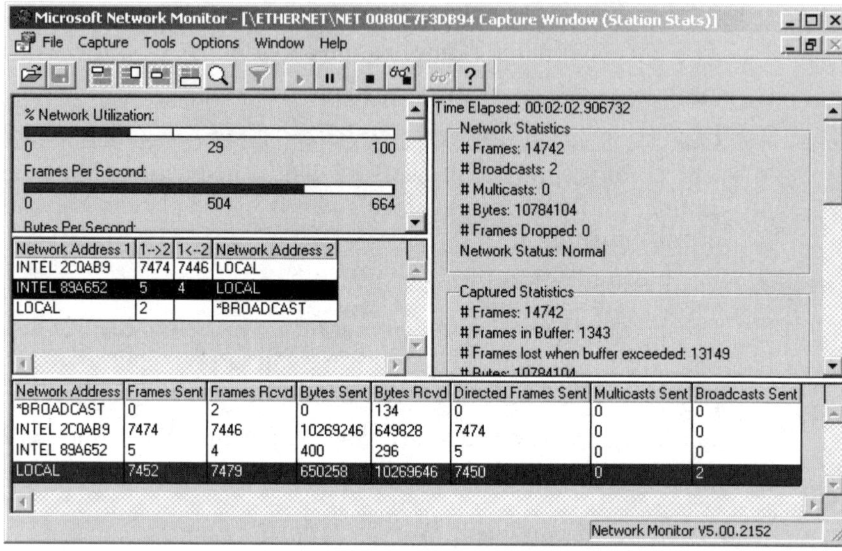

The Network Monitor lets you capture network packets and monitor network traffic. The Network Monitor will capture incoming and outgoing packets, placing a time stamp on each based on the elapsed time since you started the capture. In addition to capturing packets, the Network Monitor will decode them. This will make it easy for you to view information about packets, such as their source address, destination address, type, and so forth.

Summary network and capture statistics will be displayed while the capture is running. The Network Monitor Driver captures the data from the network adapter and passes the data to the Network Monitor. The version of Network Monitor that ships with Windows 2000 can only capture local incoming and outgoing traffic but is still useful for checking traffic for specific systems. For example, you could use Network Monitor to monitor traffic for a server that is providing network services to determine the usage levels.

The version of Network Monitor that ships with Microsoft's Systems Management Server (SMS) allows you to capture traffic from any system with the Network Monitor Driver loaded. The Network Monitor Driver will forward the data to the system acting as a remote monitor. This will increase the amount of background traffic on your network.

TCP/IP Utilities

You were introduced to several TCP/IP management utilities at the beginning of this course. As a quick review, these were as follows:

- Ipconfig

  After implementing your new network design, Ipconfig can be very helpful in troubleshooting DHCP-related problems. You can use Ipconfig to release and renew automatic IP address assignments.

- Ping

  An obvious use for Ping is to simply test for connectivity, in other words, to see if you can get a packet transmitted between a source and destination host. This is a good quick check to see if a system is running and available. Another place where you can use Ping is to look for latency in your network, more in WAN connections than in LAN connections. Ping sends a packet to the remote host and waits for a reply. Part of the information reported on return is the round-trip time, which will give you an idea of links where latency could be a potential problem.

- Pathping

  Pathping is useful for tracing the path that a packet is taking through your private intranet or even through the Internet. This is a good way of checking to see if your router design is working like you expect.

- Tracert

  Tracert is another option for tracing the path between source and destination hosts. Once again, this is a way of checking how your router design is working.

It is likely that, if not already familiar with these utilities, you will become very familiar with their use while managing a TCP/IP network.

Other Monitoring Devices

The additional monitoring devices listed here are the same as you saw earlier in the course. They are as follows:

- Time-Domain Reflectometer (TDR)

  A TDR can be especially helpful during and immediately after implementation if you are running new network cabling. It can identify any problems you might have introduced through imperfect or improperly installed cables. Keep in mind that just because you received a cable as new, it doesn't guarantee that it's good. You are going to want to make sure that you've corrected any potential hardware problems before you start additional network testing and analysis.

- Network monitors

  You may choose to use a non-Microsoft network monitor product due to features or functionality not supported by Microsoft. As with the Microsoft Network Monitor product, you can use a network monitor to monitor bandwidth usage. Most have the ability to filter traffic so that you can monitor specific types of traffic.

- Protocol analyzer

  Protocol analyzers perform a wide range of real-time network traffic analysis tasks. You may be more familiar with the term *network analyzers*. Both terms refer to the same type of monitoring device. A protocol analyzer provides all of the functionality described for network monitors and TDRs. In addition, it lets you identify system activity, track performance trends, and identify network bottlenecks. You can also set alerts and monitor for specific network conditions. In a large network, you may find that your traffic monitor requirements justify the cost of investing in a protocol analyzer.

Choose monitoring tools specific to your network requirements. If you have only periodic monitoring requirements, you may find it cost effective to outsource some monitoring activities.

Hardware Monitoring

Hardware monitoring focuses on network hardware and network traffic. Specific items that require periodic monitoring include the following:

- LAN traffic levels

  Monitor LAN traffic levels to determine when (or if) you need to further segment your network through the use of additional subnets. You may also find that you may want to move some activities off to a separate subnet or duplicate network services in other subnets. For example, if you are supporting all DNS requirements from one location and are experiencing very high levels of DNS traffic, you may want to add more DNS servers in different locations.

- WAN traffic levels

  Monitor traffic over WAN links to determine if the links provide sufficient bandwidth for your communication requirements. You may find that you need to upgrade to faster links or implement additional links. You can also reduce WAN traffic by implementing local network services and adjusting the locations of user resources.

- Cable plant condition

  This was mentioned a little earlier. Network cable quality can degrade over time or cable flaws may turn up that weren't initially visible. Substandard cable is going to result in substandard network performance.

- Router performance

  You will want to periodically monitor router performance to make sure that your routers are able to support the required traffic volume. You may need to upgrade the quality of your routers or add more routers to your network design to provide alternate paths. You may be able to avoid making changes to your routers by making changes to the underlying traffic source and making changes to server and other resource locations.

You may have a regular *spot-check* schedule that you use to verify network hardware performance. Many organizations only monitor hardware performance when they suspect a performance problem. Periodic monitoring can help you identify potential problem conditions before they impact network performance.

Software Monitoring

The term *software monitoring* is being used to refer to monitoring network activity relating to network services and application support. Though not mentioned separately for each, you will want to monitor the performance of any servers providing services to the network. One relatively painless way of doing this is through the use of alerts.

Server and service availability are not being included in this monitoring discussion. After you've worked out any initial availability problems in your network design, it will typically only become an issue when there is a failure in your network.

The following services need to be monitored:

- DNS

  You already know that DNS is used for TCP/IP name resolution. As part of this, DNS is used when clients need to find an authentication server or, in an Active Directory domain, a Global Catalog server. You will want to monitor traffic generated by name queries and zone updates.

- WINS

  WINS provides NetBIOS name resolution services for the network. Name resolution requests can also be forwarded to WINS when they cannot be resolved by your DNS name servers. There may also be some traffic generated through automatic DHCP updates to the WINS database. You will want to monitor name registration and resolution traffic. You will also need to keep an eye on the traffic generated by WINS replication.

- DHCP

  Most of the traffic generated by DHCP servers occurs as DHCP clients start and request IP addresses and configuration information. If you've enabled DHCP to provide dynamic DNS updates, there will be some additional traffic generated through this process.

- Routing and Remote Access Service (RRAS)

  Routing was listed as one of the hardware items that needs to be monitored, but routing also falls in the software category. The same general guidelines apply when watching the traffic through the router and router performance statistics. This can be especially important with Windows 2000 servers running RRAS since it is not uncommon for a server to be configured to manage multiple routing tasks such as support for both dial-in access and VPN connections.

- NAT

  The NAT protocol and NAT servers are designed for use where there are minimal Internet access requirements. You are going to want to keep an eye on the traffic volume supported by the NAT server.

- Proxy Server

  While the same guidelines apply as for other servers that have been discussed with this topic, Proxy Server is designed to help you in the monitoring process. If you've enabled logging, you can review the Proxy Server logs to view usage information.

- Application servers

  What you need to monitor for an application server somewhat depends on the server. It is obvious that you will want to monitor client traffic and traffic patterns, especially for remote access clients. With some application servers, there may be other monitoring requirements such as monitoring traffic generated by replication updates.

- Dfs

  If you decide to implement Dfs, you are going to want to monitor user access and access patterns for resources that are being managed through Dfs. This will help you to determine if and when you need to add Dfs root replicas or Dfs link replicas.

- Active Directory

  The focus for this discussion is the traffic generated through Active Directory replication. Many service updates, such as Active Directory-integrated DNS and dynamic Dfs, are implemented through Active Directory domain replication. This means that you can see increases in domain replication traffic from the number and types of services you've added. Monitor replication traffic to help you determine when you need to make changes to how replication is being managed.

- Global Catalog

  The Global Catalog includes all Active Directory objects. This includes all of the objects in all of the domains. A computer in one domain can use the Global Catalog to locate resources (and other objects) in a different domain. To help keep the Global Catalog a more manageable size, it does not include all object attributes. Only the most commonly used attributes are saved. One potential problem area is traffic levels during user logon since the Global Catalog is also involved in locating an authentication server in an Active Directory domain.

  There are also replication concerns in Active Directory networks. Changes to any domain in the forest will be replicated to all of the Global Catalog servers.

- Lightweight Directory Access Protocol (LDAP) service

  Clients use LDAP when communicating with domain controllers in general and specifically when communicating with Global Catalog servers. Some applications will also use LDAP to communicate directly with the Active Directory. You can use Network Monitor filtering to watch for LDAP traffic without having to search through other types of traffic.

- Certificate Services

  Certificate Services is responsible for issuing and managing X.509 certificates. Certificates are used for validation and public key encryption. One use of certificates is in IPSec security management. There will typically be little need for monitoring the traffic generated by Certificate Services.

Software monitoring will be especially important after making changes to network applications, resource locations, or the number or mix of users on your network.

Ongoing Management

From the discussions you've already seen in this chapter, you should have a good idea of some of the ongoing management tasks that you are going to face. Some common tasks include the following:

- Network growth

  As mentioned previously, you need to include growth and expansion plans in your network design. Compensating for network growth and changing network conditions will be an ongoing part of your network management requirements.

- User management

  There are going to be ongoing changes to your user population, including the number, type, and distribution of users. This is going to require you to revise your network design and implementation over time to provide optimal support for your user population.

- Resource management

  As your user population changes, so will the resource requirements necessary to support that population. Changes to applications, both end user and server based, are also going to impact your resource management requirements.

This list includes issues that relate directly to your network design. However, when considering ongoing network management as a whole, this list does little to even scratch the surface of the management requirements such as user and resource security, changing logon controls, physical data security requirements changes, and so forth.

Windows 2000 Administrative Tools

The focus of this course has been on network design rather than on physical implementation. Because of this, there has been only limited discussion of management tools and procedures. While an introduction to detailed procedural steps is still beyond the scope of this course, you may find an overview of commonly used management tools helpful. These include the following:

- Configure Your Server

  The Configure Your Server tool, by default, displays when you launch Windows 2000. This tool provides easy access to configuration wizards. You can use Configure Your Server to launch wizards to set up Active Directory, network services, and application services. The tool can also launch wizards to configure your server as a file, print, or Web/media server.

- Computer Management

  The Computer Management tool provides system and storage management tools. You can use this tool to manage local or remote systems. This is going to be your primary system management tool.

- Event Viewer

  The Event Viewer tool is used to view the event logs. You were shown a list of the supported event logs earlier in this chapter. The event logs can be helpful tools for both monitoring current system conditions and isolating and correcting system or software failures.

- Distributed File System

  The Distributed File System tool is used to create and manage Distributed File System (Dfs) shares. It will likely be necessary over time to make changes to your Dfs design.

- Internet Services Manager

  The Internet Services Manager tool is your Internet Information Server (IIS) management utility. This will be your primary Web and FTP server management utility.

- Performance

  The Performance tool gives you access to the System Monitor as well as performance logs and alerts.

- Routing and Remote Access

  The Routing and Remote Access tool is used to configure and manage routing and remote system access. This is one tool that should already be familiar to you. This is the tool you use to configure Routing and Remote Access options.

- Services

  The Services tool lets you view and manage server services. You can view the status of any service on a system, including the security context the service was started under. You can view and modify service properties and view dependencies. Dependencies are important because a service cannot run unless any services it depends on are already running. One use of this tool is in troubleshooting, since it lets you check and see if a service is running on a server.

- Active Directory Sites and Services

  The Active Directory Sites and Services tool is used for setting up Active Directory sites and managing Active Directory replication.

- DNS

  DNS services are managed through the DNS tool. This is the tool you will use to manage DNS properties, set up DNS zones, and manage standard DNS zone replication.

- WINS

  The is the tool for managing Windows Internet Name Service (WINS), including WINS properties. This is the tool that you'll use to add static database entries and to set up WINS replication.

- DHCP

  You will use the DHCP tool for managing DHCP scopes, including IP addresses and host configuration options. In an Active Directory domain environment, this is the tool that you use to register a DHCP server with the Active Directory.

- Internet Authentication Service

  The Internet Authentication Service tool is your Windows 2000 tool for configuring and managing RADIUS support.

This is not a full list of the Administrative Tools supported by Windows 2000. It is a list of some of the tools that most closely relate to the subjects discussed during this course and that you are most likely to use during network implementation and management.

If you look at a server's **Administrative Tools** menu, you will only see some of these tools listed. For example, a Windows 2000 server will not, by default, have any of the Active Directory tools installed. Also, it will only have service management tools such as DNS and WINS available if those services have been installed.

You may find it more convenient to make these tools available on a member server that you could then remotely manage much of your network and network services from. The source for installing additional Administrative Tools on a Windows 2000 server is copied to the server during installation. This set of tools is sometimes referred to as the Admin Pack. The path and filename for this file is as follows:

```
\%systemroot%\system32\adminpak.msi
```

Additional Tools

While on the subject of management tools, there are a couple of additional items that deserve special mention. These are as follows:

- Control Panel's Add/Remove Programs utility

  In the context of the subject at hand, the Add/Remove Programs utility is important because it is the utility used to install Windows 2000 components. As you should already know, components available for installation through this utility include DNS, WINS, and DHCP.

- Network and Dial-up Connections utility

  This is where you set up client connections, including dial-up connections. This is also the utility that you use to manage existing client connections. This utility is available through the **Start | Settings** menu. It can also be launched from the Control Panel.

These tools are available on all Windows 2000 systems.

Scenario 9-2: Network Monitoring

The purpose of this scenario is to provide a review of important points relating to network monitoring. Suggested solutions are provided in Appendix B at the end of the manual. You should review the case studies in Appendix C before starting this scenario.

Things and Stuff

1. You have upgraded both Windows NT Server systems to Windows 2000 Server. You are concerned that the servers may become a network bottleneck. How can you make sure that any problems with performance are logged automatically?

2. You want to gather performance data for a full business day for each of your Windows 2000 Server systems. How can you do this?

Barney's Bank

1. You want to monitor and capture all traffic between Corpus Christi and London. What Windows 2000 utility will let you do this?

    ....

    ....

2. You suspect WINS replication errors. Where should you check first to see if any WINS replication errors have been recorded?

    ....

    ....

OPTIMIZATION

This section takes another look at the issue of optimization. The following topics are covered in this section:

- Network Optimization
- Service Optimization

Most of the information presented in this section is a review of information seen in previous sections.

Network Optimization

Let's start by looking at optimization at the network level. Several tips and technologies have been mentioned throughout this course. This discussion pulls these together for you as a concise reference.

There are three primary keys to optimizing network performance. These are as follows:

- Available bandwidth

  The more bandwidth you have, the more traffic you can support.
- Network traffic

  As traffic levels increase, you run the risk of overloading your bandwidth and restricting network traffic.
- Router hops

  Each router hop increases latency during data transmissions. Also, there is a risk of one or more routers becoming bottlenecks when supporting high levels of network traffic.

In addition, there are some more service-specific things you can do to help improve network communications. These are discussed in the following sections.

Network Design

You've seen issues relating to optimizing network performance through your network design. Let's review the following key points:

- Maximize bandwidth.

  You already know the ways that you can increase available bandwidth. Increasing bandwidth for a LAN segment means upgrading to a higher-speed technology, such as going from 10BaseT to 100BaseT Ethernet.

  Both local and remote links benefit from this by keeping hops to a minimum. Remote link bandwidth is improved by using faster links. You can improve the effective bandwidth for remote links, as well as local links to some extent, by providing multiple paths.

- Minimize traffic.

  You want to keep traffic to a minimum. This is typically more important when looking at link traffic but can become an issue on a local LAN segment. You can reduce link traffic by keeping data resources local to the users that need to access them. Network service traffic often requires you to compare the traffic generated by servicing users with the traffic required by service updates to see which generates the least amount of traffic.

- Optimize resource locations.

  Any time you can keep resources local to your users, you are going to reduce link traffic. This will not, however, always be possible. You may want to consider using additional copies of the data located on local LANs when possible. Dfs gives you a way of setting up and managing this.

You may have a *feeling* for how your network is performing. No matter how accurate your hunches have been in the past, you need to monitor network traffic to determine if any changes you make are really effective.

Network Load Balancing (NLB)

Network Load Balancing (NLB) was mentioned earlier as a way of optimizing network service support. Specifically, it was mentioned as a way of improving how inbound traffic is managed. One application of NLB would be to improve inbound traffic through proxy servers.

NLB is a Windows 2000 networking driver that lets you organize servers into clusters. You can include up to 32 systems into an NLB cluster. The network service load is balanced between the servers in the cluster. NLB clusters also provide fault tolerance since, should one server fail, its load is automatically shared among the other hosts in the cluster.

> *NOTE:* *NLB clusters are different than the server clusters introduced earlier in the course. The servers are not connected to a shared disk device. The servers in the cluster communicate with each other through the network.*

Round-Robin DNS

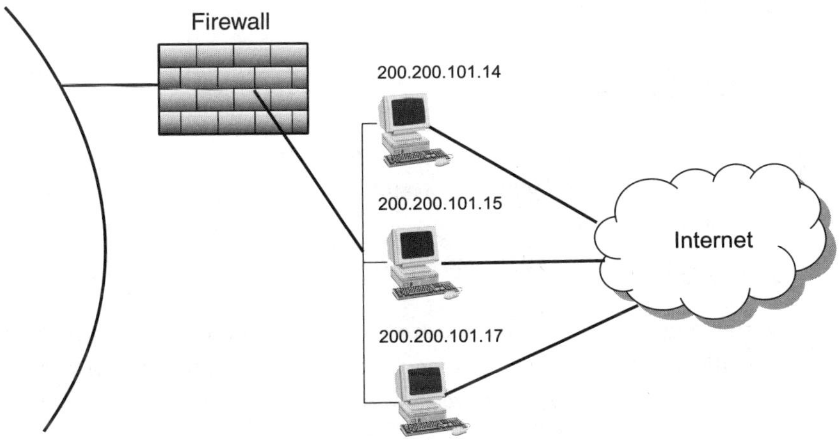

Round robin is a relatively easy way of implementing load balancing on your network. As with NLB, round robin can be especially helpful in balancing inbound traffic loads.

To implement round-robin balancing, multiple address (A) resource records are defined for a host name. DNS responses to queries for that host name will return one of the IP addresses defined by the A records, rotating through the available resource records.

In the previous figure, there are three Web servers. All three are servicing the host name www.ssclass.com. When a query comes in for www.ssclass.com, the response will send 200.200.101.14 as the IP address. The next query received will receive a response of 200.200.101.15, then the next with 200.200.101.17, and then the process will start over again.

Quality of Service (QoS)

The course introduced you to QoS earlier. As a quick review, QoS gives you a way of allocating a portion of the available bandwidth to resources and real-time applications or other applications a guaranteed bandwidth is a critical requirement for. Applications you are reserving the bandwidth for must be written to take advantage of QoS, and any router in the data path must support RSVP.

Service Optimization

Attention now turns to optimization tips for selected network services. This is a summary of a few key points to keep in mind during network design and implementation.

General Tips

Optimizing network service performance starts with optimizing your network. If your network isn't in top shape, you won't be able to get optimum performance out of your network services. You also have to optimize the server the service is running on.

There are several factors that have to be considered when placing servers that are providing network services. These include the following:

- User distribution
- User support requirements
- LAN segment bandwidth
- Link bandwidth
- Link persistence
- Routing path(s)

These considerations were introduced earlier in the course. The general rule is to place servers as near as possible to the hosts that will need access to the network services they provide. As you have already seen, there are going to be exceptions to this rule. For example, the expected traffic volume required to support multiple servers might make it more effective to support the service from a central location.

DNS

When deciding how many DNS servers you are going to need and where they are going to be deployed, you have to balance the traffic generated by name query traffic against the traffic generated by replication. You may find it necessary to do some fine-tuning after you've implemented your network design.

Replication can become an issue in a large network. If you create Active Directory-integrated zones, replication is supported as part of Active Directory replication. You may want to create sites, especially in a large WAN, to give you more control over replication. If you create or extend standard DNS zones, you have direct control over how DNS replication is managed.

WINS

The issues are similar when deciding on how you are going to support WINS. You have to balance the traffic generated by host registrations and replication to find your best design.

Remember that you can control replication by creating push and pull partners. With push replication, replication is controlled by the sending system and is based on the number of changes to the WINS database. When you use pull, the receiving system controls replication, which in this case, will occur on a set schedule. If your major concern is reducing latency (minimizing convergence), you will probably find that your best solution is to use a combination of push and pull partners. If you want to limit traffic over remote links by restricting traffic to off-peak hours, you would set up pull partners.

If you don't place a WINS server in each routed subnet, it may be necessary to set up WINS Proxy Agents in any subnet that does not have a local WINS server. This is only necessary when you have hosts that cannot be configured as WINS clients.

DHCP

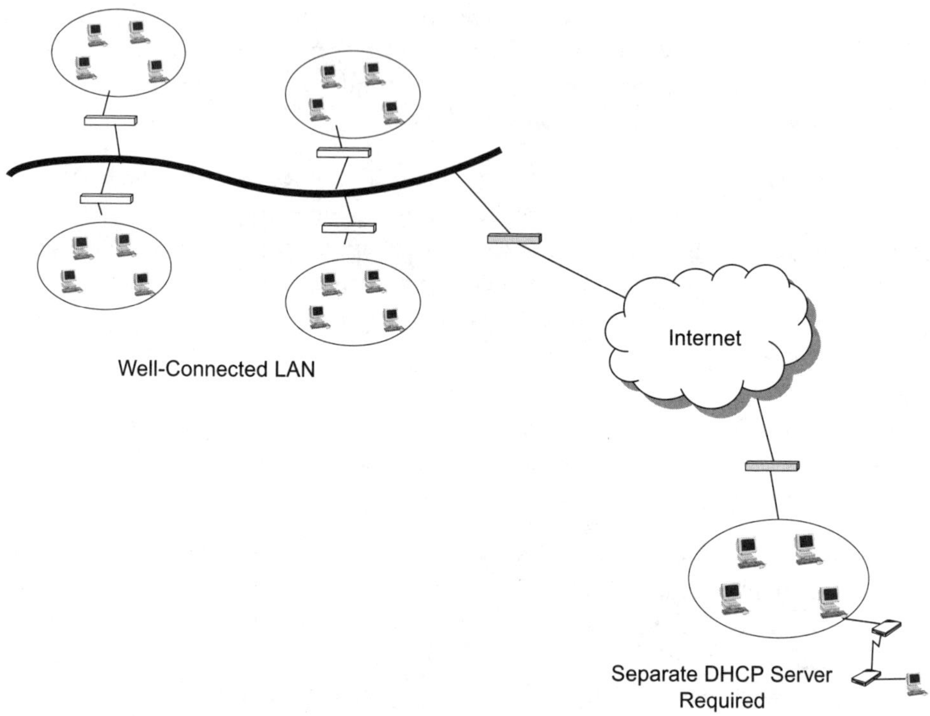

One key point to keep in mind when setting up DHCP servers is that a DHCP server should only be configured to support local and well-connected LANs or subnets. Remotely linked LANs that are linked through lower-bandwidth connections or demand-dial connections need to be supported by their own local DHCP server.

It is unlikely that you will see much difference in performance when you split an IP address range across two or more DHCP servers. What it does provide you with is a level of fault tolerance should a LAN's or cable segment's DHCP server fail.

Proxy Server

What you need to do to optimize Proxy Server depends on whether you are optimizing for inbound or outbound traffic. Outbound traffic is best served by multiple servers configured as a Proxy Array. Inbound traffic can be optimized by the use of NLB or round-robin DNS.

Scenario 9-3: Load Balancing

The purpose of this scenario is to give you practice in working with issues relating to optimization. Suggested solutions are provided in Appendix B at the end of this manual. It may be helpful to review the case studies in Appendix C at the end of this manual.

Barney's Bank

1. You are preparing to deploy a critical SQL Server application. You need to balance the transaction load across several systems running SQL Server. What load balancing method would you use to control this?

2. You are looking for a relatively easy-to-manage method of balancing the load between the four file servers that you are going to be deploying to support the Barney's Bank Web site. What load balancing method will you use?

SUMMARY

During this chapter, you were introduced to the following:

- Design implementation
- Design testing
- Deployment schedules
- Check lists
- Managing deployment
- Monitoring tools
- Hardware monitoring
- Software monitoring
- Management tools
- Network Load Balancing (NLB)
- Round-robin DNS

POST-TEST QUESTIONS

The answers to these questions are in Appendix A at the end of this manual.

1. A single host name will have multiple resource records of what type when round-robin DNS is being used to provide load balancing?

2. You are going to configure all user workstations as DHCP clients. What dependency is implied by this?

3. What systems will include a Directory Services log as an Event Viewer log?

4. What Windows 2000 Administrative Tool would be used to manage replication configuration for Active Directory-integrated DNS zones?

5. Why would an application typically use LDAP in an Active Directory domain environment?

6. Which Windows 2000 Administrative Tool can be used to view service dependencies?

7. What is the maximum number of systems that can be included in an NLB cluster?

Appendix A — Answers to Pre-Test and Post-Test Questions

CHAPTER 1

Pre-Test Answers

1. The cable plant is the physical path networked systems communicate over.
2. You have to plan for communications between your organization and other organizations.
3. Better input as to the needs of other departments and a better chance of getting your network design accepted by different departments
4. Logon security is the first line of defense against unauthorized network access.
5. A. Workgroup
6. Transport Control Protocol/Internet Protocol (TCP/IP)

Post-Test Answers

1. If the organization includes a remote location, the network design must include remote access support.
2. Current systems may not meet minimum installation or compatibility requirements for the new operating system.
3. Information gathering, design, implementation, and management
4. The network management model will need, in most cases, to reflect the business management model.
5. At the domain controllers
6. Star
7. The server needs to communicate directly with a network printer that uses DLC.
8. Upper management

CHAPTER 2

Pre-Test Answers

1. Subsidiary
2. A policy is a description of positions or practices. A procedure is the step-by-step instructions to complete a task.
3. Information flow analysis
4. Centralized and decentralized
5. There is less available bandwidth in a remote link.
6. Providing a communication link between the existing network and the acquired network
7. An acquired office will typically have an existing network that must be integrated into the existing network structure. A new office will not have a network in place but will require design and implementation of a new network.
8. Data (disk) fault tolerance

Post-Test Answers

1. Operational (or ongoing)
2. When the resources are not available internally or when outsourcing is more cost effective than using internal resources
3. Archival storage of documents and other information relating to the product
4. Decentralized IT management tends to result in a lack of standardization in network implementations.
5. A written change-management process
6. This is a policy because it describes a task but gives no details as to how the task will be accomplished.
7. Regional

CHAPTER 3

Pre-Test Answers

1. A nonrouted LAN will have a single network address. A routed LAN will have multiple network addresses.
2. It provides a high-speed communication path between the LANs.
3. Network Monitor
4. Security log
5. 10 Mbps
6. Domain Name System (DNS) and Windows Internet Name System (WINS)
7. 1.544 Mbps
8. By logging on to the local LAN
9. You need to know the support structure that is in place to determine what changes will need to be made with the new network design.
10. User logons are validated by the local machine.
11. NTFS
12. Proxy server
13. Winmsd

Post-Test Answers

1. 56 Kbps
2. Router
3. Category 5
4. 4 Mbps and 16 Mbps
5. Higher availability of the network services, reduced latency, and reduced traffic across wide-area links
6. Basic Rate ISDN (BRI) and Primary Rate ISDN (PRI)
7. Increased bandwidth and fault tolerance for availability should one link become unavailable
8. Power users typically need access to more data files and larger data files than other users.
9. For added access security between subnetworks

CHAPTER 4

Pre-Test Answers

1. RG-58 family cable
2. 1,024
3. 4 Mbps and 16 Mbps
4. A. NetBEUI
5. When connecting with Novell NetWare servers or clients using the IPX/SPX protocol
6. Traffic destined for a host (computer) in a different subnetwork will be routed through the default gateway.
7. Whenever possible, user workstations and servers, providing resources that they need, should be placed on the same subnetwork.
8. This may generate excessive link traffic due to updates through replication.
9. Provide the computer with a modem and dial-up line.
10. For security, to isolate your LAN from direct contact with the Internet

Post-Test Answers

1. Improved availability and a higher effective bandwidth
2. Fifteen links
3. 72
4. 100 meters (328 feet)
5. TCP/IP
6. The subnet mask identifies the host address and network address in the IP address.
7. To improve availability and minimize traffic between subnetworks
8. To allow multiple users to connect to the Internet through a single connection

CHAPTER 5

Pre-Test Answers

1. DHCP service
2. The sending host's default gateway
3. NetBIOS name to IP address resolution
4. You can use private IP addresses if your network does not connect to the Internet or connects through address translation.
5. The maximum number of hops between subnets
6. Five
7. The process of combining consecutive Class C addresses to provide support for additional hosts
8. Open Shortest Path First (OSPF)
9. To make sure the subnet isn't generating more traffic than its bandwidth can support
10. Gateway Service for NetWare
11. Host Integration Server (SNA Server)

Post-Test Answers

1. When connecting directly to the Internet
2. 254
3. Pathping and Tracert
4. Local broadcast
5. Fourteen
6. Packet filtering
7. Add a second router and balance the traffic between the two routers.
8. You have either not entered a value for the default gateway or have entered an incorrect value for the default gateway.
9. Install NWLink and CSNW on both Windows 2000 Professional systems.
10. TCP/IP, NWLink, NetBEUI, Banyan VINES IP, and AppleTalk

CHAPTER 6

Pre-Test Answers

1. NetBIOS name-to-IP address resolution
2. SRV (Service record)
3. Replication is managed as part of Active Directory replication.
4. One
5. Install a caching-only server in the remote location.
6. Active-Directory integrated
7. You cannot. The entry must be deleted and then re-created.
8. You would configure the receiving WINS server as a pull partner.
9. None. The name resolution requirements can be met through NetBIOS broadcasts.
10. All servers that receive the request and have a valid IP address will respond.
11. The client has a locally configured value for the primary WINS server.
12. To provide fault tolerance in case one of the DHCP servers should fail and to provide load balancing
13. Network traffic will increase.
14. You can configure your DNS server to forward unresolved name queries to a WINS server for resolution.

Post-Test Answers

1. Create an alert on the DHCP server to monitor process performance counters and to inform you if the alert triggers.
2. Full zone transfer
3. A and PTR
4. An A record
5. Place a DNS server in each LAN.
6. If possible, configure the DNS server as a standard secondary zone name server. Use a firewall to control traffic between the DNS server and the Internet.
7. Set up WINS Proxy Agents.
8. Name registration traffic, name resolution requests and responses, and WINS replication traffic

9. L2TP with IPSec
10. Place a WINS server in each LAN.
11. You haven't authorized the DHCP server.
12. The network routers have not been configured as DHCP Relay Agents.
13. Four, one in each office
14. Shortening the period increases traffic; lengthening the period decreases traffic.

CHAPTER 7

Pre-Test Answers

1. The connection between the NAT server and the LAN will be a persistent connection.
2. Your routers must be configured as DHCP Relay Agents.
3. IP and IPX
4. Point-to-Point Protocol (PPP)
5. EAP-TLS, MS-CHAP, or MS-CHAP v2
6. It is used to combine multiple physical connections into one logical connection with a higher effective bandwidth.
7. Internet Authentication Service (IAS)
8. Never. The remote access client will connect to a RADIUS client. The RADIUS client forwards the authentication request to the RADIUS server.
9. Two
10. Proxy Server
11. Address pools and special port mappings
12. TCP/IP and IPX/SPX
13. One
14. When you want to provide network systems with anonymous access to the Internet. This is sometimes used when configuring Proxy Server for use in a heterogeneous network.
15. Voluntary tunnel
16. IPSec
17. The requests will be denied.

Post-Test Answers

1. A direct, point-to-point persistent connection
2. An encrypted VPN connection
3. Internet Connection Sharing (ICS) and Network Address Translation (NAT)
4. Connect to a private network through the Internet
5. TCP/IP, IPX, NetBEUI, and AppleTalk
6. RADIUS
7. Other hosts can access the remote network through the client.
8. A password used by a RADIUS server and client for mutual authentication
9. Active Directory domains and Windows NT 4.0 domains
10. Disable DHCP Relay Agent on the router connecting the screened subnet to the rest of the network.
11. TCP/IP and IPX/SPX
12. Nothing is wrong; a Proxy Array will not improve inbound performance.
13. L2TP
14. The Web server should be deployed as part of your private network. The exact location will depend on user access requirements.

CHAPTER 8

Pre-Test Answers

1. NAT server protocol support is limited. Make sure that your applications do not require any protocols not supported by NAT.
2. File open, file save, and autosave
3. A high-bandwidth, high-availability connection
4. With centralized storage, data is typically backed up on a more regular basis.
5. One
6. Through Active Directory replication
7. When your network is not an Active Directory domain

Post-Test Answers

1. WINS
2. Your firewall must be configured to pass protocols and data packets required by the server-based application.
3. You must configure local access security to prevent unauthorized access.
4. RSVP
5. Share the folder from the new server and update the link.
6. Set up local alternates for commonly accessed files.
7. Domain Dfs root

CHAPTER 9

Pre-Test Answers

1. You want to correct any current problems so that they will not impact your implementation.
2. Check lists will help you assure that no steps are skipped and that you have consistent installations.
3. The process for installing systems is simplified, and you are assured consistent installations.
4. Counter logs in the Performance tool
5. Ipconfig
6. Lightweight Directory Access Protocol (LDAP)
7. Internet Authentication Service
8. Enter multiple address (A) resource records for a single host name. Each A record will have the IP address of a different server.

Post-Test Answers

1. Address (A)
2. You must set up one or more DHCP servers.
3. Active Directory domain controllers
4. Active Directory Sites and Services
5. To communicate directly with the Active Directory
6. Services
7. 32

Appendix B — Solutions

CHAPTER 1

Things and Stuff

1. Retail sales
2. From the information given, there are no remote access requirements.

Barney's Bank

1. Centralized management
2. Phased implementation

Fairco Manufacturing

1. Invoice posting. The network could be enabled to allow field salespeople to post invoices electronically through remote access.
2. Unless there is a need that hasn't been stated for NWLink, remove NWLink from the systems and run TCP/IP only.

CHAPTER 2

Scenario 2-1

Things and Stuff

1. Retail sales
2. Regional
3. Invoices are posted by users. Invoice information is written to an Access database. Reports are generated from the access database.

Barney's Bank

1. Service based
2. International
3. Centralized management
4. Branch offices

Fairco Manufacturing

1. A combination of manufacturing, product development, and wholesale warehousing
2. National
3. The procedures and information flow involved in processing customer orders

Scenario 2-2

1. Barney's Bank, for information used to compile periodic reports
2. Barney's Bank and Fairco Manufacturing
3. Barney's Bank

Scenario 2-3

1. All three (Things and Stuff, Barney's Bank, and Fairco Manufacturing)
2. Barney's Bank
3. Barney's Bank
4. Barney's Bank, since remote offices and subsidiaries are making undocumented changes to their networks
5. Things and Stuff

Scenario 2-4

1. Because Barney's Bank is a financial service organization and because it falls under both United States and international regulations
2. Things and Stuff is most likely to need outside assistance. Things and Stuff is the only case study company that is not currently supporting remote communications and has the smallest, least-experienced technical staff.
3. Use data fault tolerance to protect against hard disk failure.
4. Barney's Bank
5. Point-of-sale posting performance

CHAPTER 3

Scenario 3-1

Things and Stuff's Current Network

1. This is a nonrouted LAN. You know this because all of the systems can communicate, and the only protocol used, NetBEUI, is a nonroutable protocol.
2. 10 Mbps
3. None
4. Each system will locally validate each logon attempt.

Barney's Bank's Current Network

1. TCP/IP, since TCP/IP is required when installing Active Directory services
2. DNS
3. Logon performance may be less than optimal since all logon attempts from the subnetworks wired with a star topology must be routed to the subnetwork wired with a bus topology.

Fairco Manufacturing's Current Network

1. 10 Mbps
2. The use of HOSTS files becomes progressively harder to manage as the size of the network increases.
3. The PDC and BDC can both validate user logons.

Scenario 3-2

1. Across the demand-dial links between Corpus Christi and the U.S. branch offices
2. All U.S. offices and the London and Dublin offices

Scenario 3-3

1. Things and Stuff, because a number of the users have blank passwords
2. From the information provided, Fairco Manufacturing. It is the only company supporting any kind of remote access.
3. Barney's Bank, with delays in getting data from other LANs
4. Barney's Bank
5. Things and Stuff and Fairco Manufacturing
6. Implement higher bandwidth links between the main and remote warehouses.

Scenario 3-4

1. Things and Stuff
2. Barney's Bank, due to the geographic scope and number of systems involved
3. All servers and a representative sampling of user workstations

CHAPTER 4

Scenario 4-1

1. The entire cable plant will have to be replaced and hubs purchased and installed. It will probably be necessary to replace the current network adapters.
2. Star topology

Scenario 4-2

Barney's Bank's Current Network

1. TCP/IP is definitely in use. There is nothing to imply the use of other protocols.
2. You will need to add TCP/IP support to the new office's LAN. There should be no other changes required at any of the other offices.

Fairco Manufacturing's Current Network

1. None. TCP/IP is already supported on the network.
2. From the information provided, there is no justification for requiring NWLink.

Scenario 4-3

Things and Stuff

1. A nonrouted LAN would be best suited because of the small number of systems in the network.
2. Since the network is already configured as a nonrouted LAN, no changes would be required.

Fairco Manufacturing

1. Routed LAN
2. A router, and there would possibly be a need for one or more additional hubs for reconfiguring the network.
3. You would need to place a BDC in the warehouse subnetwork.

Scenario 4-4

Barney's Bank's Network Goals

1. From what you have been told, your best solution is to place network servers in Corpus Christi and London. With the small user populations in the other LANs, they shouldn't require separate servers.

2.

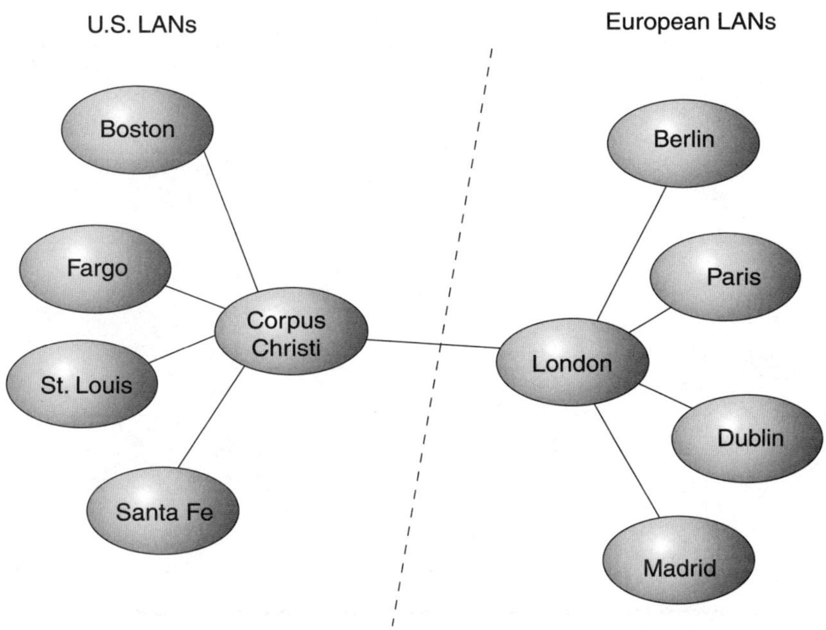

Fairco Manufacturing's Network Users

1. Set up a small LAN in each of the remote warehouses. Provide either a full-time connection or a higher-speed demand-dial connection between the remote warehouses and the main office.
2. Provide a higher-speed link from the warehouses to the main office.
3.

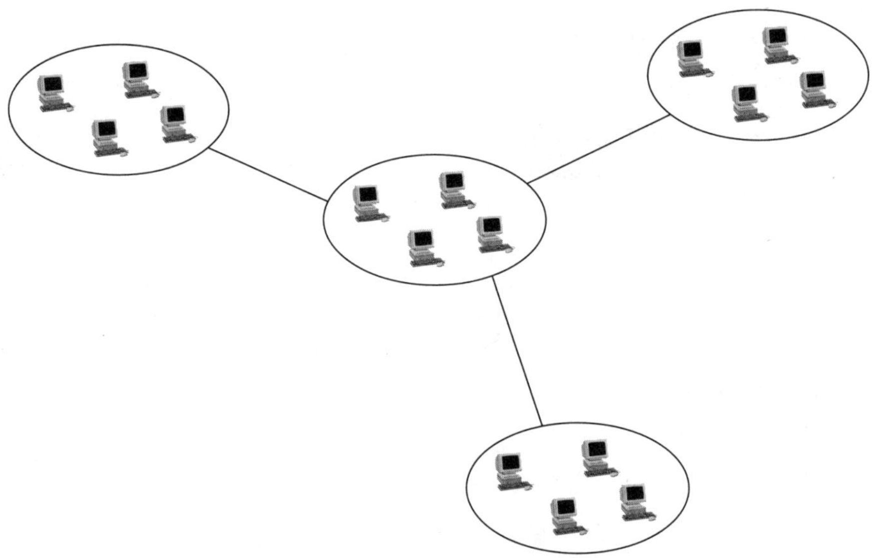

CHAPTER 5

Scenario 5-1

Barney's Bank

1. Twelve–three for Corpus Christi and one for each of the remaining offices
2. Three. Using a subnet mask of 255.255.255.192, you can get two subnets with up to 62 hosts from each of the Class C addresses. This will support the five European offices with one network left not used and will provide more than enough support for growth.
3. A router must support RIP version 2, OSPF, or BGP.

Fairco Manufacturing

1. 255.255.255.224
2. 30

Exercise 5-1

1. You received four successful replies from 192.168.105.1.
8. You receive a message that the destination host is unreachable.
9. Alpha and Beta are now on different subnets, and there is no router available.

Scenario 5-2

1.

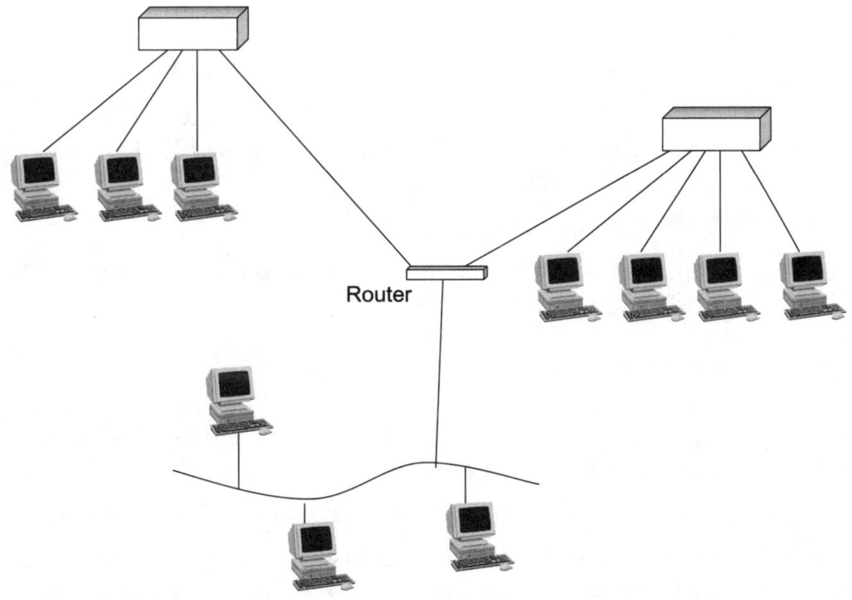

2. Place a domain controller in each of the star-routed subnetworks.

Exercise 5-2

20. The request times out because Alpha has not been configured with a default gateway.
21. The destination host is unreachable because Alpha does not have a default gateway.
27. The command works without errors and you receive a reply.

Scenario 5-3

Scenario 1

1. Install GSNW on one or both of the domain controllers.
2. None
3. The solution does not change routing requirements.

Scenario 2

1. One
2. None

CHAPTER 6

Scenario 6-1

Things and Stuff

1. None. Since the network is currently using NetBEUI as its only protocol, there are no DNS servers in place.
2. Active Directory-integrated zone
3. Implement DHCP, configure the clients as DHCP clients, and have DHCP dynamically update the DNS database.

Barney's Bank

1. The U.S. and European systems are going to be set up as separate Active Directory domains. That means that each will have a separate DNS namespace, and you can configure each as a separate zone.
2. Whether the existing DNS servers support SRV resource records
3. Since the remote offices connect to Corpus Christi through demand-dial links, any query that cannot be resolved locally would force a connection to Corpus Christi. Instead, place a DNS server in each of the remote offices. (This would also minimize bandwidth usage.)
4. L2TP with IPSec

Fairco Manufacturing

Use caching-only servers at the remote warehouses.

Scenario 6-2

Things and Stuff

1. None. Since this is a nonrouted LAN, name resolution requests can be resolved through NetBIOS broadcasts.
2. All of the current systems can be configured as WINS clients.

Barney's Bank

1. Place the WINS servers in the Corpus Christi and London offices.
2. You will want to replace the demand-dial links with persistent links.

Scenario 6-3

Barney's Bank

1. All routers on the European links must be configured as DHCP Relay Agents.
2. One, since the subnets are connected through high-speed persistent connections
3. Five, one for Corpus Christi and one for each remote office. Each remote office will need its own DHCP server since it connects to Corpus Christi through a demand-dial connection.

Fairco Manufacturing

1. Since DHCP is running on Windows NT, it won't be necessary to make any changes. The DHCP service will be able to start even if the DHCP server has not been authorized.
2. With the small number of hosts in the remote locations, you should use manually assigned IP addresses. Otherwise, you would probably need to place a DHCP server in each warehouse LAN.

Scenario 6-4

Barney's Bank

1. Add the DHCP servers to the Active Directory DnsUpdateProxy group.
2. Configure the DNS servers to forward unresolved queries to one of the WINS servers.

CHAPTER 7

Scenario 7-1

Fairco Manufacturing

1. In the main office LAN
2. Set up the remote access server as a VPN server with a single connection to the Internet. Salespeople will be configured as VPN clients and dial in through the Internet to connect to the remote access server.
3. Set up a remote access policy to define the conditions for accepting a connection.

Scenario 7-2

Fairco Manufacturing

1. You won't need to make any changes. Windows NT 4.0 domains are supported by RADIUS.
2. In your main office LAN
3. You would place a RADIUS client in each remote warehouse LAN.
4. VPN

Scenario 7-3

Things and Stuff

1. All network hosts would have to support TCP/IP either in addition to or in replacement of NetBEUI.
2. You would select a private IP address for LAN host addresses.

Scenario 7-4

Barney's Bank

1. Place the proxy servers in Corpus Christi and London.
2. Enable the Guest account on the proxy server and in Active Directory in the European domain.
3. You will configure the proxy server with a single network adapter.

Scenario 7-5

Barney's Bank

1. None. The requests will be denied by default.
2. The firewall should be located between the Web server and the Internet.

CHAPTER 8

Scenario 8-1

1. Fairco Manufacturing
2. Barney's Bank
3. You should expect traditional application requirements for all of the case study companies.

Scenario 8-2

1. Barney's Bank, due to its growth through acquisition plans
2. Things and Stuff, as a peer-to-peer workgroup
3. None of the companies have identified applications that would significantly benefit from QoS.
4. Things and Stuff

Scenario 8-3

Barney's Bank

1. Stand-alone or domain Dfs roots
2. Set up a domain Dfs in Corpus Christi and Dfs replicas in the remote offices. Set up links to alternate copies of the data that are local to the remote LANs.

Fairco Manufacturing

1. Stand-alone Dfs roots
2. None

CHAPTER 9

Scenario 9-1

Things and Stuff

1. At least one of the systems, probably one of the Windows NT servers, will have to be upgraded to Windows 2000 Server.
2. DNS

Barney's Bank

Install the upgrades using unattended installations.

Scenario 9-2

Things and Stuff

1. Set up alerts to write to the event logs when performance counters exceed your defined limit.
2. Set up a counter log to record the performance data.

Barney's Bank

1. Network Monitor
2. Check the Application log on the WINS server that you suspect is having the replication errors.

Scenario 9-3

Barney's Bank

1. Network Load Balancing
2. Round-robin DNS

Appendix C—Case Studies

INTRODUCTION TO CASE STUDIES

The following case studies are used in conjunction with scenario-based training activities and are referenced at various times during the course. References appearing with the scenario-based activities are abbreviated, focusing on information relating to that specific scenario only. This appendix includes the full text of each of the case studies.

Things and Stuff

Things and Stuff is a retail sales outlet with a single location. The owner hopes to expand to different locations eventually, but there are no definite plans to do so at this time. All sales are walk-in, point-of-sale transactions. Sales information is written to an Access database that daily and weekly reports are generated from.

Current Network

The current network has two Windows NT server systems, nine Windows NT workstations, and three Windows 98 systems. The systems are currently configured as a workgroup. One person is responsible for network management and spends most of his time fixing problems introduced by users attempting to *improve* the network. The network administrator has a set budget but is given free reign to manage the network within that budget.

The network is configured as a 10Base2 Ethernet network. The only protocol in use on the network is NetBEUI. Users logged on to any system can access shared resources from other systems.

Current IT Structure

The current IT structure is informal and limited. The one network administrator is self-taught. This is one of the reasons why there has been no attempt before now to change from a workgroup configuration. The network administrator is responsible for all network management tasks.

Change management procedures are also informal. The network administrator has free reign to make changes as long as they remain within the network budget. Additional funding must be approved directly by the business owner.

Network Users

Network users are familiar with the applications that they use on a regular basis. They have been provided with step-by-step instructions for activities such as sharing folders to the network.

Network Security

Network security is very lax. Some users have assigned themselves blank passwords to make it easier to log on. There are no restrictions on local access security. When folders are shared, all users are given full control over the shared folders.

Users are responsible for their own backups. The Windows NT server systems are backed up weekly by the network administrator. The server that holds the Sales tracking Access database is backed up daily with differential backups. None of the network systems use disk fault tolerance.

Network Goals

The owner would like to upgrade all systems to Windows 2000 Server and Workstation but hasn't decided whether he wants to make any changes to the current LAN configuration.

The network administrator is of another opinion about network design. He wants to upgrade to a 100BaseT network.

Barney's Bank

Barney's Bank is a full-service financial institution with branch offices in various locations in the United States. Barney's Bank also has several wholly owned subsidiaries, with five different locations in Europe. The organization has traditionally grown through acquisition and plans to continue to use this as its primary growth model.

Each of the remote offices has limited control over day-to-day decisions, but all major decisions are made from the main office in Corpus Christi, Texas. There is currently no central repository for corporate data. Most periodic reports are compiled from e-mail attachments and hard-copy data sent to the main office weekly.

Current Network

From an IT standpoint, the organization is best described as a mismatched and patched-together mess. As new locations have been acquired, the existing networks have been left in place, resulting in a network management and communications nightmare. The network management staff is short-handed and overworked.

The main corporate LAN located in the home office is a routed LAN configured as an Active Directory domain. It consists of three subnetworks, all Ethernet, one using a bus topology, and the other two using star topologies. The bus topology subnetwork uses RG-48 A/U coaxial cable. The two subnetworks using a star topology are wired with Category 4 UTP cable. At present, there are two domain controllers in the corporate LAN, both located on the bus topology subnetwork.

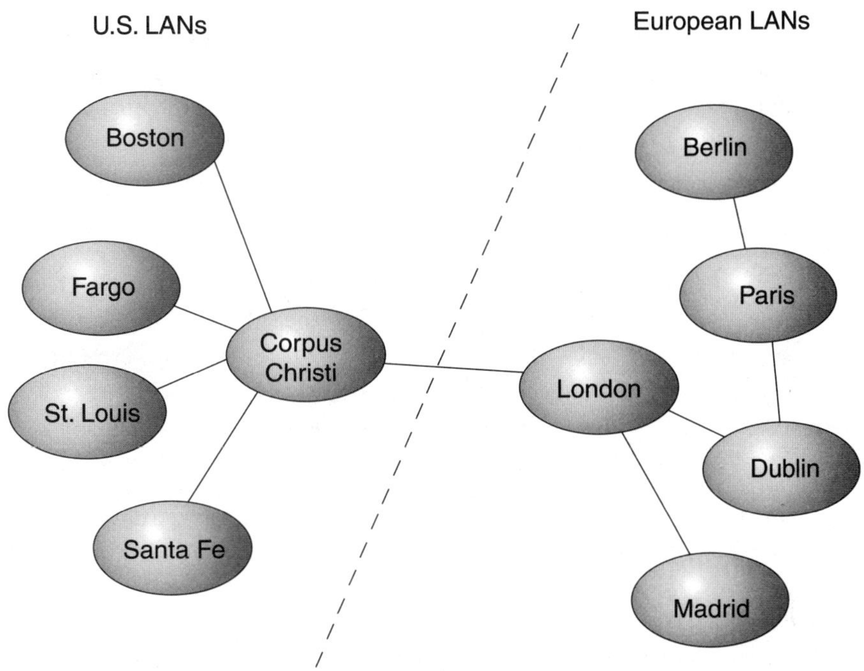

The previous figure is a schematic representation of the current WAN configuration. Except for the LAN in Corpus Christi, all of the LANs are nonrouted LANs. There is an X.25 connection between Corpus Christi and London. The U.S. branch offices connect to the Corpus Christi office through demand-dial ISDN connections. There are E1 connections between all of the European offices. In addition to the domain controllers in Corpus Christi, there are domain controllers in each of the U.S. offices, in London, and in Dublin. There are DNS servers in Corpus Christi and London. At present, address assignments are managed manually.

Current IT Structure

The current IT staff includes one IT manager, four network administrators who work out of the Corpus Christi office, and two or more network technicians in each branch and subsidiary office. There have been plans for a 24/7 user Help Desk for over 5 years, but as of yet, there have been no efforts to implement these plans. Network technicians spend more time working with users than working with the network. Network failures are common and costly.

The network is managed as a separate department. Its funding comes as a prorated amount from other departmental budgets. Any changes to the network that will require additional expenditures must be approved by the executive finance committee. Rather than going through this process, many remote offices *hid* network expansion costs in other departmental budgets to make what they saw as critical changes.

Network Users

As is common with most companies, there are users at all different levels of skills and experience. Users need access to all of the other LANs at different times to get the information that they need. Most corporate data is stored on servers in each of the LANs, but some data is located on user systems. The policy for shared data states that the data must be saved to a network server for sharing. Users are not authorized to share data directly from their own systems.

Users are complaining about delays in being able to get the data that they need. There have been intermittent problems with not being able to locate or access the data at all.

Network Security

An attempt has been made to centralize security management, but the results have been mixed at best. Group Policy has been used to enforce password guidelines, but the network administrators suspect there have been attempts by some users to log on with other users' names and passwords. Because of differences in time zones and work schedules, users can be logging on to the network at any time.

Network servers are backed up with full backups weekly. Servers containing financial data are backed up with differential backups daily. Disk mirroring has been implemented on domain controllers but not on any other servers. Users are responsible for their own backups, through there have been some requests for over-the-network backups by some users.

Network Goals

The organization wants to standardize its network operations, implementing two Active Directory domains configured as part of the same forest. The company will have separate domain namespaces for the United States and Europe.

In response to its competition, Barney's Bank wants to give its users access to account information via the Internet. It is also considering using a Virtual Private Network (VPN) to connect the main offices in the United States and Europe via the Internet.

Fairco Manufacturing

Fairco Manufacturing designs, manufactures, and distributes a wide variety of items for department stores in the United States. Sales are wholesale only to retail outlets. The organization employs a large number of outside salespeople who travel to the major customers on established routes. There are plans in the near future to spin warehouse operations off as a separate subsidiary.

Current Network

Fairco Manufacturing has a large LAN configured as a Windows NT domain. Dial-in access is provided to remote warehouses in strategic locations around the country. This is the only remote communication currently in place. Field salespeople either call in, fax, or hand deliver orders to the main office, where they are manually posted. Shipping delays can run from 3 to 20 days, and there is a constant problem with back orders due to out-of-stock items.

The LAN is configured as a nonrouted LAN running NWLink and TCP/IP protocols. It is wired in a star topology and was recently rewired using Category 5 UTP. The systems currently have 10 Mbps or 10/100 Mbps Ethernet adapters, about an equal number of each spread evenly around the LAN. The Windows NT domain is set up with one PDC and one BDC. IP name resolution is supported through the use of HOSTS files.

Current IT Structure

Fairco Manufacturing currently has one network administrator working with five network technicians. The network technicians also provide Help Desk assistance to network users. The network falls under the Operations department, and any network changes must be approved by the Operations manager. Decisions that require additional funding must be approved by the owner.

Network change decisions are seldom documented. The process is typically managed entirely through verbal approval. The budget for network operations is considered part of the general Operations department budget. There is an ongoing push to keep network expenses for daily operations to a minimum.

Network Users

Users on the corporate LAN have few complaints about the network. Most of the data they need is located local to the corporate LAN.

Warehouse users are less happy with the way things are currently run. The warehouses currently have two or more stand-alone systems. Only one of the systems in each location, a Windows NT server running SQL Server 6.5, is provided with a modem for remote access. Users use this system periodically during the day to check stock in the main warehouse. These systems also dial in automatically each night to send and receive database changes through SQL Server replication. Sometimes the replication is still running when users are in the morning.

Network Security

Logon security has been kept simple by user request. There are restrictions on minimum password length and reuse of old passwords, but users are not required to change passwords on any type of periodic schedule.

The SQL Server system on the corporate LAN is backed up on a regular basis. Other servers are backed up intermittently, usually when someone remembers to run them, but not on any set schedule. User workstations are not backed up. None of the network systems are using disk fault tolerance.

Network Goals

The organization wants to update and upgrade its network. In the process, it wants to streamline its operations and improve its business processes. One critical requirement is finding a way to reduce the delay between when an order is taken by an outside salesperson and when it is shipped to the customer.

Glossary

[ROOT] object

An object in the directory tree that provides the highest point to access different Country and Organization objects and allow trustee assignments granting rights to the entire directory tree. Country, Organization, and Alias objects are created at the [ROOT] object. It is a place holder and contains no information.

16-bit application

An application native to Windows 3.1 or Windows for Workgroups 3.11.

32-bit application

An application native to Windows NT or Windows 95.

2000rkst.msi

Source file for installing Windows 2000 Support Tools. This file is located in the \Support\Tools\ directory of the Windows 2000 Installation CD-ROM.

Accelerated Graphics Port (AGP)

A bus specification that allows 3D graphics to be displayed rapidly and smoothly on personal computers.

Access Control

The method of authenticating user accounts when users log on to a Windows 2000 or NT domain. Users are granted or denied access to network resources through the use of security descriptors.

Access Control Entry (ACE)

An access privilege assigned to a user or group. With Windows NT/2000 Server, the ACE is stored with the object being protected.

Access Control List (ACL)

1. A list of trustees who have been granted rights to an object or rights to the properties of an object. Each object in the NDS contains an Access Control List.

2. Under Windows NT/2000, the Access Control List contains user and group Access Control Entries.

Access Control List and Access Control Entry

When discussing Windows NT Server security, the discretionary Access Control List (ACL) contains an entry for each user or group for which access privileges or restrictions have been defined. The format of each Access Control Entry (ACE) is that of an access mask containing all values appropriate for the type of resource.

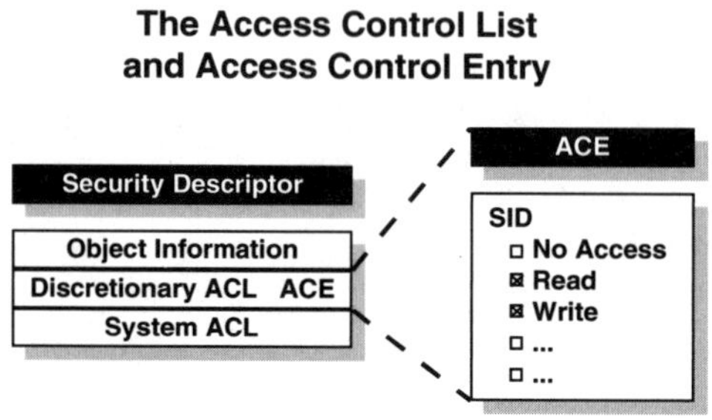

The order in which the entries are listed is significant. SIDs (Security IDs) that have a permission of "No Access" assigned are listed first. This is to ensure that any users or groups specifically restricted from the resource do not accidentally gain access.

Access token

Security token generated during the logon process. The access token includes the user's Security ID (SID), the SIDs of any groups the user belongs to, and explicit user rights assignments.

Accessibility

The level at which the application's user interface supports interaction by users with special needs.

Accessories

Microsoft Windows or Windows NT applets.

Acknowledgment (ACK)

A response by the receiver of a communications message indicating the message was received correctly.

Active Directory

The Windows 2000 directory service. Active Directory treats users, files, directories, applications, and other items as objects. It allows system administratiors to modify the properties of objects. Objects and their properties are described in the Active Directory schema.

Active Directory Installation Wizard

Windows 2000 utility used for promoting a Windows 2000 system to domain controller.

Active Directory Restore Mode Administrative Password

Password required for starting a domain controller in the Active Directory Restore Mode.

Active Directory Services

Microsoft incorporated its automated directory service called Active Directory Services (ADS) into Windows 2000. ADS is a highly integrated set of APIs and protocols that extends its services across multiple servers and name spaces. It also will collect and show resource information that is across LAN and WAN connections.

ADSI allows applications to communicate with Active Directory and provides the means for directory service clients to use one set of interfaces to communicate with any namespace that provides an ADSI implementation. Instead of API calls, ADSI makes it simple to access a namespace's services.

Active Directory Services Interface (ADSI)

A COM-based service that allows developers to create Web-based applications that interact with and manage Active Directory from a single interface.

Active Directory-integrated zone

Zone information is stored in the Active Directory database. There is no text file associated with the zone information. The Active Directory replication process performs the replication.

Active Server Pages

A script that can be compiled and run by Internet Information Server. It is written using an ActiveX scripting language, such as VBScript or JScript. Its output is usually plain HTML that can be displayed by any browser.

Address

A unique designation for the location of data, the identity of an intelligent device, or a logical network address. An address allows each device on a single communications line to respond to its own message.

Address resolution

A means for mapping logical addresses to physical addresses.

Address Resolution Protocol (ARP)

A protocol used between routers and nodes to determine the MAC or OSI physical layer address when the Network layer (IP) address is known.

Addressing

The method by which numbers are assigned to identify hardware resources or disk channels. Each controller must have a unique address. The documentation shipped with the controller will list the physical address settings.

Add/Remove Hardware Wizard

Wizard launched by the Control Panel Add/Remove Hardware utility that lets you install, uninstall, and troubleshoot hardware devices.

Adminpak.msi

Source file for installing additional Administrative Tools on a Windows 2000 system. This file is located in the \%systemroot%\system32 folder.

Advanced Configuration and Power Interface (ACPI)

The system interface that enables a motherboard to describe its power management interface, as well as attached devices and their configuration, to the operating system.

Agent

In the client/server model, the part of the system that performs information preparation and exchange on behalf of a client or server application.

Alert

1. Windows 2000 method for monitoring and detecting performance counter limits.
2. An error message sent to the system control point at the host system.
3. A defined response to an event occurring in SQL Server.

Algorithm

The steps that must be performed in order to complete a particular action.

Alias (CNAME) resource record

Resource record used for creating an alias name for a host record already in file, mapping multiple names to a single IP address.

Allocation

Associating a memory address with a block of data and setting aside physical memory to back it.

Analog

The representation of a continuously changing physical variable (sound, for example) by another physical variable (such as electrical current).

Answer file

A text file containing answers to Setup prompts for a Windows NT or Windows 2000 unattended installation. Answer files can be created by using the Windows 2000 Setup Manager Wizard found in the Windows 2000 Resource Kit Deployment Tools.

Applet

A Java program that is embedded in an HTML page and run in a Java-enabled browser.

Application

The use to which an information processing system is put. For example, a payroll application, an airline reservation application, or a network application.

Application layer

OSI Layer 7 providing an interface with user or application programs.

Application Programming Interface (API)

An interface application developers use to invoke the services provided by the operating system or another application. For example, the ODBC API allows developers to use call functions provided by the ODBC library. The WIN32 API allows developers to call functions to interface with 32-bit Windows operating systems.

Application Server Mode

Terminal Services server mode optimized for support of multiuser applications.

Architecture

The specific design and construction of a computer. Architecture usually refers to the hardware makeup of the central processing unit and the size of the byte or set of bytes it processes, such as 8-bit, 16-bit, or 32-bit architecture.

Archive

Storing files on a long-term medium, such as optical disks or magnetic tape.

Area

One part of an autonomous system in OSPF that is used to combine routes to reduce the size of routing tables.

Asynchronous

1. A form of communication where each transmitted character is preceded by a start bit and followed by a stop bit. This eliminates the need for a particular spacing or timing scheme between characters. Personal computers communicate asynchronously via a serial port.

2. An adjective used to describe a method that returns control to the consumer before it completes execution. An asynchronous component cannot return a value.

Asynchronous Transfer Mode (ATM)

A high-speed (155 to 162 Mbps) communications transport facility capable of carrying voice, data, and video signaling. ATM forms the backbone for broadband ISDN networks.

Attribute

A characteristic that defines an Active Directory (AD) object. Most AD objects are defined by a set of attributes that make the object unique.

Audit policy

Security policy settings that identify security events that will generate Security log entries. Events can be based on the success and/or failure of an action.

Authentication

1. A way to verify that an object sending messages or requests to an NDS is permitted to act on or receive those messages or requests.

2. Login or resource access validation.

Authentication (Connection)

The process by which connection credentials are verified before accepting the connection.

Author mode

Microsoft Management Console (MMC) mode that allows users to modify MMC custom consoles.

Authorization (Connection)

The process by which a connection attempt is verified to ensure that it is allowed.

Automatic Private IP Addressing (APIPA)

An automatic IP configuration process where a client computer that is configured to automatically obtain an IP address can assign itself an IP address when a DHCP server is not available. The APIPA address range is from the 169.254.0.0 network, with a subnet mask of 255.255.0.0.

Autonomous system

The entire OSPF network and routers that are under the control of one corporation.

Autostatic routes

Routes that are learned using a routing protocol like RIP, but the actual process of collecting the routing information only happens when initiated by an administrator.

Backup

Pertaining to a system, device, file, or facility that can be used to recover data in the event of a malfunction or loss of data.

Backup Domain Controller (BDC)

Windows NT domain controller that serves as a backup/failover to the Primary Domain Controller (PDC).

Bandwidth

1. The range of frequencies that can be transmitted through a particular circuit.

2. The speed at which data travels over a particular media. Bandwidth is measured in bits per second.

Bandwidth throttling

Limiting the amount of network or Internet connection bandwidth that will be made available to a Web site or Web server.

Basic disk

A hard disk configured for industry-standard disk storage. Basic disks are supported by MS-DOS, all Windows versions, all Windows NT versions, and Windows 2000.

Basic Rate ISDN

ISDN connection using two 64-Kbps channels.

Batch

A method of computer job processing where input is collected and run through the processing programs all at once and outputs are produced in the form of files and reports. Batch is the opposite of interactive job processing in which an operator at a terminal interacts with the processing program directly during data entry. Most personal computers employ interactive processing. Mainframes use batch processing.

Batch program

A text file that contains operating system commands. When you run a batch program, the operating system carries out the commands in the file as if you had typed them at the command prompt.

Binary

Having two components or possible states. Usually represented by a code of zeros and ones.

Binding

The process by which an object's type library is located.

Binding and unbinding

Binding assigns a communication protocol to network boards and LAN drivers. Unbinding removes the protocol. Each network board needs at least one communication protocol bound to its LAN driver to process packets. Multiple protocols can be bound to the same LAN driver and board. You can also bind the same protocol stack to more than one LAN driver on the server. Workstations with different protocols can be cabled on the same scheme.

Boot

To start or restart your computer, loading the operating system from a disk drive.

Boot Information Negotiation Layer (BINL)

Service that responds to client requests, controls file downloads, and manages other processes during remote installations using RIS.

Border routing

The practice of splitting a large network into multiple areas with combined IP routes. Usually implemented using OSPF areas.

Break

An interruption in program execution or data transmission; a loss of communication between sender and receiver. Also a keyboard key that enables the interruption.

Bridge

Bridges are network devices that are more intelligent than repeaters, in that they can read the specific physical address of devices on one network and filter information before passing it on to another network segment.

Bridge Functionality

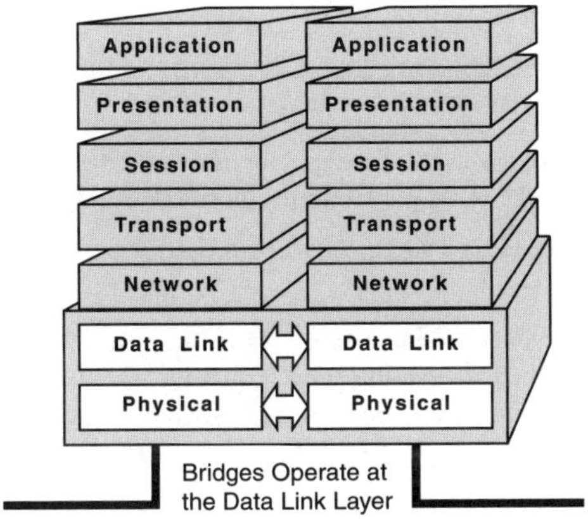

Bridges operate at the Data Link layer of the OSI Model or, more precisely, at the Media Access Control (MAC) sublayer. Bridges go beyond simply amplifying the signal and are able to regenerate the signal. This prevents the duplication and spread of line noise. Only a clean signal is sent. This allows bridges to expand a network beyond that which can be accomplished with only repeaters.

In general, bridges are transparent to higher-level protocols. Segments connected through a bridge remain part of the same logical network. Bridges can filter traffic based on addresses. This allows a bridge to reduce traffic between segments and can also be used to improve security by selecting the packets that can be passed between segments.

Broadcast

1. A transmission of a message intended for general reception rather than for a specific station.

2. In LAN technology, a transmission method used in bus topology networks that sends all messages to all stations even though the messages are addressed to specific stations.

3. A NetWare console command that transmits a message to all network nodes or list of nodes.

Browser

1. This client program (software) is used to look at various Internet resources and retrieve information.

2. Windows service that collects and organizes shared network resources in a hierarchical manner.

3. A NetWare console command that transmits a message to all network nodes or list of nodes.

Browsing

1. Allows you to find objects in the NetWare Directory, which is arranged in hierarchical order.

2. Viewing and retrieving data from the Internet.

3. Viewing available network resources in hierarchical order.

Buffer

A temporary storage place for information. Many times it is a device used to compensate for a difference in either the rate of data flow or the time of occurrence of events in transmission from one device to another.

Built-in Domain users

User accounts created when Active Directory services are installed and the Active Directory is created.

Built-in Local users

User accounts created when Windows 2000 is installed.

Bus

1. A pathway on which data travels. Examples of buses in a typical Macintosh computer include the expansion bus (NuBus or PCI), Apple Desktop Bus (ADB), and SCSI bus.

2. LAN data pathway based on a single cable terminated at both ends.

Bus topology

A bus network topology consists of a linear transmission medium that is terminated at both ends. Nodes attach directly to the bus, making failures difficult to troubleshoot. Any break in the bus causes the entire network to become inoperable. Difficulty in troubleshooting is considered the biggest drawback for a bus topology.

Simple Bus Network

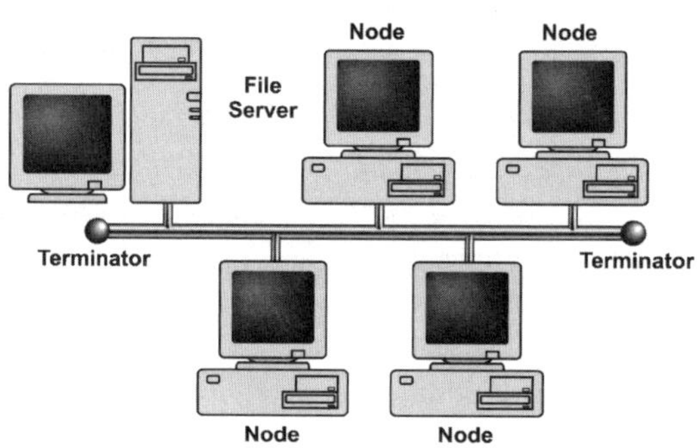

Although a bus normally is drawn as a straight line in pictures and diagrams, most bus networks represent cables that snake, weave, and wrap their way through building's conduits and corridors. This can make the overall length of buses grow rapidly.

Bus topologies commonly use coaxial cable as their transmission medium. Traditionally, Ethernet has used a bus topology.

Byte

Short for "binary digit eight." A unit of information consisting of usually 8 bits. A file's size is measured in bytes or potential storage capacity is measured in bytes, but when dealing with very large numbers, the terms kilobyte, megabyte, or gigabyte are used.

Cache

An area of computer memory set aside for frequently used data to speed operations. Some caches are general purpose, while others are for specific operations. A disk cache is an area of system memory reserved for caching disk reads and writes. A CPU cache is a dedicated, high-speed memory array used to cache pending instructions.

Cell

1. This is a fixed length data element that can be transmitted in asynchronous transfer mode (ATM).
2. Cellular transmission boundary.

Certificate

The document (usually digital) issued by a Certificate Authority that includes the Certificate Authority's digital signature, the user's public and private key, and user information.

Certificate Authority (CA)

A server that issues certificates for the purpose of authenticating users and computers or securing data transmission.

Chart view

System Monitor view displaying real-time performance counter data as a line chart.

Checksum

Used in data communications to monitor the number of bits being transmitted between communication devices by means of a simple mathematical algorithm. The checksum is used to ensure that the full complement of bits is received successfully by the receiving device.

Cipher

A Windows 2000 command used for managing data encryption.

Classless Interdomain Routing (CIDR)

A new way of designing IP address configuration; used on the Internet to aggregate blocks of addresses together in order to make more addresses available and to group routing information to ease the load on Internet routers.

Clean installation

Refers to a new installation of Windows 2000 as opposed to an upgrade.

Cleanup

SQL Server replication process-distributed updates and sync information are removed.

Client

1. A workstation that requests services of another computer (server).
2. The portion of a client/server application providing the end-user interface (front-end).

Client Access License (CAL)

Microsoft software license allowing one client connection for either per-server or per-seat licensing.

Client Installation Wizard (CIW)

Installation wizard downloaded to the remote client during RIS installation. CIW is also known as the OSChooser.

Client software

A software program used to contact and obtain data from a server software program on another computer, often across a great distance. Each client program is designed to work with one or more specific kinds of server programs, and each server requires a specific kind of client.

Clock/Calendar

Used to identify the date and time of computer transactions. Certain software programs utilize the date and time functions more than others.

Cluster

1. A group of data stored together on one or more sectors of a floppy disk or hard disk. (A sector usually contains 512 bytes of data.) When DOS stores data on a disk, it usually breaks the data into smaller sections, which it writes to various places on the disk as appropriate.

2. A group of servers that perform the same service. A cluster of servers can be used to provide load balancing and for fault tolerance.

CMOS RAM

This memory stores system configuration data, for example, the number of drives, types of drives, and amount of memory. It is battery-powered, so it can retain the date, time, and other information that must be stored when the computer is turned off.

Code

A set of rules that specify the way data is represented, such as ASCII or EBCDIC. Code is also used to describe lines of instructions for the computer, as in program code.

Collision

In some networking schemes, any station may transmit when it senses that the carrier is free. A collision occurs when two stations transmit simultaneously. If a collision is detected, each station will wait for a randomly determined interval before retransmitting the data.

Collision

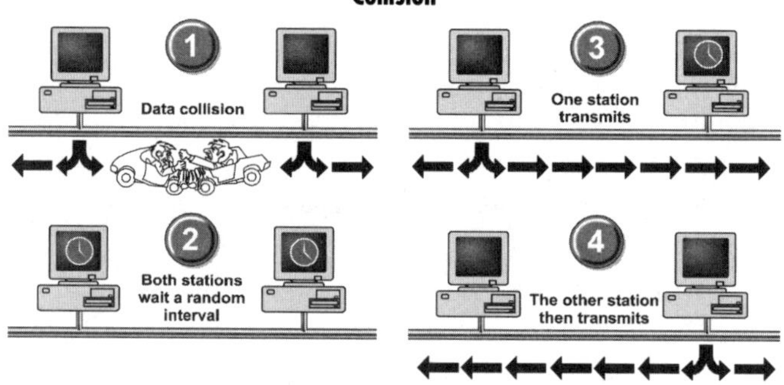

Most network operating systems track retransmissions, which is a good indication of the number of collisions occurring on the network.

Column

Vertical section of a table that stores one attribute for many entities.

Com

An extension for Internet addresses representing commercial enterprises. For example, galedsl@msen.com.

Command

Any executable statements.

Command prompt

A displayed symbol, such as C:>, that informs the user that a DOS system is idle. It represents that the command-line interface is ready to receive input.

Common Name (CN)

Refers to a leaf object in the NDS tree. This could be a user's login name, a printer object, or a server object.

Any name that points to a leaf object, usually seen as CN=leafobject.

Compact

Windows 2000 command-line command for managing data compression.

Compact Disc Read-Only Memory (CD-ROM)

A read-only optical disc commonly used to distribute applications software or archive data.

Complete Trust Model

In Microsoft Windows NT's complete trust model, each domain can act as both a master domain and a resource domain. In most cases, each domain is managed separately, with access to other domains granted through two-way trust relationships.

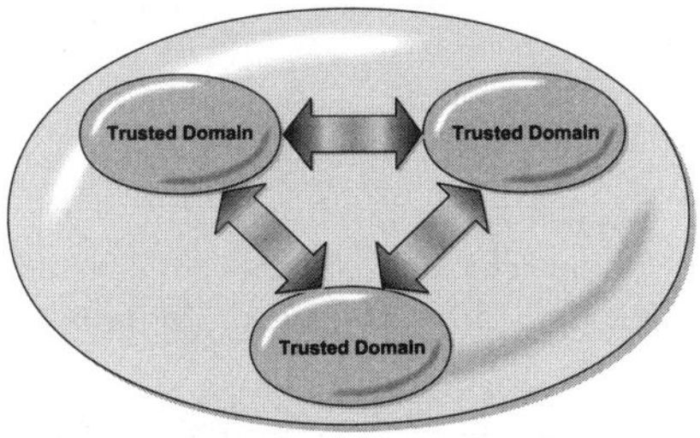

The complete trust model is a mix of independence and interdependence—independent in that each domain has its own users and groups. Each domain sets its own access, rights, and permission policies. Each domain administrator is responsible for his or her domain and must be trusted to manage that domain properly.

The model is interdependent because, unless there is a need to share resources between domains, there would be no reason for setting up a complete trust model. Domain administrators must work together to provide resource access while ensuring that security is not compromised.

This model is most appropriate to organizations that do not have a central MIS department available to manage master domains. It often fits well into organizations made up of somewhat independent departments or divisions. Companies must be ready, however, to accept the potential risks inherent in a noncentralized management structure.

Component

Hardware or software that is part of a functional unit.

Component Load Balancing

Allows middle-tier components to run on a cluster of servers. This provides fault tolerance and scalability.

Component Object Model (COM)

A binary specification that allows unrelated objects to communicate with each other. Also known as COM, the Component Object Model is the foundation of the OLE and ActiveX technologies.

Compulsory tunnel

A tunnel created by an intermediary system or device that a client can communicate through with the target server.

Computer Emergency Response Team (CERT)

This organization was formed by DARPA in November 1988 to work with the Internet community to improve its response to computer security events for Internet hosts, to raise awareness of computer security issues, and to improve the security of existing systems. CERT products and services include 24-hour technical assistance for computer security incidents, product vulnerability assistance, technical documents, and tutorials. In addition, the team has a number of mailing lists (including one for CERT Advisories) and has an anonymous FTP server at cert.org, where security-related documents and tools are archived. The CERT may be reached by e-mail at cert@cert.org and by telephone at +1-412-268-7090 (24-hour hotline).

Computer object

A leaf object representing a computer on the network. Its properties can store data, such as the name of the person the computer is assigned to or the computer's serial number.

CONFIG.NT

The replacement for CONFIG.SYS for DOS programs running under Windows NT.

CONFIG.SYS

The DOS environment is set up and configured by loading device drivers. This is done through two system configuration files: AUTOEXEC.BAT and CONFIG.SYS. When DOS is booted, these two files are executed.

CONFIG.SYS is a text file. It must be located at the root directory of the boot drive. The CONFIG.SYS is called by the IO.SYS file and contains commands to configure hardware and load device drivers.

It is always a good idea to make a backup of this file prior to installing a new application. Many applications will automatically make changes to this file during the installation process. It is wise to make note of these changes in case of system errors. Applications that alter this file typically make a backup copy. Refer to the application's documentation for details.

Changes to the CONFIG.SYS file will not take effect until the system is rebooted.

Mistakes in the CONFIG.SYS file may cause system startup errors. You can bypass the execution of CONFIG.SYS by pressing the *F5* key when you see the "Starting DOS" message. Using ***F8*** instead of *F5* will allow you to selectively bypass commands in the CONFIG.SYS file. This can help isolate problem lines within the configuration file.

CONFIG.SYS is still supported with Windows 95 to provide backward compatibility.

Configuration partition

Replication partition containing information about Active Directory structure. The configuration partition replicates to all domain controllers in a forest.

Connection object

An object representing a potential source server for Active Directory replication.

Connection-oriented

The model of interconnection in which communication proceeds through three well-defined phases: connection establishment, data transfer, and connection release. Examples include X.25, Internet TCP and OSI TP4, and ordinary telephone calls.

Connectionless

The model of interconnection in which communication takes place without first establishing a connection. Sometimes called datagram. Examples: LANs, Internet IP and OSI CLNP, UDP, ordinary postcards.

Constant

A name used to refer to a value that does not change during application execution.

Consumer

The application or component that uses the services provided by another component. For example, if an application uses the Spell Search functionality exposed by Microsoft Word, that application is a consumer of Microsoft Word.

Container

Special type of object within Windows 2000 Active Directory that is used to hold other objects.

Container object

1. Active Directory object that is able to contain other objects. Container objects are used in organizing the Active Directory's logical structure.

2. The type of object in NetWare's NDS used to organize other objects on the network into groups such as workgroups, departments, or divisions. A container object will contain other objects.

3. A Visual Basic object defining a set of objects as a group.

Context

The context points to where you are located in the NDS tree. This serves as a logical pointer to an object such as a user, printer, or server.

Context switch

The immediate switching from one program to another without first closing the files, allowing users to operate several programs concurrently, such as a graphics program and a word processing program. With context switching, unlike multitasking, when one program is being used, the other halts. Advantages of context switching are rapid switching, exchange of clipboard files, and fast data transfer. In a multiple loading operating system such as Macintosh, the programs are held in random access memory.

Control

Visible Visual Basic object used to generate an event or display on-screen information.

Control Panel

1. On a Macintosh, the Control Panel is a system software utility stored in the Control Panels folder (found in the System Folder). Panels are used to configure various services such as AppleTalk and user preferences such as desktop patterns and wallpaper.

2. Windows-family utility containing management tools.

Controller

An application that can be used to build solutions using ActiveX objects. Visual Basic is a controller.

Counter log

A log used for collecting performance counter data over time.

Crash

A system failure or *bomb*. A system crash requires that the user perform a reboot to restart the computer.

Crop

Cut the edges off an object so that it can fit in a particular area. Typcally used in reference to graphics.

Cscript

Windows Script Host component that hosts a script in a command-line environment.

Cursor

1. An indicator that keeps track of the current position in the result set.
2. Visual cue provided for data input or user interaction.

Cyclic Redundancy Check (CRC)

A mathematically calculated value that is attached to a network packet at the Physical layer, which is used to do low-level error checking on network packets. If any bit of the packet has changed during transmission, the CRC will no longer be valid and the packet will have to be retransmitted.

Data

1. In a database, facts about places, individuals, objects, events, concepts, and so on.
2. Used to refer to any stored information.

Data compression

A process by which a sampling algorithm is used to reduce the size of a data file. Windows 2000 supports data compression on NTFS volumes only.

Data integrity

The data quality that exists as long as accidental or malicious destruction, alteration, or loss of data does not occur.

Data modification

Changing data. Under SQL Server, this is through the SQL Statements INSERT, DELETE, and UPDATE.

Data stream

All data transmitted through a data channel in a single read or write operation. Also, a continuous stream of data elements being transmitted, or intended for transmission, in character or binary-digit form, using a defined format.

Data Transfer Rate

Determines how fast a drive or other peripheral can transfer data with its controller. The data transfer rate is a key measurement in drive performance.

Database

A collection of interrelated data stored together that is fundamental to a system or enterprise. A data structure for accepting, storing, and providing on-demand data for multiple independent users.

Database server

1. A server running database management system software.
2. The Microsoft SQL Server that houses the SMS site database.

Datagram

A message transmitted in a network, requiring no response or acknowledgment.

Dcpromo.exe

Windows 2000 command-line utility that launches the Active Directory Installation Wizard for promoting and demoting domain controllers.

Debugger

An application that allows a programmer to see the statement that is being executed and the contents of variables or registers to facilitate the location of programming errors.

Default

1. One of a set of operating conditions that is automatically used when a device such as a printer or computer is turned on or reset. Pertaining to an attribute, value, or option when none is explicitly specified.

2. An access modifier that limits access to a class's variables and methods to other classes in the same package.

Default domain controller policy

Group Policy Object (GPO) created automatically during Active Directory installation and linked to the domain controller's container.

Default domain policy

Group Policy Object (GPO) created automatically during Active Directory installation and linked at the domain level.

Default drive

The drive the workstation is currently using. It is identified by a drive prompt, such as A:> or F:>.

Delegation

Assignment of administrative permissions and control to selected users and groups.

Demand-dial router

A router that can open a modem, ISDN, or VPN connection to a remote network when packets need to be routed to the remote network.

Desktop

Most Graphical User Interfaces (GUIs) refer to the work area on the computer screen as the desktop. All window items appear and are moved around on this desktop area.

Device

Any computer peripheral or hardware component (such as printer, mouse, monitor, or disk drive) capable of receiving and/or sending data, generally through the use of a device driver.

Device driver

Hardware-specific software that acts as an interface between the operating system and the hardware attached to a computer. Device drivers allow applications to communicate with hardware in a controlled and orderly fashion. A device driver is installed when the system is initialized, either by the operating system or through an installable device driver. Some examples of installable device drivers are mouse, graphical/video monitor, communications port, printer, and network interface card.

Device Driver Interface (DDI)

A set of functions a driver provides to allow communication between the device driver and the operating system.

Device Manager Snap-in

MMC snap-in that lets you view and manage hardware devices.

Dfs link

Dfs association with an existing network share.

Dfs link replica

Copy of a Dfs link hosted on a different server. It provides redundancy for failover and load balancing and is only supported under domain Dfs roots.

Dfs root

Topmost point (root) of a Dfs hierarchy.

Dfs root replica

Copy of a Dfs root hosted on a different server. It provides redundancy for failover and load balancing and is only supported for domain Dfs roots.

DHCP Relay Agent

A special function that can be configured on a Windows 2000 server. It configures the computer to forward DHCP broadcast traffic across the router.

DHCPAck

DHCP server response verifying a DHCP client's acceptance of an IP address and containing a valid lease. The broadcast may include client configuration parameters.

DHCPDiscover

DHCP client broadcast used to locate a DHCP server and request an IP address.

DHCPNAck

DHCP server response for an unsuccessful lease attempt.

DHCPOffer

DHCP server broadcast used to offer an IP address and lease to a DHCP client.

DHCPRequest

DHCP client broadcast used to accept an offered IP address and lease.

Dial-in router

Windows 2000 RRAS configuration that supports IP and IPX WAN connections over dial-up or persistent links.

Dialog box

An on-screen window used to display information. Generally used when user intervention is required, such as clicking on the **OK** or **Cancel** buttons.

Digital

Devices that represent data in the form of digits, based on the binary system where the binary digits (bits) are zero or one. Also, pertaining to data that consists of digits.

Digital, Intel, Xerox (DIX)

A type of Ethernet connector.

Digital signature

1. An arithmetic function that uses a user's private key to create a unique signature that can only be read using the user's public key. The digital signature ensures that the data is coming from the correct user and that it has not been tampered with.

2. Verifies that the sender of a package is who he claims to be. A digital signature is encrypted with the private key and verified using the corresponding public key.

Digital Subscriber Line (DSL)

A digital service that can be run on normal phone lines that provides very fast (up to 10 Mbps) and, in most cases, inexpensive access to the Internet. The two most common forms of DSL are Asymmetric Digital Subscriber Line (ADSL) and Symmetric Digital Subscriber Line (SDSL). DSLs require specialized equipment and are limited by distances to central connection points, so DSL technology is not available everywhere.

Digital to Analog Converter (DAC)

DAC chips are found on analog adapters. Because the PC operates digitally, it sends digitized information to the adapter. If the device accepts analog input only, the DAC on the adapter must convert the digital data into analog instructions for the device.

Digital Video Disc (DVD)

An optical storage device that can store up to 17 GB of data. It is typically used for storing video and other types of multimedia. A DVD player can read standard CD-ROMs.

Direct replication partner

A direct source for Active Directory replication.

Directory

1. Part of a structure for organizing files on a disk. A directory can contain files and subdirectories. The structure of directories and subdirectories on a disk is called a directory tree. The top-level directory in a directory tree is the root directory. In Windows 2000, the Active Directory provides the methods for storing directory data and making this data available to network users and administrators.

2. In NetWare, the highest organizational level is the file server. Each server's main directory is called a VOLUME, and subdirectories are called directories.

Directory and file permissions

These permissions, assigned to users and groups, set user access level.

Directory permissions

Access permissions assigned to users or groups.

Directory services

Services utilized within Active Directory that store information about network resources in one centralized location in order to simplify administrative management of the domain.

Directory structure

Most computers use a tree or filing system to organize volumes, directories, files, and data on their hard disks.

Directory tree

A hierarchical structure of objects, based on a logical or physical organization of objects, in the Directory database.

Directory User Agent (DUA)

The software that accesses the X.500 Directory Service on behalf of the directory user. The directory user may be a person or another software element.

Discretionary ACL (DACL)

The DACL lists the Security IDs (SIDs) for all users and groups granted or denied access to an object.

Disk

A circular object with a magnetic surface used to store files (programs and documents) on a computer. For example, a floppy or hard disk.

Disk Cleanup

Utility that can be used to locate and remove temporary and other unused or unneeded files.

Disk Defragmenter

MMC snap-in used to analyze and defragment disk partitions, logical drives, and volumes.

Disk drive

A magnetic or optical device used to store files and folders. Types of disk drives include fixed (hard) disks, floppy disks, and removable media such as Syquest, Jaz, Zip, and magneto-optical (MO) disks.

Disk Management

MMC snap-in used for managing hard disks, disk partitions, and disk volumes.

Disk mirroring

Disk mirroring is an implementation of Redundant Arrays of Independent Disks (RAID) Level 1. It uses two disk drives configured with equal-sized partitions and connected to the same disk controller. During each data write, the same data is written to both disk partitions.

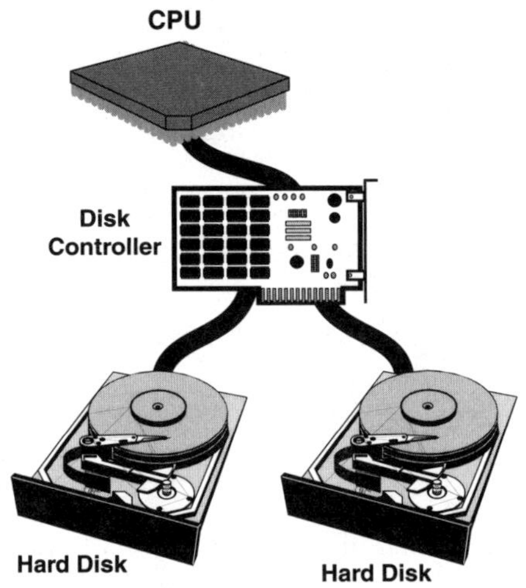

With disk mirroring, disk utilization is 50% of the dedicated storage space. I/O performance generally is better than when using disk striping with parity. A mirrored pair can be split without loss of data.

Disk mirroring is designed to keep the computer operational in spite of disk errors or loss of a hard disk. If a read error occurs, data from the other disk is used. If one drive fails, the server will continue running by using the other drive.

Use disk mirroring when data must be protected against drive failures, and hard disk resources are and will be plentiful as system requirements grow.

Disk mirroring is normally used on peer-to-peer networks and smaller LANs to protect critical data files. Due to the amount of storage lost through redundancy, it is not commonly used on larger LANs.

Disk Operating System (DOS)

The software programs that control the operation of the computer and the movement of information throughout the computer system.

DOS is the medium by which the user communicates with the computer system and manipulates data.

Disk quota

Windows 2000 feature allowing limits to be set on users' available disk space. Disk quotas are set by volume and by user. Disk quotas are only supported on NTFS volumes.

Diskperf

Command-line command that is used to activate and deactivate disk performance counters.

Distance-vector protocol

A routing protocol that uses a routing table that consists of routes that are configured with a distance (hop count) and a vector (the gateway to the destination network).

Distributed database

This collection of information files or databases resides at different sites yet appears to the user to be a single database.

Distributed File System (Dfs)

A hierarchical file display that consists of logical links to shared folders. Dfs displays a logical file system to users, allowing them to see and access all shared available network resources in a way that makes their physical location on the network transparent to the user.

Distribution folder

Shared folder used as the installation source during Windows NT and Windows 2000 over-the-network installations.

Distribution group

Active Directory domain group used for distribution management.

Domain

1. In NetWare, DOMAIN is used as a console command that will create a protected operating system domain for running untested NLMs in Ring 3. This prevents a module from interfering with the core operating system.

2. In the Internet, a domain is a part of the naming hierarchy. The domain name is a sequence of names (separated by periods) that identify host sites. For example: galenp@mail.msen.com.

Domain Controller

Server within a domain and storage point for domainwide security information. This also refers to a partition of the Active Directory the Windows NT Server holds.

Domain controller (Windows 2000)

A Windows 2000 Server that has been promoted into the domain controller role. Each domain controller has a copy of the Active Directory domain database and SYSVOL folder.

Domain Dfs root

Dfs root hosted by a server but stored in Active Directory services. Root and link replicas are supported.

Domain Global group

Active Directory domain group scope. In mixed mode, members can include user accounts from the same domain. In addition, Global groups from the same domain are supported in native mode.

Domain Local group

Active Directory domain group scope. In mixed mode, members can include user accounts from any domain in the forest or Global groups from any domain in the forest. In addition, Domain Local groups from the same domain and Universal groups from any domain in the forest are supported in native mode.

Domain Model

A method of organizing Windows NT Server domains for security and management.

Domain name

A unique domain name designates a location on the Internet. Domain names always have two or more parts separated by periods. The leftmost part is the most specific, and the part on the right is the most general. A given machine may have more than one domain name, but a given domain name points to only one machine.

Domain Name System (DNS)

A hierarchical, distributed method of organizing systems and network names on the Internet. DNS administratively groups hosts (systems) into a hierarchy of authority that allows addressing and other information to be widely distributed and maintained. A big advantage of DNS is that using it eliminates dependence on a centrally maintained file that maps host names to addresses.

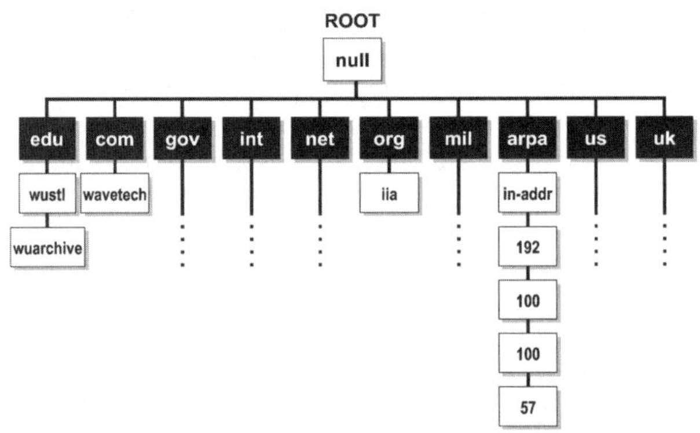

The diagram shows the hierarchical organization of domain names. The bottom level of the tree structure contains the names of companies or even machines within a company. For example, consider wuarchive.wustl.edu. The bottom of the tree is wuarchive. This is the name of a particular piece of equipment within the wustl domain, which is under the edu domain.

The name of a particular domain is read from the bottom of the tree up to the root. The root is unnamed and is represented with just a period. For example, wavetech.com is a particular domain. If we were to give the fully qualified domain name (FQDN), we would include the unnamed root, so it would be written as "wavetech.com." The final period at the end of the name specifies the root of the tree. The root must always be specified for the host equipment. To make it easy, most software will convert a domain name to an FQDN for the user by appending any missing domain names all the way to the root.

The top of the tree lists the top-level domains. These are reserved names. Every domain will have a top-level domain by type or country.

Domain Naming master

Forest-wide operations master role responsible for addition of domains to the forest or removal of domains from the forest.

Domain partition

Replication partition containing domain objects and attributes. The domain partition fully replicates to all domain controllers in a domain.

Domain Universal group

Active Directory domain group scope that is only supported in native mode. Members can include users from any domain in the forest, Global groups from any domain in the forest, and Universal groups from any domain in the forest.

Domain user account

A user account created as an Active Directory object and used for domain logon and resource access verification.

Domainwide master roles

Operations master roles implemented at the forest level. These are Relative ID master, PDC emulator, and Infrastructure master.

Dotted decimal notation

The syntactic representation for a 32-bit integer that consists of four 8-bit numbers written in base 10 with periods (dots) separating them. Used to represent IP addresses in the Internet, as in 192.67.67.20.

Download

A process where a file is transferred from a host computer to a user's computer. Download is the opposite of upload.

Driver

Software used to allow the operating system to communicate with an add-on hardware device such as a disk controller or display adapter.

Drop

Individual connections (sometimes called nodes) on a multipoint (also called multidrop) circuit.

Dynamic

Pertaining to a priority of a process that is varied by the operating system. Contrasts with absolute priority.

Dynamic Data Exchange (DDE)

A process that allows two applications to exchange information.

Dynamic disk

A Windows 2000 disk configuration that supports disk volumes rather than industry-standard disk partitions.

Dynamic DNS (DDNS)

A newer standard of DNS where client hosts can automatically register A (host) and PTR (pointer) resource records. DDNS allows clients with a dynamically assigned address to register directly with the Windows 2000 DNS server and update the DNS table dynamically.

Dynamic Drive

Dynamic attach and release of network drives under Microsoft Mail.

Dynamic Host Configuration Protocol (DHCP)

A TCP/IP application-layer protocol that provides for dynamic address assignment on a network.

Dynamic-Link Library (DLL)

A module that is linked at load time or run time.

Dynamic linking

Using an update command to ensure that all data changed in one program is automatically changed in another program, thereby keeping the data consistent. Dynamic linking is particularly useful in database management.

Dynamic Random Access Memory (DRAM)

The most commonly used memory type for personal computers. Because of its passive componentry design, DRAM requires a periodic refresh signal to maintain valid data.

Echo

The reflection of transmitted data back to its source. Also a phenomenon in voice circuits.

Electronic Frontier Foundation (EFF)

A foundation established to address social and legal issues arising from the increasingly pervasive use of computers as a means of communication and information distribution.

Electronic Mail (e-mail)

The most popular Internet application and the driving force behind the Internet's rapid growth. While controlling another computer remotely or transferring files from one computer to another may be useful, neither is as exciting as being able to communicate with millions of Internet users around the globe. Many users join the Internet just for e-mail access.

Fortunately, it is possible to exchange e-mail with people that are not directly part of the Internet. For example, by using gateways to other public e-mail networks, Internet e-mail can reach users with commercial service provider accounts such as CompuServe, BITNET, America Online, Prodigy, and the Microsoft Network. E-mail can also reach users who work at companies that get their mail access from corporate network providers such as MCImail, Applelink, and uuNet.

E-mail is popular because it works very quickly, while traditional mail can take a day or two to cross town or weeks to reach an international destination. E-mail can travel from sender to receiver within hours (sometimes minutes) despite the distance between them. If the network is extremely busy or if an administrator configures a user's system to send e-mail once a day (as opposed to every few minutes), the e-mail may take a little longer to arrive. In general, however, e-mail moves around the world at a rapid pace. It is possible for a person in the U.S. to send a message to West Africa, receive a response, and send another message, all in the space of an hour.

E-mail is also very flexible. Users can attach different types of files to their e-mail messages. Marketing can embed audio and video clips within text messages, co-workers can transfer spreadsheets or project updates, families can share pictures and birthday messages.

Electronic mail address

Designation given to an individual or domain that directs messages or other information over computers in general to a specific person or destination.

Emulation

The imitation of all or part of one system by another. This can be accomplised either in hardware or software. The imitating system accepts the same data, executes the same programs, and achieves the same results as the imitated system.

Products such as SoftWindows and Virtual PC allow Macintosh computers to emulate the Windows or Windows 95 operating system and an Intel-based PC.

Apple designed the "68K" emulator for the PowerPC processor in order to allow Power Macintosh computers to run older 680x0-specific software.

Encapsulated PostScript File (EPS or EPSF)

A file format used by graphics and publishing applications.

Encapsulation

In object-oriented programming (OOP), encapsulation defines a data structure of attributes and a group of member functions as a single unit called an object. In networking, encapsulation is the process of enclosing packets of one type of protocol by another.

Encrypting File System (EFS)

Windows 2000 data encryption service based on a user's public and private keys. Data encryption is only supported on NTFS volumes.

Encryption

Involves encoding a packet's data prior to transmission to ensure data security. The Data Encryption Standard (DES) is an algorithm used for coding and decoding data for security purposes.

End-to-end

Governs the interaction from the source computer to the destination device and vice versa; i.e., a program in the source machine exchanges messages with a similar program in the destination machine. The transport layer (fourth layer) of the International Standards Organization (ISO) reference model of open systems interconnection (OSI) is an end-to-end process, as are layers five to seven. In contrast, layers one to three of the ISO model specify intermediate, or subnetwork, interactions between a device and its immediate neighbor. Layers one to three are referred to as chained.

Enhanced Graphics Adapter (EGA)

Introduced as an enhancement to the first color display for PCs (CGA). The EGA was equipped with two more wires providing intensity for each of the three primary colors and the ability to produce more color combinations. Also, the horizontal scanning frequency was synchronized for a much clearer output display.

Entity

1. OSI terminology for a layer protocol machine. An entity within a layer performs the functions of the layer within a single computer system, accessing the layer entity below and providing services to the layer entity above at local service access points.

2. A definable object during database definition.

Errors

A term used to refer to errors or messages generated by DB-Library, the OS, or the network software.

Ethernet

A Carrier Sense, Multiple Access with Collision Detection (CSMA/CD) specification.

Ethernet was originally developed by Xerox, Intel, and Digital Equipment Corporation in the late 1970s, with specifications first released in 1980. The standard defines the cabling, connectors, and other characteristics for the transmission of data, voice, and video over local area networks at 10 Mbps. Recent improvements have increased the speed to 100 Mbps.

There are four types of Ethernet frames defined: 802.2, 802.3, Ethernet_SNAP, and Ethernet II. These are similar but incompatible.

The types of Ethernet cables are Thin Ethernet (Thinnet), Thick Ethernet (Thicknet), Twisted Pair, and Fiber Optic.

Event

An action that results in a message being sent or activity in a program. An event can be generated by a user, an application, or the operating system.

Exceptions

An event that indicates that something unexpected occurred. An exception can be generated by hardware, by the operating system, or by an application.

Expanded Memory (EMS)

Created when PC processors were limited to 1 MB of Random Access Memory (RAM). Spreadsheet users needed a way to create extremely large spreadsheets and could not do this in the 640 KB available in PCs of that era. A way to work around this memory limitation was needed.

To answer this need, Lotus, Intel, and Microsoft (LIM) developed the Expanded Memory Specification.

This specification utilized a special EMS adapter board to store additional memory where data could be stored for later use. When needed, data is moved from the EMS board to system memory by *paging* the data through a 64-KB page frame in the Upper Memory Area (UMA). The page frame is made up of four 16-KB pages. An expanded memory manager, such as EMM386.EXE, is used to control the paging of data between the EMS board and system memory.

LIM Expanded Memory

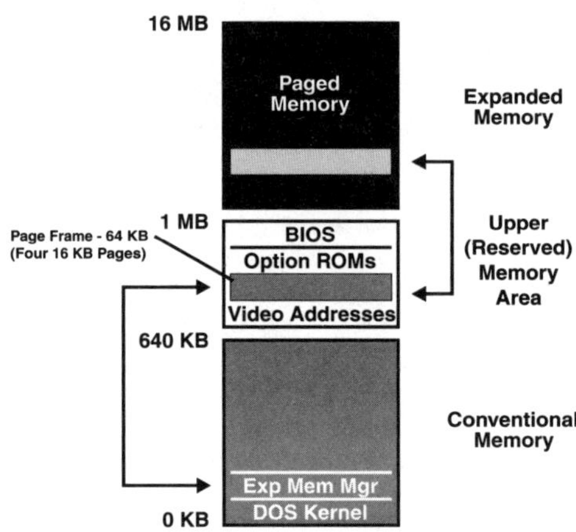

Eventually, the special EMS board was entirely emulated in software, making the special hardware requirement obsolete.

EMS is typically only used by older DOS applications.

Extended partition

A basic disk partition. An extended partition can have multiple logical drives. An extended partition is not bootable. A basic disk can have one extended partition.

Extension snap-in

A snap-in designed to add additional administrative features to another snap-in. Also referred to as an extension.

Extranet

Extends the intranet to include other users, such as customers or partner organizations, who will be able to access some part of the intranet. The extranet is configured to give access to only a small part of the information that exists on the intranet, and in most cases, the users must be authenticated before they can get access to the information.

Fault tolerance

Operating-system features designed to accommodate failures, therefore improving disk reliability and application accessibility. Related terms are "Disk Mirroring," "Disk Duplexing," "Disk Striping with Parity," "Clustering," and "Load Balancing."

File

A sequence of bytes stored on a secondary storage medium such as a floppy disk or hard disk. Generally, a computer file contains either a program or data.

Program files contain instructions or commands that are to be executed by the computer. Data files that contain only ASCII characters are text files, while files containing binary data, i.e., data other than ASCII characters, are called binary files. Bytes that comprise a file are not necessarily stored on contiguous disk blocks and may be scattered across a disk due to fragmentation.

Macintosh files generally consist of a Data Fork (the file contents) and a Resource Fork (a pointer to the application that created the file).

File caching

This improves file access time by using the RAM memory to store recently accessed files.

File compression

More data can be stored on server hard disks by compressing files that are not being used. NetWare and Windows NT support identifying files and directories to be compressed. With DOS, Windows, and Windows 95, disk partitions are identified for compression.

File format

The arrangement of information in a file. There are many standard and nonstandard file formats used on various computing platforms. The use of standard formats for information such as vector graphics, bitmapped graphics, audio, word processing, and spreadsheets allows information to be accessed by applications from multiple vendors.

File Format API (FFA PI)

API sets supporting message transfer between Microsoft Mail and foreign mail systems.

File server

A computer that stores files and provides access to them from workstations. File servers generally contain large hard disks and high amounts of memory.

If a computer is used exclusively as a file server, it is a dedicated file server. If a computer is used as a workstation and a file server simultaneously, it is a nondedicated file server.

The NOS (Network Operating System) runs on the file server and controls access to files, printers, and other network resources.

File server protocol

A communications protocol that allows application programs to share files.

File transfer

The process of copying a file from one computer to another over a network. FTP is a popular program used to copy files over the Internet.

File Transfer Protocol (FTP)

A part of the TCP/IP suite that is used to transfer files between any two computers, provided they support FTP. The two computers do not have to be running the same operating system.

In general, people use FTP to move files from one account or machine to another or to perform what is called an "anonymous FTP." For example, if storage space on a particular machine is low, the user can free up storage space by using FTP to move the files to a machine with more space. Another reason to move a file to a different account is to print a file to a particular printer. If the file is on a machine that cannot access the desired printer, it must be moved to a machine that does have access.

Whatever the reason for the transfer, FTP requires the user to know the proper login name and the password for both computers to move files between them.

While an anonymous FTP also moves from one computer to another, it has two main differences. An anonymous FTP session usually involves gathering files that a user does not have. Anonymous FTP does not require the user to know a login name and password to access the remote computer.

The Internet has many anonymous FTP sites. Each site consists of an FTP server, a large number of files, and guest login names such as "anonymous" or "FTP." This allows any user to visit these systems and copy files from the FTP site to their personal computer. With the appropriate authority, users can copy files from their system to an anonymous FTP site.

Despite the variety of FTP servers and clients on the Internet and the different operating systems they use, FTP servers and clients generally support the same basic commands. This standard command set allows users to accomplish tasks such as looking at a list of files in the current directory of the remote system, regardless of the operating system in use. Other common commands allow users to change directories, get specific file information, copy files to a local machine, and change parameters.

Graphical Web browsers transform the traditional character-based, command-line FTP interface into a point-and-click environment. The only way a user may know that they are in the middle of an FTP session is that the Universal Resources Locator (URL) box in the browser will change from an address that begins with "http://..." to "ftp://...".

Filter

A device or program that separates data, signals, or material in accordance with specified criteria.

Filtering (Group Policy Object)

A way of controlling whether a Group Policy Object (GPO) is processed and assigned based on security group membership.

Firewall

Used as a security measure between a company's local area network (LAN) and the Internet. The firewall prevents users from accessing certain address Web sites. A firewall also helps to prevent hackers from accessing internal resources on the network. A combination of hardware and software that separates a LAN into two or more parts for security purposes. Today, firewalls are commonly used to prevent unauthorized access to a network from the Internet.

FireWire

A high-speed serial interface designed by Apple Computer to allow communications between a Macintosh computer and peripherals such as scanners, disk drives, printers, digital cameras, etc.

Flag

A variable indicating that a certain condition holds.

Focus

Term used to refer to the active screen object or control.

Folder

A directory. The Macintosh operating system uses folders as an analogy for directories. Folders may contain files and other folders.

Folder Redirection

A process whereby user profile information is redirected to a network share location.

Foreground category

A classification of processes that consists of those associated with the currently active screen group.

Foreground process

A process that can receive user input.

Forest

A collection of two or more trees. They do not share a common namespace but do share a Global Catalog and a common schema.

Forestwide master roles

Operations master roles implemented at the forest level. These are Schema master and Domain Naming master.

Forward

A feature of electronic mail transmission that enables a message recipient to re-address the mail and send it to a third party.

Forward Lookup query

DNS query used for mapping host names to IP addresses.

Forward Lookup Zone

DNS zone used for host name-to-IP address resolution.

Fragment

Part of an IP message.

Frame

In IEEE (Institute of Electrical and Electronics Engineers) terminology, the unit of data transferred at the OSI (Open Systems Interconnection) data link layer.

Frame type

A data-link level specification describing the packet structure on a network. Different frame types are incompatible with each other.

Frequency

The number of times one complete incident or function occurs. In electronics, frequency usually refers to the number of waveforms that are repeated per second, measured in Hertz.

From

The field in an electronic mail header that contains the return address of the message originator.

Full-text database

A computer file that holds the complete text of original sources, such as newspaper or periodical articles, books, court decisions, and directories.

Full-text search

The SQL Server 7.0 feature that allows you to create a catalog of the text contained in particular fields. A column with full-text search enabled and the catalog populated allows users to search for records based on a field containing certain words.

Full zone transfer

Zone transfer method requiring transfer of the full DNS database from the source name server to the destination name server.

Function Key

"Extra" keys on a computer keyboard. PCs and Macintosh keyboards generally have 12 function keys. Other types of computers have more.

Function keys are used for various purposes by the operating system and applications software.

Gateway

The primary linkage between mixed environments such as PC-based LANs and host environments such as SNA.

Gateways generally operate at all seven layers of the OSI Reference Model. They may provide full content conversion between two environments, such as ASCII to EBCDIC, as well as other application and presentation layer conversions.

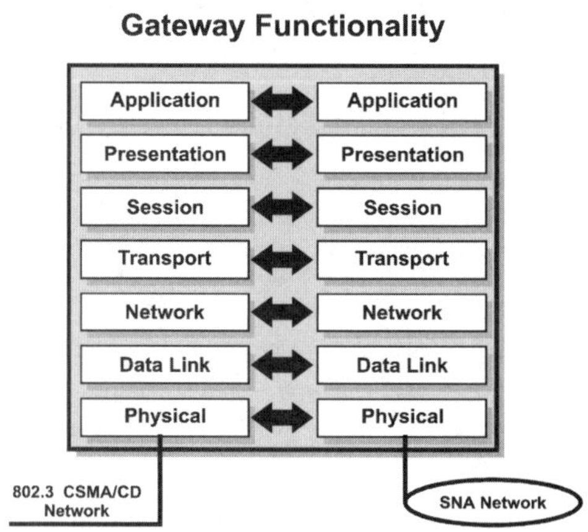

Other types of gateways include fax gateways, which allow users to send and receive faxes from their workstations. These may also be integrated with mail service gateways, which allow communications between users of different mail systems.

Generic Routing Encryption (GRE) protocol

A protocol used by PPTP to encapsulate the encrypted packets that are being transmitted across the Internet.

Global Catalog (GC)

A database containing scaled-down attributes of every Active Directory object from every domain in a tree or forest. The GC replies to queries so that users in one domain can locate resources in another domain.

Global Catalog server

The first domain controller created in a tree that, by default, stores the Global Catalog.

Global group

A group definition allowing permission assignments to local machines or other domains through local group membership of the Global group.

Gov

A governmental organization is identified by this Internet address suffix. For example, whitehouse.gov.

Graphical Identification and Authentication (GINA)

Windows 2000 component that collects logon information that it packages and sends to the Local Security Authority.

Graphical User Interface (GUI)

A program that executes commands given by the user to the computer. A GUI uses graphic representations of commands and/or a menu format to display commands that the user may execute with a mouse or similar device.

The graphical user interface makes using a computer easier, especially for the beginner. Mosaic is a Graphical User Interface for the Internet. Microsoft Windows, OS/2, and the Macintosh operating system are examples of graphical user interfaces for personal computers.

Group

Collection of users used for security management or distrubtion management. Windows 2000 groups can contain other objects such as computers.

Group nesting

A term referring to one group being a member of another group.

Group object

A leaf object that represents several User objects. It provides collective, rather than individual, network administration. Group objects are created based on the use of applications, printers, or print queues. Group objects may also be created based on users who perform similar tasks or need similar information, or to simplify trustee assignments.

Group Policy (GP)

Windows 2000 feature that allows administrators to assign security settings and additional properties to domain members based on their personal accounts or group memberships.

Group Policy Container (GPC)

Active Directory object that stores Group Policy Object (GPO) attributes.

Group Policy Object (GPO)

An Active Directory object that contains configuration information on desktop environments, servers, users, and other objects. GPOs can be applied to domains, sites, or OUs for the purpose of simplifying administrative control over Active Directory objects. Each Windows 2000 computer, regardless of if it is a member of an Active Directory domain, will also have a local GPO.

Group Policy Snap-in

Utility for editing Group Policy Object (GPO) policy settings.

Group Policy Templates (GPT)

Folder created each time a new Group Policy Object (GPO) is created. The GPT contains policy settings for the GPO.

Handle

1. In draw programs and similar object-oriented graphics programs, handles are the small black squares that appear around a selected object so the object can be resized, moved, copied, or scaled by using a mouse or similar pointing device.

2. An operating system object that contains a reference to an object like a window or printer.

Hard disk

A peripheral mass-storage device that uses sealed, rotating, nonflexible, magnetically coated disks to store data and program files. Hard disk types include SCSI, IDE, and EIDE.

Hardware

All electronic components of a computer system, including peripherals, circuit boards, and input and output devices. Hardware is the physical equipment, as opposed to software consisting of programs, data procedures, rules, and associated documentation.

Hardware Abstraction Layer (HAL)

Windows NT module that isolates the operating system kernel from the hardware platform.

Hardware Compatibility List (HCL)

A list of systems and adapters maintained by Microsoft. The HCL is a list of systems tested and verified as compatible with a specific operating system version.

Header

Contains identifying information.

Electronic mail message headers contain the message originator's name and address, receiver, subject, date, etc.

A packet header carries the source and destination addresses along with other information.

Heap

1. A block of memory that is set aside for dynamic allocation.

2. SQL Server term for the collection of all pages containing all rows in a table.

High-Density (HD)

The density refers to how tightly data can be recorded on the media. This is usually used to describe floppy diskettes. Using a magnetic medium that has much finer (smaller) magnetic particles, more data can be recorded on the media. HD diskettes require high-density drives.

Histogram view

System Monitor view displaying average performance counter data as a bar chart.

Hive files

Component files making up the Windows NT Registry.

Home directory

1. The topmost (root) directory for Web sites using IIS. Serves as the default location for a Web site's content pages.

2. On Local Area Networks, a directory that belongs to a single user for storage of data. Normally, the user is the only person with access to this directory. On most networks, the supervisor or administrator can also access any user's home directory.

Home page

A document coded in HTML (HyperText Markup Language) that acts as a top-level document for an Internet site or a topic. A home page contains hypertext links to related documents.

Hop

Describes routing through a network. A hop is a data packet moving through routers from the point of origination to the destination.

Hop count

The number of cable segments a message packet passes through between its source and network or internetwork destination. The destination can be no more than 16 hops from the source.

Host

A computer that is remotely accessible and provides information or services for users on a network. It is quite common to have one host machine provide several services, such as WWW and USENET. A host computer on the Internet can be accessed by using an application program such as electronic mail, telnet, or FTP. A host computer may also be a bulletin board.

Host (A) resource record

Forward zone host name-to-IP address mapping record.

Host Information (HINFO) resource record

Resource record identifying a host's CPU and operating system.

Hostname

The name given to a computer that identifies it as an Internet or other site.

Hub

1. In disk drives, the hub is the central mechanism within the drive that causes the disk to rotate and keeps it centered during the rotation. On floppy diskettes, the hub fits into the hole in the center of the diskette to keep it level and balanced during rotation.

2. In networking, a central connecting point for network wiring.

Hypertext

Allows users to move from one site or place in a document to another. Hypertext links in World Wide Web documents link the user from terms in one document to the site referenced in the original document.

Hypertext Transfer Protocol (HTTP)

A set of directions for Web servers that tells them how to respond to various events initiated by users. HTTP is the most important protocol used in the World Wide Web (WWW).

The simplest example is clicking on a link to another part of the same file. The server receives the information that the link has been activated and sends back the designated part of the file for display.

An HTTP client program is required on one end, and an HTTP server program on the other.

I/O

I/O (Input/Output) refers to the sending and receiving of data from the central processing unit (CPU) to other peripheral devices such as disk drives. The input/output channel carries out all transfer of data so as to free up the CPU. The keyboard is the most common input device, and the monitor is the most common output device.

I/O address

Space used to access I/O hardware such as I/O adapters, buses, and special registers used by I/O devices known as control status registers (CSR). I/O address space is one of two equal parts of primary memory, or addressable memory. The other equal part is memory address space.

I/O privilege mechanism

A facility that allows a process to ask a device driver for direct access to the device's I/O ports and any dedicated or mapped memory locations it has. The I/O privilege mechanism can be used directly by an application or indirectly by a dynamic link package.

Icon

A graphical picture used to represent an application, folder, file, disk drive, or printer.

Identifier

The name of a database or database object.

Incremental Zone server (IXFR)

Zone transfer method where only changes are transferred from the source name server to the destination name server.

Index

A database object that provides efficient access to rows in a table, based on key values.

Infrastructure master

Domainwide operations master role responsible for updating user-to-group references in a multidomain environment.

Inheritance

1. The means by which a child object can get information from its parent.
2. The process by which Access Control Entries are passed from a parent object to a child object.
3. The process by which permissions are passed from a group to its members.

Inheritance chain

The path from a particular class to its superclasses in the class hierarchy.

Inheritance hierarchy

The collection of all subclasses that extend from a common parent class. Each subclass inherits the properties of its parent class.

INI Files in Windows for Workgroups

WIN.INI contains environmental information, while SYSTEM.INI contains system configuration information. The settings for the desktop, color schemes, and multimedia information are located in CONTROL.INI. PROGMAN.INI contains Program Manager appearance and configuration information, and WINFILE.INI contains the settings for File Manager's appearance and operation. The network drivers and protocol information is found in PROTOCOL.INI. MSMAIL.INI contains information for the Mail program. EFAXPUMP.INI is only present if the fax is installed and contains information about fax modems, security, and received faxes. SCHDPLUS.INI contains information about Schedule+'s appearance and behavior. Finally, there is SHARED.INI, which contains settings that allow users in the same workgroup to share custom commands and messages for Mail.

Many Windows applications create their own .INI files during installation. Others will add entries to the WIN.INI file.

The contents of the .INI files are read during Windows for Workgroups startup. After editing the files, restart Windows for Workgroups to activate the changes.

INSTALL

1. Common software installation filename.

2. A NetWare 3.x and 4.x loadable module used to install, modify, or update the NetWare operating system. The module is contained in the INSTALL.NLM file and is loaded with the LOAD console command. NetWare 3.12 and 4.x also have DOS INSTALL programs that are used to initialize the original install process.

Instance

An occurrence of an object in memory.

Institute of Electrical and Electronics Engineers (IEEE)

A professional ANSI-accredited body of scientists and engineers based in the U.S. IEEE promotes standardization and consults to the American National Standards Institute on matters relating to electrical and electronic development. The IEEE 802 Standards Committee is the leading official standard organization for LANs (Local Area Networks).

Integrated Drive Electronics (IDE)

The standard interface for a hard disk drive. Controller electronics are integrated into the drive. The controller connects to a paddleboard that may be external to, or on, the system board. The paddleboard then interfaces with the bus to the CPU. An IDE bus can be identified by its 40-pin connector, as opposed to the 50-pin connector of a SCSI bus.

Integrated Services Digital Network (ISDN)

A special kind of telecommunications network designed to handle more than just data. Digital network operating over PSTN local loop wiring. Multiple services, including video, text, voice, data, facsimile images, and graphics, are supported over 64-Kbps channels. Standard configurations combine multiple channels to provide higher transfer rates.

Integrity

Data consistency and accuracy.

IntelliMirror

The Microsoft technology that stores a mirror image of a client computer on a server. In Microsoft 2000, the umbrella term for a collection of technologies designed to reduce the cost of network ownership.

Interactive

The exchange of information and control between the user and a computer process.

Interactive also refers to time-dependent (real-time) data communications. Typically communications in which a user enters data and then waits for a response message from the destination before continuing.

Interface

1. A shared boundary between two functional units, defined by functional characteristics, signal characteristics, and other characteristics, as appropriate. Also, any of the electrical and logical devices that permit computers and peripherals to be interconnected.

2. A contract between an object and its users.

Interfaces

A set of methods that can be implemented by Java classes.

Interior Gateway Protocol (IGP)

The protocol used to exchange routing information between collaborating routers in the Internet. Router Information Protocol (RIP) and Open Shortest Path First (OSPF) are examples of IGPs.

International Standards Organization (ISO)

Founded in 1946, the ISO promotes the development of international standards for the computer, communications, and other fields. ISO members are the standards organizations of 89 countries. The United States representative is the American National Standards Institute (ANSI).

Internet

An international computer network of networks that connect government, academic, and business institutions. Networks on the Internet include MILNET, NSFnet, and other backbone networks, as well as mid-level networks and stub (local) networks.

Internet networks communicate using TCP/IP (Transmission Control Protocol/Internet Protocol). The Internet connects colleges, universities, military organizations and contractors, corporations, government research laboratories, and individuals.

Although parts of the Internet operate under single administrative domains, the Internet as a whole reaches around the globe, connects computers (from personal computers to supercomputers), and is not administered by any single authority. The Internet in July 1995 roughly connected 60,000 independent networks into a vast global Internet.

Used as a descriptive term, an internet is a collection of interconnected packet-switching networks. Any time you connect two or more networks together, you have an internet—as in *inter*national or *inter*state.

Internet Activities Board (IAB)

The IAB is the technical body that oversees the development of the Internet suite of protocols commonly referred to as "TCP/IP." It has two task forces, the IRTF and the IETF, each charged with investigating a particular area.

Internet address

A 32-bit value written or displayed in numbers that specify a particular network and node on that network.

Internet Connection Server

RRAS configuration within Windows 2000 Server that enables you to share a single Internet connection with other computers on the network.

Internet Connection Sharing (ICS)

A service available in Windows 2000 Professional and Server that allows the sharing of a single connection to the Internet or a remote network with multiple network clients. ICS is very easy to configure but also limited to using a single small network.

Internet Control Message Protocol (ICMP)

Used for error reporting and recovery, and is a required component of any IP implementation.

Internet Engineering Task Force (IETF)

One of the task forces of the IAB, the IETF is responsible for solving short-term engineering needs of the Internet. It has more than 40 Working Groups.

Internet Group Management Protocol (IGMP)

Part of the TCP/IP protocol suite. Provides multicasting broadcasts for communications and passing management information in a multicasting group.

Internet Information Server (IIS)

Microsoft Internet Information Server is a network file and application server that transmits information in Hypertext Markup Language.

Internet Protocol (IP)

The OSI layer 3 routed protocol used to transmit packetized information on a TCP/IP network.

Internet Relay Chat (IRC)

An Internet protocol that supports real-time conversations between Internet users worldwide.

Internet Service Provider (ISP)

Companies that provide an Internet connection for educational institutions, individuals, companies, and organizations.

Internetwork

Two or more networks connected by a router.

Internetwork Packet Exchange (IPX)

Used with SPX as the resident protocol in NetWare. A router with IPX routing can interconnect local area networks (LANs) so that Novell NetWare clients and servers can communicate.

In NetWare 3.x, IPX is the name of the command-line utility used to see the versions and options of IPX.COM. This was used prior to the introduction of ODI drivers.

Internetwork Packet Exchange Open Data-Link Interface (IPXODI)

This is a module that takes the workstation requests determined to be for the network by the NetWare DOS Requester and packages them with transmission information (such as their destination), then transfers them to the Link Support Layer (LSL). IPXODI requires that each packet have an initialized header specifying information targeting network delivery and announcing from where the packet came, where it is going, and what happens after delivery.

InterNIC

The Internet Network Information Center (InterNIC) was developed in 1993 by General Atomics, AT&T, and NSI to provide information services to Internet users. It offers a reference desk that provides networking information, referrals to other resources, and associate users with their local NICs. It also provides coordination to share information and activities with U.S. and international organizations, as well as education services to train mid-level and campus NICs, and to end users to promote Internet use.

Interoperability

The ability to use products from different vendors in the same system. Communication protocols, such as IP or AFP, can be used in ODI to process information from the network. The user does not have to know each protocol's required method of packet transmission. Interoperability also means an application can share files, even when running on different platforms, such as Macintosh or UNIX.

Intersite replication

Replication occurring between Active Directory sites, between direct connections, and across site links.

Intranet

1. A network or series of networks that is private to an organization. In some cases, the definition of an intranet or extranet is limited to using Internet technologies to provide and access resources. This is the most accurate description of intranets and extranets, but the meaning is often extended to include other technologies such as simple file and print sharing.

2. A private internet, usually within a company, for facilitating information sharing. It looks and acts just like the public Internet.

Intrasite replication

Replication occuring within an Active Directory site.

IP address

Each host in the network is assigned a unique IP address for each network connection (installed network adapter). The IP address is used to identify packet source and destination hosts.

An IP address is a 32-bit address, written as 4 octets (bytes) separated by periods. For example, 195.143.67.2.

This way of representing an IP address is also known as dotted decimal notation. Each address will also have an associated subnet mask, dividing the address into its network prefix and host suffix. For example, you might have the following defined as a subnet mask: 255.255.255.0. The subnet mask is used to identify the network and host portions of the address.

The network portion identifies where the host is located, and the host portion identifies the device connected to that network.

When dealing with a network the size of the Internet, address assignments must be carefully coordinated. With millions of hosts operating on thousands of networks, the potential for duplicate addresses is significant. The job of coordinating Internet IP addresses is given to the Network Information Center.

An assigned address is only required if your network is connected to the Internet. If connected to the Internet, your network address will be assigned through the Internetwork Network Information Center, or InterNIC.

To get an Internet address, contact the InterNIC at InterNIC Registration Services, c/o Network Solutions, Inc., 505 Huntmar Park Drive, Herndon, Virginia 22070, (703) 742-4777, or at hostmaster@internic.net.

An organization is assigned a network address. The organization can further divide this into its own subnets and assign the host addresses.

Rather than going to the InterNIC, it is more likely that an organization will work through a local provider for address assignment. The organization will then subdivide the address, if necessary, and assign host addresses.

IP datagram

The fundamental unit of information passed across the Internet. It contains source and destination addresses along with data and a number of fields that define the length of the datagram, the header checksum, and flags to indicate whether the datagram can be (or has been) fragmented.

IP number

Sometimes called a *dotted quad*, it is a unique number consisting of four parts separated by periods. For example, 109.123.251.2. Each value in the dotted quad ranges from 0 to 255, representing the decimal form of an 8-bit binary number.

Every machine that is on the Internet has a unique IP number. If a machine does not have an IP number, it is not really *on* the Internet. Most machines also have one or more Domain Names so that they are easier for people to remember.

IP Security (IPSec)

A part of TCP/IP standards in which all IP traffic between two computers is encrypted so that the packets cannot be captured on the network and read by unauthorized users.

IPSec transport mode

An implementation of IPSec where the data is encrypted for the whole path from one computer to another.

IPSec tunnel mode

An implementation of IPSec where the data on the network is encrypted for only part of the entire path. Usually implemented on routers connected to public networks.

IPX external network number

A network number that uniquely identifies a network cable segment. An IPX external network number is a hexadecimal number, one to eight digits (1 to FFFFFFFE). When the IPX protocol is bound to a network board in the server, the number is assigned. IPX can be bound with multiple frame types or protocols to the same network board. Network number and network address are two terms used to refer to the IPX external network number.

IPX internal network number

A logical network number that identifies an individual NetWare server. During installation, the service is assigned an IPX internal network number. It is a hexadecimal number, 1 to 8 digits (1 to FFFFFFFE), that is unique to each server on a network. The IPX internal network number must also be different from any IPX external network number on the internetwork.

IPX internetwork address

A 12-byte number (represented by 24 hexadecimal characters) divided into three parts: the 4-byte (8-character) IPX external network number, the 6-byte (12-character) node number, and the 2-byte (4-character) socket number.

Iterative query

A query usually made by one DNS server to another asking for the IP address of a specific host name. The responding DNS server either provides the IP address or it refers the first DNS server to another DNS server that might have the information.

Job

Contains instructions for actions that will be performed. This replaces the SQL Server 6.5 term task.

Join

A relational operator that produces a single table from two tables, based on a comparison of particular column values (join columns) in each of the tables. The result is a table containing rows formed by the concatenation of the rows in the two tables. The values of the join columns compare or, if specified, include nonmatching rows.

Kerberos

Default authentication protocol for Windows 2000 clients and services.

Kernel

A set of essential operating routines used by the operating system (usually hidden from the user) to perform important system tasks such as managing the system memory or controlling disk operations.

Kernel mode

Lower-level Windows NT or Windows 95 operating system functions.

Key Distribution Center (KDC)

Kerberos protocol authentication server and ticket-granting service.

Keyboard

The device that allows the user to input data into the computer or to execute commands. Most keyboards resemble a typewriter. The standard is a 101-key keyboard.

Keys

Attribute columns that show a unique value for each entity.

Knowledge Consistency Checker (KCC)

A Windows 2000 service that uses site and subnet information, provided by domain administrators, for the purpose of generating a replication topology. The KCC uses its topology information to calculate the best connections for Active Directory replication.

Landscape

A document orientation that has a vertical dimension greater than its horizontal dimension.

Latency (replication latency)

The delay between when a change is made to an object attribute on one domain controller and when the change is replicated to other domain controllers in the domain.

Layer 2 Tunneling Protocol (L2TP)

A protocol that provides authentication services over public networks. Often used in conjunction with IPSec to create secure VPN connections.

Leaf Object

A type of NetWare object that does not contain other objects. Examples are user, printer, or server objects.

Legacy hardware

Term referring to hardware devices that require continued support in a new operating system environment.

Library

A group of programs or objects in a file.

Lightweight Directory Access Protocol (LDAP)

Modeled from X.500 and Directory Access Protocol (DAP), LDAP is a scaled-down version of its predecessor, DAP, which was unsuccessful because it was too inefficient (heavy) with thin clients, personal computers, and Internet use. Active Directory directly supports the Lightweight Directory Access Protocol.

Lines per inch (lpi)

Lpi dictates how many typewritten lines will be placed in the height of an inch on the paper.

Link

Any part of a Web page that is connected to something else. Clicking on or selecting a link will make that something else appear. (This is one major difference between virtual reality and real reality.) The first part of the URL named in a link denotes the method or kind of link. The methods include file (for local files), ftp, gopher, http, mailto, news, and wais (for some kinds of searches).

Linking

The process of associating a Group Policy Object (GPO) with a site, domain, OU, or container.

Link State Announcement (LSA)

The process used by OSPF routers to announce their routing tables to adjacent routers.

LMHOSTS

The LMHOSTS file lists the IP address and NetBIOS name for each network machine with which the local machine may need to communicate.

Local account

A Windows NT Server user account not authorized for interactive logon but supporting resource access.

Local Area Network (LAN)

A group of computers running specialized communications software and joined through an external data path.

A LAN will cover a small geographic area, usually no larger than a single building. The computers have a direct high-speed connection between all workstations and servers, and share hardware resources and data files. A LAN has centralized management of resources and network security.

PC-based networks can trace their heritage back to what are now often referred to as legacy systems. These systems were mainframe and minicomputer hosts accessed through dumb terminals.

There are a number of similarities between LANs and these legacy systems, such as centralized storage and backup, access security, and central management of resources. There are, however, a number of differences.

Traditional host systems are characterized by centralized processing, dumb terminals, custom applications, and high expansion costs and management overhead. LANs are characterized by distributed processing, intelligent workstations (PCs), and off-the-shelf applications. LANs are modular, are inexpensive to expand, and have more moderate management costs.

Local drive

The common name for a physical drive attached to a workstation.

Local group

1. Group scope supported by Windows 2000 that defines its members as being local to the machine. Local groups are valid only on nondomain/stand-alone servers and workstations.

2. When discussing Windows NT server domains, it is a group definition supporting local domain resource management. When discussing workstations, it is a group definition supporting local management of a Windows NT workstation.

Local Group Policy Object

Group Policy Object used for setting and managing policies for stand-alone and workgroup member Windows 2000 systems. A system will have only one local Group Policy Object.

Local printer

A printer directly connected to one of the ports on the computer. The opposite is one connected through a network, which would be a remote printer.

Local Security Authority (LSA)

Windows 2000 component that maintains information about local system security and the local security policy.

Logical Unit (LU)

The element within a network based on IBM's System Network Architecture (SNA) by which a user (terminal or program) attaches to the network. LUs are described by type to indicate their functional capabilities. LU2, for example, is a 3270-type device.

Local user account

A user account created on a workstation, member server, or stand-alone system and used for local logon authentication.

Logoff script

Executable file that runs when a user logs off.

Logon script

DOS or NT batch file or executable that may run when a user logs on to a computer system. Logon scripts can be used to map drives and search drives to directories, display messages, set environment variables, and execute programs or menus.

Loop

1. A series of program statements running in cyclic repetition.
2. An iterative programming construct. Loops are used to repeatedly execute a block of code.

Low Entry Networking (LEN)

A form of IBM's System Network Architecture (SNA) that permits PCs and minicomputers to communicate when a network does not contain an IBM mainframe.

LPT port

Also known as a parallel port, it is a connection on the computer, usually LPT1, where the cable for a parallel printer is connected. Generally, LPT1 through LPT3 can exist on a personal computer. Special equipment can be added to extend this capability.

Mail Exchanger (MX) resource record

Resource record identifying a mail server for a specific domain.

Mailbox

An area on a computer used to receive and store electronic mail messages.

Mailing list

A list of electronic mail addresses. A mailing list can be maintained by an individual user to send messages to groups of people. The mailing list is also used by listserv and other mail exploder programs to forward electronic mail messages on a specific topic to the listserv subscriber list.

Mailing lists are like newsletters except that any subscriber may contribute. A message sent to the list will automatically be sent to everyone who has subscribed to the list. A series of messages with the same subject line is called a thread.

Mainframe

A legacy computer that is capable of multitasking and other robust operations. It is generally used as a host for a large number of users.

Makeboot.exe

A utility used to create Setup boot disks for Windows 2000. Makeboot.exe runs on MS-DOS and 16-bit Windows-family systems.

Makebt32.exe

A utility used to create Setup boot disks for Windows 2000. Makebt32.exe runs on 32-bit Windows-family operating systems.

Mandatory user profile

Roaming user profile that does not allow the user to save changes made to the profile while logged on.

Manufacturing Automation Protocol (MAP)

A token-passing bus designed for factory environments by General Motors; standard IEEE 802.4 is nearly identical to MAP.

Mapping

1. The transferring of data between a disk and a computer's RAM.
2. Attaching to a server-based directory using the local drive ID.

Master

An instance where the highest privileges reside in a device (usually a computer) where they have control of other devices or servers.

Master Boot Record (MBR)

The physical section of a hard drive closest to the spindle where configuration and partition information is stored.

Master Domain Model

Windows NT Server domain model where one domain provides user and global group management for a set of trusting domains. Resources and local groups are managed individually at the trusting domains.

Master replica

The Directory replica that is used to create a new Directory partition in the Directory database. It also allows users to read and update Directory information. Although many Directory replicas of the same partition can exist, only one can be the master replica.

Media

A generic term for the medium that is used to record data. Media can be a floppy diskette, a hard disk, or other similar recording surface (an audio tape, for instance).

Media Access Control Sublayer (MAC)

The level of the IEEE 802 data station that controls and mediates access to media.

Megabit (Mb)

1,048,576 bits.

Megabits per second (Mbps)

Millions of bits per second (bps).

Megabyte (MB)

1,048,576 bytes.

Megabytes per second (MBps)

Millions of bytes per second (Bps).

Megahertz (MHz)

A million cycles per second. A CPU that operates at 200 Mhz uses a clock oscillator that runs at 200 million cycles per second.

Memory

A hardware component of a computer system that can store information and applications for later retrieval. Types of memory are RAM (Random Access Memory), ROM (Read-Only Memory), conventional, expanded, and extended memory.

Menu

1. A displayed list of items from which a user can make a selection.

2. A NetWare menu utility in 3.x that allows for the use of customized menus created as ASCII text files.

Menu bar

The bar of selections found at the top of a Macintosh application or the Finder.

Message

A notification from one object to another that some event has occurred.

Messages

A term used to refer to errors or messages generated by SQL Server.

Messaging API (MAPI)

One of the primary ways that people use the computer to communicate with each other. This is accomplished by sending messages and documents to each other via an electronic mail system.

Most companies are using at least one type of electronic mail system. Unfortunately, many companies are not using a single unified mail system for all of their employees, and other companies need interconnectivity with users who work for different companies.

Traditionally, corporations have installed gateways to get around this problem. However, gateways are highly specialized and can only be used to connect a particular pair of mail systems. Corporations often need a number of gateways to handle the different combinations of mail systems used by their employees and other contacts.

To resolve this problem, an API was developed that allowed for connectivity between various mail service providers and mail-aware/mail-enabled client applications. The result was the Messaging API, otherwise known as MAPI.

MAPI has a layered architecture that allows various client applications to communicate with multiple messaging systems. The main components are the client application, the MAPI subsystem, the MAP spooler, service providers, and the messaging system.

The client application is a front-end application that makes MAPI calls.

The MAPI subsystem, also known as the messaging subsystem, handles the client application's calls and provides standard user interface objects, such as dialog boxes and forms.

The MAPI spooler is responsible for forwarding the message to the appropriate transport service provider.

Service providers are responsible for translating MAPI methods to a format the messaging system can understand.

The messaging system is a back-end application that is responsible for routing messages over the network or across phone lines. Messaging systems currently available include Microsoft Mail, cc:Mail, IBM PROFS, X.400, and Novell MHS.

Method

A defined behavior for a particular interface. An object that owns an interface must implement its methods.

Metric

The cost assigned to a route in a routing table based on the bandwidth and availability of the network link.

Metropolitan Area Network (MAN)

A complete communications network set up by a local telephone company. This network services customers in regional locations, providing them with microwave and satellite relay stations, fiber optics, and cellular radio services with a 50-kilometer range operating at speeds from 1 megabit per second to 200 megabits per second.

A MAN is larger than a LAN (Local Area Network) but smaller than a WAN (Wide Area Network). A MAN may be made up of several LANs. MANs provide an integrated set of services for real-time voice, data, and image transmission.

Microsoft Management Console (MMC)

A framework that hosts Microsoft and third-party management tools, called snap-ins, that are used to administer computers, services, networks, users, and other components of the Windows system. The MMC does not provide any management functionality itself, but instead hosts the tools (snap-ins) that do.

The MMC provides the user with a simplified, single interface to the snap-ins. An MMC can be customized and the administrative tasks delegated with limited or full functionality of the included snap-ins.

Microsoft Point-to-Point Encryption (MPPE) protocol

Protocol used for data encryption between RAS servers and clients. Encryption is supported for the MS-CHAP and EAP-TLS remote access protocols.

Microsoft Software Installer file

Microsoft Software Installer (MSI) file type used with the Windows Installer Service. This type of file contains installation instructions and is capable of actively tracking and repairing application installation.

Migration

1. Conversion of NetWare servers from NetWare 2, NetWare 3, or from another operating system, to NetWare 4. Operating system migration is different from data migration, which is the moving of files to near-line or offline storage devices.

2. Transfer of users, groups, directories, and files from a NetWare Server to a Windows NT Server.

3. Transfer of users, groups, and application data from one application to another.

Milliseconds (ms)

A thousandth of a second. Access rates are expressed in milliseconds.

Mirror

Copying a hard disk's partition and data and duplicating it on another hard disk at the same time it is written on the original disk. Mirroring is set up during installation.

Mirror set

Basic disk fault-tolerant configuration using two physical hard disks with identical data. This is an implementation of RAID 1.

Mirrored volume

Dynamic disk fault-tolerant configuration using two physical hard disks with identical data. This is an implementation of RAID 1.

Mixed mode

A domain mode that includes a PDC upgraded to Windows 2000 and BDCs that have not been upgraded. Mixed mode also refers to the upgraded PDC and upgraded BDCs but without the native mode switch turned on.

Modem

An abbreviation for modulator/demodulator. A modem is a peripheral device that permits a personal computer, microcomputer, or mainframe to receive and transmit data in digital format across voice-oriented communications links such as telephone lines.

Monitors

Enforce mutually exclusive access to methods, particularly synchronized methods.

Motherboard

The electronic circuit board containing the primary computer components such as CPU, RAM, ROMs, etc.

Mounting point

A folder in one volume that another volume's data may be accessed through. The folder specified as a mounting point must be empty.

MS-DOS

MS-DOS is Microsoft's version of the DOS operating system.

Mud, Object Oriented (MOO)

One of several kinds of multiuser role-playing environments. MOO is a text-based environment.

Multicast

A special form of broadcast where copies of the packet are delivered to only a subset of all possible destinations.

Multicasting

When packets are sent from one server and received by many computers at the same time. Multicasting uses Class D IP addresses.

Multihomed host

A computer connected to more than one physical data link. The data links may or may not be attached to the same network.

Multimedia

In computing, multimedia refers to the presentation of information using sound, graphics, animation, and text.

Multiple Master Domain Model

Windows NT Server domain model when multiple trusted domains provide user and global group administration for a set of trusting domains. Resources and local groups are managed individually at the trusting domains.

Multiple Master Replication Model

Replication model used for Active Directory replication in which no domain controller is authoritative.

Multiprotocol routing

Windows 2000 RRAS configuration supporting any combination of IP routing, IPX routing, and AppleTalk routing.

Multitasking

A mode of operation that provides for the concurrent performance or interleaved execution of two or more tasks.

Multiuser

The ability of a computer that can support several interactive terminals at the same time.

Name server

Server running DNS server services and able to service queries for at least one zone.

Name server (NS) resource record

Resource record identifying a domain's name servers.

Name resolution

The process of mapping a node name into the corresponding network address. The name of a file can be resolved to the file itself through the Windows NT file system forming a namespace.

Namespace

TCP/IP term for a given subnet assigned by an authoritative body and referring to a group of addresses within a given range associated with a name. There can be only one authoritative DNS server for each domain namespace.

Native mode

Domain mode that only has Windows 2000 domain controllers and doesn't contain any PDC or BDCs.

NDS container object types

There are three container object types in the NDS: Country, Organization, and Organizational Unit.

It is important to note that in the [ROOT], you can create only Country, Organization, or Alias objects.

A Country container object identifies the name of the country. This allows multiple countries to be identified for Wide Area Networks (WANs). A Country container object can contain only Organization and Alias objects. The Country object is a two-character field and is identified by "C=."

An Organization container object identifies the name of the company, divisions within a company, or departments. Each [ROOT] of the NDS requires a minimum of one Organization object. An Organization container object can only contain Organizational Units and Leaf objects. The Organization object name can be up to 64 characters and is identified by "O=."

The Organizational Unit container object identifies different divisions or departments within the company. The Organizational Unit is a sublevel of the Organization container object and can only contain Leaf objects or other organizational units. Organizational Unit objects are optional within the directory tree. The Organizational Unit can be up to 64 characters and is identified by "OU=."

Net

An Internet domain designated for networks that include network service centers, network information centers, and others items. Examples are nyser.net or concentric.net.

NetBIOS

Standard programming interface for the development of distributed applications.

NetBIOS Extended User Interface (NetBEUI)

This is a nonroutable transport protocol written to the NetBIOS interface.

NetBIOS name

Microsoft networks, including workgroups and NT Server domains, always use NetBIOS names to identify workstations and servers. Machines recognize each other through unique machine names. Shared resources, files, and printers are accessed using NetBIOS names. For example, resources are identified by their Universal Naming Convention (UNC) name, which uses the format \\server\share_name.

In a UNC name, "server" is the NetBIOS name of the machine where the resource is physically located, and "share_name" is the name uniquely identifying the resource.

Microsoft NetBIOS names may contain up to 15 characters and are used to identify entities to NetBIOS. These entities include computers, domain names, workgroup names, and users.

In an internetwork TCP/IP environment, it is necessary to support resolution between NetBIOS names and IP addresses. Microsoft provides two methods of supporting this name resolution: LMHOSTS and Windows Internet Name Service (WINS).

LMHOSTS name resolution is based on a locally stored ASCII text file.

WINS Name resolution is based on WINS servers.

When designing your network, you will need to select the most appropriate method for your organizational requirements.

NetWare Client for DOS and MS Windows

Software that connects DOS and MS Windows workstations to NetWare networks and allows their users to share network resources.

Network

A group of computers and other devices connected together so they can communicate with each other.

Network adapter

The card that allows a computer to interface with the network. Also known as a Network Interface Card (NIC).

Network address

1. A network number that uniquely identifies a network cable segment. It may be referred to as the IPX external network number.

2. A network address can also be the network portion of an IP address. For a Class A network, the network address is the first byte of the IP address. For a Class B network, the network address is the first two bytes of the IP address. For a Class C network, the network address is the first three bytes of the IP address. In each case, the remainder is the host address.

Network Address Translation (NAT)

1. A component that is included with Windows 2000 Server that allows multiple users to share one connection, such as a modem or DSL connection, to the Internet. NAT is designed for mid-sized networks and offers more configuration flexibility than ICS. NAT operates as a router forwarding all requests to the Internet as well as supporting address translation. This means that the computers inside the network do not have to have Internet-compatible addresses.

2. A service available through RRAS on a Windows 2000 Server that allows the sharing of a single connection to the Internet or a remote network with multiple network clients. NAT is more difficult to configure than ICS but can also operate in more complex environments.

3. Routing protocol available through an Internet Connection Server (ICS) configuration that allows a home network or small office to share a single Internet connection. This protocol requires that your client computers be configured as DHCP clients.

Network application

A computer program housed on a server and designed to run over the network instead of being installed and run locally.

Network drive

The common name for a logical drive.

Network Driver Interface Specification (NDIS)

A specification that is part of the Windows 2000 networking architecture, which provides a boundary layer between the network protocols and the network card drivers. NDIS makes it possible to run multiple protocols and multiple network cards on one computer as long as all of them are designed to work with NDIS.

Network File System (NFS)

Software developed by Sun Microsystems that allows you to use files on another computer or network as if they were on your local computer.

Network Information Center (NIC)

A resource providing network administrative support as well as information services and support to users. The most famous of these on the Internet is the InterNIC, which is where new domain names are registered.

Network Interface Card (NIC)

Workstations communicate with each other and the network server via this circuit board, which is installed in each computer. It can also be referred to as an NIC, LAN card, or network card.

Network Monitor

An SMS utility that functions as a *sniffer* and is used to capture, transmit, and display network packets.

Network printer

A printer shared by multiple computers over a network.

Network server

A network node that provides file management, printing, or other services to other nodes or workstations. A node can function as a file server exclusively or as both a file server and a workstation.

New Technology File System (NTFS)

A fast and reliable file system provided with Windows NT. It is fully recoverable and allows the implementation of local security.

Node

A device at a physical location that performs a control function and influences the flow of data in a network. Node can also refer to the points of connection in the links of a network. Any single computer connected to a network.

Node address

A number that uniquely identifies a network board. It is also referred to as the node number.

Node number

A number that uniquely identifies a network board. It may also be referred to as a station address, physical node address, or node address. Every node must have at least one network board connecting it to the network. Each board must have a unique node number to distinguish it from other network boards on the network.

Non-Domain Local group

Any group created on a Windows 2000 system configured as a stand-alone system, workstation member, or domain member will be created as a Local group.

Nonresident Attribute

An attribute that is not stored in the NTFS directory entry but elsewhere on the hard disk.

Non-Windows application

An application designed to run with DOS but not specifically with Microsoft Windows. The application may not be able to take full advantage of all Windows features, such as memory management.

NT Lan Manager (NTLM) protocol

Authentication protocol used with Windows NT and earlier Windows-family products.

NWLink

The IPX/SPX-compatible protocol provided with Windows 2000. It is used primarily to connect to NetWare servers that support IPX/SPX.

Object

1. In Novell networking, an object contains information about network resources. An object is made up of categories of information, called properties, and the data in those properties. Some objects represent physical entities, like a user or printer. Others represent logical entities, like groups and print queues.

2. In SQL Server, objects are tables, data types, views, stored procedures, indexes, triggers, rules, and constraints.

3. Objects can be compound documents that incorporate data of different formats.

4. An object can also be any program, file, or utility that can be accessed by the user.

5. In some environments, an object is an item that is contained in the site database.

Object attributes

A set of characteristics defining and describing an Active Directory object.

Object Linking and Embedding (OLE)

Microsoft's specification that allows applications to transfer and share data.

Object ownership

The login username of the object's creator becomes the object owner. The owner has full privileges on that object. The system administrator can set up aliases for object creators to ensure that all objects within a database have the same owner's name.

Object permissions

Available permissions (standard permissions and special permissions) for managing Active Directory object access and security.

Object-oriented programming (OOP)

Component-based application development. C++ is a popular object-oriented language, providing classes that combine data and functionality in a single object.

Octet

A set of 8 bits or one byte.

OLE Automation controller

An application that calls the exposed methods of automation servers to perform various tasks.

OLE container

An application that can accept OLE objects and/or controls.

OLE server

An application that provides and manages OLE objects.

One-Way Trust

A trust relationship where trust exists in one direction only.

Open Network Computing (ONC)

A distributed applications architecture promoted and controlled by a consortium led by Sun Microsystems.

Open Shortest Path First (OSPF) protocol

A routing protocol used in larger internetworks. It is more complex to administer than RIP and requires more processing power on the routers, but it is also more efficient for a large internetwork.

Open Systems Interconnection (OSI)

To support international standardization of network terminology and protocols, the International Standards Organization (ISO) proposed a reference model of open systems interconnection. Currently under development, OSI ensures that any open system will communicate with any other OSI-compliant system.

Operating system

The software program that controls all system hardware and provides the user interface.

Operations Master

Active Directory operations that are not permitted to occur at different places in the network at the same time (i.e., single-master).

Operations master roles

Special roles assigned as single-master roles to domain controllers.

Organizational Unit (OU)

Windows 2000 Active Directory container object.

OSI Network Address

The address, consisting of up to 20 octets, used to locate an OSI Transport entity. The address is formatted into an Initial Domain Part, which is standardized for each of several addressing domains, and a Domain Specific Part, which is the responsibility of the addressing authority for that domain.

OSI Presentation Address

The address used to locate an OSI Application entity. It consists of an OSI Network Address and up to three selectors, one each for use by the Transport, Session, and Presentation entities.

OSI Transport Protocol Class 0 (TP0)

Also known as Simple Class, this is the simplest OSI Transport Protocol, useful only on top of an X.25 network (or other network that does not lose or damage data).

OSI Transport Protocol Class 4 (TP4)

Also known as Error Detection and Recovery Class, this is the most powerful OSI Transport Protocol, useful on top of any type of network. TP4 is the OSI equivalent to TCP.

Over-the-network installation

Windows NT and Windows 2000 installations where a shared network directory is used as the installation source.

Owner

An object that creates and/or manages some other object. For example, a dialog box is the owner of the controls that appear on it.

Package

1. An object that contains software installation information. Used to distribute software to client computers.

2. Data Transformation Service (DTS) object defining tasks to be executed.

Packet

A unit of data transmitted at the OSI network layer; or any addressed segment of data transmitted on a network.

Packet Assembler/Disassembler (PAD)

Device that accepts dial-in access for a client system over the PSTN and connects the client to the X.25 public data network.

Packet Internet groper (Ping)

A program used to test reachability of destinations by sending them an ICMP echo request and waiting for a reply. The term is used as a verb: "Ping host X to see if it is operational!"

Parallel ports

In a parallel interface, eight data bits of data are sent at the same time, in parallel, on eight separate wires. Therefore, parallel transmissions are faster than serial transmissions.

Parallel ports, also called LPT ports, were originally used to connect line printers and terminals. Most systems have at least one parallel port, which is called LPT1.

There are two parallel standards: Bi-Tronics and Centronics (IEEE 1284). Centronics cables support a higher data rate. The Centronics connector is a 25-pin D-shell connector and is considered the standard.

Printers generally use parallel communications, as do some early notebook PC network adapters. Devices are available that allow the connection of SCSI devices to a parallel port.

Parity bit

A check bit that is added to each byte to signal the computer that the bits in a byte have transmitted correctly.

Parity check

A technique used to quickly check the integrity of data received after a transmission, or from memory. Parity checking can apply to bytes, words, long words, and other units of information.

Partition

1. An area of storage on a fixed disk that contains a particular operating system or a logical drive where data and programs can be stored.

2. The NetWare Directory database is divided into these logical divisions. A partition represents a distinct unit of data in the Directory tree that can store and replicate Directory information. Each Directory partition has a container object. All objects and data about the objects are contained in it. Directory partitions do not include any information about the file system, directories, or files located therein.

Partition management

A method of management that allows users to divide the Directory into partitions and manage various Directory replicas of these Directory partitions.

Password

A word or set of letters and numbers allowing access to a facility, computer, or network. A password may be accompanied by some other unique identifier before the user is allowed to log in.

Path

1. In hierarchical data structures, such as operating system directories, the path is the chain from a root directory (as in MS-DOS) or volume (as in NetWare) to a specific subdirectory or file.

2. In data communications, the path is the transmission route from sending node to receiving node.

Pathname

The pathname is information that uniquely designates an item on a server. Pathnames have the form "volume/folder/.../name," where the volume is the storage device (typically a hard disk) on which the file resides, and "folder/.../" designates the series of nested folders (or, in the DOS and UNIX worlds, directories) containing the file.

Because pathnames use the slash (/) to separate the labels they contain, it is a good idea not to use slashes in the names of HTML files even when, as on Macs, it is legal to do so. A URL will typically include a pathname.

PDC Emulator

Domainwide operations master role that supports client systems that do not have the Windows 2000 client software and Windows NT domain Backup Domain Controllers (BDCs)

Peer

A Windows Socket application that functions as both a server and a client.

Peer-to-peer

Communication in which two communications systems communicate as equal partners sharing the processing and control of the exchange, as opposed to host-terminal communication in which the host does most of the processing and controls the exchange.

Permissions

Authority to run certain actions on certain database objects or to run certain commands. SQL Server permissions are generated using Grant and Revoke commands.

Per-seat licensing

Microsoft software licensing option where license tracking is based on individual client systems with unlimited server connections supported.

Per-server licensing

Microsoft software licensing option where license tracking is based on concurrent server connections.

PICS

A file format used by some animation applications.

Ping

This utility is used to test the presence of other computers on the network. You can use IP addresses or NetBIOS names if you have a WINS server running or have made the appropriate entry in the LMHOSTS file.

Plug and Play

The specification for a hardware and software architecture that allows automatic device identification and configuration.

Point-to-point

Data communications links are divided into two main categories, depending on how the line is structured: either point-to-point or multipoint. Point-to-point describes a channel that is established between two, and only two, stations. The link may be a dedicated or a dial-up line connecting a processor and a terminal, two processors, or two terminals.

Point-to-Point Protocol (PPP)

The successor to the SLIP protocol, PPP allows a computer to use a regular telephone line and a modem to make IP connections. PPP can also carry other routable protocols such as IPX.

Point-to-Point Tunneling Protocol (PPTP)

Network technology that gives clients using TCP/IP, IPX, or NetBEUI the ability to create a secure VPN over a public TCP/IP network, such as the Internet.

Pointer

Represents the memory address of a data variable.

Pointer (PTR) resource record

Resource record used for reverse lookup zone IP address-to-host name mapping.

Policy

A set of rules regarding resources that are applied to individuals or groups.

Port

1. A memory address that identifies the physical circuit used to transfer information between a microprocessor and a peripheral.

2. On the Internet, *port* often refers to a number that is part of a URL, appearing after a colon (:) immediately after the domain name. Every service on an Internet server listens on a particular port number on that server. Most services have standard port numbers. Web servers normally listen on port 80. Services can also listen on nonstandard ports, in which case the port number must be specified in a URL when accessing the server. You might see a URL of the form: gopher://peg.cwis.uci.edu:7000/, which shows a gopher server running on a nonstandard port (the standard gopher port is 70).

3. Port also refers to translating a piece of software from one type of computer system to another, for example, translating a Windows program to run on a Macintosh.

Portrait

The orientation setting in which the vertical dimension is longer than the horizontal dimension.

Post

To send a message to a network newsgroup or electronic bulletin board.

Preboot Execution Environment (PXE)

Extensions to the DHCP protocol that provide support for RIS to enable Windows 2000 Professional deployment through remote installation.

Preferences

A folder contained in the Macintosh System folder. This folder holds application software preferences established by the system's user.

Preferred Bridgehead server

A site's preferred domain controller for receiving replication data through intersite replication.

Presentation layer

OSI Layer 6. It is the OSI layer that determines how application information is represented (i.e., encoded) while in transit between two end systems.

Prestaging clients

The process of creating a computer account object in the Active Directory that contains the account GUID to uniquely identify the computer. Prestaged clients can be assigned to specific RIS servers as a way of enforcing load balancing between the servers.

Primary Domain Controller (PDC)

The first domain controller created in a Windows NT domain.

Primary partition

A basic disk partition that will have one logical drive ID. A primary partition marked Active is a bootable partition. A basic disk can have multiple primary partitions, but only one may be marked as Active.

Primary Rate ISDN

ISDN connection providing one or more of up to 23 64-Kbps channels.

Print device

Term used to refer to a physical printer, fax, or other device that can be associated with a logical printer.

Print queue

A network directory that stores print jobs. The print server takes the print job out of the queue and sends it when the printer is ready. It can hold as many print jobs as disk space allows.

Print server

A network computer, either dedicated or nondedicated, used to handle the printing needs of workstations.

Print server object

A Leaf object that represents a network print server in the Directory tree.

Print spooler

A program that allows background printing so that a computer may be used for other processing tasks while a print job is in progress.

Printer

A peripheral hardware device that produces printed material. In Windows 2000, refers to a logical printer created on a Windows 2000 system. The logical printer will be associated with one or more physical print devices.

Printer driver

A program that translates the printed file into the language the printer understands. A printer cannot be used unless the correct driver is installed.

Printer object

A Leaf object that represents a physical printing device on the network.

Printer port

A communications port located on the rear panel of a computer, designed for the connection of a printer.

Priority

Sometimes abbreviated as PRI, PRIO, or PRTY; a rank assigned to a task that determines its precedence in receiving system resources.

Private

An access modifier that specifies class members to be accessible only by other members of the class in which they are defined.

Private key

The second part of the key pair. The private key is held by only one person or computer.

Procedure

1. A block of program code with or without formal parameters (the execution of which is invoked by means of a procedure call).

2. A set of executable Visual Basic program steps.

Process

1. Once a 32-bit application is launched, it is loaded into memory. It receives a block of memory addresses. A process cannot execute any commands and does not use any processor time.

2. To perform operations on data in a process; or, a course of events defined by its purpose or by its effect, achieved under given conditions. A course of events occurring according to an intended purpose or effect.

Process throttling

Limiting the amount of processor time that will be made available to a Web site's applications.

Processor

In a computer, the processor, or Central Processing Unit (CPU); this is a functional unit that interprets and executes instructions. A processor contains at least an instruction control unit and an arithmetic and logic unit.

Profile

The group of settings that define a user's working environment. These settings are contained in a Registry file and within the Documents and Settings folder on a Windows 2000 computer.

Program Information File (PIF)

A file used by Microsoft Windows, Windows NT, and Windows 2000 to provide parameters necessary for running non-Windows applications.

Properties

Values related to an object.

Property

A variable containing information about a particular object. Properties can be exposed or private.

Protected

An access modifier that specifies class members to be accessible only to methods in that class and in subclasses of that class.

Protocol

1. A set of strict rules (usually developed by a standards committee) that govern the exchange of information between computer devices. Also, a set of semantic and syntactic rules that determine the behavior of hardware and software in achieving communication.

2. PROTOCOL is also a NetWare 3.x console command that displays the protocols registered on a file server along with the names of their frame types and protocol identification numbers as included by the LAN driver when it is installed.

Proxy

1. The mechanism whereby one system *fronts for* another system in responding to protocol requests. Proxy systems are used in network management to avoid implementing full protocol stacks in simple devices, such as modems.

2. A copy of an out-of-process component's interfaces. Its role is to marshal method and property calls across process boundaries.

Proxy server

A server that is positioned between an internal network and the Internet. The proxy server can be configured to limit which users have access to the Internet, which sites users are allowed to connect to, what protocols users are allowed to use, and to cache Internet requests. Some proxy servers also provide some firewall capability.

Public

An access modifier that specifies class variables and methods to be accessible to objects both inside and outside the class. Public class members have global visibility.

Public key

One of the key pair used for PKI. The public key for each certificate is made available to all users and computers who request the key from the correct source.

Public Key Infrastructure (PKI)

1. A system that is used to provide distributed security to the network. PKI services include Internet Security, logon authentication security, private and public key encryption, and Certificate Services.

2. A method of distributed security that uses certificates and public and private keys to authenticate users and computers, and to secure communication between computers.

3. An encryption scheme that uses a shared key for encryption and decryption of files.

Published printer

This is a printer that has been published in the Active Directory. A printer must be shared before it can be published.

Published resource

A resource that has been published in the Active Directory as an Active Directory object.

Queue

A holding area in which items are removed in a first in, first out (FIFO) manner. In contrast, a stack removes items in a last in, first out (LIFO) manner.

Quota entries

Disk quota limits set for individual users.

RAID 5 volume

Dynamic disk fault-tolerant configuration using multiple disks with data and parity striped across multiple disks. This is an implementation of RAID 5.

Random Access Memory (RAM)

The computer's storage area to write, store, and retrieve information and program instructions so they can be used by the central processing unit. The contents of RAM are not permanent.

Rbfg.exe

Utility used to create an RIS client boot diskette.

Reboot

The process of restarting a computer system.

Recovery Console

Windows 2000 administrative tool that can be launched instead of launching Windows 2000 at startup.

Recursive query

A query made by a client to a DNS server asking that a host name be resolved to an IP address. The DNS server can respond with either the IP address that a client is looking for or with the notification that the host name cannot be resolved to an IP address.

Redirector

Another name for the networking client. The redirector is responsible for redirecting file requests to the network when a client computer is accessing a file that is located on another server.

Registry

Windows NT and Windows 95 configuration database.

Relation

The formal term for a table.

Relationship

The *verb* part of a statement describing the association between two different entities. For example, the relationship between an author and a book is that an author writes books. There is a direct relationship between the two entities. This relationship would be described as many-to-many.

Relative ID master

Domainwide operations master role responsible for managing relative IDs for the domain.

Remote access

The ability of a computer to access an offsite or distant computer using telephone lines or a network.

Remote Access Service (RAS)

In most networks, clients are connected directly to the network. In some cases, however, remote connections are needed for your users. Microsoft provides RAS to let you set up and configure client access.

Users connecting to a RAS server, generally through a modem, can be limited to accessing only that server or can be given access to the entire network. Effectively, this is the same as a local connection to the network except that any type of data transfer runs significantly slower. You will need to select connection options appropriate to your access requirements, available support, and budgetary constraints.

Remote Administration Mode

Terminal Services server mode optimized for support of remote server management.

Remote Authentication Dial-In User Service (RADIUS)

Client/server-based authentication and authorization service for remote access. Connection criteria are passed from the remote access server to the RADIUS server, which will inform the remote access server whether access is allowed or declined.

Remote client

Remote Microsoft Mail user.

Remote Desktop Protocol (RDP)

Protocol used for communication between Terminal Services servers and clients.

Remote Installation Services (RIS)

Windows 2000 services that support remote installation. RIS is based on PXE extensions to DHCP.

Remote management

Use of a remote console by a network supervisor or by a remote console operator to perform file server tasks.

Remote Procedure Call (RPC)

A protocol that standardizes initiation and control processes on remote computers.

Replica

A copy of the data defined by a NetWare Directory partition. The Directory database must be stored on many servers to be distributed across a network. Rather than storing a copy of the entire Directory database at each server, replicas of each Directory partition are stored on many servers. An unlimited number of Directory replicas for each Directory partition can be created and stored on any server.

Replication

The process of copying Active Directory object state to all domain controllers.

Replication partitions

Partitions within the Active Directory database. Each replication partition replicates separately.

Reply

An electronic mail program feature that enables a message receiver to automatically respond to a received message without manually addressing the message.

Resolution

In monitors, this refers to the sharpness of the displayed image or text on a monitor and is a direct function of the number of pixels in the display area. Resolution is the number of pixels across one line of the monitor by the number of lines down the screen (for example, 800x480). The greater the pixel count, the higher the resolution and the clearer the screen image.

Resource record

DNS database entry associating host names with network resources.

Resources

Objects an application needs, such as icons, cursors, and regions.

Restore

To bring back computer data or files that have been lost through tampering or other corruption or through hardware malfunction. Files should be backed up frequently to protect against such loss.

Reverse Address Resolution Protocol (RARP)

Used to map the MAC, or hardware address, to a host's IP, or software address.

If the only thing a station knows at initialization is its own MAC address (usually from configuration information supplied by the manufacturer), how can it learn its IP address? The RARP protocol serves this purpose.

RARP allows a station to send out a broadcast request in the form of a datagram that asks, "Who am I?" or "What is my IP address?" Another host (typically a RARP server) must be prepared to do the inverse of ARP, f. For example, taking the MAC address and mapping it into an IP network and node number. This only happens at startup. RARP is not run again until the next time the device is reset or restarted.

A value of 0x8035 in the Ethernet Type field indicates that the datagram is a RARP datagram. There must be a RARP server on each segment because broadcasting is used, and broadcasts are not normally forwarded by IP routers. All machines on the network receive the request, but only those authorized to supply the RARP service will process the request and send a reply. Such machines are known as RARP servers.

Reverse Lookup query

DNS query used for mapping IP addresses to host names.

Reverse Lookup Zone

DNS zone used for IP address-to-host name resolution.

Ring topology

Provides a closed-loop transmission medium. Repeaters at each node connection duplicate the signal. This is done to minimize signal degradation.

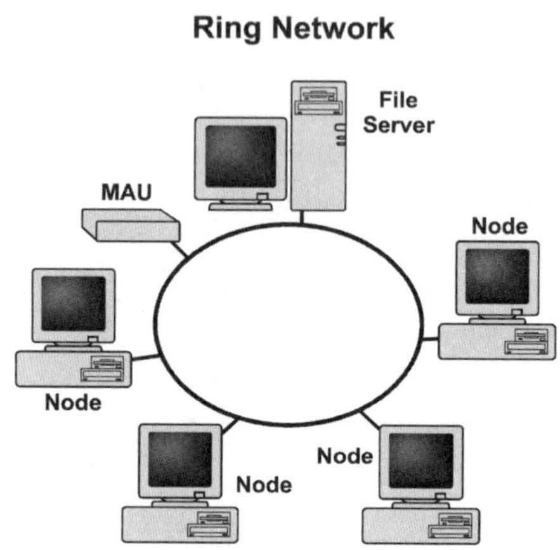

Traditional rings have the same failure risk as a bus topology. Any break brings down the entire network. To prevent this type of failure, most ring implementations (such as Token Ring) are wired in a star topology with an out loop and a return loop from each workstation to the wiring hub.

The Fiber Distributed Data Interface (FDDI) design specification calls for a dual fiber-optic ring. Should a break occur in either ring, it automatically converts to a bus topology.

Riprep.exe

Utility used for creating RIS installation images.

RIPrep image

Installation source image for use with RIS. An RIPrep image is created from an existing Windows 2000 Professional system.

Roaming User Profile (RUP)

User profile that is stored in a network location and made available to the user when logging on to any system in the domain.

Rollback

Cancels a SQL transaction and returns the result set to the state it was in prior to the beginning of the transaction.

Round robin

A DNS configuration option which can be used if multiple computers with different IP addresses have the same host name. The DNS server will provide load balancing by rotating through the IP addresses for successive client requests.

Route

To move data between multiple connected networks.

Router

1. A connection between two networks that specifies message paths and may perform other functions, such as data compression.

2. In early versions of NetWare, the term bridge was sometimes used interchangeably with the term router.

Router configuration

The settings and parameters that configure a NetWare 4 server as a router. They are set through internetwork utilities.

Routing and Remote Access Service (RRAS)

Windows 2000 service that enables a Windows 2000 server to simultaneously support multiprotocol routing, demand-dial routing, and remote access. RRAS supports clients running Windows 2000, Windows NT, Windows 9x, UNIX variants, and Macintosh.

Routing Information Protocol (RIP)

A routing protocol used in small- to medium-sized internetworks. It is easy to configure but not efficient in large internetworks (more than 20 subnets).

Row

The set of data values associated with one instance of the entity that the table describes; one set of columns.

RS-232-C

A low-speed serial interface used to connect data communications equipment (such as modems and terminals) defined as a standard by the Electronic Industries Association. All standards recommended by the EIA have an RS prefix.

Rule

SQL Server referential integrity feature ensuring that a value either falls within a specific range, matches a specified pattern, or matches a value from a specified list.

Scale

Stretch or shrink the contents to fit inside a specific area.

Scheduler

Also known as a dispatcher. The part of the operating system that determines which thread should run and the relative priority of each executing thread.

Schema master

Forestwide operations master role that controls schema updates and modifications.

Schema partition

Replication partition containing the Active Directory schema. The schema partition replicates to all domain controllers in a forest.

Scope

1. A group of IP addresses as well as other TCP/IP configuration information that the DHCP server can provide for DHCP clients.

2. Variable scope refers to where in the application a variable can be seen. Scope can be limited to a procedure, a module, or global (visible throughout the application).

3. Project scope refers to the definition of features, requirements, schedule, and budget for a project.

Screensaver

A system utility used to prevent monitor damage by powering the video monitor down or displaying a moving graphic.

Script

Set of executable statements written in a scripting language supported by Windows Script Host (WSH).

Search engine

A search engine is a computer or group of computers that provides search capabilities for resources on the Internet.

Sector

In disk drives, each track is divided into sectors. Sectors resemble pieces of a pie.

Sector sparing

Disk fault tolerance feature that allows remapping of bad sectors to an alternate sector when disk I/O errors occur.

Secure MIME (S/MIME)

An Internet standard used to digitally sign and encrypt e-mail messages.

Secure Sockets Layer (SSL)

An authentication and encryption standard that uses PKI to authenticate users when connecting to a secure Web site and encrypts all data that flows between the Web server and client.

Security Association (SA)

A security agreement between two computers using IPSec that defines the levels of encryption supported by both computers.

Security Configuration and Analysis

MMC snap-in that can be used to review and analyze local security policy, edit local security policy, and import and apply a security template on a stand-alone or workgroup member Windows 2000 system.

Security descriptor

A structure that contains information about which users can access an object and for what purpose. Only objects created under Windows NT can have security descriptors.

Security Identifier (SID)

Unique identifier value used in Windows NT Workstation and NT Server security management.

Security group

At the time of their creation, the three kinds of groups–Local, Global, and Universal–can be classified within Active Directory as a security group or a distribution group. The security classification allows rights and permissions to be assigned to the group. Distribution groups, on the other hand, are nonsecure groups that are primarily used for e-mail distribution lists or other means of nonsecure communication.

Security Template

File representing a security configuration defined as a group of security settings. Security templates can be applied to domain or local Group Policy Objects.

Segment

1. A self-contained portion of a computer program that may be executed without the entire computer program necessarily being maintained in internal storage at any one time.

2. In computer graphics, a segment is a collection of display elements that can be manipulated as a unit. A segment may consist of several and separate dots, line segments, or other display elements.

3. In TCP/IP, a segment is a message block.

4. Named collection of SQL Server disk storage pieces.

Sender

A component within the SMS Executive service that is used to send data from one site to another.

Serial communication

The transmission of data between devices over a single line, one bit at a time.

Serial interface

A connection point through which information is transferred one digital bit at a time. The term serial interface is sometimes applied to interfaces in which the data is transferred serially via one path, but some control signals can be transferred simultaneously via parallel paths.

Serial Line IP (SLIP)

An Internet protocol used to run IP to connect two systems over serial lines such as telephone circuits or RS-232 cables. SLIP is now being replaced by PPP.

Serial multitasking

The process by which multiple programs execute, but only one at a time.

Serial port

In a serial interface, bits of information are sent in a series, one at a time. Data bits are typically surrounded by starting and ending flags, which provide synchronization.

Serial ports are also called communications (COM) ports and referenced by number; COM1 is serial port 1. Most systems come with two COM ports.

The standard serial port connector is a 9-pin D-shell connector, but some systems still have older 25-pin D-shell connectors. Adapters are available to convert between the two standard connectors. With either connector, only 9 connector pins are soldered to 9 wires inside the cable.

Most serial cables are no longer than 50 feet. Use of longer cables can result in transmission errors.

Modems, serial printers, and serial mice use serial communications.

A new bus type, the Universal Serial Bus (USB), will become more prevalent in the future. The concept behind the USB is to consolidate all desktop peripherals into a single high-speed (12-Mbps) access route.

The USB allows up to 64 devices to be daisy-chained together. The single USB connector type will support many devices, including some that in the past used the serial, parallel, keyboard, mouse, or game ports.

The USB will usher in a new set of hardware peripherals and accessories, including products such as digital cameras and virtual-reality gloves.

More information about USB can be found at the Universal Bus Implementers Forum Home Page: www.usb.org.

Serial transmission

Transmission in which data (binary digits) can be transmitted only one bit at a time using only one communications line. In contrast, parallel transmission sends each byte simultaneously using separate lines. Connections exceeding one meter in distance typically use serial transmission.

Server

A computer or a software package that provides services to client software running on other computers on a network. Possible services include file sharing, printer sharing, or communications services.

Server Manager

In Windows NT Server, the Server Manager lets you manage domain members and provides a quick way of viewing information about your domain. With Server Manager, you can view system properties or view and manage shared directories and services running on Windows NT Workstations and Servers. It will also allow you to add member systems to, or remove member systems from, the domain, promote a backup domain controller into the role of domain controller, and broadcast messages to the domain. You can also view and manage trusting domains.

DOS, Windows 3.x, and Windows for Workgroups stations will be listed while active on the domain but are not registered as domain members.

Server Message Block (SMB)

The protocol used by Microsoft servers to exchange data, such as files and print jobs, across a network connection.

Service provider

A DLL that interfaces with a device or third-party application. A service provider is generally developed by the developer of the device or application it supports.

Service (SRV) resource record

Resource record identifying a server hosting a particular service.

Session

1. That group of processes or tasks associated with an application.

2. A NetWare 3.1x menu utility used to change a user's environment while logged in to the server. It can be used to change file servers, log out, view a list of network groups or users, or send a message to a group or user. It can display, add, delete, or modify drive mappings.

Session key

Encrypts and decrypts the contents of a message. In most PKI implementations, the public key is used to encrypt the session key. Also called a symmetric or bulk encryption key.

Session Layer

OSI Layer 5, which is the OSI layer that provides means for dialogue control between end systems.

Session ticket

Ticket granted in a Kerberos authentication providing access to a network resource.

Sets

Groups of rows to which aggregates apply.

Setup Manager

Utility that can be used to automatically create answer files and distribution folders for unattended Windows 2000 installations.

Setupact.log

File created during Windows 2000 Setup listing all file operations taking place during GUI mode Setup.

Setuperr.log

File created during Windows 2000 Setup listing errors reported by devices or services during Setup.

Setuplog.txt

File created during Windows 2000 Setup listing each driver and service loaded and each DLL registered by Setup.

Share name

The name given to a shared resource. The universal naming convention references machine name and share name.

Share Point

A shared resource identified by a UNC name.

Shared printer

This is a printer that has been shared to the network and can be accessed by its UNC path.

Shell

A portion of a program that responds to user commands, also called user interface. The shell is loaded as a Terminate-and-Stay Resident program (TSR).

Shortcut

A technique that allows a Windows 95 or Windows NT user to create a link to a file or program in an alternative location.

Signed driver

A device driver that has been digitally signed by Microsoft certifying that the driver has passed the WHQL Windows 2000 certification tests. The digital signature is recognized natively by Windows 2000 systems.

Simple Mail Transfer Protocol (SMTP)

The Internet standard protocol for transferring electronic mail messages between computers.

Simple Network Management Protocol (SNMP)

One of the most comprehensive tools available for TCP/IP network management. It operates through conversations between SNMP agents and management systems. Through these conversations, the SNMP management systems can collect statistics from and modify configuration parameters on agents.

The agents are any components running the SNMP agent service and are capable of being managed remotely. Agents can include minicomputers, mainframes, workstations, servers, bridges, routers, gateways, terminal servers, and wiring hubs.

Management stations are typically more powerful workstations. Common implementations are Windows NT or UNIX stations running a product such as HP OpenView, IBM Systemview/6000, or Cabletron Spectrum. The software provides a graphic representation of the network, allowing you to move through the network hierarchy to the individual device level.

There are three basic commands used in SNMP conversations: GET, SET, and TRAP.

The GET command is used by the management station to retrieve a specific parameter value from an SNMP agent. If a combination of parameters is grouped together on an agent, GET-NEXT retrieves the next item in a group. For example, a management system's graphic representation of a hub includes the state of all status lights. This information is gathered through GET and GET-NEXT.

The management system uses SET to change a selected parameter on an SNMP agent. For example, SET would be used by the management system to disable a failing port on a hub.

SNMP agents send TRAP packets to the management system in response to extraordinary events, such as a line failure on a hub. When the hub status light goes red on the management systems representation, it is in response to a TRAP.

An SNMP management station generates GET and SET commands. Agents are able to respond to SET and GET and to generate TRAP commands.

Simple volume

Dynamic disk configuration with all disk space coming from one hard disk. Disk space assigned to the volume does not have to be contiguous.

Single Domain Model

Simplest Windows NT Server domain model where only one domain exists on the network.

Site

1. (Active Directory) A group of domain controllers defined by a set of one or more subnet addresses. Sites are used in managing Active Directory replication, logon, and the Distributed File System (Dfs).

2. Any location of Internet files and services.

3. A group of domains and/or computers. A site can be either a Primary or Secondary site. The Central site is the highest site in the heirarchy and can administer all sites in the system.

Site link

A communication path between two or more servers.

Site link bridge

Object used for bridging site links when the IP transport transitive link feature is turned off.

Site link cost

A relative value used for identifying faster and slower site links. The site link cost is used to determine a preferred path for replication data when multiple paths are available.

SLIP

An Internet protocol used to run IP over serial lines such as telephone circuits or RS-232 cables interconnecting two systems. SLIP is now being replaced by PPP.

Slipstreaming

A process whereby a Windows 2000 service pack is applied to an installation file set. This allows the service pack to be applied automatically to the destination system during installation.

Smart

Containing microprocessor intelligence. A modem or adapter is smart if it has its own computer chip. A dumb device is limited in functions and features and takes processing power from a high-level system.

Smart card

A device used to authenticate users on a network. Within PKI, the smart card contains the user's certificates and private keys.

Snap-in

A management tool designed to run in the Microsoft Management Console (MMC) environment.

Socket

1. Information that is used when two computers are connecting to each other across an IP network. A socket consists of the IP address of the intended computer, a protocol number (TCP or UDP), and a port number.

2. The destination of an IPX packet is represented by this part of an IPX internetwork address in a network node. Some sockets are reserved by Novell for specific applications; all NCP request packets are delivered to socket 451h. By registering those numbers with Novell, third-party developers can reserve socket numbers for specific purposes.

Software

A computer program, or a set of instructions written in a specific language, that commands the computer to perform various operations on data contained in the program or supplied by the user.

Spanned volume

Dynamic disk configuration using disk space from multiple hard disks.

Spooler

System software used to provide background printing.

SRV resource records

A new type of resource record used in Windows 2000 to identify servers on the network that provide network resources, such as domain controllers and LDAP servers.

Stamp

A set of values used for conflict resolution during replication. The stamp includes three values: the USN version number (Version), the time when the change was made (Originating Time), and the originating domain controller (originating DSA).

Stand-alone Dfs root

Dfs root hosted on a server and stored in the server's Registry. Root and link replicas are not supported by a stand-alone Dfs root.

Stand-alone snap-in

A single management utility designed to run in the Microsoft Management Console (MMC) environment.

Standard primary

Zone name server configuration option where the zone database is stored locally as a text file.

Standard secondary

Zone name server with a replica of a standard zone database file.

Start menu

The pop-up menu containing Windows 95 functions that is accessed by pressing the **Start** button on the Taskbar.

Start of Authority (SOA) resource record

Resource record identifying the primary name server or authoritative source for a zone.

Station

A term used as a shortened form of workstation, but it can also refer to a server, router, printer, fax machine, or any computer device connected to a network by a network board and communication medium.

Stream transmission

A connection-oriented transfer of data between two sockets.

Stream-oriented

A type of transport service that allows its client to send data in a continuous stream in the same order as sent and without duplicates.

String

A sequence of characters, whether they make sense or not. For example, "dogcow" is a string, but so is "z@x#tt!." Every word is a string, but relatively few strings are words. A search form will sometimes ask you to enter a search string, meaning a keyword or keywords to search on. Sometimes string means a sequence that does not include space, tab, return, and other blank or nonprinting characters.

Stripe set

Basic disk configuration using multiple disks with data striped across the disks for performance improvement. This is an implementation of RAID 0.

Stripe set with parity

Basic disk fault-tolerant configuration using multiple disks with data and parity striped across multiple disks. This is an implementation of RAID 5.

Striped volume

Dynamic disk configuration using multiple disks with data striped across the disks for performance improvement. This is an implementation of RAID 0.

Structured Query Language (SQL)

An ISO data-definition and data-manipulation language for relational databases. Variations of SQL are offered by most major vendors for their relational database products. SQL is consistent with IBM's Systems Application Architecture and has been standardized by the American National Standards Institute (ANSI).

Subdirectory

This is a directory that lies below another in the file system structure. For example, in SALES/NEW, NEW is a subdirectory of SALES.

Subnet

The primary reason to divide a network into subnets is network performance and available bandwidth. Without separate networks, each transmission would be broadcast across the entire internetwork, waiting for the destination system to respond. As the network grows, this causes increases in traffic until it exceeds the available bandwidth.

Subnets

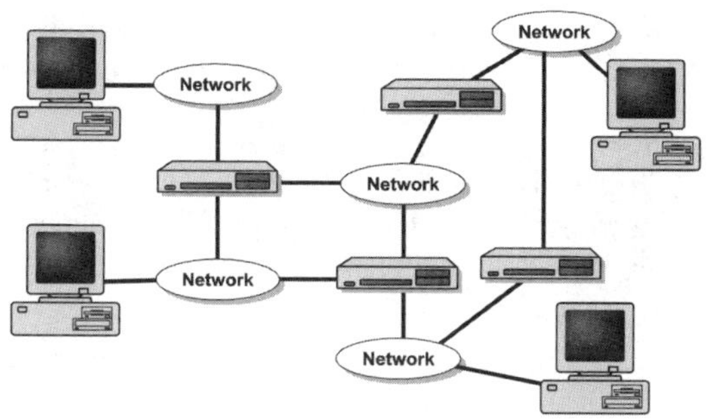

Routers divide, as well as provide, communications between the networks. Packets bound for a destination within the local network are kept local. Only packets bound for other networks are broadcast across the network, moving from router to router. Overall traffic levels are reduced.

Subnet mask

A filter that separates subnetted addresses into network and local entities. Local systems have subnet masks so they can restrict the broadcast to be received on the local network only.

Subnetting

When a complex network is recognized as a single address from outside of the network.

Subnetwork

A collection of OSI end systems and intermediate systems under the control of a single administrative domain and utilizing a single network access protocol. For example, private X.25 networks amid a collection of bridged LANs.

Superscopes

A configuration option in WINS that can be used to combine multiple scopes into one logical scope.

Switch

A statement that selects an action from a number of alternatives. Switch compares the value of an integer test-expression with each of several case labels.

Symmetric Multiprocessing (SMP)

In an SMP operating system such as Windows NT, the operating system can run on any processor or can share tasks between several processors. User and applications threads can also be shared between processors, making best use of processor time and reducing bottlenecks.

Synchronization

1. Replica synchronization is a way to ensure that replicas of a NetWare Directory partition have the same information as other replicas of the same partition. Time synchronization is a way to ensure all servers in a NetWare Directory tree register the same time.

2. Under SQL Server replication, this is the process of copying database schema and data from a publishing server to a subscription server.

3. When discussing the Internet, it is the process of setting the same clock or data rate in the receiving terminal as in the sending terminal. This is a requirement to enable the receiving device to read the incoming bits and to translate them into characters. Synchronization, accomplished by a signal from the sending terminal, enables the receiving band to recognize any single bit and to identify which group of bits belongs in which characters. Once the first bit of a character is recognized, the receiver can count off the required number of bits and identify each character if it learns the number of bits in the character and the speed at which the bits are coming. Two common approaches to synchronized transmission between devices are synchronous transmission and asynchronous transmission.

Synchronous

Pertaining to two or more processes that depend upon the occurrence of a specific event such as a common timing signal.

Sysprep

A Windows 2000 utility that prepares the hard drive of a fully configured master computer for duplication and deployment. Sysprep requires that the master and target computers have identical HALs, ACPI support, and mass storage controllers.

A third-party disk-imaging tool is necessary to both create the actual image of the installation and deploy it to other computers.

Sysprep.inf

Answer file used by the Mini-Setup Wizard as an unattended installation of a Windows 2000 image created using Sysprep.

System ACL (SACL)

The System ACL controls auditing messages to be generated for the object and written to the Security log in the Event Viewer.

System configuration

A process that specifies the devices and programs that form a particular data-processing system.

System Default Profile

A Windows NT profile defining background color, screen saver, and wallpaper settings when no user is logged on.

System Information Snap-in

MMC snap-in that displays system information including, but not limited to, the system configuration summary, resource usage, and resource conflicts.

System Monitor Snap-in

MMC snap-in that is used to view and record activity from performance counters.

System software

The operating system software.

System state data

Critical Windows 2000 local system components such as the Registry and system boot files.

Sysvol folder

Shared folder installed on each Active Directory domain controller. The folder contains scripts and part of the domain's Group Policy Objects.

T1

A leased-line connection capable of carrying data at 1,544,000 bits per second. At maximum theoretical capacity, a T1 line could move a megabyte in less than 10 seconds. That is still not fast enough for full-screen, full-motion video, for which you need at least 10,000,000 bits per second. T1 is the fastest speed commonly used to connect networks to the Internet.

T2

A leased-line connection capable of carrying data at 6,312,000 bits per second.

T3

A leased-line connection capable of carrying data at 45,000,000 bits per second. This is more than enough to do full-screen, full-motion video.

Table

A rectangular display of data values shown as horizontal rows and vertical columns.

Table list

The list of tables, views, or both following the From keyword in a Select statement.

Tape backup device

This internal or external tape drive backs up data from hard disks.

Target

Any server, workstation, or service on the network that has a Target Service Agent loaded. The data can be backed up or restored on a target. When backing up and restoring to the host server, the target and host become the same.

Task

In a multiprogramming or multiprocessing environment, one or more sequences of instructions created by a control program as an element of work to be accomplished by a computer.

Telnet

1. The Telnet protocol is a part of the TCP/IP protocol suite. Many Internet nodes support Telnet, which is similar to UNIX's rlogin program. Telnet lets users log in to any other computer on the Internet, provided that the target computer allows Telnet logins, and the user has a valid login name and password. The computers do not have to be of the same type to Telnet between them.

Some systems expect external access, and a special software package is set up to handle outside calls. This eliminates the need to *log in* once a user reaches the remote host.

The most popular reason to log in to a remote computer is to run software that is available only on the remote computer. Another reason is when a user's computer is incompatible with a particular program, operating system, available memory, or doesn't have the necessary processing power.

People with several Internet accounts can use Telnet to switch from one account to the other without logging out of any of the accounts.

Users can use Telnet as an information-gathering tool by searching databases for information. These databases include LOCIS (the Library of Congress Information System), CARL (Colorado Association of Research Libraries), ERIC (Educational Resources Information Center), and CIJE (Current Index to Journals in Education).

2. An Internet standard user-level protocol that allows a user's remote terminal to log in to computer systems on the Internet. To connect to a computer using Telnet, the user types Telnet and the address of the site or host computer.

Terminal

A device that allows you to send commands to a computer somewhere else. At a minimum, this usually means a keyboard and a display screen and some simple circuitry. Usually you will use terminal software in a personal computer. The software pretends to be ("emulates") a physical terminal and allows you to type commands to a computer somewhere else.

Terminal emulation

The use of hardware and software on a personal computer to duplicate the operation of a terminal device at both the operator and communications interface sides of the connection so that a mainframe computer capable of supporting the emulated terminal will also support the PC.

Terminal emulator

A program that allows a computer to act like a terminal when logged in to a remote host. The VT100 terminal is emulated by many popular communications packages.

Terminal server

A special-purpose computer that has places to plug in many modems on one side and a connection to a LAN or host machine on the other side. Thus, the terminal server does the work of answering the calls and passes the connections on to the appropriate node. Most terminal servers can provide PPP or SLIP services if connected to the Internet.

Terminal Services

Windows 2000 service providing a Windows 2000 desktop environment for clients with Win32 operating systems that are unable to fully support a local installation of Windows 2000.

Text fields

An input box where a user accepts a single line of text.

Thread

The object of a process that is responsible for executing a block of code. A process can have one or multiple threads.

Threads

Each process must have at least one thread. Threads are responsible for executing code.

Ticket-Granting Ticket (TGT)

Ticket granted by a Key Distribution Center (KDC) in Kerberos that is used to request session tickets.

Time out

When two computers are talking and, for whatever reason, one of the computers fails to respond.

Time to Live (TTL)

The amount of time between when a packet of data leaves its point of origin and when it reaches its destination. The TTL is encoded in the IP header and is used as a hop count (to measure the route to the packet's destination).

Title bar

A line displayed at the top of a window or dialog box.

Token

In a LAN (Local Area Network), the symbol of authority that is passed successively from one data station to another to indicate the station temporarily in control of the transmission medium. Each data station has an opportunity to acquire and use the token to control the medium.

Token bus

A form of network, usually a local area network (LAN), in which access to the transmission medium is controlled by a token. The token is passed from station-to-station in a sequence. A station wishing to transmit will do so by removing the token from the bus and replacing it with the data to be transmitted. When transmission is complete, the transmitting station will reinitiate the token-passing process.

Token Ring

IBM originally created Token Ring (IEEE 802.5). Over the last few years, it has steadily gained popularity.

It is a network that runs as a logical ring but is usually wired as a physical star. It has a 4-Mbps or 16-Mbps transfer rate and runs on Unshielded Twisted Pair, Shielded Twisted Pair, or Fiber Optic cabling.

A Token (data frame) passes from system to system. A system can attach data to a token if the token is free (empty). In turn, each system on the ring receives, regenerates, and passes the token.

Token Passing in a Token Ring Network

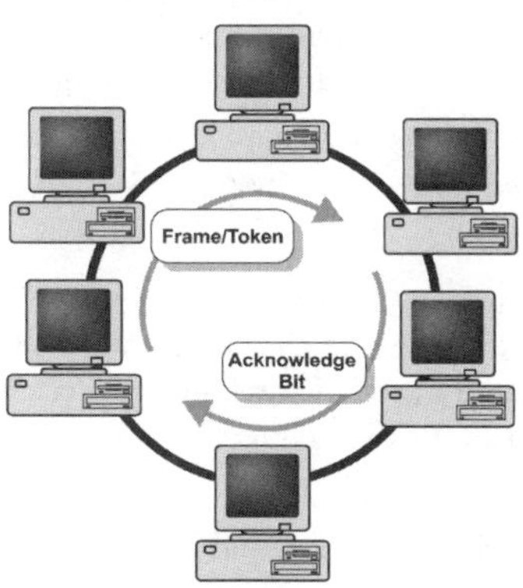

With Token Ring, it is possible to predict the passage of the token. The predictability inherent in Token Ring makes it a popular choice for timing-critical and control applications.

Topology

Refers to the physical layout of network components (such as cables, stations, gateways, and hubs).

Tracks

On a disk, data is organized into concentric circles, or tracks, on the disk medium. One complete circle represents one track. Tracks on disks are analogous to the tracks you might see on a record used in a record player (curving lines on the record surface). Tracks are typically numbered from the outermost track to the innermost, or from the outer edge of the medium to the inner hub area. To figure out the number of tracks on a fixed disk drive, multiply the number of cylinders by the number of heads.

Traffic

The total information flow in a communications system.

Transitive replication partner

An indirect source for Active Directory replication.

Transitive trust

Trust relationships that are propagated to all domains in a Windows 2000 network. Transitive trust rules state, "If A trusts B, and A trusts C, then B trusts C."

Transmission

The electrical transfer of a message signal from one location to another.

Transmission Control Protocol (TCP)

The reliable connection-oriented protocol used by DARPA (Defense Advanced Research Projects Agency) for their internetworking research. TCP uses a three-way handshake with a clock-based sequence number selection to synchronize connecting entities and to minimize the chance of erroneous connections due to delayed messages. TCP is usually used with IP (Internet Protocol), the combination being known as TCP/IP.

Transmission Control Protocol/Internet Protocol (TCP/IP)

1. Originally designed for WANs (Wide Area Networks), TCP/IP was developed in the 1970s to link the research center of the U.S. Government's Defense Advanced Research Projects Agency. TCP/IP is a protocol that enables communication between the same or different types of computers on a network. TCP/IP can be carried over a wide range of communication channels. The Transmission Control Protocol is connection-oriented and monitors the correct transfer of data between computers. The Internet Protocol is stream-oriented and breaks data into packets.

2. The preferred protocol for Windows 2000 networks. In order for Windows 2000 client computers to communicate with Windows 2000 servers, both must have TCP/IP configured correctly.

Transmit

To send data from one place for reception elsewhere. Also, moving an entity from one place to another, as in broadcasting radio waves, dispatching data via a transmission medium, or transferring data from one data station to another via a line.

Transport layer

OSI Layer 4, which is responsible for reliable end-to-end data transfer between end systems.

Tree

A collection of one or more domains that share a common namespace.

Tunneling

A method of encapsulating data for transmission between two authenticated end points.

Unattend.txt

Default name for an answer file used during over-the-network unattended Windows NT and Windows 2000 installations.

Unattended installation

An operating system installation run without end-user interaction. Answers to Setup prompts are supplied by text files called answer files.

Uniform Resource Locator (URL)

A URL is the pathname of a document on the Internet. URLs can be absolute or relative. An absolute URL consists of a prefix denoting a *method* (http for Web sites, gopher for gophers, and so forth). The prefix is followed by a colon, two slashes (://), and an address. The address consists of a domain name followed by a slash and a pathname (or "username@domain name" for mailto). The last part is an optional anchor, which is preceded by a #. The # symbol points to a place within the Web page.

Uniqueness Database File (UDF)

A text file containing unique responses used to override answer file responses during Windows NT and Windows 2000 unattended installations.

Universal group

An Active Directory group available only in native mode that can contain domain users from anywhere within a tree or forest.

Universal Naming Convention (UNC)

A file-naming convention that uses the *machine_name**share_name* format.

Universal Serial Bus (USB)

A standard promoted by Intel for communication between an IBM PC and an external peripharal over an inexpensive cable using biserial transmission.

USB works at 12 Mbps with specific cost consideration for low-cost peripherals. It supports up to 127 devices and both isochronous and asynchronous data transfers. Cables can be up to 5 m long, and it includes built-in power distribution for low power devices. It supports daisy-chaining through a tiered multidrop topology.

Before March 1996, Intel started to integrate the necessary logic into PC chip sets and encourage other manufacturers to do likewise, so currently there is widespread availability and support.

Because of its relatively low speed, USB is intended to replace existing serial ports, parallel ports, keyboard and monitor connectors, and be used with keyboard, mice, monitors, printers, and possibly some low-speed scanners and removable hard drives. For faster devices, existing IDE, SCSI, or emerging FC-AL or FireWire interfaces can be used.

UNIX

A computer operating system originally developed at AT&T's Bell Research Laboratories and later at the University of California Berkeley. It is implemented in a growing number of minicomputer and microcomputer systems.

UNIX is *multi-user* because it is designed to be used by many people at the same time and has TCP/IP built into the operating system. It is the most common operating system for servers on the Internet.

Update Sequence Number (USN)

Value used to track changes made to Active Directory objects.

User

1. An individual permitted to access a computer, network, or other system.

2. SQL Server database access account.

User account

Security object used for logon authentication and resource access verification.

User interface

A program operated by a computer user to interact with the computer. Also known as user agent.

User login script

This login script sets environment specifics for a user. It is optional but most often used for items that cannot be included in a system or profile login script. If used, it will run after container and profile login scripts.

User mode

1. The default Microsoft Management Console (MMC) mode that allows users to use, but not modify, MMC custom consoles. Three modes of varying restrictions are available for setting.

2. Higher-level Windows NT, Windows 95, or Windows 98 operating system functions. The user mode includes the protected subsystems and application sessions.

User object

A leaf object in NDS that represents a person with access to the network and stores information about this person.

User profile

Collection of folders containing information about a user's desktop environment, application settings, and other personal data that is applied when a user logs on.

Username

The name by which a login ID is known within the context of a database.

Utility

The capability of a system, program, or device to perform the functions it was designed for.

Value

A single data element, such as contents of one column-one row intersection.

Variable

In programming, a variable is used for temporary data storage. Each variable will have an identifying name, a data type, and an assigned (or assumed) value.

The term declaration is used to refer to the statement that causes a variable to be created.

The two types of variable declarations in Visual Basic are explicit and implicit.

An explicit declaration is when a variable is defined or created before it is needed. This is normally a better method of defining variables because it forces better planning and control.

With implicit declaration, the variable is defined *on the fly.* You define the variable by referring to it as part of a program statement. Any time Visual Basic encounters a name in your code that is not defined elsewhere, a new variable is created using that name.

Video card

The hardware board that contains the electronic circuitry to drive a video display monitor.

View

A method of creating custom presentation of data stored in database tables.

Virtual directory

Web site directory linked to a different physical directory location that serves as a means to extend the home directory.

Virtual machine

The Windows technique used to execute an application. Virtual machines include a virtual address space, processor registers, and privileges.

Virtual Private Network (VPN)

Remote access configuration where users and remote networks connect to network servers across the Internet. A tunnel is created through the Internet and all of the data that crosses the Internet is encrypted. Windows 2000 supports two protocols for setting up VPNs: Point-to-Point Tunneling Protocol (PPTP) or Layer 2 Tunneling Protocol/IPSec (L2TP/IPSec).

Virus

A program that can destroy data and change itself to escape detection. A virus can move into other computer systems by incorporating itself into programs or files that are shared among computer systems.

Visual Basic

A general purpose programming language for the Microsoft Windows family of products.

Volume set

Multiple basic disk partitions joined as one logical drive.

Voluntary tunnel

A tunnel created by a client computer to a target server.

WebDAV

Protocol that, when used with IIS, supports Web folders. This allows clients to manage remote folders and files through the Internet using an HTTP connection. File and folder maintenance can be performed using Internet Explorer 5, a Microsoft Office 2000 application, or any network connection using Windows 2000. WebDAV is an extention of the HTTP 1.1 standard.

WebDAV Publishing Directory

Special virtual directory that supports client read, write, delete, copy, move, and search operations. The WebDAV Publishing Directory is created by using the IIS Snap-in.

Well-connected sites

Sites that communicate through high-speed connections.

Wide Area Network (WAN)

Expands the basic LAN model by linking Local Area Networks (LANs) and allowing them to communicate with each other. By traditional definition, a LAN becomes a WAN when it crosses a public right-of-way, requiring a public carrier for data transmission. More current usage of the term usually includes any situation where a network expands beyond one location/building. A WAN is characterized by low- to high-speed communication links and usually covers a wide geographic area. The remote links may be operational LANs or only groups of workstations. With the exception of a WAN's wider area of operation, the benefits and features of LANs and WANs are the same.

Win32 Driver Model (WDM)

Specification defining device driver file architecture for Windows 2000 family- and Windows 98-compatible device driver files.

Windows (Microsoft)

A graphical shell operating environment that runs on top of DOS. It contains many accessories and features that access DOS functions, such as file, program, and printer management. Windows is referred to as a GUI (Graphical User Interface).

Windows Hardware Quality Labs (WHQL)

Testing entity for certifying WDM device drivers for digital signing.

Windows NT (NT)

An acronym for New Technology.

Windows Script Host (WSH)

Environment for running scripts without the need of a container application.

Winnt.exe

Windows NT and Windows 2000 Setup program. Winnt.exe runs on MS-DOS and 16-bit Windows-family operating systems.

Winnt.sif

Answer file used when running an unattended installation of Windows 2000 by booting from the Installation CD-ROM.

Winnt32.exe

Windows NT and Windows 2000 Setup program. Winnt32.exe runs on 32-bit Windows-family operating systems.

WINS proxy

A special function that can be assigned to a Windows 2000 server that enables the server to forward registration and name resolution requests from non-WINS clients to a WINS server.

Workgroup

A defined set of Windows for Workgroups, Windows 95, or NT stations that are able to communicate and share file and print resources.

Workstation

A personal computer that is connected to a network. It can perform tasks through application programs or utilities. The term client or station may also be used.

World Wide Web (WWW)

A recent, and the fast-growing, addition to the Internet.

In 1991, Tim Berners-Lee developed the World Wide Web for the European Council for Nuclear Research (CERN). It was designed as a means of communicating research and ideas between members of the high-energy physics community.

Browsers are the client tools that allow users to view the contents of the Web. The Web at that time had no easily accessible viewing capabilities. The browsers were text-only, line-mode tools that offered no graphical capabilities and few navigation links.

Early in 1993, a team at the National Center for Supercomputing Applications (NCSA) at the University of Illinois at Champaign-Urbana developed an Internet browsing program called Mosaic. The NCSA had no way to disseminate or market the program.

Later that year, a former NCSA graduate student (Tim Krauskopf) offered the University of Illinois a business plan and was given the rights to license Mosaic. The company is called Spyglass. Another company, with the help of former NCSA programmers, created its own Internet browser company and wanted to call it Mosaic Communications, but the NCSA would not allow this. The company was renamed Netscape, and their graphical Web browser was named Netscape Navigator. Netscape markets its browsers and servers directly to consumers, while Spyglass markets Mosaic to component suppliers such as AT&T, IBM, and Microsoft.

Because the Mosaic project initiated the graphical browser implementation, the term Mosaic is sometimes still used to describe any graphical Web browser.

The Web unifies many of the existing network tools with hypertext (also called hyperlinks). Hypertext gives users the ability to explore paths of information in nonlinear ways. Instead of reading through files in a preplanned sequential arrangement, users can move from item to item in any order they choose.

Some hyperlinks lead to ftp sites, newsgroups, gopher sites, and other Web sites that house additional graphical Web documents. To navigate these Web sites and find links, search engines are available. While current engines can only identify sites that meet the user's criteria, second-generation search engines will use artificial intelligence to report to users on information that exactly meets their needs.

The graphical interfaces make the Internet much more appealing, powerful, and simple. Besides being more intuitive than text-based tools, graphical browsers offer full hypermedia support. As recently as 1994, few trade journals mentioned the Web.

Today, Web addresses (URLs) are included in television, radio, magazine, and movie advertisements and on billboards. By 1995, Web traffic was doubling every four months and was growing more than twice as fast as general Internet traffic. Entire businesses now reside on the Web, and millions of people use it for communications and educational resources.

Wscript

Windows Script Host component that hosts a script in a Windows GUI environment.

X.25

A data communications interface specification that describes how data passes into and out of packet-switching networks. The protocol suite approved by the CCITT and International Standards Organization (ISO) defines the origination, termination, and use of virtual circuits that connect host computers and terminals across the network.

ZAP file

A file type used with the Windows Installer Service. ZAP files are similar to INI files and provide installation instructions.

Zone

A grouping of logical devices on one or more networks based on DNS domain namespace.

Zone delegation

The process by which an authoritative server is identified for a subdomain, creating a new zone. The procedure will create a new DNS database with initial SOA and NS resource records.

Zone Information Protocol (ZIP)

Responsible for linking users and resources on the network with the appropriate zone.

Zone integration

The process of integrating Active Directory and non-Active Directory domains for interoperability.

Zone List

A list of zones (up to 255).

Zone Root Domain

Topmost zone in a DNS zone hierarchy.

Zone transfer

The process by which standard secondary zone server database copies are updated.

ACRONYMS

—A—

AAL	ATM Adaptation Layer
Abend	Abnormal end
ABR	Automatic Baud Rate Detection
ACDI	Asynchronous Communications Device Interface
ACE	Access Control Entry
ACF/VTAM	Advanced Communications Function/Virtual Telecommunications Access Method
ACK	Acknowledgment
ACL	Access Control List
ACPI	Advanced Configuration and Power Interface
ACSE	Association Control Service Element
AD	Administrative Domain
ADB	Apple Desktop Bus
ADMD	Administration Management Domain
ADO	ActiveX Data Objects
ADSI	Active Directory Services Interface
ADSP	AppleTalk Data Stream Protocol
AEP	AppleTalk Echo Protocol
AFP	AppleTalk Filing Protocol
AGP	Accelerated Graphics Port
AIFF	Audio Interchange File Format
ANI	Automatic Number Identification
ANSI	American National Standards Institute
AOW	Asia and Oceania Workshop
APA	All Points Addressable
API	Application Programming Interface
APM	Advanced Power Management
APPC	Advanced Program-to-Program Communications
ARA	AppleTalk Remote Access
ARP	Address Resolution Protocol
ARPA	Advanced Research Project Agency
ARPANET	Advanced Research Projects Agency Network
ARQ	Automatic Request for Retransmission
ASCII	American Standard Code for Information Interchange
ASD	Automatic Skip Driver Agent
ASMP	Asymmetric Multiprocessing
ASN.1	Abstract Syntax Notation One
ASP	Active Server Pages
ASP	AppleTalk Session Protocol

ATM	Asynchronous Transfer Mode
ATP	AppleTalk Transaction Protocol
AUI	Attachment Unit Interface
AUP	Acceptable Use Policy
AWG	American Wire Gauge

—B—

BBS	Bulletin Board System
bcp	Bulk Copy Program
BDC	Backup Domain Controller
BER	Basic Encoding Rules
BIOS	Basic Input/Output System
BISDN	Broadband ISDN
bit	Binary Digits
BITNET	Because It's Time Network
BNC	British Naval Connector
BOC	Bell Operating Company
Bps	Bytes per second
bps	Bits per second
BRI	Basic Rate Interface
BSC	Binary Synchronous Communications
BSD	Berkeley Software Distribution
BTAM	Basic Telecommunications Access Method

—C—

CAL	Client Access License
CAP	Competitive Access Provider
CATV	Community Antenna Television
CBR	Constant Bit Rate
CBT	Computer-Based Training
CCITT	International Consultative Committee for Telegraphy and Telephony
CCL	Common Command Language
CCR	Commitment, Concurrency, and Recovery
CCTV	Closed-Circuit Television
CD-ROM	Compact Disc Read-only Memory
CDF	Channel Definition Format
CERN	European Laboratory for Particle Physics
CERT	Computer Emergency Response Team
CGA	Color Graphics Adapter
CGI	Common Gateway Interface
CICS	Customer Information Control System
CIR	Committed Information Rate
CISC	Complex Instruction Set Computer
CIX	Commercial Internet Exchange

CLBS	Component Load Balancing Service
CLNP	ConnectionLess Network Protocol
CLTP	ConnectionLess Transport Protocol
CMIP	Common Management Information Protocol
CMOS	Complementary Metal Oxide Semiconductor
CMOT	CMIP Over TCP
CN	Common Name
CO	Central Office
COM	Component Object Model
CONP	Connection Oriented Network Protocol
COS	Corporation for Open Systems
COSINE	Cooperation for Open Systems Interconnection Networking in Europe
CPE	Customer Premise Equipment
CPI	Common Programming Interface
cps	Characters per second
CPU	Central Processing Unit
CRC	Cyclic Redundancy Check
CREN	Corporation for Research and Educational Networking
CRT	Cathode Ray Tube
CSMA	Carrier Sense Multiple Access
CSMA/CA	Carrier Sense Multiple Access with Collision Avoidance
CSMA/CD	Carrier Sense Multiple Access with Collision Detection
CSNET	Computer Science Network
CSP	Cryptographic Service Provider
CSU	Customer Service Unit
CU	Control Unit

—D—

DAC	Digital to Analog Converter
DACS	Digital Access Cross Connects
DARPA	Defense Advanced Research Projects Agency
DAO	Data Access Objects
DAV	Digital Audio Video
DB2	IBM Data Base 2
DBCS	Double Byte Character Set
DBMS	Database Management System
DBO	Database Owner
DBOO	Database Object Owner
DCA	Defense Communications Agency
DCE	Distributed Computing Environment
DCE	Data Communications Equipment
DCOM	Distributed COM
DD	Double Density

DDE	Dynamic Data Exchange
DDI	Device Driver Interface
DDL	Data Definition Language
DDM	Distributed Data Management Architecture
DDN	Defense Data Network
DDNS	Dynamic DNS
DDP	Datagram Delivery Protocol
DES	Data Encryption Standard
DET	Directory Entry Table
Dfs	Distributed File System
DFT	Distributed Function Terminals
DHCP	Dynamic Host Configuration Protocol
DHTML	Dynamic HTML
DID	Direct Inward Dial
DIMM	Dual, In-line Memory Module
DISA	Defense Information Systems Agency
DIX	Digital, Intel, Xerox
DLC	Data Link Control
DLCI	Data Link Connection Identifier
DLL	Dynamic-link library
DMA	Direct Memory Access
DMI	Digital Multiplexed Interface
DML	Data Manipulation Language
DNA	Distributed interNet Application
DNS	Domain Name System
DOS	Disk Operating System
dpi	Dots per inch
DQDB	Distributed Queue Dual Bus
DRAM	Dynamic Random Access Memory
DS	Data Set
DS	Double-Sided
DS1	Digital Signaling Level 1
DS2	Digital Signaling Level 2
DS3	Digital Signaling Level 3
DSA	Directory System Agent
DSDD	Double-Sided, Double-Density
DSE	Data Service Equipment
DSHD	Double-Sided, High-Density
DSP	Digital Signal Processor
DSU	Data Service Unit
DTC	Distributed Transaction Coordinator
DTE	Data Terminal Equipment

DTR	Data Terminal Ready
DTS	Data Transformation Service
DUA	Directory User Agent
DVD	Digital Video Disc or Digital Versatile Disc
DXF	Drawing Exchange Format
DXI	Data Exchange Interface

—E—

E-mail	Electronic mail
EARN	European Academic and Research Network
EBCDIC	Extended Binary-Coded Decimal Interchange Code
ECF	Enhanced Connectivity Facilities
ECP	Extended Capabilities Port
EDI	Electronic Data Interchange
EEHLLAPI	Entry Emulator High-Level Language Application Program Interface
EFF	Electronic Frontier Foundation
EFS	Encrypting File System
EGA	Enhanced Graphics Adapter
EGP	Exterior Gateway Protocol
EIDE	Enhanced IDE
EMF	Enhanced Metafile
EMS	Expanded Memory
EPS or EPSF	Encapsulated PostScript File
ER Model	Entity/Relationship Model
ES-IS	End System-Intermediate System
ESDI	Enhanced Industry Standard Architecture
ESF	Extended Super Frame
EUnet	European UNIX Network
EUUG	European UNIX Users Group
EWOS	European Workshop for Open Systems

—F—

FAQ	Frequently Asked Questions
FARNET	Federation of American Research NETworks
FAT	File Allocation Table
FCB	File Control Block
FCC	Federal Communications Commission
FCS	Frame Check Sequence
FDDI	Fiber Distributed Data Interface
FEP	Front-End Processor
FFAPI	File Format API
FIPS	Federal Information Processing Standard
FM	Frequency Modulation
FNC	Federal Networking Council

FPU	Floating Point Unit
FQDN	Fully Qualified Domain Name
FRICC	Federal Research Internet Coordinating Committee
FT1	Fractional T1
FT3	Fractional T3
FTAM	File Transfer, Access, and Management
FTP	File Transfer Protocol
FYI	For Your Information

—G—

GDI	Graphics Device Interface
GIF	Graphics Interchange Format
GINA	Graphical Identification and Authentication
GOSIP	Government OSI Profile
GP	Group Policy
GPO	Group Policy Object
GUI	Graphical User Interface

—H—

HAL	Hardware Abstraction Layer
HCL	Hardware Compatibility List
HCSS	High Capacity Storage System
HD	High Density
HDLC	High-level Data Link Control
HDX	Half-duplex
HFS	Hierarchical File System
HID	Human Interface Device
HLLAPI	High-Level Language Application Program Interface
HMA	High Memory Area
HPFS	High Performance File System
HTML	HyperText Markup Language
HTTP	HyperText Transfer Protocol
Hz	Hertz

—I—

IAB	Internet Activities Board
ICM	Image Color Management
ICMP	Internet Control Message Protocol
ICS	Internet Connection Server
IDE	Integrated Drive Electronics
IEEE	Institute of Electrical and Electronics Engineers
IESG	Internet Engineering Steering Group
IETF	Internet Engineering Task Force
IFS	Installable File System
IGP	Interior Gateway Protocol

IGRP	Internet Gateway Routing Protocol
IIS	Internet Information Server
IMHO	In My Humble Opinion
INTAP	Interoperability Technology Association for Information Processing
IONL	Internal Organization of the Network Layer
IP	Internet Protocol
IPX	Internetwork Packet Exchange
IPXODI	Internetwork Packet Exchange Open Data link Interface
IRC	Internet Relay Chat
IrDA	Infrared Developers Association
IRF	Inherited Rights Filter
IRQ	Interrupt Request Lines
IRTF	Internet Research Task Force
IS-IS	Intermediate System-Intermediate System
ISAPI	Microsoft Internet Server Application Programming Interface
ISDN	Integrated Services Digital Network
ISO	International Standards Organization
ISODE	ISO Development Environment
ISP	Internet Service Provider
IXC	Inter-exchange Carrier

—J—

JANET	Joint Academic Network
JPEG	Joint Photographic Experts Group
JUNET	Japan UNIX Network

—K—

KB	Kilobyte
Kb	Kilobit
KBps	Kilobytes per second
Kbps	Kilobits per second
KCC	Knowledge Consistency Check
KDC	Key Distribution Center

—L—

L2PDU	Layer Two Protocol Data Unit
L3PDU	Layer Three Protocol Data Unit
LAN	Local Area Network
LAPB	Link Access Protocol Balanced
LAPD	Link Access Protocol Device
LAPS	LAN Adapter and Protocol Support
LATA	Local Access and Transport Area
LCD	Liquid Crystal Diode
LDAP	Lightweight Directory Access Protocol
LDT	Local Descriptor Table

LEC	Local Exchange Carriers
LEN	Low Entry Networking
LLAP	LocalTalk Link Access Protocol
LMI	Local Management Interface
lpi	Lines per inch
LSA	Local Security Authority
LSL	Link Support Layer
LU	Logical Unit

—M—

MAC	Media Access Control Sublayer
MAN	Metropolitan Area Network
MAP	Manufacturing Automation Protocol
MAPI	Messaging API
MAU	Media Access Unit
MB	Megabyte
Mb	Megabit
MBps	Megabytes per second
Mbps	Megabits per second
MBR	Master Boot Record
MCGA	Multi-Color Gate Array
MDI	Multiple Document Interface
MHS	Message Handling System
MHz	Megahertz
MIB	Management Information Base
MIDI	Musical Instrument Digital Interface
MILNET	Military Network
MIME	Multipurpose Internet Mail Extensions
MIPS	Million Instructions Per Second
MLID	Multiple Link Interface Driver
MMC	Microsoft Management Console
MOO	Mud, Object Oriented
MPEG	Moving Pictures Experts Group
MPPE	Microsoft Point-to-Point Encryption
ms	Milliseconds
MSAU	MultiStation Access Unit
MSI	Microsoft Software Installer
MTA	Message Transfer Agent
MTU	Maximum Transmission Unit
MUD	Multi-User Dungeon or Dimension
MVS	Multiple Virtual Storage
MVS-CICS	Multiple Virtual Storage-Customer Information Control System
MVS/TSO	Multiple Virtual Storage/Time-Sharing Option

—N—

NAK	Negative AcKnowledgment
NAT	Network Address Translation
NBP	Name Binding Protocol
NCC	NetWare Control Center
NCP	NetWare Core Protocol
NCP	Network Control Point
NCSA	National Center for Supercomputing Applications
NDS	NetWare Directory Services
NetBEUI	NetBIOS Extended User Interface
NetWare DA	NetWare Desk Accessory
NFS	Network File System
NIC	Network Information Center
NIC	Network Interface Card
NIST	National Institute of Standards and Technology
NLM	NetWare Loadable Module
NLQ	Near Letter Quality
NLSP	NetWare Link Services Protocol
NMS	Network Management Station
NNS	NetWare Name Service
NNTP	Network News Transfer Protocol
NOC	Network Operations Center
NREN	National Research and Education Network
NSAP	Network Service Access Point
NSEPro	Network Support Encyclopedia Professional Volume
NSEPro	Network Support Encyclopedia Professional Edition
NSF	National Science Foundation
NSFnet	National Science Foundation Network
NT	Windows NT
NT1	Network Termination 1
NT2	Network Termination 2
NTAS	Windows NT Advanced Server
NTFS	New Technology File System
NTLM	NT Lan Manager
NTP	Network Time Protocol
NWADMIN	Network Administrator

—O—

OBS	Optical Bypass Switch
ODI	Open Datalink Interface
OHCI	Open Host Controller Interface
OIW	Workshop for Implementors of OSI
OLE	Object Linking and Embedding

ONC	Open Network Computing
OOP	Object-oriented programming
OPAC	Online Public Access Catalog
OpenHCI	Open Host Controller Interface
OSI	Open Systems Interconnection
OSPF	Open Shortest Path First

—P—

PAD	Packet Assembler/Disassembler
PAP	Printer Access Protocol
PBX	Private Branch Exchange
PCI	Peripheral Component Interconnect
PCI	Protocol Control Information
PCL	Printer Control Language
PCM	Pulse Code Modulation
PCMCIA	Personal Computer Memory Card International Association
PDC	Primary Domain Controller
PDF	Printer Definition Files
PDN	Packet Data Network
PDS	Processor-Direct Slot
PDU	Protocol Data Unit
PID	Process Identification Number
PIF	Program Information File
Ping	Packet internet groper
PKI	Public Key Infrastructure
PMMU	Paged Memory Management Unit
POP	Point of Presence
POP	Post Office Protocol
POSI	Promoting Conference for OSI
POST	Power On Self Test
POTS	Plain Old Telephone Service
ppm	pages per minute
PPP	Point-to-Point Protocol
PPTP	Point-to-Point Tunneling Protocol
PRAM	Parameter RAM
PRI	Primary Rate Interface
PRMD	Private Management Domain
PROFS	Professional Office System
PSN	Packet Switch Node
PU	Physical Unit
PUC	Public Utility Commission
PVC	Permanent Virtual Circuit

—Q—

QMF	Query Manager Facility
QoS	Quality of Service

—R—

RADIUS	Remote Authentication Dial-In User Service
RAID	Redundant Array of Independent Disks
RAM	Random Access Memory
RARE	Reseaux Associes pour la Recherche Europeene
RARP	Reverse Address Resolution Protocol
RAS	Remote Access Service
RAS	Remote Access Server
RBOC	Regional Bell Operating Company
RDP	Remote Desktop Protocol
REM	REMARK
RFC	Request For Comments
RFS	Remote File System
RIP	Raster Image Processor
RIP	Router Information Protocol
RIPE	Reseaux IP Europeene
RISC	Reduced Instruction Set Computer
ROM	Read-Only Memory
ROSE	Remote Operations Service Element
RPC	Remote Procedure Call
RRAS	Routing and Remote Access Service
RTF	Rich Text Format
RTMP	Routing Table Maintenance Protocol
RTSE	Reliable Transfer Service Element
RUP	Roaming User Profile

—S—

SAA	Systems Application Architecture
SAP	Service Access Point
SAP	Service Advertising Protocol
SAPI	Service Access Point Identifier
SAPS	Service Access Point Stations
SAR	Segmentation and Reassembly protocol
SCSI	Small Computer Systems Interface
SDH	Synchronous Digital Hierarchy
SDI	Storage Device Interface
SDLC	Synchronous Data Link Control
SDN	Software Defined Network
SDU	SMDS Data Unit
SFT	System Fault Tolerance

SGML	Standard Generalized Markup Language
SGMP	Simple Gateway Management Protocol
SID	Security Identifier
SIMM	Single, In-line Memory Module
SIP	SMDS Interface Protocol
SLIP	Serial Line Internet Protocol
SMDS	Switched Multimegabit Data Service
SMI	Structure of Management Information
SMP	Symmetric Multiprocessing
SMS	Storage Management Services
SMTP	Simple Mail Transfer Protocol
SNA	System Network Architecture
SNMP	Simple Network Management Protocol
SONET	Synchronous Optical Network
SPAG	Standards Promotion and Application Group
SPE	Synchronous Payload Envelope
SPX	Sequenced Packet Exchange
SQL	Structured Query Language
SRAM	Static RAM
SRPI	Server Requester Programming Interface
SS7	Signaling System 7
SSL	Secure Sockets Layer
STDM	Statistical Time Division Multiplexing
STI	Still Image Interface
STM	Synchronous Transport Module
STS	Synchronous Transport Signal
SVC	Switched Virtual Circuit
Sysop	Systems Operator

—T—

TA	Terminal Adapter
TAC	Terminal Access Controller
TCP	Transmission Control Protcol
TCP/IP	Transmission Control Protocol/Internet Protocol
TDM	Time-Division Multiplexor
TE1	Terminal Equipment Type 1
TE2	Terminal Equipment Type 2
Telex	Teleprinter Exchange
TIFF	Tagged Image File Format
TLI	Transport Layer Interface
TNX	Teletypewriter Exchange Service
TP0	OSI Transport Protocol Class 0
TP4	OSI Transport Protocol Class 4

TSA	Target Server Agent
TSR	Terminate and Stay Resident program
TTF	TrueType fonts
TTL	Time to Live
TTS	Transaction Tracking System
TWX	Teletypewriter Exchange Service

—U—

UA	User Agent
UDP	User Datagram Protocol
UMA	Upper Memory Area
UMBs	Upper Memory Blocks
UNC	Universal Naming Convention
UPS	Uninterruptible Power Supply
URL	Uniform Resource Locator
USB	Universal Serial Bus
UUCP	UNIX-to-UNIX Copy Program

—V—

VBR	Variable Bit Rate
VCI	Virtual Connection Identifier
VDM	Virtual DOS Machine
Veronica	Very Easy Rodent-Oriented Netwide Index to Computerized Archives
VGA	Video Graphics Array
VLM	Virtual Loadable Module
VLSI	Very Large-Scale Integration
VM/CMS	Virtual Machine/Conversational Monitor System
VMM	Virtual Memory Manager
VNET	Virtual Network
VPI	Virtual Path Identifier
VPN	Virtual Private Network
VRAM	Video RAM
VRC	Vertical Redundancy Check
VRML	Virtual Reality Modeling Language
VSE/CICS	Virtual Storage Extended/Customer Information Control System
VT	Virtual Terminal

—W—

WAIS	Wide Area Information Servers
WAN	Wide Area Network
WATS	Wide Area Telephone Service
WDM	Win32 Driver Model
WHQL	Windows Hardware Quality Labs
WWW	World Wide Web
WYSIWYG	What You See Is What You Get

—X—

XDR	External Data Representation
XMS	Extended Memory
XNS	Xerox Network System

—Z—

ZAW	Zero Administration Initiative for Windows
ZIP	Zone Information Protocol

Index

H

I

L

O

P

S

W

X

Z

SPECIAL SUPPLEMENTAL EXERCISES

KEY TERMS

Chapter 1 – Introduction

Backup Domain Controller (BDC)

Windows NT domain controller that serves as a backup/failover to the Primary Domain Controller (PDC).

Client

1. A workstation that requests services of another computer (server).
2. The portion of a client/server application providing the end-user interface (front-end).

Domain

1. In NetWare, DOMAIN is used as a console command that will create a protected operating system domain for running untested NLMs in Ring 3. This prevents a module from interfering with the core operating system.
2. In the Internet, a domain is a part of the naming hierarchy. The domain name is a sequence of names (separated by periods) that identify host sites. For example: galenp@mail.msen.com.

Ethernet

A Carrier Sense, Multiple Access with Collision Detection (CSMA/CD) specification. Ethernet was originally developed by Xerox, Intel, and Digital Equipment Corporation in the late 1970s, with specifications first released in 1980. The standard defines the cabling, connectors, and other characteristics for the transmission of data, voice, and video over local area networks at 10 Mbps. Recent improvements have increased the speed to 100 Mbps.

There are four types of Ethernet frames defined: 802.2, 802.3, Ethernet_SNAP, and Ethernet II. These are similar but incompatible. The types of Ethernet cables are Thin Ethernet (Thinnet), Thick Ethernet (Thicknet), Twisted Pair, and Fiber Optic.

NetBIOS

Standard programming interface for the development of distributed applications.

NWLink

The IPX/SPX-compatible protocol provided with Windows 2000. It is used primarily to connect to NetWare servers that support IPX/SPX.

Primary Domain Controller (PDC)

The first domain controller created in a Windows NT domain.

Protocol

1. A set of strict rules (usually developed by a standards committee) that govern the exchange of information between computer devices. Also, a set of semantic and syntactic rules that determine the behavior of hardware and software in achieving communication.
2. PROTOCOL is also a NetWare 3.x console command that displays the protocols registered on a file server along with the names of their frame types and protocol identification numbers as included by the LAN driver when it is installed.

Server

A computer or a software package that provides services to client software running on other computers on a network. Possible services include file sharing, printer sharing, or communications services.

Transmission Control Protocol/Internet Protocol (TCP/IP)

1. Originally designed for WANs (Wide Area Networks), TCP/IP was developed in the 1970s to link the research center of the U.S. Government's Defense Advanced Research Projects Agency. TCP/IP is a protocol that enables communication between the same or different types of computers on a network. TCP/IP can be carried over a wide range of communication channels. The Transmission Control Protocol is connection-oriented and monitors the correct transfer of data between computers. The Internet Protocol is stream-oriented and breaks data into packets.
2. The preferred protocol for Windows 2000 networks. In order for Windows 2000 client computers to communicate with Windows 2000 servers, both must have TCP/IP configured correctly.

Topology

Refers to the physical layout of network components (such as cables, stations, gateways, and hubs).

Workgroup

A defined set of Windows for Workgroups, Windows 95, or NT stations that are able to communicate and share file and print resources.

Review Questions

1. Updating the network gradually over time is called:
   a. Turn-key implementation
   b. Phased Implementation
   c. Interim Implementation
   d. Dynamic Implementation

2. Which of the following are features of a workgroup? Select all that apply.
    a. Each system manages its own security and resources
    b. There is central logon authentication
    c. Decentralized management
    d. Designed for small organizations
    e. Complex to set up and maintain
    f. Also known as peer-to-peer networks
3. Which of the following are features of a Windows 2000 network? Select all that apply.
    a. Directory information is stored in a multi-master central directory
    b. There is only one PDC
    c. Domain structure is organized around a logical design
    d. One DC stores a writeable copy of the directory database - other DCs store read-only copies of the directory database
    e. A Windows 2000 network cannot contain Windows NT domain controllers
4. Which of the following topologies uses coaxial cabling?
    a. Star
    b. Bus
    c. Ring
    d. Mesh
5. Which topology is the easiest to isolate for problem solving?
    a. Star
    b. Bus
    c. Ring
6. Which protocol does not support routing?
    a. TCP/IP
    b. NWLink IPX/SPX
    c. AppleTalk
    d. NetBEUI
7. Which protocol is most often used to connect HP printers to the network? Select 2 from the list.
    a. TCP/IP
    b. NWLink IPX/SPX
    c. DLC
    d. AppleTalk
    e. NetBEUI

8. How many network protocols can be bound to any single network adapter running Windows 2000?
   a. 1
   b. 2
   c. 4
   d. 8
   e. 16
   f. Unlimited
9. Which of the following factors may influence the design of a network? Select all that apply.
   a. Company organizational structure
   b. Total number of employees
   c. Physical location of employees
   d. IT management model - centralized vs. decentralized
   e. Number of IT staff
   f. Client operating systems
   g. Relationship with suppliers and partners
10. Put the following processes in the proper order for a successful network implementation.
    a. Design
    b. Management
    c. Information Gathering
    d. Implementation
11. List the three primary goals of any network design.
12. Which network model uses domains as a security boundary? Select all that apply.
    a. Windows 2000
    b. Windows NT
    c. Windows 2000 workgroup
    d. Windows 98 peer-to-peer network
13. Which network topology is the easiest to expand?
    a. Bus
    b. Ring
    c. Star
14. Which of the following is not an access protocol?
    a. Ethernet

b. Token Ring
c. ArcNet
d. AppleTalk
e. FDDI

15. Which access protocol provides the highest transmission speed?
    a. Ethernet
    b. ArcNet
    c. AppleTalk
    d. FDDI
16. Which transport protocol can only be used for short, line of site transmissions?
    a. DLC
    b. IPX/SPX
    c. IrDA
    d. AppleTalk
    e. NetBEUI
17. Which network topology requires hubs, repeaters, or MSAUs for connectivity? Select all that apply.
    a. Bus
    b. Star
    c. Ring
18. What is the function of a protocol?
    a. Describes how computers are linked together
    b. Specifies the language used for communication between computers
    c. Specifies the physical connection between computers in a network
    d. Provides users access to network resources and services
    e. All the above
19. Which of the following is an advantage of decentralized IT management?
    a. Policies are defined at the organization level
    b. Central control of security
    c. The ability to respond quickly to changing conditions
    d. Consistency of policies throughout the organization
    e. None of the above
    f. All the above

20. All Windows 2000 domain controllers store a writeable copy of the directory database. True or False?
21. What is the maximum number of Windows 2000 BDCs that can be supported in native mode?
    a. 10
    b. 32
    c. 255
    d. Unlimited
    e. None of the above
22. Which network topologies are based on a loop? Select all that apply.
    a. Ethernet
    b. Token Ring
    c. ArcNet
    d. FDDI
    e. IrDA
23. IrDA is typically used to connect what devices? Select all that apply.
    a. Keyboards
    b. Mouse
    c. Printers
    d. PDAs
    e. Laptop computers
    f. Scanners
24. The Star network topology typically uses which cabling?
    a. 10Base2
    b. 10BaseT
    c. 10Base10
    d. Coaxial
25. Explain FDDI's built-in fault tolerance.

CASE PROJECTS

Case 1

You have been asked to gather data regarding the current network infrastructure for your company, a law firm. Currently the network consists of:

-1 file and print server

- 1 e-mail server
- 1 Web server
- 32 client computers

What specific information would you gather for each server/workstation that will be used to help create a new network design?

Case 2

You work for a small insurance company that currently has a few computers that are not networked. The owner has asked you to design an infrastructure consisting of 15 new client computers. Users need only to share files and printers. Outline the advantages and disadvantages of implementing a workgroup and a Windows 2000 domain.

Case 3

You have been asked to help upgrade networking cabling for Applied Engineering, a manufacturer of electronic components. They are located in an industrial park and occupy three separate buildings. One building contains the administration, one building is manufacturing, and the other contains the warehouse. Currently all buildings are connected in an Ethernet bus topology using 10Base2 cabling.

The director of IT has asked you for a proposal on upgrading the cabling. The proposed solution must meet the following criteria:

- The cabling solution must be able to support 100 Mbps transmission rates
- The cabling solution must be easy to expand and troubleshoot
- A break in a single cable should not affect the entire network
- What cabling would you recommend for each building? What cabling would you recommend to connect each building? What additional hardware is required?

KEY TERMS

Chapter 2 - Business Environment Questions

Active Directory

The Windows 2000 directory service. Active Directory treats users, files, directories, applications, and other items as objects. It allows system administrators to modify the properties of objects. Objects and their properties are described in the Active Directory schema.

Application

The use to which an information processing system is put. For example, a payroll application, an airline reservation application, or a network application.

Internet Service Provider (ISP)

Companies that provide an Internet connection for educational institutions, individuals, companies, and organizations.

Migration

1. Conversion of NetWare servers from NetWare 2, NetWare 3, or from another operating system, to NetWare 4. Operating system migration is different from data migration, which is the moving of files to near-line or offline storage devices.
2. Transfer of users, groups, directories, and files from a NetWare Server to a Windows NT Server.
3. Transfer of users, groups, and application data from one application to another.

Software

A computer program, or a set of instructions written in a specific language, that commands the computer to perform various operations on data contained in the program or supplied by the user.

Review Questions

1. Explain the difference between policies and procedures.
2. The primary goal of a centralized IT administration model is:
   a. Ability to adapt to changes quickly
   b. Need for standardization
   c. Reduce the number of IT staff required
   d. All the above
3. Centralized IT administration requires Active Directory in a Windows 2000 network. True or False?
4. Fail-over clustering is also known as?
   a. Redundant servers
   b. Load balancing
   c. Round robin clustering
   d. Server clustering
5. Which of the following is a characteristic of a branch office? Select all that apply.
   a. A branch office tends to have a high level of autonomy.
   b. A branch office is an extension of the organization.
   c. A branch office is a wholly owned entity.
   d. A branch office receives its directions from head office.
   e. All the above

6. Competing standards is usually a problem found at what level of geographical scope?
   a. Regional
   b. National
   c. International
   d. All the above
7. Which part of the product life cycle applies to Windows NT Server?
   a. Product birth
   b. Product growth
   c. Product reproduction
   d. Product death
8. What is the largest concern when supporting a WAN environment?
   a. Available bandwidth
   b. Competing network standards
   c. Lack of competent IT staff
   d. Politics
   e. All the above
9. What components of Active Directory are designed for decentralized administration? Select all that apply.
   a. Forests
   b. Child domains
   c. Organizational Units
   d. Global Catalog
10. Explain the difference between information flow and communication flow.
11. Which part of the product life cycle applies to Windows 2000?
    a. Product birth
    b. Product growth
    c. Product reproduction
    d. Product death
12. List three design constraints that you might encounter when planning network infrastructure upgrades.

13. Which of the following is not a business goal?
    a. Increase sales
    b. Reduce IT administration costs
    c. Open additional offices
    d. Upgrade all workstations to high-performance computers
    e. None of the above
14. Government regulations may affect which of the following network policies? Select all that apply.
    a. Cable type used
    b. Backup policies
    c. Data encryption policies
    d. Workspace design policies
    e. Network protocol policies
15. Which of the following is not an example of internal growth?
    a. Adding new network connections
    b. Installing additional computers
    c. Opening a new office
    d. Hiring additional support staff
16. List two features of Windows 2000 that help reduce Total Cost of Ownership (TCO).
17. Which of the following does not increase network availability?
    a. RAID 5 volumes
    b. Server clustering
    c. FDDI
    d. Multiple domain controllers
    e. Round robin DNS
18. Which of the following costs should be included in a network upgrade budget? Select all that apply.
    a. System upgrades
    b. Software upgrades
    c. Network cabling upgrades
    d. End user training
    e. IT staff training
    f. Outsourced services
    g. IT salaries

19. The company you work for is looking at implementing streaming video for internal training. What influence will this have on the network design?
20. A company with a single office falls under which geographic scope?
    a. Regional
    b. National
    c. International
    d. Local
21. Why is it difficult to accurately measure information flow within an organization?
22. Why is planning for growth difficult?
23. To control data access, where should data be stored?
    a. Local workstation
    b. Network share
    c. Network DFS root
    d. On a RAID 5 volume
24. In a retail sales environment, which should be the primary goal of the network design?
    a. Performance
    b. Security
    c. Inbound communication
    d. Outbound communication
25. If a remote link to a WAN cannot be upgraded, what can be done to increase effective bandwidth? Select all that apply.
    a. Install domain controllers in each remote site
    b. Install DNS servers in each remote site
    c. Install WINS Proxy Agents in each remote site
    d. Configure each remote site as a separate domain

HANDS-ON PROJECTS

Project 2-1

Hands-on Project

In this hands-on activity you will install and configure a Windows 2000 Server. This exercise assumes the computer is configured to boot from a CD.

1. Insert the Windows 2000 Server CD into the CD ROM drive and boot from the CD ROM. The Windows 2000 Setup screen will appear.
2. Press **Enter** at the Welcome to Setup screen to begin the installation.

3. Press **F8** to agree to the licensing agreement.
4. Press **C** to create a partition.
5. Use **Backspace** to erase the current size and type **2000** as the partition size and press **Enter**.
6. Press **Enter** again to install Windows 2000 on the new partition.
7. Select **Format the partition using the NTFS file system** and press **Enter**. Once the partition has been formatted, Setup will copy the necessary files to the partition. Once complete the computer will reboot.
8. Press **Enter** at the Welcome screen. Setup will now install devices.
9. Select **Next** at the Regional Settings screen to accept the defaults.
10. Type your name and organization and press **Enter**.
11. Enter the product key listed on the CD, and click on **Next**.
12. Press **Enter** at the Licensing Mode screen.
13. Type **Server1** as the computer name.
14. Type **password** as the password.
15. Retype **password** in the Confirm password text box and click on **Next**.
16. Click on **Next** to install the default Windows 2000 components.
17. Verify the current date and time.
18. Select the time zone and click on **Next**.
19. Select **Typical Settings** and click on **Next**.
20. Select **This computer is not on a network**. Ensure WORKGROUP is entered as the workgroup name and click on **Next**.
21. When done, click on **Finish**. The computer will reboot.

Project 2-2

In this hands-on activity you will configure a static IP address on Server1

1. Log on the computer as Administrator with a password of password.
2. Close the Configure your Server window.
3. Right-click on **My Network Places** and click on **Properties**.
4. Right-click on **Local Area Connection** and click on **Properties**.
5. Double-click on **Internet Protocol (TCP/IP)**.
6. Enable the radio button for **Use the following IP address**.
7. Enter **192.168.0.1** as the IP Address.
8. Enter **255.255.255.0** as the subnet mask and click on **OK** twice.
9. Close the Network and Dial-up Connections window.

Project 2-3

In this hands-on activity you will install and configure a second Windows 2000 Server. This exercise is based on the assumption that the computer is configured to boot from a CD.

1. Insert the Windows 2000 Server CD into the CD ROM drive and boot from the CD ROM. The Windows 2000 Setup screen will appear.
2. Press **Enter** at the Welcome to Setup screen to begin the installation.
3. Press **F8** to agree to the licensing agreement.
4. Press **C** to create a partition.
5. Use **Backspace** to erase the current size and type **2000** as the partition size and press **Enter**.
6. Press **Enter** again to install Windows 2000 on the new partition.
7. Select **Format the partition using the NTFS file system** and press **Enter**. Once the partition has been formatted, Setup will copy the necessary files to the partition. Once complete the computer will reboot.
8. Press **Enter** at the Welcome screen. Setup will now install devices.
9. Select **Next** at the Regional Settings screen to accept the defaults.
10. Type your name and organization and press **Enter**.
11. Enter the product key listed on the CD; click on **Next**.
12. Press **Enter** at the Licensing Mode screen.
13. Type **Server2** as the computer name.
14. Type **password** as the password.
15. Retype **password** in the Confirm password text box and click on **Next**.
16. Click on **Next** to install the default Windows 2000 components.
17. Verify the current date and time.
18. Select the time zone and click on **Next**.
19. Select **Typical Settings** and click on **Next**.
20. Select **This computer is not on a network**. Ensure WORKGROUP is entered as the workgroup name and click on **Next**.
21. When done, click on **Finish**. The computer will reboot.

Project 2-4

In this hands-on activity you will configure a static IP address on Server2

1. Log on the computer as Administrator with a password of password.
2. Close the Configure your Server window.
3. Right-click on **My Network Places** and click on **Properties**.
4. Right-click on **Local Area Connection** and click on **Properties**.

5. Double-click on **Internet Protocol (TCP/IP)**.
6. Enable the radio button for Use the following IP address.
7. Enter **192.168.0.2** as the IP Address.
8. Enter **255.255.255.0** as the subnet mask and click on **OK** twice.
9. Close the Network and Dial-up Connections window.

Project 2-5

In this hands-on activity you will configure Server1 as a domain controller for the domain AD2000.com.

1. On Server1, click on **Start**, point to **Programs**, point to **Administrative Tools,** and click on **Configure Your Server**.
2. Click on **Active Directory**.
3. Click on **Start the Active Directory Wizard**.
4. Click on **Next**.
5. Select **Domain controller for a new domain** and click on **Next**.
6. Select **Create a new domain tree** and click on **Next**.
7. Click on **Create a new forest of domain trees** and click on **Next**.
8. Type **AD2000.com** as the full DNS name and click on **Next**.
9. Type **AD2000** as the domain NetBIOS name and click on **Next**
10. Click on **Next** to accept the default locations for the database and log files.
11. Click on **Next** to accept the default SYSVOL folder location.
12. Click on **OK** to accept the message stating a DNS server cannot be contacted.
13. Select **Yes, install and configure DNS on this computer** and click on **Next**.
14. Click on **Next** to use pre-Windows 2000 permissions.
15. Type **password** as the Administrator account password. Retype **password** to confirm the password and click on Next.
16. Click on **Next**. The process of promoting the server to an Active Directory controller will begin. If prompted, insert the Windows 2000 Server CD and click on **OK**.
17. When done, click on **Finish**.
18. Click on **Restart Now**.

Project 2-6

In this hands-on activity you will configure Server 2 as a second domain controller for the domain AD2000.com.

1. On Server 2, click on **Start**, point to **Programs**, point to **Administrative Tools,** and click on **Configure Your Server**

2. Click on **Active Directory**.
3. Click on **Start the Active Directory Wizard**.
4. Click on **Next**.
5. Select **Additional domain controller for an existing domain** and click on **Next**.
6. Type **Administrator** as the user name.
7. Type **password** as the password.
8. Type **AD2000.com** as the domain and click on **Next**.
9. Click on the **Browse** button and click on **AD2000.COM**. Click on **OK**.
10. Click on **Next**.
11. Click on **Next** to accept the default locations for the database and log files.
12. Click on **Next** to accept the default SYSVOL folder location.
13. Click on **OK** to accept the message stating a DNS server cannot be contacted.
14. Type **password** as the Administrator account password. Retype **password** to confirm the password and click on **Next**.
15. Click on **Next**. The process of promoting the server to an Active Directory controller will begin. If prompted, insert the Windows 2000 Server CD and click on **OK**.
16. When done, click on **Finish**.
17. Click on **Restart Now**.

CASE PROJECTS

Case 1

Barkman & Associates, a medium-sized insurance firm with 150 employees in three cities (Dallas, Chicago, and Seattle) currently has their e-mail hosted by their ISP. Management has asked you to prepare a report concerning hosting the email system internally.

In this report, include the following:

- Advantages and disadvantages of hosting e-mail internally
- Additional hardware that would be required
- Network infrastructure upgrades that would be required
- Training costs

Case 2

The IT manager has decided to implement a formal change management procedure regarding the network. All requests to modify the network must now be made in writing and have approval from the IT manager. You have been asked to create the change management form that must be filled out and approved. This form will also be used to document all changes made to the network. What information will you include on the change management form?

Case 3

Your company is looking into hiring additional IT support staff to help with the network upgrade to Windows 2000. The Human Resources department has asked you for help in writing the advertisements. Write an advertisement for each of the following IT support positions: Network Administrator; Technical Support; and End User Support. Include in each advertisement the degree or diploma required, the number of years experience required, tasks to be performed, and a salary range.

KEY TERMS

Chapter 3 - Technical Environment Analysis

Alert

1. Windows 2000 method for monitoring and detecting performance counter limits.
2. An error message sent to the system control point at the host system.
3. A defined response to an event occurring in SQL Server.

Asynchronous Transfer Mode (ATM)

A high-speed (155 to 162 Mbps) communications transport facility capable of carrying voice, data, and video signaling. ATM forms the backbone for broadband ISDN networks.

Bandwidth

1. The range of frequencies that can be transmitted through a particular circuit.
2. The speed at which data travels over a particular media. Bandwidth is measured in bits per second.

Counter log

A log used for collecting performance counter data over time.

Domain Name System (DNS)

A hierarchical, distributed method of organizing systems and network names on the Internet. DNS administratively groups hosts (systems) into a hierarchy of authority that allows addressing and other information to be widely distributed and maintained. A big advantage of DNS is that using it eliminates dependence on a centrally maintained file that maps host names to addresses.

The bottom level of the tree structure contains the names of companies or even machines within a company. For example, consider wuarchive.wustl.edu. The bottom of the tree is wuarchive. This is the name of a particular piece of equipment within the wustl domain, which is under the edu domain.

The name of a particular domain is read from the bottom of the tree up to the root. The root is unnamed and is represented with just a period. For example, wavetech.com is a particular domain. If we were to give the fully qualified domain name (FQDN), we would include the unnamed root, so it would be written as "wavetech.com." The final period at the end of the name specifies the root of the tree. The root must always be specified for the host equipment. To make it easy, most software will convert a domain name to an FQDN for the user by appending any missing domain names all the way to the root.

The top of the tree lists the top-level domains. These are reserved names. Every domain will have a top-level domain by type or country.

Encryption

Involves encoding a packet's data prior to transmission to ensure data security. The Data Encryption Standard (DES) is an algorithm used for coding and decoding data for security purposes.

Firewall

Used as a security measure between a company's local area network (LAN) and the Internet. The firewall prevents users from accessing certain address Web sites. A firewall also helps to prevent hackers from accessing internal resources on the network. A combination of hardware and software that separates a LAN into two or more parts for security purposes. Today, firewalls are commonly used to prevent unauthorized access to a network from the Internet.

Host (A) resource record

Forward zone host name-to-IP address mapping record.

Integrated Services Digital Network (ISDN)

A special kind of telecommunications network designed to handle more than just data. Digital network operating over PSTN local loop wiring. Multiple services, including video, text, voice, data, facsimile images, and graphics, are supported over 64-Kbps channels. Standard configurations combine multiple channels to provide higher transfer rates.

Local Area Network (LAN)

A group of computers running specialized communications software and joined through an external data path.

A LAN will cover a small geographic area, usually no larger than a single building. The computers have a direct high-speed connection between all workstations and servers, and share hardware resources and data files. A LAN has centralized management of resources and network security.

PC-based networks can trace their heritage back to what are now often referred to as legacy systems. These systems were mainframe and minicomputer hosts accessed through dumb terminals.

There are a number of similarities between LANs and these legacy systems, such as centralized storage and backup, access security, and central management of resources. There are, however, a number of differences.

Traditional host systems are characterized by centralized processing, dumb terminals, custom applications, and high expansion costs and management overhead. LANs are characterized by distributed processing, intelligent workstations (PCs), and off-the-shelf applications. LANs are modular, are inexpensive to expand, and have more moderate management costs.

LMHOSTS

The LMHOSTS file lists the IP address and NetBIOS name for each network machine with which the local machine may need to communicate.

Network

A group of computers and other devices connected together so they can communicate with each other.

Network address

1. A network number that uniquely identifies a network cable segment. It may be referred to as the IPX external network number.
2. A network address can also be the network portion of an IP address. For a Class A network, the network address is the first byte of the IP address. For a Class B network, the network address is the first two bytes of the IP address. For a Class C network, the network address is the first three bytes of the IP address. In each case, the remainder is the host address.

Network Monitor

An SMS utility that functions as a *sniffer* and is used to capture, transmit, and display network packets.

Proxy server

A server that is positioned between an internal network and the Internet. The proxy server can be configured to limit which users have access to the Internet, which sites users are allowed to connect to, what protocols users are allowed to use, and to cache Internet requests. Some proxy servers also provide some firewall capability.

Public Switched Telephone Network (PSTN)

Refers to the international telephone system based on copper wires carrying analog voice data.

Remote access

The ability of a computer to access an offsite or distant computer using telephone lines or a network.

Router

1. A connection between two networks that specifies message paths and may perform other functions, such as data compression.

2. In early versions of NetWare, the term bridge was sometimes used interchangeably with the term router.

System Monitor Snap-in

MMC snap-in that is used to view and record activity from performance counters.

Virtual Private Network (VPN)

Remote access configuration where users and remote networks connect to network servers across the Internet. A tunnel is created through the Internet and all of the data that crosses the Internet is encrypted. Windows 2000 supports two protocols for setting up VPNs: Point-to-Point Tunneling Protocol (PPTP) or Layer 2 Tunneling Protocol/IPSec (L2TP/IPSec).

Wide Area Network (WAN)

Expands the basic LAN model by linking Local Area Networks (LANs) and allowing them to communicate with each other. By traditional definition, a LAN becomes a WAN when it crosses a public right-of-way, requiring a public carrier for data transmission. More current usage of the term usually includes any situation where a network expands beyond one location/building. A WAN is characterized by low- to high-speed communication links and usually covers a wide geographic area. The remote links may be operational LANs or only groups of workstations. With the exception of a WAN's wider area of operation, the benefits and features of LANs and WANs are the same.

Windows Internet Naming Service (WINS)

A system that determines the IP address associated with a particular network computer. This is called *name resolution*.

Review Questions

1. A network that is divided into small segments, each with their own network address, is called a:
   a. Non-Routed LAN
   b. WAN
   c. MAN
   d. Routed LAN
2. Which Windows 2000 tool allows an administrator to view types of network packets sent on the network?
   a. Windows Diagnostics
   b. Event Viewer
   c. Network Monitor
   d. IPSec
   e. Performance Monitor
   f. All the above

3. You would like to be notified when free disk space on your server is less than 100 MB. What feature of Performance Monitor would you use?
   a. Trace log
   b. Report
   c. Alert
   d. Counter log
4. Which command displays the current TCP/IP configuration of a Windows 2000 client?
   a. PATHPING
   b. TRACERT
   c. IPCONFIG
   d. WINIPCFG
   e. PING
5. Which tool can be used to locate breaks and shorts in the network cabling?
   a. Protocol analyzer
   b. Time-Domain Reflectometer
   c. Multimeter
   d. Network Monitor
6. Which cabling type utilizes a central conducting core that is surrounded by copper mesh to reduce crosstalk?
   a. STP
   b. UDP
   c. Coaxial
   d. FDDI
7. What is the maximum data transmission rate for CAT 5 cabling?
   a. 4 Mbps
   b. 10 Mbps.
   c. 16 Mbps.
   d. 100 Mbps
   e. Unlimited
8. Which services can be used to resolve names to IP addresses? Select 2 from the list.
   a. DHCP
   b. DNS
   c. WINS

d. RAS

e. NAT

9. What is the data transmission rate of a T1 line?

a. 56 Kbps.

b. 64 Kbps.

c. 256 Kbps.

d. 512 Kbps

e. 1.544 Mbps.

10. Which WAN connectivity requires a Packet Assembler/Disassembler on each end of the line?

a. PSTN

b. ISDN

c. X.25

d. ATM

e. DSL

11. Which disaster protection solution provides automatic fail-over support and load balancing?

a. Disk mirroring

b. Disk duplexing

c. Server Cluster

d. Redundant servers

e. All the above

12. Which protocol is responsible for data encryption in a Windows 2000 network?

a. EAS

b. IPSec

c. BAP

d. ESMTP

13. What disaster protection solution protects a server against a hard disk controller crash?

a. Disk mirroring

b. Disk duplexing

c. Server cluster

d. RAID 5

e. All the above

14. Which WAN connectivity uses a dial-up connection over high-quality telephone lines?
    a. ATM
    b. X.25
    c. ISDN
    d. IrDA
15. Which file resolves host names to IP addresses?
    a. LMHOSTS
    b. LMHOSTS.SAM
    c. HOST.TXT
    d. HOSTS
    e. NETWORKS
16. In which situation is plenum-rated cabling required? Select all that apply.
    a. Cables routed near fluorescent lights
    b. All exposed cabling
    c. Cabling vertically run through walls and suspended ceilings
    d. Cables longer than 20 feet
    e. Only from computer to wall bracket
17. How many pairs of wires does CAT 3 wiring have?
    a. 1
    b. 2
    c. 3
    d. 4
    e. 5
18. What is the purpose of the twists in UTP?
    a. Provide strength to the cabling
    b. Extends the effective range of the cabling
    c. Reduces interference between the cables
    d. All the above
19. What are the reasons for breaking up a LAN into multiple subnets, each connected by a router? Select all that apply.
    a. Isolate traffic
    b. Increase effective bandwidth
    c. Propagate broadcasts

d. Filter traffic between subnets

e. Increase effective cabling range

20. Which System Monitor view allows you to view average values of selected counters?

a. Chart

b. Report

c. Log

d. Histogram

e. All the above

21. What is the major difference between trace logs and counter logs in System Monitor?

a. Trace logs display real-time counters while counter logs display counter values over time

b. Trace logs record events from start to finish

c. Counter logs display real-time counters while trace logs display counter values over time

d. Counter logs record more detail than trace logs and are therefore larger in size

22. Which troubleshooting tool is new in Windows 2000?

a. IPCONFIG

b. PING

c. TRACERT

d. PATHPING

e. HOSTNAME

23. What is another name for 10Base2 cabling?

a. Thicknet

b. Thinnet

c. UTP

d. STP

e. FDDI

24. Generally, which service has the biggest impact on network performance?

a. Logon authentication

b. Access files/printers

c. Host name resolution

d. IP Address renewal

25. Which of the following are required for DNS support in Windows 2000? Select all that apply.
    a. Dynamic DNS updates
    b. Secure DNS updates
    c. SRV records
    d. Active Directory Integrated Zones

Hands-on Projects

Project 3-1

In this hands-on activity, you will install Network Monitor and capture packets sent from Server1 to Server2 for analysis.

1. Log on to Server1 as Administrator.
2. Click on **Start**, point to **Settings**, and then click on **Control Panel**.
3. Double-click on **Add/Remove Programs**.
4. Click on **Add/Remove Windows Components**.
5. Click on **Management and Monitoring Tools** and click on **Details**.
6. Enable **Network Monitor Tools** and click on **OK**.
7. Click on **Next**. Insert the Windows 2000 CD in the CD ROM drive and click on **OK**.
8. Click on **Finish**.
9. Close all open windows.
10. Click on **Start**, point to **Programs**, point to **Administrative Tools**, and click on **Network Monitor**.
11. Click on **OK**.
12. Select the network that matches the MAC address of the network card attached to the network.
13. Click on the **Capture** menu and click on **Start. Network Monitor** will now capture all packets to and from Server1.
14. On Server2, start a command prompt. Type **ping 192.168.0.1** and press Enter.
15. On Server1, click on the **Capture** menu and click on **Stop and View**. A list of the captured packets is displayed. What protocol is used by the echoes?
16. Log off on Server2.
17. On Server1, switch to Network Monitor. Select **File, Close** from the menu.

18. Click on **Capture**, click on **Start**.
19. On Server 2, log onto the computer as Administrator.
20. Once logged on to Server2, switch to Server1 and click on **Capture**, click on **Stop and View**.
21. Scroll through the list and find all broadcast based traffic. What is the destination IP address?
22. Exit Network Monitor. Do not save the capture if prompted.

Project 3-2

In this hands-on activity, you will modify LMHOSTS and HOST files for name resolution.

1. On Server1, start Windows Explorer.
2. Expand the folder C:\WINNT\SYSTEM32\DRIVERS\ETC.
3. Right-click on the file HOSTS and select **Open With**.
4. Select **Notepad** from the list and click on **OK**.
5. Scroll to the end of the file. What entry is listed?
6. Below the entry type **127.0.0.1** and press **Tab**.
7. Type **www.acme.com**.
8. Save and close the file.
9. Start a Command Prompt.
10. Type **ping www.acme.com** and press Enter. What IP address did it resolve?
11. Switch back to Windows Explorer.
12. Rename the file LMHOSTS.SAM to LMHOSTS (no period).
13. Right-click on the file LMHOSTS and select **Open With**.
14. Select **Notepad** from the list and click on **OK**.
15. Scroll to the end of the file.
16. Start a new line at the end of the file.
17. Type **127.0.0.1** and press Tab
18. Type **Fido**.
19. Save and close the file.
20. Switch to the command prompt.
21. Type **ping fido** and press Enter. What reply do you get back?
22. Close command prompt.
23. Close Windows Explorer.

Project 3-3

In this hands-on activity, you will configure System monitor on Server1 to display an alert when the %Processor counter is over 50% utilization.

1. On Server1, click on **Start**, point to **Programs**, point to **Administrative Tools**, and click on Performance.
2. Expand Performance Logs and Alerts.
3. Click on **Alerts**.
4. Right-click on **Alerts** and click on **New Alert Settings**.
5. Type **Processor Utilization** and click on **OK**.
6. Click on the **Add** button.
7. Select **%Processor Time** from the list of counters and click on **Add**.
8. Click on **Close**.
9. Click on the list box for Alert when the value is and select **Over**.
10. Type **50** in the Limit text box.
11. Specify **1** as the Interval.
12. Click on the **Action** tab.
13. Enable the **Send a network message to** check box and type **Administrator**.
14. Click on **OK**.
15. Minimize the Performance window.
16. Right click on the desktop and click on **Properties**.
17. Click on the **Screen Saver** tab.
18. Select **3D Maze** as the screen saver and click on **Preview**. Do not move the mouse or touch the keyboard until the alert message is displayed. Click on **OK**.
19. Switch to Performance.
20. Right click on the **Processor Utilization** alert and click on **Stop**.
21. Close all open windows.

Project 3-4

In this hands-on activity, you will back up the system state on Server1.

1. On Server1, click on **Start**, point to **Programs**, point to **Accessories**, point to **System Tools**, and click on **Backup**.
2. Click on the **Tools** menu and select **Options**.
3. Click on the **Backup Log** tab.
4. Enable **Detailed** and click on **OK**.
5. Click on the **Backup Wizard** button.

6. Click on **Next**.
7. Select **Only back up the System State data** and click on **Next**.
8. Type **c:\system state.brf** in the Backup media or file name text box and click on **Next**.
9. Click on **Finish**. The backup will start. It will take a few minutes to complete the backup. Notice the size of the data to be backed up.
10. Click on the **Report** button. Scroll through the backup log and note what is included in the System State.
11. Close the report window.
12. Click on **Close**.
13. Click on the **Restore** tab.
14. Expand File.
15. Expand The Media created on today's date.
16. Double-click on **System State**.
17. Type **c:\system state.brf** and click on **OK**. Notice what was included in the system date backup.
18. Close Backup.

Project 3-5

In this hands-on activity, you will view system configuration information using System Information.

1. On Server1, click on **Start**, point to **Programs**, point to **Accessories**, point to **System Tools**, and click on **System Information**. The system information will be displayed.
2. What version of Windows 2000 is installed?
3. What is the total amount of physical memory?
4. What is the total amount of virtual memory?
5. Expand Hardware Resources.
6. Click on **IRQs**. What IRQ is assigned to the network card? What IRQ is assigned to the mouse?
7. Expand Software Environment.
8. Click on **Running Tasks**. What tasks are running in the background?
9. Press **Ctrl + Alt + Del**.
10. Click on **Task Manager**.
11. Click on **Processes**. Are the same tasks listed as those in step 8?
12. Close Windows Task Manager.
13. Close System Information.

Case Projects

Case 1

You have been asked to configure a new file and print server's hard drives for fault tolerance. The new server consists of 5 - 9 GB SCSI drives. The server will be a domain controller for logon authentication, as well as storing users home folders and shared data folders. In addition, the server will also function as a print server for 3 high-speed printers attached to the network.

The IT director for the company would like the new server configured as follows:

- The operating system and boot drive should be protected from a controller failure or a hard disk failure.
- Data must be always available even in the event of a single hard disk failure.
- The data partition must have the ability to grow as new hard disks are added.
- Disk space must be organized as efficiently as possible.

1. Design the hard disk partitions according to the information presented above.
2. Which partition would contain the user's home folders?
3. Which partition would contain the shared data folders?
4. Which partition would store the print spool files?

Case 2

Acme Insurance has hired you to help the company design a WAN infrastructure that will allow its offices to communicate and share resources. Offices are located in Dallas, Chicago, Seattle, and Omaha. The company has asked you to prepare a report outlining the advantages and disadvantages of each connectivity option:

- Analog Dial-up
- DSL
- ISDN

Case 3

The president of the company is concerned about security and theft of data and e-mail. In Windows 2000, which security options would you configure to:

- Prevent viewing e-mail or data transfers
- Prevent unauthorized users from accessing network shares
- Enable secure traffic between all domain controllers
- Allow users to log onto the network only from their computer

Key Terms

Chapter 4 - Network Environment Design

AppleTalk

An inexpensive local-area network (LAN) architecture built into all Apple Macintosh computers and laser printers.

Bus topology

A bus network topology consists of a linear transmission medium that is terminated at both ends. Nodes attach directly to the bus, making failures difficult to troubleshoot. Any break in the bus causes the entire network to become inoperable. Difficulty in troubleshooting is considered the biggest drawback for a bus topology.

Although a bus normally is drawn as a straight line in pictures and diagrams, most bus networks represent cables that snake, weave, and wrap their way through building's conduits and corridors. This can make the overall length of buses grow rapidly.

Bus topologies commonly use coaxial cable as their transmission medium. Traditionally, Ethernet has used a bus topology.

Data Link Control (DLC)

The second lowest layer in the OSI reference model. Every network interface card (NIC) has a *DLC address* or *DLC identifier (DLCI)* that uniquely identifies the node on the network.

For networks that conform to the IEEE 802 standards (e.g., Ethernet), the DLC address is usually called the Media Access Control (MAC) address.

File server

A computer that stores files and provides access to them from workstations. File servers generally contain large hard disks and high amounts of memory.

If a computer is used exclusively as a file server, it is a dedicated file server. If a computer is used as a workstation and a file server simultaneously, it is a nondedicated file server.

The NOS (Network Operating System) runs on the file server and controls access to files, printers, and other network resources.

Internet Connection Sharing (ICS)

A service available in Windows 2000 Professional and Server that allows the sharing of a single connection to the Internet or a remote network with multiple network clients. ICS is very easy to configure but also limited to using a single small network.

Latency (replication latency)

The delay between when a change is made to an object attribute on one domain controller and when the change is replicated to other domain controllers in the domain.

Network Address Translation (NAT)

1. A component that is included with Windows 2000 Server that allows multiple users to share one connection, such as a modem or DSL connection, to the Internet. NAT is designed for mid-sized networks and offers more configuration flexibility than ICS. NAT operates as a router forwarding all requests to the Internet as well as supporting address translation. This means that the computers inside the network do not have to have Internet-compatible addresses.
2. A service available through RRAS on a Windows 2000 Server that allows the sharing of a single connection to the Internet or a remote network with multiple network clients. NAT is more difficult to configure than ICS but can also operate in more complex environments.
3. Routing protocol available through an Internet Connection Server (ICS) configuration that allows a home network or small office to share a single Internet connection. This protocol requires that your client computers be configured as DHCP clients.

Print server

A network computer, either dedicated or nondedicated, used to handle the printing needs of workstations.

Ring topology

Provides a closed-loop transmission medium. Repeaters at each node connection duplicate the signal. This is done to minimize signal degradation. Traditional rings have the same failure risk as a bus topology. Any break brings down the entire network. To prevent this type of failure, most ring implementations (such as Token Ring) are wired in a star topology with an out loop and a return loop from each workstation to the wiring hub.

The Fiber Distributed Data Interface (FDDI) design specification calls for a dual fiber-optic ring. Should a break occur in either ring, it automatically converts to a bus topology.

Systems Network Architecture (SNA)

A set of network protocols developed by IBM. Originally designed in 1974 for IBM's mainframe computers, SNA has evolved over the years so that it now also supports peer-to-peer networks of workstations.

Star topology

All devices are connected to a central hub. The logical layout of this topology resembles a star. Star networks are relatively easy to install and manage, but bottlenecks can occur because all data must pass through the hub.

Review Questions

1. What is the maximum cable segment length of 10Base2 cabling?
   a. 100 meters
   b. 150 meters
   c. 185 meters
   d. 200 meters
   e. Unlimited
2. Which of the following cable types support 10BaseT? Select all that apply.
   a. CAT 1
   b. CAT 2
   c. CAT 3
   d. CAT 4
   e. CAT 5
3. Which of the following cabling types provides the highest security against signal tapping?
   a. Coaxial
   b. UTP
   c. STP
   d. Infrared
   e. Fiber-optic
4. Which topology uses a token passing architecture? Select all that apply.
   a. Ethernet
   b. Token Ring
   c. FDDI
   d. AppleTalk
   e. All the above
5. Which is the default protocol for Windows NT and Microsoft LAN Manager?
   a. NetBEUI
   b. TCP/IP
   c. NwLink IPX/SPX
   d. SNA

6. Which is the default frame type supported by NetWare 4?
   a. 802.2
   b. 802.3
   c. 802.4
   d. 802.5
7. Which TCP/IP protocol is responsible for router-based error messages?
   a. ARP
   b. ICMP
   c. IGMP
   d. TFTP
   e. SNMP
8. What is the maximum number of workstations supported in a 10BaseT star topology?
   a. 260
   b. 512
   c. 1024
   d. 2000
   e. Unlimited
9. Your Windows 2000 network consists of Mac clients, NetWare 3.11 servers, and Windows 2000 Professional clients connected to the Internet. Which protocols would you install on the server to allow communication with all clients? Select all that apply.
   a. NetBEUI
   b. NWLink IPX/SPX
   c. TCP/IP
   d. DLC
   e. AppleTalk
   f. SNA
10. Which service provides a way of sharing an internet connection among multiple client computers? Select all that apply.
    a. DHCP
    b. DNS
    c. ICS
    d. NAT
    e. RAS

11. Which cabling type connects to the computer using an RJ-45 connector? Select all that apply.
    a. 10Base2
    b. 10BaseT
    c. 10Base5
    d. 100BaseT
    e. FDDI
12. List three reasons to upgrade network cabling.
13. If Windows 2000 detects multiple NWLink frame types on the network, which frame type will it set as the default?
    a. 802.2
    b. 802.3
    c. 802.5
    d. Ethernet II
    e. SNAP
14. Which TCP/IP protocol is used to resolve IP addresses to MAC addresses?
    a. PING
    b. TCP
    c. IP
    d. ARP
    e. UDP
15. You have a Windows 2000 Server with 2 network cards connected to 2 subnets. One subnet uses TCP/IP as the protocol and the other subnet uses NWLink IPX/SPX. How would you configure the binding order for each network card to prevent unnecessary network traffic?
16. Each remote network in a WAN requires its own domain controller for logon authentication. True or False?
17. Which is the default protocol installed in a Windows 2000 Typical installation?
    a. NetBEUI
    b. NWLink IPX/SPX
    c. AppleTalk
    d. TCP/IP
    e. DLC
    f. IrDA

18. How many bits does IPv6 use for addressing?
    a. 32
    b. 64
    c. 128
    d. 256
    e. 512
19. What is the purpose of a secondary DNS server?
20. Which protocol is non-routable? Select all that apply.
    a. NetBEUI
    b. NWLink IPX/SPX
    c. TCP/IP
    d. DLC
    e. AppleTalk
21. How many bits are used for Ipv4 IP addressing?
    a. 8
    b. 16
    c. 32
    d. 64
    e. 128
22. In a Token Ring network, what is the maximum distance from MAU to MAU?
    a. 45 meters
    b. 100 meters
    c. 152 meters
    d. 2.5 meters
    e. 260 meters
23. What are the two most common methods of remote access? Select two from the list.
    a. X.25
    b. Dial-up
    c. VPN
    d. ISDN
24. Where does the system send a packet destined for a different subnet?
    a. Default gateway
    b. Primary DNS server

c. WINS server

d. Proxy server

25. What is the maximum number of computers in an Ethernet 10Base2 bus LAN?

a. 200

b. 500

c. 72

d. 90

e. 160

Hands-on Projects

Project 4-1

In this hands-on activity, you will install and configure NWLink IPX/SPX to support both 802.2 and 802.3 frame types on Server1.

1. Right-click on **My Network Places** and select **Properties**.
2. Right-click on **Local Area Connection** and select **Properties**.
3. Click on **Install**.
4. Select **Protocol** and click on **Add**. Which protocols are listed?
5. Select **NWLink IPX/SPX/NetBIOS Compatible Transport Protocol** and click on **OK**. If required, point to the location of the Windows 2000 Server setup files.
6. Once installed, select **NWLink IPX/SPX/NetBIOS Compatible Transport Protocol** from the list of installed components and click on **Properties**.
7. Type **A** as the internal network number
8. Select **Manual frame type detection** and click on **Add**.
9. Select **802.2** as the frame type.
10. Type **A1A1A1A1** as the network number and click on **OK**.
11. Click on **Add**.
12. Select **802.3** as the frame type.
13. Type **B2B2B2B2** as the network number and click on **OK**.
14. Click on **OK**.
15. Start a Command Prompt.
16. At the command prompt, type **ipxroute config** and press **Enter**. What information is displayed?
17. Close all open windows.

Project 4-2

In this hands-on activity, you will configure the binding order so that TCP/IP is the first protocol in the binding order.

1. Right click on **My Network Places** and select **Properties**.
2. Click on **Advanced** from the menu and click on **Advanced Settings**.
3. Click on **Internet Protocol (TCP/IP)** under Client for Microsoft Networks.
4. Click on the **Up** arrow.
5. Click on **OK**.
6. Close the window.

Project 4-3

In this hands-on activity, you will configure Server1 to provide Internet Sharing Connection. The procedure will be cancelled at the last step because of hardware limitations.

1. On Server1, click on **Start**, point to **Settings**, and click on **Network and Dial-up Connections**.
2. Double-click on **Make New Connection**.
3. If prompted for location information, select your country from the list and enter the area code for your city. Click on **OK**.
4. Click on **OK** again.
5. Click on **Next**.
6. Click on **Dial-up to the Internet** and click on **Next**.
7. Click on **I want to set up my Internet Connection manually** and click on **Next**.
8. Click on **I connect through a local area network (LAN)** and click on **Next**.
9. Turn off **Automatic discovery of proxy server** and click on **Next**.
10. Click on **No** and click on **Next**.
11. Deselect the **To connect to the Internet immediately** check box.
12. Click on **Finish**.
13. Right-click on **Local Area Connection** and click on **Properties**.
14. Click on the **Sharing** tab.
15. Enable the **Enable Internet Connection Sharing for this connection** check box and click on **OK**.
16. Read the message displayed on the window and click on No.
17. Click on **Cancel**.
18. Close the Network and Dial-up Connections window.

CASE PROJECTS

Case 1

The small firm you work for has asked you to set up internet access for all 15 users through a DSL line attached to a Windows 2000 server. Would you implement ICS or NAT? What factors will influence your decision?

Case 2

In preparation for upgrading your existing network to Windows 2000, you have identified and documented the physical cabling in your building. Your current network consists of 25 computers attached in a bus topology using 10Base2 cabling running at 10 Mbps. After talking with the owner, plans are to increase staff and computers by 20 within the next year and move the accounting department (10 computers) to another floor within the same office building. As well, all new computers will be configured with 10/100 Mbps network cards.

1. Will the current network cabling be able to handle the future growth?
2. What recommendations would you make regarding upgrading the network cabling?
3. What factors would influence your decision?

Case 3

Southdale Property Management manages apartments building. Its office consists of 60 users connected using Token Ring on IBM Type 1 cabling running at 4 Mbps. They would like to upgrade to 10 Mbps Ethernet. What cabling would you recommend? What additional hardware must be purchased? Prepare a report outlining the total cost of the upgrade.

KEY TERMS

Chapter 5 - TCP/IP Implementation

Dynamic Host Configuration Protocol (DHCP)

A TCP/IP application-layer protocol that provides for dynamic address assignment on a network.

File Transfer Protocol (FTP)

A part of the TCP/IP suite that is used to transfer files between any two computers, provided they support FTP. The two computers do not have to be running the same operating system.

In general, people use FTP to move files from one account or machine to another or to perform what is called an "anonymous FTP." For example, if storage space on a particular machine is low, the user can free up storage space by using FTP to move the files to a machine with more space. Another reason to move a file to a different account is to print a file to a particular printer. If the file is on a machine that cannot access the desired printer, it must be moved to a machine that does have access.

Whatever the reason for the transfer, FTP requires the user to know the proper login name and the password for both computers to move files between them.

While an anonymous FTP also moves from one computer to another, it has two main differences. An anonymous FTP session usually involves gathering files that a user does not have. Anonymous FTP does not require the user to know a login name and password to access the remote computer.

The Internet has many anonymous FTP sites. Each site consists of an FTP server, a large number of files, and guest login names such as "anonymous" or "FTP." This allows any user to visit these systems and copy files from the FTP site to their personal computer. With the appropriate authority, users can copy files from their system to an anonymous FTP site.

Despite the variety of FTP servers and clients on the Internet and the different operating systems they use, FTP servers and clients generally support the same basic commands. This standard command set allows users to accomplish tasks such as looking at a list of files in the current directory of the remote system, regardless of the operating system in use. Other common commands allow users to change directories, get specific file information, copy files to a local machine, and change parameters.

Graphical Web browsers transform the traditional character-based, command-line FTP interface into a point-and-click environment. The only way a user may know that they are in the middle of an FTP session is that the Universal Resources Locator (URL) box in the browser will change from an address that begins with "http://..." to "ftp://...".

Internet Engineering Task Force (IETF)

One of the task forces of the IAB, the IETF is responsible for solving short-term engineering needs of the Internet. It has more than 40 Working Groups.

IPCONFIG

A command line utility used to display IP information. The purpose of this utility is to provide the user with diagnostic information related to TCP/IP network configuration.

IP Security (IPSec)

A part of TCP/IP standards in which all IP traffic between two computers is encrypted so that the packets cannot be captured on the network and read by unauthorized users.

Layer 2 Tunneling Protocol (L2TP)

A protocol that provides authentication services over public networks. Often used in conjunction with IPSec to create secure VPN connections.

PATHPING

A route tracing tool that combines features of the *ping* and *tracert* commands with additional information that neither of those commands provides. The *pathping* command sends packets to each router on the way to a final destination over a period of time, and then computes results based on the packets returned from each hop.

Ping

This utility is used to test the presence of other computers on the network. You can use IP addresses or NetBIOS names if you have a WINS server running or have made the appropriate entry in the LMHOSTS file.

Point-to-Point Tunneling Protocol (PPTP)

Network technology that gives clients using TCP/IP, IPX, or NetBEUI the ability to create a secure VPN over a public TCP/IP network, such as the Internet.

Request for Comment (RFC)

Documentation about an internet standard, standardized through the Internet Engineering Task Force (IETF).

Route

To move data between multiple connected networks.

Subnet

The primary reason to divide a network into subnets is network performance and available bandwidth. Without separate networks, each transmission would be broadcast across the entire internetwork, waiting for the destination system to respond. As the network grows, this causes increases in traffic until it exceeds the available bandwidth.

Routers divide, as well as provide, communications between the networks. Packets bound for a destination within the local network are kept local. Only packets bound for other networks are broadcast across the network, moving from router to router. Overall traffic levels are reduced.

Telnet

A terminal emulation program for TCP/IP networks such as the Internet.

Traceroute (Tracert)

A utility that traces a packet from your computer to an Internet host, showing how many hops the packet requires to reach the host and how long each hop takes.

REVIEW QUESTIONS

1. Which transport protocol provides guaranteed delivery of a packet?
   a. UDP
   b. TCP
   c. IP
   d. ICMP
2. Explain the difference between selective acknowledgement and normal acknowledgement.
3. Which command displays TCP/IP connection information for the system?
   a. IPCONFIG
   b. TRACERT
   c. PATHPING
   d. NETSTAT
   e. NBTSTAT
4. What is the command to display the computer's routing table?
   a. ROUTE PRINT
   b. ROUTE VIEW
   c. ROUTE -P
   d. ROUTE -F
5. List 3 advantages to configuring DHCP to lease IP Addresses over assigning static IP addresses.
6. What is the default subnet mask for a Class C IP Address?
   a. 255.0.0.0
   b. 255.255.0.0
   c. 255.255.255.0
   d. 255.255.255.255
7. Which IP class can support only 254 workstations maximum per subnet?
   a. Class A
   b. Class B
   c. Class C
   d. Class D
   e. All the above
8. List 3 reasons to divide a large network into smaller subnets.

9. You have assigned the IP range 10.X.X.X to the internal computers. You would like to divide the network into 10 subnets. What subnet mask would you use?
   a. 255.0.0.0
   b. 255.192.0.0
   c. 255.224.0.0
   d. 255.240.0.0
   e. 255.248.0.0
   f. 255.252.0.0
10. Your computer has been assigned the IP address 192.168.72.12 with a subnet of 255.255.224.0. Which of the following IP addresses are on your local subnet? Select all that apply.
    a. 192.168.60.200
    b. 192.168.95.253
    c. 192.168.32.17
    d. 192.168.64.1
    e. 192.168.100.142
    f. 192.168.96.96
11. Which protocol is responsible for routing packets?
    a. IP
    b. TCP
    c. UDP
    d. ICMP
    e. ICMP
    f. ARP
12. When is the Time-To-Live (TTL) of a packet decremented by one?
    a. Each time the packet is fragmented
    b. Each time the packet received by the default gateway
    c. Each time the packet is resent
    d. Each time the packet crosses a router
    e. All the above
13. The RIP protocol is the most efficient routing protocol for a large, subnetted network consisting of 20 subnets. True or False?

14. In order to use Quality of Service, all routers must support what protocol?
    a. WINS forwarding
    b. RSVP
    c. DNS
    d. BAP
    e. EAS
15. You are viewing the Processor Queue Length counter in System Monitor and notice that the value is 2. What does that indicate?
    a. More RAM is required
    b. The processor needs to be upgraded
    c. The hard drives are too slow
    d. The network is a bottleneck
    e. A and B
    f. A and C
    g. There is no problem
16. Which service provides access to Windows 2000 file and print services for NetWare clients?
    a. GSNW
    b. CSNW
    c. FPNW
    d. NWLink
17. What three IP address ranges are reserved for internal use only?
18. What application layer protocol provides remote terminal emulation?
    a. FTP
    b. Telnet
    c. HTTP
    d. SMTP
    e. SNMP
19. Reliable communication between systems is provided at which layer of the DARPA model?
    a. Network
    b. Internet
    c. Transport
    d. Application

20. What IP address range is used for Automatic Private IP Addressing?
    a. 10.X.X.X
    b. 172.31.X.X
    c. 192.168.X.X
    d. 169.254.X.X
21. You noticed your computer is not able to connect to any network resources. You discover the IP address assigned to your computer through DHCP is 0.0.0.0. List three possible reasons you were not assigned a valid IP address.
22. What is the maximum number of workstations a Class B IP address can support?
    a. 16,777,214
    b. 128,426
    c. 65,534
    d. 254
23. What does the IP address 255.255.255.255 indicate?
24. What PING switch is used to specify a different echo count?
    a. –v
    b. –t
    c. –n
    d. –i
25. What IP Class does the address 224.200.200.12 belong to?
    a. Class A
    b. Class B
    c. Class C
    d. Class D

Hands-on Projects

Project 5-1

In this hands-on activity, you will configure Server1 and Server2 for Automatic Private Addressing. The following procedure is to be performed on both computers.

1. Right-click on **My Network Places** and select **Properties**.
2. Right-click on **Local Area Connection** and select **Properties**.
3. Double-click on **Internet Protocol (TCP/IP)**.
4. Enable the **Obtain IP address automatically** radio button and click on **OK**.

5. Start a command prompt.
6. Type **ipconfig /renew** and press **Enter**. After a few minutes an error message will display indicating that a DHCP server is unavailable.
7. Type **ipconfig** and press **Enter**. What addresses was assigned to the network adapter?
8. On Server1 at the command prompt, type **ping server2** and press Enter. What reply do you receive? Ping Server2's new IP address. Were you successful?
9. Reconfigure the proper IP addresses for Server1 (192.168.0.1) and Server2 (192,168.0.2) with a subnet mask of 255.255.255.0.
10. Close all open windows.

Project 5-2

In this hands-on activity, you will configure Server1 as a network router supporting both RIP and OSPF routing protocols.

1. On Server1, click on **Start**, point to **Programs**, point to **Administrative Tools**, and click on **Routing and Remote Access**.
2. Right-click on **Server1** and click on **Configure and Enable Routing and Remote Access**.
3. Click on **Next**.
4. Select **Network Router** and click on **Next**.
5. Click on **Next** to route all protocols.
6. Select **No** to not configure a dial-on demand router and click on **Next**.
7. Click on **Finish**.
8. Expand Server1(local).
9. Expand IP Routing.
10. Right-click on **General** and click on **New Routing Protocol**.
11. Click on **Open Shortest Path First (OSPF)** and click on **OK**.
12. Right-click on **OSPF** and click on **Properties**. Click on each tab and view its configuration. Click on **Cancel**.
13. Right-click on **General** and click on **New Routing Protocol**.
14. Click on **RIP Version 2 for Internet Protocol** and click on **OK**.
15. Right-click on **RIP** and click on **Properties**. Click on each tab and view its configuration. Click on **Cancel**.
16. Close Routing and Remote Access.

CASE PROJECTS

Case 1

Your network currently consists of 100 workstations and servers divided into 5 subnets of 20 computers. Each subnet is connected to a router. Each subnet is assigned the following IP range addresses:

Subnet 1	172.16.32.1 - 172.16.32.20	subnet mask 255.255.224.0
Subnet 2	172.16.64.1 - 172.16.64.20	subnet mask 255.255.224.0
Subnet 3	172.16.96.1 - 172.16.96.20	subnet mask 255.255.224.0

What is the maximum number of subnets the subnet mask of 225.225.224.0 can support?

Case 2

You are designing a new network infrastructure to support 25 subnets using the 10.0.0.0 internal address range.

What Class A subnet mask supports up to 25 subnets?

What are the ranges of valid IP addresses for each subnet?

Case 3

A call center consisting of 200 workstations has been assigned a Class C subnet range of 200.12.172.0. They are planning to install an additional 100 workstations within the next week. The call center director does not want to subnet the workstations. How can the call center support 300 workstations on a Class C subnet? What subnet mask would they use? What are the valid ranges of IP addresses that can be assigned to the call center's workstations?

KEY TERMS

Chapter 6 - TCP/IP Services

Bootstrap Protocol (BootP)

An Internet protocol that enables a diskless workstation to discover its own IP address, the IP address of a BOOTP server on the network, and a file to be loaded into memory to boot the machine. This enables the workstation to boot without requiring a hard or floppy disk drive. The protocol is defined by RFC 951.

Direct replication partner

A direct source for Active Directory replication.

Dynamic Host Configuration Protocol (DHCP)

A TCP/IP application-layer protocol that provides for dynamic address assignment on a network.

Dynamic DNS (DDNS)

A newer standard of DNS where client hosts can automatically register A (host) and PTR (pointer) resource records. DDNS allows clients with a dynamically assigned address to register directly with the Windows 2000 DNS server and update the DNS table dynamically.

Incremental Zone server (IXFR)

Zone transfer method where only changes are transferred from the source name server to the destination name server.

Media Access Control (MAC) Address

A unique number hard coded into every network interface card to uniquely identify it on a network.

Multicast

A special form of broadcast where copies of the packet are delivered to only a subset of all possible destinations.

Scope

1. A group of IP addresses as well as other TCP/IP configuration information that the DHCP server can provide for DHCP clients.
2. Variable scope refers to where in the application a variable can be seen. Scope can be limited to a procedure, a module, or global (visible throughout the application).
3. Project scope refers to the definition of features, requirements, schedule, and budget for a project.

Time to Live (TTL)

The amount of time between when a packet of data leaves its point of origin and when it reaches its destination. The TTL is encoded in the IP header and is used as a hop count (to measure the route to the packet's destination).

WINS proxy

A special function that can be assigned to a Windows 2000 server that enables the server to forward registration and name resolution requests from non-WINS clients to a WINS server.

Zone

A grouping of logical devices on one or more networks based on DNS domain namespace.

Review Questions

1. DNS resolves ________________ to ________________.
2. WINS is a requirement of Active Directory. True or False?
3. The root domain in DNS is represented by a:

   a. /

b. .

c. \

d. Domain name

4. The maximum number of characters in a domain name is:

a. 16

b. 32

c. 63

d. 254

e. 255

5. A name resolution query that maps an IP address to a host name is called a:

a. Forward lookup

b. Reverse lookup

c. Interative lookup

d. Recursive lookup

6. List two differences between an Active Directory integrated DNS zone and a Standard Primary DNS zone.

7. Standard Primary DNS zone files are stored in which folder by default?

a. \%systemroot%\dns.

b. \%systemroot%\system\dns

c. \%systemroot%\system32\dns

d. \%systemroot%\config\dns

e. \%systemroot%\system32\config

8. At what three intervals will a WINS client attempt to refresh its name registration with a WINS server?

9. After how many unsuccessful attempts to contact the primary WINS server for a name resolution will a WINS client try to resolve the name with a secondary WINS server?

a. 2

b. 3

c. 5

d. 6

e. Randomly

10. In a network divided into 5 subnets, what is the minimum number of WINS servers required for name resolution across subnets?
    a. 1
    b. 2
    c. 5
    d. 6
11. Explain the differences between a push WINS partner and pull WINS partner.
12. What is the default DHCP lease duration in Windows 2000?
    a. 24 hrs
    b. 48 hrs
    c. 72 hrs
    d. 144 hrs
    e. 192 hrs
13. You install and configure a DHCP server on the local subnet but cannot start the service. You confirm that the DHCP server is configured properly, clients are configured for DHCP, and there are no network problems. What is a possible cause?
    a. The clients do not have a DNS server configured
    b. The DHCP server is not authorized in Active Directory
    c. There is no DHCP Proxy Agent configured
    d. The subnet mask configured in the scope is incorrect
14. You have a single DHCP server to lease addresses to 5 subnets. What must be configured on each subnet to support a single DHCP server?
    a. DHCP Proxy Agent
    b. DHCP Relay Agent
    c. DNS Forwarder
    d. WINS Node Type
15. When will a DHCP client attempt to renew its IP address from the DHCP server? Select all that apply.
    a. The computer is rebooted
    b. At 50% of its lease duration
    c. When the IP address lease has expired
    d. At 85% of its lease duration
16. Why is the DHCPDiscover message sent as a broadcast and not as a directed packet?
17. Explain burst handling with respect to name registration and the consequences of not enabling burst handling.

18. What solutions are available in a Windows 2000 network to provide NETBIOS name resolution to non-WINS clients? Select all that apply.
    a. Secondary WINS servers
    b. WINS Proxy Agent
    c. LMHOST
    d. WINS client software
    e. Install NetBEUI.
19. When replicating between WINS servers, a push partner is generally configured in which situations? Select all that apply.
    a. The WINS servers have high-speed connectivity
    b. The WINS servers have low speed connectivity
    c. WINS replication occurs during off-peak hours
    d. Latency is to be kept to a minimum.
20. Network traffic when replicating Active Directory-integrated DNS zones is not encrypted and poses a security risk. True or False?
21. Which DNS record maps a computer host name to its IP address?
    a. A record
    b. SRV record
    c. MX record
    d. CNAME record
    e. PTR record
22. What is the reverse lookup zone for the network address 200.204.17.0?
    a. 200.204.17.in-addr.arpa
    b. 17.204.200.in-addr.arpa
    c. 200.in-addr.arpa
    d. 200.204.in-addr.arpa
23. Which of the following is not a requirement of DNS servers in a Windows 2000 network? Select all that apply.
    a. SRV records
    b. Dynamic updates
    c. Secure updates
    d. Incremental zone transfers
    e. None of the above

24. Microsoft.com is an example of what type of domain?
    a. Root domain
    b. Top-level domain
    c. Second-level domain
    d. Subdomain
25. A DHCP server is configured, but client has an incorrect default gateway. The DHCP server has the proper default gateway configured. Why is the client configured incorrectly?
    a. The client does not have a DNS server configured
    b. The DHCP server is not authorized in Active Directory
    c. There is no DHCP Proxy Agent configured
    d. The client is configured with a static IP address

Hands-on Projects

Project 6-1

In this hands-on activity, you will install WINS and configure Server1 to resolve NetBIOS name requests WINS.

1. Log on to Server1 as Administrator.
2. Click on **Start**, point to **Settings**, and then click on **Control Panel**.
3. Double-click on **Add/Remove Programs**.
4. Click on **Add/Remove Windows Components**.
5. Select **Networking Services** from the list and click on **Details**.
6. Scroll through the list and find **Windows Internet Naming Service**.
7. Enable the check box for Windows Internet Naming Service and click on **OK**.
8. Click on **Next**. If prompted, specify the path to the Windows 2000 installation CD and select **OK**.
9. Click on **Finish**.
10. Click on **Close**.
11. Click on **Start**, point to **Programs**, point to **Administrative Tools**, and then click on **WINS**.
12. Expand **Server1**.
13. Right click on **Server1** and click on **Properties**.
14. Click on the **Intervals** tab. What is the renewal interval for each WINS entry?
15. Click on the **Advanced** tab. Where is the WINS data stored?

16. Click on **OK**.
17. Right-click on **My Network Places** and click on **Properties**.
18. Right-click on **Local Area Network** and click on **Properties**.
19. Double-click on **Internet Protocol (TCP/IP)**.
20. Click on the **Advanced** button.
21. Click on the **WINS** tab.
22. Click on **Add**.
23. Type **192.168.0.1** and click on **Add**.
24. Click on **OK** three times.
25. Close the Network and Dial-Up Connections window.

Project 6-2

In this hands-on activity, you will configure Server2 to forward all NetBIOS name requests to Server1.

1. On Server2, right-click on **My Network Places** and click on **Properties**.
2. Right-click on **Local Area Network** and click on **Properties**.
3. Double-click on **Internet Protocol (TCP/IP)**.
4. Click on the **Advanced** button.
5. Click on the **WINS** tab.
6. Click on **Add**.
7. Type **192.168.0.1** and click on **Add**.
8. Click on **OK** three times.
9. Close the Network and Dial-Up Connections window.

Project 6-3

In this hands-on activity, you will view the computer names registered in WINS.

1. On Server1 switch to WINS.
2. Expand Server1.
3. Right-click on **Active Registrations** and click on **Find by Owner**.
4. Select **All owners** and click on **Find Now**. Which computers are listed in the WINS database?
5. Right-click on the WINS server name and select **Display Server Statistics**. How many queries have been made? How many of those queries have been successful?
6. Switch to Server2 and start a command prompt. Type **ping server5** and press **Enter**. Was the ping successful? Why or why not?

7. Switch back to Server1. Does the number of WINS queries change?
8. Switch back to Server2 and type **ping server1** and press **Enter**. Does the number of queries change? Was the ping successful? Why or why not?
9. Close all windows

Project 6-4

In this hands-on activity, you will view the DNS configuration that was created when Active Directory was installed.

1. On Server1, click on the **Start** button, point to **Programs**, point to **Administrative Tools**, and click on **DNS**.
2. Expand Server1.
3. Expand Forward Lookup Zones. Which zones have been defined? What does the **.** zone indicate?
4. Click on the **AD2000.com** zone. What records were created when Active Directory was installed?
5. Right-click on **AD2000.com** and click on **Properties**. What type of zone is it?
6. Click on **Cancel**.

Project 6-5

In this hands-on activity, you will configure a standard primary DNS zone for the domain TwoThousand.net.

1. Right-click on **Server1** and click on **New Zone**.
2. Click on **Next**.
3. Ensure that **Standard primary is selected** as the zone type and click on **Next**.
4. Ensure that **Forward Lookup Zone** is selected and click on **Next**.
5. Type **twothousand.net** and click on **Next**.
6. Accept the default file name and click on **Next**.
7. Click on **Finish**.
8. Click on **twothousand.net**. What records are automatically created?

Project 6-6

In this hands-on activity, you will configure a reverse lookup zone for the network address 192.168.0.0.

1. Right-click on **Server1** and click on **New Zone**.
2. Click on **Next**.
3. Ensure that **Standard primary** is selected as the zone type and click on **Next**.

4. Select **Reverse Lookup Zone** and click on **Next**.
5. Ensure that **Network ID** is selected and type **192.168.0**.
6. Click on **Next**.
7. Notice the name of the DNS zone and click on **Next**.
8. Click on **Finish**.
9. Expand Reverse Lookup Zones.
10. Click on **192.168.0.x subnet**. What records are created by default?
11. Right-click on **twothousand.net** and click on **New Host**.
12. Type **server1** as the name.
13. Type **192.168.0.1** as the IP address.
14. Enable the **Create associated pointer (PTR) record** check box and click on **Add Host**.
15. Click on **OK** to confirm the record was successfully added.
16. Click on **Done**.
17. Click on **192.168.0.x subnet**. Is there a pointer record for 192.168.0.1?

Project 6-7

In this hands-on activity, you will install DNS on Server2 and configure secondary DNS zones for TwoThousand.NET and for the reverse lookup zone.

1. Log on to Server2 as Administrator.
2. Click on the **Start** button, point to **Settings**, click on **Control Panel**.
3. Double-click on **Add/Remove Programs**.
4. Click on **Add/Remove Windows Components**.
5. At the Windows components screen, scroll down to Networking Services. Click on **Networking Services** and click on the **Details**.
6. In the Networking Services dialog box, click on the checkbox next to **Domain Name System (DNS)**.
7. Click on **OK**.
8. Click on **Next**. If prompted, insert the Windows 2000 Server CD into the CD-ROM drive and click on **OK**.
9. Click on **Finish**.
10. At the Add/Remove Programs window click on **Close**.
11. Close Control Panel.
12. Click on the **Start** button, point to **Programs**, point to **Administrative Tools**, and click on **DNS**.

13. Right-click on **Server2** and click on **New Zone**.
14. Click on **Next**.
15. Select **Standard secondary** and click on **Next**.
16. Select **Forward lookup zone** and click on **Next**.
17. Type **twothousand.net** and click on **Next**.
18. Type the IP address **192.168.0.1** and click on **Add**.
19. Click on **Next**.
20. Click on **Finish**.
21. Expand Server2.
22. Expand Forward Lookup Zones. Is TwoThousand.net listed?
23. Click on **twothousand.net**. What records are displayed?
24. Switch back to Server1.
25. Right-click on **twothousand.net** and click on **New Host**.
26. Type **server2** as the name.
27. Type **192.168.0.1** as the IP address.
28. Enable the **Create associated pointer (PTR) record** check box and click on **Add Host**.
28. Switch back to Server2.
30. Right-click on **twothousand.net** and click on **Transfer from Master**. Did the Server2 records get transferred?
31. Right-click on **Reverse Lookup Zones** and click on **New Zone**.
32. Click on **Next**.
33. Select **Standard secondary** and click on **Next**.
34. Select **Reverse lookup zone** and click on **Next**.
35. Select Reverse Lookup zone name and type **0.168.192.in-addr.arpa** and click on **Next**.
36. Click on **Finish**.
37. Right-click on **192.168.0.x subnet** and click on **Transfer from Master**. Did the pointer records get transferred?
38. Close all open windows on Server1 and Server2.

Project 6-8

Hands-on Project

In this hands-on activity, you will integrate WINS and DNS resolution.

1. Switch to Server1.
2. Click on the **Start** button, point to **Programs**, point to **Administrative Tools**, and click on **DNS**.

3. Expand Server1.
4. Expand Forward lookup Zones.
5. Right-click on **ad2000.com** and click on **Properties**.
6. Click on the **WINS** tab.
7. Enable the check box for **Use WINS forward lookup**.
8. Click in the IP address text box, type **192.168.0.1**, and click on **Add**.
9. Click on **OK**.
10. Close **DNS**.
11. Start a command prompt.
12. At the command prompt, type **nslookup** and press **Enter**.
13. At the > prompt, type **server2.ad2000.com** and press **Enter**. What address does the name resolve?
14. At the > prompt, type **server2** and press **Enter**. Does it resolve the computer name?
15. Type **exit** and press **Enter**.
16. Close the command prompt.

CASE PROJECTS

Case 1

You have been hired by Acme Insurance to help implement DNS for their network. Offices are located in Dallas, Chicago, Seattle, and Omaha. Each office is on a separate subnet connected to the head office (Dallas) by ISDN. The company has registered Acme-Insurance.com. The IT Director in Dallas has asked you to evaluate two methods for implementing DNS.

Method 1

- Configure a Standard Primary DNS zone for Acme-Insurance.com in Dallas.
- Configure a secondary DNS server in Dallas and configure replication between the primary and secondary DNS servers.
- Configure all clients in each subnet to point to Dallas as both primary and secondary DNS servers.

Method 2

- Configure a Standard Primary DNS zone for Acme-Insurance.com in Dallas.
- Configure secondary DNS servers in Chicago, Seattle, and Omaha.
- Configure replication between the primary and secondary DNS servers.
- Configure clients to point to their local DNS server as the primary DNS server and configure the DNS server in Dallas as the secondary server.

Document the advantages and disadvantages of each method. Which method would you implement? Why?

Case 2

Acme Insurance has opened up a small office in Montreal, Canada. Currently there are 20 employees there and no IT staff. Head office in Dallas has registered the domain name Acme-Insurance.ca. Montreal is connected to Dallas using DSL.

Where would you create the primary DNS zone for Acme-Insurance.ca?

Which server(s) would be configured as secondary DNS servers for Acme-Insurance.ca?

How would you configure replication between the primary and secondary server(s)?

What factors influenced your decision?

Case 3

Your company has 100 valid IP addresses that it assigns through DHCP. Out of a total of 80 employees in the company, approximately half are laptop users who connect to the network once a week to check e-mail and print files. Currently the DHCP lease is set to the default duration of 8 days. Occasionally a laptop user does not receive an IP address from the DHCP server even though you have more IP addresses than users. What could be the cause? What two things can be done to prevent the problem from happening again?

Key Terms

Chapter 7 - Wide Area Design

Authentication

1. A way to verify that an object sending messages or requests to an NDS is permitted to act on or receive those messages or requests.
2. Login or resource access validation.

Dynamic Host Configuration Protocol (DHCP)

A TCP/IP application-layer protocol that provides for dynamic address assignment on a network.

Domain Name System (DNS)

A hierarchical, distributed method of organizing systems and network names on the Internet. DNS administratively groups hosts (systems) into a hierarchy of authority that allows addressing and other information to be widely distributed and maintained. A big advantage of DNS is that using it eliminates dependence on a centrally maintained file that maps host names to addresses.

The diagram shows the hierarchical organization of domain names. The bottom level of the tree structure contains the names of companies or even machines within a company. For example, consider wuarchive.wustl.edu. The bottom of the tree is wuarchive. This is the name of a particular piece of equipment within the wustl domain, which is under the edu domain.

The name of a particular domain is read from the bottom of the tree up to the root. The root is unnamed and is represented with just a period. For example, wavetech.com is a particular domain. If we were to give the fully qualified domain name (FQDN), we would include the unnamed root, so it would be written as "wavetech.com." The final period at the end of the name specifies the root of the tree. The root must always be specified for the host equipment. To make it easy, most software will convert a domain name to an FQDN for the user by appending any missing domain names all the way to the root.

The top of the tree lists the top-level domains. These are reserved names. Every domain will have a top-level domain by type or country.

Encryption

Involves encoding a packet's data prior to transmission to ensure data security. The Data Encryption Standard (DES) is an algorithm used for coding and decoding data for security purposes.

Firewall

Used as a security measure between a company's local area network (LAN) and the Internet. The firewall prevents users from accessing certain address Web sites. A firewall also helps to prevent hackers from accessing internal resources on the network. A combination of hardware and software that separates a LAN into two or more parts for security purposes. Today, firewalls are commonly used to prevent unauthorized access to a network from the Internet.

Internet Connection Sharing (ICS)

A service available in Windows 2000 Professional and Server that allows the sharing of a single connection to the Internet or a remote network with multiple network clients. ICS is very easy to configure but also limited to using a single small network.

Network Address Translation (NAT)

1. A component that is included with Windows 2000 Server that allows multiple users to share one connection, such as a modem or DSL connection, to the Internet. NAT is designed for mid-sized networks and offers more configuration flexibility than ICS. NAT operates as a router forwarding all requests to the Internet as well as supporting address translation. This means that the computers inside the network do not have to have Internet-compatible addresses.
2. A service available through RRAS on a Windows 2000 Server that allows the sharing of a single connection to the Internet or a remote network with multiple network clients. NAT is more difficult to configure than ICS but can also operate in more complex environments.

3. Routing protocol available through an Internet Connection Server (ICS) configuration that allows a home network or small office to share a single Internet connection. This protocol requires that your client computers be configured as DHCP clients.

Packet Filtering

Controlling access to a network by analyzing the incoming and outgoing packets and letting them pass or halting them based on the IP addresses of the source and destination.

Proxy server

A server that is positioned between an internal network and the Internet. The proxy server can be configured to limit which users have access to the Internet, which sites users are allowed to connect to, what protocols users are allowed to use, and to cache Internet requests. Some proxy servers also provide some firewall capability.

Remote Authentication Dial-In User Service (RADIUS)

Client/server-based authentication and authorization service for remote access. Connection criteria are passed from the remote access server to the RADIUS server, which will inform the remote access server whether access is allowed or declined.

Remote access policies

A set of rules that define the conditions under which users are allow to connect via remote access. Policies commonly incorporate rules based on time of day, callback, and callerID.

Remote Access Service (RAS)

In most networks, clients are connected directly to the network. In some cases, however, remote connections are needed for your users. Microsoft provides RAS to let you set up and configure client access.

Users connecting to a RAS server, generally through a modem, can be limited to accessing only that server or can be given access to the entire network. Effectively, this is the same as a local connection to the network except that any type of data transfer runs significantly slower. You will need to select connection options appropriate to your access requirements, available support, and budgetary constraints.

Routing and Remote Access Service (RRAS)

Windows 2000 service that enables a Windows 2000 server to simultaneously support multiprotocol routing, demand-dial routing, and remote access. RRAS supports clients running Windows 2000, Windows NT, Windows 9x, UNIX variants, and Macintosh.

Virtual Private Network (VPN)

Remote access configuration where users and remote networks connect to network servers across the Internet. A tunnel is created through the Internet and all of the data that crosses the Internet is encrypted. Windows 2000 supports two protocols for setting up VPNs: Point-to-Point Tunneling Protocol (PPTP) or Layer 2 Tunneling Protocol/IPSec (L2TP/IPSec).

Wide Area Network (WAN)

Expands the basic LAN model by linking Local Area Networks (LANs) and allowing them to communicate with each other. By traditional definition, a LAN becomes a WAN when it crosses a public right-of-way, requiring a public carrier for data transmission. More current usage of the term usually includes any situation where a network expands beyond one location/building. A WAN is characterized by low- to high-speed communication links and usually covers a wide geographic area. The remote links may be operational LANs or only groups of workstations. With the exception of a WAN's wider area of operation, the benefits and features of LANs and WANs are the same.

Windows Internet Naming Service (WINS)

A system that determines the IP address associated with a particular network computer. This is called *name resolution*.

WINS proxy

A special function that can be assigned to a Windows 2000 server that enables the server to forward registration and name resolution requests from non-WINS clients to a WINS server.

Review Questions

1. Which protocol in Windows 2000 is required for smart card authentication?
   a. EAP
   b. BAP
   c. PPTP
   d. MS-CHAP
   e. SPAP
2. MS-CHAP authentication sends the user's name and password in clear text to the server for authentication. True or False?
3. Which protocol dynamically assigns additional bandwidth if available to a connection?
   a. EAP
   b. BAP
   c. PPTP
   d. Multilink
4. Windows 2000 Server can only be configured as a RADIUS server. True or False?

5. Which protocols are supported by NAT? Select all that apply.
   a. IP
   b. NWLink IPX/SPX
   c. Kerberos v5
   d. IPSec
   e. LDAP
   f. RPC
6. All clients connecting to the Internet through Microsoft Proxy must have TCP/IP installed. True or False?
7. Which of the following are properties of L2TP? Select all that apply.
   a. Can only be used on IP internetworks
   b. Can be used on IP, X.25, Frame Relay, and ATM
   c. Supports tunnel authentication
   d. Supports PPP data encryption
   e. Uses a TCP connection for tunnel maintenance
   f. Uses a UDP connection for tunnel maintenance
8. RRAS can be configured as a multiprotocol router. Which protocols can RRAS route? Select all that apply.
   a. TCP/IP
   b. NWLink IPX/SPX
   c. NetBEUI
   d. AppleTalk
   e. DLC
9. List three options for client side remote access security settings.
10. Which of the following features in Remote Routing and Access server protect the private network from outsiders?
    a. NAT
    b. IP filtering
    c. Port mappings
    d. Address pools
    e. All the above
11. Proxy Server allows the administrator to control Internet access on a user-by-user basis. True or False?

12. IP in IP VPN protocol is used to tunnel what type of traffic?
    a. IPSec packets
    b. PPP packets
    c. Multicast
    d. IP datagrams
13. Combining multiple physical connections into one logical connection is a function of which protocol?
    a. BAP
    b. PPP
    c. Multilink
    d. PPTP
    e. L2TP
14. Which type of tunnel is initiated by a remote access server?
    a. Compulsory
    b. Voluntary
    c. Both
15. Per-user remote access policies are supported on which type of domains?
    a. Windows 2000 native and mixed mode
    b. Windows NT only
    c. Windows NT and Windows 2000 mixed mode.
    d. Windows 2000 native mode only.
16. A Windows 2000 RADIUS server is provided by which service?
    a. VPN
    b. IAS
    c. NAT
    d. EAP
    e. Active Directory
17. What two services does RADIUS provide?
18. RADIUS authentication can be done through what three methods?
19. Security policies on a RADIUS server are applied when?
    a. A remote access user establishes a connection
    b. A remote user is authenticated
    c. A remote user accesses a resource

20. What protocol (s) translates one or more private IP address to a public IP address? Select all that apply.
    a. NAT
    b. ICS
    c. BAP
    d. PPP
    e. DHCP
21. You would like to provide shared internet access and IP address translation on a network with a combination of Windows 2000 and Netware clients. Which solution would you implement?
    a. NAT
    b. ICS
    c. Demand-dial routing
    d. Proxy server
    e. All the above will work
22. Which of the following is not a data access recommendation?
    a. Use groups to manage security
    b. Enable the Guest account
    c. Grant only required permissions
    d. Enable auditing on confidential files.
23. A Windows 2000 server can be configured as a VPN server, dial-on demand router, and configured as a NAT server at the same time. True or False?
24. Windows 2000 RRAS can support which dial-in policies? Select all that apply.
    a. Disconnect automatically if the connection is idle for a specified amount
    b. Restrict access based on time of day
    c. Limit dial-in access to a single phone number
    d. Limit the maximum length of time for a session.
25. By default, what level of encryption is enabled for remote access?
    a. Clear-text
    b. Smart card
    c. MS-CHAP
    d. SPAP

HANDS-ON PROJECTS

Project 7-1

In this hands-on activity, you will implement NAT on a Windows 2000 Server. NAT will be configured to lease IP addresses in the 192.168.10.x range. The Microsoft Loopback adapter will be configured as the external interface.

Installing the Microsoft Loopback Adapter

1. Log on to Windows 2000 Server as Administrator.
2. Click on **Start**, point to **Settings**, and then click on **Control Panel**.
3. Double-click on **Add/Remove Hardware**.
4. Click on **Next**.
5. Select **Add/Troubleshoot a Device** and click on **Next**.
6. Select **Add a new device** and click on **Next**.
7. Select **No, I want to select the hardware from a list** and click on **Next**.
8. Click on **Network Adapter** and click on **Next**.
9. Select **Microsoft** as the manufacturer.
10. Select **Microsoft Loopback Adapter** and click on **Next**.
11. Click on **Next**.
12. Click on **Finish**.
13. Right-click on **My Network Places** and click on **Properties**.
14. Right-click on **Local Area Connection 2** and click on **Rename**.
15. Type **External**.
16. Close the Network and Dial up Connections window.

Project 7-2

Configuring NAT

1. Click on **Start**, point to **Programs**, point to **Administrative Tools**, and then click on **Routing and Remote Access**.
2. Expand Routing and Remote Access.
3. Right-click on the server name and click on **Configure and Enable Routing and Remote Access**.
4. Click on **Next**.
5. Select **Manually Configured Server** and click on **Next**.
6. Click on **Finish**.
7. Click on **Yes** to start the service.

8. Expand the server name.
9. Expand IP Routing.
10. Right-click on General and click on **New Routing Protocol**.
11. Click on **Network Address Translation (NAT)** and click on **OK**.
12. Right-click on **Network Address Translation** and click on **New Interface**.
13. Click on **External** and click on **OK**.
14. Select **Public Interface connected to the Internet**.
15. Enable the check box for Translate TCP/UDP headers and click on **OK**.
16. Right-click on **Network Address Translation** and click on **New Interface**.
17. Click on **Local Area Connection** and click on **OK**.
18. Select **Private Interface connected to private network** and click on **OK**.
19. Click on **Network Address Translation** under IP Routing.
20. Double-click on **External**.
21. Click on the **Address Pool** tab.
22. Click on **Add**.
23. Enter **192.168.10.1** as the starting address.
24. Enter **255.2155.255.0** as the mask.
25. Enter **192.168.10.254** as the ending address.
26. Click on **OK** twice.
27. Close all open windows.

Project 7-3

In this hands-on activity, you will view the options available using RADIUS authentication.

1. On Server1, click on the **Start** button, point to **Programs**, point to **Administrative Tools**, and click on Routing and Remote Access.
2. Right-click on **Server1** and click on **Properties**.
3. Click on the **Security** tab.
4. Click on the **Authentication provider** drop list and click on **RADIUS Authentication**.
5. Click on the **Configure** button.
6. Click on **Add**.
7. Type **server2** in the Server name text box and click on **OK**.
8. Click on **OK**.

9. Click on **OK** to accept the message regarding restarting Routing and Remote Access.
10. Click on the **Authentication Methods** button.
11. Click on the **EAP Methods** button. What options are available?
12. Click on **OK**.
13. Click on **Cancel**.
14. Click on **OK**.
15. Click on **Yes** to restart Routing and Remote Access.
16. Close Routing and Remote Access.

CASE PROJECTS

Case 1

Your manager is concerned that remote user's username and passwords are being sent over the phone lines in clear text. He has asked you to evaluate secure methods of authenticating remote users. What other authentication methods are available in Windows 2000 that provide secure authentication? Prepare a report outlining the advantages and disadvantages of each method.

Case 2

Acme Insurance would like to provide its sales people with remote access for e-mail, accessing and updating on-line client files, and submitting expense forms. The IT Director has asked you to prepare a report comparing dial-up access to VPN access. In this report, include the following:

- Equipment requirements on the server side and client side for each type of remote access.
- Approximate costs of each access in total.
- Pros and cons of each remote access method.
- Methods of controlling remote access.

Which remote access method would you choose? What factor(s) influenced your decision?

Case 3

You are configuring a Proxy server for a small company. The owner wants to ensure that they cannot get hacked from the outside but should still be able to perform their work. In particular she would like to implement packet filtering. Only the following traffic should be allowed:

- HTTP in and out
- DNS name resolutions out

- POP3 traffic in and out allowed
- SMTP traffic allowed in and out.

What ports need to be opened on the Proxy server?

KEY TERMS

Chapter 8 - Designing Resource Availability

Bandwidth

1. The range of frequencies that can be transmitted through a particular circuit.
2. The speed at which data travels over a particular media. Bandwidth is measured in bits per second.

Distributed File System (Dfs)

A hierarchical file display that consists of logical links to shared folders. Dfs displays a logical file system to users, allowing them to see and access all shared available network resources in a way that makes their physical location on the network transparent to the user.

Dfs link

Dfs association with an existing network share.

Dfs root

Topmost point (root) of a Dfs hierarchy.

Filtering (Group Policy Object)

A way of controlling whether a Group Policy Object (GPO) is processed and assigned based on security group membership.

Firewall

Used as a security measure between a company's local area network (LAN) and the Internet. The firewall prevents users from accessing certain address Web sites. A firewall also helps to prevent hackers from accessing internal resources on the network. A combination of hardware and software that separates a LAN into two or more parts for security purposes. Today, firewalls are commonly used to prevent unauthorized access to a network from the Internet.

Network application

A computer program housed on a server and designed to run over the network instead of being installed and run locally.

Quality of service

Quality of Service (QOS) is a protocol used to guarantee a certain amount of bandwidth for a particular user or a particular type of network traffic. It is often used in conjunction with Voice over IP, streaming audio and streaming video.

Review Questions

1. List three factors that might influence the application environment design.
2. A solution for time-critical applications that allocates a portion of bandwidth for a specific application is called:
   a. Bandwidth Application Protocol
   b. Quality of Service
   c. Multilink
   d. SAP
3. Which of the following are benefits of Distributed File System (DFS)? Select all that apply.
   a. Fault tolerance
   b. Load balancing
   c. Transparency
   d. Centralized backups
   e. Increased performance
4. What is the maximum number of DFS roots per server?
   a. 1
   b. 2
   c. 16
   d. 32
   e. Unlimited
5. List three differences between a Stand-Alone DFS root and a Domain DFS root.
6. In order to implement QoS in your organization, routers must support which protocol?
   a. BAP
   b. SAP
   c. RSVP
   d. PPTP
7. Which clients by default can access DFS without installing additional software? Select all that apply.
   a. Windows 95
   b. Windows 98
   c. Windows NT
   d. Windows 2000
   e. Windows 3.11

8. Active Directory is required to create a domain DFS root. True or False?
9. A copy of a DFS root created on another server is called a:
    a. Stand-alone replica
    b. Domain replica
    c. Active directory integrated replica
    d. Root replica
10. Client/server applications generally require what type of network connection? Select two from the list.
    a. High bandwidth
    b. Low bandwidth
    c. High availability
    d. Fault tolerance
    e. Clustered servers
11. Generally, centralized data storage should be used for which type of data? Select all that apply.
    a. Shared data
    b. Personal data
    c. Data that is difficult to re-create
    d. Easily re-created data.
    e. Mission-critical data
    f. Non-critical data
    g. Confidential data
12. Windows 98 can function as an application server. True or False?
13. What is the maximum number of DFS roots per domain?
    a. 1
    b. 8
    c. 16
    d. 32
    e. 255
    f. Unlimited
14. By default, an accessed DFS link is cached locally at the client for how long?
    a. 600 seconds
    b. 1000 seconds
    c. 1500 seconds

   d. 1800 seconds
   e. 2500 seconds

15. List three potential problems associated with centrally stored data.
16. A Stand Alone DFS root must be created on an NTFS volume. True or False?
17. A VPN is a good solution for remote applications that require:
    a. Data encryption
    b. High bandwidth
    c. High availability
    d. Firewalls
18. Which of the following are options for improving remote application performance? Select all that apply.
    a. Upgrading to faster links
    b. Installing a local application server
    c. Implementing multiple connections
    d. Implementing DFS
    e. Installing local domain controllers
    f. Installing local DNS servers
19. DFS is installed by default in Windows 2000 Server and Advanced Server. True or False?
20. In domain DFS with root replicas, which server contains the master copy of data?
    a. The first root replica created
    b. The first root replica with replication enabled
    c. User defined
    d. None of the above
21. Whenever possible, place resources local to users that require access to them. True or False?
22. What is the UNC path to access a DFS root named Public located on the server named DATASRV1 in the SoutdaleMgmt.com domain?
    a. \\Southdalemgmt\Public
    b. \\ Southdalemgmt\DFS\Public
    c. . \\ DATASRV1\DFS\Public
    d. . \\ DATASRV1\Public
23. List the three bursts of bandwidth requirements that traditional applications use.

24. You have configured domain DFS with three root replicas. One of the servers that stores a root replica is not available. What must you do to provide users with access to the DFS share?
    a. Modify the root replica to point to another server.
    b. Re-create the root replica on another server
    c. Re-map a drive letter on each client to a new root replica
    d. None of the above.
25. Client/Server applications that use RPCs cannot be run through NAT. True or False?

Hands-on Projects

Project 8-1

In this hands on activity, you will create a stand alone DFS on Server1.

1. Logon as Administrator on Server1.
2. Create the following folders and shares:
   C:\EMPDATA shared as Employee Data
   C:\PERSONNEL shared as Personnel
   C:\EXPENSE shared as Expense Forms
   C:\DATA shared as Data
3. Click on **Start**, point to **Programs**, point to **Administrative Tools**, and then click on **Distributed File System**.
4. Right-click on **Distributed File Systems** and click on **New Dfs Root**.
5. Click on **Next**.
6. Select **Create a Standalone Dfs root** and click on **Next**.
7. Select **Next**.
8. Select **Data** as the existing share and click on **Next**.
9. Type **Shared Data** as the comment and click on **Next**.
10. Click on **Finish**.
11. Browse the network and locate the share named Data. What is available in the share?
12. Switch back to Distributed File System.
13. Right-click on the **Data DFS root**.
14. Click on **New Dfs Link**.
15. Type **Shared Employee Data** as the link name.
16. In the Send the user to this shared folder, click on **Browse** and select the Employee Data share.

17. Select **OK**.
18. Switch back to My Network Places and browse the Data share. What is available now?
19. Switch back to Distributed File System.
20. Right-click on the **Data DFS root**.
21. Click on **New Dfs Link**.
22. Type **Expense Forms** as the link name.
23. In the Send the user to this shared folder, click on **Browse** and specify the Expense Forms share.
24. Select **OK**.
25. Right-click on the **Data DFS root**.
26. Click on **New Dfs Link**.
27. Type **Personnel Forms** as the link name.
28. In the Send the user to this shared folder, click on **Browse** and specify the Personnel share.
29. Select **OK**.
30. Switch back to My Network Places and browse the Data share. What is available now?
31. Close all open windows.

Project 8-2

In this hands-on activity, you will remove the DFS root from Server1.

1. On Server1, click on **Start**, point to **Programs**, point to **Administrative Tools**, and then click on **Distributed File System**.
2. Right-click on **Distributed File Systems** and click on **Delete Dfs Root**.
3. Click on **Yes** to confirm the removal.

Project 8-3

In this hands-on activity, you will create a Domain DFS hosted on Server2.

1. On Server 2, create the folder C:\DFS DATA. Create a text file named DFS.TXT in C:\DFS DATA.
2. Click on **Start**, point to **Programs**, point to **Administrative Tools**, and then click on **Distributed File System**.
3. Right-click on **Distributed File Systems** and click on **New Dfs Root**.
4. Click on **Next**.
5. Select **Create a domain Dfs root** and click on **Next**.
6. Ensure AD2000.COM is the host domain for the DFS root and click on **Next**.

7. Click on **Browse** and double-click on Server2 from the list. Click on **Next**.
8. Select **Create a new share**.
9. Type **C:\DFS DATA** as the path to share
10. Type **Domain DFS Data** as the comment and click on **Next**.
11. Click on **Next** to accept the DFS root name.
12. Click on **Finish**.
13. Switch to Server1. Browse My Network Places and locate the DFS share on Server2. Do you see the file DFS.TXT?

Project 8-4

In this hands-on activity, you will create a root replica hosted on Server1.

1. On Server 2, switch to Distributed File System.
2. Right-click on **\\AD2000.com\Domain DFS Data** and click on **New Root Replica**.
3. Click on **Browse** and double-click on Server1 from the list. Click on **Next**.
4. Select **Create a new share**.
5. Type **C:\DFS DATA** as the path to share
6. Type **Domain DFS Data** as the comment and click on **Next**.
7. Click on **Yes** to have the system create the folder on Server1.
8. Switch to Server1 and start Windows Explorer. Does the folder C:\DFS DATA exist? Does it contain the file DFS.TXT? Why or Why not?

Project 8-5

In this hands-on activity, you will replicate the contents of the domain dfs data share from Server2 to Server1.

1. On Server 2, switch to Distributed File System.
2. Right-click on **\\AD2000.com\Domain DFS Data** and click on **Replication Policy**. What are the current settings?
3. Click on **\\SERVER2\Domain DFS Data** and click on **Enable**.
4. Click on **\\SERVER1\Domain DFS Data** and click on **Enable**.
5. Click on **OK**. Wait a few minutes for replication to occur.
6. Switch to Server1. Start Windows Explorer. Browse the folder C:\DFS DATA. Does it contain the file DFS.TXT?
7. Close all open windows on Server1 and Server2.

CASE PROJECTS

Case 1

Southdale Property Management has a single office in Austin, which manages properties across the US. They will be opening sales offices in Denver and New York within the next six months. The sales offices will be connecting to the office in Austin using dial-on demand VPNs. All shared data is stored centrally on servers in Austin. What DFS solution should they implement? Why?

Case 2

Southdale Property Management manages properties across the U.S. with head office in Austin and sales offices in Denver and New York. The sales offices will be connecting to the office in Austin using VPNs. The company is looking into implementing a client/server application located in Austin for managing property information. Prepare a report outlining the pros and cons of the solution. What recommendations would you make regarding the networking infrastructure before the solution is implemented?

Case 3

You have been hired by Acme Insurance to help implement shared folders on the network. Offices are located in Dallas, Chicago, Seattle, and Omaha. Each office is on a separate subnet connected to head office (Dallas) by ISDN. Currently employees access shared data stored on three separate servers in Dallas and one in Seattle. However, new employees find it difficult to remember server names. In addition the ISDN lines connecting to Dallas are running at 90% capacity.

The IT Director has asked you to implement a DFS which specifically addresses the following concerns:

- Employees do not need to know the server name where the share is stored
- The solution is fault tolerance
- The solution is load balancing
- Employees can access all shared data using one drive mapping
- The solution reduces the network traffic during peak hours.

How would you implement DFS?

Key Terms

Chapter 9 - Implementation and Management

Active Directory

The Windows 2000 directory service. Active Directory treats users, files, directories, applications, and other items as objects. It allows system administrators to modify the properties of objects. Objects and their properties are described in the Active Directory schema.

Application

The use to which an information processing system is put. For example, a payroll application, an airline reservation application, or a network application.

Distributed File System (Dfs)

A hierarchical file display that consists of logical links to shared folders. Dfs displays a logical file system to users, allowing them to see and access all shared available network resources in a way that makes their physical location on the network transparent to the user.

Domain Name System (DNS)

A hierarchical, distributed method of organizing systems and network names on the Internet. DNS administratively groups hosts (systems) into a hierarchy of authority that allows addressing and other information to be widely distributed and maintained. A big advantage of DNS is that using it eliminates dependence on a centrally maintained file that maps host names to addresses.

The diagram shows the hierarchical organization of domain names. The bottom level of the tree structure contains the names of companies or even machines within a company. For example, consider wuarchive.wustl.edu. The bottom of the tree is wuarchive. This is the name of a particular piece of equipment within the wustl domain, which is under the edu domain.

The name of a particular domain is read from the bottom of the tree up to the root. The root is unnamed and is represented with just a period. For example, wavetech.com is a particular domain. If we were to give the fully qualified domain name (FQDN), we would include the unnamed root, so it would be written as "wavetech.com." The final period at the end of the name specifies the root of the tree. The root must always be specified for the host equipment. To make it easy, most software will convert a domain name to an FQDN for the user by appending any missing domain names all the way to the root.

The top of the tree lists the top-level domains. These are reserved names. Every domain will have a top-level domain by type or country.

Domain Controller

Server within a domain and storage point for domainwide security information. This also refers to a partition of the Active Directory the Windows NT Server holds.

Domain controller (Windows 2000)

A Windows 2000 Server that has been promoted into the domain controller role. Each domain controller has a copy of the Active Directory domain database and SYSVOL folder.

Dynamic Host Configuration Protocol (DHCP)

A TCP/IP application-layer protocol that provides for dynamic address assignment on a network.

File server

A computer that stores files and provides access to them from workstations. File servers generally contain large hard disks and high amounts of memory. If a computer is used exclusively as a file server, it is a dedicated file server. If a computer is used as a workstation and a file server simultaneously, it is a nondedicated file server.

The NOS (Network Operating System) runs on the file server and controls access to files, printers, and other network resources.

Global Catalog (GC)

A database containing scaled-down attributes of every Active Directory object from every domain in a tree or forest. The GC replies to queries so that users in one domain can locate resources in another domain.

Ipconfig

A command line utility used to display IP information. The purpose of this utility is to provide the user with diagnostic information related to TCP/IP network configuration.

Lightweight Directory Access Protocol (LDAP)

Modeled from X.500 and Directory Access Protocol (DAP), LDAP is a scaled-down version of its predecessor, DAP, which was unsuccessful because it was too inefficient (heavy) with thin clients, personal computers, and Internet use. Active Directory directly supports the Lightweight Directory Access Protocol.

Network Address Translation (NAT)

1. A component that is included with Windows 2000 Server that allows multiple users to share one connection, such as a modem or DSL connection, to the Internet. NAT is designed for mid-sized networks and offers more configuration flexibility than ICS. NAT operates as a router forwarding all requests to the Internet as well as supporting address translation. This means that the computers inside the network do not have to have Internet-compatible addresses.
2. A service available through RRAS on a Windows 2000 Server that allows the sharing of a single connection to the Internet or a remote network with multiple network clients. NAT is more difficult to configure than ICS but can also operate in more complex environments.

3. Routing protocol available through an Internet Connection Server (ICS) configuration that allows a home network or small office to share a single Internet connection. This protocol requires that your client computers be configured as DHCP clients.

Network Monitor

An SMS utility that functions as a *sniffer* and is used to capture, transmit, and display network packets.

Pathping

A route tracing tool that combines features of the *ping* and *tracert* commands with additional information that neither of those commands provides. The *pathping* command sends packets to each router on the way to a final destination over a period of time, and then computes results based on the packets returned from each hop.

Ping

This utility is used to test the presence of other computers on the network. You can use IP addresses or NetBIOS names if you have a WINS server running or have made the appropriate entry in the LMHOSTS file.

Proxy server

A server that is positioned between an internal network and the Internet. The proxy server can be configured to limit which users have access to the Internet, which sites users are allowed to connect to, what protocols users are allowed to use, and to cache Internet requests. Some proxy servers also provide some firewall capability.

Round robin

A DNS configuration option that can be used if multiple computers with different IP addresses have the same host name. The DNS server will provide load balancing by rotating through the IP addresses for successive client requests.

Systems Management Server (SMS)

A set of tools from Microsoft that assists in managing PCs connected to a local-area network (LAN) SMS enables a network administrator to create an inventory of all the hardware and software on the network and to store it in an SMS database.

Time Domain Reflectometry (TDR)

Used to pinpoint flaws and problems in underground and aerial wire, cabling, and fiber optics.

Traceroute (Tracert)

A utility that traces a packet from your computer to an Internet host, showing how many hops the packet requires to reach the host and how long each hop takes.

Windows Internet Naming Service (WINS)

A system that determines the IP address associated with a particular network computer. This is called *name resolution*.

Review Questions

1. Which event log stores failed logon events?
   a. Application log
   b. System log
   c. Security log
   d. Directory services log
2. The Global Catalog stores what type of information?
   a. All attributes for all objects in the domain
   b. All attributes for the most commonly accessed objects in the domain
   c. All attributes for all objects in the forest
   d. The most common attributes for all objects in the forest
   e. All attributes for the most commonly accessed objects in the forest
3. Which port does LDAP use?
   a. 110
   b. 25
   c. 119
   d. 389
   e. 53
4. What is the maximum number of servers that can be included in a Network Load Balancing cluster?
   a. 2
   b. 4
   c. 8
   d. 16
   e. 32
   f. Unlimited
5. Round-robin balancing is implemented by:
   a. Assigning multiple address records for a single host name in DNS
   b. Assigning multiple MX records for a single host name in DNS
   c. Assigning multiple host records for a single address record in DNS
   d. Assigning multiple host records incremental priorities in DNS
   e. None of the above.
6. List three advantages to using check lists during the implementation phase.

7. Which protocol can be used to query computers and routers for status information?
   a. DHCP
   b. SNMP
   c. SMTP
   d. RVSP
8. Which of the following options should reduce traffic across the WAN? Select all that apply.
   a. Subnet the network
   b. Install domain controllers in each subnet
   c. Install local DNS servers
   d. Update the WAN links
   e. Install DHCP Relay Agents in each subnet
9. DNS is queried to find domain controllers or global catalog servers when a user attempts to log on to the domain. True or False?
10. Which application level protocol is used to query the global catalog?
    a. IP
    b. SAP
    c. RVSP
    d. LDAP
    e. SMTP
11. The source path for installing additional administration tools on a Windows 2000 server is:
    a. \%systemroot%\system\admin.msi
    b. \%systemroot%\system32\admin.msi
    c. \%systemroot%\system\adminpak.msi
    d. \%systemroot%\system32\adminpak.msi
12. Upgrading network cabling from 10BaseT to 10Base5 will increase network bandwidth. True or False?
13. What is the maximum number of hops a packet can go through before it is declared undeliverable for RIP-based routing?
    a. 8
    b. 12
    c. 15
    d. 16
    e. Unlimited

14. Which type of network traffic can be optimized by implementing a proxy array?
    a. Outbound
    b. Inbound
    c. Both inbound and outbound
15. Which internet sharing solution also provides caching of accessed web sites?
    a. NAT
    b. ICS
    c. Proxy server
    d. All the above
    e. NAT and ICS
16. Which tool is used to manage replication of standard secondary DNS zones?
    a. Active Directory Sites and Services
    b. Active Directory Domains and Trusts
    c. File Replication Service
    d. DNS
17. In a Windows 2000 LAN with one root domain and four child domains connected by routers, how many global catalog servers are required for user logon authentication?
    a. 1
    b. 2
    c. 4
    d. 5
18. Which administration tool can be used to identify DHCP packets on the local subnet?
    a. System Monitor
    b. Network Monitor
    c. DNS Server log
    d. Event Viewer
19. Which event viewer logs are installed by default on all Windows 2000 systems? Select all that apply.
    a. Application log
    b. Security log
    c. Directory Service log
    d. System log

   e. File Replication log
   f. DNS log

20. Which Windows 2000 tools can be used to install and configure client workstations? Select all that apply.
    a. RIS
    b. Group Policies
    c. Windows Installer Service
    d. Computer Management
    e. Component Services
21. Supported SNMP components are stored in what files?
    a. Management Information Bases
    b. SNMP communities
    c. SNMP agents
    d. SNMP traps
22. The version of Network Monitor that ships with Windows 2000 can only trap incoming and outgoing local traffic. True or False?
23. Certificate Services is responsible for issuing and management of what version of certificates?
    a. X.500
    b. X.509
    c. Kerberos V2
    d. Kerberos V4
24. What Windows 2000 service is responsible for configuring and managing RADIUS support?
    a. Internet Security and Acceleration service
    b. Routing an Remote Access service
    c. Internet Authentication Service
    d. Internet Security and Authentication service
25. LANs connected through lower-bandwidth connections or dial-up connections should have their own local DHCP server. True or False?

CASE PROJECTS

Case 1

Fleetwood Credit union is a financial services firm that serves the needs of its members in the city of Fleetwood, Iowa. There is a WAN in place to connect all eight branches of Fleetwood Credit Union. Each branch has 20 to 30 workstations and a single server providing dial-on demand access to head office in Fleetwood. All data is centrally stored on a server in Fleetwood. In addition, all internet access is through a fiber connection at head office. The board of directors has asked you to evaluate methods of reducing the amount of traffic going through the VPN to head office. Prepare a report outlining methods of reducing WAN traffic and their associated costs.

Case 2

Applied Solutions, a manufacturing company with head office in Minneapolis, has contracted you to migrate their offices from Windows NT to Windows 2000 Active Directory. In addition to Minneapolis, there are manufacturing plants in Phoenix, Atlanta, and Denver. Each plant maintains their own equipment, has their own IT staff, and operates as a profit center. Each office has a PDC providing DNS, WINS, and DHCP and two BDCs. In addition, there is a member server running SQL and Microsoft Exchange for e-mail. Client computers are a mixture of Windows 95, Windows 98, and Windows NT workstations.

Connectivity between the plants and Minneapolis is frame relay. Management would like to replace the frame relay with a fast internet connection and implement a VPN solution for accessing files between plants.

Management has asked you to create an implementation plan that addresses the following issues:

- No downtime is permitted at the plants.
- All client computers are to be upgraded to Windows 2000 professional without data loss.
- To simplify administration, all DNS and WINS management will be centralized in Minneapolis. However each plant must be able to resolve host names and NETBIOS names if the link to Minneapolis is down.
- During the upgrade, e-mail must always be accessible.
- The new active directory root will be created in Minneapolis with each plant location being a child domain.

Create an implementation plan for the physical upgrade of Windows 2000 and the implementation of active directory. The plan should include a network diagram, deployment schedule, and check lists for each plant location.

Case 3

Starlight Auction Inc. has asked you to design a fault tolerance solution for their internet auction site. Starlight has three IIS servers running Windows 2000 Advanced Servers, which host their online auction web site. When a user connects to the web site, Starlight would like to have the user connect to a less-used server. Additionally, the solution should provide fault tolerance in the event a web server is unavailable. What solution would you implement?